Multinational Business Finance

SIXTH EDITION

SINGAPORE

BAHRAIN

HONG KONG

TOKYO AND SYDNEY

TOKYO

BAHRAIN

HONG KONG

SINGAPORE

SYDNEY

| 1000 | 0900 | 0800 | 0700 | 0600 | 0500 | 0400 | 0300 | 0200 | 0100 | 2400 | 2300 |

Greenwich Mean Time

| +2 | +3 | +4 | +5 | +6 | +7 | +8 | +9 | +10 | +11 | +12 |

Hours different from GMT

Reprinted by permission of HarperCollins Publishers. Data from *Euromoney*, April 1979, p.14.

Multinational Business Finance

SIXTH EDITION

David K. Eiteman
UNIVERSITY OF CALIFORNIA, LOS ANGELES

Arthur I. Stonehill
OREGON STATE UNIVERSITY

Michael H. Moffett
OREGON STATE UNIVERSITY

▲▼▲ **ADDISON-WESLEY PUBLISHING COMPANY**

READING, MASSACHUSETTS ■ MENLO PARK, CALIFORNIA ■ NEW YORK
DON MILLS, ONTARIO ■ WOKINGHAM, ENGLAND ■ AMSTERDAM ■ BONN
SYDNEY ■ SINGAPORE ■ TOKYO ■ MADRID ■ SAN JUAN ■ MILAN ■ PARIS

Executive Editor: Barbara Rifkind
Managing Editor: Mary Clare McEwing
Production Supervisor: Sarah Hallet
Production Services: Barbara Pendergast
Text Designer: Gary Fujiwara
Cover Designer: Sametz Blackstone Associates, Inc.
Technical Art Consultant: Dick Morton
Illustrator: Scot Graphics
Permissions Editor: Mary Dyer
Manufacturing Supervisor: Roy Logan

Library of Congress Cataloging-in-Publication Data

Eiteman, David K.
    Multinational business finance. — 6th ed. / David K. Eiteman,
Arthur I. Stonehill, Michael H. Moffett, with a contribution by Cheol S. Eun.
    p.   cm.
    Includes bibliographical references and indexes.
    ISBN 0-201-53899-7
    1. International business enterprises—Finance.   I. Stonehill,
Arthur I.   II. Moffett, Michael H.   III. Title.
HG4027.5.E36   1991
658.15'99—dc20   91-27508
                                                     CIP

Reprinted with corrections, March 1992

Copyright © 1992 by Addison-Wesley Publishing Company, Inc.

3 4 5 6 7 8 9 10–HA–95949392

Preface

As the field of international finance has evolved, so has the content of *Multinational Business Finance*. In this sixth edition we continue to identify three major trends and themes that differentiate international financial management from its domestic counterpart.

As in previous editions, we perceive the multinational firm to be a unique institution that acts as a catalyst and facilitator of international trade and as an important producer and distributor in host countries where its affiliates are located. The success of a multinational firm continues to be dependent on its ability to recognize and benefit from imperfections in national markets for products, factors of production, and financial assets.

Also carried over from earlier editions is the theme that volatile exchange rates may increase risk, but they also create great opportunities for both investors and firms to profit, given a proper understanding of exchange-risk management.

The sixth edition continues to recognize the increasing importance of global integration of money and capital markets, a trend that is creating expanded opportunities for both investors and organizations that need to raise capital. Although global integration of financial markets removes some market imperfections, which impede the flow of capital internationally, excellent opportunities continue to exist for investors to increase their returns while lowering their risks through international portfolio diversification and for firms to lower their cost of capital by sourcing it internationally.

NEW TO THE SIXTH EDITION

The sixth edition of *Multinational Business Finance* has been revised to reflect changes in the field of international finance occurring since the end of 1988. In particular:

- We have added separate chapters on sourcing debt internationally (Chapter 11), and sourcing equity internationally (Chapter 12).

- We have combined and expanded our discussion of forecasting and parity conditions (Chapter 6).

- Corporate strategy and direct foreign investment has been completely revised (Chapter 15).

- Certain topics have been given expanded coverage due to their current importance.
    1. The financial implications of the Single European Market and the possibility of a single European currency have been expanded in Chapter 2.
    2. The coverage of swaps has been expanded in Chapter 11.

3. Corporate strategy with respect to mode of entry into foreign markets has been revised to focus on strategic alliances and takeovers as well as the more traditional strategies in Chapter 15.

■ A brand-new feature of the sixth edition is the inclusion at the end of half of the chapters of an *anecdote*, an *illustrative case,* or a proprietary *decision case.*

■ Another new feature is the expansion and revision of the end-of-chapter problems to feature spreadsheet applications. A disk containing all spreadsheet templates comes with the *Instructor's Manual.*

AUDIENCE

The sixth edition of *Multinational Business Finance* is appropriate for the same audiences as the first five editions. Earlier editions have been widely used in international financial management courses in university degree programs, university-run executive programs, and company management development programs.

Readers will find *Multinational Business Finance* most meaningful if they have the background knowledge or experience equivalent to a basic finance course. A previous course in international economics is desirable, but the text is designed to cover sufficient economic material so that a separate background is not essential.

ACKNOWLEDGMENTS

The authors are very grateful to the numerous persons who have provided critical comments and suggestions to improve both the current and earlier editions of this book. The sixth edition has benefited immensely from comments we received on the fifth edition, both from formal reviews and from colleagues' replies to a questionnaire. We take this opportunity to thank the following respondents for their detailed comments and answers:

James Baker
Kent State University

Morten Balling
Aarhus School of Business

Nancy Bord
University of Hartford

Tom Brewer
Georgetown University

J. Markham Collins
University of Tulsa

William R. Folks, Jr.
University of South Carolina

Robert Grosse
University of Miami at Coral Gables

Laurent Jacque
University of Minnesota

Fred Kaen
University of New Hampshire

Robert Kemp
University of Virginia

Seung Kim
St. Louis University

Martin Lawrence
William Paterson College

Jeanette Medewitz
University of Nebraska at Omaha

Robert Mefford
University of San Francisco

Eloy Mestre
American University

Gregory Noronha
Old Dominion University

John Olienyk
Colorado State University

Lars Oxelheim
Industriens Utredningsinstitut,
Sweden

Yoon S. Park
George Washington University

Lee Remmers
INSEAD, France

David Rubenstein
University of Houston

Hamid Shomali
Golden Gate University

Kishore Tandon
CUNY - Bernard Baruch College

Russell Taussig
University of Hawaii at Manoa

Richard Wright
Willamette University

Alexander Zampieron
Bentley College

Colleagues who have been especially helpful in the sixth edition revision are Morten Balling (Aarhus School of Business, Denmark), J. Markham Collins (University of Tulsa), Steven Ford (Hewlett-Packard), Veikko Jaaskelainen (Helsinki School of Economics and Business Administration, Finland), Aage Jacobsen (Gudme Raaschou Investment Bank, Denmark), Chuck Kwok (University of South Carolina), and Russell Taussig (University of Hawaii at Manoa).

The final product is also the end result of the many valuable reviews and suggestions received on earlier editions, all of which have guided us as our thoughts evolved over the years. Particularly helpful have been comments from:

Paul Adair
Philadelphia Stock Exchange

Hossein G. Askari
George Washington University

Robert T. Aubey
University of Wisconsin, Madison

David Babbel
University of Florida

James Baker
Kent State University

Morten Balling
Aarhus School of Business, Denmark

Barbara Block
Tektronix, Inc.

Holly Bowman
Bankers Trust

Finbarr Bradley
New York University

Michael Brooke
University of Manchester, England

Robert Carlson
Wake Forest University

Payson Cha
The Cha Group, Hong Kong

Robert Chia
National University of Singapore

Frederick D. S. Choi
New York University

Mark Ciechon
University of California, Los Angeles

Alan N. Cook
Baylor University

Robert Cornu
Cranfield School of Management, UK

Steven Dawson
University of Hawaii at Manoa

John A. Deuchler
Private Export Funding Corporation

Gunter Dufey
University of Michigan

Käre Dullum
Gudme Raaschou Investment Bank, DK

Vihang Errunza
McGill University

Cheol S. Eun
University of Maryland

William R. Folks, Jr.
University of South Carolina

Lewis Freitas
University of Hawaii at Manoa

Ian Giddy
University of Pennsylvania

Manolete Gonzales
Oregon State University

David Heenan
Theo Davies

Sharyn H. Hess
Foreign Credit Insurance Association

Alfred Hofflander
University of California, Los Angeles

Ronald A. Johnson
Northeastern University

Ira G. Kawaller
Chicago Mercantile Exchange

Gordon Klein
University of California, Los Angeles

Kenneth Knox
Tektronix, Inc.

Steve Kobrin
University of Pennsylvania

Eric Y. Lee
Fairleigh Dickinson University

Donald Lessard
Massachusetts Institute of Technology

Rita Maldanado-Baer
New York University

Arthur J. Obesler
Eximbank

Edmund Outslay
Michigan State University

Lee Remmers
INSEAD, France

Alan Rugman
University of Toronto

R. J. Rummel
University of Hawaii at Manoa

Lemma Senbet
University of Wisconsin

Alan Shapiro
University of Southern California

Hany Shawky
State University of New York, Albany

Russell Taussig
University of Hawaii at Manoa

I. Barry Thompson
Continental Bank

Norman Toy
Columbia University

Harald Vestergaard
Copenhagen Business School

Joseph D. Vu
University of Illinois, Chicago

Gerald T. West
Overseas Private Investment Corporation

Willem Winter
First Interstate Bank of Oregon

Richard Wright
Willamette University

Alexander Zampieron
Bentley College

Cheol Eun deserves a special thanks for allowing us to continue using his contributions carried over from the fifth edition.

Inevitably woven into the fabric of this book are ideas received from faculty and students at institutions where we have taught. These include our home universities of University of California, Los Angeles, and Oregon State University. Our visiting stints have been at the University of California, Berkeley; Cranfield School of Management, U.K.; University of Hawaii at Manoa; Northern European Management Institute, Norway; Copenhagen Business School, Denmark; Aarhus School of Business, Denmark; Helsinki School of Economics and Business Administration, Finland; Institute for the Development of Executives, Argentina; National University of Singapore; International Center for Public Enterprises, Yugoslavia; Beijing Institute of Chemical Engineering Management, People's Republic of China; and Dalian University of Science & Technology, People's Republic of China. Further ideas came from consulting assignments in Argentina, Belgium, Canada, Denmark, Hong Kong, Indonesia, Japan, Malaysia, Mexico, the Netherlands, Norway, People's Republic of China, Taiwan, the United Kingdom, and Venezuela.

We would also like to thank all those with Addison-Wesley who have worked so diligently on this sixth edition: Barbara Rifkind for her continuing support and enthusiasm, Kari Heen for handling all details with a smile, Mary Clare McEwing for making sure things got done, and Barbara Pendergast for her excellent editorial and production services.

Finally, we would like to rededicate this book to our parents, the late Wilford Eiteman, Sylvia Eiteman, the late Harold Stonehill, Norma Stonehill, Hoy Moffett, and Bennie Ruth Moffett, who gave us the motivation to become academicians and authors. We thank our wives, Keng-Fong, Kari, and Megan, for their patience through the years spent preparing this edition. Thanks to Megan Murphy for her construction of the spreadsheet templates for the *Teacher's Manual*. Melody Brown deserves special thanks for her excellent help in researching and producing the many drafts and final manuscript.

Pacific Palisades, California	D.K.E.
Corvallis, Oregon	A.I.S.
Corvallis, Oregon	M.H.M.

About the Authors

David K. Eiteman is Professor of Finance at the John E. Anderson Graduate School of Management at UCLA. He has been a member of the faculty at UCLA since 1959. He has also held teaching or research appointments at the National University of Singapore, Dalian University (China), the Helsinki School of Economics and Business Administration (Finland), University of Hawaii at Manoa, University of Bradford (UK), Cranfield School of Management (UK), and IDEA (Argentina). He has served a term as President of the Western Finance Association.

Professor Eiteman received a B.B.A. (Business Administration) from the University of Michigan, Ann Arbor (1952), an M.A. (Economics) from the University of California, Berkeley (1956), and a Ph.D. (Finance) from Northwestern University (1959).

He has authored or co-authored four books and twenty-nine other publications. His articles have appeared in *The Journal of Finance, Financial Analysts Journal, Journal of International Business Studies, California Management Review, Columbia Journal of World Business, Management International, Business Horizons, MSU Business Topics, Public Utilities Fortnightly,* and others.

Arthur I. Stonehill is currently a Professor of Finance and International Business with three-year split appointments at Oregon State University, University of Hawaii at Manoa, and Copenhagen Business School (Denmark). He has been a member of the faculty at Oregon State University since 1966. He has also held teaching or research appointments at the University of California, Berkeley, Cranfield School of Management (UK), and the North European Management Institute (Norway). He is presently serving as President of the Academy of International Business.

Professor Stonehill received a B.A. (History) from Yale University (1953), an M.B.A. from Harvard Business School (1957), and a Ph.D. from the University of California, Berkeley (1965). In 1989 he was awarded an honorary doctorate from the Aarhus School of Business (Denmark).

He has authored or co-authored seven books and twenty-three other publications. His articles have appeared in *Financial Management, Journal of International Business Studies, California Management Review, Journal of Financial and Quantitative Analysis, Journal of International Financial Management and Accounting, The Investment Analyst (UK), Nationaløkonomisk Tidskrift (Denmark), Sosialøkonomen (Norway), Journal of Financial Education,* and others.

Michael H. Moffett is an Assistant Professor of Finance and International Business at Oregon State University, but currently a visiting Assistant Professor of International Business at the University of Michigan, Ann Arbor. He has been a member of the faculty at Oregon State University since 1985. He has also held teaching or research appointments at the Brookings Institution, the University of Hawaii at Manoa, the Aarhus School of Business (Denmark), the Helsinki School of Economics and Business Administration (Finland), and the University of Ljubljana (Yugoslavia).

Professor Moffett received a B.A. in Economics from the University of Texas at Austin (1977), an M.S. in Resource Economics from Colorado State University (1979), an M.A. in Economics from the University of Colorado, Boulder (1983), and a Ph.D. in Economics from the University of Colorado, Boulder (1985).

He has authored or co-authored two books and seven other publications. His articles have appeared in *Journal of Financial and Quantitative Analysis, Journal of International Money and Finance, Journal of International Financial Management and Accounting, Journal of Contemporary Policy Issues, Brookings Discussion Papers in International Economics,* and others.

Contents

Chapter 7
Managing Operating Exposure   185

Chapter 8
Managing Transaction Exposure   203

Chapter 9
Managing Accounting Exposure   244

PART 3
Financing from a Global Perspective   277

Chapter 10
International Banking   279

Chapter 11
Sourcing Debt Internationally   313

PART 4
Direct Foreign Investment Decisions   433

Chapter 15
Corporate Strategy and Direct Foreign Investment   435

Chapter 16
Political Risk Management   466

Chapter 17

PART 5

Chapter 18

Chapter 19

PART 1

THE INTERNATIONAL FINANCIAL ENVIRONMENT

After an introductory Chapter 1 on trends and themes in international financial management, the rest of Part 1 describes the international financial environment. Chapter 2 describes the evolution of the international monetary system. Chapter 3 explains the significance of balance of payments imbalances, as well as aberrations such as the persistent U.S. balance of payments deficits and the developing country debt problem. Chapter 4 describes the foreign exchange market. Chapter 5 describes the recently developed derivative markets for foreign exchange futures and options, including an illustration of how speculators operate in the spot, forward, and derivative markets.

CHAPTER 1

Trends and Themes

During the past 20 years the study of international finance has exploded in popularity. This is due in part to at least three major trends in the business world, and corresponding opportunities to benefit from these trends. Briefly, the trends may be summed up as follows.

1. The multinational firm has become increasingly important as a facilitator of international trade and as a manufacturer in host countries where its affiliates are located. The emergence of the multinational firm as a major actor in international affairs has stimulated the creation of international business courses in business and management schools. Throughout the world the finance version of these courses is typically called international financial management or multinational business finance in order to distinguish it from the traditional international finance course taught by economics departments.

2. The advent of floating exchange rates in 1973, and subsequent volatility of exchange rates, has added considerable uncertainty to the environment in which business firms, investors, and governments operate. Floating exchange rates, with their impact on the return and riskiness of a firm's cash flows, as well as on the return and riskiness of portfolio investments, have piqued the interest of mainline finance theorists. As a result, courses that previously were taught as part of an international business program are now more often taught from a corporate finance perspective.

3. During the 1980s, and continuing into the 1990s, global integration of money and capital markets increasingly became a reality, creating expanded opportunities for both investors and organizations that need to raise capital. Global integration of money and

capital markets has accelerated the interest of both finance and economics theorists and practitioners. New courses and books have sprung forth to explain international portfolio investment and how financial markets are linked internationally.

Although it is impossible to do justice fully to each of these three trends, we hope to give you a thorough introduction to each so that you can follow the exciting developments in international finance that are literally unfolding each day.

The trends we have identified create opportunities for firms and investors to benefit from them. Three corresponding themes highlight the most important benefits.

1A. Multinational firms will continue to grow profitably because they are able to benefit from imperfections in national markets for products, factors of production, and financial assets.

2A. Volatile exchange rates may increase risk but they also create opportunities for both firms and investors to profit, given a proper understanding of exchange risk management.

3A. Although the trend toward global integration of money and capital markets tends to remove market imperfections that impede the flow of capital internationally, excellent opportunities will continue to exist for firms to lower their cost of capital by sourcing it internationally, and for investors to increase their return while lowering their risk through international portfolio diversification.

In the sections that follow we will elaborate on these three themes and the three trends that underlie them. The chapter will conclude by giving a preview of the rest of the book, with an emphasis on how international finance differs from domestic finance.

MARKET IMPERFECTIONS: A RATIONALE FOR THE CONTINUED PROSPERITY OF MULTINATIONAL FIRMS

For several centuries economists have used the classical economic theory of comparative advantage to explain trade movements between nations. Springing from the writings of Adam Smith and David Ricardo in the eighteenth and nineteenth centuries, the theory in simple terms states that everyone gains if each nation specializes in the production of those goods that it produces relatively most efficiently and imports those goods that other countries produce relatively most efficiently. The theory has supported free-trade arguments. Appendix A explains the theory of comparative advantage for readers who need a review.

The doctrine of comparative advantage made an initial assumption that although the products of economic activity could move internationally, the factors of production were relatively fixed in a geographic sense. Land, labor, and capital were assumed to be internationally immobile. Although the early economists did not go beyond their initial three factors, by implication such other factors as managerial skills, worker education, and research and development abilities were assumed to be largely attributes of particular nations.

The still-growing post–World War II wave of direct foreign investment and the growth of multinational business enterprises is perhaps the major economic phenomenon of the last half of the twentieth century. This development, which holds such potential for the economic betterment of the world's population, runs counter to the postulates of Smith and Ricardo in that it is based on international mobility of the most important factors of production in the twentieth century. Capital raised in London by a Belgium-based corporation may finance the acquisition of machinery by a subsidiary located in Australia. A management team from French Renault may take over a U.S.-built automotive complex in the Argentine. Clothing for dolls, sewn in Korea on Japanese-manufactured sewing machines according to U.S. specifications, may be shipped to northern Mexico for assembly with other components into dolls being manufactured by a U.S. firm for sale in New York and London during the Christmas season. A California-manufactured air bus, the Lockheed L-1011, was powered by British Rolls-Royce engines, while a competing air bus, the Douglas DC-10, flies on Canadian wing assemblies. A Hong Kong bank originally developed with British management and capital buys control of a major upstate New York banking chain, which in turn finances the construction in Korea of ships intended for the Greek merchant marine.

Virtually every very large firm in the world has become multinational to at least a limited extent. Appendices B and C provide a brief summary of the 50 largest U.S. and 50 largest non-U.S. multinational firms. These are the real world actors to which we will refer throughout the book.

Rate of Return

Multinational firms strive to take advantage of imperfections in national markets for products, factors of production, and financial assets. Imperfections in the market for products translate into market opportunities for multinational firms. Large international firms are better able to exploit such competitive factors as economies of scale, managerial and technological expertise, product differentiation, and financial strength than are their local competitors. In fact, multinational firms thrive best in markets characterized by international oligopolistic competition, where these factors are particularly critical. In addition, once multinational firms have established a physical presence abroad, they are in a better position than purely domestic firms to identify and implement market opportunities through their own internal information network.

Multinational firms are also well positioned to identify and exploit imperfections in the market for factors of production. For example, their own internal information network can identify countries in which labor is inexpensive relative to its productivity, because multinational firms possess comparative, realized manufacturing costs from their own affiliates. Domestic firms typically are unaware of specific opportunities to reduce costs by manufacturing in foreign locations. Once aware of this factor, though, they still must rely on costly, ad hoc field studies starting from a low base of market knowledge. Multinationals are also able to develop and utilize those raw material sources that host country firms cannot develop because of a lack of technological or managerial expertise, economies of scale, or sufficient financial strength.

In some cases the common stock of multinational firms may serve as a vehicle for investors who wish to hold internationally diversified portfolios but are prevented from achieving diversification because of perceived and real imperfections in the market for financial assets. For example, international portfolio investors can be frustrated by foreign exchange controls, withholding taxes on dividends, capital market controls, lack of full disclosure, and lack of knowledge about foreign securities markets. The multinational firms' common stock may be perceived as a convenient proxy for international diversification without the headaches involved in dealing with foreign securities markets.

Risk

Multinational firms are particularly well suited to the task of managing risk from the perspectives of all interest groups. Geographical and currency diversification allow multinational firms to minimize fluctuations in returns due to business cycles, to maintain or improve their competitive positions in the face of foreign exchange rate changes, to reduce the impact of political interference, to diversify the risk of technological obsolescence, and to minimize their cost of capital.

Geographical diversification of operations permits multinational firms to reduce fluctuations in their earnings, cash flow, and perhaps stock market value. Their financial performances are a weighted average of results from markets that are seldom perfectly correlated with each other. The lower the correlation, the better the chance for reducing bankruptcy risk and the more valuable the firms might be in a portfolio theory context if securities market imperfections exist.

Unexpected changes in foreign exchange rates can create disequilibria, which, if properly understood by firms, can lead to opportunities for increased profit. For example, a country that undervalues its currency creates a foreign exchange risk for those firms that export to that country. However, the same undervaluation creates an opportunity to increase operating profits on exports from that country, an opportunity that would be beneficial to multinational or host country firms with a manufacturing base in that country. In effect, geographical diversification by multinational firms reduces the chance that their financial performance will be overly dependent on the exchange rate policy of any single country, or that their real asset values will erode because of hyperinflation in any one country.

Another advantage of diversification is that it increases the bargaining power of multinational firms when they negotiate investment agreements with potential host countries. It also allows them to make the best deal possible when bargaining over residual benefits from an investment that has failed or is being nationalized. Although purely domestic firms are not subject to political risk abroad, they are not immune from political interference or even expropriation at home. In that sense multinational firms have the advantage of being potentially stateless. Expropriation of "parent" firms may not mean the end of the multinationals as entities, because management can be relocated and continue to run surviving affiliates.

Firms in high-technology industries can remain internationally competitive only if they have continuous access to the latest research and development. Such activities are often concentrated geographically in a few centers of excellence. For example, to be at the frontier of knowledge in the electronics industry, a firm should, ideally, maintain a physical presence or strong contacts with the centers of excellence that have developed in the United States in the "Silicon Valley" south of San Francisco or in similar areas in Massachusetts, Texas, and Florida. Additional centers of excellence exist in Japan, the United Kingdom, France, Italy, the Netherlands, South Korea, Singapore, Hong Kong, Sweden, Switzerland, and Germany. Although one cannot predict which center of excellence or which researcher will produce the next exciting breakthrough, a firm that has diversified internationally by locating in each of these centers has a high probability of maintaining a competitive technological position in the electronics industry.

Financing risk can be considerably reduced for multinationals in comparison to domestic firms. Multinationals have access to both international and national debt and equity markets. Other things being equal, this added availability of capital reduces their cost of capital in comparison to firms that are restricted to raising funds from only one capital market. In addition, when foreign exchange markets are in disequilibrium, multinational firms have the option to finance in different currencies, some of which may offer temporarily lower costs of debt or equity than would be justified by expected changes in exchange rates.

Multinational Firms and Host Countries: The Potential for Goal Conflict

From an economic perspective host countries welcome multinational firms because they are viewed as agents of technology transfer and host country economic development. From a business perspective multinational firms are eager for opportunities to invest in geographic locations where they can earn a rate of return high enough to compensate them for the perceived level of risk. National and international market imperfections provide these opportunities.

Although a strong economic and business rationale exists for the success of multinational firms, they must live with host country economic, political, social, and religious goals and the potential for conflict with such goals. Thus, maximizing the value of the multinational firms for the benefit of their shareholders may conflict with concepts of national sovereignty, which nearly always override the rights of individual firms, multinational or domestic. Therefore, in choosing operational financial goals and making policy decisions to implement these goals, financial executives of multinational firms must recognize the institutional, cultural, and political differences among host countries, which in turn lead to different national perceptions of the "proper" goals of a business entity.

Differing viewpoints on financial goals can cause friction within a multinational firm if local managers are citizens of the host country. Such managers are often experienced only in local business norms. Additionally they will have, quite naturally and correctly, a degree of loyalty to host country aspirations. The suitability of merger or joint-venture partners across national borders depends partly on how the importance of market value is perceived by the potential partners. Other corporate goals may be preferred by a firm located in a country where equity markets are very imperfect and market value nearly impossible to determine, and where society does not appropriately value the contribution of the stockholder. Indeed, the choice between stockholder wealth maximization and other goals of financial management is a value judgement that differs among managers in different countries.

FLUCTUATING EXCHANGE RATES

An understanding of foreign exchange risk is essential for managers and investors in today's environment of volatile foreign exchange rates. The present international monetary system is characterized by a mix of floating and managed exchange rate policies pursued by each nation in its own best interest. As we will describe in Chapter 2, some currencies are tied to the U.S. dollar, some to the European Economic Community (EEC) currencies, some to the Japanese yen, some to the U.K. pound, and some are floating freely without a reference currency. This rather complex system has led to violent shifts in the relative value of various currencies, with a consequent gain or loss in relative purchasing power.

When a currency increases in relative value, such as was the case for the U.S. dollar between 1981 and 1985, exports from the United States decline because their prices become too high when converted to the currency of the foreign importer. Likewise, imports into the United States increase because they cost less in U.S. dollar terms when converting from a foreign currency. The loss of exports hurts gross national product and employment in the United States, but low-cost imports benefit consumers and help keep a lid on inflation. Thus any firm that exports or imports, or even a domestic firm that competes against imports, is directly affected by changes in the value of the U.S. dollar. All firms must understand foreign exchange risk in order to anticipate increased competition from imports or to realize increased opportunities for exports.

Multinational firms have the advantage of being geographically diversified. They need to understand foreign exchange risk in order to shift production to countries with relatively undervalued currencies and to promote sales in countries with overvalued currencies. They also typically have access to international sources of funds. The relative cost of these funds, after considering exchange rate effects, is likely to change, thereby giving multinational firms an opportunity to lower their cost of capital.

An understanding of foreign exchange risk is also important for portfolio investors. As will be shown in Chapter 13, opportunities exist to diversify a portfolio internationally to take advantage of exchange rate changes and differing security market performances in other countries. The net result of international portfolio diversification has often meant an improved portfolio return and a reduction in portfolio risk.

GLOBAL MONEY AND CAPITAL MARKET INTEGRATION

During the past decade an explosive growth has occurred in international portfolio investment. This growth has been fueled in part by a trend toward liberalizing securities markets in the most important world capital markets. The United States was the first to liberalize, after the Securities and Exchange Commission pressured the investment community to adopt negotiated rather than fixed commissions when executing securities trades. Subsequently the EEC countries have adopted rules that should eventually lead to an integrated money and capital market, although their capital markets are not yet liberalized to the extent of those in the United States. The "Big Bang" of October 1986 was the U.K. version of capital market liberalization. Not only were commissions to be negotiated but the basic structure of the market was made more competitive. This change included encouraging competition from foreign securities firms located in the United Kingdom.

Even the Japanese capital market, which now equals or exceeds the U.S. market in size in some categories (equity markets, for example), has been slowly liberalized. Foreign firms have been admitted to the Tokyo Stock Exchange. Japanese banks and securities firms have been permitted almost free rein to compete abroad. Restrictions on the use of yen as an international currency have been eased and foreign firms may raise capital in Japan.

Although global integration is well started, many restrictions on the free flow of capital still exist. Furthermore, performances of stock and bond markets vary widely among countries and over time. Therefore opportunities still exist for a portfolio investor to benefit from diversifying internationally.

ORGANIZATION OF THE BOOK

The material in this book is organized in five parts, which are briefly described in the following pages.

The International Financial Environment

Part 1 describes the international financial environment in order to provide the background needed for understanding how to manage foreign exchange risk arising from volatile exchange rates.

Chapter 2 describes the international monetary system as it has evolved since World War II. The historical volatility of exchange rates (trend 2) is illustrated. Contemporary exchange rate realities, such as the European Monetary System (EMS) and world monetary system reform are explained.

The first part of Chapter 3 explains how the balance of payments is measured and how to interpret various measures of the surplus or deficit. The second part of the chapter covers imbalances in trade and capital accounts for both developed and developing countries. The chapter concludes with a discussion of the external debt problem of a number of developing countries, particularly those located in Latin America.

Chapter 4 describes the institutions and processes which collectively comprise the foreign exchange market. The Eurocurrency market is introduced. The linkage between interest rates and exchange rates, known as *interest rate parity*, is explained.

Chapter 5 describes the foreign exchange futures and options markets and their use by traders and speculators. (Their use for commercial hedging purposes is analyzed later, in Chapter 8.)

Foreign Exchange Risk Management

Part 2 covers all aspects of foreign exchange risk management from the viewpoints of the multinational firm, importers, exporters, and investors.

Chapter 6 explains how one might, in theory and in practice, forecast changes in exchange rates for both the short-run and long-run time horizons. It also continues the explanation of the economic parity conditions, which link prices, interest rates, and exchange rates.

Chapter 7 explains how the multinational firm should measure and manage operating (economic) exposure—the potential for the firm's value to change as the result of an unexpected change in exchange rates, as it affects future cash flows.

Chapter 8 analyzes the various ways of managing transaction exposure, or the potential impact of an exchange rate change on obligations already incurred. It describes hedging in the forward, money, futures, options and swap markets. Also covered are operating strategies that act as hedges.

Chapter 9 explains how a multinational firm measures and manages accounting (translation) exposure, which is the potential for accounting-derived changes in owners' equity. Various foreign exchange translation methods are described and compared.

Financing from a Global Perspective

Part 3 analyzes how multinational firms can lower their cost of capital by sourcing funds in global money and capital markets.

Chapter 10 describes the role played by international banks in providing access to short and medium term debt, particularly in the Eurocurrency market, and how excesses in this activity led to the so-called "LDC debt problem." The chapter also includes a description of the types of banking offices and services which are available to service multinational firms.

Chapter 11 describes how firms can tap international debt markets. Major sources of funds include syndicated loans, Euronotes, international bonds, and swaps. The effect of foreign exchange risk on the cost of debt is analyzed.

Chapter 12 describes how firms can tap international equity markets. The trend toward global integration, compared to still existing equity market differences, is discussed.

Chapter 13 analyzes the investor strategy of international portfolio diversification. It includes a discussion of the theoretical rationale for such a strategy and an example of historical results. This chapter was written by Cheol Eun, who is an expert in this field. For nonfinance majors it may be a little heavy going, but it is well worth the effort. It is also the only chapter in the book written from the perspective of an investor, rather than from that of a multinational firm.

Chapter 14 prescribes how a multinational firm can take advantage of the international availability of capital, and lingering market segmentation, to reduce its cost of capital. A firm's optimal overall consolidated financial structure, as well as the financial structures of its foreign affiliates, are analyzed.

Direct Foreign Investment Decisions

Part 4 covers all aspects of the direct foreign investment decision, including corporate foreign entry strategy, political risk assessment, and capital budgeting for a foreign project.

Chapter 15 describes what motivates firms to invest abroad. It analyzes various foreign entry strategies including exports, licensing, management contracts, joint ventures, cross-border acquisitions, and "greenfield" direct investments.

Chapter 16 analyzes how firms assess political risk prior to entry to a foreign market. Potential goal conflicts between multinational firms and host countries are analyzed. Various strategies to minimize political risk are described.

Chapter 17 analyzes how capital budgeting for a foreign project differs from capital budgeting for a domestic project. The main differences are caused by foreign exchange risk, political risk, and taxes. Another complication is the need to evaluate two rates of return. One is the local return from the viewpoint of the foreign project itself. The other is the parent's return from repatriated cash flows.

Management of Ongoing Operations

Part 5 covers how to manage ongoing operations of the multinational firm.

Chapter 18 covers all aspects of trade financing. This topic includes documentation, such as letters of credit, drafts, and bills of lading. Also covered are specialized trade financing topics, such as export credit insurance and countertrade.

Chapter 19 covers all aspects of working capital management. It analyzes how firms move funds internationally, given such constraints as differential taxes, political risk, and foreign exchange risk. The concept of unbundling cash transfers in the form of royalties, fees, and overhead is described. Also analyzed are the transfer pricing problem, how to deal with blocked funds, how to manage cash balances with centralized depositories and multilateral netting centers, how to manage receivables, and how to control inventory.

Chapter 20 analyzes the complexities of international performance evaluation and control. The impact of foreign exchange rate changes and inflation on performance evaluation is emphasized. The chapter also covers comparative accounting and financial statement analysis. International differences in accounting practices, degree of disclosure, and auditing standards are discussed. The use and misuse of international ratio analysis is highlighted.

Chapter 21 analyzes the influence of taxes on international decision-making. The discussion includes comparative corporate tax rates, exclusions, and the wide use of value-added taxes outside the United States. The chapter concludes with a description of parent country taxation of foreign-source income and an Appendix which describes the U.S. system as revised in 1986.

Economic Focus: "Come Back Multinationals"*

The flow of foreign direct investment by multinational companies was five times greater, at $50 billion, in 1986 than it was 15 years earlier. In the early 1970s any prediction of such growth would have provoked fresh demands for a United Nations "code of conduct" to control the behaviour of what were then widely labeled as exploitative giants.

No longer. The UN still wants such a code, but its most recent report on the activities of what it calls "transnational corporations" stresses the good that such companies do. Third-world governments are coming to appreciate the employment, skills, exports and import-substitutes that they deliver.

The developing world's resentment of the direct investment of multinationals once stemmed from these companies' very rationale for setting up factories broad. One of their reasons was to gain better access to foreign markets: this was construed as a threat to crowd-out local firms. Their second reason was the quest for lower manufacturing costs: this was exploitation. The fact that a search for fickle comparative advantage led such companies to invest abroad was taken to imply a lack of commitment to the society and employment of the host country.

The UN report debunks many of these bogeyman assumptions. One old bogey was *size*—the idea that multinationals are always big, powerful and liable to abuse their power. Although giant corporations certainly account for a large share of the world economy, smaller companies are nowadays just as likely as big ones to invest abroad.

The 600 biggest companies in the world—the "billion dollar club" because their annual sales exceed $1 billion—still create a fifth of the world's total value-added in manufacturing and agriculture. But half of the world's companies that have operations abroad are small or medium-sized. Japan and Britain were two of the world's largest exporters of capital in the first half of the 1980s: 23% of Japanese "multinationals" employed fewer than 300 people in 1984; and in 1981 78% of the British firms with direct investments overseas employed fewer than 500. The smallest company in the billion-dollar club (America's Pennwalt Corporation) has, in contrast, nearly 10,000 employees.

Multinationals increase *employment* in their host countries. The UN's conservative estimate of direct employment by multinationals is 65m, or 3% of the world's labour force. Add indirect employment, such as jobs created by suppliers and by the general lift to an economy that multinationals can provide—and such companies may generate 6% of world employment. American multinationals employed almost 6.5m people abroad in 1984, 32% of these in developing countries, 42% in Europe, 5% in Japan, and 14% in Canada.

Foreign investors increase a host country's *output* and *exports*. This is especially important for developing, or newly industrialising, countries which need fast growth and foreign exchange to service bank debt. Foreign-owned companies accounted for 55% of Singapore's employment in manufacturing industry in 1982, 63% of its manufacturing output and 90% of its exports of manufactured goods. They produced 70% of Zimbabwe's industrial output. In 1983 nearly 30% of Argentina's manufacturing output and exports came from multinationals. It is often easier for a multinational to export than for an indigenous firm to do so. It has better distribution and marketing networks overseas, and can sometimes circumvent protectionism in other countries more effectively.

Such truths are hitting home; but there is still some third-world resistance to multinationals in the service industries. This is a pity, because the UN report shows that services are taking an increasing share of multinationals' foreign direct investment—particularly, but not only, within the rich countries. Services' share of America's outward investment rose from 24% in 1975 to 34% in 1985; from 29% to 35% of Britain's; and from 36% to 52% of Japan's. They accounted for 19% of Mexico's inward foreign investment in 1971, then 23% in 1981; for 20% of foreign investment in Nigeria in 1975, then 37% in 1982.

Exportable Services

Why the sensitivity? Despite huge foreign earnings from hotels, services often seem less exportable than goods. Although services like insurance can be exported, meals in restaurants, health care and local transport network cannot. Investment in services by a foreign company then appears to offer the prospect of outflows of profit, not accompanied by an increase in exports or inflows of high-tech skills. The UN also reports a "widespread impression that service industries consist largely of technologically stagnant, small-scale personal services based on unskilled labour working with little capital in ways that have not changed for many years."

The impression is wrong. The UN says that service multinationals bring with them what it calls "soft technology"—the skills required to run an efficient business. They train much of the skilled labour that they need locally, rather than import it. They often give these workers more of the sorts of skills that can usefully be hired by indigenous rival companies. By contrast, skills taught in manufacturing are sometimes appropriate only to a sophisticated multinational. The local subsidiaries of service multinationals are, the UN finds, more "complete and free-standing" than those in manufacturing, precisely because they add their value *in situ*.

The report shows how often exporting industries can be hobbled by inefficient services. A study of 17 developing countries found that, while the average price of a range of labour-intensive services was only 60% that in America, the prices of high-technology services (such as electricity, air transport and telecommunications) were often over twice the American level, despite subsidies. This handicaps industry. While these countries had an average GDP per head that was 20% of the American level, their spending per head on telecoms was only 1% of America's.

Slowly the message is registering: the best multinational code for the third world may well be the one that you can dial, and that gets you through.

1. Multinational Firms in the Local Area

Make a list and try to find some facts about the most important multinational firms in your state, province, or other local political entity. How important is international business (sales, assets, profit, etc.) to these firms?

2. Global Money, Capital Market Integration and Local Firms

With reference to your list of multinational firms identified in question 1, try to discover the extent to which they have used international capital markets to raise funds.

3. Imports and Exports

Identify the major imports and exports of your state, province, or other local political entity. List the countries with which you trade in order of importance.

4. Come Back Multinationals: The Crowding-Out Effect

The anecdote at the end of Chapter 1 entitled "Come Back Multinationals" discussed the changing world attitude toward multinational corporations. What evidence is cited which sheds new light on the old attitudes that multinational companies crowd-out local firms and exploit their host countries?

5. Come Back Multinationals: Exportable Services

Many of the industrialized countries in the world saw a shift in employment from the manufacturing to the service sector in the 1980s. What are the arguments for and against the role played by multinational firms in promoting direct foreign investment in host-country service sectors?

BIBLIOGRAPHY

Aliber, Robert F., *The International Money Game*, 5th ed., New York: Basic Books, 1987.

Choi, Frederick D. S., "International Data Sources for Empirical Research in Financial Management," *Financial Management*, Summer 1988, pp. 80–98.

Curhan, J. P., W. H. Davidson, and R. Suri, *Tracing the Multinationals*, Cambridge, Mass.: Ballinger, 1977.

Dufey, Gunter, and Ian Giddy, *50 Cases in International Finance*, Reading, Mass.: Addison-Wesley, 1986.

George, Abraham, and Ian H. Giddy, *International Finance Handbook*, Vols. 1 and 2, New York: Wiley, 1983.

Holland, John, *International Financial Management*, New York and Oxford, U.K.: Basil Blackwell, 1986.

Investing, Licensing and Trading Conditions Abroad, New York: Business International, a reference service that is continually updated.

Learner, Edward E., *Sources of International Comparative Advantage*, Cambridge, Mass.: MIT Press, 1986.

Lessard, Donald R., *International Financial Management*, 2nd ed., Theory and Application, New York: Wiley, 1987.

——, "Global Competition and Corporate Finance in the 1990s," *Journal of Applied Corporate Finance*, vol. 3, no. 4, Winter 1991, pp. 59–72.

Levi, Maurice, *International Finance: Financial Management and the International Economy*, 2nd ed., New York: McGraw-Hill, 1990.

Levich, Richard M., "Recent International Financial Innovations: Implications for Financial Management," *Journal of International Financial Management and Accounting*, volume 1, no. 1, Spring 1989, pp. 1–14.

Madura, Jeff, *International Financial Management*, 2nd ed., St. Paul, Minn.: West Publishing, 1989.

Recent Trends in International Direct Investment, Washington, D.C.: OECD, 1987.

Robbins, Sidney M., and Robert B. Stobaugh, *Money in the Multinational Enterprise*, New York: Basic Books, 1973.

Robock, Stefan H., and Kenneth Simmonds, *International Business and Multinational Enterprises*, 3rd ed., Homewood, Ill.: Irwin, 1987.

Root, Franklin R., *International Trade and Investment*, 6th ed., Cincinnati: Southwestern, 1987.

Shapiro, Alan C., *Multinational Financial Management*, 4th ed., Boston: Allyn and Bacon, 1989.

Solnik, Bruno, *International Investments*, 2nd ed., Reading, Mass.: Addison-Wesley, 1991.

Stonehill, Arthur, Theo Beekhuisen, Richard Wright, Lee Remmers, Norman Toy, Antonio Parés, Alan Shapiro, Douglas Egan, and Thomas Bates, "Financial Goals and Debt Ratio Determinants: A Survey of Practice in Five Countries," *Financial Management*, Autumn 1975, pp. 27–41.

Stonehill, Arthur, and David Eiteman, *Finance: An International Perspective*, Homewood, Ill.: Irwin, 1987.

Toyne, Brian, "International Exchange: A Foundation for Theory Building in International Business," *Journal of International Business Studies*, Spring 1989, pp. 1–17.

Vernon, Raymond, *Storm over the Multinationals*, Cambridge, Mass.: Harvard University Press, 1977.

——, and Louis T. Wells, Jr., *Manager in the International Economy*, 4th ed., Englewood Cliffs, N.J.: Prentice-Hall, 1987.

Walmsley, Julian, *Dictionary of International Finance*, 2nd ed., New York: Wiley, 1985.

Wilkins, Mira, *The Maturing of Multinational Enterprise*, Cambridge, Mass.: Harvard University Press, 1974.

Zenoff, David B., ed., *Corporate Finance in Multinational Companies*, London: Euromoney Publications, 1987.

DIRECTORIES OF MULTINATIONAL FIRMS

American Export Register, New York: Thomas International Publishing, Annual.

American Register of Exporters and Importers, New York: American Register of Exporters and Importers Corporation, Annual.

Angel, Juvenal L., *Directory of American Firms Operating in Foreign Countries*, periodic editions, New York: Uniworld Business Publications.

Directory of United States Importers, New York: The Journal of Commerce, Biannual.

The Theory of Comparative Advantage

The theory of comparative advantage and its corollary, the theory of factor proportions, provide a basis for explaining and justifying international trade in a model world assumed to enjoy free trade, perfect competition, no uncertainty, costless information, and no government interference. The theory contains the following features:

- Exporters in country A sell goods or services to unrelated importers in country B (any other country).

- Firms in country A specialize in making products that can be relatively efficiently produced, given country A's endowment of factors of production, that is, land, labor, capital, and technology. Firms in country B do likewise, given the factors of production found in country B. In this way the total combined output of A and B is maximized.

- Since the factors of production cannot be freely moved from country A to country B, the benefits of specialization are realized through international trade.

- How the benefits of the extra production are shared depends on the terms of trade. Each share is determined by supply and demand in perfectly competitive markets in the two countries. Neither country A nor B is worse off than before trade, and typically both are better off, albeit perhaps unequally.

For an example of the benefits of free trade based on comparative advantage, assume that country A is relatively efficient at producing food and country B is relatively efficient at producing cloth. Assume that each unit of production (land, labor, capital, and technology) in country A can produce either 6 tons of food or 12 yards of cloth, whereas each unit of production in country B can produce either 2 tons of food or 10 yards of cloth. In other words, a production unit in A has an absolute advantage over a production unit in B in both food and cloth. Nevertheless, country A has a larger relative advantage over country B in producing food (6 to 2) than cloth (12 to 10). As long as these ratios are unequal, comparative advantage exists.

Assume that both countries have one million units of production and the production and consumption situations before trade are as follows.

	Units of Production	Total Production (millions of tons or yards)	Total Consumption (millions of tons or yards)
Country A			
Food	700,000 X 6 =	4.2	4.2
Cloth	300,000 X 12 =	3.6	3.6
Country B			
Food	700,000 X 2 =	1.4	1.4
Cloth	300,000 X 10 =	3.0	3.0

Now assume that trade is allowed, with the barter ratio between food and cloth being 4 yards of cloth equal 1 ton of food. The barter ratio must end up between the ratios in each of the countries, since without trade nobody in country A would pay more than 2 yards of cloth for 1 ton of food, while in country B nobody would pay more than 5 yards of cloth for 1 ton of food. Assume that country A transfers all units of production from producing cloth to producing food and country B transfers all units of production from producing food to producing cloth. The resulting output is then bartered so that both countries consume more food or cloth than they consumed before trade was allowed. The new production and consumption situations after trade could be as follows.

	Units of Production	Total Production (millions of tons or yards)	Trade (millions of tons or yards)	Total Consumption (millions of tons or yards)
Country A				
Food	1,000,000 x 6 =	6.0	−1.6	4.4
Cloth	—	—	+6.4	6.4
Country B				
Food	—	—	+1.6	1.6
Cloth	1,000,000 x 10 =	10.0	−6.4	3.6

Both countries have benefitted from specializing and trading. Country A consumes 200,000 tons more of food and 2.8 million yards more of cloth. Country B consumes 200,000 tons more of food and 600,000 yards more of cloth. Total combined production of both food and cloth has increased through the specialization process, and it only remains for the exchange ratio to determine how the larger output is distributed between the countries.

Although international trade might have approached the comparative advantage model during the nineteenth century, it certainly does not today, for the following reasons:

- Countries do not appear to specialize only in those products that could be most efficiently produced by that country's particular factors of production. Instead, governments interfere with comparative advantage for a variety of economic and political reasons, such as full employment, economic development, national self-sufficiency in defense-related industries, and protection of an agricultural sector's way of life. Government interference takes the form of tariffs, quotas, and other nontariff restrictions.

- At least two of the factors of production, capital and technology, flow directly between countries rather than only indirectly through traded goods and services. This direct flow occurs between related affiliates of multinational firms, as well as between unrelated firms via loans, licenses, and management contracts.

- Although the terms of trade are ultimately determined by supply and demand, the process by which this trade occurs is different from that visualized in traditional trade theory. The terms of trade are determined partly by administered pricing in oligopolistic markets.

- Comparative advantage shifts over time as less developed countries become more developed and realize their latent opportunities. For example, comparative advantage in producing cotton textiles shifted from the United Kingdom to the United States, to Japan, to Hong Kong, to Taiwan, and to Thailand.

- The classical model of comparative advantage did not really address certain other issues such as the effect of uncertainty and information costs, the role of differentiated products in imperfectly competitive markets, and economies of scale.

Nevertheless, although the world is a long way from the classical trade model, the principle of comparative advantage is still valid. The closer the world gets to true international specialization, the more world production and consumption can be increased, provided the problem of equitable distribution of the benefits can be solved to the satisfaction of consumers, producers, and political leaders. Complete specialization, however, remains an unrealistic limiting case, just as perfect competition is a limiting case in microeconomic theory.

The 50 Largest U.S. Multinational Firms

1989 rank	Company	Revenue Foreign ($mil)	Revenue Total ($mil)	Revenue Percent foreign	Net Profit Foreign ($mil)	Net Profit Total ($mil)	Net Profit Percent foreign	Assets Foreign ($mil)	Assets Total ($mil)	Assets Percent foreign
1	Exxon	63,429	86,656	73.2	2,888	2,975	97.1	46,417	83,219	55.8
2	IBM	36,965	62,710	58.9	4,145	3,758	110.3	37,793	77,734	48.6
3	General Motors	33,768	126,932	26.6	2,952	4,224	69.9	43,576	172,899	25.2
4	Mobil	33,003	50,976	64.7	1,648	2,663	61.9	19,972	39,080	51.1
5	Ford Motor	31,964	96,146	33.2	2,208	3,835	57.6	43,218	160,695	26.9
6	Citicorp	19,877	37,970	52.3	−416	498	D-P	87,168	221,002	39.4
7	EI du Pont de Nemours	14,152	35,534	39.8	896	2,881	31.1	10,244	34,715	29.5
8	Texaco	13,710	32,416	42.3	2,054	2,942	69.8	6,827	25,636	26.6
9	ITT	10,944	25,271	43.3	453	985	46.0	11,502	48,725	23.6
10	Dow Chemical	9,516	17,600	54.1	1,127	2,499	45.1	9,943	22,166	44.9
11	Proctor & Gamble	8,529	21,398	39.9	355	1,206	29.4	5,260	16,351	32.2
12	Philip Morris Cos	7,630	39,011	19.6	560	2,946	19.0	5,714	38,528	14.8
13	Eastman Kodak	7,529	18,398	40.9	540	529	102.1	6,628	23,648	28.0
14	Digital Equipment	6,893	12,742	54.1	690	1,073	64.3	4,719	10,668	44.2
15	General Electric	6,769	54,574	12.4	773	5,703	13.6	11,346	128,344	8.8
16	United Technologies	6,501	19,757	32.9	377	763	49.4	3,901	14,598	26.7
17	Amoco	6,354	24,379	26.1	322	1,610	20.0	9,960	30,430	32.7
18	Hewlett-Packard	6,338	11,899	53.3	486	829	58.6	3,897	10,075	38.7
19	Xerox	6,093	17,635	34.6	385	856	45.0	7,657	30,088	25.4
20	Chevron	6,047	29,443	20.5	793	251	315.9	7,653	33,884	22.6
21	Chase Manhattan	6,013	13,904	43.2	−943	−665	141.8	30,948	107,369	28.8
22	American Intl Group	5,432	14,150	38.4	893	1,754	50.9	18,510	46,143	40.1
23	Minn Mining & Mfg	5,389	11,990	44.9	485	1,274	38.1	3,712	9,776	38.0
24	Unisys	4,961	10,097	49.1	44	−639	P-D	3,353	10,751	31.2
25	Motorola	4,910	9,620	51.0	304	646	47.1	2,605	7,686	33.9
26	JP Morgan & Co	4,888	10,394	47.0	−1,693	−1,275	132.8	38,663	88,964	43.5
27	Coca-Cola	4,886	8,966	54.5	819	1,193	68.7	2,840	8,283	34.3
28	Johnson & Johnson	4,876	9.757	50.0	600	1,082	55.5	3,656	7,919	46.2
29	American Express	4,859	25,047	19.4	171	1,157	14.8	28,201	130,855	21.6
30	Goodyear Tire & Rubber	4,448	10,869	40.9	95	189	50.3	3,162	8,460	37.4
31	Tenneco	4,285	14,083	30.4	198	584	33.9	4,884	17,381	28.1
32	Chrysler	4,172	34,922	11.9	181	315	57.5	5,615	51,083	11.0
33	Sears, Roebuck	4,135	53,794	7.7	67	1,509	4.4	3,171	86,972	3.6

The 50 Largest U.S. Multinational Firms (continued)

1989 rank	Company	Revenue			Net Profit			Assets		
		Foreign ($mil)	Total ($mil)	Percent foreign	Foreign ($mil)	Total ($mil)	Percent foreign	Foreign ($mil)	Total ($mil)	Percent foreign
34	Woolworth	3,790	8,820	43.0	117	329	35.6	1,697	3,907	43.4
35	Bristol-Myers Squibb	3,685	9,189	40.1	149	747	19.9	2,104	8,497	24.8
36	Bankers Trust New York	3,657	7,258	50.4	−1,188	−980	121.2	34,991	55,658	62.9
37	NCR	3,514	5,956	59.0	313	412	76.0	1,824	4,500	40.5
38	K mart	3,512	32,753	10.7	NA	323	NA	1,217	13,538	9.0
39	Aluminum Co America	3,416	10,910	31.3	1,051	1,367	76.9	4,899	11,541	42.4
40	American Brands	3,360	7,265	46.2	310	631	49.1	2,683	11,394	23.5
41	Colgate-Palmolive	3,211	5,039	63.7	157	280	56.1	1,672	3,536	47.3
42	Sara Lee	3,201	11,718	27.3	190	410	46.3	2,854	6,523	43.8
43	BankAmerica	3,195	11,389	28.1	−477	820	D-P	21,268	98,764	21.5
44	Bank of Boston	3,114	6,844	45.5	97	70	138.6	6,185	36,492	16.9
45	Monsanto	3,091	8,681	35.6	294	679	43.3	2,449	8,604	28.5
46	Merck	3,064	6,551	46.8	397	1,495	26.6	2,146	6,757	31.8
47	Whirlpool	3,032	6,808	44.5	93	215	43.3	1,944	5,436	35.8
48	Manufacturers Hanover	2,996	8,300	36.1	−919	−588	156.3	24,067	60,479	39.8
49	Caterpillar	2,993	11,126	26.9	97	968	10.0	2,116	10,926	19.4
50	Union Carbide	2,951	8,744	33.7	91	573	15.9	3,250	8,546	38.0

Source: Excerpted by permission of *Forbes* magazine, July 23, 1990. © Forbes Inc., 1990.

The 50 Largest Non–U.S. Multinational Firms

1989 rank	Company	Country	Rev. ($mil)	Net Inc. ($mil)	Assets ($mil)	Market Value ($mil)	Empl. (thou)
1	Sumitomo Corp	Japan	158,221	350	35,681	9,331	13.0
2	C Itoh & Co Ltd	Japan	147,106	246	48,156	8,904	10.0
3	Mitsui & Co Ltd	Japan	136,578	255	61,169	10,455	10.8
4	Marubeni Corp	Japan	131,419	235	51,889	8,256	7.3
5	Mitsubishi Corp	Japan	129,689	423	74,288	16,719	32.0
6	Nissho Iwai Corp	Japan	108,118	129	28,077	4,799	7.2
7	Royal Dutch/Shell	Holland	85,536	6,483	90,503	66,933	135.0
8	Toyota Motor Corp	Japan	61,052	2,634	49,639	50,477	91.8
9	Hitachi Ltd	Japan	49,557	1,477	49,650	33,066	290.8
10	British Petroleum Co	UK	48,602	2,860	50,758	29,495	119.9
11	Toyo Menka Kaisha	Japan	45,055	47	13,480	3,690	3.3
12	Nichimen Corp	Japan	42,989	64	13,872	2,237	2.8
13	Nippon Tel & Tel	Japan	42,166	1,917	72,655	118,881	283.3
14	Matsushita Electric	Japan	42,030	1,652	49,944	29,655	198.3
15	Daimler-Benz Group	Germany	40,633	3,420	36,952	22,498	368.2
16	Nissan Motor Co Ltd	Japan	39,525	812	36,546	19,941	129.5
17	Kanematsu Corp	Japan	39,219	61	11,144	1,312	2.7
18	Fiat Group	Italy	38,044	2,412	40,492	17,850	289.3
19	Volkswagen Group	Germany	34,760	523	33,496	11,358	250.6
20	Siemens Group	Germany	32,676	787	34,470	21,214	365.0
21	Unilever	Holland	31,256	1,532	20,720	22,081	300.0
22	Toshiba Corp	Japan	29,757	924	32,960	22,926	125.0
23	Dai-Ichi Kangyo Bank	Japan	29,628	1,015	437,437	49,606	18.5
24	Nestlé	Switz	29,341	1,473	22,897	22,666	196.9
25	Tokyo Electric Power	Japan	28,636	518	77,645	41,709	39.6
26	Sanwa Bank Ltd	Japan	27,587	1,134	399,980	45,632	13.6
27	Mitsubishi Bank Ltd	Japan	27,019	998	354,290	47,199	14.5
28	Honda Motor Co Ltd	Japan	26,976	572	18,090	11,366	57.2
29	Philips Group	Holland	26,972	646	28,708	4,992	304.8
30	Sumitomo Bank Ltd	Japan	26,815	1,620	409,448	55,854	16.0
31	VEBA Group	Germany	26,174	672	20,362	11,087	94.7
32	Barclays Plc	UK	25,571	741	204,861	10,631	116.5
33	BASF Group	Germany	25,328	1,072	20,689	9,923	137.0
34	Hoechst Group	Germany	24,413	1,026	19,637	9,595	169.3
35	NEC Corp	Japan	24,113	597	23,435	20,465	114.6

The 50 Largest Non–U.S. Multinational Firms (continued)

1989 rank	Company	Country	Rev. ($mil)	Net Inc. ($mil)	Assets ($mil)	Market Value ($mil)	Empl. (thou)
36	National Westminster	UK	24,067	382	186,559	9,426	113.0
37	Crédit Lyonnais	France	24,003	491	210,727	4,222	61.5
38	Peugeot Groupe SA	France	23,981	1,614	16,151	7,209	158.1
39	Elf Aquitaine Group	France	23,510	1,129	33,181	13,685	78.0
40	Banco do Brasil	Brazil	23,120	97	82,694	598	134.3
41	Bayer Group	Germany	23,031	1,108	21,967	11,954	78.2
42	Générale d'Elec	France	22,570	774	30,943	11,404	210.0
43	Suez Group	France	22,538	636	125,163	9,702	75.0
44	Fuji Bank Ltd	Japan	22,353	1,420	367,187	53,207	15.0
45	Imperial Chemical	UK	21,595	1,525	18,096	13,997	133.8
46	BNP Group	France	21,235	535	231,463	5,019	60.3
47	RWE Group	Germany	20,995	339	21,967	11,954	78.2
48	Mitsubishi Electric	Japan	20,839	537	20,492	13,960	85.7
49	Nippon Steel Corp	Japan	20,543	609	26,285	28,193	57.2
50	Asea Brown Boveri	Switz	20,442	586	24,051	14,099	189.5

Source: Excerpted by permission of *Forbes* magazine, July 23, 1990. © Forbes Inc., 1990.

The International Monetary System

The increased volatility of exchange rates since 1973 was identified in Chapter 1 as one of the three main economic trends of the past 20 years. Under the current system of partly floating and partly fixed exchange rates, the earnings of multinational firms, banks, and individual investors have been subjected to significant real and paper fluctuations as a result of changes in relative exchange rates. Policies to forecast and react to exchange rate fluctuations are still evolving as understanding of the functioning of the international monetary system grows, as accounting rules for foreign exchange gains and losses become clarified, and as the economic effect of exchange rate changes on future cash flows and market values becomes recognized.

One of the three main themes outlined in Chapter 1 was that while volatile exchange rates may increase risk, they also create profit opportunities for both firms and investors, given a proper understanding of exchange risk management. However, in order to manage foreign exchange risk, management must first understand how the international monetary system has evolved over time and how it functions today. The international monetary system is defined in this book as the structure within which foreign exchange rates are determined, international trade and capital flows accommodated, and balance of payments adjustments made. These topics are analyzed in the remainder of this chapter, as well as the following three chapters.

HISTORY OF THE INTERNATIONAL MONETARY SYSTEM

The Gold Standard, 1876–1913

From the days of the Pharaohs (about 3000 B.C.) gold was used as a medium of exchange and a store of value. The Greeks and Romans used gold coins and passed on this tradition through the mercantile era to the nineteenth century. The great increase in trade during the free-trade period of the late nineteenth century led to a need for a more formalized system for settling international trade balances. Although there were no multilateral agreements such as exist today, one country after another declared a par value for its currency in terms of gold and then tried to adhere to the so-called "rules of the game" of what came to be known later as the classical gold standard. The gold standard as an international monetary system gained acceptance in Western Europe in the 1870s. The United States was something of a latecomer to the system, not officially adopting the standard until 1879.

The "rules of the game" under the gold standard were clear and simple. Each country would establish the rate at which its currency (paper or coin) could be converted to a weight of gold. The United States for example, declared the dollar to be convertible to gold at a rate of $20.67/ounce of gold (in effect until the beginning of World War I). The British pound was pegged at £4.2474/ounce of gold. Therefore the dollar-pound exchange rate could be determined as follows:

$$\frac{\$20.67/\text{ounce of gold}}{£4.2474/\text{ounce of gold}} = \$4.86656/£.$$

Each country's government then agreed to buy or sell gold at its own fixed parity rate on demand. This served as a mechanism to preserve the value of each individual currency in terms of gold, and therefore the fixed parities between currencies. Under this system it was therefore very important for a country to maintain adequate reserves of gold in order to back its currency's value. The system also had the effect of implicitly limiting the rate at which any individual country could expand its supply of money. The growth in money was limited to the rate at which additional gold could be acquired by official authorities. The gold standard worked adequately until World War I interrupted trade flows and the free movement of gold. This caused the main trading nations to suspend the operation of the gold standard.

The Inter-War Years, 1914–1944

During World War I and the early 1920s, currencies were allowed to fluctuate over fairly wide ranges in terms of gold and each other. Theoretically it was expected that supply and demand for a country's exports and imports would cause moderate changes in its exchange rate about a central equilibrium value. This was the same function that the gold flow performed under the previous gold standard. Unfortunately, flexible exchange rates did not work in an equilibrating manner. On the contrary, international speculators sold the weak currencies short, causing them to fall further in value than warranted by the real economic factors. The reverse happened with strong currencies. Fluctuations in currency values could not be offset by the relatively thin forward exchange market except at exorbitant cost. The net result was that the volume of world trade did not grow in the 1920s in proportion to world gross national product (GNP) and declined to a very low level with the advent of the Depression in the 1930s.

Several attempts were made to return to the gold standard. The United States returned to gold in 1919, the United Kingdom in 1925, and France in 1928. The revaluation of the

British pound in April of 1925 to \$4.86656/£ (pre-war parity) resulted in increased unemployment and economic stagnation in the U.K., all in order to restore confidence in the exchange rate system. The problem of finding reasonably stable new parity values for gold was never really solved before the collapse of the Austrian banking system in 1931 caused most trading nations to abandon the gold standard once again.

The United States returned to a modified gold standard in 1934 when the U.S. dollar was devalued to \$35/oz. of gold from the previous \$20.67/oz. in effect prior to World War I. Although the U.S. returned to the standard, gold was traded only with foreign central banks, not private citizens. From 1934 to the end of World War II, exchange rates were theoretically determined by each currency's value in terms of gold. During World War II and its immediate aftermath many of the main trading currencies lost their convertibility into other currencies. The dollar was the only major trading currency that continued to be convertible.

The Bretton Woods Agreement, 1944

A so-called gold exchange standard was adopted by the Allied Powers as a result of negotiations at Bretton Woods, New Hampshire, in 1944. The agreement established an international monetary system which was in essence a dollar-based system. The agreement also provided for the establishment of institutions for aiding countries in their balance of payments and exchange rate policies (The International Monetary Fund (IMF)) and in general economic development (the International Bank for Reconstruction and Development (World Bank)).[1]

Under the provisions of the Bretton Woods Agreement, all countries were to fix the value of their currencies in terms of gold but were not required to exchange their currencies for gold. Only the dollar remained convertible into gold (at \$35 per ounce). Therefore all countries decided what they wished their exchange rates to be vis-à-vis the dollar, then calculated what the gold par value of their currencies should be to give the desired dollar exchange rate. All participating countries agreed to try to maintain the value of their currencies within 1% of par by buying or selling foreign exchange or gold as needed. Devaluation was not to be used as a competitive trade policy, but if a currency became too weak to defend, a devaluation of up to 10% would be allowed without formal approval by the IMF. Larger devaluations required the IMF's approval.

The International Monetary Fund

The IMF was established to render temporary assistance to countries trying to defend their currencies against cyclical, seasonal, or random occurrences. The IMF can also assist a country having structural trade problems if the country is taking adequate steps to correct its problems. However, if persistent deficits occur, the IMF cannot save a country from eventual devaluation. The Soviet Union participated in the Bretton Woods meeting, as one of the Allied Powers, but eventually it chose not to join either the International Monetary Fund or the World Bank.

To carry out its task, the IMF was originally funded by each member subscribing to a quota based on expected post-World War II trade patterns.[2] The quotas have since been expanded and the distribution revised a number of times to accommodate the growth in overall world trade, new additions to IMF membership, and growth in importance of the exporting countries. The original quotas were paid 25% in gold or dollars and 75% in local currencies. Any member could borrow back up to its original 25% gold or convertible-currency payment, called the "gold tranche," in any 12-month period, plus 100% of its total quota. Thus a member was able to borrow 125% of its quota in convertible currencies or gold even though it only paid in 25% in convertible currencies or gold. The IMF imposed restrictions on borrowing beyond the first 25% of quota to ensure that steps were being taken to correct the borrower's currency problems.

Over the years access to IMF loans has been gradually liberalized. Under the guidelines presently in effect, each of the 151 member countries can borrow annually up to 150% of its quota, or up to 450% during a three-year period. Cumulative access, net of scheduled repayments, could be up to 600% of a member's quota.

Relative distribution of quotas is important as a determinant of the relative distribution of voting power. The industrialized countries have always maintained voting control, since they have subscribed to a majority of the quotas. At the present time the United States holds a little over 19.1% of voting control. Other large voting rights are held by the United Kingdom (6.6%), West Germany (5.8%), France (4.8%), Japan (4.5%), Saudi Arabia (3.5%), and Canada (3.2%).[3]

In addition to its quota resources, which were expanded to $180 billion in 1990, the IMF currently has access under certain circumstances to funds that it can borrow from the major industrialized countries. Under the General Arrangements to Borrow (GAB) and associated agreements, the IMF can use the borrowed funds not only to help the GAB members over temporary exchange problems but also to assist nonmembers, such as countries with heavy external debt burdens.

Convertible Currencies and Reserves

During the post-World War II era the various central banks held gold, dollars, pounds sterling, other convertible trading currencies, and "special drawing rights" (to be explained shortly) as reserves to help them maintain their currency value. Since a country's gold tranche could be withdrawn automatically from the IMF, countries considered it part of their reserves. Since the supply of monetary gold and the gold tranche remained virtually constant after 1949, most of the growth in world monetary reserves from $46 billion in 1949 to $117 billion in 1971 was due to increased holdings of foreign exchange (mainly dollars).

Formation of the EEC in 1957 and the European Free Trade Area (EFTA) in 1959, as well as the concurrent return of the major trading nations to full convertibility, caused a rapid increase in trade and direct foreign investment. The year 1959 also marked the beginning of large deficits in the U.S. balance of payments, but it was not until the early 1960s that an international monetary reserve dilemma was recognized.[4] Virtually all the newly mined gold (about $1 billion per year) was being absorbed by commercial users or lost to hoarders. The only way that international monetary reserves could increase in step with the increase in trade and foreign investment was for the reserve-currency countries to run deficits in their balance of payments so that other countries received more reserve currencies than they paid out.

Unfortunately, as some of the reserve-currency countries ran deficits, especially the United States, the United Kingdom, and France, a credibility gap developed. Monetary speculators and central bankers began to doubt the ability of these reserve-currency countries to continue to convert their currency into gold (in the case of dollars) and dollars (in the case of nondollar reserve currencies). Evidence of this distrust manifested itself on the London free market in wide fluctuations in the price of gold above the $35 per ounce official rate and in the drain of gold and foreign exchange from the deficit countries.

The United Kingdom was forced to devalue the pound by over 14% in 1967 after several years of crisis and rumored devaluation. The pound fell from $2.80/£ to $2.40/£. France devalued the franc in 1969. The United States reacted to its continuing balance of payments deficits in 1963 by levying an interest equalization tax on foreign borrowing in U.S. capital markets. This tax effectively forced foreign borrowers to raise long-term capital elsewhere and hastened the development of the Eurobond market. As U.S. balance of payments deficits continued, voluntary controls on new dollar capital outflows from U.S. firms were imposed in 1965. These controls were followed in 1968 by mandatory controls on direct foreign investment by U.S. firms and credit restraint on foreign lending by U.S. banks. Despite these precautions the U.S. balance of payments position continued to worsen and credibility deteriorated until the crisis of 1971.

Official Currency Swaps. Official currency swaps provided a temporary supplement to international monetary reserves during the 1960s.[5] Swap agreements were negotiated among the central banks of the "Group of Ten" most industrialized countries. Instant reserves were created by a swap of credit lines between central banks. For example, if the United Kingdom were losing gold to West Germany, the Bank of England could create a pound sterling credit in favor of the Bundesbank (Germany's Central Bank) and the Bundesbank in turn would create a Deutschemark credit in favor of the Bank of England. The Bank of England would then use the Deutschemarks to buy pounds, but the Bundesbank would not draw on its pound line of credit. Thus there would be an upward buying pressure on the pound and an excess supply of Deutschemarks, causing, it was hoped, a return flow of gold or dollars to the United Kingdom. When this return flow occurred, the Deutschemarks were repaid to the Bundesbank and the swap retired. The problem of a need for growth in permanent reserves to maintain the ratio of reserves to world trade was not solved, however.

Special Drawing Rights. A more lasting solution to the need for growth in world monetary reserves was started with the creation of "special drawing rights" on the IMF. In late 1967, at Rio de Janeiro, agreement was reached in principle on a system whereby the IMF would create new reserves called special drawing rights (SDRs) and distribute them to each member country in proportion to that member's quota. Creation of these reserves would be in an amount sufficient to maintain the proportion of reserves to world trade. SDRs would be exchanged only among central banks, and would be convertible into other currency but not directly into gold. The IMF issued the first SDRs in 1970, and by mid-1990 a total of a little more than SDR 20 billion (U.S. $26 billion) were outstanding, representing about 4% of world international reserves other than gold.

The SDR's value was originally based on the average value of a basket of 16 major trading currencies weighted according to their importance in world trade. The first SDR unit was equal to one U.S. dollar, but the SDR fluctuates in value relative to the U.S. dollar, depending on the relative performance of the individual currencies.

On January 1, 1981, the basket of currencies was officially reduced from 16 to 5. One SDR unit equaled $1.27174 both before and after conversion to the new valuation system. Once the U.S. dollar/SDR exchange rate is established, the value of any other currency in terms of the SDR can be determined by using its market rate vis-à-vis the dollar and then converting to SDRs using the U.S. dollar/SDR rate. SDR rates for more than 40 currencies are calculated and announced daily by the IMF. As of June 1991 one SDR was worth a little over $1.32.

Eurodollars and Other Eurocurrencies

A Eurodollar is a U.S. dollar time deposit in a bank legally resident outside the United States. The bank may be a foreign bank, the overseas branch of a U.S. bank, or a special entity called an International Banking Facility (IBF). IBFs will be described in more detail in Chapter 10. For the moment it is sufficient to note that they are physically located in the United States in parent bank facilities but are treated by both federal and state governments as if they were located abroad.

Eurodollar time deposit maturities range from call money and overnight funds to longer periods; certificates of deposit are usually for three months or more and in million-dollar increments. Note that a Eurodollar deposit is not a demand deposit; it is not created on the bank's books by writing loans against required fractional reserves, and it cannot be transferred by a check drawn on the bank having the deposit. Eurodollar deposits are transferred by wire or cable transfer of an underlying balance held in a correspondent bank located within the United States. A domestic analogy would be the transfer of deposits held in savings and loan associations, which is done by having the association write a check on a commercial bank. The appendix to this chapter illustrates how a Eurodollar is created, loaned to a customer via the interbank market, and then eventually repaid.

Any convertible currency can exist in "Euro-" form. Thus there are Euromarks (Deutschemarks deposited in banks outside Germany), Eurosterling (British pounds deposited outside the United Kingdom), and Euroyen (Japanese yen deposited outside Japan), as well as Eurodollars.

The banks in which Eurocurrencies are deposited are often referred to as "Eurobanks." Dufey and Giddy define a Eurobank as "a financial intermediary that simultaneously bids for time deposits and makes loans in a currency other than that of the country in which it is located."[6] Eurobanks are major world banks that, in addition to their Eurobusiness, generally conduct a domestic banking business. Thus the Eurocurrency operation that qualifies a bank for the name "Eurobank" is in fact a department of a large commercial bank, and the name "Eurobank" springs from the function performed.

The Eurocurrency market serves three valuable purposes: (1) Eurocurrency deposits are an efficient and convenient money market device for holding excess corporate liquidity; (2) the Eurocurrency market is a major source of short-term bank loans to finance corporate working capital needs, including the financing of imports and exports; (3) the market is useful for arbitrage purposes.

The exact size of the Eurocurrency market is difficult to measure because it varies with daily decisions by depositors on where to hold readily transferable liquid funds, and particularly on whether to deposit dollars within or outside the United States. Eurocurrency statistics are provided both in the *Annual Report of the Bank for International Settlements (BIS)*, in Basle, Switzerland, and by Morgan Guaranty Trust Company of New York in its bimonthly *World Financial Markets*. Based on these publications, it is estimated that the Eurocurrency market had grown to over $5 trillion by the end of 1990. About 80% of the deposits are interbank, so the net size of the market is considerably smaller. At least 65% of the deposits and claims are denominated in U.S. dollars.

Development of the Eurodollar Market

Historically, the Eurodollar market was born shortly after World War II, when Eastern European holders of dollars, including the various state trading banks of the Soviet Union, were afraid to deposit their dollar holdings in the United States because these deposits might be attached by U.S. residents with claims against communist governments. Therefore Eastern European holders deposited their dollars in Western Europe, particularly with two Soviet banks: the Moscow Narodny Bank, in London, and the Banque Commerciale pour l'Europe du Nord, in Paris. These two banks redeposited the funds in other Western banks, especially in London. Additional dollar deposits came from various central banks in Western Europe, which elected to hold part of their dollar reserves in this form to obtain a higher yield. Commercial banks also placed their dollar balances in the market for the same reason as well as because specific maturities could be negotiated in the Eurodollar market. Additional dollars came to the market from European insurance companies with a large volume of U.S. business (who found it financially advantageous to keep their dollar reserves in the higher-yielding Eurodollar market) and from the various holders of international refugee funds.

These historical precedents sometimes distract observers from the forces that have led to the strong and large market of the present time. The modern Eurodollar market "represents the highly efficient response of international banks to the needs of businesses and governments for low-cost funds with assured availability."[7] Although the basic causes of the growth of the Eurodollar market are economic efficiencies, a number of unique institutional events during the 1950s and 1960s helped its growth. In 1957 British monetary authorities responded to a weakening of the pound by imposing tight controls on U.K. bank lending in sterling to nonresidents of the United Kingdom. Encouraged by the Bank of England, U.K. banks turned to dollar lending as the only alternative that would allow them to maintain their leading position in world finance. Although New York had the advantage of being "home base" for the dollar, as well as having a large domestic money and capital market, international trading in the dollar centered in London because of that city's expertise in international monetary matters and its proximity in time and distance to major customers.

Additional support for a European-based dollar market came from the balance of payments difficulties of the United States during the 1960s, which temporarily segmented the U.S. domestic capital market from that of the rest of the world. Passage of the U.S. interest equalization tax in 1963 effectively closed the U.S. capital markets to foreign issues. This action encouraged the creation of alternative sources of medium- and long-term funds in the Eurocurrency and newly created Eurobond markets. The Federal Reserve System's foreign credit restraint program prevented foreign borrowers, including U.S.-owned foreign affiliates, from medium-term borrowing in the United States, thus reinforcing the need for banking alternatives in Europe. Finally, restrictions on U.S. foreign direct investment, which began on a voluntary basis in 1965 but became mandatory in 1968, forced U.S. multinational firms to source funds needed for overseas operations outside the United States, that is, in the Eurocurrency and Eurobond markets, and provided an impetus for an early version of the Euro-commercial paper market. Although these restrictions were removed in 1974, their effect at the time was to direct attention to the efficiency of the Eurodollar market.

THE TRANSITION TO FLOATING EXCHANGE RATES

The Crisis of August 1971

Lack of confidence in the international monetary system, and the dollar in particular, reached a peak in August 1971, when it became obvious that the United States was heading toward an all-time high balance of payments deficit, which ultimately reached $29.6 billion for 1971 on a reserve transactions basis. On August 15, 1971, President Richard Nixon was forced to suspend official purchases or sales of gold by the U.S. Treasury after the United States suffered outflows of roughly one-third of its official gold reserves in the first seven months of the year. Furthermore, in what was termed "Phase I" of a series of policy changes, the United States temporarily imposed a 10% surcharge on all imports, and all domestic U.S. prices were frozen at existing rates.

Because the price of gold at $35 per ounce was theoretically left unchanged, there was no immediate impact on the amount of international monetary reserves. Nevertheless, the United States served notice to the world that the dollar could no longer be used as the basis for the gold exchange standard. In the meantime, exchange rates of most of the leading trading countries were allowed to float in relation to the dollar and thus indirectly in relation to gold. By the end of 1971 most of the major trading currencies had appreciated vis-à-vis the dollar. This amounted to a de facto devaluation of the dollar.[8]

Smithsonian Agreement of December 1971

Multilateral bargaining sessions among the world's leading trading nations, namely the Group of Ten, reached a compromise agreement at the Washington, D.C., meeting of December 17–18, 1971, later known as the Smithsonian Agreement. The United States agreed to devalue the dollar to $38 per ounce of gold (an 8.57% devaluation). In return, the other members of the Group of Ten agreed to revalue their own currencies upward in relation to the dollar by specified amounts. Actual revaluations ranged from 7.4% by Canada to 16.9% by Japan. Furthermore, the trading band around par value was expanded from the existing 1% band to plus or minus 2.25 %, which meant a maximum movement of 4.5% with respect to the U.S. dollar.

By the second half of 1972, new currency alignments were already being tested. The dollar was weak because of the continued U.S. balance of payments deficit. Moreover, convertibility of the dollar into gold was still suspended, with little prospect for a return to convertibility in the near future. In fact, the price of gold on the London free market in August 1972 was $70 per ounce rather than $38 per ounce.

The Smithsonian Agreement was less than a year old before market pressures forced changes in the new rates. The U.K. pound was floated in June 1972 and the Swiss franc in January 1973. In early 1973 the U.S. dollar came under attack once again, thereby forcing a second devaluation on February 12, 1973, this time by 10% to $42.22 per ounce. By late February 1973 a fixed-rate system appeared no longer feasible given the extreme surges of speculative flows of currencies. The major foreign exchange markets were actually closed for several weeks in March 1973, and when they reopened, most currencies were allowed to float to levels determined by market forces. Par values were left unchanged. The dollar had floated downward an average of 10% by June 1973.

Members who signed the Smithsonian Agreement in December 1971 recognized that the time was ripe for some major changes in the international monetary system devised at Bretton Woods in 1944, but no agreement existed on what changes would be desirable. Some felt a return to fixed rates was imperative, but the majority believed that some sort of managed float would be needed to control the huge increase in potential "hot money," particularly the immense "dollar overhang" held by central banks, the commercial banking systems of the world, and individuals. In September 1972 the IMF appointed the so-called Committee of 20, an expanded version of the Group of Ten, to suggest revisions to the international monetary system by July 1974. The reality of the oil crisis that immediately followed and sharp differences within the committee caused it to fail in its mission, but it laid the groundwork for the IMF meeting at Jamaica in January 1976.

Jamaica Agreement of January 1976

At Jamaica an agreement was reached that provides the rules of the game for today's system. Highlights of the Jamaica Agreement are as follows:

- Floating rates were declared acceptable, although member countries are permitted to interfere to even out unwarranted fluctuations caused by sheer speculation. In other words, member countries are no longer expected to maintain a band around par value.

- Gold was demonetized as a reserve asset. The IMF agreed to return 25 million ounces to its members and to sell another 25 million ounces at the going market price (around $2 billion). The proceeds of the sale were to be placed in a trust fund to help the poorer nations. Members could also sell their own gold reserves at market price rather than at the previous par value price.

- IMF quotas were increased to $41 billion. Subsequently they were increased to the present equivalent of $180 billion. The non-oil-exporting less developed countries were given improved access to borrowing at the IMF. Voting rights were adjusted to reflect the new distribution of trade and reserves, including a total of 10% of voting power to OPEC countries.

Fixed Versus Flexible Exchange Rates

Most observers thought that economists had finally resolved their disagreements about exchange rate flexibility when freely floating rates were adopted by many countries in 1973 and confirmed by the Jamaica Agreement in 1976. The fact that some countries have chosen to maintain fixed rates, others use adjustable pegs, and still others manage floating rates certainly clouds the issue and complicates the task of forecasting.

The traditional arguments for and against flexible rates are as follows:

For Flexible Rates:

- Flexible exchange rates permit a smoother adjustment to external shocks. No need exists to inflate or deflate the whole economy as might occur under fixed rates.

- Central banks do not need to maintain large, sterile international reserves to defend a fixed rate.

- Central banks do not need to lose money trying to defend an inappropriate rate for too long a period.

- Countries can maintain independent monetary and fiscal policies without being overly worried about their effect on the exchange rate.

- Forward markets provide an efficient and inexpensive means to eliminate foreign exchange risk for those who choose to buy such insurance.

Against Flexible Rates:

- Increased volatility under flexible exchange rates increases price uncertainty. This might lead to a reduction in international trade and a lowering of the world living standard.

- Flexible rates are inherently inflationary because they remove the external discipline imposed on a government's monetary and fiscal policy. This is particularly important to monetarists who are presently advocating a return to fixed rates.

- Flexible rates lead to destabilizing speculation that causes the exchange rate to "overshoot" its natural equilibrium level.

- Small open economies do not have efficient forward markets to enable a firm to offset exchange risk. This creates a bias against trade and an incentive for foreign direct investment in such economies.

- Temporarily misaligned rates can cause faulty decisions on resource allocation. Some industries expand or contract when they should not because they misinterpret the duration of exchange rate levels. This might create unnecessary temporary unemployment, wasted production capacity, and calls for protectionism.

THE EXPERIENCE UNDER FLOATING EXCHANGE RATES, 1973–PRESENT

Since March 1973 exchange rates have become much more volatile and less predictable than they were during the "fixed" exchange rate period, when changes occurred infrequently. This volatility was due in part to a number of unexpected shocks to world monetary order. The most important shocks were, in chronological order, the oil crisis of late 1973, loss of confidence in the U.S. dollar in 1977 and 1978, the second oil crisis in 1979, formation of the European Monetary System in 1979, diversification of foreign exchange reserves by central banks starting in 1979, the surprising strength of the U.S. dollar during the period 1981 to 1985, followed by a rapid decline in the value of the U.S. dollar from February 1985 until early 1988. Since the 1980–1988 swing of the U.S. dollar, world currency values have stabilized to a certain degree, except for a brief flurry caused by the Persian Gulf War of 1990–1991.

Exhibit 2.1 summarizes graphically the roller coaster volatility experienced by the U.S. dollar during the period 1971–1990. The Morgan Guaranty Index depicted in Exhibit 2.1 is the *nominal effective exchange rate* of the U.S. dollar compared with a weighted basket of the currencies of 15 other industrial countries. This index is weighted by the size

Exhibit 2.1   U.S. Dollar Movement Under Floating Exchange Rates

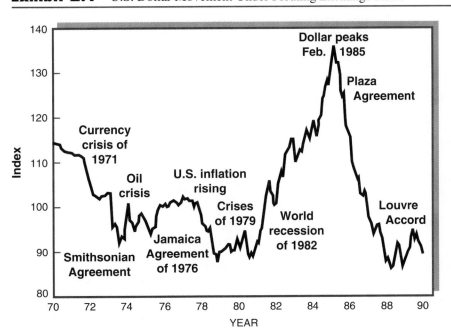

Source: 15-country nominal exchange rate index of the U.S. dollar, Morgan Guaranty, *World Financial Markets*, various issues. 1980–1982=100.

of the United States bilateral trade in manufactured goods with 15 other industrial countries during the year 1980. The weighted average exchange rates for the years 1980–1982 are fixed at an index value of 100. Most other countries also experienced significant currency volatility once rates were floated. Exhibit 2.2 provides a summary of currency events from 1971 to 1990. An analysis of those key events that caused currency volatility follows.

Exhibit 2.2   Currency Events 1971–1990

Date	Event	Impact
August 1971	Nixon closes the U.S. gold window	Suspends purchases or sales of gold by the U.S. Treasury; temporary imposition of 10% surcharge on all imports.
December 1971	Smithsonian Agreement	Group of Ten reaches a compromise whereby the US$ is devalued to $38/oz of gold; most other major currencies are appreciated versus the US$
June 1972	British pound floated	Bank of England allows pound to float.
January 1973	Swiss franc floated	Swiss central bank allows franc to float.
February 1973	U.S. dollar devalued	Devaluation pressure increases on US$, forcing further devaluation to $42.22/oz of gold.
Feb–March 1973	International currency markets in crisis	Fixed exchange rates no longer considered defensible; speculative pressures force closure of international foreign exchange markets for nearly two weeks; markets reopen on floating rates for major industrial currencies.
June 1973	U.S. dollar depreciation	Floating rates continue to drive the now freely-floating US$ down by about 10% by June.
Fall 1973–1974	OPEC oil embargo	Organization of Petroleum Exporting Countries (OPEC) impose oil-embargo eventually quadrupling the price of oil worldwide; because world oil prices are stated in US$, value of US$ recovers some former strength.
January 1976	Jamaica Agreement	IMF meeting in Jamaica results in the acknowledgment or "legalization" of the floating exchange rate system already in effect; gold is demonetized as a reserve asset; IMF quotas are increased.
1977–1978	U.S. inflation increases	Carter administration reduces unemployment at the expense of inflation increases; rising U.S. inflation causes continued deterioration in the dollar.
March 1979	EMS created	The European Monetary System is created, establishing a cooperative exchange rate system for participating members of the EEC.
Summer 1979	OPEC raises prices	OPEC nations raise price of oil once again.
Fall 1979	Iranian assets frozen	Carter responds to Iranian hostage crisis by freezing all Iranian assets held in U.S. financial institutions.
Spring 1980	U.S. dollar begins rise	Worldwide inflation and early signs of recession coupled with real interest differential advantages for dollar-denominated assets contribute to increased demand for dollars.
August 1982	The Debt Crisis	Mexico informs U.S. Treasury on Friday 13, 1982, that it will be unable to make debt service payments; Brazil and Argentina follow in the following months; what is now termed the "debt crisis" begins.

continued

Exhibit 2.2 *continued*

Date	Event	Impact
February 1985	U.S. dollar peaks	The U.S. dollar peaks against most major industrial currencies, hitting record highs against the Deutschemark and other European currencies.
September 1985	Plaza Accord	The Group of Ten members meet at the Plaza Hotel in New York to sign an international cooperative agreement to control the volatility of world currency markets and to establish currency target zones.
February 1987	Louvre Accord	The Group of Five members state they will "intensify" economic policy coordination to promote global growth and reduce external imbalances; members agree that current exchange rates are "consistent with underlying economic fundamentals."
Fall 1990	U.S. dollar hits bottom	The U.S. dollar reaches its weakest point in post World War II history, hitting ¥120/$ and falling below DM1.50/$.
Spring 1991	U.S. dollar recovers	The successful conclusion of the Persian Gulf War restores confidence in the United States. The U.S. dollar strengthens to DM1.68/$ and ¥138/$, its prewar level.

Oil Crisis of 1973–1974

Starting in October 1973 oil prices began to rise precipitously, followed by the oil embargo and its aftermath, the quadrupling of oil prices by 1974. These events cast a new light on the long-run balance of payments strength of the industrial countries. It appeared that the United States, being more self-reliant in energy sources, would fare better in making the adjustment to higher energy costs and lower energy availability than most European countries and Japan. North Sea oil and gas discoveries also placed the United Kingdom, Norway, and the Netherlands in a more favorable energy position than the other European countries. In fact, by the end of 1973 the U.S. dollar had recovered its summer losses and the U.S. balance of payments position was strengthening because of the increased competitiveness of U.S. goods and services at the lower value for the dollar.

On January 29, 1974, the United States removed all controls on capital flows, including the interest equalization tax, direct foreign investment program, and the Federal Reserve's foreign credit restraint program. This was done partly to reflect improvement in the U.S. balance of payments and subsequent strengthening of the U.S. dollar but also in anticipation of the growth of U.S. dollars held by petroleum-exporting countries, the so-called petrodollars. By removing capital controls, the United States hoped to encourage petrodollar holders to maintain their newfound wealth in dollars and to recycle these dollars through the U.S. capital market.

OPEC's success at raising oil prices led to a rapid shift in wealth from the industrialized countries to the oil-exporting countries. Although a large proportion of the incremental oil revenues were recycled by the exporters through increased imports of goods and services for ambitious development plans (Iran, Indonesia, Venezuela, and Nigeria), very large dollar reserves were accumulated by Saudi Arabia and Kuwait because they did not have the population base to justify huge increases in imports. These surplus dollars were by and large reinvested in U.S. dollar bank deposits and government securities.

The oil price shock led to new instability in foreign exchange rates. The rates fluctuated rather severely during the period 1974–1977 in response to differential national rates of inflation, interest rates, structural shifts in the balance of payments, and outright speculation. The increased exchange rate pressures affected all currencies worldwide, including the relatively new attempt at coordinated policies among six of the European countries known as "the snake" (discussed in detail in the following section).

Most of the non-OPEC world suffered a severe slowdown in economic growth rates during 1974 and 1975 before it absorbed the impact of the oil shock. Although growth rates picked up in 1976 and 1977, so did rates of inflation. This combination resulted in restrictive monetary and fiscal policies, particularly in Europe and Japan but also to a lesser degree in the United States. The Carter administration continued to give full employment priority over inflation. As a result, the U.S. balance of payments began to deteriorate in 1976, with the situation worsening in 1977.

U.S. Dollar Crisis of 1977-1978

During the period 1977–1978, expansionary policies of the Carter administration led to a substantial rate of growth in GNP and a reduction in unemployment in the United States but also to an increased rate of inflation and a deterioration of the U.S. balance of payments. Germany, Japan, Switzerland, and the Netherlands, which were pursuing a more conservative growth policy with lower rates of inflation, ran rather large surpluses in their balance of payments. As a result, their currencies appreciated vis-à-vis the U.S. dollar. The situation worsened throughout 1978 as the U.S. government followed a policy of "benign neglect." This meant ignoring the depreciation of the dollar because domestic economic goals were accorded a higher priority. Such a policy led to worldwide loss of confidence in the dollar. Central bankers who had previously absorbed excess dollars in the marketplace in order to cushion its fall began to shift their official reserves out of dollars into Deutschemarks and Swiss francs. They were joined by wealthy investors, particularly the Saudi Arabians. The market for dollar-denominated Eurobonds dried up as investors demanded issues denominated in other currencies.

By October 1978 the dollar had depreciated about 20% on a trade-weighted basis compared to early 1977. This depreciation was well beyond what could be predicted by economic analysis of inflation and interest rate differentials (a subject to be covered in Chapter 6). The dollar's decline worsened domestic U.S. inflation as the prices of imports rose. OPEC members considered switching the pricing of oil from dollars to a more stable currency, such as the SDR, in response to the decline in the real value of their oil exports and monetary reserves.

The Carter administration finally reacted on November 1, 1978, with a program designed to restore confidence in the dollar. The program included a sharp increase in interest rates, a promised reduction in the federal budget deficit, and creation of a $30 billion fund of foreign currencies to be used to support the dollar in foreign exchange markets. The latter was to be raised by sales of foreign-currency-denominated bonds, borrowing from the IMF, and expanding the existing swap agreements with foreign central banks.

The Carter program worked temporarily. Its shock value changed short-term expectations and signaled a switch in U.S. policy to one of concern rather than neglect for the dollar's international value. However, by February 1979 the dollar was again under pressure because of turmoil in Iran, low U.S. interest rates relative to inflation, and the ominous trend toward central bankers' diversifying their foreign currency reserves into Deutschemarks, Japanese yen, and Swiss francs. This trend was aided by a newfound willingness on the part of Germany, Japan, and Switzerland to issue the appropriate interest-bearing securities as a means of financing their dramatically increasing oil import bills.

Crises of 1979

In addition to diversifying their reserves, OPEC members reacted to the dollar's weakness by enforcing a doubling of oil prices during 1979. As a result, the industrial countries once again slipped into recession, just as they had in 1974–1975. The higher price of oil increased inflationary pressures for all countries, including the United States and Japan, who imported large proportions of their petroleum needs.

Foreign exchange market conditions became more unsettled in November 1979 when President Carter froze all Iranian assets in the United States as well as in U.S. banks abroad. Other OPEC members, especially Saudi Arabia, were naturally alarmed at this action because they could visualize the same thing happening to their assets under the wrong circumstances in the future. As a result, their dollar funds were discreetly moved out of U.S. banks into non-U.S. banks in the Eurodollar market. In addition, some dollars were converted into other reserve currencies in order to keep assets safe from any potential future U.S. unilateral actions.

Rising inflationary pressures, coupled with credit pressures fostered by the OPEC price shock, resulted in the institution of tight monetary policies in September 1979 by the newly appointed Chairman of the U.S. Federal Reserve System, Paul Volker. The relatively tight monetary policies which Volker subsequently maintained were focused on the elimination of inflation, this time at the expense of employment. The United States and other major industrial countries moved into recession. This recession fostered rapid swings in both interest and exchange rates. For example, a credit crunch in the United States caused historically high interest rates toward the end of 1979, followed by a precipitous decline in the middle of 1980, when Treasury bills fell below 8%. Still another credit crunch occurred at the end of 1980, when Treasury bills climbed to 15%.

The Rise of the U.S. Dollar, 1980–85

The period 1980–1985 was characterized by unexpected strength of the U.S. dollar and by its counterpart, unexpected weakness of the European currencies. The strength of the U.S. dollar was due to a combination of favorable factors that overcame the unfavorable effect of a large and growing U.S. balance of payments deficit on current account. Strong growth in the United States attracted heavy inflows on capital account from investors seeking higher returns on real asset investments. High real returns (adjusted for inflation) on financial assets also attracted foreign inflows to purchase debt securities. Political turmoil in other parts of the world reinforced the common perception of the United States as a safe political haven for personal wealth. U.S. banks sharply curtailed their lending to less developed countries, which were overburdened with external debt. More attractive opportunities caused by growth with low inflation in the United States also motivated U.S. banks and international portfolio investors to divert funds from other markets back to the U.S. market. The U.S. rate of inflation was kept under control despite the huge U.S. government budget deficit because a growing stream of imports, motivated by the relatively high price of the U.S. dollar, provided stiff price competition for U.S.-made goods. In addition, a worldwide glut of oil and other basic commodities reduced the U.S.-dollar costs of these necessary imports.

The Fall of the U.S. Dollar, 1985–1987

The rapid decline in value of the U.S. dollar from 1985 until the end of 1987 was caused by a combination of government intervention and natural market forces. The strengthening dollar from 1980 to 1985 had precipitated a rapid deterioration of the U.S. balance of trade, leading to cries for protection from U.S. business sectors that were hurt by a rising tide of imports, as well as from U.S. labor union leaders, who were reacting to jobs lost to imports. This threat of protectionism led to a willingness on the part of most major industrial countries to more closely coordinate economic policies. The object was for other countries to foster more rapid rates of growth in order to absorb more imports from the United States. Simultaneously the United States would reduce its real interest rates to the level of those in other countries in order to stem the inflow of capital, which was supporting the value of the dollar. Reduction of U.S. interest rates was made feasible by the prospect of more fiscal restraint, as evidenced by passage of the Gramm-Rudman-Hollings Balanced Budget Act in late 1985.

Plaza Agreement and Louvre Accords

In September 1985, the finance ministers and central bank governors of the so-called Group of Five industrial countries (France, Japan, West Germany, the United Kingdom, and the United States) met at the Plaza Hotel in New York City and reached what was later referred to as the Plaza Agreement. They announced that it would be desirable for most major currencies to appreciate vis-à-vis the U.S. dollar and pledged to intervene in exchange markets to accomplish this objective. Since the dollar had already started to weaken in value during the spring and summer of 1985, this announcement further accelerated the dollar's decline.

The dollar declined rapidly throughout the rest of 1985, all of 1986, and on into early 1987. In fact, it showed signs of overshooting its purported "natural level" given the changed economic conditions. Therefore in February 1987 the major industrial countries again met and reached a new agreement known as the Louvre Accords. They agreed that exchange rates had been realigned sufficiently and pledged to support stability of exchange rates around their current levels. Although the dollar declined further during 1987, it rallied in early 1988, thereby ending for the moment its dramatic rise and fall during the period 1980–1987.

The dollar maintained this relative position over the period from early 1988 until mid-1990, when the Persian Gulf Crisis sent the dollar falling. Successful conclusion of the Persian Gulf war restored confidence in the United States and the dollar recovered to its prewar levels in the spring of 1991.

CONTEMPORARY EXCHANGE RATE REALITIES

Contemporary Currency Regimes and Spheres

The present system of international exchange rate arrangements is summarized in the IMF table depicted in Exhibit 2.3. The U.S. dollar continues to be used as a base currency for many countries (about 25 at end-of-year 1990), many of which depend on their trading relationship with the United States for economic growth. In addition to the dollar the French franc acts as a base currency for many countries, most of whom were previously French possessions. In addition to the single-currency rate-bases of the U.S. dollar, French franc, and the IMF's SDR, Exhibit 2.3 provides an overview of those currencies managed cooperatively, currencies managed in accordance with baskets of other currencies ("indicators"), and those currencies classified simply as "managed floats."

The global economy is increasingly dominated by three major currency "blocs." The U.S. dollar, the Japanese yen, and the German mark each represent "spheres of influence" on other currencies, many of whom are geographically, politically, and, most importantly, economically related to these three industrial powers. The rapid growth of the Japanese economy and the increasingly strong leadership role which it is accepting on world markets has forced the yen into a major world role, whether it was the intent of the Japanese authorities or not. Once more the markets have made many of the currency decisions without the cooperation of governments. The rise of the German mark is also a reflection of rapid economic growth; its role will be further consolidated as Europe moves toward increasing economic integration resulting from the 1992 Single European program and the reunification of West and East Germany itself. We now turn to the consideration of the world's major formalized currency cooperation system, the European Monetary System.

The European Monetary System (EMS)

European exchange rate cooperation began slowly after the international monetary crisis of 1971. Starting in April 1972, members of the EEC, plus prospective members Denmark, Ireland, Norway, and the United Kingdom, entered into the European Joint Float Agreement. This agreement became known as "the snake." Under this arrangement values of members' currencies were to be held within a 2.25% trading band with respect to each other. Jointly they were allowed to float within a 4.5% band with respect to the U.S. dollar, as permitted under the Smithsonian Agreement. This float within a float earned the name

Exhibit 2.3 International Monetary Fund Currency Arrangements (as of December 3, 1990)[1]

Currency Pegged to				Flexibility Limited in Terms of a Single Currency or Group of Currencies			More Flexible		
U.S. dollar	French franc	Other currency	SDR	Other composite[2]	Single currency[3]	Cooperative arrangements[4]	Adjusted according to a set of indicators[5]	Other managed floating[5]	Independently floating
Afghanistan	Benin	Bhutan (Indian Rupee)	Burundi	Algeria	Bahrain	Belgium	Chile	China, P.R.	Argentina
Angola	Burkina Faso	Kiribati (Australian Dollar)	Iran, I. R. of	Austria	Qatar	Denmark	Colombia	Costa Rica	Australia
Antigua and Barbuda	Cameroon	Lesotho (South African Rand)	Libya	Bangladesh	Saudi Arabia	France	Madagascar	Ecuador	Bolivia
Bahamas, The	C. African Rep.	Swaziland (South African Rand)	Myanmar	Botswana	United Arab Emirates	Germany	Mozambique	Egypt	Brazil
Barbados	Chad	Tonga (Australian Dollar)	Rwanda	Bulgaria		Ireland	Zambia	Greece	Canada
Belize	Comoros	Yugoslavia (deutsche mark)	Seychelles	Cape Verde		Italy		Guinea	El Salvador
Djibouti	Congo			Cyprus		Luxembourg		Guinea-Bissau	Gambia, The
Dominica	Côte d'Ivoire			Czechoslovakia		Netherlands		Honduras	Ghana
Dominican Rep.	Equatorial Guinea			Fiji		Spain		India	Guatemala
Ethiopia	Gabon			Finland		United Kingdom		indonesia	Jamaica
Grenada	Mali			Hungary				Korea	Japan
Guyana	Niger			Iceland				Lao P.D. Rep	Lebanon
Haiti	Senegal			Israel				Mauritania	Maldives
Iraq	Togo			Jordan				Mexico	Namibia
Liberia				Kenya				Nicaragua	New Zealand
Oman				Kuwait				Pakistan	Nigeria
Panama				Malawi				Portugal	Paraguay
St. Kitts and Nevis				Malta				Singapore	Peru
St. Lucia				Mauritius				Somalia	Phillippines
St. Vincent and the Grenadines				Morocco				Sri Lanka	Sierra Leone
Sudan				Nepal				Tunisia	South Africa
Suriname				Norway				Turkey	United States
Syrian Arab Rep.				Papua New Guinea				Viet Nam	Uruguay
Trinidad and Tobago				Poland					Venezuela
Yemen, Republic of				Romania					Zaïre
				Sao Tome & Principe					
				Solomon Islands					
				Sweden					
				Tanzania					
				Thailand					
				Uganda					
				Vanuatu					
				Western Samoa					
				Zimbabwe					

[1] Excluding the currency of Democratic Kampuchea, for which no current information is available. For members with dual or multiple exchange markets, the arrangement shown is that in the major market.

[2] Comprises currencies which are pegged to various "baskets" of currencies of the members' own choice, as distinct from the SDR basket.

[3] Exchange rates of all currencies have shown limited flexibility in terms of the U.S. dollar.

[4] Refers to the cooperative arrangement maintained under the European Monetary System.

[5] Includes exchange arrangements under which the exchange rate is adjusted at relatively frequent intervals, on the basis of indicators determined by the respective member countries.

Source: International Monetary Fund, International Financial Statistics, Washington, D.C., March 1991, p. 22.

"the snake within the tunnel." To top it off, the Dutch and Belgians agreed to maintain a still narrower 1% trading band with respect to each other. Naturally this arrangement achieved the ultimate distinction of being known as "the worm within the snake within the tunnel." Within two months, however, market pressures forced the United Kingdom to withdraw from the snake, followed quickly by Denmark. Although Denmark rejoined the snake in October 1972, Italy withdrew in February 1973.

Chaotic conditions in foreign exchange markets in 1978 hastened the need to create mechanisms that would foster more stability. One of these mechanisms arose from the ashes of the all-but-defunct snake cooperation. In March 1979 the nine members of the EEC established the European Monetary System (EMS). The EMS was constructed of three basic elements: (1) the Exchange Rate Mechanism (ERM); (2) the set of central rates of exchange among member currencies; (3) the European Currency Unit (ECU).

The Exchange Rate Mechanism (ERM) is the process by which the member countries maintain the managed exchange rates. The ERM presently consists of ten countries who actively manage their currencies in order to maintain the EMS parities. Only Greece and Portugal remain non-ERM participants. The ERM has three features: (1) the stipulation that there is a bilateral responsibility for the maintenance of exchange rates: (2) the availability of additional support mechanisms which provide the means and resources for maintaining the parities; (3) a last-resort or safety valve of agreed upon realignments when currencies irretrievably diverge from parity.

The central rates of the EMS are the specified bilateral exchange rates among all member currencies; this actually constitutes a grid of bilateral exchange rates among all members. Each currency is then allowed to range ± 2.25% around these central rates. If the currencies approach these bilateral bounds, "indicators of divergence" are encountered which mandate bilateral actions for the maintenance of the central rates.[9] For example, when the United Kingdom recently joined the ERM, the pound was given a central rate of £.338983/DM. The pound, unlike other EMS members, was officially allowed a 6% range (± 3% band) about this central rate.

The third feature, the ECU, is a basket or index currency created from a weighted average of all member currencies. Each member currency is defined in terms of units per ECU. The weights are based on each member's share of intra-European trade and the relative size of its GNP. The ECU was originally worth $1.40, but its value varies over time as the members' currencies float jointly with respect to the U.S. dollar and other nonmember currencies. Exhibit 2.4 demonstrates how the value of the ECU is determined in terms of the U.S. dollar.

Members intervene in the foreign exchange markets through the system of mutual credit facilities. Each member can borrow almost unlimited amounts of foreign currency from other members for periods that can be extended up to three months. A second line of defense includes loans that can be extended to nine months, but the total amount available is limited to a pool of credit, originally about 14 billion ECUs, and the size of the member's quota in the pool. Additional funds are available for maturities of from two to five years from a second pool, originally about 11 billion ECUs, but to use these funds, the borrowing member must correct domestic economic policies that are causing its currency to deviate.

Exhibit 2.4   The European Monetary System

Country	Currency	per ECU[2]	$/unit[3]	$ Value[4]	% of Total[5]
Germany	Mark	.6242	0.5919	0.3695	30.43
France	Franc	1.332	0.1716	0.2286	18.82
Italy	Lira	151.8	.000808	0.1227	10.08
United Kingdom[1]	Pound	.08784	1.7095	0.1502	12.35
Denmark	Krone	0.1976	0.1558	0.0308	2.53
Belgium	Franc	3.301	.02886	0.0953	7.84
Luxembourg	Franc	0.13	.02886	0.0038	0.31
Netherlands	Guilder	0.2198	0.5269	0.1158	9.52
Ireland	Pound	.008552	1.5767	0.0135	1.11
Greece[1]	Drachma	1.44	.006072	0.0087	0.72
Spain	Peseta	6.885	.009611	0.0662	5.44
Portugal[1]	Escudo	1.393	.006734	0.0094	0.77
Total $ Value			$1.216/ECU		100.0%

[1] The United Kingdom became an active member in the Exchange Rate Mechanism in October, 1990; the group of EMS countries which actively work to maintain EMS parity rates. Greece and Portugal are not members of the ERM, although both are members of the EEC and EMS. Although these currencies are included in the definition of the ECU, neither country accepts responsibility for maintaining any specific value of their currency relative to other EMS currencies.

[2] The ECU is a basket or index currency unit created by a weighted average of the member currencies. The units of currency per ECU reflect the central rates of the EMS's bilateral grid. The EMS has undergone 11 realignments of its central rates (not ECU weights) since its inception in March of 1979: (1) September 24, 1979; (2) November 30, 1979; (3) March 23, 1981; (4) October 5, 1981; (5) February 22, 1982; (6) June 14, 1982; (7) March 21, 1983; (8) July 22, 1985; (9) April 7, 1986; (10) August 4, 1986; (11) January 12, 1987.

[3] Spot rates of exchange versus the U.S. dollar, Friday June 16, 1990, from the *Wall Street Journal*.

[4] The subsequent dollar value reflects currency per ECU at the current spot dollar exchange rate at that point in time. The "value" of the ECU then changes continually with respect to an outside currency (external to EMS).

[5] The proportion of value which each member currency constitutes is its current U.S. dollar value divided by the U.S. dollar value of the ECU itself. Columns may not sum to stated totals due to rounding.

The European Monetary Cooperation Fund (EMCF) was established in 1982 as an institution to administer the various credit facilities and issue an initial supply of ECUs to the member countries similar to the way the IMF issues SDRs. The members deposit 20% of their gold and dollar reserves with it in return for a corresponding amount of ECUs.

Although many outside the EMS debate the actual success of the EMS in establishing and preserving exchange rate parities, the present membership continues to be supportive. All evidence indicates that the cooperative structure of the EMS has resulted in less exchange rate volatility than would have been experienced in its absence.

A second area of contention is over the increasing dominance demonstrated by the German mark within the EMS. Often termed the "DM-Zone" rather than the EMS, the mark makes up over 30 percent of the ECU and is the only member currency other than the Dutch guilder to have continually appreciated throughout the 11 realignments of the system since its inception. Recent events surrounding the increased economic integration of Europe have prompted even long-standing critics, however, to study the possibility of monetary union.

European Monetary Integration

With the passage of the Single European Act of 1985 (SEA) the pace of European integration quickened. This Act amended the Treaty of Rome (1957) to once more pursue the creation of a true Internal Market:

> The internal market shall comprise an area without internal frontiers in which the free movement of goods, persons, services and capital is ensured in accordance with the provisions of this Treaty.[10]

The SEA stated that in order for the Community to move closer toward the formation of an Internal Market, progress would be necessary in four major areas: (1) strengthening of the European Monetary System (EMS), which allowed stable rates of currency exchange between most member countries; (2) harmonization of national supervisory structures for financial systems; (3) renewed efforts to prevent tax evasion; (4) achievement of full liberalization of capital movements. The Commission noted that all could not be achieved simultaneously, but that the liberalization of capital movements (item 4) would "create a dynamic process leading to integration," and the achievement of the other primary goals.

An area of concerted new interest, although not expressly an agreed upon part of the SEA, was that of European monetary integration, a single currency for all members. As a result of the EEC meetings in Hanover in June of 1988, the European Council stated that it wished to continue to move toward the "realization of economic and monetary union." The Council appointed then EEC President Jacque Delors to chair a committee to study the steps necessary to achieve monetary union.

The Delors Report was completed in April 1989, and recommended the following process for the accomplishment of monetary union:

Stage 1: Extend the EMS participation to all 12 EEC members and to "tighten" individual economic policies to preserve the stability of the EMS.

Stage 2: Amend the Treaty of Rome (founding document of the EEC) to create a European System of Central Banks similar to that of the United States Federal Reserve System; these banks would gradually influence independent monetary policies. This amendment would be combined with a narrowing of EMS bands and by the issuance of macroeconomic policy guidelines by the European Council of Ministers.

Stage 3: Centralized monetary and budget controls would be binding upon members. Exchange rates would be "locked-in". The Delors Committee believed that at this stage a single European currency would emerge.

The movement toward a more unified European economy will, however, constitute serious problems for the ability of the EMS to preserve stability. The present EEC structure of independent monetary policies combined with a fixed-exchange rate system, and the move to complete freedom in capital movements in the 1990–1992 period, will most likely require a new realignment of the EMS central rates. On the more stabilizing side of the debate is the probable dampening impact German monetary unification (with East Germany) will have on the continual "bullish" behavior of the mark.

There are three types of monetary integration:

1. *Currency Union*—where exchange rates are fixed and supplemental financing facilities are provided to aid in the maintenance of the fixed rates.

2. *Financial Integration*—where capital is free to move within a system of unified financial institutions and markets, but exchange rates are not necessarily fixed.

3. *Monetary Union*—where in addition to the fixing of exchange rates, there is freedom of capital movement, availability of supplemental financing facilities, and unified or at least coordinated monetary policy.

The Single European Act of 1985, in its focus on the liberalization of capital flows without directly addressing the exchange rate regime, falls within the second classification. The series of events following the 1985 Act regarding the interest by the European Council in locking-in fixed exchange rates is seemingly moving toward the third classification of true monetary union.

Whether the EEC actually will move to a single monetary system and possibly then to a single currency (increasingly termed the EMU, the European Monetary Unit), only time will tell. The complexities of establishing a central bank of Europe which effectively controls monetary policy throughout the member states will require a commitment to economic and political integration beyond that of the existing EEC governing structure.

German Currency Union

The reunification of West Germany (Federal Republic of Germany or FRG) and East Germany (German Democratic Republic or GDR) in 1990 serves as a classic case study of the intricacies of exchange rates and monetary policies. One of the first steps in the reunification process of the two Germanies was the economic unification of the two countries. Currency union was achieved on July 1, 1990, when the Deutschemark was extended to East Germany, and Ostmarks were convertible to Deutschemarks at government decreed rates of exchange depending on the nature and amount of the conversion.

Within specified limits, the currency and savings of East German residents were convertible on a one-to-one basis. For existing claims and liabilities beyond those specified limits, the conversion rate was two Ostmarks per Deutschemark. It was thought that at these conversion rates the currency unification would result in an increase of approximately 10% of the West German money supply. Although this in isolation would be cause for inflation (more money chasing the same quantity of goods), the added economic output of the GDR was also roughly equivalent to 10% of that of the FRG. The result, if all the estimates are accurate, should be a larger economic unit all operating with a common currency—the DM—with few new inflationary pressures. In the brief period since German currency union, the Deutschemark has remained relatively stable, and if anything, has strengthened against other major world currencies.

WORLD CURRENCY REFORM

Emergence of the Triad Currency System

With the joint float of the EMS, the continued strength of the Japanese yen, and the reemergence of gold as a key reserve asset, the international monetary system has gradually evolved into a series of currency blocs. Within each currency-bloc, currencies float within a narrow band. The currency blocs themselves float with respect to each other, typically pulled by the strongest currency in each bloc. The main blocs are anchored by the Deutschemark (EMS), the U.S. dollar, and the Japanese yen.

To reduce exchange risk, the world's central bankers have diversified their portfolios of reserve assets to include one or more key currencies from each currency bloc, as well as Swiss francs, gold, ECUs, and SDRs. In the long run the use of a multicurrency reserve system may stabilize the value of each individual central bank's portfolio of reserve assets. On the other hand, decisions by central bankers and a few OPEC countries to switch the composition of portfolios could be very destabilizing for individual currencies. Under these circumstances the burden of domestic adjustment to international monetary pressures will be shared by the United States, Germany, Japan, and Switzerland rather than fall on the United States alone, which was the case up until 1978. All these countries, except the United States, have previously tried to avoid having their currencies used as reserve assets because of the fear that it would limit their ability to conduct independent economic policies. It will now be increasingly difficult for all major industrial countries to conduct independent monetary and fiscal policies without regard to international consequences.

Exchange Rate Volatility

To what extent have floating rates increased the actual volatility of exchange rates? Under the floating rate system, exchange rates adjust a little every day instead of the large one-time adjustments characteristic of the prior fixed exchange rate period. If the balance of payments adjustment mechanism is working correctly, exchange rates should eventually tend toward the same level under either floating or fixed rates, but the path taken creates different challenges for managers who must forecast exchange rates and for government officials who must manage the economy.

John Williamson has identified the problem of assessing exchange rate variability as follows:

> It is important to distinguish between short-term volatility and persistent misalignments. By volatility is meant the amount of short-run variability in the exchange rate from hour to hour, day to day, week to week, or month to month. By misalignment is meant a persistent departure of the exchange rate from its long run equilibrium level.[11]

There are signs that the increased cooperation on the part of the major industrial powers is starting to have some success in the management of exchange rates. Exhibit 2.5 depicts the three major world currencies and their movements over the 1980s. The volatility of the currencies is obvious; the range over which the yen-dollar and mark-dollar have moved is considerable. What is encouraging is the fact that the yen and mark have seemingly moved in unison since 1985, when the dollar was at its peak (of overvaluation). First the Plaza Agreement of September 1985 did by all accounts aid in the continued depreciation of the dollar through coordinated macroeconomic policies and exchange market intervention by the Group of Five. The later Louvre Accord of 1987 was seemingly the start of the relatively stable period of tri-currency movements depicted in Exhibit 2.5. Although the international currency markets have grown to such a magnitude that central bank interventions are not solely capable of "pegging rates," the coordination of macroeconomic policies (fiscal, monetary, and international) appears to be having some success.

Exchange Rate Tradeoffs

Exhibit 2.6 provides an exchange rate "map" of the major issues which all exchange rate regimes must trade off, exchange rate rules versus discretion, and cooperative versus noncooperative systems.[12] Regime structures like that of the gold standard require no cooperative policies among countries, only the assurance that all will abide by the "rules of the game." In the gold standard this translated into the willingness of governments to buy or sell gold at parity rates on demand. The Bretton Woods Agreement required more in the way of cooperation in that gold was no longer the "rule," and countries were then required to cooperate to a higher degree to maintain the dollar-based system. Contemporary systems like that of the EMS constitute hybrids of these cooperative and rule regimes.

Exhibit 2.5 Exchange Rate Convergence in the Late 1980s: $, DM, ¥

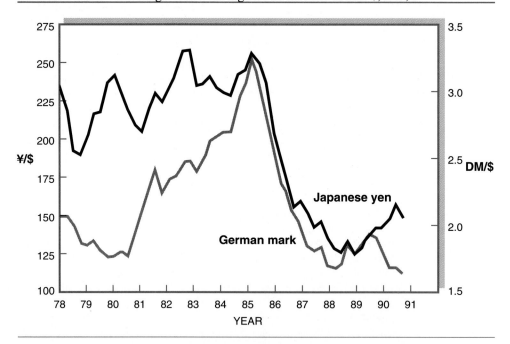

Source: *Federal Reserve Bulletin*, U.S. Federal Reserve Board, monthly period average exchange rate.

Exhibit 2.6 The Economist's "Exchange Rate Map"

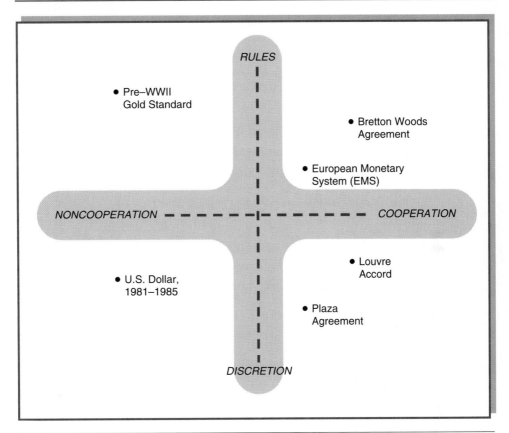

Source: Drawn from the series of *The Economist*, May 21 and May 28, 1988. The axes of the diagram represent the two separate sets of trade-off decisions a country has under alternative exchange rate systems. Vertically, different exchange rate arrangements may dictate whether the country's government has strict intervention requirements (RULES) or whether it may choose if, when, and to what degree to intervene in the foreign exchange markets (DISCRETION). Horizontally, the trade-off is whether the countries who are participants in a specific system must consult and act in unison (COOPERATION) or may simply operate as a member of the system, but act on their own (NONCOOPERATION).

The present international monetary system is one which is characterized by no rules, with varying degrees of cooperation. The Plaza Agreement and the Louvre Accord both represent attempts by the major industrial countries (Group of Five) to come to some agreement about cooperative policies, although nonbinding. As the regime or system moves into the lower left quadrant or upper right quadrant of Exhibit 2.6, however, exchange rate stability decreases. This is what is generally believed to have been the case for the U.S. dollar on its roller-coaster ride in the 1980s. Any future proposals for reform of the international monetary system will have to address these two critical tradeoffs, often considered by many governments the choice between two evils.

 *Edouard Balladur, France's finance minister in Jacques Chirac's government between March 1986 and June 1988, has recently expressed inquietude over the persistent weakness of the U.S. dollar. Mr. Balladur, who these days directs the Association pour le Liberalisme Populaire, a group dedicated to promoting free-market liberalism in Paris, for some years has advocated the institution of a true international monetary system, including on this page Feb. 23, 1988. Following are excerpts from his responses, translated from French, to questions posed by The Wall Street Journal.*

Editorial: "A Stronger Dollar, a New Money Order"*

Why does the decline of the dollar bother you?

For several years the dollar in terms of its purchasing power has settled in a permanent fashion at a level below the European currencies. This relative weakness is understandable if we take into account all at once the considerable economic problems of America and the desire of the U.S. to secure a competitive advantage before making a concerted effort to remedy these problems.

It remains to be seen whether this policy is correct. The example of Germany and of Japan shows that the best way to fight inflation, as well as to have a favorable trade balance, isn't necessarily to allow the erosion of a currency in response to internal economic imbalances.

The international arrangements of recent years on the economic and monetary front reflect the following notion: Let's help the Americans redress their balance-of-payments problems, but with the assurance that they'll help themselves by reducing their own budget deficits.

The American administration's inability to solve its budgetary problems reflects without a doubt the persistent cause underlying its difficulties, the essential reason for which is the dollar's weakness, which has prevented the government from resolving these problems.

A dollar that is too weak poses only disadvantages, as there is a limit to what North America can gain from monetary competition. Beyond this limit everyone loses: Europe, naturally, whose industries will be directly threatened; and the U.S. itself, which risks throwing into doubt its entire anti-inflationary strategy by "importing" inflation through an excessively undervalued dollar.

Is the decline of the dollar contrary to the Louvre Accords?

Yes, an excessive decline of the dollar runs contrary to the spirit of the Louvre Accords—just as, for that matter, an excessive rise of the dollar does, and just as excessive drops and rises of each of the currencies concerned do.

The spirit of the Louvre Accords is the initiation of a collective strategy to coordinate the ... policies of the major industrialized countries and to reduce ... possible uncertainties in economic and monetary matters.

Allow me to add one thing, even though I am one of the authors of the Louvre Accords. They were necessary, and they still should be observed, but they were not sufficient. The world suffers from the lack of a true international monetary system, one with built-in ... constraints independent of the will of governments.

If the U.S. suffers another period of serious inflation, what will the effects be on the world economy?
The world dreads an American recession. As long as the major countries do not wish to see the Federal Reserve boost interest rates because of their concerns over a recession, they have no choice but to put up with a weaker dollar. The situation would be wholly different if a robust American economy allowed rates on the American market to rise without harming the country's economic health. That isn't the case now.

Inflation in the 1970s proved . . . destructive. Rarely has American economic policy required such delicate handling [as now]. The Fed must avoid worsening the recession and fueling inflation simultaneously.

Is it time for the G-7 to consider seriously the establishment of a more stable monetary order? How would you propose to approach the task?
I have always favored establishing a more stable monetary order. I have proposed, if you recall, three systems in the order of increased constraints on the freedom of governments:

- Perfecting the Louvre Accords in the direction of closer cooperation among governments.
- Establishing a system similar to the European Monetary System but on a global scale.
- Finally, adopting a standard of value around which all the currencies would be defined.

I am convinced that the world can make a true recovery only by adopting such a standard. It would serve as a reserve currency for all central banks and would enable the establishing of a grid of parities. The central banks would have to commit themselves to hold reserves composed in part by this new standard. All the currencies, on the external level, would become convertible in the standard. The International Monetary Fund would manage the system.

The European Monetary System appears to be proving its worth. Does this strengthen the argument for reestablishing a broad international system?
Yes. I am convinced that the success of the European Monetary System—which in a certain sense is what remains of the former world system and Bretton Woods—argues for establishing a broad international system that includes major currencies.

Nevertheless, one observation is in order. The European countries would not have felt the need for the European Monetary system if we had a strong and stable international monetary system. The stability of monetary values and of trade inside the Community is very important; it cannot in itself suffice to assure global balance. [W]e need a system in which the dollar would stop serving as reference.

One problem is that the German mark is the anchor currency for the EMS. But we imagine that the U.S. would be reluctant to fix to the mark, just as Europe would be reluctant to fix to the dollar.

The true anchor of the EMS is the exchange mechanism itself, which guarantees the coherence of the whole system and which provides the incentive to each of the participating economies to perform at its best.

Would you envision a role for gold in a future monetary system?

I don't see how a true world system that by necessity must create a new monetary standard could avoid a reference to gold. I don't see either how we can avoid reform of the banking and credit system. Thus I welcome the plans of the American Treasury secretary, Nicholas Brady, to design new American banking regulations.

If, in order to reestablish monetary order, we want to withdraw from the central banks the right to act at will, without constraints and sanctions, we must also withdraw the power to create anarchy from the commercial banks. For me freedom without order is inconceivable.

Does the pursuit of a single European currency advance or retard efforts to establish a new worldwide monetary order?

In Europe we have already done what we had to do to protect ourselves from monetary fluctuations. But this is not enough because world trade and world financial balance depend on the relationship among the dollar, the yen and the European currencies.

We must henceforth concentrate on that. I would like the European countries to take the initiative of asking the U.S. and Japan to work with them on worldwide monetary reform. [The Europeans'] silence and passivity surprises me.

SUMMARY

- The international monetary system has evolved from the gold standard at the beginning of the century to the floating rate system that is used today.

- The Jamaica Agreement of January 1976 provided the rules for today's floating rate system.

- The global experience under a system of floating exchange rates (for the major industrial countries) has been largely an unstable one. The series of events we have recounted for the 1973–1991 period constitute a series of shocks to a system which somehow survived such battering.

- The European Monetary System was formed in March 1979. The EMS has combined the elements of rules and cooperation in a new version of currency exchange which to date has been relatively successful.

- The world monetary system has shown a movement toward regional currency blocs, forming what is commonly referred to as a "triad" (United States, Japan, Germany) dominance of currencies.

1. Fixed Versus Flexible Exchange Rates

The French government has repeatedly suggested that the international monetary system return to a system of fixed exchange rates. Discuss the pros and cons of this idea.

2. Managed Exchange Rates

Under the present system of floating and managed exchange rates, many countries have chosen to tie their currencies to a key currency or to a basket of currencies. On what basis do you believe they pick the key currency or basket? What are the advantages and disadvantages of such policies?

3. The U.S. Dollar Fluctuations

The U.S. dollar experienced a sharp increase in its value during the period 1981–1985, followed by a steep decline during the period 1985–1987, and then a recovery in 1988. What caused these sharp fluctuations? Do you think this is likely to happen again in the near future? If so, what is likely to be the cause? If not, why do you expect stability?

4. The EMS is an attempt to reduce exchange rate fluctuations between the currencies of its members.

Why do they think this is desirable? How successful has the EMS been in reducing internal fluctuations?

5. SDRs and ECUs

SDRs and ECUs are artificial currencies that are held as part of the reserves of central banks. What is the backing behind these currencies? Why do central banks accept them as payment instead of demanding circulating currencies such as dollars, deutsche marks, pounds, francs, and yen?

6. The value of the ECU (CO2A.WK1)

Exhibit 2.4 demonstrated the valuation of the European Currency Unit (ECU) versus the U.S. dollar. The dollar value of the ECU will change constantly as its component currencies change in value relative to the dollar. Using current spot exchange rate quotations listed in *The Wall Street Journal*, find the ECU's value in U.S. dollars today.

7. The IMF as a World Central Bank

The IMF was originally envisaged by John Maynard Keynes, the father of many current theories of macroeconomics, as a world central bank. To what extent has the IMF fulfilled this vision? What steps must be taken for the IMF to become a true central bank? What are the obstacles to this evolution?

NOTES

1. For a detailed analysis of the immediate post–World War II international monetary system, see Robert Triffin, *Europe and the Money Muddle*, New Haven, Conn.: Yale University Press, 1957.

2. Current international financial statistics covering the IMF and member countries appear in the current month's issue of IMF, *International Financial Statistics*, Washington, D.C.

3. International Monetary Fund, *Annual Report*, Washington, D.C.: International Monetary Fund, 1989.

4. A widely read pioneering analysis of the adequacy of international reserves appears in Robert Triffin, *Gold and the Dollar Crisis*, New Haven, Conn.: Yale University Press, 1961.

5. Current reports on official currency swaps and other operations of central banks in the foreign exchange markets are published several times a year in the monthly Federal Reserve Bulletin, Board of Governors of the *Federal Reserve System*, Washington, D.C.

6. Gunter Dufey and Ian H. Giddy, *The International Money Market*, Englewood Cliffs, New Jersey: Prentice-Hall, 1978, p. 10.

7. ———, *Credit Creation and the Growth of the Eurodollar Market*, Research Paper No. 127, New York: Columbia University Graduate School of Business, 1976.

8. A definition of terms used in reporting changes in exchange rates is appropriate, if for no other reason than that newspaper accounts often use the word devaluation incorrectly. The term devaluation in a narrow and semantically correct sense refers only to a drop in foreign exchange value of a currency that is pegged to gold or to another currency. The opposite of devaluation is revaluation. The terms weakening, deterioration, or depreciation refer to a drop in the foreign exchange value of a floating currency. The opposite of weakening is appreciating or strengthening, which refers to a gain in the exchange value of a floating currency. A currency is considered "soft" if it is expected to be devalued or to depreciate relative to major currencies, or if its exchange value is being artificially sustained by its government. A currency is considered "hard" if it is expected to revalue or appreciate relative to major trading currencies.

9. Professor H. Lee Remmers of INSEAD (Fontainebleau, France) has sent us the following clarification: "The divergence is measured as the difference between the ECU market value of each currency and its ECU parity. The point at which a currency reaches its threshold is 75% of the maximum divergence possible. This maximum will be different for each currency in the ECU in proportion to its weight. Therefore, the German mark will have the lowest threshold (about 1.06%) since it is the most important component of the ECU, and the Irish punt will have the highest (1.67%) since it accounts for the smallest weight. There is at least one currency advisory service (as well as the Financial Times) that publishes the 'divergence indicator' on a regular basis—this indicator being a sort of early warning signal that pressure is building on a currency foreshadowing a possible realignment."

10. The Single European Act, Section II, Subsection I, Article 13, Article 8a, 1985, *Treaty Establishing the European Communities*, abridged edition, Office for Official Publications of the European Communities, Luxembourg, 1987.

11. John Williamson, *The Exchange Rate System*, 2nd ed., Washington, D.C.: Institute for International Economics, June 1985.

12. This section borrows from the analysis presented in *The Economist*, "Economics Focus," in consecutive issues dated May 21 (p. 77) and May 28 (p. 65), 1988.

BIBLIOGRAPHY

Agmon, Tamir, Robert G. Hawkins, and Richard M. Levich, eds., *The Future of the International Monetary System*, Lexington, Mass.: Lexington Books, 1984.

Coffey, Peter, *The European Monetary System— Past, Present and Future*, second edition, Dordrecht, the Netherlands; Lancaster, UK: Kluwer Academic Publishers, 1987.

Cooper, Richard N., *The International Monetary System: Essays in World Economics*, Cambridge, Mass.: MIT Press, 1987.

Dornbusch, Rudiger, "Exchange Rate Economics: 1986," *The Economic Journal*, March 1987, pp. 1–18.

Friedman, Irving, *Reshaping the Global Money System*, Lexington, Mass.: Lexington Books, 1987.

Genberg, Hans, "The European Monetary System," in *The Handbook of International Financial Management*, Robert Z. Aliber, ed., Dow Jones-Irwin, Homewood, Il., 1987, pp. 732–758.

Haberler, Gottfried, "The International Monetary System in the World Recession," in William J. Fellner, ed., *Contemporary Economic Problems*, 1983–84, Washington, D.C.: American Enterprise Institute, 1983.

International Monetary Fund, *The European Monetary System: Recent Developments*, Washington, D.C.: IMF, 1986.

Jurgensen Report, *Report of the Working Group on Exchange Market Intervention*, Washington, D.C.: U.S. Treasury, 1983.

Koromzay, Val, John Llewellyn, and Stephen Potter, "The Rise and Fall of the Dollar: Some Explanations, Consequences and Lessons," *The Economic Journal*, March 1987, pp. 23–43.

McKibben, Warwick J., and Jeffrey D. Sachs, "Comparing the Global Performance of Alternative Exchange Agreements," *Journal of International Money and Finance*, 7, no. 4, December 1988, pp. 387–410.

Makin, John H., "Fixed versus Floating: A Red Herring," *Columbia Journal of World Business*, Winter 1979, pp. 7–14.

Scammel, W.M., *Stability of the International Monetary System*, Totowa, NJ: Rowman and Littlefield, 1987.

Schinasi, Garry J., "European Integration, Exchange Rate Management, and Monetary Reform: A Review of the Major Issues," *International Finance Discussion Papers*, Board of Governors of the Federal Reserve System, Number 364, October 1989.

Shafer, Jeffrey R., and Bonnie E. Loopesko, "Floating Exchange Rates after Ten Years," *Brookings Papers on Economic Activity*, Washington, D.C.: Brookings Institution, 1983.

Taylor, Dean, "Official Intervention in the Foreign Exchange Market, or Bet against the Central Bank," *Journal of Political Economy*, April 1982, pp. 356–368.

Williamson, John, "A Survey of the Literature on the Optimal Peg," *Journal of Development Economics*, September 1982.

——, *The Open Economy and the World Economy*, New York: Basic Books, 1983.

——, *The Exchange Rate System*, Washington, D.C.: Institute for International Economics, September 1983.

Creation and Use of Eurodollars

A Eurodollar is not a currency separate from a dollar in the United States. Similarly, every Eurocurrency has an exchange value identical with its domestic or home currency counterpart. If the domestic counterpart devalues or revalues, the rate of exchange between its corresponding Eurocurrency and other foreign currencies changes by the same amount.

Eurocurrency deposits differ from their domestic money market counterparts only in terms of their geographic location and in terms of the interest rates that might be paid on deposits or loans relative to home currency interest rates.

The process by which Eurocurrencies come into existence can be illustrated with dollars. Eurodollars are created when a dollar deposit is transferred from a bank within the United States to a bank outside the country, or when someone outside the United States acquires dollars, perhaps because of a commercial transaction or a purchase in the foreign exchange market, and deposits those dollars in a bank outside the United States. Eurodollar creation can be illustrated by following "T-account" entries that arise when U.S. dollars are deposited in foreign banks.

Step 1.   Assume that before the creation of any Eurodollars a Dutch multinational corporation acquires $100 on demand deposit in a New York bank. Eurodollar transactions are usually $500,000 or more, but we are using $100 to simplify the presentation. The demand deposit of the Dutch corporation would be reflected on the books of the New York bank, the Dutch corporation, and the Federal Reserve Bank of New York as follows:

(1) New York bank

	Demand deposit due Dutch corporation	$100

(2) Dutch corporation

Demand deposit held with N.Y. bank $100	

(3) Federal Reserve Bank of New York bank

	Reserve deposit due N.Y. bank as part of its reserve requirement (assume 20% reserve requirement)	$20

Step 2.   Assume that the Dutch corporation decides to convert its dollar demand deposit into an interest-earning form. The corporation might instruct the New York bank to invest the sum in money market instruments such as U.S. Treasury bills or time

certificates of deposit with the New York bank. Possibly for reasons of higher yield, however, the Dutch corporation decides to deposit its dollars in a dollar-denominated time deposit at a London bank. The result is as follows:

(4) New York bank

	Demand deposit due Dutch corporation −$100
	Demand deposit due London bank +$100

(5) London bank

Demand deposit in N.Y. bank +$100	Time deposit due Dutch corporation +$100

(6) Dutch corporation

Demand deposit held with N.Y. bank −$100	
Time deposit in London bank +$100	

By this step a Eurodollar, that is, a U.S. dollar-deposit liability of a foreign bank, has been created. Note, however, that the $100 liability of the London bank is matched by the bank's $100 claim on a demand deposit in New York. Total deposit levels in the United States have not changed, but ownership of the U.S. deposit has shifted from a foreign corporation to a foreign bank. The reserve requirement at the Federal Reserve Bank and the U.S. money supply are unchanged.

Step 3. Because the London bank is paying interest on its dollar time-deposit liability to the Dutch corporation, it wishes to invest the underlying dollars to earn a return on them. Assume that the London bank decides, as a matter of prudence, to retain $10 of its deposit in the New York bank as a liquid reserve and to loan $90 to a Paris bank. This is an interbank loan and will usually take the physical form of the London bank instructing the New York bank by wire to transfer funds out of its own account and into the account of the Paris bank. It will be noted that because Eurodollars are not demand deposits they are transferred by orders given to the New York bank and not by writing checks or other transfer of the Eurodollar deposit balances on the books of the European bank.

The London bank's loan to the Paris bank is reflected in the T-accounts that follow:

(7) London bank

Demand deposit in N.Y. bank −$90	
Loan to Paris bank +$90	

(8) Paris bank

Demand deposit in N.Y. bank +$90	Dollar loan repayable to London bank +$90

(9) New York bank

	Demand deposit due London bank	−$90
	Demand deposit due Paris bank	+$90

No change has occurred in the amount of demand-deposit liabilities of the New York bank. However, title to $90 of such deposits has been shifted from the London bank to the Paris bank. Contrary to some views of the Eurodollar market, there has not been a pyramiding or expansion of Eurodollar deposits within Europe. Total Eurodollar deposits remain at $100, the time deposit of the Dutch corporation. Additionally, ownership of a New York based deposit has been transferred to a new owner, and a repayment obligation (the Eurodollar loan) created in Europe.

Step 4.   Assume that the Paris bank reloans its $90 to a French importer, who is seeking a dollar loan to pay for imports from the United States. The transactions to record the loan would be as follows:

(10) Paris bank

Demand deposit in N.Y. bank	−$90	
Dollar loan to French importer	+$90	

(11) French importer

Dollar check drawn on N.Y. bank	+$90	Loan payable in dollars to Paris bank	+$90

If the French importer owned a New York bank account, the importer might deposit the loan proceeds in New York rather than hold the physical check as has been assumed in this example. The French importer might also instruct the Paris bank to wire dollar funds directly to the New York exporter, thus combining T-account transaction (11) with transaction (12) below. For simplicity we will assume separate transactions and the holding of the physical check by the French importer as an asset.

Assume that the New York exporter has a bank account in the same New York bank and deposits all receipts in that bank. When the French importer pays the New York exporter, the transaction would be recorded thus:

(12) French importer

Dollar check drawn on N.Y. bank	− $90	
Inventory	+$90	

(13) New York exporter

Demand deposit in N.Y. bank from deposit of check received	+$90		
Inventory	− $90		

(14) New York bank

	Demand deposit due Paris bank	− $90
	Demand deposit due N.Y. exporter	+$90

Use of the proceeds of the Paris bank's Eurodollar loan to the French importer to pay the U.S. exporter does not cause any change in the volume of demand deposits of U.S. banks. The only change is that an obligation to a foreigner (the Paris bank) is changed to an obligation to a domestic business (the New York exporter).

Step 5. Eventually the French importer must accumulate or acquire dollars to repay its Eurodollar loan from the Paris bank, possibly by selling the imported goods for dollars or by selling them for francs and using the francs to buy dollars on the foreign exchange market. Assume, for our example, that the goods have been sold for French francs and the French importer now buys $90 of U.S. currency with accumulated French francs and uses the $90 to repay the loan. The resulting transactions would be as follows (accounting for the sale within France is ignored, as is interest on the loan):

(15) French importer

(a) French francs (dollar equivalent)	− $90	(b) Loan payable in dollars to Paris bank	− $90
(a) U.S. currency	+$90		
(b) U.S. currency	− $90		

(16) Paris bank

Dollar loan to French importer	− $90	
Dollar deposit in N.Y. bank (to reflect deposit of dollar currency received)	+$90	

(17) New York bank

	Demand deposit due Paris bank	+$90
Currency	+$90	

Step 6. Finally the Paris bank repays its loan from the London bank by wiring a transfer of New York funds held by the Paris bank (the example ignores interest):

(18) Paris bank

Dollar deposit in N.Y. bank	– $90	Loan from London bank	– $90

(19) London bank

Dollar deposit in N.Y. bank	+$90		
Loan to Paris bank	– $90		

(20) New York bank

		Demand deposit due London bank	+$90
		Demand deposit due Paris bank	– $90

Summary. Most of these transactions cancel out, as shown in Exhibit 2A.1, in which each of them is summarized in T-account form and the ending balance indicated.

At the end of the series of transactions, the New York bank owes the London bank $100, this demand deposit having originally been acquired from the Dutch corporation and then transferred first to the London bank, then to the Paris bank, and then back to the London bank. Additionally, the New York bank received $90 in currency to match the eventual increase in demand deposits due the exporter. This transaction is no different from one resulting if the exporter sells its merchandise for cash on Manhattan Island and deposits the sales proceeds.

The London bank ended where it started, owning a $100 demand deposit in New York and owing a $100 time deposit to the Dutch corporation. Similarly, the Paris bank, which started with no dollar balances or loans, ended up with all its accounts closed out.

The Dutch corporation ended with a $100 time deposit in London rather than a $100 demand deposit in New York. The French importer ended up with an additional $90 of inventory purchased and with its French franc cash balances reduced by the equivalent of US$90. Had the French importer sold the acquired inventory for US$90 or more of French francs, the ending balance would have been cash sales proceeds less whatever French francs were needed to acquire the dollars to repay the Eurodollar loan from the Paris bank.

The New York exporter ended with $90 of additional cash in the New York bank from the proceeds of the sale. In the example inventory was reduced by $90, implying a sale at cost with no profit. In fact, inventory might have been reduced by some (lesser) cost and the balance shown as an increase in retained earnings.

Throughout the entire example reserve balances at the New York Federal Reserve Bank remained at $20, the backing required for the single $100 of demand deposit balances which circulated among various European holders. No additional reserve balance is shown for the additional deposit of the New York exporter because that balance is matched 100% by currency deposited.

Exhibit 2A.1 T-Accounts Summarizing Eurodollar Transactions

New York Bank

(4)	DD Dutch corp.	100	(1)	DD Dutch corp.	100
(9)	DD London bank	90	(4)	DD London bank	100
(14)	DD Paris bank	90	(9)	DD Paris bank	90
(17)	Dollar currency	90	(14)	DD NY exporter	90
(20)	DD Paris bank	90	(17)	DD Paris bank	90
			(20)	DD London bank	90
	Dollar currency	90		DD London bank	100
				DD NY exporter	90

London Bank

(5)	DD NY bank	100	(5)	TD Dutch corp.	100
(7)	Loan Paris bank	90	(7)	DD NY bank	90
(19)	DD NY bank	90	(19)	Loan Paris bank	90
	DD NY bank	100		DD Dutch corp.	100

Paris Bank

(8)	DD NY bank	90	(8)	Loan London bank	90
(10)	Loan Paris importer	90	(10)	DD NY bank	90
(16)	DD NY bank	90	(16)	Loan Paris bank	90
(18)	Loan London bank	90	(18)	DD NY bank	90

Dutch Corporation

(2)	DD NY bank	100			
(6)	TD London bank	100	(6)	DD NY bank	100
	TD London bank	100			

French Importer

(11)	Dollar check	90	(11)	Loan Paris bank	100
(12)	Inventory	90	(12)	Dollar check	90
(15a)	US$ currency	90	(15a)	French francs	90
(15b)	Loan Paris bank	90	(15b)	US$ currency	90
	Inventory	90		French francs	90

continued

Exhibit 2A.1   *continued*

New York Exporter

(13) DD NY bank	90	(13) Inventory	90
DD NY bank	90	Inventory	90

Federal Reserve Bank of New York

(3) Reserves, NY bank	20
Reserves, NY bank	20

Note: DD means demand-deposit balance; TD means Eurodollar time-deposit balance.

CHAPTER 3

Balances and Imbalances of Payments

The balance of payments is an accounting system that measures all economic transactions between residents of one country and residents of all other countries. Economic transactions include exports and imports of goods and services, capital inflows and outflows, gifts and other transfer payments, and changes in a country's international reserves.

A country's own balance of payments is important to business managers, investors, consumers, and government officials because it influences, and is influenced by, other key macroeconomic variables such as gross national product, employment, price levels, exchange rates, and interest rates. As a result, monetary and fiscal policy must take the balance of payments into account.

Managers and investors are vitally interested in the balance of payments of foreign countries for the following reasons.

- The balance of payments helps to forecast a country's market potential, especially in the short run. A country experiencing a serious balance of payments deficit is not likely to import as much as it would if it were running a surplus.

- The balance of payments is an important indicator of pressure on a country's foreign exchange rate, and thus on the potential for a firm trading with or investing in that country to experience exchange gains or losses.

- Continuing deficits in a country's balance of payments may signal future controls on outgoing capital movements, such as payments of dividends, fees, and interest to foreign firms and investors.

In this chapter we will first describe how the balance of payments is measured. We then discuss a number of summary measures or aggregates often used to describe the balance of payments. The second major section details trade and current account imbalances, as well as capital account imbalances. We then proceed to detail current issues: the persistent imbalances in trade and capital of some developing countries (The Debt Crisis), and imbalances in capital flows among the industrial countries.

MEASURING THE BALANCE OF PAYMENTS

Balance of payments accounts are a systematized procedure for measuring, summarizing, and stating the effect of all financial and economic transactions between residents of one country and residents of the remainder of the world during a particular time period. If expenditures abroad by residents of one nation exceed what the residents of that nation can earn or otherwise receive from abroad, that nation is generally deemed to have a "deficit" in its balance of payments. However, if a nation earns more abroad than it spends, that nation incurs a "surplus." Balance of payments accounts are intended to show the size of any deficit or surplus and to indicate the manner in which it was financed.

Debits and Credits

In dealing with the rest of the world, a country earns foreign exchange on some transactions and expends foreign exchange on others. Transactions that earn foreign exchange are recorded in the balance of payments statistics as a "credit" and are marked by a plus (+) sign. As a general matter, credits are obtained by selling to nonresidents either real or financial assets or services. For example, the export of U.S.-made machinery earns foreign exchange and is therefore a credit. The sale to a foreigner of a service, such as an airline trip on a U.S. carrier, also earns foreign exchange and is a credit. Conceptually the sale of the trip to the foreigner is an export of a U.S. service to a nonresident of the United States—even though the trip may have taken place between New York and San Francisco, or between Bombay and Cairo, rather than between a U.S. and a foreign city.

Borrowing abroad earns foreign exchange and is therefore recorded as a credit. This type of transaction may be viewed as though it were the export of U.S. securities (shares of stock, bonds, promissory notes, etc.) to foreigners; thus it generates foreign exchange in a manner analogous to the export of such tangible merchandise as machines.

Transactions that expend foreign exchange are recorded as debits and are marked with a minus (−) sign. The foremost example is the import of goods from foreign countries. When U.S. residents buy coffee from Latin America, foreign exchange is expended and the import is recorded as a debit. Similarly, when U.S. residents purchase foreign services, such as insurance policies taken out with Lloyds of London or ship merchandise in a vessel owned by a Korean shipping company, foreign exchange is used. Lending to foreigners also uses foreign exchange and is recorded as a debit; foreign lending may be considered as equivalent to the importing of foreign securities. A useful format for balance of payments data appears in Exhibit 3.1, which is taken from the IMF's monthly publication, *Balance of Payments Statistics*. This source is valuable for comparing various countries, because a comparable format is used for the balance of payments statistics of each nation.

Exhibit 3.1 United States Balance of Payments Statistics, Aggregated Presentation: Transactions data, 1982–1989 (billions of U.S. dollars)

	1982	1983	1984	1985	1986	1987	1988	1989
A. Current Account, excl. Group F	**−5.86**	**−40.18**	**−98.99**	**−122.25**	**−145.42**	**−162.22**	**−128.99**	**−110.04**
Merchandise: exports f.o.b.	211.20	201.81	219.90	215.93	223.36	250.28	320.34	360.46
Merchandise: imports f.o.b.	−247.64	−268.89	−332.41	−338.09	−368.41	−409.77	−447.31	−475.33
Trade balance	−36.44	−67.08	−112.51	−122.16	−145.05	−159.49	−126.97	−114.87
Other goods, services, and income: credit	144.86	142.06	159.45	150.21	160.60	181.75	213.08	242.71
Reinvested earnings	*4.69*	*13.46*	*17.22*	*14.11*	*10.02*	*19.71*	*12.61*	*22.41*
Other investment income	*80.66*	*68.51*	*75.73*	*68.16*	*70.95*	*70.82*	*97.41*	*105.14*
Other	*59.51*	*60.09*	*66.50*	*67.94*	*79.63*	*91.22*	*103.06*	*115.16*
Other goods, services, and income: debit	−104.51	−105.19	−133.32	−134.82	−145.08	−170.15	−200.04	−223.12
Reinvested earnings	*2.38*	*−.09*	*−2.91*	*1.37*	*2.30*	*−1.48*	*−6.56*	*.10*
Other investment income	*−59.48*	*−54.47*	*−66.66*	*−67.51*	*−72.30*	*−83.76*	*−101.95*	*−128.52*
Other	*−47.41*	*−50.63*	*−63.75*	*−68.68*	*−75.08*	*−84.91*	*−91.53*	*−94.70*
Total goods, services, and income	3.91	−30.21	−86.38	−106.77	−129.53	−147.89	−113.93	−95.28
Private unrequited transfers	−1.43	−1.28	−1.77	−2.06	−1.86	−1.84	−1.77	−1.33
Total, excl. official unrequited transfers	2.48	−31.49	−88.15	−108.83	−131.39	−149.73	−115.70	−96.61
Official unrequited transfers	−8.34	−8.69	−10.84	−13.42	−14.03	−12.49	−13.29	−13.43
Grants (excluding military)	*−6.09*	*−6.49*	*−8.68*	*−11.28*	*−11.87*	*−10.28*	*−10.74*	*−10.95*
Other	*−2.25*	*−2.20*	*−2.16*	*−2.14*	*−2.16*	*−2.21*	*−2.55*	*−2.48*
B. Direct Investment and Other Long-Term Capital, excl. Groups F through H	**−10.73**	**−7.98**	**29.77**	**78.33**	**81.87**	**46.14**	**94.07**	**87.93**
Direct investment	12.83	5.26	13.80	5.87	15.40	15.85	42.24	40.50
In United States	*13.80*	*11.96*	*25.39*	*19.03*	*34.09*	*46.89*	*58.45*	*72.23*
Abroad	*−.97*	*−6.70*	*−11.59*	*−13.16*	*−18.69*	*−31.04*	*−16.21*	*−31.73*
Portfolio investment	−.88	4.73	28.76	64.43	71.60	31.06	40.31	44.79
Other long-term capital								
Resident official sector	−6.65	−4.65	−4.25	−.97	−.47	−1.39	.94	2.48
Disbursements on loans extended	*−8.59*	*−8.16*	*−7.80*	*−5.90*	*−7.14*	*−4.85*	*−5.82*	*−3.87*
Repayments on loans extended	*3.80*	*4.58*	*4.07*	*4.30*	*5.65*	*7.20*	*9.94*	*6.10*
Other	*−1.86*	*−1.07*	*−.52*	*.63*	*1.02*	*−3.74*	*−3.18*	*.25*
Deposit money banks	−16.03	−13.32	−8.54	9.00	−4.66	.62	10.58	.16
Other sectors	—	—	—	—	—	—	—	—
Total, Groups A plus B	**−16.59**	**−48.16**	**−69.22**	**−43.92**	**−63.55**	**−116.08**	**−34.92**	**−22.11**
C. Other Short-Term Capital, excl. Groups F through H	**−18.05**	**32.71**	**42.58**	**29.86**	**13.92**	**52.54**	**7.00**	**16.32**
Resident official sector	7.15	5.59	1.57	−1.44	−.52	−1.96	−.17	1.84
Deposit money banks	−26.24	28.98	27.54	24.30	26.76	45.88	5.49	8.01
Other sectors	1.04	−1.86	13.47	7.00	−12.32	8.62	1.68	6.47
D. Net Errors and Omissions	**36.67**	**11.40**	**27.36**	**19.86**	**15.85**	**6.68**	**−8.35**	**22.58**
Total, Groups A thorugh D	**2.03**	**−4.05**	**.72**	**5.80**	**−33.78**	**−56.86**	**−36.27**	**16.79**

continued

Exhibit 3.1   *continued*

	1982	1983	1984	1985	1986	1987	1988	1989
E. Counterpart Items	**−1.12**	**−1.65**	**−2.15**	**4.37**	**5.43**	**6.56**	**−2.13**	**1.55**
Monetization/demonetization of gold	−.03	−.28	−.24	−.04	−.24	.15	−.23	.02
Allocation/cancellation of SDRs	—	—	—	—	—	—	—	—
Valuation changes in reserves	−1.09	−1.37	−1.91	4.41	5.67	6.41	−1.90	1.53
Total, Groups A thorugh E	**.91**	**−5.70**	**−1.44**	**10.17**	**−28.35**	**−50.30**	**−38.40**	**18.33**
F. Exceptional Financing	**—**	**—**	**—**	**—**	**—**	**—**	**—**	**—**
Total, Groups A through F	**.91**	**−5.70**	**−1.44**	**10.17**	**−28.35**	**−50.30**	**−38.40**	**18.33**
G. Liabilities Constituting Foreign **Authorities' Reserves**	**2.95**	**5.25**	**2.41**	**−1.96**	**33.46**	**47.72**	**40.19**	**8.48**
Total, Groups A through G	**3.86**	**−.45**	**.97**	**8.21**	**5.11**	**−2.58**	**1.79**	**26.81**
H. Total Change in Reserves	**−3.86**	**.45**	**−.97**	**−8.21**	**−5.11**	**2.58**	**−1.79**	**−26.81**
Monetary gold	.03	.27	.24	.05	.25	−.15	.23	−.01
SDRs	−1.15	.22	−.62	−1.65	−1.10	−1.89	.65	−.31
Reserve position in the Fund	−2.29	−3.96	−.23	−.41	.22	.38	1.60	.70
Foreign exchange assets	−.44	3.92	−.37	−6.20	−4.47	4.24	−4.28	−27.19
Other claims	—	—	—	—	—	—	—	—
Credit from the Fund and Fund administered resources	—	—	—	—	—	—	—	—

Source: International Monetary Fund, *Balance of Payments Statistics*, March 1991.

Exhibit 3.1 is based on the IMF's presentation of the balance of payments of the United States for the period 1982–1989.

Analytical Arrangement

In any balance of payments presentation all transactions between residents and nonresidents are conceptually divided into two analytical categories, the sum of which is zero. Thus in one sense the balance of payments always balances. One can visualize the statement as having an imaginary horizontal line drawn across the list of accounts such that all transactions "above the line" are financed by all transactions "below the line." This imaginary line may be drawn higher or lower, depending on the analytical need of the person evaluating the accounts.

The IMF presentation in Exhibit 3.1 is intended to facilitate a variety of analytical perspectives, with a user able to regard as "above the line" any cumulative partial balance from Group A down through Group G. Most of the partial balances from Group A down have a name and particular analytical use, as will be discussed later in this chapter.

Trade Balance. The *trade balance* is defined as the net balance on *merchandise trade*. The first two lines under Group A of Exhibit 3.1 show exports and imports of merchandise such as wheat, machinery, automobiles, bananas, aircraft, and oil. In each year the United States ran a deficit on its trade balance, as shown on the third line under Group A.

Although the merchandise trade balance is an often-quoted summary measure, it is not necessarily the most important. Countries like the United States and Japan have relatively large service sectors, so that international trade in services (banking, construction, etc.) constitute significant proportions of the overall balance of payments. The United States, for example, continues to run a sizable annual surplus in its balance on service trade.

Balance on Current Account. The concept of *current account* expands the trade balance concept to include earnings and expenditures for services and "invisible" trade items, such as transportation, tourism, investment income including earnings from foreign affiliates, and military expenditures. The name of the account reflects the definition that the payments occurring are a result of current trade and service activity. When the net effect of these items is added to the merchandise trade balance, the resultant balance on "goods, services, and income" measures the net transfer of real resources between the United States and the rest of the world.

Special note must be made that the investment income component of the current account is the flow of earnings from different forms of capital or portfolio investments made in prior periods. For example the current income a U.S. corporation earns on a manufacturing facility constructed in Canada in previous years would fall into the current account. The initial investment of capital, however, would be termed a "capital flow" and fall into the capital accounts to be defined next.

As shown in Exhibit 3.1 on the twelfth line under Group A (Total: goods, services, and income), the current account balance deteriorated badly from 1983–1987 due to the exceptional strength of the dollar. Analysis of the balance of payments presumes that the balance down through "goods, services, and income" is determined autonomously because of pricing, quality, or similar factors.

The remaining items in Group A, private and official unrequited transfers, measure unilateral transfers not matched by a quid-pro-quo transaction. Unrequited transfers include sums sent home by migrant workers, parental payments to students studying abroad, private gifts, pension payments to retirees living abroad, and governmental gifts or grants.

The net sum of all merchandise, service, income, and unrequited transfers is the balance on "current account," shown at the top of Group A. The balance on current account is the measure most frequently used in economic policy analysis since it comes closest to measuring the effect of the international sector on a nation's GNP. It is also the measure most often cited in the news media when reporting the balance of payments results.

Basic Balance. The *basic balance* is the net result of activities in Groups A and B. Group B measures long-term capital flows, including direct foreign investments. Long-term capital flows are presumed to be autonomous because of fundamental desires to invest for the long run. The basic balance is useful in evaluating long-term trends in the balance of payments, since it does not include the volatile, easily reversible, short-term capital flows. The United States had a deficit on its basic balance account throughout the period 1982–1989.

Overall Balance, or Official Settlements Balance. The *overall balance*, sometimes called the *official settlements balance*, is the net result of activities in Groups A, B, C, and D. Group C measures short-term capital movements, such as transactions in money market instruments and bank deposits. In one sense these are autonomous in that they occur for their own sake. From another perspective, however, they are often induced by the monetary policies of various countries. For this reason short-term capital movements are sometimes regarded as volatile and readily reversible rather than as fundamental and stable in nature.

Group D measures errors and omissions. This account comprises transactions that are known to have occurred but for which no specific measure was made. The account arises because balance of payments statistics are gathered on a single-entry basis, rather than on a double-entry basis as in corporate accounting, from statistics collected when goods move through customhouses or funds flow through the banking system. Many transactions are not recorded but are known to have occurred because other components of the statistical series reveal an imbalance. For example, one large unrecorded account is the illegal drug trade. Because most errors and omissions are in current account or capital items, the errors and omissions balance is placed before striking the balance labeled "Total, Groups A through D," which is the overall balance.

The overall balance is one of the most frequently used measures because it represents the sum of all autonomous transactions that must be financed by the use of official reserves or of other nonreserve official transactions that are often viewed as being a substitute for reserve transactions. It is a comprehensive balance often used to judge a country's overall competitive position in terms of all private transactions with the rest of the world. Deficits or surpluses in the overall balance are frequently used to judge pressure for exchange rate changes. The overall balance of the United States turned positive in 1989 after being negative for the previous three years.

Other Adjustments. Groups E, F, and G in Exhibit 3.1 constitute transactions that have official attributes but are not counted in official reserves. Counterpart items are transactions that create or destroy official reserves. The monetization or demonetization of gold arises because gold is a commodity when held by private parties but a monetary reserve item when held by the central authorities. Monetization of gold means gold has moved from private hands to official accounts. Allocation or cancellation of SDRs represents a change in official holdings. Exceptional financing refers to financing mobilized by authorities outside of reserve transactions. Typical examples are postponing debt repayments or drawing on loans to finance transactions that would otherwise have depleted the country's reserve assets.

Changes in Reserves. The net result of activities in Groups A through G in Exhibit 3.1 must be financed by changes in official monetary reserves. Group H shows changes in the reserve holdings of the United States. These consist of monetary gold, SDRs, the U.S. reserve position with the IMF, and U.S. holdings of foreign exchange assets.

Balance of Payment Interpretation

Exhibit 3.2 provides a brief "qualitative guide" to the interrelationships of the summary measures discussed above. The sample year utilized in this case for the United States is 1985, a rather pivotal year for the U.S. dollar. The merchandise trade balance for 1985 was a deficit of $122.2 billion. This is the account balance which is the most well-recognized and publicized of the various BOP summary statistics. The merchandise trade balance, when supplemented with the balance on international services, income, and official and private unrequited transfers, results in the current account balance. The current account balance for 1985 was a deficit of $122.3 billion.

Although the current account was at a substantial deficit in 1985, note the surplus in the long-term capital account (+78.3). The basic balance of –$43.9 billion results from long-term capital inflows compensating for a large portion of the merchandise trade net outflows in 1985. With the additions of short-term capital flows and errors and omissions, the final measure utilized, the overall balance, was a surplus of $5.8 billion in 1985.

Exhibit 3.2 The United States Balance of Payments: Commonly Used Summary Measures (billions of dollars)

Group	Category Component	Balance in 1985	Cumulative Total	Popular Name
A	Merchandise Trade	–122.2		
	Other current items	0.1		
	Current Account	–122.3	–122.3	"Current Balance" (A)
B	Direct Investment	5.9		
	Portfolio Investment	64.4		
	Other long-term items	8.2		
	Long-Term Capital	+78.3	–43.9	"Basic Balance" (A+B)
C	Short-Term Capital	+29.9	–14.1	
D	Errors and Omissions	+19.9	+5.8	"Overall Balance" (A+B+C+D)

Source: *Balance of Payments Statistics*, International Monetary Fund, March 1991.

IMBALANCES IN THE BALANCE OF PAYMENTS

The meaning of a deficit or surplus in the balance of payments (BOP) has changed since the advent of floating exchange rates. Traditionally, these measures were used as evidence of pressure on a country's foreign exchange rate. Pressure was measured by transactions that were compensatory in nature, that is, forced on the government to settle the deficit.[1]

Exchange Rate Impacts

The relationship between the balance of payments and exchange rates can be illustrated by use of a simplified model that summarizes balance of payments data as follows:

Current Account Balance		Capital Account Balance		Official Forex Balance		Balance of Payments
$(X - M)$	+	$(CI - CO)$	+	FXB	=	BOP

Where X is exports, M is imports, CI is capital inflows, CO is capital outflows, and FXB is the foreign exchange reserve balance of the country.

Under a fixed exchange rate system it is the government's responsibility to assure a BOP of zero. If the sum of the current and capital accounts do not equal zero, the government is responsible for foreign exchange market intervention through its official foreign exchange reserves account (*official forex balance*). If the sum of the first two accounts is greater than zero, this represents a surplus demand for the domestic currency. Government must intervene in the market and sell domestic currency for foreign currencies and gold to reattain an equilibrium BOP of zero. If the sum of the current and capital accounts is negative, excess supply of domestic currency on world markets, the government must intervene by buying the domestic currency with its reserves of foreign currencies and gold. It is obviously important for a government to maintain significant foreign exchange reserve balances to allow it to intervene effectively.

Under a floating exchange rate system, the government of a country has no such responsible role. Under floating exchange rates, the fact that the current and capital account balances do not sum to zero would automatically (theoretically) alter the exchange rate in the direction necessary to obtain a BOP of zero. For example a country running a sizable current account deficit ($(X-M)<0$), with a capital account balance of zero (CI–CO=0) would have a net BOP in deficit. This means that there is an excess supply of the domestic currency on world markets, and like all goods in excess supply, the market rids itself of the imbalance by lowering the price. Thus the domestic currency would fall in value, depreciate, and the BOP would move back towards zero. As we will see in Chapter 6, exchange rate markets do not always follow the theories.

As noted earlier (Chapter 2), when a currency's value changes under floating rates, it is termed *appreciation* or *depreciation*. A change in the value of a currency whose exchange rate is set and defended by government, a fixed exchange rate regime, is termed *revaluation* or *devaluation*.

Managed Floats

Although still relying on market conditions for day-to-day exchange rate determination, countries operating with managed floats often find it necessary to take actions to maintain their desired exchange rate values. They therefore seek to alter the market's valuation of a specific exchange rate by influencing the motivations of market activity, rather than through direct intervention in the foreign exchange markets.

The primary action taken by governments at the present time is to change relative interest rates, thus influencing the economic fundamentals of exchange rate determination. As we will discuss in detail in Chapter 6, the power of interest rate changes on international capital and exchange rate movements can be substantial. A country wishing to "defend its currency" in today's markets under a managed float may choose to raise domestic interest rates to attract additional capital from abroad. This alters market forces and creates additional market demand for the domestic currency. In this process, the government "signals" exchange market participants that it intends to take measures to preserve the currency's value within certain ranges.

Economic Development Impacts

Apart from implications for pressure on foreign exchange rates, the balance of payments has also been used for economic development analysis. In that context a deficit or surplus in the current account is not necessarily good or bad for a country. From a national income viewpoint, a deficit on current account could have a negative effect on GNP and employment if underemployment exists, whereas a surplus could have a positive effect. However, if full employment exists, a current account deficit that can be financed abroad would allow the import of investment goods that would not have been possible otherwise.

From a program viewpoint, economic development usually requires a net import of goods and services (deficit in the current account) financed by foreign savings. Less developed countries find it nearly impossible to generate sufficient domestic savings or technical and managerial know-how to reach the "takeoff" point without external aid.

Finally, from a liquidity viewpoint, a deficit could mean that a country is building up a net long-term creditor position vis-à-vis the rest of the world through direct foreign investments and long-term loans while simultaneously building up its short-term liabilities to the rest of the world.

The BOP and the Sources and Uses of Foreign Currency Funds

The balance of payments is to a large degree the income statement of an individual country, but actual "cash flows" of the country are not summarized so simply. Whereas all business and economic activity which occurs within a country is normally denominated in its own currency, much of international trade and financial transactions are denominated in foreign currencies. Although these foreign currencies can potentially include any currency in the world, the majority of world financial transactions are increasingly denominated in the major trading currencies: the U.S. dollar, the German mark, and the Japanese yen.

These currencies are obtainable through two major avenues: (1) the exporting of merchandise and services which are then paid for in a foreign currency, for example the

U.S. dollar; (2) the borrowing of capital which is denominated in foreign currency. The uses of these foreign currency earnings include imports of goods and services and the servicing of prior debt obligations denominated in foreign currencies. Governments also require large foreign currency reserves in order to intervene in foreign currency markets. Although it is not unusual for a country or firm to borrow the capital necessary for debt-service payments (not a policy we normally encourage in finance courses), the long-term stable source of foreign exchange earnings is through exports.

The Debt Crisis

On Friday August 13, 1982, the Finance Minister of Mexico, Silva Herzog, placed a telephone call to then U.S. Secretary of the Treasury Baker informing him that Mexico would be unable to make debt-service payments due on Monday August 16th. The *debt crisis* officially began. In the following months other major countries with large international debt burdens such as Brazil and Argentina followed suit, announcing their inability to meet debt-service obligations.

The origins of the debt crisis appear simple with the benefit of 20–20 hindsight. Many of the developing countries of the world believed in the late 1970s that by borrowing on world markets they could accelerate their rate of economic development. Given that most of these countries had abundant natural resources and primary commodities of various kinds, capital was the only major factor of production which they felt they needed for more rapid development. Not unlike any private firm operating in a domestic market, they believed that the products and earnings of the enterprises financed by the borrowing would provide the funds necessary for servicing the debt. If the capital borrowed was as fruitful for these countries as they had hoped, and the lending banks and institutions believed, there would have been little trouble in servicing the debt burdens. Unfortunately for all parties involved, this was not to be the case.

Although there are many factors which contributed to the problems of the debt-ridden countries, we believe there are two primary financial focal points for the debt crisis. First, it is estimated that approximately 90% of the debt acquired by these countries was denominated in U.S. dollars. This required each country to service its obligations in a currency which was obtainable only through three avenues: (1) exports which were paid for in convertible currencies; (2) the borrowing of additional convertible currencies; and (3) direct foreign investment. The debtor countries obviously preferred to service their debt through export earnings rather than additional borrowing. However, on a number of occasions additional capital was necessary for the completion of export-related projects, or simply to allow the country to meet its obligations until export market performance improved. Direct foreign investment was more than offset by capital flight.

The second major financial factor contributing to the debt crisis was the world-wide economic turmoil, primarily in the form of dollar-based inflation, which occurred in the late 1970s and continued into the 1980s. The second oil crisis (1979) induced new waves of imported oil-inflation throughout the industrialized countries. As inflation increased, so did interest rates. Rising interest rates resulted in rapidly escalating debt-service obligations for the borrowing countries as a majority of the debt acquired was at variable rates.

The major industrial nations then chose to fight the inflationary conditions with substantial restrictive measures, measures which contributed to the inception of a major world recession in the early 1980s. A world recession translated into depressed markets for the very exports the developing countries were dependent upon. This in combination with the dollar-denominated debt resulted in the inability of the most heavily indebted countries to meet their debt-service obligations. The debt crisis was the result.

Since the inception of the crisis many of the indebted countries have been able to restructure much of their existing debt, acquire additional funds needed for continued economic growth, and successfully re-establish export earnings. Exhibit 3.3 provides a status report on the continuing efforts by these debt-burdened countries to grow and service their obligations. As of 1989, Brazil topped the list with a debt level of $112.7 billion, with Mexico close behind at $102.6 billion. Looking further, for Brazil this requires interest payments alone of $17.4 billion in 1989–1990, which represent 36.1% of all export earnings of the country. The columns in Exhibit 3.3 listing average annual growth of major components of the national economies aid in highlighting the less than desired rates of economic growth over the 1982–1988 period. Note the continuing difficulties of several countries including Bolivia, Costa Rica, and Poland, in achieving higher export than import growth. Finally, the one indicator of the table which is most disheartening is the negative signs on the average annual growth of per capita consumption in 11 of the debt-burdened countries listed. This is an indication of a falling standard of living for the residents of these countries.

Issues in International Capital Flows

International economic and financial problems in the 1980s were not confined to the current account. The capital account and its subject financial flows moved to the forefront of much of the concern over "imbalances."

Capital flows across countries are typically classified in terms of maturity, short-term and long-term, and whether the investment represents some degree of control over the target investment. Short-term capital flows respond primarily to interest rate differentials and expectations of interest rate changes across countries. As will be detailed in Chapter 6, speculators and arbitragers are able to move massive quantities of capital around the world in moments in search of the highest returns. This allows small interest differentials to be exploited by the astute investor.

Short-Term Capital Flows. Short-term debt instruments, such as the U.S. treasury bill (maturities of 13, 26, and 52 weeks), have at different times in the 1980s represented relatively high rates of return and low levels of risk for investors worldwide. Their relatively high yields during the early 1980s, combined with the "safe haven" argument that the United States constituted one of the most stable political and economic environments, induced significant capital flows from abroad (particularly from Japan). It is this portfolio investment which is the subject of much of the debate over foreign financing of the U.S. government budget deficit.

Exhibit 3.3 Debt, Debt Service, and Growth in Severely Indebted Middle Income Countries

Country	Debt Outstanding, 1989[a] Total (US$ bill.)	From private sources (%)[b]	Debt Service, 1989–90 Total (US$ bill.)	Interest (US$ bill.)	Debt Ratios (percent) Debt–GNP 1988	Interest–exports, 1988	Average Annual Growth Rates, 1982–88 (percent) GDP	Exports	Imports	Investment	Per capita consumption
Argentina	61.9	74.3	14.7	9.0	60.5	27.5	0.9	2.3	0.6	-2.7	-0.1
Bolivia	5.8	12.2	1.0	0.4	135.5	17.2	-1.0	1.5	4.6	-5.0	-2.7
Brazil	112.7	75.2	30.4	17.4	30.7	36.1	4.7	5.6	-1.4	2.6	2.4
Chile	18.5	68.8	4.5	3.1	96.6	15.1	4.6	7.0	4.6	15.4	0.4
Congo	4.2	53.4	1.7	0.5	238.3	13.3	-0.7	3.3	-10.2	-15.2	-2.8
Costa Rica	4.6	47.4	1.4	0.4	100.0	13.4	3.8	1.9	9.3	9.1	3.5
Cote d'Ivoire	14.0	61.6	4.2	1.8	161.8	15.7	0.5	-3.0	-7.0	-7.6	-3.4
Ecuador	11.5	51.1	3.9	1.6	113.3	12.7	2.2	6.6	-1.0	-20.0	-1.5
Honduras	3.4	22.3	0.7	0.3	81.9	15.6	2.8	2.9	4.6	7.7	-1.0
Hungary	17.9	87.4	4.9	2.2	65.2	10.1	1.4	3.9	3.0	0.4	1.4
Mexico	102.6	76.0	28.4	16.3	58.0	27.3	0.2	4.7	1.6	-5.0	-1.5
Morocco	20.8	26.2	5.6	2.4	105.9	15.3	4.1	6.1	1.1	0.1	0.9
Nicaragua	8.6	19.6	1.5	0.6	0.0	25.0	-0.7	-12.9	0.8	2.0	-1.5
Peru	19.9	43.0	4.4	1.1	47.3	5.6	2.1	-1.8	-4.5	-2.4	0.6
Philippines	28.5	56.1	7.3	4.1	72.9	18.6	-0.2	6.3	2.5	-10.7	-0.2
Poland	40.1	31.2	12.5	4.5	63.9	5.6	4.5	5.5	6.3	3.5	3.8
Senegal	3.6	15.5	0.8	0.3	76.6	12.1	2.5	-1.3	-3.5	1.7	-1.5
Uruguay	4.5	79.1	1.1	0.6	50.1	18.3	1.8	4.6	1.5	-4.0	1.3
Venezuela	34.1	94.7	11.9	5.8	57.7	24.1	2.1	6.0	1.2	2.1	-2.1
Total[c]	**517.5**	**65.4**	**142.0**	**72.3**	**53.6**	**22.3**	**2.5**	**4.8**	**1.3**	**-0.7**	**0.4**

a. Estimated total external liabilities, including the use of IMF credit.

b. Debt service is based on all external debt at end of 1988. It does not take into account new loans contracted or debt reschedulings signed after that date.

c. Based on recent data Egypt would be classified as severely indebted instead of moderately indebted. For purposes of this report, Egypt is classified as moderately indebted.

Source: The World Bank, *World Debt Tables*, 1989–1990, Washington, D.C., 1990, p. 30.

Long-Term Capital Flows. Long-term capital flows play a significant role in the balance of payments structure of many nations. Whereas short-term capital tends to follow interest rates, long-term capital is typically attracted to economic and business environments representing significant long-run stability and economic growth.

The classification of international capital flows is also premised on the degree of control over a target investment by a foreign investor. In the United States, the acquisition of 10% or more of the equity of a U.S. enterprise is considered sufficient for a foreign investor to exercise some influence on the management and operations of the firm. It is then categorized as direct foreign investment (DFI), and the firm itself is reclassified as the U.S. affiliate of a foreign company. The definitional requirement for DFI varies across countries, with West Germany requiring 25%, and both Great Britain and France specifying 20% as the point of "foreign control." If ownership is less than the DFI threshold level, or the investment is a debt instrument, it is summarily classified as portfolio investment.

DFI is often further subdivided into the nature of the investment itself: (1) "greenfield" projects in which the capital is used for the construction of new production, sales or commercial facilities; (2) "acquisitions" investments which are essentially the purchase of pre-existing enterprises or operations. Greenfield investments are looked upon by most governments as a strong potential contributor to economic welfare, and are normally encouraged and courted. Acquisitions, however, are increasingly a source of emotional and political concern as foreign residents buy the land and resources of domestic enterprises. This has become a topic of emotional "sovereignty" as residents of the countries experiencing these capital inflows worry over the potential loss of home-control.

Capital Flight

A final issue is that of capital flight. Although no single accepted definition of capital flight exists, Ingo Walter's discussion has been one of the more useful.

> International flows of direct and portfolio investments under ordinary circumstances are rarely associated with the capital flight phenomenon. Rather, it is when capital transfers by residents conflict with political objectives that the term "flight" comes into general usage.[2]

Although not limited to heavily indebted countries, the rapid and sometimes illegal transfer of convertible currencies out of a country poses significant economic and political problems. Many of the heavily indebted countries have suffered significant capital flight, which has compounded their problems of debt service.

There are four primary mechanisms by which capital may be moved from one country to the next. Transfers via the usual international payments mechanisms, regular bank transfers, are obviously the easiest, lowest cost, and legal. Transfers by cash movements by bearer are more costly and for most transfers internationally, illegal. The third form of movement is the transfer of cash into collectibles or precious metals, which are then in turn transferred across borders. The fourth form of transfer and the one most typically associated with capital flight, is that of the false invoicing of international trade transactions. Capital is successfully moved through the under-invoicing of exports or the over-invoicing of imports, where the illegally relocated balances are normally deposited in banking institutions in the country of choice. It has been suspected that some of the dollar loans originally extended to Latin American countries have been redeposited in the same lending banks, but under the ownership of new identities.

Emerging Trends in Trade and Capital Flows

Exhibits 3.4, 3.5, and 3.6 provide graphical representations of the current account balances and overall balances of the United States, Japan, and West Germany for the past two decades. A number of trends are evident.

Exhibit 3.4 shows balances on current account and overall balance for the United States. The magnitude of the current account deficit of the United States, beginning in 1983, is striking. It was over $100 billion each year 1985–1989. Yet, the overall balance of

Exhibit 3.4   United States Balance of Payments (billions of U.S. dollars)

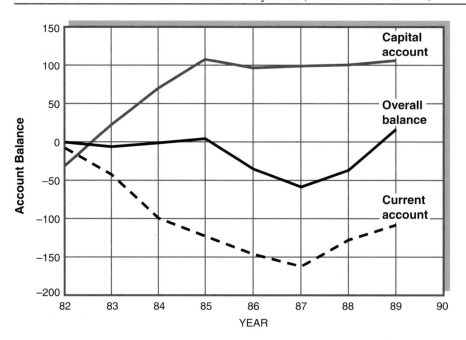

Source: Adapted from *Balance of Payments Statistics*, International Monetary Fund, Washington, D.C., March 1991.

Exhibit 3.5   Japanese Balance of Payments (billions of U.S. dollars)

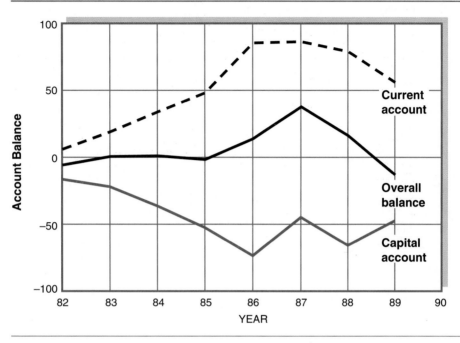

Source: Adapted from *Balance of Payments Statistics*, International Monetary Fund, Washington, D.C., March 1991.

payments was supported to a large degree by massive net capital inflows. The improvement in the overall balance of payments for the United States, 1987–1989, coincides with the fall of U.S. interest rates and the dollar over this period.

For Japan and West Germany over the same period, a largely reciprocal relationship is evident. The massive U.S. current account deficit's growth coincides with the rapid development of Japan's current account surplus in 1982, continuing into 1990. The Japanese overall balance of payments also went into considerable surplus in the late 1980s, while the yen doubled in value versus the U.S. dollar over this same period.

The current account balance of Germany has shown a considerable amount of volatility. The current account surplus which Germany has enjoyed continues to be something of a stabilizing force given the volatility of its overall balance. The institution of a withholding tax on foreign portfolio investment in Germany in 1988 is purported to have been one of the major reasons for the massive net capital outflow in that year. The tax was quickly dropped!

Exhibit 3.6   German Balance of Payments (billions of U.S. dollars)

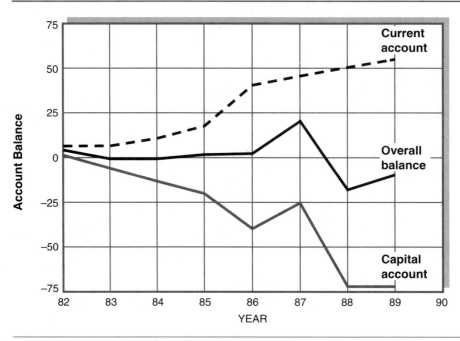

Source: Adapted from *Balance of Payments Statistics*, International Monetary Fund, Washington, D.C., March 1991.

Ecuadorian Debt for Development*

Jack is nervous. Jack Van de Water is the Director for International Education Programs at Oregon State University, and therefore responsible for managing the financing of all study-abroad programs. It is May 1991 and one of the causes of Jack's nervousness is the need to decide whether or not the University is to take part in the "Debt for Development" program (hereafter DFD) in financing its study programs in the country of Ecuador. The DFD program is designed to aid not-for-profit entities like universities in increasing their spending capabilities abroad while contributing to the reduction of large foreign debt levels suffered by many developing countries.

Ecuador and Debt

Ecuador is another in the long line of Latin American countries attempting to deal with large levels of foreign debt. This debt is made up of loans taken out by the government of Ecuador and other semi-government institutions in Ecuador (like utilities, railroads, etc) during the late 1970s and early 1980s when the prospects for economic development in

---

* Michael H. Moffett, Oregon State University, May 1991. Reprinted with permission.

that part of the world were quite strong. Ecuador, like Brazil and Mexico, went to the international capital markets to obtain funds, to speed up its rate of industrialization. The debt was primarily in the form of U.S. dollars, a currency with wide international purchasing power at the time. The capital was intended to improve the internal infrastructure and manufacturing industries of Ecuador to allow it to generate increased earnings— particularly in export markets where it could be paid in U.S. dollars—so that the debt could be serviced and eventually repaid. Things, however, did not quite work out that smoothly.

The internal and external sectors of the Ecuadorian economy did not grow sufficiently to generate the large amounts of foreign currency earnings needed for debt service during the 1980s. By 1987, a large amount of Ecuadorian debt was classified as in arrears, and by 1988 a substantial secondary market had developed for the sale of dollar debt owed by Ecuador to commercial banks throughout the world. Ecuador, like other heavily indebted countries, was faced with few alternatives to service dollar-denominated debt: (1) export (or run a net export surplus); (2) borrow additional dollars. The second alternative was not considered overly attractive by either the borrower or the lenders. The export market was relatively stable, but not growing sufficiently to service the existing levels of debt. A new alternative arose: miss the debt-service payments!

The term "debt," as normally used in reference to developing countries, consists of long-term borrowings by government or semigovernment entities from the international capital markets. The lenders are governments, international aid and development organizations like the International Monetary Fund (IMF), and large commercial banks worldwide. Although the first two organizations do not operate on the basis of profit, the commercial banking sector does operate in an increasingly competitive mode. As the debt crises of the early 1980s came and stayed, many of the commercial banks tried to either reschedule their loans to foreign borrowers (thus effectively redefining the loan as not being in arrears on servicing its obligations), or to rid themselves of their foreign debt completely. It is this dumping of debt, in which the commercial banks are willing to sell their loans to nonrelated third parties, which feeds the growing secondary market for third-world debt. Since the loans are often not currently being serviced by the borrowing country, and the prospects for payment in full are often poor, the banks are willing to sell the loans at a considerable discount from the face value of the loan.

The Debt for Development Program
The DFD program is described in its own literature as follows:

> The Debt for Development Coalition, Inc., represents not-for-profit organizations committed to finding ways to turn the international debts of countries into economic development opportunities.

If a portion of the external debt of developing nations can be converted—by donation or purchase—into local currencies, not-for-profit organizations can use the funds for development projects needed to help spur economic growth in Latin America, Africa, Asia, and the Pacific.

Coalition members are U.S. colleges and universities, cooperatives, private volunteer organizations, and research institutes engaged in economic development programs overseas. The coalition also maintains close cooperation with various U.S. environmental organizations.

The coalition works closely with private organizations in debtor nations to identify programs important to each country's economic priorities such as education, public health, nutrition, agriculture, small business enterprises, research, housing, credit, and natural resource management programs.

The DFD program arose from the growing activity in what is called debt for equity swaps. Many of the indebted countries wished to alter the nature of their obligations from debt to participating equity, where the holder would see returns tied to the profits (or losses) of the enterprises associated with the capital. The idea was to encourage long term equity involvement in the country, rather than the debt repayment at any cost posture of most debt holders.

The Debt for Development swap is something akin to a debt for equity swap. The dollar-debt is swapped for sucre-denominated debt in this case, however, rather than into the equity ownership of a sucre-denominated enterprise. Most debt holders have traditionally opposed debt redenomination schemes due to the weakness and inconvertibility of many of the developing country currencies. A country heavily indebted in dollars might reissue all debt in its own currency, essentially printing money to repay the debt. This is commonly thought to be too dangerous for all parties, resulting in depreciated values in repayment and inducing the country to undertake inflationary policies not in its own best interest. The DFD program, however, altered this process substantially by limiting the actual sucre to be swapped, and by requiring a debt swap with a repayment schedule matching that of the initial debt obligation. The first and foremost concern on the part of an indebted country like Ecuador is that the debt and debt service is in a foreign currency, in this case U.S. dollars. This swap program would allow Ecuador to exchange sucre debt for dollar debt.

Ecuadorian Debt for Development
The DFD program would work in the following way. Commercial banks holding Ecuadorian debt would sell their loans to the DFD program participant. The debt would be sold at a discount, with the banks receiving partial repayment in dollars, and writing the remainder of the loans off as bad debt obligations. The U.S. government, as well as the governments of several other large industrial countries having banks with third world debt, have provided tax relief to aid commercial banks to write off these loans through "advantaged loan loss reserves."

Ecuadorian debt has been quoted at between $0.16 and $0.20 per dollar of face value debt throughout late 1990 and early 1991. The third party—Oregon State University— would purchase dollar-denominated debt. The debt would then be swapped, with the Ecuadorian government crediting Oregon State with $0.50 for every dollar in debt face value. The Ecuadorian government would then exchange this discounted dollar value for the domestic currency, Sucre, at the official government exchange rate, sucre 970/$.

Several other countries follow a slightly different procedure whereby the country would swap the debt at 100 percent face value, but then exchange the dollar debt to domestic currency at a significantly altered (overvalued) exchange rate. The indebted country thus gains one way or the other in the actual exchange of dollar-debt for domestic currency. Ecuador thus succeeds in reducing its dollar-denominated debt obligations to foreign banks, and essentially assures that the proceeds of the conversion will be spent in the domestic economy (sucre do not buy anything anywhere else)!

There is, however, a final twist to this specific program. Ecuador, although anxious to retire or replace existing dollar-denominated debt with domestic currency, does not wish to add to inflationary pressures by pumping up its money supply. The government of Ecuador therefore will swap the debt as described, but for sucre-denominated bonds, not cash. These bonds would then be serviced by sucre-denominated cash flows (coupons) to be paid quarterly until maturity on October 31, 1996. The payment schedule and maturity matches the schedules of the original debt.

This last feature poses a problem for Jack (he is to the point of facial "ticks" now; twitching). Given the limited resources a university possesses in conducting study-abroad programs, he needs all the sucre value possible for use in the current period. Jack inquires as to the liquidity of these government bonds, and is told that the market is "thin", but the bonds will likely be able to be sold at discounts ranging from 10 to 30 percent depending on financial and inflationary conditions.

Jack's Dilemma

Jack was now running short of time. He had to decide whether to commit his resources and his study-abroad program financing, approximately $50,000 for the 1991-92 academic year, to the DFD program or not. Jack then summarized the major points which he needed to weigh in the pro and con columns of the dog-eared Big Chief tablet on his desk.

SUMMARY

- Although termed a "balance of payments," the BOP is actually an income statement which summarizes all economic transactions between residents of one country and residents of all other countries.

- The balance of payments consists of three major components: (1) the current account balance; (2) the capital account balance; (3) the official foreign currency reserves balance. The current account balance, which includes imports and exports of merchandise and service trade, has traditionally been the focus of attention. However, the 1980s saw a massive growth in the level of capital flows internationally, resulting in increased interest in the capital account balance and its subcomponents.

- The capital account balance combines both short-term capital flows and long-term capital investment. Short-term flows often follow the highest and yet safest real returns on short-term debt instruments, for example, the U.S. treasury bill in the mid-1980s. Long-term capital flows are normally attracted to countries thought to offer more stable and profitable business environments for longer periods of time.

- The plight of many of the world's heavily indebted countries is more easily understood when viewed from the perspective of the current and capital accounts of the balance of payments. In order for countries with continued capital account deficits (net borrowers) to be able to service their outstanding debt and prevent their currencies from weakening, it is necessary that they manage their current account and trade balances to create surpluses.

- The chapter concluded with a brief overview of the major balance of payment accounts of the United States, Japan, and Germany. The United States experienced a continuing surplus in its capital account while suffering a record deficit in the current account during the 1980s. Both Japan and Germany, however, exhibited opposite positions with large surpluses in the current account and deficits in their capital account balances.

1. The U.S. Balance of Payments

The United States had a large and growing balance of payments deficit on current account throughout the period 1981–1985. Yet, the U.S. dollar strengthened greatly during this period. Why was this the case?

2. Latin American Balance of Payments

Most Latin American countries were suffering balance of payments deficits on current accounts during the period 1981–1985. Unlike the United States, however, their currencies rapidly weakened in value. Why did the Latin American currencies' experience differ so markedly from the U.S. experience?

3.   Mexico's Balance of Payments

Find the most recent balance of payments data for Mexico. Explain the main trends in Mexico's balance of payments performance using whatever articles you can find. If you were advising Mexico about how to improve its balance of payments, what would you suggest? Be sure to consider the political ramifications of your suggested policies.

4.   FDI Versus Portfolio Investment

The topic of FDI in the United States and in many countries has become one which generates as much emotion as it does economic analysis. Discuss the business and nonbusiness issues of foreign ownership of companies within a country.

5.   Redefining Imports and Exports

Many people argue that the traditional measures of imports and exports no longer provide accurate indicators of how well a country's businesses are doing. They suggest that the exports of a country's companies to noncountry companies, regardless of whether the operations in question are located at home or not (just owned by a parent enterprise domiciled in the country in question) should be considered exports. Evaluate this alternative in regard to the international financial and economic concerns which the traditional balance of payments measures were designed to track.

◨ **6. U.S. Balance of Payments and Subaccounts in the 1980s (CO3A.WK1)**

Using Exhibit 3.1 (or the CO3A.WK1 template) answer the following questions regarding the behavior of sub-accounts in the 1980s:

    a)   What was the basic balance for the United States in 1987?

    b)   What was the level of merchandise imports and exports in the worst year of the U.S. trade balance?

    c)   What was the "balance of payments" for the United States in 1987, and which measure is most appropriate?

7. Coalition Financing of the Persian Gulf War

How will the financial contributions of the United Nations coalition members to the United States be entered in the U.S. balance of payments accounts for 1990 and 1991? Will it help or hurt the U.S. balance of payments?

NOTES

1. See Patricia Hagen Kuwayama, "Measuring the United States Balance of Payments," *Monthly Review*, Federal Reserve Bank of New York, August 1975, pp. 183–194. Also see Charles N. Stabler, "'Bottom Line' Data on Payments Balance Held Meaningless by U.S. Advisory Board," *Wall Street Journal*, December 10, 1975, p. 6.

2. Ingo Walter, "The Mechanisms of Capital Flight," in *Capital Flight and Third World Debt*, edited by Donald R. Lessard and John Williamson, Institute for International Economics, Washington D.C., 1987, p. 104.

BIBLIOGRAPHY

Bergsten, Fred C., *Trade Policy in the 1980s*, Washington, D.C.: Institute for International Economics, November 1982.

Bergsten, Fred C., and Shafique Islam, *The United States as a Debtor Country*, Washington, D.C.: Institute of International Economics, 1990.

Brown, Brendan, *The Flight of International Capital: A Contemporary History*, New York and London: Croom Helm, 1987.

Carvounis, Chris C., *The United States Trade Deficit of the 1980s*, Westport, Conn.: Quorum Books, 1987.

Corden, W. Max, "An International Debt Facility?" *IMF Staff Papers*, 35, no. 3, September 1988, pp. 401–421.

de Vries, Margaret Garritsen, *Balance of Payments Adjustment, 1945–1986: The IMF Experience*, Washington, D.C.: IMF, 1987.

Eichengreen, Barry, and Peter H. Lindert, *The International Debt Crisis in Historical Perspective*, Cambridge, MA: MIT Press, 1990.

Ganitsky, Joseph, and Gerardo Lema, "Foreign Investment Through Debt-Equity Swaps," *Sloan Management Review*, 29, no. 2, Winter 1988, pp. 21–29.

Graham, Edward, and Paul Krugman, *Foreign Direct Investment in the United States*, Washington, D.C.: Institute for International Economics, 1989.

Hooper, Peter, and Steven W. Kohlhagen, "The Effect of Exchange Rate Uncertainty on the Prices and Volume of International Trade," *Journal of International Economics*, November 1978, pp. 483–511.

Hufbauer, Gary Clyde, Diane T. Berliner, and Kimberly Ann Elliott, *Trade Protection in the United States: 31 Case Studies*, Washington, D.C.: Institute for International Economics, 1986.

Hutchinson, Michael, and Charles Piggott, "Budget Deficits, Exchange Rates and the Current Account: Theory and U.S. Evidence," Federal Reserve Bank of San Francisco, *Economic Review*, Fall 1984, pp. 5–25.

International Trade: The U.S. Trade Deficit: Causes and Policy Options for Solutions, Washington, D.C.: U.S. General Accounting Office, 1987.

Korteweg, Pieter, "Exchange-Rate Policy, Monetary Policy, and Real Exchange-Rate Variability," *Essays in International Finance*, No. 140, Princeton, N.J.: Princeton University, December 1980.

Millman, Gregory J., "Financing the Uncreditworthy: New Financial Structures for LDCs," *Journal of Applied Corporate Finance*, vol. 3, no. 4, Winter 1991, pp. 83–89.

Ohmae, Kenichi, "Lies, Damned Lies, and Statistics: Why the Trade Deficit Doesn't Matter in a Borderless World," *Journal of Applied Corporate Finance*, vol. 3, no. 4, Winter 1991.

Tavis, Lee A., ed., *Rekindling Development: Multinational Firms and World Debt*, Notre Dame, IN: Notre Dame Press, 1988.

Williamson, John, *Voluntary Approaches to Debt Relief*, Washington, D.C.: Institute for International Economics, 1988.

Williamson, John, and Donald Lessard, eds., *Capital Flight and Third World Debt*, Washington, D.C.: Institute for International Economics, 1987.

The Foreign Exchange Market

The foreign exchange market provides the physical and institutional environment in which foreign exchange is traded, exchange rates are determined, and foreign exchange management is implemented. In this chapter the operation of the spot and forward markets is described. In Chapter 5 the operation of the derivative futures and options markets is described. Together, these four markets comprise the foreign exchange market in its broadest interpretation.

In the first part of the chapter we describe the following features of the foreign exchange market:

- The geographical extent of the foreign exchange market.
- The three main functions performed by the market.
- The market's participants.
- The immense transaction volume that takes place daily in the foreign exchange market.
- Types of transactions, including spot, forward, and swap transactions.
- Exchange rates and quotations.
- The process of intermarket arbitrage.

In the second part of the chapter we explain the theory of interest rate parity as well as how covered interest arbitrage guarantees that this theory will nearly always hold true.

83

GEOGRAPHICAL EXTENT OF THE FOREIGN EXCHANGE MARKET

Geographically the foreign exchange market spans the globe, with prices moving and currencies traded somewhere every hour of every business day. Major world trading starts each morning in Wellington and Sydney, moves west to Tokyo, Hong Kong, and Singapore, passes on to Bahrain, shifts to the main European markets of Frankfurt, Zurich, and London, jumps the Atlantic to New York, and ends up in San Francisco and Los Angeles. The market is deepest, or most liquid, early in the European afternoon, when markets of both Europe and the U.S. East Coast are open. This period is regarded as the best time to ensure the smooth execution of a very large order.

At the end of the day in California, when traders in Tokyo and Hong Kong are just getting up for the next day, the market is thinnest. During these hours, when the U.S. West Coast is awake and Europe sleeps, aggressive speculators or central banks sometimes try to move prices by trading large blocks, and thus influence attitudes in Europe the following morning about particular currencies. Many of the largest international banks operate foreign exchange trading rooms in each major geographic trading center in order to serve important commercial accounts on a 24-hour-a-day basis.

In some countries, a portion of the foreign exchange trading is conducted on an official trading floor by open bidding. Closing prices are published as the official price, or "fixing," for the day, and certain commercial and investment transactions are based on this officially published price. In some countries local firms, including affiliates of multinational corporations that earn foreign exchange from exports, surrender that foreign exchange to the central bank at the daily fixing price.

Banks engaged in foreign exchange trading are connected by a highly sophisticated telecommunications network. Professional dealers and brokers obtain exchange rate quotes on desk-top video monitors and communicate with one another by telephone, telefax, and telex. In fact, a foreign exchange trading room physically resembles a stock brokerage office. The foreign exchange departments of many nonbank business firms also have video monitors that they use to keep in touch with the market and to decide which banks are making the best quotations. The two leading suppliers of foreign exchange information systems are Telerate and Reuters.

FUNCTIONS OF THE FOREIGN EXCHANGE MARKET

The foreign exchange market is the mechanism by which one may transfer purchasing power between countries, obtain or provide credit for international trade transactions, and minimize exposure to the risks of exchange rate changes.

Transfer of Purchasing Power

Transfer of purchasing power is necessary because international trade and capital transactions normally involve parties living in countries with different national currencies. Usually each party wants to hold its own currency, although the trade or capital transaction can be invoiced in any convenient currency. For example, a Japanese exporter may sell Toyota automobiles to a Brazilian importer. The exporter could invoice the Brazilian importer in Japanese yen, Brazilian cruzeiros, or a third-country currency such as U.S. dollars. The currency would be agreed upon beforehand.

Whichever currency is used, one or more of the parties must transfer purchasing power to or from its own national currency. If the transaction is in yen, the Brazilian importer must buy yen with its cruzeiros. If the transaction is in cruzeiros, the Japanese exporter must sell the cruzeiros received for yen. If U.S. dollars are used, the Brazilian importer must first exchange cruzeiros for dollars, and the Japanese exporter must then exchange dollars for yen. The foreign exchange market provides the mechanism for carrying out these purchasing power transfers.

Provision of Credit

Since the movement of goods between countries takes time, a means must be devised to finance inventory in transit. In the case of the Toyota automobile transaction, somebody would need to finance the automobiles while they are being shipped to Brazil and also while they are "floored" with the Toyota dealers in Brazil before final sale to a customer. The elapsed time typically might be anywhere from a few weeks to six months, depending on the kind of shipment.

In the case of automobiles, the Japanese exporter may agree to provide credit by carrying the accounts receivable of the Brazilian importer, with or without interest. Alternatively, the Brazilian importer may pay cash on shipment from Japan and finance the automobiles under its normal inventory financing arrangement. The foreign exchange market provides a third source of credit. Specialized instruments, such as bankers' acceptances and letters of credit, are available to finance trade. (These documents are explained in Chapter 18.)

Minimizing Foreign Exchange Risk

Neither the Brazilian importer nor the Japanese exporter may wish to carry the risk of exchange rate fluctuations. Each may prefer to earn a normal business profit on the automobile transaction rather than risk an unexpected change in anticipated profit should exchange rates suddenly change. The foreign exchange market provides "hedging" facilities for transferring the foreign exchange risk to someone else. (These facilities are explained in Chapter 8).

MARKET PARTICIPANTS

The foreign exchange market consists of two tiers, the interbank or wholesale market, and the client or retail market. Individual transactions in the interbank market are usually for large sums that are multiples of a million U.S. dollars or the equivalent value in other currencies. By contrast, contracts between a bank and its clients are usually for specific amounts, sometimes down to the last penny.

Five broad categories of participants operate within these two tiers: bank and nonbank foreign exchange dealers, individuals and firms conducting commercial or investment transactions, speculators and arbitragers, central banks and treasuries, and foreign exchange brokers.

Bank and Nonbank Foreign Exchange Dealers

Banks, and a few nonbank foreign exchange dealers, operate in both the interbank and client markets. They profit from buying foreign exchange at a "bid" price and reselling it at a slightly higher "offer" (also called "ask") price. Competition among dealers worldwide keeps the spread between bid and offer thin, and so contributes to making the foreign exchange market "efficient" in the same sense as in securities markets.

Dealers in the foreign exchange departments of large international banks often function as "market makers." They stand willing at all times to buy and sell those currencies in which they specialize. Market-making dealers usually maintain an "inventory" position in such currencies. They trade with other banks in their own monetary centers and in other centers around the world in order to maintain inventories within the trading limits set by bank policies. Trading limits are important because foreign exchange departments of many banks operate as profit centers, and individual dealers are compensated on a profit incentive basis. Unauthorized violations of trading limits by dealers under profit pressure have occasionally caused embarrassing losses to major banks.

Small- to medium-sized banks are likely to participate but not be market makers in the interbank market. Instead of maintaining significant inventory positions, they buy from and sell to larger banks to offset retail transactions with their own customers. Of course, even market-making banks do not make markets in every currency. They trade for their own account in those currencies of most interest to their customers and become participants when filling customer needs in less important currencies.

Individuals and Firms Conducting Commercial and Investment Transactions

Individuals and firms use the foreign exchange market to facilitate execution of commercial or investment transactions. This group consists of importers and exporters, international portfolio investors, multinational firms, and tourists. Their use of the foreign exchange market is necessary but nevertheless incidental to the underlying commercial or investment purpose. Some of these participants use the market to "hedge" foreign exchange risk.

Speculators and Arbitragers

Speculators and arbitragers profit from trading within the market itself. Their motive differs from that of dealers in that speculators and arbitragers are operating only in their own interest, without a need or obligation to serve clients or to ensure a continuous market. Whereas dealers seek profit from the spread between bid and offer and only incidentally seek to profit from general price changes, speculators seek all of their profit from a change in general price levels. Arbitragers seek to profit from simultaneous price differences in different markets.

A large proportion of speculation and arbitrage is conducted by traders in the foreign exchange departments of banks, on behalf of the bank. Thus banks act both as exchange dealers and as speculators and arbitragers. (Banks seldom admit to speculating; instead they see themselves as "taking an aggressive position"!)

Central Banks and Treasuries

Central banks and treasuries use the market to acquire or spend foreign exchange reserves as well as to influence the price at which their own currency is traded. They may act to support the value of their own currency because of policies adopted at the national level or because of commitments entered into through membership in such joint float agreements as the EMS. Consequently their motive is not to earn a profit as such, but rather to influence the foreign exchange value of their currency in a manner that will be beneficial to the interests of their citizens. In many instances they will be doing their job best when they willingly take a loss on their foreign exchange transactions.

Foreign Exchange Brokers

Foreign exchange brokers are matchmakers who facilitate trading between dealers without themselves becoming principals in the transaction. For this service they charge a small commission. They maintain instant access to hundreds of dealers worldwide via open telephone lines. At times a broker may maintain a dozen or more such lines to a single client bank, with separate lines for different currencies and for spot and forward markets.

It is the broker's business to know at any moment exactly which dealers want to buy or sell any currency. This knowledge enables the broker to find quickly an opposite party for a client without revealing the identity of either party until after a transaction has been arranged. Dealers use brokers because they want to remain anonymous, since the identity of participants may influence short-term quotes. For example, if Citibank is trying to reduce a large long position in Deutschemarks, it will not want to identify itself to potential buyers because that information might influence their quotes.

New York has 14 foreign exchange brokerage firms. Most of these are British owned, and they operate in conjunction with European and Asian offices of their parent firms. About 44% of foreign exchange transactions in New York City, in April of 1989, were estimated to have been arranged by foreign exchange brokers.[1]

SIZE OF THE MARKET

In April of 1989, 21 central banks and monetary authorities around the world conducted surveys of the foreign currency trading activity occurring within their countries. The survey included both commercial banks and private dealers of currencies. The Bank for International Settlements (BIS) has compiled these detailed surveys, attempted to eliminate all double counting, and estimated activity which was not covered by the survey. The BIS now estimates that daily foreign currency trading amounts to over $640 billion worldwide. Exhibit 4.1 provides a detailed summary of the foreign exchange activity survey results.[2]

Exhibit 4.1   Foreign Exchange Market Activity in April 1989 (billions of U.S. dollars)

Countries	(1) Total Net Turnover[a]	(2) With Customers[b]	(3) Interbank (domestic)[b]	(4) Interbank (crossborder)[b]	(5) Net Spot Turnover[a]	(6) Percent of which U.S. dollars
United Kingdom	187[c]	26	54[c]	107[c]	(119)	89.6
United States	129[c]	10	45[c]	71[c]	81	96.0
Japan	115	34	31	47	46	95.2
Switzerland[d]	57	9	11	36	30	75.0
Singapore	55	(6)	8	(41)	(31)	95.2
Hong Kong	49	5.4	11	33	(30)	93.2
Australia	30	6.0	7.0	15.0	18	97.3
France[d]	26[c]	5.0	6.0[c]	15	(15)	71.9
Canada	15	4.0	2.7	7.8	6.1	94.4
Netherlands	13	1.5	3.1[c]	8.5[c]	7.2	68.8
Denmark[d]	13	1.3	1.8	10	(6.4)	80.0
Sweden	13	1.6	1.4	8.7	9.5	100.0
Belgium	10	1.3	1.6	7.6	5.2	81.7
Italy[d]	10	1.4	0.8	8.0	7.6	53.6
Others[e]	22	1.6	4.4	15	16	80.7
Total	744	114	189	431	428	89.9
Adjustment for double-counting	−204				−123	
Total Reported Net Turnover	540				305	
Estimated Gaps in Reporting	100				55	
Estimated Global Turnover	640				360	

a The figures for individual countries indicate turnover net of double counting arising from local interbank business. The totals at the foot of the table are estimates of turnover net of double counting arising from both local and cross-border interbank business. Figures in parentheses are rough estimates.

b Columns (2) + (3) + (4) = (1). The items do not always sum to total net turnover because the classification is not exhaustive.

c Based on estimates of domestic and cross-border interbank business arranged through brokers.

d No adjustment for less than full coverage; estimated market coverage is the following: Switzerland, 85%; France, 95%; Denmark, 90%; Italy, 75%.

e Bahrain, Finland, Greece, Ireland, Norway, Portugal, and Spain.

Source: Bank for International Settlements, *60th Annual Report*, June 11, 1990, p. 209; taken from Survey of Foreign Exchange Market Activity, BIS, February 1990.

The survey results yield a number of important characteristics. First, the unadjusted total net turnover, estimated at $744 billion, is dominated by trading in the United Kingdom, United States, and Japan (totaling $431 billion, or 58% of all trading). Secondly, of total net turnover of foreign exchange, 58% is between banks internationally, with 25% being between banks domestically, and the remaining 17% with customers of the banks and dealers surveyed. Finally, of all transactions covered by the survey, approximately 90% included the U.S. dollar as one of the currencies in the transaction. The U.S. dollar obviously still serves as the central currency (the "numeraire") through which most world foreign exchange trading occurs.

The most recent survey by the Federal Reserve Bank of New York, for April 1989 (part of the larger BIS survey), reveals the size of the market in the United States in more detail. The survey was based on 123 banking institutions in addition to 14 nonbank financial institutions and 13 brokers located in the United States. After eliminating double counting, institutions had an average daily turnover totaling $128.9 billion (a 120% increase over 1986 alone). After adjustment for double counting (for trades among the reporting financial institutions), the average daily foreign currency turnover was:

Commercial Banking Institutions	$110.5 billion
Nonbank Financial Institutions	$ 18.4 billion
Brokers and others	$ 56.9 billion
Total Average Daily Turnover	$128.9 billion

As illustrated in Exhibit 4.2, the major currency traded by banks was German marks (32.9% of gross trading), followed by Japanese yen (25.2%), British pounds (14.6%) and Swiss francs (11.8%). Next in importance were Canadian dollars (4.0%), French francs (3.2%), and Australian dollars (2.7%). Among the currency shares, the British pound, Canadian dollar, and French franc all demonstrated markedly smaller shares of currency exchange since the prior survey of March 1986. Although the Australian dollar and the Swiss franc both increased their market shares, the German mark and Japanese yen increased their combined market share from 57.2% in March 1986 to 58.1% in April of 1989. This gives additional support to our belief in the increasing triad world market ($,¥,DM) discussed in Chapter 2.

TYPES OF TRANSACTIONS

Transactions in the foreign exchange market are executed on a "spot," "forward," or "swap" basis. A spot transaction requires almost immediate delivery of foreign exchange. A forward transaction requires delivery of foreign exchange at some future date. A swap transaction is a simultaneous purchase and sale of a foreign currency.

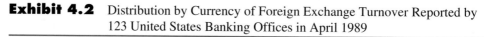

Exhibit 4.2   Distribution by Currency of Foreign Exchange Turnover Reported by
123 United States Banking Offices in April 1989

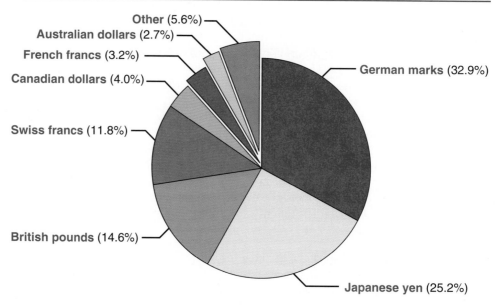

Source: Federal Reserve Bank of New York, *"Summary of Results of U.S. Foreign Exchange Market Turnover Survey Conducted in April 1989."* Released September 13, 1989.

As described above, most foreign exchange trading in the interbank market is between the U.S. dollar and other currencies. Thus a transaction involving the exchange of, say, yen for Mexican pesos will usually be carried out by exchanging yen for dollars and dollars for Mexican pesos.

Spot Transactions

A spot transaction in the interbank market is the purchase of foreign exchange, with delivery and payment between banks to be completed, normally, on the second following business day. One-day settlement is normal between the U.S. and Canadian dollars. The date of settlement is referred to as the "value date." On the value date, most dollar transactions in the world are settled through the computerized Clearing House Interbank Payments Systems (CHIPS) in New York, which provides for calculation of net balances owed by any one bank to another and for payment by 6:00 P.M. that same day in Federal Reserve Bank of New York funds.

A typical spot transaction in the interbank market might involve a U.S. bank contracting on a Monday for the transfer of £10,000,000 to the account of a London bank. If the spot exchange rate were $1.6984/£, the U.S. bank would transfer £10,000,000 to the London bank on Wednesday, and the London bank would transfer $16,984,000 to the U.S. bank at the same time. A spot transaction between a bank and its commercial customer would not necessarily involve a wait of two days for settlement.

Spot transactions dominate the interbank market. They represented 63.9% of the transactions undertaken by U.S. banks in April 1989, according to the survey by the Federal Reserve Bank of New York.[3]

Forward Transactions

A forward transaction (also called "outright forward") requires delivery at a future value date of a specified amount of one currency for a specified amount of another currency. The exchange rate is established at the time the contract is agreed on, but payment and delivery are not required until maturity. Forward exchange rates are normally quoted for value dates of one, two, three, six, and twelve months. Actual contracts can be arranged for other numbers of months or, on occasion, for periods of more than one year. Payment is on the second business day after the even-month anniversary of the trade. Thus a two-month forward transaction entered into on March 18 will be for a value date of May 20, or the next business day if May 20 falls on a weekend or holiday.

Although most forward contracts have specific maturity dates, "forward option" contracts that permit delivery at the beginning of a month (first to tenth day of the month), at the middle (eleventh to twentieth), or at the end (twenty-first to thirty-first) can be arranged. Such contracts cost more, but are preferred when a business firm does not know the exact date of receipt of foreign funds.

Note that as a matter of terminology one can speak of "buying forward" or "selling forward" to describe the same transaction. A contract to deliver dollars for guilders in six months might be referred to as "buying guilders forward for dollars" or "selling dollars forward for guilders."

Outright forward transactions in the interbank market are normally entered into by banks to offset forward exchange contracts with nonbank customers such as business firms and individuals. These customers usually make an outright forward transaction with the bank to protect themselves against a change in home currency value of foreign funds to be received or delivered in a business transaction.

Although outright forward contracts are quite important for multinational firms, they represent a relatively small proportion of the volume of trading by banks. According to the survey by the Federal Reserve Bank of New York, outright forward contracts accounted for only 4.2% of foreign exchange transactions undertaken by the sample U.S. banks in April 1989.[4]

Swap Transactions

A swap transaction in the interbank market is the simultaneous purchase and sale of a given amount of foreign exchange for two different value dates. Both purchase and sale are with the same other bank. A common type of swap is a "spot against forward." The dealer buys a currency in the spot market and simultaneously sells the same amount back to the same bank in the forward market. Since this is executed as a single transaction with one other bank, the dealer incurs no unexpected foreign exchange risk. The difference between the spot and forward rates is known and fixed.

A more sophisticated transaction is called a "forward-forward" swap. For example, a dealer could sell £20,000,000 forward for dollars for delivery in two months at $1.6870/£ and simultaneously purchase back £20,000,000 forward for delivery in three months at $1.6820/£. The difference between the buying price and the selling price is equivalent to the interest rate differential between borrowing costs of the two currencies. A swap can be viewed as a technique for borrowing another currency on a fully collateralized basis. (Swap quotations will be discussed in the section that follows.)

Swap transactions are very important in the interbank market. They represented 27.0% of foreign exchange transactions in April 1989 for the sample U.S. banks.[5]

FOREIGN EXCHANGE RATES AND QUOTATIONS

A foreign exchange rate is the price of one currency expressed in terms of another currency. A foreign exchange quotation, or quote, is a statement of willingness to buy or sell at an announced price.

Direct and Indirect Quotes

Foreign exchange quotations are either direct or indirect. A direct quote is the home currency price of one unit of foreign currency. In the United States, $0.5487/DM is a direct quote for one German mark. An indirect quote is the price in foreign currency of one unit of the home currency. In the United States a quotation of DM1.8225/$ is an indirect quote for the German mark. Direct and indirect quotations are reciprocals: 1 divided by 1.8225 equals 0.5487, and 1 divided by 0.5487 equals 1.8225. Since Germany is the home country of the mark, the quote of DM1.8225/$, which is an indirect quote in New York, is a direct quote for one dollar in Frankfurt.

Foreign exchange selling rate quotations are reported daily in the financial section of most major newspapers. Typical *Wall Street Journal* quotes are shown on the inside back cover of this book. The data are provided by Bankers Trust Company as of 3 P.M. U.S. Eastern time and are valid for interbank transactions in amounts of $1,000,000 or more. For smaller interbank and retail transactions the rates would be a little less favorable for the bank's customers. The two right-hand columns in the *Wall Street Journal* quotes give foreign currency units per U.S. dollar; these are indirect quotes from a U.S. viewpoint. The two left-hand columns give direct quotes, which are reciprocals of those on the right.

European and American Terms

Most interbank quotations around the world are stated in "European terms," which means the foreign currency price of one U.S. dollar. Thus the normal way throughout the world of quoting the relationship between the mark and the dollar is DM1.8225/$; this may also be called "German terms." A Japanese yen quote of ¥132.00/$ is called "Japanese terms." European terms were adopted as the universal way of expressing foreign exchange rates for most (but not all) currencies in 1978 to facilitate worldwide trading through telecommunications.

The alternative way of expressing exchange rates, the dollar price of one unit of foreign currency, is referred to as "American terms." American terms are normally used in the interbank market for quotations of the U.K. pound sterling, Australian dollar, New Zealand dollar, and Irish punt. Sterling is quoted as the foreign currency price of one pound for historical reasons: For centuries the British pound sterling was divided into 20 shillings, each of which had 12 pence. Multiplication and division with this nondecimal currency were difficult, so the custom evolved for foreign exchange prices in London, then the undisputed financial capital of the world, to be stated in foreign currency units per pound. This practice remained even after sterling changed to decimals in 1971. The other three currencies are quoted on American terms because of their close historical ties to Great Britain.

The relationship between European and American terms, on the one hand, and direct and indirect, on the other, can be summarized as follows.

European Terms:	*American Terms:*
Foreign currency price of one U.S. dollar.	U.S. dollar price of one unit of foreign currency.
For example, DM1.8225/$	For example, $0.5487/DM
A direct quote in Europe.	A direct quote in the U.S.
An indirect quote in the U.S.	An indirect quote in Europe.

American terms are used in many retail markets, such as those found in airports for tourists, and are also used on the foreign currency futures market in Chicago and the foreign exchange options market in Philadelphia. These derivative markets are discussed in the following chapter.

Bid and Offer Quotations

Interbank quotations are expressed as a bid and an offer (also referred to as ask). A bid is the rate at which a dealer is willing to buy another currency, and an offer is the rate at which a dealer is willing to sell that currency. Dealers bid (buy) at one price and offer (sell) at a slightly higher price, making their profit from the spread between the buying and selling prices. Note that the quotes on the inside back cover of this book are offer (sell) quotes.

Bid and offer quotations are complicated in the foreign exchange markets by the fact that the bid for one currency is also the offer for the other currency in which a trader wishes to deal. For example, a trader who wants to buy dollars at DM1.8215 is simultaneously offering to sell marks. Assume a bank makes the quotations shown in the top half of Exhibit 4.3 under the heading "DM/$." The spot quotations on the first line indicate that the bank's foreign exchange trader will "buy dollars" (that is, "sell marks") at the bid price of DM1.8215 per dollar. The trader will "sell dollars" (that is, "buy marks") at the offer price of DM1.8225 per dollar.

Exhibit 4.3   Foreign Exchange Quotations for the German Mark (DM)

	Quotations as Given in Interbank Market European Terms (DM/$)		Reciprocals Calculated for Convenience of Retail Customers American Terms ($/DM)	
	Bid	Offer	Bid	Offer
Outright quotations				
Spot	1.8215	1.8225	0.5487	0.5490
One month forward	1.8157	1.8169	0.5504	0.5526
Three months forward	1.8040	1.8056	0.5538	0.5543
Six months forward	1.7873	1.7891	0.5589	0.5595
Points quotations				
One month forward	58–56			
Three months forward	175–169			
Six months forward	342–334			

The heading "outright quotations" means that the full price to all of its decimal points is given. Traders, however, tend to abbreviate when talking on the phone or putting quotations on a video screen. The first term, the bid, of a spot quotation may be given in full: that is, "1.8215." However, the second term, the offer, will probably be expressed only as the digits that differ from the bid. Hence the bid and offer for spot marks would be printed 1.8215—25 on a video screen or spoken as "1.8215 (pause) 25" or "1.8215 to 25" on the telephone. On the telephone the trader may simply say "15 (pause) 25" or "15 to 25," assuming that the leading digits are known.

Note that when quotations in European terms are converted to American terms, bid and offer reverse: The reciprocal of the bid becomes the offer, and the reciprocal of the offer becomes the bid. In Exhibit 4.3, the reciprocal of the bid of DM1.8215/$ becomes the offer of $0.5490/DM, while the reciprocal of the offer of DM1.8225/$ becomes the bid of $0.5487/DM. For a bank to make a profit, the bid must be smaller than the offer; that is, the bank must buy foreign exchange for less than it sells it. In the indirect quotes above, the trader will buy one dollar for DM1.8215 and then resell it at a higher DM1.8225, making a profit. Using reciprocals, the trader will buy one mark for $0.5487 and then resell it for $0.5490, also making a profit.

In actuality currency markets are rarely so docile that traders can expect to profit by simultaneously buying at their bid and selling at their offer. If a trader quotes 1.8215—25 and buys dollars at 1.8215, the dealer's next quote may be 1.8220—30 if the market is going up or 1.8210—20 if it is going down. A trader's profitability depends more on ability to time purchases and sales in each instance. Additionally, since each dealer is a market maker (that is, stands ready to buy or sell at any time for a price) a counterparty may "hit the bid" or force the dealer to buy when the dealer's preference is to sell, or the offer may be "lifted" when the dealer would prefer to buy.

Expressing Forward Quotations on a Points Basis

The spot and forward quotations given in the top half of Exhibit 4.3 are outright: DM1.8215/$ for the spot bid and DM1.7873/$ for the six-month forward bid. Among themselves foreign exchange traders usually quote forward rates in terms of points, also referred to as swap rates. The bottom part of Exhibit 4.3 shows forward quotations as they would be given on a points basis. A quotation in points is not a foreign exchange rate as such. Rather it is the difference between the forward rate and the spot rate. Consequently the spot rate itself cannot be given on a points basis.

A point is the last digit of a quotation, and convention dictates the number of digits in each quotation. German marks and most other currency prices for the U.S. dollar are expressed to four decimal points. Hence a point is equal to 0.0001 of most currencies. Some currencies, such as the Japanese yen and Italian lira, are traditionally quoted only to two decimal points. The point is used in foreign exchange quotations without the decimal point or the leading zeros. A point quotation refers to the number of points away from the outright spot rate, with the first number referring to points away from the spot bid and the second number to points away from the spot offer. A slash (/) or a dash (—) is often used to separate the bid and offer point quotations on video screens or in print. A pause or the word "to" is used in voice communication.

In the mark/dollar interbank quotations in Exhibit 4.3, the forward dollar is at a discount relative to the spot dollar. Hence points must be subtracted from the spot quotation to obtain the lower forward quotation. The six-month forward outright mark/dollar quotation is derived as follows.

A trader might say that the six-month forward dollar is at a "discount of 342 to 334 points," indicating that the points should be subtracted from the spot rate. Usually, however, traders follow an operational rule that indicates whether the forward quote is at a premium or a discount. When the bid in points is larger than the offer in points, as in the mark example above, the trader knows that the points should be subtracted and the forward quotation is at a discount. If the bid in points is smaller than the offer in points the trader knows that the points should be added and the forward quotation is at a premium.

A forward bid and offer quotation expressed in points is often called a swap rate. Many forward exchange transactions in the interbank market involve the simultaneous purchase for one date and sale (reversing the transaction) for another date. This "swap" is a way to borrow one currency for a limited time while giving up the use of another currency for the same time; that is, it is a short-term borrowing of one currency combined with a short-term loan of an equivalent amount of another currency. The two parties could, if they wanted, charge each other interest at the going rate for each of the currencies. However it is easier for the party with the higher-interest currency to simply pay the net interest differential to the other. The swap rate expresses this net interest differential on a points basis rather than as an interest rate. A points quotation and an interest rate differential are equivalent, as will be explained in the following section.

Forward Quotations in Percentage Terms

Forward quotations are sometimes expressed in terms of a percent-per-annum deviation from the spot rate. This method of quotation facilitates comparing premiums or discounts in the forward foreign exchange market with interest rate differentials. When quotations are on an indirect basis, a formula for the percent-per-annum premium or discount is as follows.

With Indirect Quotes:

$$\text{Forward premium or discount } = \frac{\text{Spot } - \text{ Forward}}{\text{Forward}} \times \frac{12}{n} \times 100,$$

where n = the number of months in the contract. If quotations are on a direct basis, the formula is as follows.

With Direct Quotes:

$$\text{Forward premium or discount } = \frac{\text{Forward } - \text{ Spot}}{\text{Spot}} \times \frac{12}{n} \times 100.$$

In Exhibit 4.4 the spot exchange rate of ¥158.65/\$ is greater than the three-month forward rate of ¥158.04/\$. The yen is therefore selling forward at a premium. If the opposite was true, that the three-month forward rate was greater than the spot exchange rate, the yen would be selling forward at a discount (and the dollar selling forward at a premium). The annualized three-month forward premium on the yen ($f^{¥}$) using the indirect quote in Exhibit 4.4 is calculated as follows:

$$f^{¥} = \frac{\left(S - F_n\right)}{F_n} \times \frac{12}{n} \times 100$$

Then substituting the spot and forward rates, as well as the number of months forward (3),

$$f^{¥} = \frac{158.65 - 158.04}{158.04} \times \frac{12}{3} \times 100$$

$$f^{¥} = +1.54\%.$$

Exhibit 4.4   Forward Rate Quotations

Quotation	¥/$	% Per Annum
Spot Rate	158.65	—
Forward 1 month	158.46	−1.44
3 months	158.04	−1.54
6 months	157.50	−1.46
12 months	156.06	−1.66

(Closing bid rates, May 4, 1990; *Harris Bank Weekly Bulletin*, Harris Bank and Trust Company of Chicago.)

The premium value is positive, signifying that the yen is selling forward at a premium. A negative premium in the case of an indirect quote would indicate a currency selling forward at a discount.

Cross Rates

Many currency pairs are only inactively traded, so their exchange rate is determined through their relationship to a widely traded third currency. For example, an Australian tourist wants to purchase Danish currency to pay for a visit to Copenhagen. The Australian dollar (symbol A$) is not actively traded with the Danish krone (symbol DKr). However, both currencies are actively traded with the U.S. dollar. Assume the following quotes.

Australian dollar   A$1.3806/US$

Danish krone   DKr6.4680/US$

The Australian tourist can exchange 1.3806 Australian dollars for one U.S. dollar, and with that dollar buy 6.4680 Danish kroner (the plural of krone). The cross rate calculation would be

$$\frac{\text{Australian dollars} / \text{U.S. dollar}}{\text{Danish kroner} / \text{U.S. dollar}} = \frac{\text{A\$1.3806} / \text{US\$}}{\text{DKr6.4680} / \text{US\$}}$$
$$= \text{A\$0.2135} / \text{DKr.}$$

In many countries quotations are in terms of the home currency price of 100 units of the foreign currency, expressed to four decimal points. Thus a posted rate might read "A$21.3451 per 100 Danish kroner."

Cross rates are used by businesses to validate the internal consistency of separate foreign exchange forecasts. A mark/dollar exchange rate for next year's forecast by a firm's German staff may be divided by a franc/dollar forecast by the French staff to see whether the cross rate is reasonable. If the implied cross rate lies outside of the bounds set by the European Monetary System, for example, both forecasts can come true only if European Monetary System parities are changed, which may not appear likely for reasons not considered in the original dollar forecasts. This point is important for maintaining consistency across foreign affiliates when drawing up corporate-wide performance budgets or setting interaffiliate transfer prices.

Intermarket Arbitrage

Cross rates can be used to check on opportunities for intermarket arbitrage. Suppose the following exchange rates are available.

Dutch guilders (symbol *fl*) per U.S. dollar   *fl*1.9025/US$

Canadian dollars per U.S. dollar   C$1.2646/US$

Dutch guilders per Canadian dollar   *fl*1.5214/C$

Exhibit 4.5   Intermarket Triangular Arbitrage

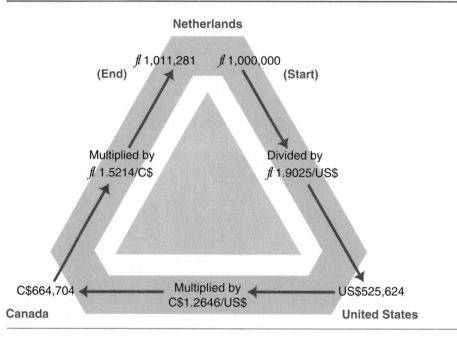

The cross rate between Dutch guilders and Canadian dollars is

$$\frac{\text{Dutch guilders / U.S. dollar}}{\text{Canadian dollars / U.S. dollar}} = \frac{\mathit{fl}1.9025 / \text{US\$}}{\text{C\$}1.2646 / \text{US\$}} = \mathit{fl}1.5044 / \text{C\$}.$$

However, the cross rate is not the same as the actual quotation of fl1.5214/C$. An opportunity for profit from arbitrage between these three markets (triangular arbitrage) exists. Exhibit 4.5 shows the steps.

A Dutch investor with fl1,000,000 can exchange it in the spot market for US$525,624. Simultaneously that investor can change the U.S. dollars for C$664,704, and at the same time exchange the Canadian dollars into fl1,011,281, making a risk-free profit of fl11,281, before transaction costs, on one "turn." Intermarket arbitrage should continue until exchange rate equilibrium is reestablished, that is, when the calculated cross rate equals the actual quotation, less a margin for transaction costs.

Measuring a Change in Spot Exchange Rates

Assume that the German mark, which has been quoted at DM2.00/$, suddenly strengthens to DM1.50/$. What is the percent increase in the dollar value of the mark, and thus in the value of mark-denominated accounts receivable or payable held by Americans?

The following formula expresses the change in the spot value of the mark from a U.S. perspective.

With Indirect Quotes:

$$\text{Percent change} = \frac{\text{beginning rate} - \text{ending rate}}{\text{ending rate}} \times 100$$

$$= \frac{2.00 - 1.50}{1.50} \times 100 = +33.33\%.$$

If exchange rates are given on a direct basis, the formula is altered similar to that of the forward premium calculation. Using the same exchange rates, but in this case their reciprocals ($.6667/DM instead of DM1.5/$), the formula for the percentage change is as follows.

With Direct Quotes:

$$\text{Percent change} = \frac{\text{ending rate} - \text{beginning rate}}{\text{beginning rate}} \times 100$$

$$= \frac{0.6667 - 0.5000}{0.5000} \times 100 = +33.33\%.$$

INTEREST RATE PARITY (IRP)

The theory of interest rate parity (IRP) provides the linkage between the foreign exchange markets and the international money markets. The theory states: *The difference in the national interest rates for securities of similar risk and maturity should be equal to, but opposite in sign to, the forward rate discount or premium for the foreign currency, except for transaction costs.* The theory is applicable only to securities with maturities of one year or less, since forward contracts are not routinely available for periods longer than one year.

To illustrate the theory, assume that an investor has $1,000,000 and several alternative but comparable monetary investments. If the investor chooses to invest in a dollar money market instrument, the investor would earn the dollar rate of interest. This results in $(1 + i^\$)$ at the end of the period, where $i^\$$ is the dollar rate of interest in decimal form. The investor may, however, choose to invest in a nondollar money market instrument of identical risk and maturity for the same period. This would require that the investor change the dollar to another currency at the spot rate of exchange, invest that currency in a money market instrument, and at the end of the period convert the resulting proceeds back to dollars. The box diagram in Exhibit 4.6 depicts these alternative monetary investments for a dollar-yen case.

A dollar-based investor would evaluate the relative returns of starting in the top left corner and investing in the dollars (straight across the top of the box) compared to

Exhibit 4.6   Interest Rate Parity (IRP)

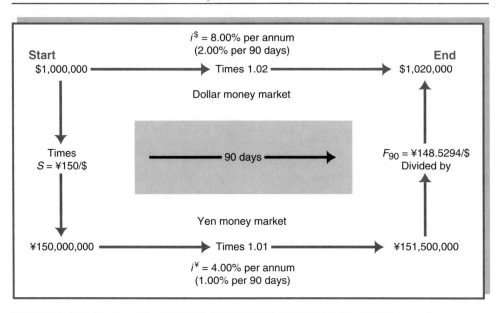

investing in the yen market (going around the box to the top right corner). The comparison of returns would be:

$$\left(1+i^{\$}\right) = S \times \left(1+i^{¥}\right) \times \frac{1}{F},$$

where S = the spot rate of exchange and F = the forward rate of exchange. Substituting the spot and forward exchange rates and respective interest rates from Exhibit 4.6 then yields:

$$\left(1+.02\right) = 150.0 \times \left(1+.01\right) \times \frac{1}{148.5}.$$

The left-hand side of the equation is the gross return the investor would earn by investing in dollars. The right-hand side is the gross return the investor would earn by exchanging dollars for yen at the spot rate, investing the yen proceeds in the yen money market, and simultaneously selling the principal plus interest in yen forward for dollars at the current 90 day forward rate.

Ignoring transaction costs, if the returns in dollars are equal between the two alternative money market investments, it is termed interest rate parity (IRP). The transaction is "covered" because there is a guaranteed exchange rate back to dollars at the end of the 90 day period. Therefore, as in Exhibit 4.6, in order for the two alternatives to be equal, any differences in interest rates must be exactly offset by the difference between the spot and forward exchange rates:

$$\frac{F}{S} = \frac{\left(1 + i^{¥}\right)}{\left(1 + i^{\$}\right)}, \text{ or } \frac{¥148.5294}{¥150.0000} = \frac{1.01}{1.02} = 0.99 = 1\%.$$

Covered Interest Arbitrage (CIA)

The spot and forward exchange markets are not, however, constantly in the state of equilibrium described by interest rate parity. When the market is not in equilibrium, the potential for "riskless" or arbitrage profit exists. The arbitrager who recognizes such an imbalance will move to take advantage of the disequilibrium by investing in whichever currency offers the higher return on a covered basis. This is called *covered interest arbitrage* (CIA).

Exhibit 4.7 describes the steps which a currency trader, most likely working in the arbitrage division of a large international bank, would implement to perform a CIA transaction. The currency trader, William Wong, may utilize any of a number of major Eurocurrencies which his bank possesses to conduct arbitrage investments. The morning conditions indicate to William Wong that a CIA transaction which exchanges Japanese yen for U.S. dollars, invested in a six month Eurodollar account, and sold forward back to yen, will yield a profit of ¥1,505,000 over and above that available from a Euroyen investment.

Conditions in the exchange markets and Euromarkets change rapidly, however, so that William Wong may find a different set of conditions requiring an opposite CIA transaction in the afternoon. The second CIA transaction uses the disequilibrium existing in the currency markets (the forward rate alone is changed in the exhibit) to use U.S. dollars for a covered investment in Japanese yen. Once again William Wong profits, in this case $8,295 on the initial $1,000,000 investment, over and above that currently available in Eurodollar accounts. Note that all profits are stated in terms of the currency in which the transaction was initialized, but that a trader (in this case in Hong Kong) may conduct investments denominated in U.S. dollars, Japanese yen, or any other major convertible currency.

It is this process of covered interest arbitrage which drives the international currency and money markets towards the equilibrium described by interest rate parity. Slight deviations from equilibrium provide opportunities for arbitragers like William Wong to make small riskless profits. This provides the supply and demand forces which will move the market back toward parity (equilibrium).

Covered interest arbitrage should continue until interest rate parity is reestablished, because the arbitragers are able to earn risk-free profits by repeating the cycle as often as possible. Their actions, however, nudge the foreign exchange and money markets back

Exhibit 4.7   Covered Interest Arbitrage (CIA)

Morning. William Wong, an arbitrager for Hong Kong & Shanghai Banking Corporation, Hong Kong, arrives at work Tuesday morning to be faced with the currency quotations shown in the "Morning Quotation Box" below. He has access to several major Eurocurrencies for arbitrage trading. On the basis of the quotations below he decides to execute the following CIA transaction:

Step 1: Convert ¥135,000,000 at the spot rate of ¥135.00/$ to $1,000,000 (see "START").

Step 2: Invest the proceeds, $1,000,000, in a Eurodollar account for six months, earning 8.00% per annum, or 4% for six months.

Step 3: Simultaneously sell the proceeds ($1,040,000) forward for yen at the six month forward rate of ¥134.50/$. This "locks-in" gross yen revenues of ¥139,880,000 (see "END").

Step 4: Calculate the cost (opportunity cost) of funds used at the Euroyen rate of 5.00% per annum, or 2.50% for six months, with principal and interest then totaling ¥138,375,000. Profit on CIA at the "end" is: ¥139,880,000 (proceeds) – ¥138,375,000 (cost) = ¥1,505,000.

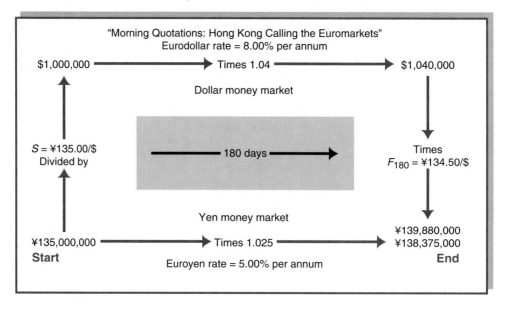

continued

toward equilibrium for the following reasons.

1. Purchase of yen in the spot market and sale of yen in the forward market (the afternoon case) narrows the premium on the forward yen. This is because the spot yen strengthens from the extra demand and the forward yen weakens because of the extra sales. A narrower premium on the forward yen reduces the foreign exchange gain previously captured by investing in yen.

2. The demand for yen-denominated securities causes yen interest rates to fall, while the higher level of borrowing in the United States causes dollar interest rates to rise. The net result is a wider interest differential in favor of investing in the dollar.

Exhibit 4.7 *continued*

Afternoon. After returning from a quick lunch, William Wong once more examines the spot and forward quotations for the U.S. dollar and the Japanese yen, as well as the Eurodollar and Euroyen interest rates. He notes that the 180 day forward rate on the U.S. dollar is dropping. By 2 P.M. he feels that it has fallen as far as it is likely to go, and jumps back into the arbitrage markets, this time with Eurodollars.

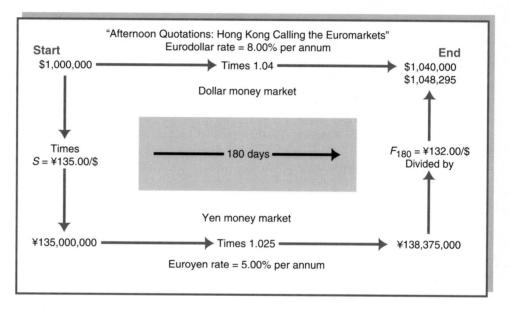

Step 1: Convert $1,000,000 at the spot rate of ¥135.00/$ to ¥135,000,000 (see "START").

Step 2: Invest the proceeds, ¥135,000,000, in a Eurodollar account for six months @ 5.00% per annum, or 2.50% for six months.

Step 3: Simultaneously sell the proceeds (¥138,375,000) forward for U.S. dollars at the new 180 day forward rate of ¥132.00/$. This "locks-in" gross yen revenues of $1,048,295 (see "END").

Step 4: Calculate the cost (opportunity cost) of funds used at the Eurodollar rate of 8.00% per annum, or 4.00% for six months, with principal and interest then totaling $1,040,000. Profit on CIA at the "END" is: $1,048,295 − $1,040,000 = $8,295.

Equilibrium

Exhibit 4.8 illustrates the conditions necessary for equilibrium. The vertical axis shows the difference in interest rates in favor of the foreign currency, and the horizontal axis shows the forward premium or discount on that currency. The interest rate parity line shows the equilibrium state, but transaction costs cause the line to be a band rather than a thin line. Transaction costs arise from foreign exchange and investment brokerage costs on buying and selling securities. Typical transaction costs in recent years have been in the range of 0.18% to 0.25% on an annual basis. For individual transactions like William Wong's arbitrage activity in the previous example, there is no explicit transaction cost per trade;

Exhibit 4.8   Interest Rate Parity and Equilibrium

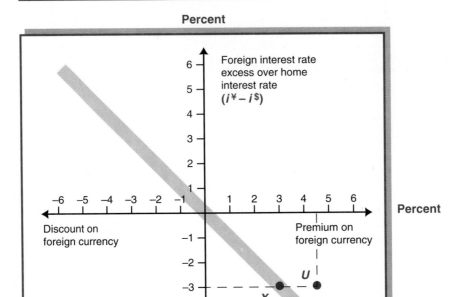

rather the costs of the bank in supporting Wong's activities are the transaction costs. Point X shows one possible equilibrium position, where a 3% lower rate of interest on yen securities would be offset by a 3% premium on the forward yen.

The disequilibrium situation, which encouraged the interest rate arbitrage in the afternoon example of William Wong, is illustrated by point U. It is located off the interest rate parity line because the lower interest on the yen is 3% (annual basis), whereas the premium on the forward yen is slightly over 4.5% (annual basis). Using the forward premium calculation presented earlier, the premium on the yen is:

$$\frac{\text{Spot rate} - \text{forward rate}}{\text{forward rate}} \times \frac{12}{6} \times 100 = \frac{135 - 132}{132} \times 200 = 4.545\%.$$

The situation depicted by point U is unstable because all investors have an incentive to execute the same covered interest arbitrage. Except for a bank failure, the arbitrage gain is virtually risk free.

Some observers have suggested that political risk does exist, since one of the governments might apply capital controls that would prevent execution of the forward contract.[6] This risk is fairly remote for covered interest arbitrage between the major financial centers of the world, especially since a large portion of funds used for covered interest arbitrage is in Eurodollars. The concern may be valid, however, for pairings with countries not noted for political and fiscal stability.

The net result of the disequilibrium is that fund flows will narrow the gap in interest rates and/or decrease the premium on the forward yen. In other words, market pressures will cause point U in Exhibit 4.8 to move toward the interest rate parity band. Equilibrium might be reached at point Y, or at any other locus between X and Z, depending on whether forward market premiums are more or less easily shifted than interest rate differentials.

SUMMARY

- Geographically the foreign exchange market spans the globe, with prices moving and currencies traded somewhere every hour of every business day.

- The three functions of the foreign exchange market are to transfer purchasing power, provide credit, and minimize foreign exchange risk.

- The foreign exchange market is composed of two tiers: the interbank market and the client market. Participants within these tiers include bank and nonbank foreign exchange dealers, individuals and firms conducting commercial and investment transactions, speculators and arbitragers, central banks and treasuries, and foreign exchange brokers.

- Transactions within the foreign exchange market are executed either on a spot basis, requiring settlement two days after the transaction, or on a forward or swap basis, which requires settlement at some designated future date.

- Quotations are given in American terms, the dollar price of another currency, or in European terms, the foreign currency price of a dollar.

- Quotations are defined as direct, meaning the home currency price of foreign currency, or indirect, meaning the foreign currency price of the home currency.

- Forward quotations may be stated on an outright basis, on a points basis, or as an annual percent deviation from the spot rate.

- A cross rate is an exchange rate between two currencies, calculated from their common relationship with a third currency. When cross rates differ from the direct rates between two currencies, intermarket arbitrage is possible.

- The relationship between forward exchange rates and interest rates is explained by the theory of interest rate parity. It states that the percentage difference between a spot and a forward quotation is determined by the difference between the interest rates in the two countries. Covered interest arbitrage is the process which ensures that interest rate parity holds even if it strays from equilibrium in the short run.

1. Luxembourg Francs
The spot Luxembourg franc is quoted, "European terms," as follows:

Bid: LF35.67/$ Ask: LF35.85/$

What are the bid and ask on a direct basis (i.e., "American terms")?

2. Currency Trading Computer Screen
The quotation screen in a foreign exchange trader's office shows the following:

Exch	Spot	1-Month	2-Month	3-Month	6-Month
DM	169 38-18	54-60	102-110	150-162	300-324
STG	161 30-18	4-6	8-10	13-15	23-25
YEN	142 05-95	63-60	81-75	184-179	373-368

where DM, STG, and YEN are the computer symbols for the Deutschemark, British pound sterling, and Japanese yen.

    a) What are the outright bid and ask quotations? (Refer to a local newspaper, if necessary, to determine the location of the decimal point.)

    b) You want to buy marks one month forward with yen. What is your effective exchange rate?

    c) You read in the financial press that the British pound has dropped 16% in value over the last decade. What was the spot quote a decade ago?

    d) What are the forward mark/dollar quotes as a percent per annum, from a U.S. perspective?

3. Forward Rates on the Swiss Franc
The following outright foreign exchange quotations are given for the Swiss franc:

	Bid (SF/$)	Ask (SF/$)
Spot rate	1.2510	1.2520
One month forward	1.2514	1.2528
Three months forward	1.2530	1.2550
Six months forward	1.2550	1.2580

    a) Calculate forward quotes for both bid and ask in terms of points.

    b) Assume you are in the United States. Calculate forward quotes for the Swiss franc as an annual percentage premium or discount. Would a foreign exchange trader in Switzerland get a different answer if asked to calculate the annual percentage premium or discount for each forward rate on the U.S. dollar? Why?

4. Calculating Forward Premiums (C04A.WK1)
Given the following spot and forward quotes, calculate the forward premiums on the German mark.

	Spot (DM/$)	Forward (DM/$)	Days Forward
a)	1.6000	1.6200	30
b)	1.6000	1.6200	90
c)	1.4800	1.6000	180
d)	1.6640	1.6260	360

5. Triangular Arbitrage

The following quotations are available to you. (You may either buy or sell at the stated rates.)

Wells Fargo, US$ quote for Canadian dollar:	US$ 0.85/C$
Dresdner Bank, US$ quote for German marks:	US$ 0.60/DM
Royal Bank, DM quote for Canadian dollars:	DM 1.43/C$

Given this information, is triangular arbitrage possible? If so, explain the steps and compute the profit if you had an initial US$1,000,000 to use.

6. Percentage Changes in Exchange Rates

If the following currencies change in value relative to the dollar as indicated, calculate the ending exchange rate in terms of local currency units per dollar:

Currency	Initial Exchange Rate	Change Relative to U.S. Dollar
Chilean peso	Ps 312.50/$	devalues 20%
Singapore dollar	S$ 1.7000/US$	appreciates 6%

7. Covered Interest Arbitrage (C04B.WK1)

William Wong, the currency trader described in Exhibit 4.7, returns to work the following day to find the following exchange rates and interest rates in the market. Explain how William Wong may make CIA profit.

Spot rate:	135.60 ¥/$
Six-month forward rate:	136.38 ¥/$
Six-month Euro$ interest rate:	10.6 % per annum
Six-month Euro¥ interest rate:	8.4 % per annum

8. Covered Interest Arbitrage in Malaysia

As a resident of Malaysia you have M$100,000 (M$ = Malaysian ringgits) which you are free to invest in any currency. Exchange rates and interest rates are as follows:

Spot rate, ringgits per U.S. dollar:	M$ 2.7000/US$
Six-month forward rate for ringgits:	M$ 2.7200/US$
Six-month Malaysia interest rate:	8.00% per annum
Six-month U.S. interest rate:	6.00% per annum

Given this information, is covered interest arbitrage worthwhile? Explain your answer, and calculate the financial advantage of one method over the other.

9. Covered Interest Arbitrage in Singapore: Morning

Patricia Yamada, a trader in the foreign exchange department of Sanwa bank, Singapore office, specializes in arbitraging U.S. dollars against Deutschemarks. She observes the following rates at 9:10 A.M. Singapore time:

Spot rate:	DM1.8200 = $1.0000
Three-month forward rate:	DM1.8000 = $1.0000

Yamada can borrow or invest U.S. dollars for three months at 9% per annum or Deutschemarks for three months at 5% per annum. She is allowed to borrow $5,000,000 or an equivalent amount in Deutschemarks.

   a) Ignoring transaction costs, how can Patricia Yamada make a risk-free profit? Assume she prefers to make her profit in dollars.

   b) If the dollar three-month interest rate should increase to 10% per annum, other conditions remaining the same, would she still make a profit using the same strategy as she uses in your answer to part a above?

   c) If transaction costs in part (a) above were $8,000 and were to be paid out of the final proceeds, how would this change her strategy, if at all?

10. Covered Interest Arbitrage in Singapore: Afternoon

At 2:15 P.M. Singapore time, Patricia Yamada (see question 9) observes a new set of rates as follows:

Spot rate:	DM1.8280 = $1.0000
Three-month forward rate:	DM1.8120 = $1.0000
Three-month dollar interest rate:	9% per annum
Three-month Deutschemark interest rate:	5% per annum

   a) Diagram (box) the new situation.

   b) Show on your diagram how Patricia Yamada can make a covered interest arbitrage profit. Ignore transaction costs.

   c) List the actions necessary to complete this arbitrage.

11. London Exchange Rate Quotes

A foreign exchange dealer in London normally provides quotes for spot, one month, three months, and six months. When you ask over the telephone for current quotations for the Finish markka (FIM) against the U.S. dollar, you hear:

"4.0040 to 200, 120 to 110, 350 to 312, 680 to 620"

Answer the following, based on the above quotation:

   a) What would you receive in dollars if you sold FIM1,000,000 spot?

   b) What would it cost you to purchase FIM15,000,000 forward three months for dollars. When would you make payment?

   c) In New York, three-month treasury bills yield 8% per annum. Using offer quotes only (for simplicity), what should be the yield on Finish three-month bills?

   d) Verify your answer to part (c) with a hypothetical investment of $10,000,000 for three months in both countries. Use only offer quotes for simplicity and ignore charges and taxes.

12. CIA in Montreal

Harry Johnson, an arbitrager with Bank of Montreal, faces the following Canadian dollar/ U.S. dollar quotes:

Spot rate:	C$1.1520 = $1.0000
Six-month forward rate:	C$1.1635 = $1.0000
Six-month Canadian interest rate:	10.00% per annum
Six-month U.S. interest rate:	7.50% per annum

Harry Johnson is authorized to use C$10,000,000 or its U.S. dollar equivalent. Transactions costs would be $1,700 paid at the end of six months. The ending profit, if any, should be held in Canadian dollars. Assuming Harry can borrow or invest at the above interest rates, how can he complete a covered interest arbitrage? What is his profit?

NOTES

1. Federal Reserve Bank of New York, *"Summary of Results of U.S. Foreign Exchange Market Turnover Survey Conducted in April 1989 by the Federal Reserve Bank of New York."* Released September 13, 1989.

2. The size of the world foreign currency market has been something of a problem for measurement until this most recent relatively comprehensive survey. The rate of growth in world trading may reflect the relatively poor estimates made previously. For example *The New York Times* (March 23, 1987) estimated world trading value at about $200 billion per trading day for early 1987 and $188 billion per day for 1986. Of the $188 billion, $90 billion (48%) was in London, $50 billion (27%) was in New York, and $49 billion (26%) was in Tokyo. *Euromoney* (Octo-

ber 1987) reported that in the first eight months of 1987 Tokyo passed New York to become the second largest foreign exchange trading market, with an average daily value of $55 billion, compared with New York's $52 billion.

3. Federal Reserve Bank of New York, *"Summary of Results of U.S. Foreign Exchange Market Turnover Survey Conducted in April 1989 by the Federal Reserve Bank of New York."* Released September 13, 1989.

4. *Ibid.*

5. *Ibid.*

6. Robert Z. Aliber, "The Interest Rate Parity Theorem: A Reinterpretation," *Journal of Political Economy*, December 1973, pp. 1451–1459.

BIBLIOGRAPHY

Adler, Michael, and Bernard Dumas, "Portfolio Choice and the Demand for Forward Exchange," *American Economic Review*, May 1976, pp. 332–339.

Aliber, Robert Z., "The Interest Rate Parity Theorem: A Reinterpretation," *Journal of Political Economy*, December 1973, pp. 1451–1459.

Askari, Hossein, and Franco Modigliani, "A Note on Capital Movements and the Relation of Spread in Spot and Forward Rates to Variations in the Short-Term Interest Differential," *Kyklos*, no. 1, 1977, pp. 38–50.

Byler, Ezra U., and James C. Baker, "S.W.I.F.T.: A Fast Method to Facilitate International Financial Transactions," *Journal of World Trade Law*, September–October 1983, pp. 458–465.

Fama, Eugene F., "Forward and Spot Exchange Rates," *Journal of Monetary Economics*, 14, 1984, pp. 319–338.

Frenkel, Jacob A., and Richard M. Levich, "Covered Interest Arbitrage: Unexploited Profits?" *Journal of Political Economy*, April 1975, pp. 325–338.

——, "Transaction Costs and Interest Arbitrage: Tranquil versus Turbulent Periods," *Journal of Political Economy*, November-December 1977, pp. 1209–1226.

Glassman, Debra, "Exchange Rate Risk and Transactions Costs: Evidence From Bid-Ask Spreads," *Journal of International Money and Finance*, 6, no. 4, December 1987, pp. 479–491.

Gregory, Ian, and Philip Moore, "Foreign Exchange Dealing," *Corporate Finance*, October 1986, pp. 33–46.

Gupta, Sanjeev, "A Note on the Efficiency of Black Markets in Foreign Currencies," *Journal of Finance*, June 1981, pp. 705–710.

Hilley, John L., Carl R. Beidleman, and James A. Greenleaf, "Does Covered Interest Arbitrage Dominate in Foreign Exchange Markets?" *Columbia Journal of World Business*, Winter 1979, pp. 99–107.

——, "Why There Is No Long Forward Market in Foreign Exchange," *Euromoney*, January 1981, pp. 94–103.

Jacque, Laurent L., "Management of Foreign Exchange Risk: A Review Article," *Journal of International Business Studies*, Spring/Summer 1981, pp. 81–101.

Kubarych, Roger M., *Foreign Exchange Markets in the United States*, rev. ed., New York: Federal Reserve Bank of New York, 1983.

Mahajan, Arvind, and Dileep Mehta, "Swaps, Expectations, and Exchange Rates," *Journal of Banking and Finance*, March 1986, pp. 7–20.

Remmers, H. L., *FORAD: International Financial Management Simulation (Players' Manual, Release 2.4)*, Fontainebleau, France: INSEAD, 1990.

Riehl, Heinz, and Rita Rodriguez, *Foreign Exchange and Money Markets*, New York: McGraw-Hill, 1983.

Sweeny, Richard J., "Beating the Foreign Exchange Market," *Journal of Finance*, March 1986, pp. 163–182.

Sweeney, Richard J., and Edward J.Q. Lee, "Trading Strategies in Forward Exchange Markets," *Advances in Financial Planning and Forecasting*, vol. 4, 1990, pp. 55–80.

Walker, Townsend, *A Guide for Using the Foreign Exchange Market*, New York: Ronald Press/Wiley, 1981.

Weisweiller, Rudi, *Introduction to Foreign Exchange*, Cambridge, England: Woodhead-Faulkner, Ltd., 1983.

Futures and Options Markets

Foreign currency futures and options are instruments that have assumed increasing importance in the marketplace in recent years. They can be used to hedge the foreign exchange risk that results from commercial transactions, and they can be used for speculative purposes. Use of foreign currency futures and options to hedge commercial transactions is covered in Chapter 8. A description of these instruments, of the markets in which they are traded, and of their use for speculation is given in this chapter. The chapter concludes with a description of the potential strategies employed by currency traders when speculating in the spot, forward, and foreign currency option markets.

FOREIGN CURRENCY FUTURES

A foreign currency futures contract is an exchange-traded agreement calling for future delivery of a standard amount of foreign exchange at a fixed time, place, and price. It is similar to futures contracts that exist for commodities (hogs, cattle, lumber, etc.), for interest-bearing deposits, and for gold.

Futures Markets

In the United States the most important marketplace for foreign currency futures is the International Monetary Market (IMM) of Chicago, organized in 1972 as a division of the Chicago Mercantile Exchange. Since 1985, contracts traded on the IMM have been interchangeable with those traded on the Singapore International Monetary Exchange (SIMEX).

A number of other currency futures markets exist, notably in New York (New York Futures Exchange, a subsidiary of the New York Stock Exchange), London (London International Financial Futures Exchange), Canada, Australia, and Singapore. So far, however, none of these rivals have come close to duplicating the trading volume of the IMM.

Contract Specifications

Contract specifications are defined by the exchange on which they are traded. The major features that must be standardized are the following:

A specific sized contract.   On the IMM, for example, a German mark contract is for DM125,000. Consequently trading can be done only in multiples of DM125,000.

A standard method of stating exchange rates.   On the IMM American terms are used; that is, quotations are the dollar cost of foreign currency units.

A standard maturity date.   IMM contracts mature on the third Wednesday of January, March, April, June, July, September, October, or December. However, not all of these maturities are available for all currencies at any given time. "Spot month" contracts are also traded. These are not spot contracts as that term is used in the interbank foreign exchange market, but are rather short-term futures contracts that mature on the next following third Wednesday, that is, on the next following standard maturity date.

A specified last trading day.   IMM contracts may be traded through the second business day prior to the Wednesday on which they mature. Therefore, unless holidays interfere, the last trading day is the Monday preceding the maturity date.

Collateral.   The purchaser must deposit a sum as an initial margin or collateral. This is similar to requiring a performance bond, and can be met by a letter of credit from a bank, Treasury bills, or cash. In addition, a maintenance margin is required. The value of the contract is marked to market daily, and all changes in value are paid in cash daily. The amount to be paid is called the variation margin.

Settlement.   Only about 5% of all futures contracts are settled by the physical delivery of foreign exchange between buyer and seller. Most often, buyers and sellers offset their original position prior to delivery date by taking an opposite position. That is, if one had bought a futures contract, that position would be closed out by selling a futures contract for the same delivery date. The complete buy/sell or sell/buy is called a "round turn."

Commissions.   Customers pay a commission to their broker to execute a round turn and only a single price is quoted. This practice differs from that of the interbank market, where dealers quote a bid and an offer and do not charge a commission.

Clearing house a counterparty.   All contracts are agreements between the client and the exchange clearing house, rather than between the two clients involved. Consequently clients need not worry that a specific counterparty in the market will fail to honor an agreement.

Exhibit 5.1 International Monetary Market Currency Contract Specifications

	Symbol	Contract Size	Minimum Price Fluct.	Margin Requirement	
				Initial	Maintenance
Currency Contracts					
Australian dollar	AD	100,000	0.0001	2,000	1,500
British pound	BP	62,500	0.0005	1,500	1,000
Canadian dollar	CD	100,000	0.0001	900	700
French franc	FR	250,000	0.00005	1,200	900
Japanese yen	JY	12,500,000	0.000001	2,000	1,500
Dutch guilder	DG	125,000	0.0001	1,200	900
Swiss franc	SF	125,000	0.0001	2,000	1,500
German mark	DM	125,000	0.0001	2,000	1,500
European Currency Unit (ECU)	ECU	125,000	0.0001	2,000	1,200
Other Contracts					
Gold, London del.	GD	100 oz	10¢/oz	1,500	1,200
Gold, New York del.	GMZ	100 oz	10¢/oz	1,500	1,500
90-day U.S. Treasury Bill	TB	$1,000,000	$0.01	1,500	1,000
Eurodollar time deposit	ED	$1,000,000	$0.01	1,500	1,000
Standard & Poor's 500 Index	SP	$500 x index	30 index points		

Source: Data from Chicago Mercantile Exchange, *Contract Specifications*, November 23, 1987.

IMM futures contracts are available in the nine currencies shown in Exhibit 5.1, as well as in gold, 90-day U.S. Treasury bills, and Eurodollar time deposits. The IMM uses its own standardized currency symbols. The symbols are shown in Exhibit 5.1.

Reading Newspaper Quotations

Futures trading on the IMM in German marks for a Tuesday was reported in Wednesday's *Wall Street Journal* as shown in Exhibit 5.2.

The first line under the headings indicates that German marks were traded on the International Monetary Market in contracts of DM125,000 each at the dollar-per-mark prices shown in the table.

The next three lines deal with contracts that expire in December, March (of 1991), and June (of 1991). These are the only maturities for mark contracts being traded.

March contracts, meaning contracts that expire on the third Wednesday in March, opened trading on Tuesday at $0.6685/DM. The highest trading price during the day was $0.6719/DM and the lowest trading price was $0.6672/DM.

Exhibit 5.2   Foreign Currency Futures Quotations

	Open	High	Low	Settle	Change	Lifetime High	Lifetime Low	Open Interest
German Mark (IMM)—125,000 marks; $ per mark								
Dec	.6701	.6739	.6685	.6695	−.0030	.6739	.5764	67,208
Mr91	.6685	.6719	.6672	.6678	−.0030	.6719	.5820	2,700
June	.6679	.6695	.6670	.6659	−.0030	.6700	.6163	108

Est vol 39,934; vol Mon 40,352; open int 70,016, −1,965.

"Settle" refers to settlement price, the daily closing price that is used by the IMM Exchange Clearing House to determine margin calls and invoice prices for deliveries. Thus the last trade for March contracts during the day was $0.6678/DM. "Change" is the difference between today's and the prior day's settlement price.

"Lifetime high and low" refers to the highest and lowest prices at which a contract has traded since its introduction. The March contract has traded as high as $0.6719 and as low as $0.5820.

The "open interest" for March contracts is 2,700 contracts. Open interest is the sum of all long (buying futures) and short (selling futures) contracts outstanding. Multiplying 2,700 by the current spot price (not shown in the table) of $0.6702 per mark suggests that the market value of outstanding June contracts was approximately 2,700 x DM125,000 x 0.6702 = $226,192,500. The open interest can be used by clients to judge ability to execute a large order. If the order were, say, 5% of the open interest, execution might be possible without a significant change in price. But if the order were, say, 25% of the open interest, execution at prices near current prices might be difficult.

The first number on the last line reports that trading volume for Tuesday was 39,934 contracts, as compared with Monday's 40,352 contracts. The open interest on Tuesday was 70,016 contracts, some 1,965 less than open interest for Monday. Tuesday's open interest can be determined by adding the three volumes shown in the open interest column: 67,208 + 2,700 + 108 = 70,016.

Foreign Currency Futures Versus Forward Contracts

Foreign currency futures contracts differ from forward contracts in a number of important ways. Exhibit 5.3 provides a comparison of the major features and characteristics of the two instruments. Nevertheless, both futures and forward contracts are used for the same commercial and speculative purposes.

Exhibit 5.3   Comparison of Foreign Currency Futures and Forward Contracts

Characteristic	Foreign Currency Futures	Forward Contracts
Size of contract	standardized contracts per currency	any size desired
Maturity	fixed maturities, the longest being typically less than one year	any maturity up to one year, sometimes longer
Location	trading occurs on the floor of an organized exchange	trading occurs between individuals and banks, and banks with each other, by telecommunications linkages
Pricing	open outcry process in the "pit" by floor traders	prices are arrived at by bid and offer quotes
Collateral	initial margin which is marked to market value on a daily basis	no explicit collateral, but standing bank "relations" necessary
Settlement	rarely delivered upon; settlement normally takes place through the purchase of an offsetting position	the contract is normally delivered upon, although the taking of offsetting positions possible
Commissions	single commission covers both purchase and later sale (roundtrip)	commissions gained through the bid-offer spreads provided to retail customers
Trading hours	traditionally traded during exchange hours; several exchanges are now moving to automated 24-hour-a-day trading	negotiated by phone 24 hours a day through bank global networks
Counterparties	unknown to each other due to the auction market structure	parties are in direct contact in setting forward specifications
Liquidity	liquid but relatively small in total sales volume and value	liquid and relatively large in sales volume compared to that of futures contracts

FOREIGN CURRENCY OPTIONS

In the last eight years the use of foreign currency options as a hedging tool and for speculative purposes has blossomed into a major foreign exchange activity. A number of banks in the United States and other capital markets offer flexible foreign currency options on transactions of $1 million or more. The bank market, or over-the-counter market as it is called, offers custom-tailored options on all major trading currencies for any time period up to one year. These provide a useful alternative to forward and futures contracts for firms interested in hedging foreign exchange risk on commercial transactions.

In December 1982, the Philadelphia Stock Exchange introduced trading in standardized foreign currency option contracts in the United States. The Chicago Mercantile Exchange and other exchanges in the United States and abroad have followed suit. Exchange-traded contracts are particularly appealing to speculators and individuals who would not normally have access to the over-the-counter market. Banks also trade on the exchanges because this is one of several alternative ways they can offset the risk of options they have transacted with clients or other banks.

Increased use of foreign currency options is a reflection of the explosive growth in the use of other kinds of options and the resultant improvements in option pricing models. The original option pricing model, developed by Black and Scholes in 1973, has been commercialized since then by numerous firms offering software programs and even built-in routines for hand-held calculators.[1] The Black and Scholes model has been modified for pricing foreign currency options.[2] Several commercial programs are available for option writers and traders to utilize.

Foreign currency option definitions are as follows.

- A foreign currency option is a contract giving the option purchaser (the buyer or holder) the right, but not the obligation, to buy or sell a given amount of foreign exchange (the underlying currency) at a fixed price per unit for a specified time period (until the expiration or maturity date).

- The seller of the option is referred to as the *writer* or *grantor*.

- A *call* is an option to buy foreign currency, and a *put* is an option to sell foreign currency.

- The *exercise* or *strike* price is the specified exchange rate for the underlying currency at which the option can be exercised.

- An *American* option gives the buyer the right to exercise the option at any time between the date of writing and the expiration or maturity date. A *European* option can be exercised only on its expiration date, not before.

- An option whose exercise price is the same as the spot price of the underlying currency is said to be *at the money*. An option that would be profitable if exercised immediately is said to be *in the money*. In-the-money calls have an exercise price below the current spot price of the underlying currency, while in-the-money puts have an exercise price above the current spot price of the underlying currency. An option that would not be profitable if exercised immediately is referred to as *out of the money*. Out-of-the-money calls have an exercise price above the current spot price of the underlying currency, while out-of-the-money puts have an exercise price below the current spot price of the underlying currency.

- The *premium* or *option price* is the cost of the option, usually paid in advance by the buyer to the seller. In the over-the-counter market, premiums are quoted as a percentage of the transaction amount. Premiums on exchange-traded options are quoted as a dollar (domestic currency) amount per unit of foreign currency.

FOREIGN CURRENCY OPTIONS MARKETS

Foreign currency options can be purchased or sold in three different types of markets:

- Options on the physical currency, purchased on the over-the-counter (interbank) market.

- Options on the physical currency, purchased on an organized exchange such as the Philadelphia Stock Exchange.

- Options on futures contracts, purchased on the IMM.

Options on the Over-the-Counter Market

Over-the-counter options are most frequently written by banks for U.S. dollars against pounds sterling, Deutschemarks, Swiss francs, Japanese yen, and Canadian dollars.[3] They are usually written in round lots of $5–10 million in New York and $2–3 million in London.[4]

The main advantages of over-the-counter options for business firms are that the size and terms of contracts can be tailored to the specific needs of the business firm and that the market is quite liquid. On the other hand, the buyer must assess the writing bank's ability to fulfill the option contract.

Options on Organized Exchanges: The Philadelphia Stock Exchange

Options on the physical (underlying) currency are traded on a number of organized exchanges worldwide, the most important of which is the Philadelphia Stock Exchange. Trading volume on the Philadelphia Stock Exchange is relatively heavy, with a single trade involving 2,000 contracts not unrealistic.

Exchange-traded options are settled through a clearing house without the buyer and seller being directly involved with each other. The clearing house is the opposite party to every option contract, and it guarantees fulfillment. Clearing-house obligations are in turn the obligation of all members of the exchange, including a large number of banks.

Foreign currency options on eight major currencies are traded on the Philadelphia Stock Exchange. Both American and European options are available for each of the currencies, except for European Currency Units (ECUs), which trade only an American option. Currency unit contract specifications in Philadelphia are shown in Exhibit 5.4.

If, for example, a person wants to buy an option on DM1,000,000, that person will purchase 16 contracts, because DM1,000,000 ÷ DM62,500 per contract = 16 contracts.

Exhibit 5.4 Currency Option Contract Specifications on Philadelphia Stock Exchange

Currency	Contract Size
Australian dollars	A$50,000 per contract
British pounds	£31,250 per contract
Canadian dollars	C$50,000 per contract
German marks	DM62,500 per contract
French francs	FF250,000 per contract
Japanese yen	¥6,250,000 per contract
Swiss francs	SF62,500 per contract
European currency units	ECU62,500 per contract

Source: From *The Wall Street Journal*, November 7, 1990. Reprinted by permission of *The Wall Street Journal*, © 1990 Dow Jones & Co., Inc. All rights reserved worldwide.

Exhibit 5.5   Foreign Currency Option Quotations

Option & Underlying	Strike Price	Calls – Last			Puts – Last		
		Nov	Dec	Mar	Nov	Dec	Mar
62,500 German Marks—cents per unit.							
67.02	58	r	r	9.13	r	0.02	r
67.02	59	r	r	8.13	r	r	r
67.02	60	r	r	7.12	r	r	r
67.02	62	r	5.15	r	r	r	r
67 ͻ2	63	r	r	r	r	0.10	r
67.02	64	r	r	3.73	r	0.18	0.79
67.02	65	r	2.43	r	0.07	0.35	r
67.02	65 1/2	r	r	s	0.10	r	s
67.02	66	1.32	1.82	r	0.18	0.65	1.53
67.02	66 1/2	r	1.38	s	0.33	0.76	s
67.02	67	0.78	1.18	2.00	r	1.02	1.83
67.02	67 1/2	r	0.95	s	r	r	s
67.02	68	r	0.67	r	1.00	r	2.38
67.02	68 1/2	0.15	r	s	r	r	s
67.02	69	r	0.47	r	r	r	r
67.02	70	r	r	0.81	r	r	r
67.02	71	r	r	0.67	r	r	r

Source: From *The Wall Street Journal*, November 7, 1990. Reprinted by permission of *The Wall Street Journal,* ©1990 Dow Jones & Co., Inc. All rights reserved worldwide.

Quotes in the *Wall Street Journal* for options on German marks are shown in Exhibit 5.5. The *Journal*'s quotes refer to transactions completed on the Philadelphia Stock Exchange on the previous day. However, the daily volume is not given. Quotations are usually available for more combinations of strike prices and expiration dates than were actually traded and thus reported in the newspaper. The letter "r" indicates that a particular contract did not trade during the previous day, while the letter "s" indicates that no option of that price and maturity is currently offered.

In Exhibit 5.5, "option & underlying" means that 67.02 cents, or $0.6702, is the spot dollar price of one German mark at the close of trading on the preceding day. "Strike price" means the price per mark that must be paid if the option is exercised. On the above date, options with 17 separate strike prices, ranging from $0.5800 to $0.7100 per mark, were available. Options are available at fixed strike prices, which prices reflect the current market price of the underlying currency at the time that option was first offered.

In Exhibit 5.5, the purchase price or premium for each option is expressed in U.S. cents per one German mark. All option premiums are expressed in *cents* per unit of foreign currency except for the French franc, which is expressed in tenths of a cent per franc, and the Japanese yen, which is expressed in hundredths of a cent per yen. In Exhibit 5.5, a

December 67 call option premium is 1.18 cents per mark. Since one option contract consists of a call of 62,500 marks, the premium for the option is DM62,500 x $0.01180/DM = $737.50. A March 67 call could be purchased for $0.0200/DM, or $1,250.00.

Each foreign currency option is introduced for trading with one, two, three, six, nine, and twelve months to run until expiration. Expiration months are March, June, September, and December, with trading also available in two additional near-term consecutive months. Thus in November, trading would occur in November, December, January, March, June, and September maturities. Finally, each option contract expires on the Saturday preceding the third Wednesday of the expiration month.

Options on Futures Contracts

Options on futures contracts can be purchased on the IMM. Options are available on quarterly (March, June, September, and December) futures only, but the options themselves expire each month. Hence, for example, one can buy three separate options on April futures, one expiring in February, one in March, and one in April. Trading in all options terminates two Fridays before the third Wednesday of the expiration month. Option prices are stated in terms of cents per unit of foreign currency.

To illustrate, consider a December futures price of $0.6695/DM, such as we saw in Exhibit 5.2. A firm wanting assurance of marks in December could buy one contract for a commission of, say, $50, plus a margin deposit of $2,000. But there is another alternative. Instead of buying December futures at $0.6695/DM, the firm could purchase any one of several call options on December futures, depending on the desired strike price. Prices, in cents per mark, for call and put options for November, December, and March, and for various strike prices, are shown in Exhibit 5.6.

Exhibit 5.6 Futures Options Prices

Strike Price	Calls – Settle			Puts – Settle		
	Nov-c	Dec-c	Mar-c	Nov-p	Dec-p	Mar-p
Deutschemark (IMM) 125,000 marks; cents per mark						
6600	1.03	1.53	2.26	0.08	0.58	1.49
6650	1.63	1.22	...	0.18	0.77	...
6700	0.33	0.95	1.74	0.38	1.00	1.96
6750	0.16	0.74	...	0.71	1.29	...
6800	0.08	0.56	1.33	1.13	1.61	2.53
6850	0.05	0.43	...	...	1.98	...

Est. vol. 9,294, Mon. vol. 9,302 calls, 16,878 puts
Open interest Mon. 72,544 calls, 97,898 puts

In Exhibit 5.6, the strike price of 6600 means $0.6600/DM, and "settle" means the price at which contracts were settled that day. Note that as the strike price increases from 6600 to 6850, the price of the call option diminishes because the likelihood of its expiring in the money decreases. The reverse is true for puts. As maturity lengthens, the price of both call and put options increases because the time value of the option is greater; that is, there exists a greater chance that the option will expire in the money.

If the firm purchased a December call option on DM125,000 at a strike price of 6700, it would pay DM125,000 x $0.00950 = $1,187.50. If by December the mark proved to be worth $0.6700 or more, the firm could exercise the option to acquire the future, and then complete the future contract to acquire marks. However, if instead the mark were to fall in value below $0.6700, the firm would abandon the option because it had expired out of the money and would purchase the now cheaper marks in the spot market.

The essential difference between using a futures contract and using an option on a futures contract is that with a futures contract the firm must deliver one currency against another, or reverse the contract on the exchange, whereas with an option the firm is protected against an adverse change in the spot value of the currency but may abandon the option and use the spot market if that is more advantageous.

Determinants of the Option Premium

The value of an option is the sum of two components, its *intrinsic value* and its *time value*. These are illustrated for a call option in Exhibit 5.7. Intrinsic value is the financial gain derived if the option is exercised immediately. It is shown by the dashed line in Exhibit 5.7. Intrinsic value will be zero when the option is out of the money, that is, when the strike price is above the market price, since no gain can be derived from exercising the option. When the spot price rises above the strike price (diagonal dashed line), the intrinsic value becomes positive because the option is always worth at least this value if exercised.

In Exhibit 5.7, when the spot price is $0.680/DM the option has an intrinsic value of $0.680–$0.670, or 1 cent per mark. Thus a DM62,500 contract would have an intrinsic value of $625. At a spot price below $0.670/DM, the option is out of the money and has no intrinsic value. Only a fool would exercise it; anyone else would buy marks more cheaply on the spot market!

The time value of an option exists because the price of the underlying currency can change between the present and the maturity date so as to make the option valuable. Time value is shown as a pink shaded area in Exhibit 5.7. (i.e., the difference between the total value line and the intrinsic value line).

An investor will usually pay something today for an out-of-the-money (i.e., zero intrinsic value) option on the chance of profit before maturity. An in-the-money option can increase in intrinsic value between the present and maturity, and an investor might pay something for this chance of increased value. Consequently the price of an option is always somewhat greater than its intrinsic value, since there is always some chance (even if minuscule) that the intrinsic value will rise between the present and the expiration date.

The total value of an option is the sum of its intrinsic value, which is easy to calculate, and its time value, which depends on the market's expectations about the likelihood that

Exhibit 5.7   Intrinsic Value, Time Value, and Total Value of a Call Option

Underlying currency: **German mark**
Contract size: **62,500**
Expiration, or maturity, date: **2 months (December)**
Exercise, or strike, price: **$0.67/DM**
Premium, or option, price: **$0.0118/DM ($737.50 per contract)**

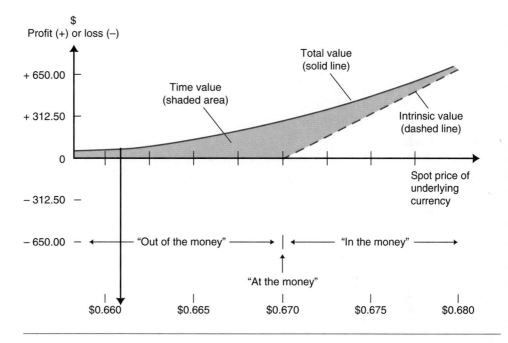

the underlying currency will rise in value (for a call option) prior to maturity. On the date of maturity an option will have a value equal to its intrinsic value, since no time remains for that intrinsic value to increase.

Option pricing models attempt to capture the combined intrinsic and time values of an option. Details of the most successful commercial versions of currency option pricing models are not disclosed to the public since these programs are sold to clients. However, most such models are derivatives of the original Black and Scholes option pricing model. In the modified version of that model the value of a foreign currency depends on the following five variables:

1.   the strike price relative to the spot exchange rate,

2.   time to maturity,

3. relative interest rates on the two currencies involved,

4. volatility of the underlying currency, and

5. supply and demand for specific options.[5]

FOREIGN CURRENCY SPECULATION

Speculation is an attempt to profit by trading on expectations about prices in the future. In the foreign exchange markets, one speculates by taking an open (unhedged) position in a foreign currency and then closing that position after the exchange rate has moved in—one hopes—the expected direction. In the remainder of this chapter we analyze the manner in which speculation is undertaken in spot, forward, and options markets. It is important to understand this phenomenon because it has a major impact on our ability to forecast future exchange rates, the subject of the next chapter.

Stabilizing and Destabilizing Speculation

Speculation is often termed stabilizing or destabilizing in its impact on market price, an impact that is particularly important in the floating exchange rate markets of the world today. Stabilizing speculations are those that reduce the volatility of markets, that is, reduce the volatility of actual prices around the currency's "natural value" or its actual trend over time. Unfortunately, "natural value" is unknown until after it has occurred, so one cannot tell in advance whether a particular speculative transaction is stabilizing or destabilizing.

Suppose that a currency has the following "natural value," and that because of market activity actual prices fluctuate above and below this value. Then speculative behavior that drives price down when price is near its peak, or up when price is near its trough, is termed stabilizing.

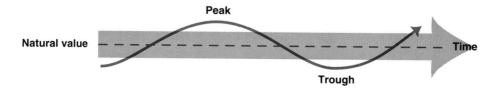

If, however, price reaches its "natural" peak and investors continue to buy in the belief the market will rise still more, their buying forces the market still farther above its "natural value." In such a case the degree of volatility and instability is increased, in that the market must eventually fall even further to get back to "natural value." This kind of increase, sometimes called a "speculative bubble," is the result of "destabilizing expectations" held by market participants, and it does not increase the efficiency of the market. Such speculatively induced volatility is usually judged bad because it creates additional uncertainty among market participants.

Speculating in the Spot Market

Willem Koopmans is a currency speculator in Amsterdam. He is therefore willing to risk money on his own opinion about future currency prices. Willem Koopmans may speculate in the spot, forward, or options markets. To illustrate, assume the German mark is currently quoted as follows.

Spot Rate: $0.6700/DM

Six-month forward rate: $0.6671/DM

Willem Koopmans has $100,000 with which to speculate, and he believes that in six months the spot rate for the mark will be $0.6800/DM. Speculation in the spot market requires only that the speculator believe the foreign currency will appreciate in value. The following steps should be taken.

1. Today use the $100,000 to buy DM149,253.7 spot at $0.6700/DM.

2. Hold the DM149,253.7 indefinitely. Although the mark is expected to rise to the target value in six months, the speculator is not committed to that time horizon.

3. When the target exchange rate is reached, sell DM149,253.7 at the new spot rate of $0.6800/DM, receiving DM149,253.7 x $0.6800/DM = $101,492.52.

4. Profit = $1,492.52, or 1.5% on the $100,000 committed for six months (3.0% per annum). This ignores interest income on the Deutschemarks and opportunity cost on the dollars for the moment.

The potential maximum gain is unlimited, while the maximum loss will be $100,000 if the marks purchased in step 1 drop in value to zero.

Speculating in the Forward Market

Forward market speculation occurs when the speculator believes that the spot price at some future date will differ from today's forward price for that same date. Success does not depend on the direction of movement of the spot rate, but on the relative position of the future spot rate and the current forward rate. Given the above data and expectations, Willem Koopmans would take the following steps.

1. Today buy DM149,903 forward six months at the forward quote of $0.6671/DM. Note that this step requires no outlay of cash.

2. In six months, fulfill the forward contract, receiving DM149,903 at $0.6671/DM for a cost of $100,000.

3. Simultaneously sell the DM149,903 in the spot market, receiving DM149,903 x $0.6800/DM = $101,934.

4. Profit: $1,934.

The profit of $1,934 cannot be related to an investment base to calculate a return on investment because the dollar funds were never needed. On the six-month anniversary Willem Koopmans simply crosses the payment obligation of $100,000 with receipts of $101,934, and accepts a net $1,934. Nevertheless, some financial institutions might require him to deposit collateral as margin to assure his ability to complete the trade.

In this particular forward speculation, the maximum loss is $100,000, the amount needed to buy marks via the forward contract. This loss would be incurred only if the value of the spot mark in six months were zero. The maximum gain is unlimited, since marks acquired in the forward market can in theory rise to an infinite dollar value.

Forward market speculation cannot be extended beyond the maturity date of the forward contract. However, if the speculator wants to close out the speculative operation before maturity, that speculator may buy an offsetting contract. In the above example, after, say, four months Willem Koopmans could sell DM149,903 forward two months at whatever forward price then existed. Two months after that he would close the matured six-month contract to purchase marks against the matured two-month contract to sell marks, pocketing any profit or paying up any loss. The amount of profit or loss would be fixed by the price at which Willem Koopmans sold forward two months.

The above example is one of four possible types of forward speculations. Exhibit 5.8 demonstrates all four forward market speculation strategies.

The examples given in this discussion have ignored any interest earned. In a spot speculation, the speculator can invest the principal amount in the foreign money market to earn interest. In the various forward speculations, a speculator who is holding cash against the risk of loss can invest those funds in the home money market. Thus relative profitability will be influenced by interest differentials.

Using Call Options for Speculation

Options differ from all other types of financial instruments in the patterns of risk they produce. The option owner has the choice of exercising the option or allowing it to expire unused. The owner will exercise it only when exercising is profitable, which means only when the option is in the money. In the case of a call option, as the spot price of the underlying currency moves up, the holder has the possibility of unlimited profit. On the down side, however, the holder can abandon the option and walk away with a loss never greater than the amount of premium paid.

The position of Willem Koopmans as a buyer of a call is illustrated in Exhibit 5.9. Assume that an option for DM62,500 is written with a strike price (exercise price) of $0.6700/DM and a maturity of two months. The cost of the option is $312.50, this being calculated as a cost of 0.5 cents per mark for DM62,500. The vertical axis measures profit or loss for the option holder at each of several different spot prices for the mark up to the time of maturity. Numerical calculations are shown beneath various spot prices.

If, for example, the spot rate were $0.6650/DM when the option expired, Koopmans would not exercise the option. (Buying marks via the option at $0.6700/DM when they

Exhibit 5.8   Alternative Speculation Strategies in the Forward
Foreign Currency Market

S_0 = spot rate today,
F = forward rate today for contract maturing one time period in the future,
S_1 = today's expectation of spot rate for one time period in the future.

Type 1: The speculator believes the spot mark *will appreciate by more* than the forward market quote.

S_1 = $0.6800/DM
F = $0.6750/DM

S_0 = $0.6700/DM

The speculator buys marks forward for dollars at $0.6750/DM, waits until maturity, delivers dollars for marks, and sells marks spot at $0.6800/DM.

Type 2: The speculator believes the spot mark *will not appreciate as much* as the forward quote.

F = $0.6750/DM
S_1 = $0.6725/DM

S_0 = $0.6700/DM

The speculator sells marks forward at $0.6750/DM, waits until maturity, covers the forward contract by buying marks on the spot market at $0.6725/DM.

Type 3: The speculator believes the spot mark *will depreciate by less* than the forward market quote.

S_0 = $0.6700/DM

S_1 = $0.6650/DM
F = $0.6600/DM

The speculator buys marks forward for dollars at $0.6600/DM, waits until maturity, delivers dollars for marks at $0.6600/DM, sells marks at spot rate of $0.6650/DM.

Type 4: The speculator believes the spot mark *will depreciate by more* than the forward quote.

S_0 = $0.6700/DM

F = $0.6600/DM
S_1 = $0.6500/DM

The speculator sells marks forward at $0.6600/DM, waits until maturity, buys the marks needed for delivery at $0.6500/DM, and delivers marks at $0.6600/DM.

---

could be bought in the market at $0.6650/DM would be highly illogical!) His total loss would be the $312.50 purchase price of the option, plus a small brokerage commission, which we will ignore throughout this illustration. At any lower price for the mark, his loss would similarly be limited to the original $312.50 cost.

Alternatively, if the ending price were $0.6850/DM, Koopmans would exercise the option, paying $41,875 to buy DM62,500 at the strike price of $0.6700/DM. The DM62,500 could be sold immediately in the spot market for $42,812.50, for a gross profit of $937.50 and a net profit, after deducting the original cost of the option, of $625. More

Exhibit 5.9   Buyer of a Call: Profit and Loss Position for
Various Ending Spot Prices

Underlying currency: German mark
Contract size: 62,500
Expiration, or maturity, date: 2 months (December)
Exercise, or strike, price: $0.6700/DM
Premium, or option, price: $0.0050/DM ($312.50 per contract)

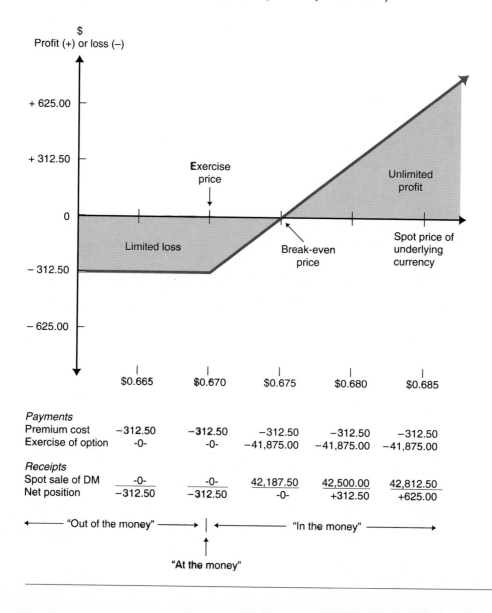

	$0.665	$0.670	$0.675	$0.680	$0.685
Payments					
Premium cost	−312.50	−312.50	−312.50	−312.50	−312.50
Exercise of option	-0-	-0-	−41,875.00	−41,875.00	−41,875.00
Receipts					
Spot sale of DM	-0-	-0-	42,187.50	42,500.00	42,812.50
Net position	−312.50	−312.50	-0-	+312.50	+625.00

←——— "Out of the money" ———→ | ←——— "In the money" ———→

↑
"At the money"

likely, he would realize the profit through executing an offsetting contract on the options exchange rather than taking delivery of the currency. Because the dollar price of a mark could rise to an infinite level, maximum profit is unlimited.

The break-even price of $0.6750/DM is the price at which Koopmans neither gains nor loses on exercise of the option. The premium cost ($312.50), combined with the cost of exercising the option ($41,875), is exactly equal to the proceeds from selling the marks in the spot market ($42,187.50). Note that at the break-even price he will exercise the option; to abandon it would be to accept a loss of $312.50. At any spot price above the exercise price and below the break-even price, the gross profit earned on exercising the option and selling the underlying currency covers part of the premium cost.

The position of the writer of the same call option is illustrated in Exhibit 5.10. If the option expires when the spot price of the underlying currency is below the exercise price, the option holder does not exercise. Consequently the writer keeps as profit the entire $312.50 paid as the option premium. Above the exercise price of $0.6700/DM, the writer of the call must deliver the underlying currency for $41,875 at a time when the value of that currency is above $41,875. If the writer wrote the option *naked*, that is, without owning the currency, that writer will now have to buy the currency at spot and take the loss. The amount of such a loss is unlimited and increases as the price of the underlying currency rises. Even if the writer already owned the currency, the writer will experience an opportunity loss, surrendering against the option the same currency that could have been sold for more in the open market.

Using Put Options for Speculation

The position of Koopmans as buyer of a put is illustrated in Exhibit 5.11. The basic terms of this put are similar to those we just used to illustrate a call. The buyer of a put option, however, wants to be able to sell the underlying currency at the exercise price when the market price of that currency drops. If the spot price of a mark drops to, say, $0.6600/DM, Koopmans will deliver DM62,500 to the writer and receive $41,875. The marks can now be purchased for $41,250 and the cost of the option was $312.50, so he will have a net gain of $312.50. At lower spot exchange rates the gain would increase, and his profit could be unlimited (up to a maximum of $41,562, when the price of a DM would be zero). At an exchange rate above $0.6700/DM, Koopmans would not exercise the option, and so would lose the $312.50 premium paid for the option.

The position of a writer of the put sold to Koopmans is shown in Exhibit 5.12. If the spot price of marks drops below $0.6700/DM, the option will be exercised by Koopmans. Below a price of $0.6600/DM, the writer will lose more than the $312.50 received from writing the option, falling below break-even. Between $0.6600/DM and $0.6700/DM the writer will lose part, but not all, of the premium received. If the spot price is above $0.6700/DM, the option will not be exercised, and the option writer pockets the entire $312.50 premium.

Earnings for the latest quarter reflected a 28% increase in non-interest income, to $461.5 million, and a lower provision for credit losses, partially offset by an increase in non-interest expenses.

In the earlier quarter, the company recorded a $670 million special provision for credit losses related to refinancing debt of developing countries.

Bankers Trust's provision for credit losses totaled $5 million in the last quarter, compared with $50 million a year earlier, excluding the special foreign-exchange provision. Net charge-offs totaled $1.4 million, compared with $46.9 million a year earlier. The allowance for credit losses as of June 30 was $1.3 billion both this year and last.

The placement on non-accrual status of about $580 million of medium-term and long-term loans to Brazilian and Ecuadorian borrowers during the first quarter of 1987 resulted in a reduction of net interest earnings of about $15 million in the latest second quarter, compared with about $16 million in the year-earlier period.

Since that action, Bankers Trust has received about $27 million of interest payments related to Brazilian loans. These interest payments have not been credited to earnings pending an agreement with Brazilian authorities.

Total assets as of June 30 were $55.5 billion, up from $54.7 billion a year earlier.

Six-month net was $300.1 million, or $3.79 a share, compared with a loss of $429.7 million a year earlier.

The year-earlier half included the $670 million special provision.

"Bankers Trust Lack of Control Cited in Move"*

Bankers Trust New York Corp.'s startling restatement of its 1987 income from foreign-exchange trading is the fallout from a lack of adequate management controls on its former star trader in foreign-currency options, Andrew J. Krieger, according to current and former bank employees.

Although Bankers Trust did impose dollar limits on Mr. Krieger's billion-dollar trading positions, few, if any, managers could really comprehend his intricate trading strategies and positions, these employees said. "Nobody understood what Andy was doing," said one former Bankers Trust trader.

While banks have long traded foreign currencies, Mr. Krieger, a 32-year-old trader who studied Sanskrit, pioneered in an embryonic product—foreign-currency options with terms of a year or longer. These over-the-counter options, which give holders the right to buy or sell currencies at a set price for a set period of time, pose special problems. They are thinly traded, making them very illiquid, and the task of valuing them is extremely complex and subjective.

Despite a lack of familiarity with the product, Bankers Trust managers allowed Mr. Krieger to take billion-dollar positions in sterling, yen, and other currencies and options

---

* From *The Wall Street Journal*, July 22–23, 1988. Reprinted by permission of *The Wall Street Journal*, © 1988 Dow Jones & Co., Inc. All rights reserved worldwide.

and to use his own assumptions about volatility and future prices to value the options, current and former employees said.

On Wednesday, that daring new product boomeranged on the bank. At the insistence of the Federal Reserve Bank of New York, Bankers slashed its previously reported $338 million in fourth-quarter foreign-exchange trading income $80 million to reflect lower values on a portfolio of foreign-currency options that was built by Mr. Krieger, who left Bankers Trust in February. He now is traveling in India, friends said, and couldn't be reached.

The restatement didn't alter Bankers' results for the year or quarter because, it said, an overfunding in its employees' bonus account of $80 million offset the lower foreign-exchange results. Bankers has told its employees that their 1988 bonuses won't be affected by the reduction.

Bankers wouldn't comment further Thursday. "We've told you what happened and what we did. We took the initiative and informed the Fed about the valuation. It wasn't until Monday that they told us to amend our call report," a spokesman said.

SUMMARY

- Foreign currency futures and options are financial instruments that are useful to businesses, banks, and individuals for both hedging and speculative purposes.

- Foreign currency futures are exchange-traded contracts that have many similarities to transactions entered into in the forward foreign exchange markets. The most important differences from the forward market are that futures contracts are for specified amounts and maturities of a foreign exchange, which means that hedging and speculation can be done only in multiples of that quantity and for the available maturities.

- Foreign currency options are financial contracts that give the holder the right, but not the obligation, to buy (in the case of calls) or sell (in the case of puts) a specified amount of foreign exchange at a predetermined price on or before a specified maturity date. Their use as a speculative device arises from the fact that an option gains in value as the underlying currency rises (for calls) or falls (for puts). Yet, the amount of loss when the underlying currency moves opposite to the desired direction is limited to the cost of the option.

- Speculation is an attempt to profit by trading on expectations about prices in the future. In the foreign exchange market, one speculates by taking an open (unhedged) position in a foreign currency and then closing that position after the exchange rate has moved; a profit results only if the rate moves in the direction that was expected. Speculative activity can be a stabilizing or destabilizing influence on the market, depending on whether it moves rates toward or away from their "natural" value.

■ 1. Willem Koopmans and Call Option Speculation (C05A.WK1)
Willem Koopmans is considering a different call option on German marks than what he bought previously (see Exhibit 5.9). He can also buy a December call option with a strike price of 66.5 cents per Deutschemark. The premium for this call option is 1.5 cents per Deutschemark. Ignore the brokerage cost on all questions 1–14.

a) Diagram the profit and loss potential for this call option as seen by Willem Koopmans.

b) What is the breakeven price for Koopmans?

c) What would Koopmans expect as the profit or loss on this call option if by December the spot exchange rate is $0.6800/DM?

■ 2. Willem Koopmans and Put Option Speculation (C05B.WK1)
Willem Koopmans is considering a different put option on German marks than what he bought previously (see Exhibit 5.11). He can also buy a December put option with a strike price of 67.5 cents per Deutschemark. The premium for this option is 1.0 cents per Deutschemark.

a) Diagram the profit and loss potential for this put option as seen by Willem Koopmans.

b) What is the breakeven price for Koopmans?

c) What would Koopmans expect as the profit or loss on this put option if by December the spot exchange rate is $0.6600/DM?

■ 3. Speculating with Call Options (C05C.WK1)
Horst Schmidt is considering buying ten call options on German marks on the Philadelphia Stock Exchange at a strike price of 54 cents per Deutschemark. Each option contract is for DM62,500. The option will expire in three months. The premium is 2.0 cents per Deutschemark. Ignore the brokerage cost. The spot rate is currently $0.5400/DM and the three-month forward rate is $0.5525/DM. Horst Schmidt believes that the most likely range for the spot Deutschemark in three months will be a low of $0.5000/DM to a high of $.6200/DM, but the most likely value will be $0.5900/DM.

a) Diagram the profit and loss position as perceived by Horst Schmidt.

b) Calculate what he would gain or lose at his expected range of future spot prices and at his expected future spot price.

c) Calculate and show on the diagram the breakeven future spot price.

■ 4. Writing Call Options (C05C.WK1)
Given the same facts as in question 3, calculate and diagram the corresponding profit, loss, and breakeven positions for the writer (seller) of the ten call options on German marks to be purchased by Horst Schmidt.

a) What is the highest spot rate expected by the writer of the call option?

b) What is the profit or loss per DM to the writer of the option if the spot rate is $0.6900/DM?

c) What is the maximum profit per DM possible for the writer of the call option?

5. Buying Futures Contracts

Horst Schmidt is also considering speculating on the Deutschemark in the futures market rather than buying the call options. He could buy five futures contracts on the Deutschemark on the IMM with a maturity date three months hence. Each contract is for DM125,000. He can buy the contracts at a price of $0.5530/DM. His margin requirements are 10% of the contract size. Given Horst Schmidt's expectations about the future spot rate for the Deutschemark, calculate his expected profit and loss position on these futures contracts. Ignore transaction costs.

6. Call Options Versus Futures Contracts

Continuing the same example from questions 3–5, prepare a summary of the advantages and disadvantages of the call options compared to the futures contracts from the viewpoint of Horst Schmidt. Be sure to include comparative risks and projected return on investment.

7. Speculating with Put Options (C05D.WK1)

Given the same facts as in question 3 above, Horst Schmidt has changed his expectation of the future spot rate of the Deutschemark. He now believes it will fall during the next three months to $0.5100/DM, but the potential range would be the same. He can purchase ten put options on the Philadelphia Stock Exchange at a strike price of 54 cents per Deutschemark, a contract size of DM62,500, an expiration three months hence, and a premium of 1.0 cents per Deutschemark.

    a) Diagram the new profit and loss position for the holder of a put option as perceived by Horst Schmidt.

    b) Calculate what he would gain or lose at his expected range of future spot prices and at his new expected future spot price.

    c) Calculate and show on the diagram the breakeven future spot price.

8. Writing Put Options (C05D.WK1)

Given the same facts as in question 7, calculate and diagram the corresponding profit, loss, and breakeven positions for the writer (seller) of the ten put options to be purchased by Horst Schmidt.

9. Selling Futures Contracts

Horst Schmidt is also considering using the futures market as an alternative to the put options. He could sell five futures contracts on the Deutschemark on the IMM with a three-month maturity, a contract size of DM125,000, 10% margin, and a selling price of $0.5530/DM. Given Horst Schmidt's new expectations about the future spot rate for the Deutschemark, calculate his expected profit and loss position on these futures contracts.

10. Put Options Versus Futures Contracts

Continuing the same example from questions 7 and 9, prepare a summary of the advantages and disadvantages of the put options compared to the futures contracts from the viewpoint of Horst Schmidt, including risks and projected return on investment.

11. Speculating on the British Pound Sterling

You have the following quotations and expectations for the British pound.

Present spot rate	$1.7800/£
Six-month forward rate	$1.8100/£
Your expectation for spot rate in six months	$1.8500/£

Six-month call options on pounds at a strike price of $1.78 sell for a premium of 4 cents per pound sterling. Assume you have $5,000,000 with which to speculate. Ignore transaction costs, taxes, and interest that might be earned on idle cash balances. If your expectations prove correct:

   a)   What would be your dollar profit from speculating in the spot market?
   b)   What risks are associated with this speculation?
   c)   How much capital must be committed?
   d)   What would be your dollar profit from speculating via the forward market?
   e)   What risks are associated with this forward speculation?
   f)   How much capital must be committed?
   g)   What would be your dollar profit from speculating via the option market?
   h)   What risks are associated with this option speculation?
   i)   How much capital must be committed?
   j)   What are the consequences for the three alternatives if interest can be earned on idle cash balances?

12. Speculating on the Movement of the Dutch Guilder

The current spot rate for Dutch guilders is:	_fl_ 1.9200/$.
The three-month forward quote is:	_fl_ 1.9000/$.

You believe that the spot Dutch guilder in three months will be _fl_ 1.8800/$, and you have $100,000 with which to speculate for three months.

Any bank with which you conduct a forward market transaction will want 100% initial margin; that is, you will be required to deposit the amount of any transaction in a certificate of deposit.

Illustrate two different ways of speculating, and calculate the dollar profit to be made by each method. Assume the three-month rate of interest for deposits or lending in the Netherlands is 4% per annum and in the U.S. is 8% per annum. For each way of speculating, explain the risks involved.

13. Trading in Madrid

Maria Cadiz, a foreign exchange trader in Madrid, sees that the 180-day forward rate for the Japanese yen against the dollar is ¥130/$. She believes that the spot yen in six months will be stronger, at ¥125/$.

What would be her expected profit on a 180-day forward speculation with $1 million? What would be her risks?

14. Laura Wong: Currency Speculator

Laura Wong (wife of William!) would like to speculate that the U.S. dollar is going to weaken compared to the Deutschemark (DM). She intends to use foreign currency options on the IMM.

The standard contract size on the IMM for DM is DM62,500. She can only afford to speculate on one contract (William has had a few bad days in a row). The most recent spot rate is \$0.6400/DM. The three-month forward rate is \$0.6500/DM. The premium for a put option on DM for three months with a strike price of \$0.6400/DM ("at-the-money") is 1.0 cents per DM. The premium for a three-month call option on DMs is 2.0 cents per DM for the same strike price.

Laura believes that the most likely range for the spot DM in three months will be a low of \$0.6000/DM and a high of \$0.6800/DM. The most likely value, in her opinion, will be \$0.6700/DM. Ignore brokerage costs.

a) Diagram the profit and loss position from Laura Wong's perspective.

b) Calculate what she would gain or lose at her expected range of future spot prices and her most likely estimate of \$0.6700/DM.

c) Calculate and show on the diagram the breakeven future spot rate for the DM.

NOTES

1. Fisher Black and Myron Scholes, "The Pricing of Options and Corporate Liabilities," *Journal of Political Economy*, May/June 1973, pp. 637–659.

2. Mark Garman and Steven Kohlhagen, "Foreign Currency Option Values," *Journal of International Money and Finance*, December 1983, pp. 231–237; J. Orlin Grabbe, "The Pricing of Call and Put Options on Foreign Exchange," *Journal of International Money and Finance*, December 1983, pp. 239–253; and Nahum Biger and John Hull, "The Valuation of Currency Options," *Financial Management*, Spring 1983, pp. 24–28.

3. Bank for International Settlements, *Recent Innovations in International Banking*, Basle, Switzerland, April 1986, p. 72. This publication contains a detailed discussion of foreign currency options.

4. *Ibid.*

5. Black and Scholes, op. cit.; and Garman and Kohlhagen, op. cit.

BIBLIOGRAPHY

Abuaf, Niso, "Foreign Exchange Options: The Leading Hedge," *Midland Corporate Finance Journal*, Summer 1987, pp. 51–58.

Adams, Paul D., and Steve B. Wyatt, "On the Pricing of European and American Foreign Currency Call Options," *Journal of International Money and Finance*, 6, no. 3, September 1987. pp. 315–338.

Agmon, Tamir, and Rafael Eldor, "Currency Options Cope with Uncertainty," *Euromoney*, May 1983, pp. 227–228.

Biger, Nahum, and John Hull, "The Valuation of Currency Options," *Financial Management*, Spring 1983, pp. 24–28.

Black, Fischer, and Myron Scholes, "The Pricing of Options and Corporate Liabilities," *Journal of Political Economy*, May/June 1973, pp. 637–659.

Bodurtha, James N., Jr., and Georges R. Courtadon, "Efficiency Tests of the Foreign Currency Options Market," *Journal of Finance*, March 1986, pp. 151–162.

——, "Tests of an American Option Pricing Model on the Foreign Currency Options Market," *Journal of Financial and Quantitative Analysis*, June 1987, pp. 153—168.

Briys, Eric, and Michel Crouhy, "Creating and Pricing Hybrid Foreign Currency Options," *Financial Management*, Winter 1988, pp. 59–65.

Chalupa, Karl V., "Foreign Currency Futures; Reducing Foreign Exchange Risk," *Economic Perspectives*, Federal Reserve Bank of Chicago, Winter 1982, pp. 3–11.

Cornell, Bradford, and Marc R. Reinganum, "Forward and Future Prices," *Journal of Finance*, December 1981, pp. 1035–1045.

Feiger, George, and Bertrand Jacquillat, "Currency Option Bonds, Puts and Calls on Spot Exchange and the Hedging of Contingent Foreign Earnings," *Journal of Finance*, December 1979, pp. 1129–1139.

Gadkari, Vilas, *Relative Pricing of Currency Options*, New York: Salomon Brothers, May 1984.

Garman, Mark B., and Steven W. Kohlhagen, "Foreign Currency Option Values," *Journal of International Money and Finance*, December 1983, pp. 231–237.

Giddy, Ian H., "Foreign Exchange Options," *Journal of Futures Markets*, Summer 1983, pp. 143–166.

——, "The Foreign Exchange Option as a Hedging Tool," *Midland Corporate Finance Journal*, Fall 1983, pp. 32–42.

Goldstein, Henry, "Foreign Currency Futures: Some Further Aspects," *Economic Perspectives*, Federal Reserve Bank of Chicago, November–December 1983, pp. 3–13.

Grabbe, J. Orlin, "The Pricing of Call and Put Options on Foreign Exchange," *Journal of International Money and Finance*, December 1983, pp. 239–253.

Grammatikos, Theoharry, and Anthony Saunders, "Stability and the Hedging Performance of Foreign Currency Futures," *Journal of Futures Markets*, Fall 1983, pp. 295–305.

Hodrick, Robert J., and Sanjay Srivastava, "Foreign Currency Futures," *Journal of International Economics*, February 1987, pp. 1–24.

Hull, John, and Alan White, "Hedging the Risks from Writing Foreign Currency Options," *Journal of International Money and Finance*, June 1987, pp. 131–152.

Miller, Merton H., "The International Competitiveness of U.S. Futures Exchanges," *Journal of Applied Corporate Finance*, vol. 3, no. 4, Winter 1991, pp. 6–20.

Philadelphia Stock Exchange, "Controlling Risk with Foreign Currency Options," *Euromoney*, February 1985. (Supplementary issue; the entire issue is devoted to foreign currency options.)

Shastri, Kuldeep, and Kishore Tandon, "Valuation of Foreign Currency Options: Some Empirical Tests," *Journal of Financial and Quantitative Analysis*, June 1986, pp. 145–160.

Shastri, Kuldeep, and Kulpatra Wethyavivorn, "The Valuation of Currency Options for Alternate Stochastic Processes," *Journal of Financial Research*, 10, no. 4, Winter 1987, pp. 283–294.

Sutton, W. H., *Trading in Currency Options*, New York: New York Institute of Finance, 1988.

Thomas, Lee R., "A Winning Strategy for Currency-Futures Speculation," *Journal of Portfolio Management*, Fall 1985, pp. 65–69.

Tucker, Alan, "Foreign Exchange Option Prices as Predictors of Equilibrium Forward Exchange Rates," *Journal of International Money and Finance*, 6, no. 3, September 1987, pp. 283–294.

Wyatt, Steve B., "On the Valuation of Puts and Calls on Spot, Forward, and Future Foreign Exchange: Theory and Evidence," *Advances in Financial Planning and Forecasting*, vol. 4, 1990, pp. 81–104.

Option-Covered Interest-Rate Parity

Cheol S. Eun
University of Maryland

The recent inauguration of the currency options market gives rise to another interest rate parity (IRP) relationship, apart from the original "forward-covered" IRP. Consequently the foreign exchange market is now linked up with international money markets via the dual IRP relationships: (i) the forward-covered interest rate parity, and (ii) the option-covered interest rate parity. In this appendix, we are going to derive the option-covered IRP, using a simple arbitrage argument in a single-period context.[1]

Before proceeding, let us first define our notation as follows:

S = currency spot exchange rate, expressed as dollars per unit of foreign currency,
S_1 = future spot exchange rate,
C = foreign currency call price,
K = exercise (striking) exchange rate,
r = 1 + the risk-free interest rate in the United States,
r^* = 1 + the risk-free interest rate in the foreign country.

The United Kingdom is taken to be the representative foreign country in the ensuing derivation.

Suppose that the current spot exchange rate between the U.S. dollar and the British pound (£) is $S = \$1.50$ per pound, and that the future spot exchange rate will be either $S = \$1.80$ or $S = \$1.20$ at the end of the period. A European call on the £ is available with an exercise exchange rate of $K = \$1.50$, expiring at the end of the period. A £ call is assumed to represent the right to buy £1,000 at the exercise exchange rate. For simplicity, the £ call is assumed to expire in 12 months. Further, individuals can borrow and lend in both U.S. and U.K. money markets at the risk-free interest rates of 10% and 8% per annum, respectively. Also, it is assumed that the U.K. Treasury is selling a pure discount bond at £925.93, paying £1,000 at maturity. Given all this information, it is possible to determine the equilibrium price of the £ call, C, which precludes covered interest arbitrage opportunities.

Consider the following portfolio, which may be called the option-covered hedge portfolio for the reason to be made clear shortly:

1. Buy a U.K. bond.
2. Write (sell) two £ calls.[2]

Exhibit 5A.1 provides the future dollar value of the hedge portfolio. As can be seen in the table, the future dollar value of the hedge portfolio is certain, irrespective of the future spot exchange rates. In fact, the hedge portfolio was designed to ensure that a change in the exchange rate would affect the values of the two separate components of the portfolio with the same magnitude, but in the opposite direction. Thus Exhibit 5A.1 demonstrates that

Exhibit 5A.1   Future Dollar Value of the Hedge Portfolio

S_1	Value of Long Position in the U.K. Bond	Value of Short Position in £ Calls	Value of the Hedge Portfolio
$1.80	$1,800	−2($300)	$1,200
$1.20	$1,200	−2($0)	$1,200

one can build a riskless portfolio in dollar terms by buying a foreign bond and writing an appropriate number of call options on the foreign currency.

Note that net (dollar) investment in the hedge portfolio is ($1.50) (925.93) − 2C. For there to be no profitable covered interest arbitrage opportunities between the U.S. and U.K. markets, the £ call must be priced in such a way that the riskless hedge portfolio yields the U.S. risk-free interest rate, that is,

$$[(\$1.50)(925.93) - 2C] (1 + 0.10) = \$1,200.$$

From the above equation we can solve for the equilibrium £ call price, that is, $C = \$149$. If the £ call were not priced at $149, it would be possible to earn arbitrage profits without bearing exchange risk.

Suppose that the £ may appreciate to $S_1 = aS$ or depreciate to $S_1 = dS$ at the end of the period. Let C_a denote the value of the £ call at the end of the period if the £ appreciates to aS, and C_d denote its value if the £ depreciates to dS. Since the £ call expires at the end of the period, we know that

$$C_a = \max [0, aS - K] \quad \text{and} \quad C_d = \max [0, dS - K].$$

Using the same covered interest arbitrage argument, we can derive the following option-covered IRP:[3]

$$C = [\phi C_a + (1-\phi)C_d]/r,$$

where

$$\phi = \frac{(r / r^*) - d}{a - d}.$$

This formula explicitly gives the equilibrium price of the currency call that precludes profitable interest arbitrage opportunities. The formula can alternatively be viewed as a single-period currency option pricing model. The formula indicates that the currency call value is ultimately determined by four factors:

1. the risk-free interest rates in the domestic and foreign countries,
2. the size of the exchange rate changes,
3. the current spot exchange rate, and
4. the exercise exchange rate.

The fact that the formula contains the foreign as well as the domestic interest rate reflects the covered interest arbitrage.

Applying our previous numerical example, we find that

$$C_a = \max[0, (\$1.80 - \$1.50) \times 1,000] = \$300,$$
$$C_d = \max[0, (\$1.20 - \$1.50) \times 1,000] = \$0,$$
$$\phi = \frac{(1.10 / 1.08) - .80}{1.20 - .80} = 0.5463.$$

Note that $aS - K$ and $dS - K$ were multiplied by 1,000 to allow for the contract size. Substituting these values into the formula, we obtain

$$C = [(0.5463)(\$300) + (1 - 0.5463)(\$0)]/1.10$$
$$= \$149.$$

This, of course, is the same result as the one we previously obtained using a more intuitive argument.

To show how to earn arbitrage profit when the option-covered IRP is in violation, let us assume that the current market price of the £ call is $180, which is higher than the equilibrium price of $149. To take advantage of the overpriced £ call, U.S. arbitragers can take the following steps.

Step 1: Write two £ calls and receive $360.

Step 2: Borrow $1,028.90, which is the difference between the dollar price of a U.K. bond and the proceeds from writing two £ calls, that is,

£925.93($1.50) - $360 = $1,028.90.

Step 3: Buy a U.K. bond for $1,388.90, which is the sum of the proceeds from the dollar loan and writing £ calls, that is,

$1,028.90 + $360 = $1,388.90.

Step 4: At the end of the period, receive $1,200, which is the certain value of the hedge portfolio, and repay $1,131.80, which is the maturity value of the dollar loan. The difference between these two dollar amounts, $68.20, is the arbitrage profit.

APPENDIX NOTES

1. Our discussion of the option-covered interest rate parity heavily draws on Eun (1987), which provides a more comprehensive analysis of the subject.

2. The number of calls to be written per U.K. bond held long was calculated from the hedge ratio H, which is equal to the range of the dollar values of the U.K. bond at maturity divided by the range of the values of the £ call at expiration. Using our numerical example, we have

$$H = \frac{\$1,800 - \$1,200}{\$300 - 0} = 2.$$

3. Refer to Eun (1987) for the derivation of this result, as well as its multiperiod generalization.

APPENDIX BIBLIOGRAPHY

Aliber, R., "The Interest Rate Parity Theorem: A Reinterpretation," *Journal of Political Economy*, November/December 1973, pp. 1451–1459.

Black, F., and M. Scholes, "The Pricing of Options and Corporate Liabilities," *Journal of Political Economy*, May/June 1973, pp. 637–654.

Cox, J., S. Ross, and M. Rubinstein, "Option Pricing: A Simplified Approach," *Journal of Financial Economics*, September 1979, pp. 229–263.

Eun, C., "Currency Options Contract and the Triangular Arbitrage Equilibria: A Synthesis," Working Paper, University of Maryland, September 1987.

Feiger, G., and B. Jacquillat, "Currency Option Bonds, Puts and Calls on Spot Exchange and the Hedging of Contingent Foreign Earnings," *Journal of Finance*, December 1979, pp. 1129–1139.

Frenkel, J., and R. Levich, "Covered Interest Arbitrage: Unexploited Profits?" *Journal of Political Economy*, April 1975, pp. 325–338.

Garman, M., and S. Kohlhagen, "Foreign Currency Option Values," *Journal of International Money and Finance*, December 1983, pp. 231–237.

Keynes, J., *Monetary Reform*, New York: Harcourt, Brace and Co. 1924.

Merton, R., "The Theory of Rational Option Pricing," *Bell Journal of Economics and Management Science*, Spring 1973, pp. 141–183.

Ross, S., "The Arbitrage Theory of Capital Asset Pricing," *Journal of Economic Theory*, December 1976, pp. 341–360.

——, "Return, Risk and Arbitrage," in I. Friend and J. Bicksler, eds., *Risk and Return in Finance*, Cambridge, Mass.: Ballinger, 1977, pp. 189–218.

Solnik, B., "International Parity Conditions and Exchange Risk," *Journal of Banking and Finance*, August 1981, pp. 281–293.

Stoll, H., "Causes of Deviations from Interest Rate Parity," *Journal of Money, Credit and Banking*, February 1972, pp. 113–117.

PART 2

FOREIGN EXCHANGE RISK MANAGEMENT

The multinational firm must identify, measure and manage three types of foreign exchange risk: (1) operating exposure; (2) transaction exposure; (3) accounting exposure. Chapter 6 analyzes how firms try to forecast exchange rates for varying time horizons and under varying exchange rate regimes. Both fundamental analysis based on economic parity conditions and technical analysis are covered. Chapter 7 analyzes operating exposure and how it can be managed. Chapter 8 shows how a firm can manage its transaction exposure with contractual hedges, swaps, and operating strategies. Chapter 9 describes how a multinational firm measures and manages accounting exposure. Accounting exposures arises from the need to translate foreign-currency-denominated statements of affiliates into the parent's reporting currency statement.

Forecasting and Parity Conditions

Are changes in exchange rates predictable? The answer to this question is critical for managers of multinational firms, international portfolio investors, and those who only export or import goods and services.

Numerous foreign exchange forecasting services exist, many of which are provided by banks and independent consultants. In addition, some multinational firms have their own in-house forecasting capabilities. Predictions can be based on elaborate econometric models, technical analysis of charts and trends, intuition, and a certain measure of gall.

Whether any of the forecasting services are worth their cost depends partly on the motive for forecasting as well as the required accuracy of the forecast. For example, long-run forecasts may be motivated by a multinational firm's desire to initiate a direct foreign investment in Japan, or perhaps to raise long-term funds denominated in Japanese yen. Or a portfolio manager may be considering diversifying for the long term in Japanese securities. The longer the time horizon of the forecast, the more inaccurate and less critical the forecast is likely to be. The forecaster will typically use annual data to display long-run trends in such economic fundamentals as Japanese inflation, growth, and the balance of payments.

Short-term forecasts are typically motivated by a desire to hedge a receivable, payable, or dividend for perhaps a period of three months. In this case the long-run economic fundamentals may not be as important as technical factors in the marketplace, government intervention, news, and passing whims of traders and investors. Accuracy of the forecast is critical since most of the exchange rate changes are relatively small even though the day-to-day volatility may be high.

Forecasting services normally undertake fundamental economic analysis for long-term forecasts, and some base their short-term forecasts on the same basic model. Others base their short-term forecasts on technical analysis similar to that conducted in security analysis. They attempt to correlate exchange rate changes with various other variables, regardless of whether there is any economic rationale for the correlation. The chances of these forecasts being consistently useful or profitable depends on whether one believes the foreign exchange market is efficient. The more efficient the market is, the more likely it is that exchange rates are "random walks," with past price behavior providing no clues to the future. The less efficient the foreign exchange market is, the better the chance that forecasters may get lucky and find a key relationship that holds, at least for the short run. If the relationship is really consistent, however, others will soon discover it and the market will become efficient again with respect to that piece of information.

Our approach will be to describe the economic fundamentals, which are known as parity conditions. We then discuss the forecasting needs of multinational firms and investors. We continue with a discussion of the various approaches to forecasting in practice, including the balance of payments approach, the asset market approach, and technical analysis. The chapter concludes with examples of practical forecasting for both short- and long-term needs.

PARITY CONDITIONS

Since the present international monetary system is characterized by a mix of freely floating, managed floating, and fixed exchange rates, no single general theory is available to forecast exchange rates under all conditions. Nevertheless, there are certain basic economic relationships, called *parity conditions*, which help to explain exchange rate movements.

Exhibit 6.1 summarizes the main parity conditions. These are:

Parity Condition	*Relationship in Exhibit 6.1*
Purchasing Power Parity	A
Fisher Effect	B
International Fisher Effect	C
Interest Rate Parity	D
Forward Rate as Unbiased Predictor of Future Spot Rate	E

Exhibit 6.1 shows that under a freely floating exchange rate system, future spot exchange rates are theoretically determined by the interplay of differing national rates of inflation, interest rates, and the forward premium or discount on each currency.

Exhibit 6.1 Integrated International Exchange Rate Parity Conditions

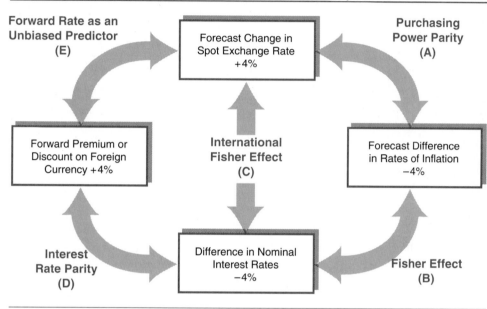

Parity relations are for any percent change in rates, or difference in rates. This example simply uses 4% for illustrative purposes.

PRICES AND EXCHANGE RATES

If the identical product or service can be sold in two different markets, and there are no restrictions on its sale or transportation costs of moving the product between markets, the product's price should be the same in both markets. This is called the *law of one price*. It is the primary principle of competitive markets that prices will equalize across markets if there are no frictions or costs of moving the products or services between markets. If the two markets are two different countries, the product's price may be stated in different currency terms, but the price of the product should still be the same. Comparison of prices would only require a conversion from one currency to the other. For example,

$$P^\$ \times S = P^\yen$$

where the price of the product in U.S. dollars ($P^\$$), multiplied by the spot exchange rate (S, yen per U.S. dollar), equals the price of the product in Japanese yen ($P^\yen$). Conversely, if the prices of the two products were stated in local currencies, and markets were efficient at competing away a higher price in one market relative to the other, the exchange rate could

Exhibit 6.2   The Law of One Price: "The McDonald's Hamburger Standard"

The hamburger standard

Four years ago *The Economist* launched its Big Mac index, a medium-rare guide to whether currencies are at their "correct" exchange rate. It is time for our annual update.

The McDonald's standard is based on the theory of purchasing-power parity (PPP), which argues that in the long run the exchange rate between two currencies should equate the price of an identical basket of goods and services in the respective countries. Our "basket" is simply a Big Mac, which has the virtue of being made locally in more than 50 countries and of tasting virtually the same from Manchester to Moscow.

In America the average price of a Big Mac (including tax) is about $2.20. In Tokyo our correspondent had to fork out ¥370 for this gastronomic delight. Dividing the yen price by the dollar price gives an implied PPP for the dollar of ¥168, compared with the current exchange rate of ¥159. So even after the recent slide in the yen, the dollar still looks to be 5% undervalued against the yen on PPP grounds. It also looks 14% undervalued against the D-mark, with a Mac-PPP of DM1.95.

Economists who have calculated PPPs by more sophisticated means come up with remarkably similar results. Professor Ronald McKinnon of Stanford University, one of the leading proponents of the theory of purchasing-power parity, comes up with mid-point estimates for the dollar's PPP of ¥165 and DM2.00.

Big MacCurrencies
Hamburger prices

Country	Price* in local currency	Implied PPP† of the dollar	Actual exchange rate 30.4.90	%over(+) or under (−) valuation of the dollar
Australia	A$ 2.30	1.05	1.32	+26
Belgium	BFr 97	44.00	34.65	−21
Britain	£ 1.40	0.64	0.61	−5
Canada	C$ 2.19	1.00	1.16	+16
Denmark	DKr 25.50	11.60	6.39	−45
France	FFr 17.70	8.05	5.63	−30
Holland	FL 5.25	2.39	1.88	−21
Hongkong	HK$ 8.60	3.90	7.79	+100
Ireland	IR£ 1.30	0.59	0.63	+7
Italy	Lire 3900	1773	1230	−31
Japan	¥ 370	168	159	−5
Singapore	S$ 2.60	1.18	1.88	+59
S.Korea	Won 2100	955	707	−26
Soviet Union	Rouble 3.75	1.70	0.60	−65
Spain	Ptas 295	134	106	−21
Sweden	SKr 10.90	10.90	6.10	−44
United States††	$2.20	–	–	–
W Germany	DM 4.30	1.95	1.68	−14
Yugoslavia	Dinar 16	7.27	11.72	+61

* Prices may vary between branches
† Purchasing-power parity: foreign price divided by dollar price
†† Average of New York, Chicago, San Francisco and Atlanta
Source: McDonald's; *Economist* correspondents

The dollar's current rate against the pound ($0.61) is close to its Mac-PPP of $0.64. But that, in turn, means that the pound is undervalued by 10% against the D-mark, giving British manufacturers a competitive edge. On the other hand most EMS currencies, especially the French franc and the lira, are still overvalued against the D-mark on PPP grounds.

Mac-currencies are now becoming truly global: the opening of the first McDonald's in Moscow has allowed us to add the rouble to our sample. Muscovites have to pay the equivalent of $6.25 (converting at the official exchange rate) for a Big Mac, which makes it the most expensive hamburger in our sample. In other words, the rouble is overvalued against the dollar to a greater degree than any other currency, with an official rate against the dollar of 0.60 roubles.

Yet this overlooks one crucial fact: in Moscow fast food comes slow, with two-to-three hour queues. If this time is valued at average Soviet hourly wages, then the true cost of gorging on a Big Mac is roughly double the cash price. This implies a "queue-adjusted" Mac-PPP of 3.40 roubles. Indigestion, Mikhail?

be deduced from the relative local product prices:

$$S = \frac{P^{¥}}{P^{\$}}$$

where S would be the spot exchange rate in yen per dollar.

Purchasing Power Parity and the Law of One Price

If the law of one price was true for all goods and services, the *purchasing power parity* (PPP) exchange rate could be found from any individual set of prices. By comparing the prices of identical products denominated in different currencies, it would be possible to determine the "real" or PPP exchange rate which should exist if markets were efficient. The "hamburger standard," as it has been christened by *The Economist* (Exhibit 6.2), is a prime example of this law of one price.

A less extreme form of this principle would be that in relatively efficient markets the price of a basket of goods would be the same in each market. This simply requires the replacement of the individual product's price with that of a price index (like that of the Consumer Price Index in the United States). The purchasing power parity exchange rate between the two countries would then be stated:

$$S = \frac{PI^{\yen}}{PI^{\$}}$$

where $PI^{\yen}$ and $PI^{\$}$ are identical price indices for Japan and the United States, respectively. This is what is known as the *absolute version of the theory of purchasing power parity*. *Absolute PPP states that the spot exchange rate is determined by the relative prices of similar baskets of goods (as represented by price indices).*

Relative Purchasing Power Parity

If the PPP theory is relaxed a bit more in its assumptions, we may observe what is termed the *relative version of the theory of purchasing power parity*. This more general idea is that PPP is not particularly helpful in determining what the spot rate is today, but that the relative change in prices between two countries over a period of time determines the change in the exchange rate over that period. More specifically, *if the spot exchange rate between two countries starts in equilibrium, any change in the differential rate of inflation between them tends to be offset over the long run by an equal but opposite change in the spot exchange rate.*

Exhibit 6.3 shows a general case of relative purchasing power parity. The vertical axis shows the percentage appreciation of the foreign currency relative to the home currency, and the horizontal axis shows the percentage higher or lower rate of inflation in the foreign country relative to the home country. The diagonal parity line shows the equilibrium position between a change in the exchange rate and relative inflation rates. For instance, point P represents an equilibrium point where inflation in the foreign country, say Japan, is 4% lower than in the home country, say the United States. Therefore, relative PPP would predict that the yen would appreciate by 4% per annum with respect to the U.S. dollar.

The theory of purchasing power parity was first popularized by the economist Gustav Cassel after World War I to answer the question of what the new exchange rate parities should be after World War I interrupted the fixed exchange rate system.

The main justification for purchasing power parity is that if a country experiences inflation rates higher than those of its main trading partners, and its exchange rate does not change, its exports of goods and services will become less competitive with comparable products produced elsewhere. Imports from abroad will also become more price competitive with higher-priced domestic products.

Empirical Tests of Purchasing Power Parity

There is an extensive literature testing both the absolute and relative versions of purchasing power parity and the law of one price.[1] The tests have, for the most part, not proven accurate in their estimates of future exchange rates. Goods and services do not in

Exhibit 6.3   Purchasing Power Parity

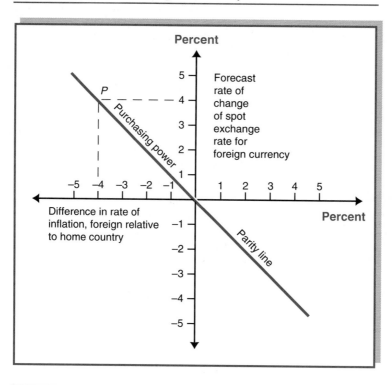

reality move at zero cost between countries, and in fact many goods are not "tradeable," for example the haircut. Many goods and services are not the same quality across countries, reflecting the differences in tastes and resources of the countries of their manufacture and consumption.

There are two general conclusions of these tests: (1) PPP holds up well over the very long run but poorly for shorter time periods; (2) the theory holds better for countries with relatively high rates of inflation and underdeveloped capital markets.[2] On the other hand, there are several problems with the tests.

Problem 1. Most of the tests use an index of prices such as the wholesale price index. This index may be misleading, since only goods that are traded directly affect supply and demand for foreign currencies. Nevertheless, even such nontraded goods as housing and medical costs indirectly affect the price of traded goods through their influence on the overall cost of living and thus on wage demands.

Problem 2. Tests of PPP should be based on comparing a similar market basket of goods in each country with all its trading partners. If purchasing power parity is working, and there are no government interferences, the effective prices for a similar basket of goods should be the same in every country once exchange rates and prices have adjusted to worldwide PPP. However, because of differences in taste, level of developments and income, it is difficult to find identical market baskets among countries. Any consumption-based index is necessarily going to compare "apples and oranges."

Problem 3. Tests of PPP require a knowledge of what the market is forecasting for differential inflation rates, but the data that are available are either realized inflation rates or existing differential interest rates used as a proxy for expected inflation.

Problem 4. There has hardly been a time period to test in which at least some government interference in the trade process did not exist.

Exchange Rate Indices: Real and Nominal

Any single country in the current global market may trade with numerous partners. This requires tracking and evaluating its individual currency value against all other currency values in order to determine relative purchasing power, that is, whether it is "overvalued" or "undervalued" in terms of PPP. One of the primary methods of dealing with this problem is the calculation of exchange rate indices. These indices are formed by trade-weighting the bilateral exchange rates between the home country and its trading partners.

The *nominal effective exchange rate index* calculates, on a weighted average basis, the value of the subject currency at different points in time. It does not really indicate anything about the "true value" of the currency, or anything related to PPP. The nominal index simply calculates how the currency value relates to some arbitrarily chosen base period. The *real effective exchange rate index* indicates how the weighted average purchasing power of the currency has changed relative to some arbitrarily selected base period.

A number of exchange rate indices are published on a frequent basis, such as the widely-used Morgan Guaranty Index, which is shown in Exhibit 6.4. It illustrates the degree to which PPP has held for four of the most important currencies during the period 1980–1990. If changes in exchange rates just offset differential inflation rates, all the real effective exchange rate indices would stay at 100. If an exchange rate strengthened more than was justified by differential inflation, its index would rise above 100, and it would be considered "overvalued" from a competitive perspective. An index value below 100 would suggest an "undervalued" currency.

As Exhibit 6.4 shows, the real effective exchange rate has varied considerably from year to year for some currencies, but the data lend some support to the concept that PPP may hold for the long run. For example, the index of the real effective exchange rate for the U.S. dollar rose from an undervalued level of 89.4 in 1980 to an overvalued level of 122.3 in 1985, only to return almost to its original level in 1990. The Japanese yen suddenly became overvalued in 1986, peaked in 1988, and returned almost to its 1980

Exhibit 6.4   Morgan Guaranty's Nominal and Real Effective
Exchange Rate Indices

Year	United States		Germany		Japan		United Kingdom	
	Nominal	*Real*	*Nominal*	*Real*	*Nominal*	*Real*	*Nominal*	*Real*
1980	90.7	89.4	100.0	103.5	95.5	103.4	99.8	99.9
1981	99.5	100.6	97.2	97.3	105.8	104.6	102.1	102.3
1982	109.8	100.6	102.8	99.2	98.6	92.3	98.0	98.6
1983	114.2	112.7	107.6	99.3	107.8	96.6	91.5	93.0
1984	122.3	119.7	107.3	98.0	112.9	97.5	88.0	90.1
1985	127.0	122.3	107.8	96.7	115.9	97.0	88.2	92.9
1986	106.0	102.4	116.1	103.4	150.1	115.4	80.7	87.4
1987	94.1	91.8	122.0	106.9	164.4	119.6	79.0	87.5
1988	88.0	87.4	121.8	106.2	181.6	125.9	83.8	94.4
1989	91.3	92.0	121.0	104.7	172.8	118.2	81.3	93.9
1990	86.6	88.2	124.9	107.1	156.9	105.8	79.3	95.3

Source: Morgan Guaranty, *World Financial Markets*, 1985–1991, New York. "Nominal Effective exchange rate is an index of its trade-weighted average value against the currencies of the corresponding country's principal trade partners. Real Effective exchange rate, which adjusts the nominal index for relative price changes, gauges the effect on the international price competitiveness of the country's manufactures due to currency changes and differential inflation. The indices should be interpreted cautiously on three counts. First, the base period (1980–1982 = 100) should not be assumed one of equilibrium in relation to purchasing power parity, the balance of payments, or other policy objectives. Second, available price indices are not fully comparable. Third, especially in LDCs, taxes and subsidies on exports, and tariffs, deposits, and special taxes on imports create de facto multiple exchange rate systems."

level in 1990. Germany and the United Kingdom showed only modest deviations from purchasing parity both in the short run and on average for the 11 year period.

Apart from measuring deviations from PPP, a country's real effective exchange rate is an important tool for predicting upward or downward pressure on its balance of payments and exchange rate, as well as an indicator of the desirability to produce for export from that country. The latter question is analyzed in Chapter 7 as part of a discussion of operating exposure.

Exchange Rate Pass-Through

Incomplete *exchange rate pass-through* is one reason that a country's real effective exchange rate index can deviate for lengthy periods from its PPP-equilibrium level of 100. The degree to which the prices of imported and exported goods change as a result of exchange rate changes is termed pass-through.[3] Although PPP implies that all exchange rate changes are passed on through equivalent changes in prices to trading partners, empirical research in the 1980s has questioned this long-held assumption. For example, the sizeable current account deficits of the United States in the 1980s did not respond to changes in the value of the dollar.

To illustrate exchange rate pass-through, assume Honda produces an automobile in Japan and pays all production expense in yen. When exporting the auto to the United States the price of the Honda in the U.S. market should simply be the yen value converted to dollars at the spot exchange rate:

$$P_{\text{Honda}}^{\$} = P_{\text{Honda}}^{\yen} \times \left(\frac{1}{S}\right),$$

where $P_{\text{Honda}}^{\$}$ is the Honda price in dollars, $P_{\text{Honda}}^{\yen}$ is the Honda price in yen, and S is the number of yen per dollar. If the yen appreciated 10% versus the U.S. dollar, the new spot exchange rate should result in the price of the Honda in the United States rising a proportional 10%. If the price in dollars increases by the same percentage change as the exchange rate, the pass-through of exchange rate changes is *complete* (or 100%).

However, if the price in dollars rises by less than the percentage change in exchange rates (as is often the case in international trade), the pass-through is *partial*, as illustrated in Exhibit 6.5. The 8.33% pass-through implies that Honda is absorbing a portion of the adverse exchange rate change. This absorption could result from smaller profit margins, cost reductions, or both. For example, components and raw materials imported to Japan cost less in yen when it appreciates. It is also likely that some time may pass before all

Exhibit 6.5 Exchange Rate Pass-Through

Pass-through is the measure of response of imported and exported product prices to exchange rate changes. Assume the price in dollars and yen of a Honda automobile produced in Japan and sold in the United States at the spot exchange rate is:

$$P_{\text{Honda}}^{\$} = \$12,000 \qquad P_{\text{Honda}}^{\yen} = \yen1,800,000 \qquad S_1 = \yen150/\$$$

Pass-through is measured by the percentage change in the dollar price following an exchange rate change. If the yen were to appreciate 10%, from ¥150/$ to ¥136.36/$, and the price of the Honda in the United States were to rise to $13,000, then the degree of pass-through is *partial*:

$$\frac{P_2^{\$}}{P_1^{\$}} = \frac{\$13,000}{\$12,000} = 1.0833.$$

This would constitute an 8.33% increase in the dollar price of the Honda resulting from a 10% appreciation of the Japanese yen against the U.S. dollar. The remaining 1.67% of the exchange rate change has been absorbed by Honda.

---

exchange rate changes are finally reflected in the prices of traded goods, including the period over which previously signed contracts are delivered upon. It is obviously in the interests of Honda to keep the appreciation of the yen from raising the price of its automobiles in major export markets.

The concept of *elasticity* is useful when determining the desired level of pass-through. A Japanese product which is relatively *price inelastic*, meaning that the quantity demanded is relatively unresponsive to price changes, may often demonstrate a high degree of pass-through. This is because a higher dollar price in the United States market would have little noticeable effect on the quantity of the product demanded by consumers, and would in fact, result in an increase in total sales revenues. However, products which are relatively *price elastic* would respond in the opposite direction. If the 10% yen appreciation resulted in 10% higher dollar prices, U.S. consumers would decrease the number of Hondas purchased. If price elasticity for Hondas in the United States was greater than one, total sales of Hondas expressed in dollars would decline. For further theoretical and quantitative details on the concept of elasticity see the appendix to this chapter.

A number of empirical studies in the late 1980s have estimated the pass-through of exchange rate changes to import prices in the United States to average between 70 and 80 percent. This partial pass-through is thought to have been a major factor in the relatively slow improvement in the U.S. trade balance following the fall of the U.S. dollar from 1985 through 1988.

INTEREST RATES, EXCHANGE RATES, AND PRICES

We have already seen how prices of goods in different countries should be related through exchange rates. We now consider how exchange rates are linked to interest rates.

The Fisher Effect

The Fisher effect, named after economist Irving Fisher, states that nominal interest rates in each country are equal to the required real rate of return plus compensation for expected inflation. More formally:[4]

$$i = r + \pi,$$

where i is the nominal rate of interest, r is the real rate of interest, and π is the expected rate of inflation over the period of time for which funds are to be lent.

The Fisher effect applied to two different countries like the United States and Japan would be:

$$i^\$ = r^\$ + \pi^\$; \quad i^¥ = r^¥ + \pi^¥,$$

where the superscripts $ and ¥ pertain to the respective nominal (i), real (r), and expected inflation (π) components of financial instruments denominated in dollars and yen, respectively. It should be noted that this requires a forecast of the future rate of inflation, not what inflation has been. Predicting the future can be difficult.

Empirical tests using ex-post national inflation rates have shown the Fisher effect to exist particularly for short-maturity government securities such as treasury bills and notes. Comparisons based on longer maturities suffer from the increased financial risk inherent in fluctuations of the market value of the bonds prior to maturity. Comparisons of private sector securities are influenced by unequal creditworthiness of the issuers. All the tests are inconclusive to the extent that the ex-post rate of inflation does not correctly measure the ex-ante expected rate of inflation.[5]

The International Fisher Effect

The relationship between the percentage change in the spot exchange rate over time and the differential between comparable interest rates in different national money markets is known as the *international Fisher effect*. "Fisher-open," as it is often termed, states that *the spot exchange rate should change in an equal amount but in the opposite direction to the difference in interest rates between two countries*. More formally:

$$\frac{S_1 - S_2}{S_2} \times (100) = i^{\$} - i^{¥},$$

where $i^{\$}$ and $i^{¥}$ are the respective national interest rates, and S is the spot exchange rate using indirect quotes at the beginning of the period (S_1) and the end of the period (S_2).

Justification for the international Fisher effect is that investors must be rewarded or penalized to offset the expected change in exchange rates. For example, if a dollar-based investor buys a one-year yen deposit earning 5% interest, compared to 9% interest in dollars, the investor must be expecting the yen to appreciate vis-à-vis the dollar by at least 4% during the year. If not, the dollar-based investor would be better off remaining in dollars. If the yen appreciates 5% during the year, the dollar-based investor would earn a bonus of 1% higher return. However, the international Fisher effect predicts that with unrestricted capital flows, an investor should be indifferent between investing in dollar or yen deposits, since investors worldwide would see the same bonus opportunity and compete it away.

Empirical tests lend some support to the relationship postulated by the international Fisher effect, although considerable short-run deviations occur. However, a more serious criticism has been posed by recent studies that suggest the existence of a foreign exchange risk premium for most major currencies. Thus the expected change in exchange rates might be consistently more than the difference in interest rates.[6]

Forward Rate as an Unbiased Predictor of the Future Spot Rate

Some forecasters believe that for the major freely floating currencies, foreign exchange markets are "efficient" and forward exchange rates are unbiased predictors of future spot exchange rates.[7]

Exhibit 6.6   Forward Rate as an Unbiased Predictor of Future Spot Rate

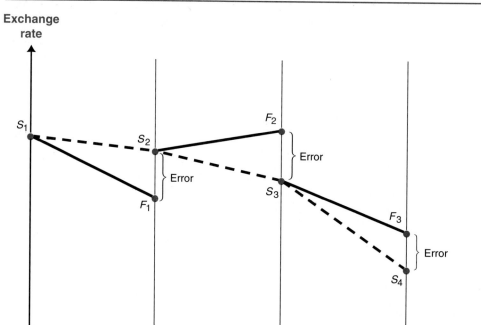

The forward rate available today (F_t), time t, for delivery at future time $t+1$, is used as a "predictor" of the spot rate of exchange which will exist on that day in the future. The forecasted spot rate for time t_2 is F_1; the actual spot exchange rate turns out to be S_2. The vertical distance between the forward rate-prediction (F_1) and the actual spot rate which does exist on that date (S_2) is the forecast error. When the forward rate is termed an "unbiased predictor of the future spot rate," it means that the forward rate overestimates and underestimates the future spot rate with relatively equal frequency and amount. It therefore "misses the mark" in a regular and orderly manner. The sum of the errors equals zero. The authors would like to thank Gunter Dufey for the original version of this clear presentation of unbiased prediction.

Exhibit 6.6 demonstrates what this concept of "unbiased prediction" means in terms of how the forward rate performs in estimating future spot exchange rates. If the forward rate is an unbiased predictor of the future spot rate, the expected value of the future spot rate at time 2 equals the present forward rate for time 2 delivery, available at time 1 (now).

$$S_2 = F_1$$

Intuitively this means that the distribution of possible actual spot rates in the future is centered on the forward rate. An *unbiased predictor*, however, does not mean that the future spot rate will actually *be equal* to what the forward rate predicts. *Unbiased prediction simply means that the forward rate will, on average, overestimate and underesti-*

mate the actual future spot rate in equal frequency and degree. The forward rate may, in fact, never actually equal the future spot rate.

The rationale for this relationship is based on the hypothesis that the foreign exchange market is reasonably efficient. Market efficiency assumes that (a) all relevant information is quickly reflected in both the spot and forward exchange markets, (b) transaction costs are low, and (c) instruments denominated in different currencies are perfect substitutes for one another.

Empirical studies of the efficient foreign exchange market hypothesis have yielded conflicting results. Nevertheless, a consensus is developing that rejects the efficient market hypothesis. It appears that the forward rate is not an unbiased predictor of the future spot rate and that it does pay to use resources to attempt to forecast exchange rates.

Early studies after exchange rates were floated in 1973 seemed to favor the efficient market hypothesis.[8] For example, Giddy and Dufey tested five different forecasting methods against foreign exchange quotations for the Canadian dollar, British pound, and French franc for the 1973–1974 period. Their results were consistent with the notion that the foreign exchange market is efficient and exchange rate forecasting is not profitable. Their major tests were on the so-called weak form of the random walk hypothesis, which asserts that successive changes in prices are independent of the sequence of past prices. Their conclusion was that "for short periods, one is able to detect a low degree of market inefficiency in the foreign exchange market. But the longer the forecasting horizon, the more evident is the inaccuracy of the time series forecasting of exchange rate changes."[9]

Kohlhagen attempted to determine whether the forward exchange market is a low-cost means of hedging exchange risks. He examined 90-day forward rates and subsequent spot rates for six countries (Canada, Denmark, France, West Germany, Switzerland, the United Kingdom) for the period of floating rates from April 1973 through December 1974, as well as for an earlier period of fixed exchange rates.[10] Among his findings was the observation that any difference between the forward rate and subsequent spot rate at the maturity of the forward contract could be attributed to random variations. Stated differently, any profit or loss from taking a consistently long or short position in the forward market was due to random forces, and the forward rates themselves were unbiased predictors of future spot rates.

Fama, who also studied the early floating rate period, concluded:

> When adjusted for variation through time in expected premiums, the forward rates of interest that are implicit in Treasury Bill prices contain assessments of expected future spot rates of interest that are about as good as those that can be obtained from the information in past spot rates. Moreover, in setting bill prices and forward rates, the market reacts appropriately to the negative autocorrelation in monthly changes in the spot rate and to changes through time in the degree of this autocorrelation. This evidence is consistent with the market efficiency proposition that in setting bill prices, the market correctly uses the information in past spot rates.[11]

If these conclusions are correct, a financial executive cannot expect to profit in any consistent manner from forecasting future exchange rates, because current quotations in the forward market reflect all that is presently known about likely future rates. While future exchange rates may well differ from the expectation implicit in the present forward market quotation, one cannot know today which way actual future quotations will differ from today's forward rate. The expected mean value of deviations is zero. The forward rate is therefore an "unbiased" estimator of the future spot rate.

More recent tests of foreign exchange market efficiency, using longer time periods of analysis, challenge the earlier findings and conclude that either exchange market efficiency is untestable or, if it is testable, the market is not efficient. Furthermore, the existence and success of foreign exchange forecasting services suggest that managers are willing to pay a price for forecast information even though they can use the forward rate as a forecast at no cost.[12]

One of the most comprehensive tests was undertaken by the Working Group on Exchange Market Intervention, which produced the so-called Jurgensen Report. They reported as follows:

> The tests provided clear evidence that consideration of readily accessible information on inflation and interest rate differentials yielded a better prediction of the future spot rate than that implied by the forward rate. Moreover, the repeated application of certain foreign exchange trading rules indicated a high probability of making some profit. However, some members thought that the results for some currencies may have been affected by the existence of capital controls, although the results were similar for the six bilateral US dollar rates tested. Other time series studies performed by the Group confirmed the existence of better predictors of the future spot rate than the forward rate.[13]

If the exchange market is not efficient, it would pay for a firm to spend resources on forecasting exchange rates. This is the opposite conclusion to the one in which exchange markets are deemed efficient.

Parity Conditions Once Again: A Numerical Illustration

The box diagram which introduced this chapter, Exhibit 6.1, is repeated here as Exhibit 6.7 with a sample set of numerical values in order to demonstrate international exchange rate linkages in practice. Each of the five relationships can be derived from relatively few actual values: spot and forward exchange rates, forecast rates of inflation in the two countries, and comparable interest rates in the two countries. Although actual market values may vary from these rather tightly integrated relationships, the size, competitiveness, and relatively low costs of international financial transactions combine to preserve these linkages over the long run.

In Exhibit 6.7, the yen is expected to strengthen 4% versus the dollar. The spot exchange rate, ¥156/$, is forecasted to change to ¥150/$ one year from now using PPP (relation A), the international Fisher effect (relation C), and the forward rate (relation E). The forecasted inflation rates for Japan (3.0%) and the United States (7.0%) result in a forecast of ¥150/$ (relative version of purchasing power parity). If the difference in nominal interest rates is used (international Fisher effect), the forecasted spot rate is also ¥150/$. Finally, the one-year forward rate on the Japanese yen, ¥150/$, if assumed to be an unbiased predictor of the future spot rate, also forecasts ¥150/$.

Exhibit 6.7   International Parity Conditions: A Numerical Example: yen/dollar

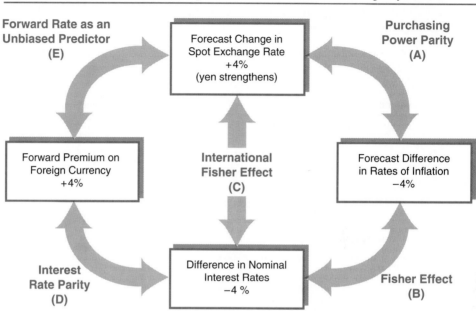

1.   Exchange Rates:

   a)   Current Spot Rate: $S_1 = ¥156/\$$
   b)   Forward Rate (one year): $F = ¥150/\$$
   c)   Expected Spot Rate: $S_2 = ¥150/\$$

   d)   forward premium on yen = $f^¥ = \dfrac{156 - 150}{150} \times 100 = +4\%$

   e)   forecast change in $S = \dfrac{S_1 - S_2}{S_2} = \dfrac{156 - 150}{150} \times 100 = +4\%$

2.   Forecast Rate of Inflation:

   a)   Japan   3 %
   b)   United States   7 %
   c)   Difference   −4 %

3.   Interest on 1 Year Govt. Security:

   a)   Japan   6 %
   b)   United States   10 %
   c)   Difference   −4 %

EXCHANGE RATE FORECASTING

Having completed the discussion of the major financial and economic forces which tie together currencies, prices, and interest rates on world markets, we next identify forecasting needs of the multinational firm. We then provide an overview of the methods of exchange rate forecasting, including examples of how exchange rate forecasts may be generated in practice.

Forecasting Needs of the Multinational Firm

A multinational firm needs exchange rate forecasts for one or more of the following purposes:

- Accounts payable and receivable. Existing and expected foreign-currency denominated payables and receivables are exposed to foreign exchange losses when converted to a firm's reporting currency. Exchange rate forecasts are helpful in deciding whether or not to protect against these potential losses. Protection is covered in Chapter 8.

- International price lists. To quote a product price in a foreign currency requires the firm to estimate what exchange rate will be in effect at the time of sale and remittance. These forecasts may extend from one day to one year into the future.

- Working capital management. A multinational firm will be constantly managing cash flows among the parent and foreign affiliates. Correct exchange rate forecasts will allow the most efficient timing of the movements of these cash flows. This is covered in Chapter 19.

- International investment analysis. The evaluation of international investments, such as portfolio investments or long-term capital projects, requires exchange rate forecasts well out into the future (1, 2, 5, or even 10 years).

Each firm's forecasting needs are characterized by a similar set of dimensions: point in time, frequency of forecast revision, and available resources for forecast construction. Exchange rate forecasts which must be continually regenerated and implemented, for example in working capital management, must be available on a short-term basis and require few resources. Long-term forecast needs, such as for multinational capital budgeting, are worthy of more in-depth analysis.

Fundamental Versus Technical Analysis

Forecasting exchange rates includes elements common to all forecasting applications. The primary methodological question is whether to construct forecasts on the basis of financial and economic theories, *fundamental analysis*, or to derive forecasts from the trend of the data series itself, *technical analysis*.

Forecasters who favor fundamental analysis are split into two schools of thought. The *balance of payments approach* emphasizes analysis of a country's balance of payments as an indicator of pressure on a managed exchange rate. The *asset market approach* postulates that the relative attractiveness of a currency for investment purposes is the main force driving exchange rates.

The Balance of Payments Approach. If a country spends more abroad in combined purchases and investments than it earns or otherwise acquires from abroad over a sustained period of time, the probability of devaluation of its currency increases. Foreigners will be building up, on balance, monetary claims against the country. If foreigners are willing to hold these claims in monetary form, the local currency need not devalue. However, if foreigners convert these monetary claims to a different currency, pressure for devaluation will increase. A country's currency might, on the other hand, appreciate if that country runs a large surplus on current account and foreigners are eager to hold its currency.

The facts and figures watched most frequently by fundamental analysts are summarized in Exhibit 6.8. This is what we term a "Users Guide." Although it is often difficult to distinguish economic forces from political forces, we have segmented the more regulatory-related factors from the economic and financial factors. Note that certain macroeconomic factors which at first glance may seem far removed from exchange rate analysis are included. The interpretation of their impacts on exchange rates usually return to basic supply and demand factors for currencies. Many of these factors (for example, government spending and money supply growth) translate to inflationary forces.

Asset Market Approach. Whether or not foreigners are willing to hold claims in monetary form depends partly on relative real interest rates and also on a country's outlook for economic growth and profitability. For example, during the period 1981–1985 the U.S. dollar strengthened despite growing current account deficits. This strength was due partly to relatively high real interest rates in the United States. However, it was also due to a heavy inflow of foreign capital to invest in the U.S. stock market and real estate, motivated by good long-run prospects for growth and profitability in the United States.

Bruno Solnik summarizes why some forecasters believe that exchange rates are more influenced by economic prospects than by the balance of payments as follows:

The asset market approach. Many economists reject the view that the short-term behavior of exchange rates is determined in flow markets. Exchange rates are asset prices traded in an efficient financial market. Indeed, an exchange rate is the relative price of two currencies and therefore is determined by the willingness to hold each currency. Like other asset prices, the exchange rate is determined by expectations about the future, not current trade flows.

A parallel with other asset prices may illustrate the approach. Let's consider the stock price of a winery traded on the Bordeaux stock exchange. A frost in late spring results in a poor harvest, in terms of both quantity and quality. After the harvest the wine is finally sold, and the income is much less than the previous year. On the day of the final sale there is no reason for the stock price to be influenced by this flow. First, the poor income has already been discounted for several months in the winery stock price. Second, the stock price is affected by future, in addition to current, prospects. The stock price is based on expectations of future earnings, and the major cause for a change in stock price is a revision of these expectations.

A similar reasoning applies to exchange rates: Contemporaneous international flows should have little effect on exchange rates to the extent they have already been expected. Only news about future economic prospects will affect exchange rates. Since economic expectations are potentially volatile and influenced by many variables, especially variables of a political nature, the short-run behavior of exchange rates is volatile.[14]

Exhibit 6.8   User's Guide to Long-Term Exchange Rate Fundamental Analysis

Political Exchange Rate Factors:

Capital Controls.   Government restrictions on the use of foreign currency for business transactions is an obvious control of exchange rates. Although governments intentionally do not publicize the imposition or removal of these restrictions, signals such as increased spreads in black market rates are often visible.

Exchange Rate Spreads.   Currencies which are not traded freely (government restrictions) will still be sold "unofficially" through external or internal black markets. An increasing spread between the official (government) exchange rate and the black market (unrestricted) rate indicates potential pressures leading to eventual devaluation or depreciation.

Macroeconomic Fundamentals:

Balance of Payments.   The BOP is in effect the supply and demand for foreign currencies. Indicators of imbalances such as the Current Account Balance and the Trade Balance are helpful in tracking forces pushing on exchange rates. A significant increase (decrease) in the Current Account Balance or Trade Balance is interpreted as an early sign of a currency appreciation (depreciation).

Foreign Exchange Reserves.   A government which is intervening in the foreign exchange markets will be using its foreign currency reserves to either push up or push down the value of its domestic currency. Efforts to support the domestic currency will result in the loss of foreign currency reserves, while efforts to depreciate the domestic currency will result in the accumulation of foreign currency reserves.

GNP or GDP Growth.   Economic growth is the largest single force affecting imports and exports. If the domestic economy is growing relatively rapidly compared to major trade partners, the level of imports is likely to rise faster than exports, trade deficits ensue, and currency depreciation is likely. A mixed signal occurs if the more rapid economic growth attracts large capital inflows, possibly offsetting the negative trade effects.

Government Spending.   Since most countries possess large government sectors, a rapid increase in government spending, particularly if financed through deficit spending, results in increased inflationary pressures on the economy. Inflation leads to depreciation.

Relative Inflation.   As described previously, a country suffering relatively higher inflation rates will, as a result of PPP forces, see its currency depreciate.

Money Supply Growth.   One of the primary causes of inflation is the rapid growth of the money supply. Many countries choose to stave off recession by increasing money supply growth to lower domestic interest rates. This usually results in a higher domestic inflation rate; currency depreciation follows.

We are left with an obvious dilemma as to which theory to follow. As others, we will compromise. To quote *The Economist*:

Now, elegantly mix the two approaches. In the long term, equilibrium exchange rates are determined by PPP; in the short term, exchange rates are determined entirely in asset markets, by interest rates and expectations.[15]

Technical Analysis. Technical analysts, traditionally referred to as *chartists*, focus on price and volume data to determine past trends which are expected to continue into the future. The single most important element of time series analysis is that future exchange rates are based on the current exchange rate. Exchange rate movements, similar to equity price movements, can be subdivided into periods: (1) day-to-day movement which is seemingly random; (2) short term movements extending from several days to trends lasting several months; (3) long term movements which are characterized by up and down long-term trends. Long-term technical analysis has gained new popularity as a result of recent research into the possibility that long-term "waves" in currency movements exist under floating exchange rates.[16]

The longer the time horizon of the forecast, the more inaccurate the forecast is likely to be. Whereas forecasting for the long-run must depend on economic fundamentals of exchange rate determination, many of the forecast needs of the firm are short- to medium-term in their time horizon and can be addressed with less theoretical approaches. Time series techniques infer no theory or causality, but simply predict future values from the recent past. We will freely mix fundamental and technical analysis in the following discussion of forecasting short-run and long-run fixed and floating exchange rates. However, please remember that forecasting is like horseshoes and hand grenades, getting close is all that counts!

FORECASTING EXCHANGE RATES IN THE SHORT RUN

Short-term forecasts are typically motivated by a desire to hedge a receivable, payable, or dividend for perhaps a period extending from one week to one year. The accuracy needs of the forecast are a high priority, as well as the ability to forecast as quickly and cheaply as possible.

The two primary alternatives for forecasting exchange rates in the short run are: (1) time series techniques which emphasize trend; (2) the use of the forward rate itself as a prediction. These alternatives are of course highly dependent on the nature of the subject exchange rate regime.

Floating Exchange Rates

The forecasting of short-term movements for floating exchange rates is dominated by isolation of trend. Short-run volatility in markets may often obscure the actual trend the rate is following. Most time series techniques for forecasting floating rates are therefore focused on the identification of the true trends, with emphasis on current exchange rates as predictors of future rates.

Since the day-to-day movements are largely unpredictable, the exchange rate is said to follow a "random walk." If the probability that the currency will appreciate is the same as the probability that it will depreciate, the forecaster expects a neutral or random outcome. The future exchange rate is then best estimated to be the same as it is today. A number of empirical studies of floating-rate currencies have shown that for periods up to 30 days, a random-walk hypothesis is often most accurate. An obvious added benefit to this approach is its zero cost, and ease of formulation.

Exhibit 6.9   Sample Short-Term Forecasting of Floating
Exchange Rate: DM/$

Goal: Forecast the DM/$ spot rate for fourth quarter, 1990
Time Increments: quarterly data and forecast[1]
Spot Rate (1990 3rd Quarter): DM1.6375/$

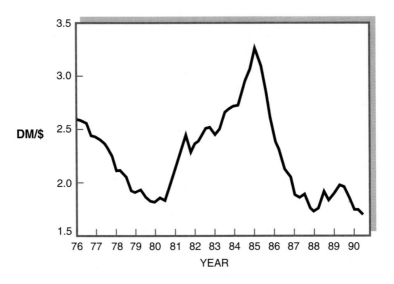

Short-Term Technique Employed	Formulation of Forecast	Forecast
Random walk hypothesis	$S_{t+1} = S_t$	1.6375
Percent change ($\pm$ 4.31%)[2]		
Dollar appreciation	$S_{t+1} = S_t * 1.0431$	1.7081
Dollar depreciation	$S_{t+1} = S_t / 1.0431$	1.5698

The technique which is considered by many to be the most accurate for forecasting periods between one and three months, is the use of the forward rate. Depending on the resources available to the individual currency forecaster, it may be one of the best bargains in currency forecasting. Forward rates for major world currencies are available in the daily business press. Forward rate quotations on other less widely traded currencies are often available by phone from the nearest international bank. It should also be noted that the forward rate forecast is actually a fundamental forecast, one derived from international interest rate differentials, as opposed to time series methods.

The forecasting of exchange rates between three months and one year is normally accomplished through combining technical and fundamental analysis. Trend analysis can

Exhibit 6.9 *continued*

Short-Term Technique Employed	Formulation of Forecast	Forecast
Weighted moving average	$S_{t+1} = (3S_t + 2S_{t-1} + S_{t-2})/6$	1.6627
Exponential smoothing		
Single		1.6375
Double		1.5906
Forward rate 90 days[3]	$S_{t+1} = F_{90}$	1.5736

Recent Spot Rates			Time Period	Mean Absolute Change[4]	Mean Percent Change[5]
1989.1:	1.8505	DM/$	1973.1–1990.3	0.1044 DM/$	0.77 %
.2:	1.9339				
.3:	1.9242		1980.1–1990.3	0.1049 DM/$	2.56 %
.4:	1.8114				
1990.1:	1.6908		1985.1–1990.3	0.1127 DM/$	2.30 %
.2:	1.6863				
.3:	1.6375		1986.2–1990.3	0.0811 DM/$	4.31 %

1. Period average exchange rates for the German mark, *Federal Reserve Bulletin*, U.S. Federal Reserve Board, monthly.

2. Dollar appreciation and depreciation utilize the mean percentage change for the latest period of stable currency rates, 1986 third quarter to 1990 third quarter, 4.31%. These values provide a statistical upper and lower bound to the spot exchange expectation for the fourth quarter of 1990.

3. Forward rate is the 90-day forward rate on the German mark quoted as of the end of September, 1990. Source: *Harris Bank Weekly Bulletin*, Harris Bank of Chicago.

4. Mean Absolute Change is the average change in the DM/$ spot exchange rate for the specified periods; absolute values are utilized to prevent "netting" impacts of positive and negative exchange rate changes from period to period.

5. Mean Percentage Change is the average percent change in the DM/$ spot exchange rate for the specified periods; absolute values of percentages are utilized to prevent "netting" of positive and negative changes.

be implemented in a variety of ways, from simple percent changes to increasingly complex computer-generated exponential smoothing and autoregressive moving-average models. Fundamental concerns such as interest rate movements, relative inflation rates, and expectations of future inflation, as well as trade and current account balances, must be considered with growing weight as the term of the forecast lengthens.

Short-Term Floating-Rate Forecasting in Practice

Exhibit 6.9 illustrates an actual short term forecasting exercise for the U.S. dollar/German mark. Using quarterly data, the goal is the prediction of the spot exchange rate for the fourth quarter of 1990. The forecast is made at the end of the third quarter of 1990. A plot of the exchange rate over time often provides the forecaster with some feel for the exchange rate's movement. Included are recent quarterly exchange rate values and percentage changes for different time periods. The plot indicates that the exchange rate has recently stabilized in a limited range. Since the beginning of the 1986 third quarter, the exchange rate has averaged a change of 4.31% per quarter.

The alternative techniques employed are all basic time series techniques which are easily implemented at little cost in time, resources, or expertise. The upper and lower bounds of the forecast may be found by calculating an average percentage change of 4.31% appreciation and depreciation. The three-period weighted moving average provides a slightly more sophisticated estimate of recent (three quarters) trend. The exponential smoothing techniques used are single exponential smoothing (applicable to stationary or "flat" data series) and double exponential smoothing (applicable to nonstationary series demonstrating positive or negative slopes over time). These techniques are normally available on personal computer statistical packages and are merely sophisticated moving average calculations.

The last but not least short-term floating-rate forecast technique is the use of the forward rate.

Regardless of which technique is chosen in the end, the essential feature of forecasting short-term rates is the low cost and relatively high degree of accuracy possible and needed.

Using the information provided in Exhibit 6.9, we chose to split the difference between the 90-day forward rate (DM1.5736/$) and the double exponential smoothing forecast (DM1.5906/$)—a forecasted spot rate of DM1.5821/$. (As we mentioned earlier, forecasting the future is frought with risks. Well, we missed. The spot rate for the fourth quarter of 1990 was DM1.5307/$!)

Fixed Exchange Rates

As opposed to floating exchange rate regimes where one assumes movements will occur, the analyst must first assume fixed-rate regimes will remain "fixed." Fixed exchange rate regimes are successful primarily because of demonstrated government success in maintaining the parity rates established. If the government is successful, few currency restrictions will exist. There will be no established black markets for domestic currency or parallel exchange markets operating for the country's currency outside of the government's sphere of influence. The forecaster must therefore look for indications of forced change, rather than assuming it will occur.

Fixed exchange rate systems do not, however, remove all responsibility of careful analysis from the currency forecaster. Many of the same characteristics which allow countries to maintain fixed exchange rates also create added pressures for occasional adjustments. Trade balances often constitute significant problems for maintaining fixed exchange rates. Unlike floating rate systems, fixed rate regimes lack automatic currency adjustments which occur gradually when imbalances arise. Problems therefore often become quite acute before currency valuation adjustments are forced upon authorities. Danger signals for impending devaluation include large and sustained trade deficits, and increasingly rapid rates of domestic inflation which exceed rates of inflation of major trading partners. Danger signals for impending revaluation include sustained trade surpluses, and relatively low rates of inflation combined with healthy economic growth.

Increased government intervention in exchange markets, including the imposition of restrictive government regulations on holding foreign currency balances, often precede devaluations. Although these factors are extremely visible, predicting the timing and magnitude of the adjustment is often impossible. The multinational firm must often minimize its exposure until fixed rates have been adjusted and stability once again achieved.

Under a fixed rate system, government foreign exchange losses can be immense, since all the other market participants can depend on government intervention to maintain parity. At some point, however, even governments must resign themselves to market pressure and allow the exchange rate to change. The tricky part of forecasting is to guess when this change will occur, since the timing and amount of exchange rate change is primarily a political decision.

FORECASTING EXCHANGE RATES IN THE LONG RUN

Forecasting exchange rates in the long run may be accomplished in a variety of ways. Forecasting methods for the long run could include computerized time series analysis, termed ARIMA (Autoregressive Integrated Moving-Average) modeling, or other types of econometric analysis using fundamental analysis such as multiple regression. These models employ the same macroeconomic fundamentals in equation form as listed in Exhibit 6.8. Although a description of these techniques is beyond the scope of this book, the student should be aware of their availability for either in-house forecasting or through professional forecasting services.

As noted in the anecdotal article at the end of this chapter, a variety of forecasting services and techniques are available commercially. Many of the professional currency advisory services provide updated currency forecasts on a daily basis, as well as personal consulting. *Euromoney* magazine has tracked and evaluated a number of the major professional currency forecasting services over the 1980s on an annual basis. The professionals have *not* on average achieved consistent success in their forecast accuracy.

Sample Long-Run Forecasting: DM/$

Exhibit 6.10 provides the basic data necessary for forecasting the dollar/mark exchange rate. The data are taken from the "Economic and Financial Indicators" section of *The Economist*, and are available on a weekly basis.

The fundamental data included in Exhibit 6.10 can be interpreted as follows:

- Economic output, although positive for both countries in the periods shown, has been distinctly stronger in Germany. Note should also be made of the rather disquieting latest month of German GDP, although some authorities were attributing this to the difficulties of German unification. The comparative economic growth rates would indicate that DM-denominated assets may be increasingly attractive in coming periods. The DM would be expected to appreciate versus the dollar.

- Prices have been rising more than twice as fast in the United States as in Germany. This is true on both the consumer and producer price levels. Producer prices reflect

Exhibit 6.10   Fundamental Data for a Sample Long Run Forecast Analysis: DM/$

	United States		Germany	
Macroeconomic Fundamentals	*Latest*	*Latest*	*Latest*	*Latest*
1. Economic Output	*Month*	*12 Mos.*	*Month*	*12 Mos.*
Industrial production (%)	+ 3.3	+ 1.5	+ 6.5	+ 5.1
GNP or GDP (%)	+ 0.4	+ 1.2	− 3.5	+ 3.4
2. Prices	*3 Mos.*	*12 Mos.*	*3 Mos.*	*12 Mos.*
Consumer prices (%)	+ 5.4	+ 5.6	+ 1.9	+ 2.9
Wholesale prices (%)	+ 3.1	+ 3.6	+ 1.7	+ 1.9
3. Trade and Exchange Rates	*Month*	*12 Mos.*	*Month*	*12 Mos.*
Trade balance ($ bn)	− 9.33	− 102.0	+ 5.06	+ 72.2
Current account balance ($ bn)	na	− 97.8	na	+ 51.6
C. Trade-weighted exchange rate (1985=100)	62.5	70.1	118.8	113.4
4. Money Supply Growth (% rise on year ago)				
Narrow, M1 (%)	+ 4.6		+ 4.2	
Broad (%)	+ 1.9		+ 3.9	
5. Interest Rates	*Gov't*	*Corp.*	*Gov't*	*Corp.*
Government bond yields, long-term (%)	9.13	9.68	9.05	9.05
Eurocurrency deposit rates, 3 month (%)	8.38	9.24	8.38	9.09
	July	*Year ago*	*July*	*Year ago*
6. Foreign Reserves ($ bn)	66.8	52.4	62.5	56.9

Source: Adapted from "Economic and Financial Indicators," *The Economist,* 29 September 1990, pp. 115–116.

labor and material expenses which will show up in the consumer prices of finished products in coming months. According to the theory of relative PPP, the DM would be expected to appreciate versus the dollar.

- Trade and current account balances for the two countries also indicate an excess supply of dollars (the U.S. trade deficit) and an excess demand for marks (the German trade surplus). Special note should be made of the lack of trade account deterioration of Germany even though economic growth has been rapid. Economic growth normally stimulates the growth of imports over exports; Germany has seemingly avoided this problem to date. The DM would be expected to appreciate versus the dollar.

- Money supply growth and interest rates are comparable between the two countries. The international Fisher effect would indicate no significant change in the exchange rate between the dollar and DM.

- Foreign exchange reserves are higher in both countries than one year ago. Although large in an absolute sense (over $60 billion in reserves in both countries), these reserves are small in relation to the estimated size of daily foreign currency trading on world markets (estimated at over $600 billion as noted in Chapter 4).

The forecaster would conclude from the above analysis that the U.S. dollar should depreciate versus the German mark over the coming one to two year period. The amount and timing of the depreciation would, however, constitute the age-old dilemma of forecasting.

The latest round of exceptional volatility in foreign exchange markets has made the need for good analysis about when to buy, sell or hedge currency risk all the more important to banks and corporations. Gavin Shreeve reports.

Forecasting: In Trends We Trust*

In a lecture to bankers and academics in London last month Bank of England governor Robin Leigh-Pemberton admitted what the market already knew.

He told his illustrious audience that there was little if anything that one central bank acting alone can do to influence the foreign exchange markets. Besides providing a short-term breathing space for interest rates the governor said candidly that for any intervention to be at all effective it would have to be 'very large indeed.' Reaction to his speech was that it was one of the most significant statements to come out of Threadneedle Street for some time.

For the practitioners it was open recognition of what really moves markets: the weight of money and emotion, not the arrogance of politicians or the divine will of central bankers. It is for this reason that talk of target zones and exchange rate bands is a pure chimera, way beyond the resources or will of finance ministers. Even the mighty and aloof Bundesbank will admit in private conversation with its fellow European central bankers the truth of this position.

Certainly the growing band of those who make a living out of second-guessing the market, the foreign exchange forecasters, have always known that the emperor had no clothes.

Said leading chartist Brian Marbour, 'At the Plaza meeting in September 1985 central bankers and the G5 states (UK, France, Japan, US, West Germany) were very arrogant about their ability to hold sway over the market and in particular the dollar. I sent my clients a telex before the meeting to close all long positions in the dollar. We did not need a Plaza statement; the dollar was going down anyway. What difference will $10 billion of intervention do in a $300 billion-a-day market?

The Banker, June 1987, pp. 83–84. Reprinted by kind permission of The Banker.

Added Paul Chertkow of Hoare Govett, 'You can't postpone the day of reckoning; however, the central banks should not abandon their efforts to smooth and control the speed of a strongly moving trend whether it be up or down.'

Andrew Smith, founder of Global Analysis Systems (GAS), told *The Banker*, 'It is the truth we have always known. All the central banks can be is a brake on the market. Intervention is not in itself influential; it is the threat of intervention that has an effect.' According to Smith central bank intervention usually signals the bottoming out of a particular cycle.

Shandi Modi, chairman and managing director of Money Market Services, one of the oldest companies in the business of foreign exchange forecasting, agrees but takes a more historical view. MMS was created in the early 1970s to do the dealer's homework for him. When MMS branched out into London in February 1981 it was, among other things, to provide the UK and European markets with an expertise on the US market and particularly on the machinations of the US Federal Reserve which did not previously exist.

Crystal Ball Analysts

Said Shandi Modi, 'In 1982 the Fed was the catalyst for most foreign exchange movement. We provided an educational service explaining the US market. Now the Fed is no longer as important; the foreign exchange market has itself replaced the Fed. Once the foreign exchange market was explained in terms of Fed behavior; now the Fed responds to the market.'

Hoare Govett's Chertkow is among the many people in the business of foreign exchange forecasting who pins his colours firmly to the mast of fundamentals. 'We are not crystal ball analysts; we try to isolate economic factors and use charts when we are looking at the short term. In fact we temper our fundamentalist analysis with charts,' he said.

And those fundamentals change. Shandi Modi points out that in the early 1980s the market clung to monitoring M1 figures from the US Fed; now M1 is almost ignored. Instead, according to Modi, the market is now much more interested in 'the real economy and in trade numbers.' He added, 'This is a mirror image of what is considered to be important to policy makers now, in determining their outlook on policy, interest rates and so on. That is why we focus on the economy.'

In assessing the present conditions in the foreign exchange markets Chertkow believes there is no substitute for what he refers to as a need for policy convergence, that is, greater cooperation among G5 governments in taking a more coordinated approach towards tackling the problems in the major economies.

For example, analysts such as Chertkow will in the next few months be looking at what if anything the Germans and the Japanese will be doing to stimulate their economies and what the US plans to do about its massive deficits; what Japan does about its massive savings will also be crucial. A close watch will be kept on the US Federal Reserve to see to what extent it will further tighten its monetary stance. This, says Chertkow, is based on the widely held assumption that nobody wants a reversal of the present downward trend in the dollar.

At Money Market Services (MMS), which provides a huge service on Telerate and is about to provide a gilts analysis service on the Reuters screen, the approach is to use a mix of technical analysis and economic fundamentals. Said MMS' Shandi Modi, 'We do not consolidate the views of the fundamentalist and chartists. In fact we do not forecast; we simply identify the factors that will be important to the traders. Chart analysis is much more relevant for the traders. It provides them with the right sort of discipline.'

Last Year's Advisor

Brian Marbour completely and emphatically disagrees. In a profession which, by its very nature, produces people with more than a fair share of self-confidence and aggression, Marbour stands out alone as a self-publicist. And not without reason. He has had a fine track record of getting the market right and has several awards to prove it.

But Marbour, who now runs his own company and has among his clients some of the world's leading banks and corporations, is a purist, a staunch adherent to the chartist credo. 'I do not read anything and I mean anything, other than charts. I have no intention of cluttering up my head with irrelevant nonsense.' He is scathing: 'Forecasting on the basis of fundamentals is very good for rationalizing the past; it is last year's best adviser.'

The forecasting business is littered with computers and econometric models stuffed with 'fundamentals' and yet, for Marbour, despite this weight of information the fundamentalist approach is nearly always wrong. The reason for this, he claims, is that there are no 'oughts' in the market.

For Marbour, whose clients are charged some $25,000 a year, the fundamentalist approach ignores the simple laws of supply and demand; for the chartist the figure on the Reuter or Telerate screen represents at any given moment the whole sum of human knowledge. Technical analysis, he says, assesses the psychology of the market in a way that the economists do not. There is, he says with a conviction bordering on the dogmatic, no such thing as value in the market; it is only a perception of value. Likewise it is not the news itself but how the market reacts to the news.

Marbour likes to quote George Bernard Shaw: 'Foreign exchange movements are like Saturday afternoons, which although occurring at regular intervals, always catch Baker Street station by surprise.'

There is no mystique about technical analysis, says Marbour; nor is it some sort of cerebral hocus pocus. It is about emotion and because of this the good technical analyst, working with his charts, 'will not leave you on the wrong side of a trend.'

According to BFP Currency Services, a specialist technical analysis firm, 'The currency exchange rate reflects not only the differing value of opinions of many appraisers but also all the hopes and fears, guesses and moods, rational and irrational, of hundreds of potential buyers and sellers.'

If there is any weakness in the chartist approach it is, Marbour is forced to admit, in the person or technician; experience is everything. Said BFP Currency Services, '...analysis of the financial market is basically analysis of behavioral psychology.'

Information Stream

Marbour produces a written report and plots his charts in the evening. His method is such that because everybody has their own time scale his clients have direct access to him.

Another approach followed by MMS and GAS is to canvas market opinion. MMS does it on a weekly basis while GAS provides 4–6 hour forecasting based on two polls a day. The poll consists of a two-minute phone call to traders at 25 of the leading banks taking in a geographical spread. GAS's Andrew Smith dismisses the notion that such a process of canvassing opinion could effectively amount to self-fulfilling prophecy. No single trading room has the power to move markets for any length of time, says Smith. Some have the clout to talk up their book in the short term but that is a very short horizon.

There is the possibility of the big players acting as a group moving the market, but again this is very much a short-term movement. Those in this category include the top-tier banks such as Citibank, Morgan, First Chicago, and Bankers Trust; Smith points out that Bankers Trust's foreign exchange operations alone contributed some $78 million to the bank's first-quarter earnings this year.

The purpose of the GAS service is to provide the traders with a barometer of the market. And he claims 75% accuracy. Now GAS is writing software to provide an options hedging strategy based on its forecasts; the package is expected to be ready in the autumn.

The GAS approach is not to evaluate the 'why' of what is happening but simply the 'what.' At MMS the weekly report is based on the same principal, that of providing the traders with what Modi calls 'a mirror of many ideas.' The report is a mix of fundamental and technical analysis and the poll. Said Modi, 'The purpose is to provide a good information stream. We help the market to operate more efficiently.' MMS has some 45 analysts and chartists worldwide; it also canvasses every week the opinion of about 100 traders, analysts, and some central bankers.

But, as might be expected, there is little unanimity in approach among foreign exchange analysts and forecasters. Hoare Govett's Chertkow, himself a contributor to the MMS poll, says the consensus approach 'is almost never right.' Added Chertkow, 'The trouble is that economists almost never know what is going to happen in the short term.'

Chertkow is part of the Hoare Govett's service which is provided by eight economists in the UK and 120 research analysts spread throughout the worldwide network of Security Pacific Corporation, the Los Angeles-based bank which owns Hoare Govett.

Said Chertkow, 'I don't look at any other currency forecasts; I simply don't want to know.' As for the fourth estate, Chertkow is dismissive: 'I take the view that newspaper people are the very last to understand what is going on.'

Nobody will be quoted referring to the foreign exchange market as a game of poker but they nearly all talk in terms of busted flushes and buying into an inside straight. But it was Winston Churchill who put his finger on the casino-like mentality and bravado of the foreign exchange markets when, still in the heady days of Bretton Woods, he said:

> There is no sphere of human thought in which it is easier to show superficial cleverness and the appearance of superior wisdom than discussing questions of currency and exchange.

SUMMARY

Exhibit 6.11 summarizes the various forecasting periods, regimes, and the authors' opinions on the preferred methodologies. Opinions, like the future itself, are subject to change without notice!

Exhibit 6.11   Exchange Rate Forecasting in Practice

Forecast Period	Regime	Recommended Forecast Methods
Short-Run	Fixed-Rate	1. Assume the fixed rate is maintained 2. Indications of stress on fixed rate? 3. Capital controls; black market rates 4. Indicators of Government's capability to maintain fixed rate? 5. Changes in official foreign currency reserves

	Floating-Rate	1. Technical methods which capture trend
		2. Forward rates as forecasts
		  a) < 30 days, assume a random walk
		  b) 30–90 days, forward rates
		  c) 90–360 days, combine trend with fundamental analysis
		3. Fundamental analysis of inflationary concerns
		4. Government declarations and agreements regarding exchange rate goals
		5. Cooperative agreements with other countries

Long-Run	Fixed-Rate	1. Fundamental analysis 2. Balance-of-Payments management 3. Ability to control domestic inflation 4. Ability to generate hard currency reserves to use for intervention 5. Ability to run trade surpluses
	Floating-Rate	1. Focus on inflationary fundamentals and PPP 2. Indicators of general economic health such as economic growth and stability 3. Technical analysis of long-term trends; new research indicates possibility of long-term technical "waves"

- Under conditions of freely floating rates the expected rate of change in the spot exchange rate, differential rates of national inflation and interest, and the forward discount or premium are all directly proportional to each other and mutually determined. A change in one of these variables has a tendency to change all of them with a feedback on the variable that changes first.

- Fixed exchange rates are determined and preserved by governments. A fixed exchange rate's major threat (change from the fixed parity rate) comes from large trade imbalances (deficit) or from ever increasing rates of domestic inflation (hyperinflation).

- Floating exchange rates are typical of the world's major industrial countries such as Japan, the United States, Germany, and the United Kingdom, all of whom have relatively large and well developed trade and capital flows.

- Time-series techniques or simple use of the forward rate are forecast alternatives. Longer-term forecasting, over one year, requires a return to the basic analysis of exchange rate fundamentals such as balance of payments, relative inflation rates, relative interest rates, and the long-run properties of purchasing power parity.

1. Wheat Trading

Two countries, the United States and Australia, produce just one good, wheat. Suppose that the price of wheat in the United States is US$2.80 per bushel and in Australia is A$3.70 per bushel.

a) According to purchasing power parity, what should be the U.S./Australian dollar spot rate of exchange?

b) Suppose the price of wheat over the next year is expected to rise to US$3.10 in the U.S. and to A$4.65 in Australia. What should be the one-year forward U.S./Australian dollar exchange rate?

c) Given your answers to (a) and (b) above, and given that the current interest rate in the United States is 10% for notes of a one-year maturity, what would you expect current Australian interest rates to be?

2. McDonald's Hamburger Standard and the Law of One Price

Exhibit 6.2, *The Economist*'s hamburger standard, demonstrated one measure of what the purchasing power parity exchange rate would be if the Big Mac was considered a standardized product around the world.

What does it mean when the value of a currency is "overvalued" or "undervalued"? Explain in the context of the U.S. dollar and the Soviet Union's ruble in the example shown.

3. Villa in Biarritz

You have just rented a villa in Biarritz for a vacation twelve months hence. Your French landlord wants to preserve real income in French francs, so the present monthly rent of FF10,000/month will be adjusted upward or downward for any change in the French cost of living between now and then.

You expect French inflation to be 3% and U.S. inflation to be 8% over the coming year. You believe implicitly in the theory of purchasing power parity, and you note from the *Financial Times* that the current spot rate is FF5.00/$. How many U.S. dollars will you need one year hence to pay your first month's rent?

4. Japan and Germany

Money and foreign exchange markets in Japan and Germany are quite efficient. You have the following information:

	Japan	*Germany*
Spot exchange rate	¥100.00/DM	DM 0.0100/¥
Expected inflation rate	2.00% p.a.	5.00% p.a.
One-year "T-bill" rate	Unknown	8.00% p.a.

a) What is your estimate of the one-year T-bill rate in Japan?

b) What is your estimate of the one-year forward exchange rate between Japanese yen and German marks?

5. Borrowing Pesos

Suppose that on January 1st the cost of borrowing Mexican pesos for one year is 20%. During the year, U.S. inflation is 4% and Mexican inflation is 15%. At the same time, the exchange rate changes from Ps3,000/$ on January 1st to Ps3,400/$ on December 31st. What is the *real* cost for an American who borrows Mexican pesos, changes them for dollars, and a year later uses dollars to repay the peso loan?

6. Swiss Interest Rates

In Switzerland the interest rate on government securities with a one-year maturity is 4%, and the expected rate of inflation for the coming year is 2%.

In the United States the interest rate on government securities with a one-year maturity is 7%, and the expected rate of inflation for the coming year is 5%.

The current spot rate for Swiss francs is SF1.4600/$. Forecast the spot rate for SF/$ one year from today. Explain your logic.

7. Your Vacation

Your spouse, an artistic photographer, has just received a $40,000 cash grant to make photographs of the Moroccan countryside for the *National Geographic.* The two of you will leave for Morocco in six months. The only thing you know about the Moroccan economy is the price elasticity of Moroccan wine sold in the United States is 1.4, and U.S. consumption of Moroccan wine is down 16.8%.

U.S. inflation is currently 6% per annum, and the current spot exchange rate is 8 Moroccan dirham for one dollar (DH8.00/$). U.S. six-month T-bills yield 8% per annum, while six-month Moroccan T-bills yield 30% per annum. You are an international finance major who believes in purchasing power parity and that forward rates are unbiased predictors of future spot rates.

You and your spouse try to answer the following questions:

a) Using the data on price elasticity, what is the current inflation rate in Morocco?

b) Using the above estimate of Moroccan inflation and the concept of Purchasing Power Parity, what should be the current six-month forward Moroccan dirham/dollar exchange rate?

c) Should you and your spouse invest your $40,000 for the next six months in the United States or in Morocco, given that you are risk adverse and intend to spend all $40,000 on the photographic expedition? What is the advantage of the best investment choice over the alternative?

8. Short-Term Forecasting of the DM/$ Exchange Rate

Exhibit 6.9 demonstrated some of the various methods for forecasting a short-term floating exchange rate.

Using the actual value of the fourth quarter DM/$ spot exchange rate, use the forecasting techniques illustrated to forecast the spot exchange rate for the first quarter of 1991.

9. Fundamental Analysis and a Long-Term Exchange Rate Forecast

Exhibit 6.10 provided a sample of the data readily available for forecasting a long-term exchange rate movement. Using the information in the exhibit, answer the following questions.

a) According to the relative version of purchasing power parity, and using the change in consumer prices in the United States and Germany, what would the DM/$ exchange rate be in one year if the spot rate in September 1990 was DM1.5200/$?

b) According to the international Fisher Effect, and using the long-term government bond yields in the United States and Germany, what would the DM/$ exchange rate be in one year if the present spot rate in September 1990 is DM1.5200/$?

10. Parity Relations: United States and France (CO6A.WK1)

Assume that in France the interest rate on government securities with a one-year maturity is 8% and the expected rate of inflation for the coming year is 5%. In the United States the one-year interest rate is 7% and the expected rate of inflation is 4%. The spot rate is FF6.0000/$ and the one-year forward rate is FF6.2000/$.

Explain the economic theories and illustrate by use of a diagram how the United States and France are linked with respect to interest rates, inflation rates, spot and forward exchange rates. Be sure to show how you calculated the premium or discount on the French franc.

11. Parity Relations: Italy and United States

Explain and diagram the theoretical equilibrium relationship between inflation rates, interest rates, current spot and forward rates, and a forecasted future spot rate. Use the following data to illustrate how your diagram works:

	United States	Italy
Expected one-year inflation rate	5%	7%
Interest rate on one-year government notes	8%	10%
Spot rate today	Lit1250/$	
One-year forward rate	Lit1275/$	

Be sure to explain in detail each economic parity relationship shown in your diagram. Show your calculation of the forward premium or discount on the Italian lira.

NOTES

1. See, for example, Lawrence H. Officer, "The Purchasing-Power-Parity Theory of Exchange Rates: A Review Article," *International Monetary Fund Staff Papers*, March 1976, pp. 1–60. Also see Richard J. Rogalski and Joseph D. Vinso, "Price Level Variations as Predictors of Flexible Exchange Rates," *Journal of International Business Studies*, Spring/ Summer 1977, pp. 71-81; Stephen P. Magee, "Contracting and Spurious Deviations from Purchasing Power Parity," in Jacob A. Frenkel and Harry G. Johnson, eds., *The Economics of Exchange Rates*, Reading, Mass.: Addison-Wesley, 1978, pp. 67–74; Lawrence Officer, Edward I. Altman, and Ingo Walter, eds., *Purchasing Power Parity and Exchange Rates: Theory, Evidence, and Relevance*, Contemporary Studies in Economic and Financial Analysis, vol. 35, London: JAI Press, 1982. Most recently, Barry K. Goodwin, Thomas Grennes, and Michael K. Wohlgenant, "Testing the Law of One Price When Trade Takes Time," *Journal of International Money and Finance*, March 1990, pp. 21-40.

2. For recent studies on the validity of PPP in the long run see Jacob Frenkel, "Purchasing Power Parity: Doctrinal Perspective and Evidence from the 1920s," *Journal of International Economics*, May 1978, pp. 169–191; and Michael R. Darby, "Movements in Purchasing Power Parity: The Short and Long Runs," in Michael R. Darby and James R. Lothian, eds., *The International Transmission of Inflation*, 1983. Two of the best recent studies questioning the validity of PPP in the long run are that of Mark Rush and Steven Husted, "Purchasing Power Parity in the Long Run," *Canadian Journal of Economics*, February 1985, pp. 137–145; and Meher Manzur, "An International Comparison of Prices and Exchanges Rates: A New Test of Purchasing Power Parity," *Journal of International Money and Finance*, March 1990, pp. 75–91.

3. This process of exchange-rate-induced price changes is a topic of relatively recent interest; the early formulation of the process beginning with Magee's analysis in the early 1970s. For a more detailed description of pass-through analysis see Stephen P. Magee, "Currency Contracts, Pass-Through, and Devaluation," *Brookings Papers on Economic Activity*, 1:1973, pp. 303–325; Stephen P. Magee, "U.S. Import Prices in the Currency-Contract Paper," *Brookings Papers on Economic Activity*, 1:1974, pp. 117–164. For more recent analyses for the United States see Catherine L. Mann, "Prices, Profit Margins, and Exchange Rates," *Federal Reserve Bulletin*, June 1986, pp. 366–379, and Michael H. Moffett, "The J-Curve Revisited: An Empirical Examination for the United States," *Journal of International Money and Finance*, 1989, pp. 425–444.

4. The actual form of the decomposed nominal exchange rate is $(1 + r)(1 + \pi) - 1$, which yields $r + \pi + r\pi$; the final compound term ($r\pi$) is normally dropped from discussions due to its relatively minor value.

5. Some relevant studies of the Fisher Effect, the International Fisher Effect, and interest rate parity are Robert E. Cumby and Maurice Obstfeld, "A Note on Exchange-Rate Expectations and Nominal Interest Differentials: A Test of the Fisher Hypothesis," *Journal of Finance*, June 1981, pp. 697–703; Frederick S. Mishkin, "Are Real Interest Rates Equal across Countries? An Empirical Investigation of International Parity Conditions," *Journal of Finance*, December 1984, pp. 1345–1357; and Fred R. Kaen, Evangelos O. Simos, and George A. Hachey, "The Response of Forward Exchange Rates to Interest Rate Forecasting Errors," *Journal of Financial Research*, Winter 1984, pp. 281–290.

6. *Ibid.*

7. For example, see Ian H. Giddy and Gunter Dufey, "The Random Behavior of Flexible Exchange Rates," *Journal of International Business Studies*, Spring 1975, pp. 1–32. Also see Dennis E. Logue, Richard J. Sweeney, and Thomas D. Willett, "The Speculative Behavior of Foreign Exchange Rates during the Current Float," *Journal of Business Research*, vol. 6, no. 2, 1978, pp. 159–173; Richard M. Levich, "Tests of Forecasting Models and Market Efficiency in the International Money Market," in Jacob A. Frenkel and Harry G. Johnson, eds., *The Economics of Exchange Rates*, pp. 129–158.

8. A good review of early foreign exchange market efficiency studies is in Stephen W. Kohlhagen, *The Behavior of Foreign Exchange Markets—A Critical Survey of the Empirical Literature*, New York: New York University Monograph Series in Finance and Economics, no. 3, 1978. An excellent summary of all the foreign exchange forecasting and management literature is in Laurent L. Jacque, "Management of Foreign Exchange Risk: A Review Article," *Journal of International Business Studies*, Spring/Summer 1981, pp. 81–101.

9. *Op. cit.* Giddy and Dufey, "Random Behavior of Flexible Exchange Rates," p. 27.

10. Stephen W. Kohlhagen, "The Performance of the Foreign Exchange Markets: 1971–1974," *Journal of International Business Studies*, Fall 1975, pp. 33–39.

11. Eugene F. Fama, "Forward Rates as Predictors of Future Spot Rates," *Journal of Financial Economics*, October 1976, pp. 361–377.

12. Three such studies are reported in the following articles: Stephen Goodman, "Foreign Exchange Forecasting Techniques: Implications for Business and Policy," *Journal of Finance*, May 1979, pp. 415–427; Richard M. Levich, "Analyzing the Accuracy of Foreign Exchange Forecasting Services: Theory and Evidence," in Clas Wihlborg and Richard Levich, eds., *Exchange Risk and Exposure: Current Development in International Financial Development*, Lexington, Mass.: Heath, 1980; John F. O. Bilson, "The Evaluation and Use of Foreign Exchange Rate Forecasting Services," in R. J. Herring, ed., *Management of Foreign Exchange Risk*, Cambridge, England: Cambridge University Press, 1983, pp. 149–179.

13. The original source is a quote from the Jurgensen Report, *Report of the Working Group on Exchange Market Intervention*, Washington, D.C.: U.S. Treasury, 1983. This particular citation was from John Williamson, *The Exchange Rate System*, Washington, D.C.: Institute for International Economics, September 1983, p. 50

14. Bruno Solnik, *International Investments*, Reading, Mass.: Addison-Wesley, 1991, p. 89. © 1991, Addison-Wesley Publishing Co., Inc. Reprinted with permission.

15. "Why currencies overshoot," *The Economist*, December 1, 1990, p. 89.

16. Charles Engel and James D. Hamilton, "Long Swings in the Dollar: Are They in the Data and Do Markets Know It?" *American Economic Review*, September 1990, pp. 689–713.

BIBLIOGRAPHY

Abuaf, Niso, and Philippe Jorion, "Purchasing Power Parity in the Long Run," *Journal of Finance*, March 1990, pp. 157–174.

Adler, Michael, and Bernard Dumas, "Portfolio Choice and the Demand for Forward Exchange," *American Economic Review*, May 1976, pp. 332–339.

Aggarwal, Raj, "The Distribution of Exchange Rates and Forward Risk Premia," *Advances in Financial Planning and Forecasting*, vol. 4, 1990, pp. 43–54.

Ang, James S., and Ali M. Fatemi, "A Test of the Rationality of Forward Exchange Rate," *Advances in Financial Planning and Forecasting*, vol. 4, 1990, pp. 3–22.

Baillie, Richard T., and Tim Bollerslev, "Common Stochastic Trends in a System of Exchange Rates," *Journal of Finance*, March 1989, pp. 167–181.

Bilson, John F.O., "The Evaluation and Use of Foreign Exchange Rate Forecasting Services," in R. J. Herring, ed., *Management of Foreign Exchange Risk*, Cambridge, England: Cambridge University Press, 1983, pp. 149–179.

Blake, David, Michael Beenstock, and Valerie Brasse, "The Performance of U.K. Exchange Rate Forecasters," *The Economic Journal*, December 1986, pp. 986–999.

Calderon-Rossell, Jorge R., and Moshe Ben-Horim, "The Behavior of Foreign Exchange Rates,"

Journal of International Business Studies, Fall 1982, pp. 99–111.

Chen, T.J., K.C. John Wei, "Risk Premiums in Foreign Exchange Markets: Theory and Evidence," *Advances in Financial Planning and Forecasting*, vol. 4, 1990, pp. 23–42.

Chiang, Thomas C., "Empirical Analysis on the Predictors of Future Spot Rates," *Journal of Financial Research*, Summer 1986, pp. 153–162.

Cornell, Bradford, and J. K. Dietrich, "Inflation, Relative Price Changes, and Exchange Risk," *Financial Management*, Autumn 1980, pp. 30–34.

Cosset, Jean-Claude, "Forward Rates as Predictors of Future Interest Rates in the Eurocurrency Market," *Journal of International Business Studies*, Winter 1982, pp. 71–83.

Cumby, Robert E., and Maurice Obstfeld, "A Note on Exchange-Rate Expectations and Nominal Interest Differentials: A Test of the Fisher Hypothesis," *Journal of Finance*, June 1981, pp. 697–703.

Darby, Michael R., "Movements in Purchasing Power Parity: The Short and Long Runs," in Michael R. Darby and James R. Lothian, eds., *The International Transmission of Inflation*, Chicago: University of Chicago Press, 1983.

Dornbusch, Rudiger, "Flexible Exchange Rates and Interdependence," *International Monetary Fund Staff Papers*, March 1983, pp. 3–30.

Dufey, Gunter, and Ian Giddy, "International Financial Planning: The Use of Market-Based Forecasts," *California Management Review*, Fall 1978, pp. 69–81.

——, "Forecasting Foreign Exchange Rates: A Pedagogical Note," *Columbia Journal of World Business*, Summer 1981, pp. 53–61.

Edison, Hali J., "Purchasing Power Parity in the Long Run: A Test of the Dollar/Pound Exchange Rate (1890–1978), *Journal of Money, Credit, and Banking*, August 1987, pp. 376–387.

Eun, Cheol S., "Global Purchasing Power View of Exchange Risk," *Journal of Financial and Quantitative Analysis*, December 1981, pp. 639–650.

Everett, Robert M., Abraham M. George, and Aryeh Blumberg, "Appraising Currency Strengths and Weaknesses: An Operational Model for Calculating Parity Exchange Rates," *Journal of International Business Studies*, Fall 1980, pp. 80–91.

Fama, Eugene F., "Forward Rates as Predictors of Future Spot Rates," *Journal of Financial Economics*, October 1976, pp. 361–377.

Finnerty, Joseph E., James Owers, and Francis J. Crerar, "Foreign Exchange Forecasting and Leading Economic Indicators: The U.S. Canadian Experience," *Management International Review*, 27, No. 2, 1987, pp. 59–70.

Folks, William R., and Stanley R. Stansell, "The Use of Discriminant Analysis in Forecasting Exchange Risk Movements," *Journal of International Business Studies*, Spring 1975, pp. 33–50.

Frenkel, Jacob A., "Flexible Exchange Rates, Prices, and the Role of 'News': Lessons from the 1970s," *Journal of Political Economy*, August 1981, pp. 665–705.

Frankel, Jeffrey, and Alan MacArthur, "Political Vs. Currency Premia in International Real Interest Rate Differentials: A Study of Forward Rates for 24 Countries," *European Economic Review*, 32, no. 5, June 1988, pp. 1083–1114.

Giddy, Ian H., "An Integrated Theory of Exchange Rate Equilibrium," *Journal of Financial and Quantitative Analysis*, December 1976, pp. 863–892.

——, and Gunter Dufey, "The Random Behavior of Flexible Exchange Rates," *Journal of International Business Studies*, Spring 1975, pp. 1–32.

Goodman, Stephen, "Foreign Exchange Forecasting Techniques: Implications for Business and Policy," *Journal of Finance*, May 1979, pp. 415–427.

Goodwin, Barry K., Thomas Grennes, and Michael K. Wohlgenant, "Testing the Law of One Price When Trade Takes Time," *Journal of International Money and Finance*, March 1990, pp. 21–40.

Gupta, Sanjeev, "A Note on the Efficiency of Black Markets in Foreign Currencies," *Journal of Finance*, June 1981, pp. 705–710.

Hansen, Lars Peter, and Robert J. Hodrick, "Forward Exchange Rates as Optimal Predictors of Future Spot Rates: An Econometric Analysis," *Journal of Political Economy*, October 1980, pp. 829–853.

Huang, Roger D., "Expectations of Exchange Rates and Differential Inflation Rates: Further Evidence on Purchasing Power Parity in Efficient Markets," *Journal of Finance*, March 1987, pp. 69–79.

Isard, Peter, "How Far Can We Push the Law of One Price?" *American Economic Review*, December 1977, pp. 942–948.

Kaen, Fred R., Evangelos O. Simos, and George A. Hachey, "The Response of Forward Exchange Rates to Interest Rate Forecasting Errors," *Journal of Financial Research*, Winter 1984, pp. 281–290.

Kohers, Theodor, "Testing the Rate of Forecasting Consistency of Major Foreign Currency Futures," *International Trade Journal*, Summer 1987, pp. 359–370.

Kohlhagen, Stephen W., *The Behavior of Foreign Exchange Markets—A Critical Survey of the Empirical Literature*, New York: New York University Monograph Series in Finance and Economics, no. 3, 1978.

Koveos, Peter, and Bruce Seifert, "Purchasing Power Parity and Black Markets," *Financial Management*, Autumn 1985, pp. 40–46.

Kwok, Chuck C.Y., and LeRoy D. Brooks, "Examining Event Study Methodologies in Foreign Exchange Markets," *Journal of International Business Studies*, Second Quarter 1990, pp. 189–224.

Lee, Cheng-Few, and Edward L. Bubnys, "The Relationship Between Inflation and Short-Term Interest Rates: An International Comparison," *Advances in Financial Planning and Forecasting*, vol. 4, 1990, pp. 123–130.

Levich, Richard M., "Tests of Forecasting Models and Market Efficiency in the International Money Market," in Jacob A. Frenkel and Harry G. Johnson, eds., *The Economics of Exchange Rates*, Reading, Mass.: Addison-Wesley, 1978, pp. 129–158.

——, "Are Forward Exchange Rates Unbiased Predictors of Future Spot Rates?" *Columbia Journal of World Business*, Winter 1979, pp. 49–61.

——, "Analyzing the Accuracy of Foreign Exchange Forecasting Services: Theory and Evidence," in Clas Wihlborg and Richard Levich, eds., *Exchange Risk and Exposure: Current Development in International Financial Development*, Lexington, Mass.: Heath, 1980.

Levin, Jay H., "Trade Flow Lags, Monetary and Fiscal Policy and Exchange Rate Overshooting," *Journal of International Money and Finance*, December 1986, pp. 485–496.

Lewis, Karen K., "Can Learning Affect Exchange Rate Behavior? The Case of the Dollar in the Early 1980s," *Journal of Monetary Economics*, vol. 23, 1989, pp. 79–100.

Magee, Stephen P., "Currency Contracts, Pass-Through, and Devaluation," *Brookings Papers on Economic Activity*, 1:1973, pp. 303–325.

——, "Contracting and Spurious Deviations from Purchasing Power Parity," in Jacob A. Frenkel and Harry G. Johnson, eds., *The Economics of Exchange Rates*, Reading, Mass.: Addison-Wesley, 1978, pp. 67–74.

Manzur, Meher, "An International Comparison of Prices and Exchanges Rates: A New Test of Purchasing Power Parity," *Journal of International Money and Finance*, March 1990, pp. 75–91.

Maldonado, Rita, and Anthony Saunders, "Foreign Exchange Restrictions and the Law of One Price," *Financial Management*, Spring 1983, pp. 19–23.

Mann, Catherine L., "Prices, Profit Margins, and Exchange Rates," *Federal Reserve Bulletin*, June 1986, pp. 366–379.

Meese, Richard, and Kenneth Rogoff, "Was It Real? The Exchange Rate-Interest Differential Relation over the Modern Floating-Rate Period," *Journal of Finance*, September 1988, pp. 933–948.

Melvin, Michael, and David Bernstein, "Trade Concentration, Openness, and Deviations from Purchasing Power Parity," *Journal of International Money and Finance*, December 1984, pp. 369–376.

Mishkin, Frederick S., "Are Real Interest Rates Equal Across Countries? An Empirical Investigation of International Parity Conditions," *Journal of Finance*, December 1984, pp. 1345–1357.

Moffett, Michael H., "The J-Curve Revisited: An Empirical Examination for the United States," *Journal of International Money and Finance*, 1989, pp. 425–444.

Officer, Lawrence H., "The Purchasing Power-Parity Theory of Exchange Rates: A Review Article," *IMF Staff Papers*, March 1976, pp. 1–60.

——, "The Productivity Bias for Purchasing Power Parity," *International Monetary Fund Staff Papers*, November 1976, pp. 545–579.

Officer, Lawrence H., Edward I. Altman, and Ingo Walter, eds., *Purchasing Power Parity and Exchange Rates: Theory, Evidence, and Relevance*, Contemporary Studies in Economic and Financial Analysis, Vol. 35, London: JAI Press, 1982.

Ohno, Kenichi, "Exchange Rate Fluctuations, Pass-Through, and Market Share," *IMF Staff Papers*, 37, no. 2, June 1990, pp. 294–310.

Oxelheim, Lars, *International Financial Market Fluctuations*, Somerset, N.J.: Wiley, 1985.

Roll, Richard W., and Bruno H. Solnik, "A Pure Foreign Exchange Asset Pricing Model," *Journal of International Economics*, May 1977, pp. 161–179.

So, Jacky C., "The Distribution of Foreign Exchange Price Changes: Trading Day Effects and Risk Measurement—A Comment," *Journal of Finance*, March 1987, pp. 181–188.

Somanath, V. S., "Exchange Rate Expectations and the Current Exchange Rate: A Test of the Monetarist Approach," *Journal of International Business Studies*, Spring/Summer 1984, pp. 131–140.

Taylor, Dean, "Official Intervention in the Foreign Exchange Market, or Bet against the Central Bank," *Journal of Political Economy*, April 1982, pp. 356–368.

Taylor, Mark P., "Covered Interest Parity: A High-Frequency, High-Quality Data Study," *Economica*, 54, no. 216, November 1987, pp. 429–438.

Wihlborg, Clas, "Interest Rates, Exchange Rate Adjustments, and Currency Risks: An Empirical Study, 1967–1975," *Journal of Money, Credit and Banking*, February 1982, pp. 58–75.

Williamson, John, *Equilibrium Exchange Rates: An Update*, Washington, D.C.: Institute for International Economics, 1990.

Wolff, Christian C. P., "Forward Foreign Exchange Rates, Expected Spot Rates, and Premia: A Signal Extraction Approach," *Journal of Finance*, June 1987, pp. 395–406.

Price Elasticity of Demand

The balance on current account is especially sensitive to changes in national price levels in both relative and absolute terms. If a country's exports increase in price faster than the same goods in competing countries, and exchange rates remain unchanged, the exports from the inflating country will probably be reduced in volume. The reverse is true of imports as relatively cheaper imports replace similar higher-priced domestic goods. The economic concept of price elasticity of demand is a relevant measure of this effect. Price elasticity of demand is a measure of the relative change in quantity sold for a given percentage change in price. More specifically,

$$E_p = \frac{\% \Delta Q}{\% \Delta P} = \frac{\Delta Q / Q}{\Delta P / P}$$

where

E_p = price elasticity of demand
ΔQ = change in quantity sold
Q = quantity sold
ΔP = change in price, and
P = original price.

For example, suppose the delivered price of British sweaters in the United States increases by 10% in dollar terms, resulting in a 20% loss in number of sweaters sold. In this case price elasticity of demand would equal 20%/10% = 2. The British sweater exporter would end up with less total dollar revenue because the loss in volume would more than offset the higher dollar price. In fact, there will be a loss in total sales revenue if price elasticity of demand is greater than one. Products of this type are price elastic.

If price elasticity of demand is less than one, a gain in total sales revenue will result from an increase in price. In this case the product is price inelastic. The point where price elasticity of demand is equal to one is called unitary elasticity. Around this point there would be no net change in sales revenue for a small change in price.

Most products in mature industries (such as textiles, machine tools, and electrical appliances) tend to be price elastic, whereas necessary products in short supply are usually price inelastic. The U.S. International Trade Committee published a study in August 1975 that estimated the relative price elasticity of imports compared to domestic substitutes. The commission studied 20 products that were being considered for U.S. tariff reductions. A tariff reduction would lower the relative price of an imported product compared to its U.S. domestic substitute. Among products with the highest import price sensitivity (all much greater than one) were footwear (leather and rubber), synthetic fibers, leather gloves, toys and games, passenger cars, and silverware. The lowest price elasticities (all less than one) were attributed to watches and clocks, veneer and plywood, fabric dress and work gloves, cutlery, and typewriters.

If a country's exports are predominantly price elastic, as is the case for the United Kingdom, a relatively high rate of inflation will cause a large negative impact on the balance of goods and services, unless offset by devaluation of the currency. Devaluation of the pound, in the U.K. example, could lower prices of U.K. exports in foreign currency terms if the prices of its exports are unchanged in pounds. On the other hand, if U.K. exporters maintain fixed foreign currency prices despite the devaluation, there would probably be no change in volume or sales revenue in foreign currency terms. Sales revenue in pounds would increase because of the more favorable exchange rate, but the pounds received would be worth less in real purchasing power because of domestic British inflation.

The same reasoning can be applied to imports. If a country's imports are price elastic, relatively high domestic inflation will cause a disproportionately large increase in imports because of the lower prices of imports in pound terms. An overvalued exchange rate, such as that experienced by the United States in 1981–1985, should have the same kind of impact on imports. They would appear to be low-priced compared to competing domestically produced goods.

Income Elasticity of Demand

In a fashion similar to price elasticity, income elasticity of demand measures the relative change in quantity sold for a given percentage change in income. More specifically,

$$E_Y = \frac{\%\Delta Q}{\%\Delta Y} = \frac{\Delta Q / Q}{\Delta Y / Y}$$

where

E_Y = income elasticity of demand,
ΔQ = change in quantity sold,
Q = original quantity sold,
ΔY = change in income, and
Y = original income.

For example, suppose that personal disposable income in the United States increased in real terms by 5%, and this situation caused a 10% increase in sweaters purchased. Income elasticity of demand is therefore 2, and we say that sales of sweaters are income elastic. In our example of the British sweater exporter, British exporters might increase sales revenue because of the income elasticity of sales of sweaters in general. Of course, if the British sweater exporter does not raise the price, it might receive the full benefit of the income effect.

In addition to the level of national income, other factors that influence a country's balance on current account include barriers to trade such as tariffs, quotas, and other "invisible" barriers. These can protect some countries from imports at the expense of others. Changes in relative productivity over the long run might change the relative price situation and through price elasticity of demand influence trade volume. New discoveries of scarce raw materials, such as oil, can have a profound effect. This was the case for the

United Kingdom, the Netherlands, and Norway, which were the prime beneficiaries of North Sea oil and gas discoveries. Technology gaps develop periodically to give some country a temporary advantage, such as the semiconductor industry in the United States or automobiles in Japan. Government subsidies, or tied development aid, can create exports that would otherwise not occur. Crop failures have occasionally given food exporters such as the United States, Canada, Australia, New Zealand, Brazil, and Argentina temporary bonanzas on exports.

BIBLIOGRAPHY

U.S. International Trade Commission, *Foreign Trade Elasticities for Twenty Industries.* Washington, D.C.: USITC Publication 738, August 1975.

CHAPTER 7

Managing Operating Exposure

Foreign exchange exposure is a measure of the potential for a firm's profitability, net cash flow, and market value to change because of a change in exchange rates. An important task of the financial manager is to measure foreign exchange exposure and to manage it in such a way as to maximize the profitability, net cash flow, and market value of the firm.

TYPES OF FOREIGN EXCHANGE EXPOSURE

What happens to a firm when foreign exchange rates change? The effect can be measured in several ways. Exhibit 7.1 shows schematically the three main types of foreign exchange exposure: operating, transaction, and accounting.

Operating Exposure

Operating exposure, sometimes called economic exposure, measures the change in the present value of the firm that results from changes in future operating cash flows caused by an *unexpected* change in exchange rates. The change in value depends on the effect of the exchange rate change on future sales volume, prices, and costs.

Transaction Exposure

Transaction exposure measures changes in the value of outstanding financial obligations incurred prior to a change in exchange rates but not due to be settled until after the

185

Exhibit 7.1   Conceptual Comparison of Difference Between Operating, Transaction, and Accounting Foreign Exchange Exposure

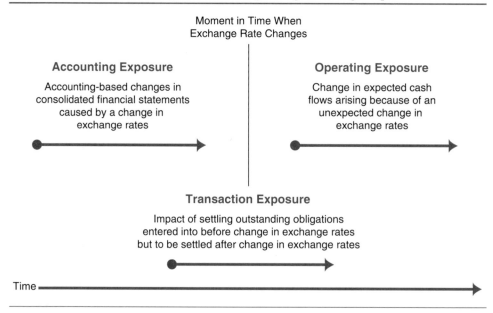

exchange rates change. Transaction exposure thus deals with changes in cash flows that result from existing contractual obligations.

Accounting Exposure

Accounting exposure, sometimes called translation exposure, measures potential accounting-derived changes in owners' equity that result from the need to "translate" foreign currency financial statements of affiliates into a single reporting currency in order to prepare worldwide consolidated financial statements.

Tax Implications of Foreign Exchange Exposure

The tax consequence of foreign exchange exposure varies by country, but as a general rule only *realized* foreign exchange losses are deductible for purposes of calculating income taxes. Similarly, only *realized* gains create taxable income. "Realized" means that the loss or gain involves cash flows.

Losses from transaction exposure usually reduce taxable income in the year in which they are realized. Losses from operating exposure reduce taxable income over a series of future years. Accounting losses, however, are not realized and so are not deductible. Some steps taken to minimize one or another of the types of exposure, such as entering into a forward exchange contract, create taxable income or loss. Other steps taken to obtain the same protection have no income tax implications. Since tax exposure is determined by the country of domicile of each affiliate, a multinational firm needs to plan its foreign exchange management policies, other things being equal, to minimize the worldwide after-tax consequences of foreign exchange losses and maximize after-tax gains.

The rest of this chapter analyzes how operating exposure is measured and how its risk is managed. Chapter 8 analyzes transaction exposure management and Chapter 9 analyzes accounting exposure measurement and management.

OPERATING EXPOSURE

Operating exposure is far more important for the long-run health of a business entity than changes caused by transaction or translation exposure. However, operating exposure is inevitably subjective because it depends on estimates of future cash flow changes over an arbitrary time horizon. Thus operating exposure does not spring from the accounting process but rather derives from operating analysis. Planning for operating exposure is a total management responsibility because it involves the interaction of strategies in finance, marketing, purchasing, and production.

An *expected* change in foreign exchange rates is not included in the definition of operating exposure because both management and investors should have factored this information into their evaluation of expected operating results and market value. From a management perspective, budgeted financial statements already reflect information about the effect of an expected change in exchange rates. For example, under equilibrium conditions the forward rate might be used as an unbiased predictor of the future spot rate. In such a case management would use the forward rate when preparing the operating budgets, rather than assume the spot rate would remain unchanged.

Another example is that expected cash flow to amortize debt should already reflect the international Fisher effect. The level of expected interest and principal repayment should be a function of expected exchange rates rather than existing spot rates.

From an investor's perspective, if the foreign exchange market is efficient, information about expected changes in exchange rates should be widely known and thus reflected in a firm's market value. Only unexpected changes in exchange rates, or an inefficient foreign exchange market, should cause market value to change.

IMPACT OF OPERATING EXPOSURE

An unexpected change in exchange rates impacts a firm's expected cash flows at four levels, depending on the time horizon used.[1]

Short Run

The first-level impact is on expected cash flows in the one-year operating budget. The gain or loss depends on the currency of denomination of expected cash flows. The currency of denomination cannot be changed for existing obligations, such as those defined by transaction exposure, or even for implied obligations such as purchase or sales commitments. Apart from real or implied obligations, in the short run it is difficult to change sales prices or renegotiate factor costs. Therefore realized cash flows will differ from those expected in the budget. However, as time passes, prices and costs can be changed to reflect the new competitive realities caused by a change in exchange rates.

Medium Run: Equilibrium Case

The second-level impact is on expected medium-run cash flows, such as those expressed in two- to five-year budgets, assuming equilibrium conditions among foreign exchange rates, national inflation rates, and national interest rates. Under equilibrium conditions the firm should be able to adjust prices and factor costs over time to maintain the expected level of cash flows. In this case the currency of denomination of expected cash flows is not as important as the countries in which cash flows originate. National monetary, fiscal, and balance of payments policies determine whether equilibrium conditions will exist and whether firms will be allowed to adjust prices and costs.

If equilibrium exists continuously, and a firm is free to adjust its prices and costs to maintain its expected competitive position, its operating exposure may be zero. Its expected cash flows would be realized and therefore its market value unchanged since the exchange rate change was anticipated. However, it is also possible that equilibrium conditions exist but the firm is unwilling or unable to adjust operations to the new competitive environment. In such a case the firm would experience operating exposure because its realized cash flows would differ from expected cash flows. As a result, its market value might also be altered.

Medium Run: Disequilibrium Case

The third-level impact is on expected medium-run cash flows assuming disequilibrium conditions. In this case the firm may not be able to adjust prices and costs to reflect the new competitive realities caused by a change in exchange rates. The firm's realized cash flows will differ from its expected cash flows. The firm's market value may change because of the unanticipated results.

Long Run

The fourth-level impact is on expected long-run cash flows, meaning those beyond five years. At this strategic level a firm's cash flows will be influenced by the reactions of existing and potential competitors to exchange rate changes under disequilibrium conditions. In fact, all firms that are subject to international competition, whether they are purely domestic or multinational, are exposed to foreign exchange operating exposure in the long run whenever foreign exchange markets are not continuously in equilibrium.

ILLUSTRATION OF OPERATING EXPOSURE

To illustrate the consequences of operating exposure in the short- and medium-run cases, we will develop a hypothetical example based on Instruments Napoleon, S.A., the wholly owned French affiliate of Washington Controls, Inc., a U.S.-based multinational firm. From the perspective of Washington Controls, dollars invested in Instruments Napoleon have a 20% required rate of return after taxes.

Instruments Napoleon manufactures in France from French material and labor. Half of production is sold within France and half is exported to other EEC countries. All sales are invoiced in French francs, and accounts receivable are equal to one-fourth of annual sales. In other words, the average collection period is 90 days. Inventory is also equal to one-fourth of annual sales and is carried at direct cost, which equals 75% of sales price. Instruments Napoleon can expand or contract production volume without any significant change in unit direct costs or in overall general and administrative expenses. Depreciation on plant and equipment is FF240,000 per year, and the corporate income tax rate in France is 50%. The December 31, 1992, balance sheet is as shown in Exhibit 7.2.

In the examples of Exhibit 7.2, we assume that on January 1, 1993, before any commercial activity begins, the French franc unexpectedly drops 20% in value, from FF6.40/$ to FF8.00/$. If no devaluation had occurred, Instruments Napoleon was expected to perform in 1993 as shown in Exhibit 7.2.

Operating exposure depends on whether an unexpected change in exchange rates causes unanticipated changes in sales volume, sales prices, or operating costs. In Chapter 4 (Appendix) we discussed the concepts of price and income elasticity of demand for a country's exports and imports. The same principles apply to a single firm, such as Instruments Napoleon. Following a devaluation of the French franc, Instruments Napoleon might choose to maintain its domestic sales prices constant in terms of French francs or try to increase domestic prices because competing imports might now be priced higher. The firm might choose to maintain export prices constant in terms of foreign currencies, or in terms of francs, or somewhere in between. The strategy followed depends to a large measure on price elasticity of demand.

On the cost side, Instruments Napoleon's costs might rise because of more expensive imported raw materials or components, or simply because all domestic prices in France have risen and labor is now demanding higher wages to compensate for domestic inflation.

Instruments Napoleon's domestic sales and costs might also be partly determined by the effect of a French devaluation on the income elasticity of demand. To the extent that the devaluation stimulates purchases of French goods in import-competing sectors of the economy as well as greater exports of French goods, both caused by initially more competitive prices of French goods, French national income should increase. This statement assumes that the favorable effect of a French devaluation on comparative prices is not immediately offset by higher French inflation. Thus Instruments Napoleon might be able to sell more goods domestically because of price and income effects and internationally because of price effects.

Exhibit 7.2   Instruments Napoleon, S.A.
Beginning Balance Sheet and Expected Cash Flows

Balance Sheet, December 31, 1992

Cash	FF 1,600,000	Accounts payable	FF 800,000
Accounts receivable	3,200,000	Short-term bank loan	1,600,000
Inventory	2,400,000	Long-term debt	1,600,000
Net plant and equipment	4,800,000	Common stock	1,800,000
		Retained earnings	6,200,000
	FF12,000,000		FF12,000,000

Expected Cash Flow, No Devaluation, 1993

Sales (1,000,000 units @ FF12.8/unit)	FF12,800,000
Direct costs (1,000,000 units @ FF9.6/unit)	9,600,000
Cash operating expenses (fixed)	1,200,000
Depreciation	240,000
Pretax profit	FF 1,760,000
Income tax expense (50%)	880,000
Profit after tax	FF 880,000
Add back depreciation	240,000
Cash flow from operations—in francs	FF 1,120,000

Existing exchange rate: FF6.40 = $1.00

Cash flow from operations—in dollars	$175,000

Expected Cash Flow, with Devaluation (Case 1)

Cash flow from operations—in francs (as above)	FF 1,120,000

New exchange rate: FF8.00 = $1.00

Cash flow from operations—in dollars	$ 140,000

To illustrate the effect of various post-devaluation scenarios on Instruments Napoleon's operating exposure, we will consider three simple cases:

1. no change in any variable;
2. increase in sales volume, other variables remain constant; and
3. increase in sales price, other variables remain constant.

To calculate the net change in present value under each of these scenarios, we will assume a five-year time horizon for any change in cash flow induced by the change in the franc/dollar exchange rate.

Case 1: No Change in Any Variable

Assume that in the five years ahead no changes occur in sales volume, sales price, or operating costs. Profits for the coming year in francs will be as expected, and cash flow from operations will be FF1,120,000. With a new exchange rate of FF8.00 per dollar, next year's cash flow measured in dollars will be FF1,120,000/8 = $140,000. The difference in first-year cash flow if a devaluation occurs at once will be:

Expected first-year cash flow, no devaluation	$175,000
Realized first-year cash flow, with devaluation	140,000
Decrease in first-year cash flow	$ 35,000

Instruments Napoleon thus experiences a drop of $35,000 in the dollar value of its French franc cash flow, and if this drop continues over the five-year time horizon, the total reduction in net cash flow will be $35,000 x 5 = $175,000. The discounted present value of this series of diminished dollar value cash flows will be considered later in this chapter.

Case 2: Volume Increases, Other Variables Remain Constant

Assume that sales within France double following the devaluation because French-made instruments are now more competitive with imports. Additionally, export volume doubles because French-made instruments are now cheaper in countries whose currencies have not weakened. The sales price is kept constant in French franc terms because management of Instruments Napoleon has not observed any change in local French operating costs.

Expected cash flow for the following year would be as described in Exhibit 7.3. The cash flow shown in the first year, however, is not available because a doubling of sales volume will require additional investment in accounts receivable and in inventory. Although a portion of this additional investment might be financed by increasing accounts payable, we will assume additional working capital is financed by cash flow from operations.

At the end of the first year accounts receivable would be equal to one-fourth of annual sales, or FF6,400,000. This amount is twice receivables of FF3,200,000 at the end of the prior year, and the incremental increase of FF3,200,000 must be financed from available cash. Year-end inventory would be equal to one-fourth of annual direct costs, or FF4,800,000, an increase of FF2,400,000 over the year-beginning level. At the end of five years these incremental cash outflows will be recaptured because any investment in current assets eventually rolls over into cash.

Assuming no further change in volume, price, or costs, cash inflows for the five years would be as described in Exhibit 7.3. In this instance the devaluation causes a change in first-year cash flow from the $175,000 anticipated in the first year without devaluation to a negative flow of $360,000. However, in the remaining four years cash flow is substantially enhanced by the operating effects of the devaluation. Over time Instruments Napoleon generates significantly more cash for its owners. The devaluation produced an operating *gain* over time, rather than an operating *loss*.

Exhibit 7.3   Instruments Napoleon, S.A.

Expected Cash Flow, Volume Increases (Case 2)

Sales (2,000,000 units @ FF12.8/unit)	FF25,600,000
Direct costs (2,000,000 units @ FF9.6/unit)	19,200,000
Cash operating expenses (fixed)	1,200,000
Depreciation	240,000
Pretax profit	FF 4,960,000
Income tax expense (50%)	2,480,000
Profit after tax	FF 2,480,000
Add back depreciation	240,000
Cash flow from operations—in francs	FF 2,720,000

New exchange rate: FF8.00 = $1.00

Cash flow from operations—in dollars	$340,000

Projected Cash Flows for 5 years

Year	Item	Francs	Dollars @FF8/$
1	Cash flow from operations	FF2,720,000	
	Less new investment in working capital	–5,600,000	
		–FF2,880,000	–$360,000
2	Cash flow from operations	2,720,000	340,000
3	Cash flow from operations	2,720,000	340,000
4	Cash flow from operations	2,720,000	340,000
5	Cash flow from operations	2,720,000	340,000
	Incremental working capital recapture in last year	5,600,000	700,000

The reason Instruments Napoleon is better off in Case 2 following the devaluation is that sales volume doubled while the per-unit dollar-equivalent sales price fell only 20%. In other words, the product faced a price elasticity of demand greater than one.

Case 3: Sales Price Increases, Other Variables Remain Constant

Assume that the franc sales price is raised 25%, from FF12.8 to FF16 per unit, in order to preserve the original dollar-equivalent unit sales price of $2.00/unit. Assume further that volume remains constant in spite of this price increase; that is, customers expect to pay the same dollar-equivalent price, and local costs do not change.

The situation would be as described in Exhibit 7.4. In this instance Instruments Napoleon is better off following the devaluation than it was before because the sales price, pegged to the international price level, increased but volume did not drop. The new level

Exhibit 7.4 Instruments Napoleon, S.A.

Expected Cash Flow, Sales Price Increase (Case 3)

Sales (1,000,000 units @ FF16.0/unit)	FF16,000,000
Direct costs (1,000,000 units @ FF9.6/unit)	9,600,000
Cash operating expenses (fixed)	1,200,000
Depreciation	240,000
Pretax profit	FF 4,960,000
Income tax expense (50%)	2,480,000
Profit after tax	FF 2,480,000
Add back depreciation	240,000
Cash flow from operations—in francs	FF 2,720,000

> New exchange rate: FF8.00 = $1.00

Cash flow from operations—in dollars	$340,000

Projected Cash Flows for 5 years

Year	Item	Francs	Dollars @FF8/$
1	Cash flow from operations	FF2,720,000	
	Less new investment in working capital	−800,000	
		FF1,920,000	$240,000
2	Cash flow from operations	2,720,000	340,000
3	Cash flow from operations	2,720,000	340,000
4	Cash flow from operations	2,720,000	340,000
5	Cash flow from operations	2,720,000	340,000
	Incremental working capital recapture in last year	800,000	100,000

of accounts receivable would be one-fourth of the new sales level of FF16,000,000, or FF4,000,000, an increase of FF800,000. No additional investment in inventory would be necessary.

Hence cash flow for the first five years would be as shown in Exhibit 7.4. Expected cash flow in every year exceeds the cash flow of $175,000 that had been anticipated with no devaluation. The increase in working capital causes net cash flow to be only $240,000 in the first year, but thereafter the cash flow is $340,000 per year.

The key to this improvement is in operating leverage. If costs are incurred in francs and do not increase after a devaluation, an increase in the sales price by the amount of devaluation will lead to sharply higher profits.

Other Possibilities

If any portion of sales revenues were incurred in other currencies, the situation would be different. The firm might leave the foreign sales price alone, in effect raising the French-

Exhibit 7.5 Summary of Operating Loss Following Devaluation for Instruments Napoleon, S.A.: Three separate cases (thousands of U.S. dollars)

	No Devaluation	Case 1	Case 2	Case 3
Exchange rate (FF/$)	6.4	8.0	8.0	8.0
Sales units (million)	1.0	1.0	2.0	1.0
Price per unit (FF)	12.8	12.8	12.8	16.0
Cost per unit (FF)	9.6	9.6	9.6	9.6

Year	Annual Cash Flows No Devaluation	CF^1	ΔCF^2	CF^1	ΔCF^2	CF^1	ΔCF^2
1	175	140	-35	-360	-535	240	65
2	175	140	-35	340	165	340	165
3	175	140	-35	340	165	340	165
4	175	140	-35	340	165	340	165
5	175	140	-35	340	165	340	165
5 wc	0	0	0	700	700	100	100

Operating Loss: Incremental Present
Value at 20% discount rate[3] | | -104.8 | | +191.7 | | +450.3 |

[1] Cash flows (CF) in thousands of U.S. dollars resulting from new set of operating assumptions.
[2] Change in cash flows (ΔCF) from base case of no devaluation.
[3] Present value of change in cash flow stream from base case.

franc-equivalent price; or it might leave the French-franc-equivalent price alone, in effect lowering the foreign sales price in an attempt to gain volume. Or, of course, it could position itself between these two extremes. Depending on elasticities and the proportion of foreign to domestic sales, total sales revenue might rise or fall.

Similarly, if some or all raw materials or components were imported and paid for in harder currencies, after-devaluation franc operating costs would increase with a drop in the value of the franc. Another possibility is that local franc costs rise after a devaluation. One cannot generalize for all countries of the world; nevertheless, local costs usually rise with some time lag following a devaluation. In each individual country, therefore, management must estimate how devaluation will affect the firm's sales revenue, sales volume, and local costs over a period of time.

Measurement of Loss

In Exhibit 7.5 the change in expected cash flows for the three cases is summarized and compared with the cash flow expected should no devaluation occur. The top portion of Exhibit 7.5 restates the expected cash flows for the three cases. The center portion shows the change in cash flow compared to the nondevaluation situation. The lowest portion shows the gain or loss from these changes in future cash flows. This should be determined by their present value, using a discount rate of 20%, which is Washington Controls' required rate of return.

In Case 1, in which nothing changes after the franc is devalued, Washington Controls incurs an operating loss of $104,800. In Case 2, in which volume doubled with no price change after the devaluation, Washington Controls experiences an operating gain of $191,700. In Case 3, in which the franc sales price was increased and volume did not change, the operating gain from devaluation was $450,300. An almost infinite number of combinations of volume, price, and cost could follow a devaluation, and any or all of them might become effective soon after a devaluation or only after the passage of some time.

MANAGING OPERATING EXPOSURE

The objective of operating exposure management is to anticipate and influence the effect of unexpected changes in exchange rates on a firm's future cash flows, rather than merely hoping for the best. To meet this objective, management must not only recognize a disequilibrium condition when it occurs, but must already have prepared the firm to react in the most appropriate way. *This task can best be accomplished if a firm diversifies internationally both its operations and its financing base.* Diversifying operations means diversifying sales, location of production facilities, and raw material sources. Diversifying the financing base means raising funds in more than one capital market and in more than one currency.

Depending on management's risk preference, a diversification strategy permits the firm to react either actively or passively to opportunities presented by disequilibrium conditions in the foreign exchange, capital, and product markets. Furthermore, such a strategy does not require management to predict disequilibrium but only to recognize it when it occurs.

Diversifying Operations

If a firm's operations are diversified internationally, management is pre-positioned both to recognize disequilibrium when it occurs and to react competitively. Consider the case where purchasing power parity is temporarily in disequilibrium. Although the disequilibrium may have been unpredictable, management can often recognize its symptoms as soon as they occur. For example, management might notice a change in comparative costs in the firm's own plants located in different countries. It might also observe changed profit margins or sales volume in one area compared to another, depending on price and income elasticities of demand and competitors' reactions.

Recognizing a temporary change in worldwide competitive conditions permits management to make changes in operating strategies. Management might make marginal shifts in sourcing raw materials, components, or finished products. If spare capacity exists, production runs can be lengthened in one country and reduced in another. The marketing effort can be strengthened in export markets where the firm's products have become more price competitive because of the disequilibrium condition.

Even if management does not actively distort normal operations when exchange rates change, the firm should experience some beneficial portfolio effects. The variability of its cash flows is probably reduced by international diversification of its production, sourcing, and sales because exchange rate changes under disequilibrium conditions are likely to increase the firm's competitiveness in some markets while reducing it in others. In that case operating exposure would be neutralized.

In contrast to the internationally diversified multinational firm, a purely domestic firm might be subject to the full impact of foreign exchange operating exposure even though it does not have foreign currency cash flows. For example, it could experience intense import competition in its domestic market from competing firms producing in countries with undervalued currencies. Domestic and Japanese personal computer manufacturers were both made aware of this problem when Korean personal computers captured a share of the U.S. market in the late 1980s. The Korean won was probably undervalued relative to both the U.S. dollar and the Japanese yen.

A purely domestic firm does not have the option to react to an international disequilibrium condition in the same manner as a multinational firm. In fact, a purely domestic firm will be mispositioned to recognize that a disequilibrium exists because it lacks comparative data from its own internal sources. By the time external data are available from published sources, it is often too late to react. Even if a domestic firm recognizes the disequilibrium condition, it cannot quickly shift production and sales into foreign markets in which it has had no previous presence.

Diversifying Financing

If a firm diversifies its financing sources, it will be pre-positioned to take advantage of temporary deviations from the international Fisher effect. If interest rate differentials do not equal expected changes in exchange rates, opportunities to lower a firm's cost of capital will exist. However, to be able to switch financing sources, a firm must already be well known in the international investment community, with banking contacts firmly established. Once again, this is not an option for a domestic firm that has limited its financing to one capital market.

In addition to diversifying capital market sources to take advantage of unexpected interest differentials, a multinational firm can reduce its default risk by matching the mix of currencies it borrows to the mix of currencies it expects to receive from operations. A number of firms use this strategy to neutralize transaction and translation exposure in addition to operating exposure. Nevertheless, this strategy is difficult to implement in practice because a firm cannot predict either magnitude or currency of denomination of cash flows very far into the future. In fact, unexpected changes in exchange rates may alter the very flows management is trying to predict, thus changing the currency mix to be matched.

Although we recommend diversification as a strategy for foreign exchange risk management, such a strategy has a potentially favorable impact on other risks as well. In particular, it could reduce the variability of future cash flows due to domestic business cycles, provided these are not perfectly correlated with international cycles. It could increase the availability of capital, also reducing its cost, by diversifying such risks as restrictive capital market policies or government borrowing competition in the capital market. It could diversify political risks such as expropriation, war, blocked funds, or just unfavorable changes in laws that reduce or eliminate profitability. The list of advantages from international diversification can even be extended to such areas as spreading the risk of technological obsolescence and reducing portfolio risk in the context of the capital asset pricing model—but now we are preempting the diversification strategy theme that appears throughout the rest of this book.

Constraints exist that may limit the feasibility of a diversification strategy for foreign exchange risk management or one of the other risks just mentioned. For example, the technology of a particular industry may require such large economies of scale that it is not economically feasible to diversify production locations. Firms in this industry could still diversify sales and financing sources, however. On the other hand, the firm may be too small or too unknown to attract international equity investors or lenders. Yet it could at least diversify its sales internationally. Thus a diversification strategy can only be implemented as far as is feasible.

"Currency Developments May Impact 1991 Results"*

(Novo Nordisk A/S, Denmark (insulin and industrial enzymes))

Novo Nordisk A/S Executive Vice President and Chief Financial Officer, Kurt Anker Nielsen, stated today in an article in the Company's monthly employee newsletter that if the exchange rates of Novo Nordisk's main invoicing currencies remain at the present low level throughout 1991, the Company's currency hedging gains will be small in 1991. That will, all other things being equal, make it more difficult to increase earnings in 1991.

Mr. Nielsen also reiterated Novo Nordisk's previously stated outlook for 1990: Novo Nordisk expects that income before tax in 1990 will exceed income before tax in 1989, provided that the value of the Danish krone against the Company's major invoicing currencies does not decrease significantly before December 31, 1990.

More than 80% of Novo Nordisk's sales are invoiced in foreign currencies, however, the majority of the Company's cost base is denominated in Danish kroner. Currency developments have had a positive impact on costs incurred in Danish kroner due to low inflation, while foreign sales translated into Danish kroner at low exchange rates have affected the Company's turnover negatively by some 400–500 million Danish kroner in the first nine months of 1990. These developments, combined with Novo Nordisk's reported gains on foreign debt in 1990 and the absence of a similar gain in 1991 under the assumption that currency exchange rates remain stable, will place heavy demands on the

*Courtesy of Novo Nordisk, Denmark.

Company's adaptability and encourage tight cost control to counteract the impact of the strong Danish krone in 1991. Following is a copy of the article in Novo Nordisk's internal employee newsletter, *Dialogue*.

Novo Nordisk is a major force in insulin production and diabetes care and is the world's largest producer of industrial enzymes. The company also manufactures and markets a variety of other pharmaceutical and bioindustrial products. Headquartered in Denmark, Novo Nordisk employs more than 8,000 people in over 30 countries and markets its products in 120 countries. Its B shares are listed on the stock exchanges in Copenhagen, London, Basel, Zurich and Geneva. Its ADSs are listed on the New York Stock Exchange under the symbol "NVO."

DIALOGUE: Currency Developments

Novo Nordisk's earnings are significantly affected by the strong Danish krone. However, owing to the company's hedging strategy, the impact will only make itself felt in the 1991 results. Tight cost control therefore is a must if the effect of the relatively high krone exchange rate is to be eliminated.

Novo Nordisk is an international company which markets its products in largely every country around the world. However, the majority of its costs are incurred in Denmark, primarily in the form of wages and salaries to staff at the Danish companies. Novo Nordisk furthermore has a large number of Danish suppliers of goods and services. This situation is characteristic of nearly all Danish export companies. As a result, these companies—including Novo Nordisk—are very sensitive to currency movements. *Dialogue* has talked with Kurt Anker Nielsen, Executive Vice President, Corporate Finance, in order to clarify how it affects Novo Nordisk and its employees.

At the beginning of 1990 Novo Nordisk's management was very pessimistic as regards realizing a better result than in 1989 because of the low currency exchange rates. Have things turned out as bad as you anticipated then?

> Yes, definitely—worse, in fact. The currency exchange rates have had a very significant impact on our results in 1990. Just look at turnover and net income for the first nine months of 1990. Our turnover would have been some DKK 400–500 million bigger if the average currency exchange rates from the first nine months of 1989 had prevailed, and this increased turnover would naturally also have increased our profit significantly.

And yet Management reiterated, both in the half year statement and in the three quarters statement that Novo Nordisk expects that income before tax for 1990 will exceed income before tax realised in 1989?

> That's correct—and we will maintain that expectation despite the present currency exchange rates, but naturally assuming that the value of the Danish krone does not decrease significantly before December 31, 1990.

Why December 31, 1990?

> Because when we finalize the accounts for 1990, we have to enter our foreign debt in terms of Danish kroner at the rates of exchange ruling on December 31, and if the value of the

Danish krone is lower then than it is now—that is, the foreign currencies increase—we'll incur a 'loss' on the foreign debt. We'll simply have to spend more money on paying off our debt.

Does that mean that Novo Nordisk is better off with a strong krone and thus "low" exchange rates of the US dollar, Japanese yen, etc.?

No, on the contrary. High dollar, yen, and sterling rates are best for Novo Nordisk, no doubt about that; but at the moment and for the next half month we would prefer stable currency exchange rates so that we can avoid a loss on our foreign debt without a chance of obtaining a similar currency 'gain' on our current payments.

So, what are your expectations for the currency exchange rates in 1991 and what impact will they have on Novo Nordisk's sales and earnings?

On the whole, we agree with the economists who expect that the present low level of Novo Nordisk's main invoicing currencies will remain stable during most of 1991, and maybe even throughout the year. If this does prove correct, the currency effect will hit Novo Nordisk hard again, because not only will we have to change, on an ongoing basis, all incomes in dollars, yen, pounds, etc., to Danish kroner at the lower exchanges rates. But the opposite effect—that is, gains—on our foreign debt will to a large extent have been entered in the accounts for 1990 and thus will not benefit us in 1991.

Kurt Anker Nielsen adds that if the currency exchange rates remain at the present low level throughout 1991 or during most of the year, the hedging gains (gains on foreign debts etc.) will be small in 1991. That will make it more difficult to increase earnings, and therefore makes heavy demands on the organization's adaptability and a tight cost control in order to counteract the impact of the strong Danish krone. It shouldn't be forgotten, though, that the currency developments have contributed to creating a very low inflation rate in Denmark. This has naturally had a positive impact on Novo Nordisk' costs incurred in Danish kroner.

SUMMARY

- Foreign exchange exposure is a measure of the potential for a firm's profitability, net cash flow, and market value to change because of a change in exchange rates. The three main types of foreign exchange risk are operating, transaction, and accounting exposures.

- Operating exposure measures the change in value of the firm that results from changes in future operating cash flows caused by an unexpected change in exchange rates.

- An unexpected change in exchange rates impacts a firm's expected cash flow at four levels. These are (1) short run; (2) medium run, equilibrium case; (3) medium run, disequilibrium case; and (4) long run.

- The objective of operating exposure management is to anticipate and influence the effect of unexpected changes in exchange rates on a firm's future cash flow, rather than being forced into passive reaction to such changes as was described in the Instruments Napoleon case. This task can best be accomplished if a firm diversifies internationally both its operations and its financing base.

1. Instruments Napoleon (C07A.WK1)

For Instruments Napoleon (see facts in the chapter), assume that the domestic sales price remains the same, because of local price controls or competition in France. Assume that the export price (in francs) rises by 25%, from FF12.8 to FF16.0, and thus preserves the original foreign-currency-equivalent sales price of $2.00/unit. Assume further that volume in both markets remains the same, because no buyer perceives that the price has changed.

a) What are the impacts on cash flow?
b) What are the impacts on working capital?
c) What are the valuation consequences?

2. Instruments Napoleon (C07A.WK1)

For Instruments Napoleon, assume that both domestic and foreign sales prices in francs increase 25% to FF16.0. Assume further that direct costs and cash operating costs also increase by 25%, possibly because of local inflation and because imported raw materials and components rise in franc terms as a result of the franc's depreciation. Volume remains the same.

    a) What are the impacts on cash flow?
    b) What are the impacts on working capital?
    c) What are the valuation consequences?

3. Operating Gains and Currency Depreciation

Explain why it is possible to have an operating gain when the currency in which a foreign affiliate operates drops in value.

4. Novo Nordisk A/S

According to Kurt Anker Nielsen, a change in value of the Danish krone versus its invoicing currencies during the next few weeks would adversely impact its 1990 earnings.

    a) Explain its effect on operating earnings during the rest of 1990.
    b) What would be its effect on Novo Nordisk's financing costs?
    c) What would Kurt Anker Nielsen like to see happen to Novo Nordisk's invoicing currency values in 1991? Why?

NOTES

1. This four-level approach is developed more fully in theory and with an extended case (Novo Industri A/S) in Arthur I. Stonehill, Niels Ravn, and Kåre Dullum, "Management of Foreign Exchange Economic Expo- sure," In Göran Bergendahl, ed., *International Finan- cial Management*, Stockholm: Norstedt & Soners, 1982, pp. 128–148.

BIBLIOGRAPHY

Abuaf, Niso, "The Nature and Management of For- eign Exchange Risk," *Midland Corporate Fi- nance Journal*, Fall 1986, pp. 30–44.

Adler, Michael, and Bernard Dumas, "Exposure to Currency Risk: Definition and Measurement," *Financial Management*, Spring 1984, pp. 41–50.

Booth, Laurence, and Wendy Rotenberg, "Assessing Foreign Exchange Exposure: Theory and Appli- cation Using Canadian Firms," *Journal of Inter- national Financial Management and Account- ing*, volume 2, no. 1, Spring 1990, pp. 1–22.

Dufey, Gunter, "Corporate Finance and Exchange Rate Variations," *Financial Management*, Sum- mer 1972, pp. 51–57.

——, "Funding Decisions in International Compa- nies," in Goran Bergendahl, ed., *International Financial Management*, Stockholm: Norstedts, 1982, pp. 29–53.

Dufey, Gunter, and S. L. Srinivasulu, "The Case for Corporate Management of Foreign Exchange Risk," *Financial Management*, Winter 1983, pp. 54–62.

Eaker, Mark R., and Dwight Grant, "Optimal Hedg- ing of Uncertain and Long-Term Foreign Ex- change Exposure," *Journal of Banking and Fi- nance*, June 1985, pp. 222–231.

Flood, Eugene, Jr., and Donald R. Lessard, "On the Measurement of Operating Exposure to Ex- change Rates: A Conceptual Approach," *Finan- cial Management*, Spring 1986, pp. 25–36.

Giddy, Ian H., "Exchange Risk: Whose View?" *Fi- nancial Management*, Summer 1977, pp. 23–33.

Hekman, Christine R., "Don't Blame Currency Values for Strategic Errors," *Midland Corporate Finance Journal*, Fall 1986, pp. 45–55.

——, "A Financial Model of Foreign Exchange Exposure," *Journal of International Business Studies*, Summer 1985, pp. 83–99.

——, "Measuring Foreign Exchange Exposure: A Practical Theory and Its Application," *Financial Analysts Journal*, September/October 1983, pp. 59–65.

Jacque, Laurent L., *Management of Foreign Ex- change Risk: Theory and Practice*, Lexington, Mass.: Heath, 1978.

——, "Management of Foreign Exchange Risk: A Review Article," *Journal of International Busi- ness Studies*, Spring/Summer 1981, pp. 81–101.

Jorion, Philippe, "The Exchange-Rate Exposure of U.S. Multinationals," *Journal of Business*, 63, no. 3, July 1990, pp. 331–345.

Kwok, Chuck C. Y. "Hedging Foreign Exchange Exposures: Independent vs. Integrative Ap- proaches," *Journal of International Business Studies*, Summer 1987, pp. 33–52.

Lessard, Donald R., and S. B. Lightstore, "Volatile Exchange Rates Can Put Operations at Risk," *Harvard Business Review*, July/August 1986, pp. 107–114.

Levich, Richard M., and Clas G. Wihlborg, eds., *Exchange Risk and Exposure*, Lexington, Mass.: Lexington Books, 1980.

Luehrman, Timothy A., "The Exchange Rate Expo- sure of a Global Competitor," *Journal of Inter- national Business Studies*, 21, no. 2, 1990, pp. 225–242.

Pringle, John J., "Managing Foreign Exchange Exposure," *Journal of Applied Corporate Finance*, vol 3, no. 4, Winter 1991, pp. 73–82.

Shapiro, Alan C., and David P. Rutenberg, "Managing Exchange Risks in a Floating World," *Financial Management*, Summer 1976, pp. 48–58.

Stonehill, Arthur I., Niels Ravn, and Kåre Dullum, "Management of Foreign Exchange Economic Exposure," in Göran Bergendahl, ed., *International Financial Management*, Stockholm: Norstedts, 1982, pp. 128–148.

Wihlborg, Clas, "Economics of Exposure Management of Foreign Subsidiaries of Multinational Corporations," *Journal of International Business Studies*, Winter 1980, pp. 9–18.

Managing Transaction Exposure

Like economic exposure, foreign exchange transaction exposure is concerned with unexpected changes in future cash flows, but over a shorter time horizon. The purpose of this chapter is to analyze how transaction exposure is measured and managed.

CAUSES OF TRANSACTION EXPOSURE

Transaction exposure measures gains or losses that arise from the settlement of financial obligations whose terms are stated in a foreign currency. Transaction exposure arises from:

1. purchasing or selling on credit goods or services whose prices are stated in foreign currencies,

2. borrowing or lending funds when repayment is to be made in a foreign currency,

3. being a party to an unperformed foreign exchange forward contract, and

4. otherwise acquiring assets or incurring liabilities denominated in foreign currencies.

The most common example of transaction exposure arises when a firm has a receivable or payable denominated in a foreign currency. Exhibit 8.1 demonstrates how this exposure is born. The total transaction exposure consists of quotation, backlog, and billing exposures. A transaction exposure is actually created at the first moment the seller quotes a price in foreign currency terms to a potential buyer (t_1). The quote can be either verbally, as in a telephone quote, or in the form of a written bid, or even a printed price list. With the placing of an order (t_2), the *potential exposure* created at the time of the quotation (t_1), is converted into that of an actual *transaction exposure* which now constitutes a

Exhibit 8.1   The "Life Span" of a Transaction Exposure

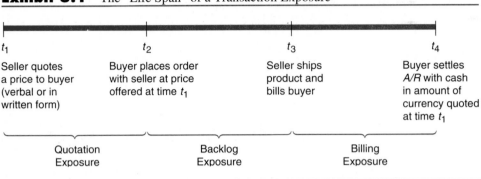

significant currency exposure to the seller. The transaction exposure exists until actual payment is received by the seller (t_4).

Purchasing or Selling on Open Account

Suppose that a U.S. firm sells merchandise on open account to a Belgian buyer for Bf700,000, payment to be made in 60 days. The current exchange rate is Bf35/$, and the U.S. seller expects to exchange the Bf700,000 for $20,000 when payment is received.

Transaction exposure arises because of the risk that the U.S. seller will receive something other than $20,000. For example, if the exchange rate were Bf38/$ when payment was received, the U.S. seller would receive only Bf700,000 ÷ Bf38/$ = $18,421, some $1,579 less than anticipated. Had the exchange rate gone to Bf33/$, however, the seller would have received $21,212, an increase of $1,212 over the amount expected. Thus, exposure is the chance of either a loss or a gain.

The U.S. seller might have avoided transaction exposure by invoicing the Belgian buyer in dollars. Of course, if it attempted to sell only in dollars it might not obtain the sale in the first place. Avoiding transaction exposure by not having sales is counterproductive to the well-being of the firm! Even if the Belgian buyer agrees to pay in dollars, transaction exposure is not eliminated. Instead it is transferred to the Belgian buyer, whose dollar account payable has an unknown cost in Belgian francs 60 days hence.

Borrowing and Lending

A second example of transaction exposure arises when funds are borrowed or loaned, and the amount involved is denominated in a foreign currency. For example, Britain's Beecham Group borrowed SF100 million in 1971 at a time when that amount of Swiss francs was worth £10.13 million. When the loan came due five years later the cost of repayment of principal was £22.73 million—more than double the amount borrowed. The London *Sunday Times*, August 22, 1976, termed this transaction loss "an expensive lump of lolly!"

Other Causes of Transaction Exposure

When a firm buys a forward exchange contract, it creates transaction exposure on purpose. This is usually done in order to hedge an existing transaction exposure. For example, a U.S. firm might want to offset an existing obligation to purchase DM1 million to pay for an import from Germany in 90 days. As will be shown in more detail in the next section, one way to hedge this payable is to purchase DM1 million in the forward market for delivery in 90 days. In this manner any change in value of the mark relative to the dollar will be neutralized. For example, if the mark increases in value, the account payable will have cost more dollars, a transaction loss; but the forward contract has already fixed the amount of dollars needed to buy the DM1 million. Thus the potential transaction loss, or gain, on the account payable has been offset by the transaction gain or loss on the forward contract.

Note that cash balances do not create transaction exposure, even though their foreign exchange value changes immediately with a change in exchange rate. This is because no legal obligation exists to move the cash from one country and currency to another. If such an obligation did exist, it would show on the books as a payable or receivable and then be counted as part of transaction exposure. Nevertheless, the foreign exchange value of cash balances does change when exchange rates change.

CONTRACTUAL HEDGES

Transaction exposure can be managed by contractual techniques and by adopting certain operating strategies. The main contractual techniques use hedges in the forward, money, futures, and options markets, as well as swap agreements, mainly back-to-back loans, currency swaps, or credit swaps. Operating strategies include the use of leads and lags in payment terms and establishment of reinvoicing centers. We will explain contractual techniques in this section, followed by operating strategies in the following section.

To illustrate how contractual hedging techniques may be used to protect against transaction exposure, consider an example in which Dayton, a U.S. manufacturing firm, sells a gas turbine generator to Crown, a British firm, in March for £1,000,000. Payment is due three months later, in June. Dayton's cost of capital is 12%. The following quotes are available.

Spot exchange rate: $1.7640/£

Three-month forward rate: $1.7540/£ (a 2.2676% per annum discount on the pound)

U.K. three-month borrowing interest rate: 10.0% (or 2.5%/quarter)

U.K. three-month investment interest rate: 8.0% (or 2.0%/quarter)

U.S. three-month borrowing interest rate: 8.0% (or 2.0%/quarter)

U.S. three-month investment interest rate: 6.0% (or 1.5%/quarter)

June put option on the Philadelphia Stock Exchange: £31,250; strike price $1.75; 2.5 cents per pound premium; brokerage cost $50 per contract

June put option in the over-the-counter (bank) market £1,000,000; strike price $1.75; 1.5% premium

Dayton's foreign exchange advisory service forecasts that the spot rate in three months will be $1.76/£.

Four alternatives are available to Dayton:

- Remain unhedged.
- Hedge in the forward market.
- Hedge in the money market.
- Hedge in the options market.

Unhedged Position

Dayton may decide to accept the transaction risk. If the firm believes its foreign exchange advisor, it expects to receive £1,000,000 x $1.76 = $1,760,000 in three months. However, that amount is at risk. If the pound should fall to, say, $1.65, Dayton would receive only $1,650,000. Exchange risk is not one-sided, however; if the transaction were left uncovered and the pound strengthened even more than forecast by the advisor, Dayton could receive considerably more than $1,760,000.

The essence of an unhedged approach is as follows.

(Today)

Do nothing.

(Three months hence)

Receive £1,000,000.
Sell £1,000,000 spot.
Receive dollars at spot
rate existing then.

Forward Market Hedge

A "forward hedge" involves a forward (or futures) contract and a source of funds to fulfill that contract. The forward contract is entered into at the time the transaction exposure is created. In Dayton's case, that would be in March, when the sale to Crown was booked as an account receivable. Funds to fulfill the contract will be available in June, when Crown pays £1,000,000 to Dayton. If funds to fulfill the forward contract are on hand or are due because of a business operation, the hedge is considered "covered," "perfect," or "square" because no residual foreign exchange risk exists. Funds on hand or to be received are matched by funds to be paid.

In some situations funds to fulfill the forward exchange contract are not already available or due later, but must be purchased in the spot market at some future date. Such a hedge is "open" or "uncovered." It involves considerable risk because the hedger must take a chance on purchasing foreign exchange at an uncertain future spot rate in order to fulfill the forward contract. Purchase of such funds at a later date is referred to as "covering." There is an old financial saying that is appropriate for an uncovered forward obligation:

> He who sells what isn't his'n
> Must buy it back or go to prison![1]

Should Dayton wish to hedge its transaction exposure in the forward market, it will sell £1,000,000 forward today at the three-month forward quotation of $1.7540 per pound. This is a "covered transaction" in which the firm no longer has any foreign exchange risk. In three months the firm will receive £1,000,000 from the British buyer, deliver that sum to the bank against its forward sale, and receive $1,754,000. This certain sum is $6,000 less than the uncertain $1,760,000 expected from the unhedged position because the forward market quotation differs from the firm's three-month forecast.

The essence of a forward hedge is as follows.

If Dayton's forecast of future rates were identical to that implicit in the forward quotation, that is, $1.7540, expected receipts would be the same whether or not the firm hedges. However, realized receipts under the unhedged alternative could vary considerably from the certain receipts when the transaction is hedged. Belief that the forward rate is an unbiased estimate of the future spot rate does not preclude use of the forward hedge to eliminate the risk of an unexpected change in the future spot rate.

Money Market Hedge

Like a forward market hedge, a money market hedge also involves a contract and a source of funds to fulfill that contract. In this instance the contract is a loan agreement. The firm seeking the money market hedge borrows in one currency and exchanges the proceeds for another currency. Funds to fulfill the contract—that is, to repay the loan—may be generated from business operations, in which case the money market hedge is "covered." Alternatively, funds to repay the loan may be purchased in the foreign exchange spot market when the loan matures. In this instance the money market hedge is "uncovered" or "open."

A money market hedge can cover a single transaction, such as Dayton's £1,000,000 receivable, or repeated transactions. Hedging repeated transactions is called *matching*. It requires the firm to match the expected foreign currency cash inflows and outflows by currency and maturity. For example, if Dayton had numerous sales denominated in pounds to British customers over a long period of time, it would have somewhat predictable U.K.

pound cash inflows. The appropriate money market hedge technique would be to borrow U.K. pounds in an amount matching the typical size and maturity of expected pound inflows. Thus, if the pound depreciates or appreciates, the foreign exchange effect on cash inflows in pounds would be offset by the effect on cash outflows in pounds from repaying the pound loan plus interest.

The structure of a money market hedge resembles that of a forward hedge. The difference is that the cost of the money market hedge is determined by differential interest rates, while the cost of the forward hedge is a function of the forward rate quotation. In efficient markets interest rate parity should ensure that these costs are nearly the same, but not all markets are efficient at all times. Furthermore, the difference in interest rates facing a private firm borrowing in two separate national markets may be different than the difference in risk-free government bill rates in these same markets. It is the latter differential that is relevant for interest rate parity.

To hedge in the money market, Dayton will borrow pounds in London at once, immediately convert the borrowed pounds into dollars, and repay the pound loan in three months with the proceeds from the sale of the generator. How much should Dayton borrow? It will need to borrow just enough to repay both the principal and interest with the sale proceeds. The borrowing interest rate will be 10% per annum, or 2.5% for three months. Therefore, assuming that x is the amount of pounds to borrow, we obtain

$$1.025x = £1,000,000$$
$$x = £975,610.$$

Dayton should borrow £975,610 and in three months repay that amount plus £24,390 of interest from the sale proceeds. Dayton should exchange the £975,610 loan proceeds for dollars at the current spot exchange rate of $1.7640/£, receiving $1,720,976 at once.

In order to compare the forward hedge with the money market hedge it is necessary to analyze how Dayton's loan proceeds will be utilized for the next three months. Remember that the loan proceeds are received today but the forward contract proceeds are received in three months. Therefore one needs to calculate either the future value in three months of the loan proceeds or the present value of the forward contract proceeds. We will use future value for pedagogical reasons, but correct use of present value would give the same comparative results.

Since both the forward contract proceeds and the loan proceeds are relatively certain, it is possible to make a clear choice between the two alternatives based on the one that yields the higher dollar receipts. This result, in turn, depends on the assumed rate of investment of the loan proceeds.

At least three logical choices exist for an assumed investment rate for the loan proceeds for the next three months. First, if Dayton is cash rich, the loan proceeds might be invested in U.S. dollar money market instruments that have been assumed to yield 6% per annum. Second, Dayton might simply use the pound loan proceeds to substitute for an equal dollar loan that it would otherwise have undertaken at an assumed rate of 8% per annum. Third, Dayton might invest the loan proceeds in the general operations of the firm, in which case the cost of capital of 12% per annum would be the appropriate rate. The future value of the loan proceeds at the end of three months under each of these three investment assumptions would be as follows.

Received today	Invested at	Future value in three months
$1,720,976	6%/yr or 1.5%/quarter	$1,746,791
$1,720,976	8%/yr or 2.0%/quarter	$1,755,396
$1,720,976	12%/yr or 3.0%/quarter	$1,772,605

Since the proceeds in three months from the forward hedge would be $1,754,000, the money market hedge would be superior to the forward hedge if Dayton used the loan proceeds to replace a dollar loan (8%) or to conduct general business operations (12%). The forward hedge would be preferable if Dayton merely invested the pound loan proceeds in dollar-denominated money market instruments at 6% annual interest.

A break-even investment rate can be calculated that would make Dayton indifferent between the forward hedge and the money market hedge. Assume that r is the unknown three-month investment rate, expressed as a decimal, that would equalize the proceeds from the forward and money market hedges. We have

$$\text{(Loan proceeds)} (1 + \text{rate}) = \text{(forward proceeds)},$$
$$\$1,720,976 (1 + r) = \$1,754,000,$$
$$r = 0.0192.$$

One can convert this three-month investment rate to an annual whole percentage equivalent as follows:

$$0.0192 \times 4 \times 100 = 7.68\%.$$

In other words, if Dayton can invest the loan proceeds at a rate higher than 7.68% per annum, it would prefer the money market hedge. If Dayton can only invest at a lower rate than 7.68%, it would prefer the forward hedge.

The essence of a money market hedge is as follows.

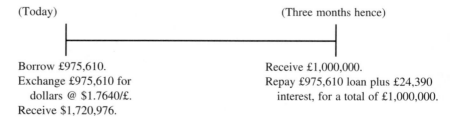

(Today)   (Three months hence)

Borrow £975,610.   Receive £1,000,000.
Exchange £975,610 for   Repay £975,610 loan plus £24,390
  dollars @ $1.7640/£.   interest, for a total of £1,000,000.
Receive $1,720,976.

Options Market Hedge

Dayton could also cover its £1,000,000 exposure by purchasing a *put* option. This technique allows Dayton to speculate on the upside potential for appreciation of the pound while limiting downside risk to a known amount.

Given the quotes shown earlier, Dayton could purchase a put option on the Philadelphia Stock Exchange having a June expiration date, a strike price of 175, a premium cost of 2.50 cents per pound, and a contract size of £31,250. The cost of this option is as follows.

Premium cost per option ($0.025 x £31,250)	$ 781.25
Brokerage cost per option	50.00
Total cost per option	$ 831.25
Option cost per pound ($831.25/£31,250)	$0.02660
Number of options needed (£1,000,000/£31,250)	32
Total cost for 32 options (32 x $831.25)	$ 26,600

Dayton could also purchase from its bank a three-month put option on £1,000,000 at a strike price of $1.75 and a premium cost of 1.50%. The cost of this option is

$$\text{(Size of option)} \times \text{(premium)} \times \text{(spot rate)} = \text{(cost of option)},$$
$$£1,000,000 \times 0.015 \times \$1.7640 = \$26,460.$$

Therefore Dayton should purchase the over-the-counter put option from its bank because that option costs $140 less than the Philadelphia put option.

Since we are using future value to compare the various hedging alternatives, it is necessary to project the premium cost of the option forward three months. Once again one could justify several investment rates. We will use the cost of capital of 12% per annum or 3% per quarter. Therefore the premium cost of the put option as of June would be $26,460(1.03) = $27,254. This is equivalent to $0.0273 per pound ($27,254 ÷ £1,000,000).

When the £1,000,000 is received in June, the value in dollars depends on the spot rate at that time. The upside potential is unlimited, the same as in the unhedged alternative. At any exchange rate above $1.75/£ Dayton would allow its option to expire unexercised and would exchange the pounds for dollars at the spot rate. If the expected rate of $1.76/£ materialized, for example, Dayton would exchange the £1,000,000 in the spot market for $1,760,000. Net proceeds would be $1,760,000 minus the $27,254 cost of the option, or $1,732,746.

In contrast to the unhedged alternative, downside risk is limited with an option. If the pound depreciated below $1.75/£, Dayton would exercise its option to sell (put) £1,000,000 at $1.75/£, receiving $1,750,000 gross, but $1,722,746 net of the $27,254 cost of the option. Although this downside result is worse than the downside of the forward or money market hedges, the upside potential is not limited the way it is with those hedges. Thus, whether the option strategy is superior to a forward or money market hedge depends on the degree to which management is risk averse.

The essence of an option market hedge is as follows.

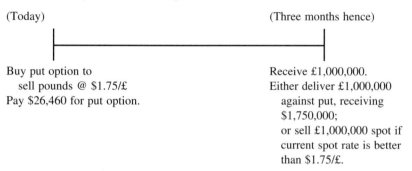

(Today)   (Three months hence)

Buy put option to   Receive £1,000,000.
  sell pounds @ $1.75/£   Either deliver £1,000,000
Pay $26,460 for put option.   against put, receiving
                                                     $1,750,000;
                                                 or sell £1,000,000 spot if
                                                 current spot rate is better
                                                 than $1.75/£.

We can calculate a trading range for the pound that defines the breakeven points for the option compared with the other strategies. The upper bound of the range is determined by comparison with the forward rate. The pound must appreciate enough above the $1.7540 forward rate to cover the $0.0273/£ cost of the option. Therefore the breakeven upside spot price of the pound must be $1.7540 + $0.0273 = $1.7813. If the spot pound appreciates above $1.7813, proceeds under the option strategy will be greater than under the forward hedge. If the spot pound ends up below $1.7813, the forward hedge would be superior in retrospect. Another way to compare the foreign currency option with the forward hedge in transaction exposure management is explained in Appendix A: Combining Puts and Calls, the Option Collar.

The lower bound of the range is determined by a comparison with the unhedged strategy. If the spot price falls below $1.75, Dayton will exercise its put option and sell the proceeds at $1.75. The net proceeds per pound will be $1.75 less the $0.0273 cost of the option, or $1.7221. If the spot rate falls below $1.7221, the net proceeds from exercising the option will be greater than the net proceeds from selling the unhedged pounds in the spot market. At any spot rate above $1.7221, the spot proceeds from the unhedged alternative will be greater.

Strategy Comparison

The four alternatives available to Dayton are shown in Exhibit 8.2. The forward hedge yields a certain $1,754,000 in three months. This would be equivalent to a money market hedge if the loan proceeds are invested at 7.68% per annum. At any higher rate, such as the 12% cost of capital, the money market hedge is preferable but at any lower rate the forward hedge is preferable.

If Dayton does not hedge, it can "expect" $1,760,000 in three months. However, this sum is at risk and might be greater or smaller. Under conditions when the forward rate is accepted as the most likely future spot rate, the expected results from an unhedged position are identical to the certain results from the forward hedge. Under such circumstances the advantage of hedging over remaining unhedged is the reduction of uncertainty.

The options market hedge has nearly the same upside potential as the unhedged alternative, except for the cost of the option, but limits the downside risk to receiving $1,722,746 net of premium cost.

Exhibit 8.2   Comparison of Alternative Hedging Strategies for Dayton

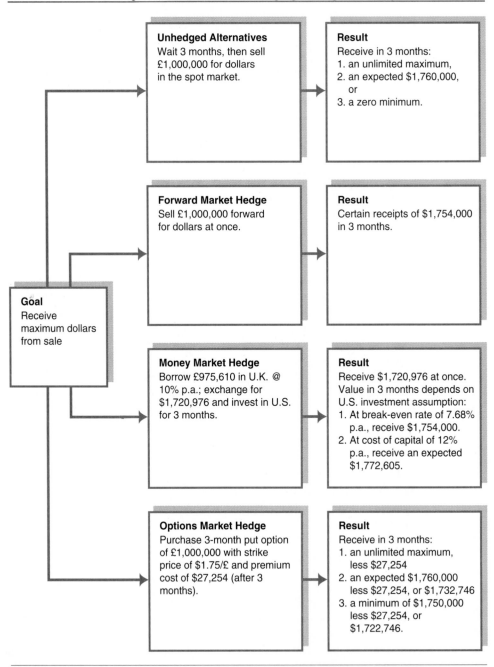

Goal
Receive maximum dollars from sale

Unhedged Alternatives
Wait 3 months, then sell £1,000,000 for dollars in the spot market.

Result
Receive in 3 months:
1. an unlimited maximum,
2. an expected $1,760,000, or
3. a zero minimum.

Forward Market Hedge
Sell £1,000,000 forward for dollars at once.

Result
Certain receipts of $1,754,000 in 3 months.

Money Market Hedge
Borrow £975,610 in U.K. @ 10% p.a.; exchange for $1,720,976 and invest in U.S. for 3 months.

Result
Receive $1,720,976 at once. Value in 3 months depends on U.S. investment assumption:
1. At break-even rate of 7.68% p.a., receive $1,754,000.
2. At cost of capital of 12% p.a., receive an expected $1,772,605.

Options Market Hedge
Purchase 3-month put option of £1,000,000 with strike price of $1.75/£ and premium cost of $27,254 (after 3 months).

Result
Receive in 3 months:
1. an unlimited maximum, less $27,254
2. an expected $1,760,000 less $27,254, or $1,732,746
3. a minimum of $1,750,000 less $27,254, or $1,722,746.

Foreign currency options have a variety of hedging uses beyond the one illustrated by Dayton. A put option can be useful to construction firms or other exporters when they must submit a fixed price bid in a foreign currency without knowing until some later date whether their bid is successful. A put option can be used to hedge the foreign exchange risk either for the bidding period alone or for the entire period of potential exposure if the bid is won. If the bid is rejected, the loss is limited to the cost of the option. In contrast, if the risk is hedged by a forward contract and the bid is rejected, the forward contract must be reversed or eventually fulfilled at an unknown potential loss or gain. The bidder has an uncovered forward contract.

Strategy Outcomes

The preceding section provided a comparison of the hedging strategies available to Dayton given its *expectations* regarding future events. Dayton, like all firms attempting to hedge transaction exposure, must decide on a strategy before the exchange rate changes occur. Exhibit 8.3 provides an evaluation of each potential strategy open to Dayton over a range of exchange rates which may occur at the end of the three month period.

The unhedged alternative's value is seen to rise at a constant rate as the £ strengthens, reflecting the actual spot rate at the end of the three month period. It's value does, however, fall substantially below all other hedge alternatives when the £ weakens (reaching $1.65 million at a future spot rate of $1.6500/£).

The value of both the money market hedge and the forward contract hedge is constant and certain. The money market hedge is, as noted previously, superior in this instance to the forward contract.

The flexibility of the foreign currency option is now obvious. The exact value of the option hedge is not known until the end of the period when the actual spot rate is known. The value of the put option is seen to rise in the same fashion as the unhedged position, thus allowing Dayton to benefit from an exchange rate moving in its favor, yet is bounded on the downside. Thus the lowest possible revenues received by Dayton never fall below $1,722,746. The option offers a compromise for the firm attempting to manage transaction exposure.

Swap Agreements

A foreign exchange swap is an agreement between two parties to exchange a given amount of one currency for another and, after a period of time, to give back the original amounts swapped. A transaction in the spot market matched by an offsetting transaction in the forward market—for example, covered interest arbitrage—is one type of swap arrangement. Other types of foreign exchange swap arrangements are the "back-to-back" or "parallel loan," the "currency swap," and the "credit swap." These are used to avoid foreign exchange transaction exposure prior to entering into a potentially risky venture. Hence they are usually negotiated before an exposed situation is created.

Back-to-Back, or Parallel, Loans. A back-to-back, or parallel, loan involves two business firms in separate countries arranging to borrow each other's currency for a

Exhibit 8.3   Valuation of Hedge Alternatives for Dayton at Ending Spot Rates

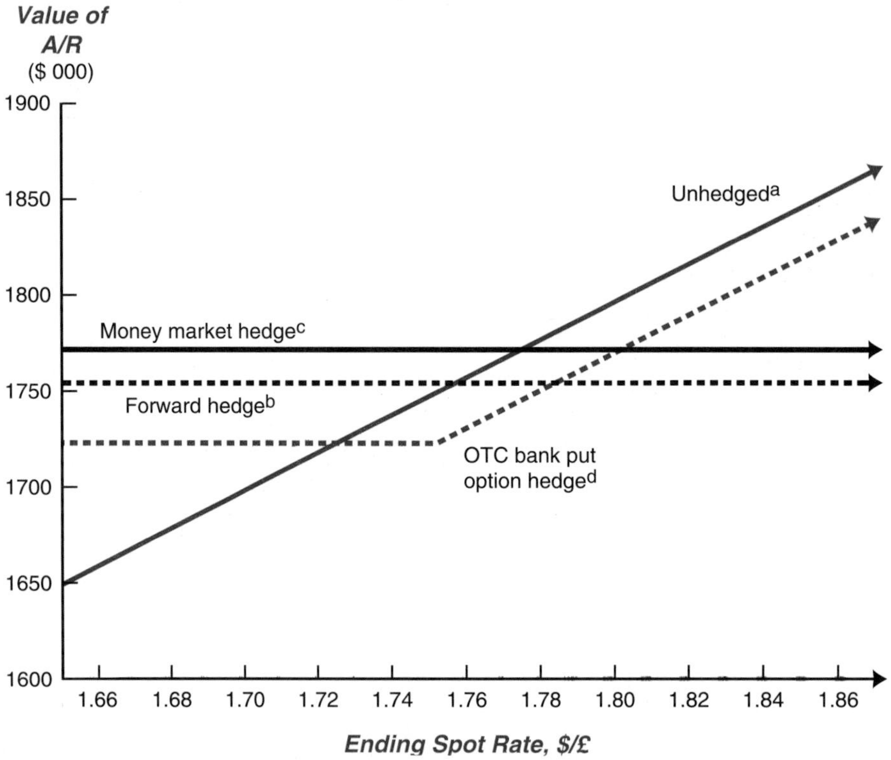

Value of
A/R
($ 000)

Unhedged[a]

Money market hedge[c]

Forward hedge[b]

*OTC bank put
option hedge[d]*

Ending Spot Rate, $/£

[a] Unhedged position of £1,000,000 varies directly with the $/£ ending spot rate.

[b] Forward contract hedge position is a constant £1,000,000 × $1.7540/£, or $1,754,000 in 90 days.

[c] Money market hedge value is a constant $1,772,605 in 90 days when carried forward at Dayton's weighted average cost of capital.

[d] OTC bank put option hedge value yields $1,732,746 in 90 days when exercised (at ending spot rates of $1.7500/£ or less). The OTC put option's value varies directly with the spot rate at ending spot rates above $1.7500/£, as Dayton exchanges its A/R of £1,000,000 at spot rates and chooses not to exercise the option, less the option's cost brought forward, $27,254.

specific period of time. At an agreed terminal date they return the borrowed currencies. The operation is conducted outside the foreign exchange markets, although spot quotations may be used as the reference point for determining the amount of funds to be swapped. Such a swap creates a covered hedge against exchange loss, since each company, on its own books, borrows the same currency it repays. Back-to-back loans are also used at a time of actual or anticipated legal limitations on the transfer of investment funds to or from either country.

The structure of a typical back-to-back loan is illustrated in Exhibit 8.4. In the basic swap, shown at the top of the exhibit, a British parent firm wanting to invest funds in its

Exhibit 8.4   Structure of a Back-to-Back, or Parallel, Loan

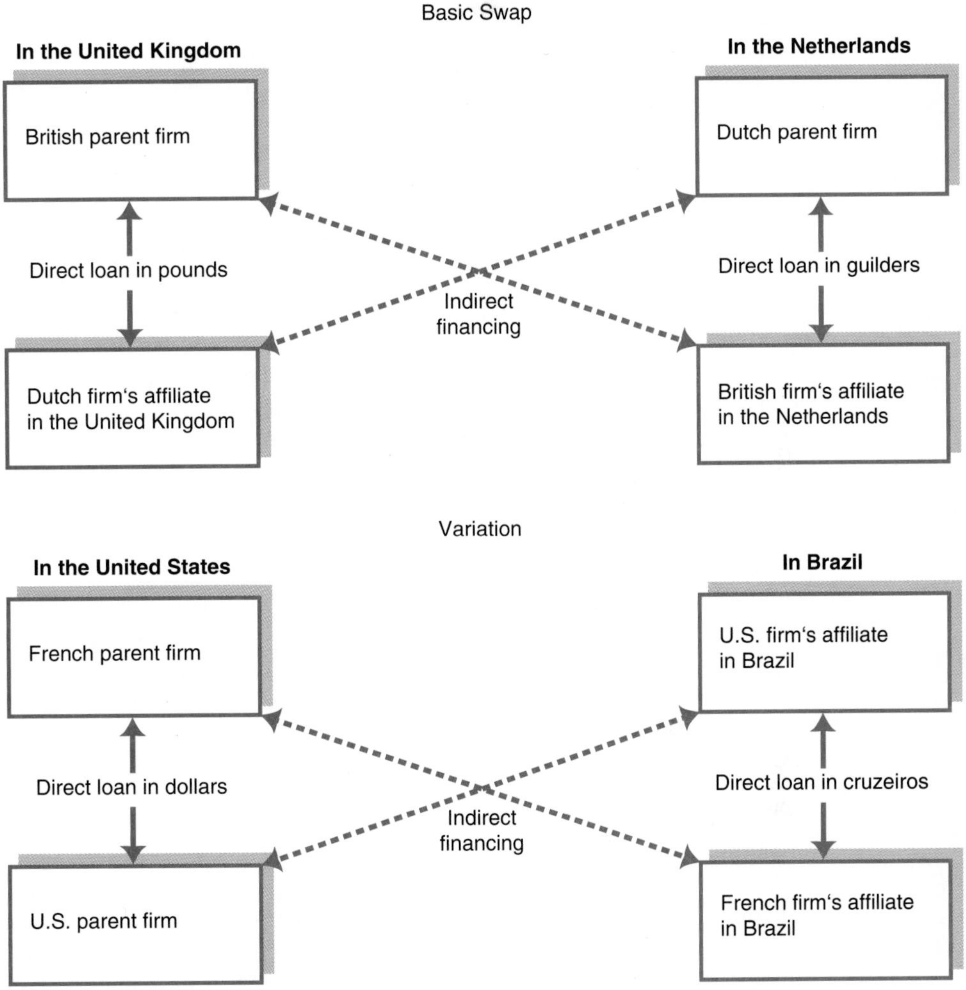

Basic Swap

In the United Kingdom   **In the Netherlands**

| British parent firm | | Dutch parent firm |

Direct loan in pounds   Indirect financing   Direct loan in guilders

| Dutch firm's affiliate in the United Kingdom | | British firm's affiliate in the Netherlands |

Variation

In the United States   **In Brazil**

| French parent firm | | U.S. firm's affiliate in Brazil |

Direct loan in dollars   Indirect financing   Direct loan in cruzeiros

| U.S. parent firm | | French firm's affiliate in Brazil |

Dutch affiliate locates a Dutch parent firm that wants to invest funds in the United Kingdom. Avoiding the exchange markets entirely, the British parent lends pounds to the Dutch affiliate in the United Kingdom, while the Dutch parent lends guilders to the British affiliate in the Netherlands. The two loans would be for equal values at the current spot rate and for a specified maturity. At maturity the two separate loans would each be repaid to the original lender, again without any need to use the foreign exchange markets. Neither loan carries any foreign exchange risk, and neither loan normally needs the approval of any governmental body regulating the availability of foreign exchange for investment purposes.

Parent company guarantees are not needed on the back-to-back loans because each loan carries the right of offset in the event of default of the other loan. A further agreement can provide for maintenance of principal parity in case of changes in the spot rate between the two countries. For example, if the pound dropped by more than, say, 6% for as long as 30 days, the British parent might have to advance additional pounds to the Dutch affiliate so as to bring the principal value of the two loans back to parity. A similar provision would protect the British if the guilder should weaken. Although this parity provision might lead to changes in the amount of home currency each party must lend during the period of the agreement, it does not increase foreign exchange risk, because at maturity all loans are repaid in the same currency loaned.

A number of variations may be developed on the basic swap theme, including use of foreign finance subsidiaries and triangular relationships. A variation involving blocked funds is shown in the bottom half of Exhibit 8.4. Assume that the Brazilian affiliate of a U.S. firm has cruzeiros in Brazil that it cannot remit to the United States because of Brazilian restrictions on the repatriation of funds. The Brazilian affiliate of the U.S. firm locates another foreign firm in Brazil that needs cruzeiros for expansion. In the example this is a French affiliate. In the example the U.S. affiliate in Brazil lends cruzeiros to the French affiliate, while in the United States the French parent lends dollars to the U.S. parent. Of course, it would be equally possible for the French parent to loan francs to the U.S. parent's affiliate in France. One can even imagine the French parent arranging for its affiliate in Egypt to loan Egyptian pounds to a U.S. affiliate in that country.

Interest may or may not be involved in a back-to-back loan, depending on whether internal interest rates in the two countries are similar or widely divergent. In one instance, for example, an interest rate differential of .75% was reported for such a loan between the United States and the United Kingdom, in comparison to a rate for hedging in the forward market of 2.75%.[2] In this particular instance a U.S.-based leasing firm loaned $10 million to a major U.S. machine tool manufacturer on behalf of a British firm that owed that sum to the U.S. equipment firm. The parallel part of the swap involved the British firm lending the pound equivalent of $10 million to the British affiliate of the U.S. leasing company. The British firm agreed to pay the U.S. leasing company 10% interest per annum in the United States, while the U.S. leasing affiliate in the United Kingdom paid interest at the rate of 10.75%. Some back-to-back loans are arranged with floating interest rates.

Currency Swap. A currency swap resembles a back-to-back loan except that it does not appear on a firm's balance sheet. Typically, two firms agree to exchange an equivalent amount of two different currencies for a specified period of time. Currency swaps can be negotiated for a wide range of maturities up to at least ten years. If funds are more expensive in one country than another, a fee may be required to compensate for the interest differential.

Accountants in the United States treat the currency swap as a foreign exchange transaction rather than as debt and treat the obligation to reverse the swap at some later date as a forward exchange contract. Forward exchange contracts can be matched against assets, but they are entered in a firm's footnotes rather than as balance sheet items. The result is that both accounting and transaction exposures are avoided, but neither a long-term receivable nor a long-term debt is created on the balance sheet. The risk of changes in currency rates to the implied collateral in a long-term currency swap can be treated with a clause similar to the maintenance-of-principal clause in a back-to-back loan. If exchange rates change by more than some specified amount, say 10%, an additional amount of the weaker currency might have to be advanced.

Credit Swap. A credit swap is an exchange of currencies between a business firm and a bank (often the central bank) of a foreign country, which is to be reversed at some future date.

The basic concept of a credit swap has been used for more than half a century between commercial banks, and between commercial banks and central banks, to satisfy temporary bank needs for foreign exchange. However, use of credit swaps between business firms and banks is a post-World War II development that arose when U.S. firms were financing affiliates in weak currency countries. The allure of a credit swap is its ability to reduce the need to finance a weak currency operation from a hard currency source.

An example would be a U.S. multinational firm wishing to finance its affiliate in Colombia. The U.S. parent deposits dollars to the account of a Colombian bank's New York correspondent, and in return, the Colombian bank in Bogota makes an equivalent loan in pesos to the U.S. firm's affiliate in Colombia. At a specified future date the transaction will be reversed; the U.S. firm's Colombian affiliate will repay the Colombian bank in Bogota the original quantity of pesos, and the Colombian bank will return the original dollar deposit in New York to the U.S. parent. Thus the U.S. parent recovers the original dollar principal advanced, regardless of what happens during the interim to the exchange rate between pesos and dollars. The Colombian bank receives an interest-free dollar deposit in its New York correspondent bank.

The swap rate at which dollars are deposited to obtain the foreign currency, and later the foreign currency exchanged to repay dollars, may or may not equal the market spot rate at the time the swap contract is negotiated. Usually the swap rate is disadvantageous to the business firm relative to the market spot rate. Thus if $1 could be exchanged for 270 pesos in the spot market, $1 might obtain only 150 pesos via the swap agreement. Consequently the dollar amount required to finance a foreign affiliate through a credit swap may substantially exceed the dollars needed to make the same investment through the foreign exchange market.

In a typical credit swap the foreign bank will charge local currency interest on the local currency loan extended to the U.S. affiliate. However, interest may or may not be paid by the foreign bank on the dollar credit made available to it.

A credit swap protects only the principal amount involved. It does not protect earnings on that principal that might be remitted to the parent, either as a return on the parent's investment or as a payment of any dollar interest charges incurred.

Foreign Exchange Contractual Hedging in Practice

Which of the various contractual hedging tools are most important to financial managers for hedging transaction exposure? A well-designed survey, undertaken in 1985 by Sarkis Khoury and K. Hung Chan, sheds some interesting light on this question.[3] Their questionnaire was designed to allow financial managers to rank the importance of each contractual hedging tool with respect to managing transaction and accounting exposure. The specific tools which were ranked, and the main characteristics of each, are presented in Appendix B. (Appendix B would also be a good summary review for readers who are feeling overwhelmed by the details of so many contractual tools.)

A total of 73 firms responded, based on a systematically selected sample of "Fortune 500" firms. Of these, 48 firms indicated they did no (contractual) hedging or minimal hedging. Another eight firms completed only part of the questionnaire. Seventeen firms completed the entire questionnaire.

The most important findings of the Khoury and Chan survey can be summarized as follows:

- A majority of the 78 firms did no or minimal contractual hedging.
- Based on the 17 completed questionnaires, the ranking of tools in order of importance was:
  1. forward contracts
  2. matching maturity and duration of exchange sensitive assets and liabilities
  3. futures contracts
  4. over-the-counter option contracts.
- Liquidity, flexibility, and certainty about cost were the most important factors in selecting a contractual hedging tool.
- Forward contracts were preferred to other tools because their cost was fixed and known, and their terms were flexible.
- Matching was also popular because of flexibility, effectiveness, liquidity, and self-reliance of the hedge.
- Futures contracts were considerably less used than forward contracts, but liquidity, cost, and profit potential of a futures hedge were desirable characteristics.
- Option contracts were used because of cost, effectiveness, flexibility, and the "optional" nature of the hedge. However, at the time of the survey, currency options were not as well understood or familiar as today.

OPERATING STRATEGIES

Transaction exposure can be partially managed by adopting operating strategies that have the virtue of offsetting existing foreign exchange exposure. The cost of adopting such strategies is less obvious than the cost of contractual arrangements because operations may become less efficient or at least distorted from what they might otherwise have been. On the other hand, sometimes rethinking operating procedures leads to new efficiencies that were previously not discovered.

Two operating strategies are particularly useful in managing transaction exposure. They are the use of leads and lags and of reinvoicing centers.

Leads and Lags: Retiming the Transfer of Funds

Firms can reduce transaction exposure by accelerating or decelerating the timing of payments that must be made or received in foreign currencies. To *lead* is to pay early. A firm holding a soft currency and having debts denominated in a hard currency will lead by using that soft currency to pay the foreign currency debts as soon as possible, before the soft currency drops in value. To *lag* is to pay late. A firm holding a hard currency and having debts denominated in a soft currency will lag by paying those debts late, hoping that less of the hard currency will be needed. If possible, firms will also lead and lag their collection of receivables, collecting soft foreign currency receivables early and collecting hard foreign currency receivables later.

Leading and lagging may be done between affiliates or with independent firms. Assuming that payments will be made eventually, leading or lagging always results in changing the cash and payables position of one firm, with the reverse effect on the other firm.

Leads and Lags Between Independent Firms

Leading or lagging between independent firms requires that the time preference of one firm be imposed to the detriment of the other firm. For example, a German firm may wish to lead in collecting its Italian accounts receivable that are denominated in lira because it expects the lira to drop in value compared with the Deutschemark. But why should the Italian customers prepay their accounts payable? Credit was part of the inducement for them to purchase from the German firm. The only way the Italians would willingly lead their accounts payable would be for the German creditor to offer them a discount about equal to the forward discount on the lira or, in equilibrium, the difference between Italian and German interest rates for the period of prepayment.

Leads and Lags Between Affiliates

Leading and lagging between related firms is more feasible because they presumably embrace a common set of goals for the consolidated group. Furthermore, periodic payments are often made between units of a multinational firm, providing the opportunity for many types of leads or lags. Reasons for such flows are shown in Exhibit 8.5. Some are for basic operational purposes, such as the shipment from one affiliate to another of raw material, goods, or partially assembled components. Payments may be made for the use of corporate facilities, such as ships, aircraft, and communication services, or for the use of technology or management services. Because opportunities for leading or lagging payments depend on the requirement for payments of this nature, the device is more readily adaptable to a company that operates on an integrated worldwide basis. If each unit functions as a separate and self-sufficient entity, opportunities for leading or lagging diminish.

Exhibit 8.5   Natural Fund Flows within a Multinational Corporate Network

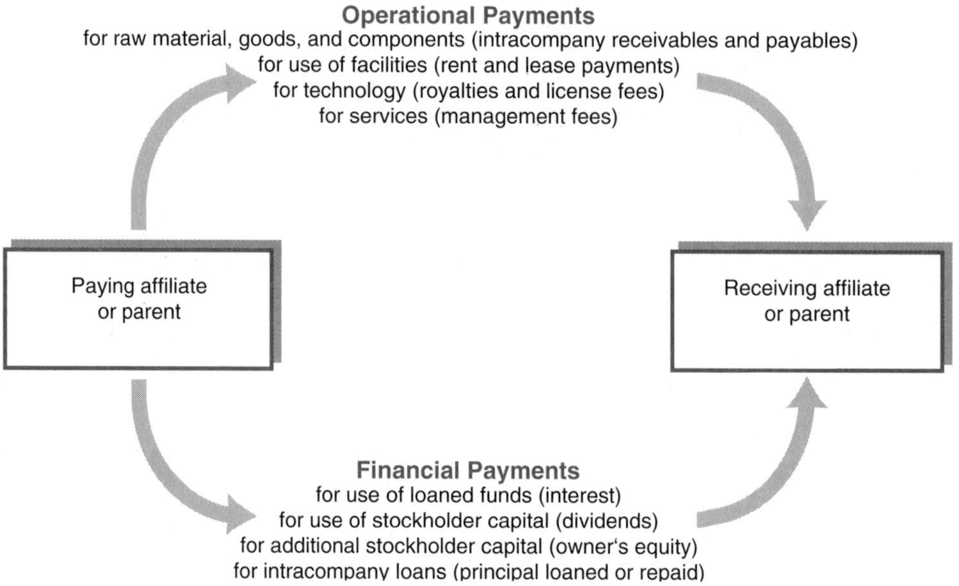

Operational Payments
for raw material, goods, and components (intracompany receivables and payables)
for use of facilities (rent and lease payments)
for technology (royalties and license fees)
for services (management fees)

| Paying affiliate or parent | | Receiving affiliate or parent |

Financial Payments
for use of loaned funds (interest)
for use of stockholder capital (dividends)
for additional stockholder capital (owner's equity)
for intracompany loans (principal loaned or repaid)

Another set of payment opportunities arises from the financing of foreign affiliates. As shown at the bottom of Exhibit 8.5, these may include interest payments, repaying principal on intracorporate loans, supplying owners' equity, and paying dividends to the owners. In addition to foreign exchange rate considerations, however, the motivation for early or late financial payments could be to position funds for liquidity reasons.

The use of leads and lags in conjunction with intracorporate family receivables is feasible only with 100% ownership of the various affiliates, because the economic effect of extended payment terms alters the relative rate of return of the various units. This practice is unfair if each unit has minority stockholders separate from the corporate family, since they do not necessarily benefit from practices that benefit the multinational firm as a whole. Inequities may also arise between various profit centers in a group of wholly owned affiliates unless adjustments are made to reflect a particular center's sacrifice. A necessary condition for efficient use of leads and lags is the ability of the parent to adjust its techniques for measuring profit or controlling investment in assets by its various affiliates so that the performance rating of units or of managers is not changed when one unit "helps" another for the good of the overall enterprise. This strategy is discussed in Chapter 20.

Because the use of leads and lags is an obvious technique for minimizing foreign exchange exposure and for shifting the burden of financing, many governments impose limits on the allowed range. *Business International*'s annual tabulation of allowed ranges is shown in Exhibit 8.6. *Business International* notes that terms allowed by governments are often subject to negotiation when a good argument can be presented. Thus, the ranges

Exhibit 8.6 Limits on Leads and Lags and Netting in Selected Countries (days)

Country	Export		Import		Netting
	lag	lead	lag	lead	
Argentina	180	360	120	120	No
Australia	Yes	Yes	Yes	Yes	Yes
Belgium	180	Yes	Yes	90	Some
Brazil	Some	Yes	180–8 yrs	No	No
Canada	Yes	Yes	Yes	Yes	Yes
Chile	90	90	120	No	No
Denmark	30	Yes	Yes	Some	Some
France	Yes	Yes	Yes	Some	Some
Germany	Yes	Yes	Yes	Yes	Yes
Greece	3 yrs	Yes	Yes	Yes	Yes
Hong Kong	Yes	Yes	Yes	Yes	Yes
India	180	Yes	180	Some	Some
Ireland	180	Yes	Yes	No	Yes
Italy	Yes	5 yrs	Yes	120	Yes
Japan	360	360	360	360	Some
Korea	180	Yes	120	No	Some
Malaysia	180	Yes	Yes	Yes	Yes
Mexico	Yes	Yes	Yes	Yes	No
Netherlands	Yes	Yes	Yes	Yes	Yes
Nigeria	No	Yes	Yes	Some	No
Norway	1 yr	Some	5 yrs	90	Some
Philippines	60	Yes	365	No	No
Singapore	Yes	Yes	Yes	Yes	Yes
South Africa	180	Yes	Yes	Some	Some
Spain	30	Yes	90	90	Some
Sweden	Yes	Yes	Yes	Some	Some
Switzerland	Yes	Yes	Yes	Yes	Yes
Taiwan	180	180	180	No	Some
Thailand	180	180	270	Yes	Some
United Kingdom	Yes	Yes	Yes	Yes	Yes
United States	Yes	Yes	Yes	Yes	Yes
Venezuela	No	No	No	No	Yes

Source: *Business International Money Report*, April 13, 1987, pp. 118–119. Reprinted with permission of the publisher, Business International Corporation, a member of the Economist Group, New York. See original source for footnotes omitted here. Unless otherwise noted, "Yes" indicates no limits on such activity. "Some" indicates specific conditions apply/permission required.

shown in Exhibit 8.6 are subject to exceptions; these are described in some 55 footnotes to the original table, which have not been reproduced in the exhibit. For example, Italy's "allowed—no limit" on export and import lags applies only to trade with other OECD countries. A 180-day limit on export lags and a five-year limit on import lags applies to trade with non-OECD countries.

Exhibit 8.7   Reinvoicing Center Structure

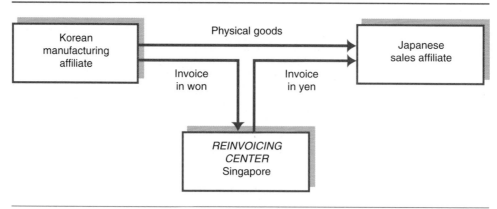

Reinvoicing Centers

A reinvoicing center is a separate corporate subsidiary that manages in one location all transaction exposure from intracompany trade. Manufacturing affiliates sell goods to distribution affiliates of the same firm only by selling to a reinvoicing center, which in turn resells to the distribution affiliate. Title passes to the reinvoicing center, but the physical movement of goods is direct from manufacturing plant to distribution affiliate. Thus the reinvoicing center handles paperwork but has no inventory.

As depicted in Exhibit 8.7, the Korean manufacturing unit of a multinational firm invoices the firm's reinvoicing center in Singapore in Korean won. The reinvoicing center in turn invoices the firm's Japanese sales affiliate in yen. Consequentially, all operating units deal only in their own currency, and all transaction exposure lies with the reinvoicing center.

To avoid charges of profit shifting through transfer pricing, most reinvoicing centers "resell" at cost plus a small commission for their services. The resale price is frequently the manufacturer's price times the forward exchange rate for the date on which payment from the distribution affiliate is expected, although other combinations are possible. The commission covers the cost of the reinvoicing center, but does not shift profits away from operating affiliates.

The reinvoicing center should avoid doing business with suppliers or customers in the country of location so that it will be able to establish nonresident status. Although the exact definition of and benefits of nonresident status vary from country to country, in general a finance subsidiary not doing any local business may be free of some taxes, such as interest withholding taxes or capital formation taxes. Nonresident firms may have greater access to external foreign exchange markets than local operating firms; they may be freer to deal in external currency markets, including Euromarkets; and they may be allowed to own bank accounts in foreign countries when that is restricted for domestic firms. Nonresident firms are usually not restricted in either borrowing from or investing with foreign banks.

The primary advantage of a reinvoicing center is that management of all foreign exchange transaction exposure for intracompany sales is centered in one location. Reinvoicing center personnel can develop a specialized expertise in choosing which hedging technique is best at any moment, and they are likely to obtain more competitive foreign exchange quotations from banks because they are dealing in larger transactions.

A second advantage is that by guaranteeing the exchange rate for future orders, the reinvoicing center can set firm local currency costs in advance. This enables distribution affiliates to make firm bids to unrelated final customers, and to protect against the exposure created by a backlog of unfilled orders. Backlog exposure does not appear on the corporate books because the sales are not yet recorded. Sales subsidiaries can focus on their marketing activities and their performance can be judged without distortion because of exchange rate changes.

A third advantage is the ability of the center to manage intra-affiliate cash flows, including leads and lags of payments. With a reinvoicing center all affiliates settle intracompany accounts in their local currencies. The reinvoicing center need only hedge residual foreign exchange exposure.

The main disadvantage is one of cost relative to benefits received. One additional corporate unit must be created, and a separate set of books must be kept. The initial setup cost can be high because existing order-processing procedures must be reprogrammed. The center will have an impact on the tax status and customs duties of all affiliates, as well as on the amount of foreign exchange business directed to local banks in each country. Establishment of a reinvoicing center is likely to bring increased scrutiny by tax authorities to be sure that it is not functioning as a tax haven. Consequently a variety of professional costs will be incurred for tax and legal advice, in addition to the costs of personnel operating the center.

Culver Radio, Inc.*

As Clyde Turner, president and owner of Culver Radio, entered his Los Angeles office on March 1, 1983, he received a cable indicating acceptance of Culver's offer to supply Klaus Pelzer, a West German distributor, with approximately one quarter million dollars of radio equipment for the remote opening of gates and garages in industrial plants and parking lots. The cable also indicated that Pelzer had wired the requested deposit of DM62,500 directly to Culver's West Los Angeles bank that same day.

Turner hoped the German order would mark the beginning of Culver's return to being profitable. Culver's 1982 net loss of $24,000 had been the combined result of a general recession in the United States and a lack of marketing effort to find new customers.

Culver Radio was formed in the mid-1960s to manufacture radio-activated controls for opening residential garage doors. California's boom in residential construction and the

---

*David K. Eiteman, University of California at Los Angeles, 1983, revised 1990. This case is based on the Dozier Industries case by Mark Eaker of the University of Virginia.

increase in suburban single family residences with two-car garages created the potential. The level of affluence of new home buyers in the 1960s and 1970s led to a willingness to spend about $400 to be able to open a garage door without having to first get out of the car. Sales rose rapidly and profits were more than adequate. In 1979, however, new housing construction tapered off. Culver's high quality meant that the replacement market was virtually zero, and sales began to slip.

Turner realized as early as 1978 that the suburban residential market would not regain its former strength, so he turned to development of an industrial version of his basic product. The industrial model was for use by delivery trucks and other vehicles entering or leaving warehouse compounds where security was important. An approaching or departing truck would notify plant security by radio of a desire to pass through the gate, but final control of the gate remained with plant security. Security could either activate the gates to open automatically on radio request from the truck, a common procedure during daylight hours; or it could control the actual gate directly, opening it after verification that the vehicle and driver were indeed authorized to enter or leave. The industrial model proved particularly useful in inner city areas where crime was a problem.

Sales of the industrial model in 1980 were good, but the recession of 1981 and 1982 caused a leveling out of sales volume while costs continued to rise with inflation. In 1981 Culver Radio experienced an operating loss, but interest income and profit from selling older equipment offset the loss. Net income for the year was positive. The 1982 operating loss was larger and was not offset by nonoperating income. Financial statements for Culver Radio for 1981 and 1982 appear in Exhibits 8.8 and 8.9.

To use idle capacity, Turner decided in 1982 to stress exports. A few foreign firms had purchased Culver's gate openers for use in their home country and had been pleased with the result. Culver Radio itself, however, had never solicited a foreign order. After discussion with the U.S. Department of Commerce International Marketing Center in Los Angeles, Turner contacted Klaus Pelzer, an industrial radio distributor in Karlsruhe, Germany. Turner flew to Frankfurt to demonstrate the Culver industrial model to Pelzer, and by Christmas of 1982 Pelzer indicated an interest in becoming the German distributor if costs seemed reasonable.

On February 1, 1983, Turner offered to sell Pelzer a shipment of radios and gate openers for DM562,500. The offer requested payment as follows:

DM 62,500	as a cash down payment at the time the offer was accepted by Pelzer.
DM 250,000	to be paid three months after the offer was accepted, by which time Culver would have shipped the first half of the order.
DM 250,000	to be paid six months after the offer was accepted, by which time Culver would have shipped the last half of the order
DM 562,500	

The price of DM562,500 was derived by pricing the order at $225,000 and multiplying this dollar price by DM2.50, the approximate exchange rate on February 1. The actual exchange rate of February 1 had been DM2.4734/$, but Turner rounded this up because of a weakness in the mark since the first of the year. Exchange quotations for the first nine weeks of 1983 are given in Exhibit 8.10.

Exhibit 8.8 Culver Radio, Inc., Statement of Income and Retained Earnings, years ending December 31, 1982, and December 31, 1981 (unaudited)

Item	1982	1981
Sales	$1,813,297	$1,855,585
Cost of Goods Sold		
Inventory, January	361,327	273,056
Purchases of materials—net	703,605	799,616
	1,065,932	1,072,672
Less inventory, December 31	438,402	361,328
Cost of materials consumed	626,531	711,344
Direct labor	247,860	222,912
Factory overhead	283,832	260,200
Cost of Goods Sold	$1,158,223	$1,194,456
Gross Profit	$ 655,074	$ 465,402
Expenses		
Selling expense	$ 466,360	$ 465,402
Warehouse and delivery expense	111,244	76,948
Administrative expense	187,616	193,138
Total Expense	$ 765,220	$ 735,488
Net (loss) from Operations	$(110,146)	$ (74,359)
Other Income		
Interest income	$ 28,339	$ 31,395
Miscellaneous income	58,349	74,178
Bad debt recovered	-0-	286
Total Other Income	$ 86,688	$ 105,959
Net Loss Before Provision for		
Federal and state taxes	$ (23,458)	$ 31,600
Provision for federal and state taxes	280	6,532
Net Loss	$ (23,738)	$ 25,068
Retained Earnings, January 1	224,805	199,737
Retained Earnings, December 31	$ 201,067	$ 224,805

Turner calculated his price of $225,000 as follows:

Raw material	$ 78,750
Direct labor	33,750
Factory overhead	36,000
Delivery expenses	6,750
Administrative overhead	22,500
Total costs	$177,750
Desired profit margin	47,250
Dollar price	$225,000
Times exchange rate	x 2.50
Deutschemark price	DM 562,500

Exhibit 8.9   Culver Radio, Inc., Balance Sheet, December 31, 1982, and December 31, 1981 (unaudited)

Assets	1982	1981
Current Assets		
Cash	$ 69,402	$170,987
Accounts receivable	99,966	104,374
Advances to employees	5,302	-0-
Due from officers	9,946	5,540
Inventory	438,402	361,327
Prepaid taxes	1,300	-0-
Total Current Assets	$624,318	$642,228
Fixed Assets		
Net fixed assets	$144,998	$121,773
Accumulated depreciation	81,579	57,089
Net Fixed Assets	$ 63,419	$ 64,642
Other Assets—deposits	$ 11,639	$ 15,361
Total Assets	$699,376	$722,231

Liabilities and Stockholders' Equity	1982	1981
Current Liabilities		
Accounts payable	$175,686	$120,798
Note payable—automobile	1,876	6,090
Accrued expenses	132,717	129,476
Accrued payroll and commissions	16,524	7,094
Payroll taxes payable	4,794	2,260
Sales taxes payable	713	3,019
Customers deposits	-0-	55,839
Income taxes due	-0-	6,250
Total Current Liabilities	$332,310	$331,426
Stockholders' Equity		
Capital stock—par value $10/share		
Authorized—70,000 shares		
Issued & outstanding 16,600 shares	$166,000	$166,000
Retained earnings	201,066	224,805
Total Stockholders' Equity	$367,066	$390,805
Total Liabilities and Equity	$699,376	$722,231

Costs were estimated on the assumption that expenses incurred in manufacturing in the United States for export would run approximately the same as for existing business. However, selling and warehousing expenses would not be incurred. Turner considered selling at cost ($177,750) in order to increase his chances of adding volume and getting a

Exhibit 8.10 German mark-U.S. dollar Exchange Quotations: Tuesdays in January, February, and March 1983 (DM/$)

Quotation Date	Spot	1-Month Forward	3-Month Forward	6-Month Forward
January 4	2.3607	2.3552	2.3491	2.3430
January 11	2.3485	2.3419	2.3354	2.3288
January 18	2.3998	2.3923	2.3793	2.3579
January 25	2.4213	2.4143	2.3992	2.3764
February 1	2.4734	2.4667	2.4498	2.4248
February 8	2.4343	2.4284	2.4131	2.3895
February 15	2.4033	2.3975	2.3827	2.3596
February 22	2.4290	2.4225	2.4079	2.3866
March 1	2.4375	2.4298	2.4153	2.3945

foothold in the German market, but eventually decided that an offer to sell for $225,000 would not lessen chances of receiving the order.

When Turner learned on March 1 that his offer had been accepted he began to think about foreign exchange risk. Although the mark had dropped in dollar value for the four weeks before the offer was made, he noted that since February 1 the mark had strengthened. The sales price of DM562,500 divided by the March 1 rate of DM2.4375/$ meant that the effective sales price was now $230,769. With jubilation, Turner noted that Culver Radio had already earned $5,769 on exchange rate changes during the bid period! Turner wondered if he should do anything now that the order was certain.

Turner called his banker, Beverly Wu, to ask her advice. She suggested four possible courses of action:

1. Hedge in the forward market.
2. Obtain protection via a money market hedge.
3. Seek protection through trading in the foreign currency option market newly created on the Philadelphia Stock Exchange.
4. Do nothing.

After explaining the alternatives, Beverly Wu read to Turner a forecast for the German mark that had been published a few weeks earlier by a London foreign exchange market advisory service:

Deutschemark. No change in this service's evaluation of the DM. Pending Germany's March 5 elections the DM will attract a following as a dollar alternative, but the following is based on its historical attractions and weight; it is more of a Pavlovian reaction than the choice of careful analysis.

The German election was between Helmut Kohl of the conservative Christian Democratic Party and Hans-Jochen Vogel, a former mayor of Munich and the leader of the Social Democrats. A major part of the election campaign centered on whether U.S. Pershing II and cruise missiles should be stationed on German soil. The Kohl forces generally favored continued close links with NATO and the U.S. military, while Vogel demanded that the U.S. and Soviets sign an arms agreement that would make it unnecessary for NATO to install the Pershing and cruise missiles. Since U.S. missiles were involved, Turner speculated that the turn of the election might influence the direction of the Deutschemark/dollar exchange rate. However, he knew he would have to make a decision before the election.

The four alternatives described by the banker were as follows:

1. Hedge in the Forward Market

In the forward market one sells marks for dollars, or vice versa, today, at a fixed price, with delivery to be accomplished at some future date, such as within one, three, or six months. The advantage of the procedure is that Turner would be assured of a fixed number of dollars when the mark sales proceeds were received. Turner noted that the three-month forward price was DM2.4153/$ and the six-month price was DM2.3945/$, meaning that more dollars would be received per mark in the future than at present. The banker explained that this was because interest rates and inflation in Germany at that moment were below comparable U.S. rates. She reported that the German bank prime rate was 12.0% while the U.S. bank prime was 15.0%. Three-month and six-month government bill rates were 10.0% in Germany and 13.6% in the United States.

2. Hedge in the Money Market

Beverly Wu explained that her bank would be able to arrange for Culver Radio to borrow marks from a bank in Germany. The rate charged would be one percentage point above the German bank prime. Should Turner want, he could borrow marks in Germany today, exchange those marks for dollars at once in the spot market, and in three or six months use the mark sales proceeds to repay the German loans.

3. Hedge with Foreign Currency Options

In December 1982 the Philadelphia Stock Exchange began trading in foreign currency options. Options were available in five currencies and in multiples of standard sized contracts:

Deutschemarks	DM	62,500 per contract
Swiss francs	SF	62,500 per contract
British pounds	£	12,500 per contract
Canadian dollars	C$	50,000 per contract
Japanese yen	¥	6,250,000 per contract

A person wanting to buy an option on £50,000, for example, would purchase four contracts: £50,000/£12,500 = 4 contracts.

Foreign currency options expire on the Saturday preceding the third Wednesday of the expiration month, and expiration months are March, June, September, and December.

Thus all contracts for June 1983 expire on June 11, 1983; and all September 1983 contracts expire on September 17, 1983. To obtain protection for September 1, Turner would have to buy contracts that expire on September 17, and then sell the contracts 17 days before they expire. This should not be a problem as a ready market existed.

Each contract has an exercise or "strike price" expressed in "U.S. terms," that is, the U.S. dollar price of the foreign currency. This is the reciprocal of "European terms," which is the way interbank trading is conducted. All strike prices are stated in two cent intervals: thus, mark options might have strike prices of 38¢, 40¢, 42¢, 44¢, etc. One strike price is usually the rounded price nearest the spot rate at the time the contract is written.

An option contract also has a purchase price or "premium." According to the *Wall Street Journal* a "Deutschemark June 42" put could be purchased for 1.17 cents (e.g., $0.0117) per mark, and a "September 42" put could be purchased for 1.48 cents ($0.0148) per mark. "June 42" means a contract that expires the following June and has a strike price of $0.42 per mark. "Put" means the option to deliver marks and receive dollars, whereas "call" means the option to deliver dollars and receive marks.

A June 42 call could be purchased for 1.60 cents, and a September 42 call could be purchased for 1.88 cents.

If the spot price of a mark were less than 42¢ in June, the holder of a put option could deliver marks and be assured of receiving 42¢ for each mark. However, if the spot price of a mark were above 42¢, a person could simply sell any available marks at the higher spot price and let the option expire.

4. Do Nothing

To do nothing would mean simply waiting until the sales proceeds were received in June and September and at that time exchange marks received for dollars at the then current spot price. The amount received might be more or less than anticipated, depending upon trends in the spot price.

Other Factors

On notification from his bank of the receipt of the DM62,500 deposit, Turner sold the marks for dollars at once, receiving $25,641 at the spot price of DM2.4375/$. Turner estimated that the long-run weighted average after-tax cost of capital for Culver Radio was 24%. Culver Radio was too small to raise long-term debt funds, so it relied mainly on its equity for long-term financing.

SUMMARY

- Transaction exposure measures gains or losses that arise from the settlement of financial obligations whose terms are stated in a foreign currency. Transaction exposure arises from (1) purchasing or selling on credit goods or services whose prices are stated in foreign currencies; (2) borrowing or lending funds when repayment is to be made in a foreign currency; (3) being a party to an unperformed forward foreign exchange contract; and (4) otherwise acquiring assets or incurring liabilities denominated in foreign currencies.

- Transaction exposure can be managed by contractual techniques and certain operating strategies.

- Contractual hedging techniques include forward, futures, money market and option hedges, as well as swap agreements, such as back-to-back loans, currency swaps, and credit swaps.

- Operating strategies include leads and lags as well as reinvoicing centers.

1. Pewter Goblets

You manufacture miniature pewter wine goblets. In mid-June you receive an order for 10,000 goblets from Schweinfurt, Germany, to be used in a sales promotion for Frankenrich wine. Payment of DM400,000 is due in mid-December. You expect the Deutschemark to rise from its present rate of DM1.5/$ to DM1.4/$ by December. You can borrow marks for six months at 6% per annum.

What should you do? Discuss issues as necessary.

2. Tucson Products

Tucson Products of Arizona is completing a new factory building in Alicante, Spain, and must make a final construction payment of Pta16,000,000 in six months. Foreign exchange and interest rate quotations are as follows:

Present spot rate:	Pta 94/$
Six-month forward rate:	Pta 97/$
Spanish six-month interest rate:	12.00% per annum
U.S. six-month interest rate:	8.00% per annum

The financial manager's own analysis suggests that in six months the following spot rates can be expected:

Highest expected rate:	Pta 102/$
Most likely rate:	Pta 98/$
Lowest expected rate:	Pta 92/$

Tucson Products has no excess cash at present, but it expects to receive adequate dollars from recovery of an overdue receivable in six months. Tucson Products's weighted average cost of capital is 20% per annum. What alternatives are available for making payment, and what are the advantages or disadvantages of each?

3. Pine Tree Lumber Company

Pine Tree Lumber Company of Portland, Oregon, sells on credit to Zaimoku, K.K., of Japan. It invoices Zaimoku in yen and is paid by Zaimoku on a quarterly basis. The next

231

payment will be for ¥300,000,000 due three months hence. Although the long-run trend of the yen has been up relative to the dollar, recent events have caused Pine Tree to worry that the yen may drop in value over the near future. The following information may be relevant to a decision on whether to hedge this risk:

Spot rate:	¥140/$
Three-month forward rate:	¥138/$
Japanese three-month interest rate:	6% per annum
U.S. three-month interest rate:	9% per annum
Three-month call option on ¥ at 140:	3% premium
Three-month put option on ¥ at 140:	1% premium

Assume that Pine Tree can borrow or invest at the given interest rates in the U.S. and Japan, and that its cost of capital is 12%. Compare alternative ways for Pine Tree to manage its exposure. Explain which one (if any) you think they should choose. Why?

4. Cleveland Tool Company

Cleveland Tool Company has received an order from a Korean manufacturing company for machinery worth Won 1,071 million. The export sale would be denominated in Korean won on a one-year open account basis. The opportunity cost of funds for Cleveland Tool Company is 14%.

The current spot rate is Won 714/$, and the forward won sells at a discount of 10% per annum. The finance staff of Cleveland Tool Company forecasts that the won will drop 8% in value over the next year. Cleveland Tool Company faces the following alternatives:

a) Wait one year to receive Won 1,071 million and then sell the won received for dollars in the spot market.
b) Sell the won proceeds of the sale forward today.
c) Borrow won from Yongsan Bank in Seoul at 20% per annum against the expected future receipts of Won.

What do you recommend, and why?

5. Dayton Manufacturing (C08A.WK1)

Dayton Manufacturing (the same U.S. manufacturer used throughout the chapter) has changed its forecast of the spot exchange rate in 90 days to $1.8050/£.

a) If all other interest rate and exchange rates remain the same, evaluate the hedging alternatives available to Dayton. Dayton's international treasurer wants all analysis to differentiate hedging alternatives which control the exchange rate risk from alternatives which eliminate the risk.
b) Dayton has concluded a second sale of two additional gas turbines to Crown (U.K.). Total payment of £2,000,000 is due in 90 days. Dayton has discovered that it will only be able to borrow in the United Kingdom at 15% per annum. Although all other interest rates have remained the same, exchange rates have

changed to the following:

| Spot rate: | $1.7620/£ |
| Forward rate, three months: | $1.7550/£ |

Dayton now forecasts a spot rate of $1.7850/£ in 90 days.

Which of the transaction exposure hedge alternatives is now probably in Dayton's best interest?

6. Hollywood Pictures, Inc.

Hollywood Pictures, Inc., is scheduled to receive a Ps 624 million dividend from its distribution affiliate in Santiago de Chile in three months. The spot rate is Ps 312/$. The three-month forward rate is Ps 340/$. Inflation in Chile is about 4.5% per month, and the Chilean peso has been devalued regularly. U.S. inflation is 0.5% per month. Hollywood Pictures' affiliate in Chile can borrow at 50% per annum.

What should Hollywood Pictures do about its forthcoming dividend?

7. Rolls Royce Limousine

You have just purchased a deluxe Rolls Royce limousine to be delivered to you in England three months from today. The purchase price is £50,000, to be paid in cash at that time.

You have enough dollars in a bank in the United States to pay cash for the car. These dollars are earning interest at 8% per annum, compounded monthly. National Westminster Bank offers 14% per annum interest on three-month time deposits, no compounding.

You want to avoid all foreign exchange risk because foreign exchange markets have been unusually volatile in recent months. The current spot rate is $1.9800/£ and the current three-month forward rate is $1.9400/£.

How should you plan to pay for your Rolls Royce?

8. O'Brien Enterprises (C08B.WK1)

O'Brien Enterprises of San Francisco has just sold merchandise for FIM 500,000 to a customer in Helsinki, with payment due in Finnish markkas three months from today. O'Brien Enterprises can borrow for three months from a California bank at 10% per annum, or from a bank in Finland at 9% per annum. O'Brien's weighted average cost of capital is 15% per annum.

Today's spot rate (direct basis) is $0.2800/FIM. Three month option contracts are available with the following characteristics:

Contract size:	FIM 125,000.
Strike price:	$0.2800/FIM.
Option premium, per contract:	$200.

a) Assume that you already hedged the transaction by the use of options contracts. On the day the option matures, the spot exchange rate is $0.2400/FIM. At this time, would you exercise the option or sell markkas in the spot market? Why? What is the dollar advantage of one choice over the other?

b) What would have been your dollar sales proceeds, three months hence, had you hedged via the money market?

c) Using today's interest rates, what should be the three-month forward exchange rate for Finnish markkas?

d) Given this rate, what would have been your dollar sales proceeds had you hedged via the forward market?

e) Given the choice, would you prefer a forward hedge or a money market hedge? Why? What is the dollar advantage of one choice over the other?

9. Mississippi Valley Power Company

Mississippi Valley Power Company (MVP) has purchased an electric power generator from Kubota Trading Company of Japan. MVP owes Kubota ¥248 million in six months. The present spot rate is ¥124/$, and the six-month forward rate is ¥122/$.

MVP can borrow or invest yen at 6% and U.S. dollars at 10% (annual rates). MPV can also purchase a six-month call option at a strike price of ¥124 for a premium of 0.014 cents per yen.

Compare the alternative ways MVP can make its payment. Which way do you recommend?

10. Hewlett-Packard

Hewlett-Packard (HP) has sold an order of calculators to a Canadian bank for C$1,000,000 (C$ is Canadian dollars). Payment is due in three months. Although HP does not usually worry about foreign exchange risk on Canadian sales it would like you to explain what alternatives for hedging exist and their costs in order to help price future sales correctly.

The following data are available:

Three-month interest rate for borrowing or investing U.S. dollars:	9% per annum
Three-month interest rate for borrowing or investing Canadian dollars:	12% per annum
Spot rate:	C$1.2000/$
Three-month forward rate:	C$1.2100/$
Three-month options from Citibank:	

Call option on C$1,000,000 at exercise price of C$1.2000, and a 1% premium
Put option on C$1,000,000 at exercise price of C$1.2000, and a 3% premium

HP's cost of capital is 12%.

a) What are the costs of each alternative? What are the advantages of each?

b) What is the breakeven reinvestment rate when comparing forward and money market alternatives? Show your calculations.

11. Pendleton Mills

Pendleton Woolen Mills of Portland, Oregon, has purchased some textile patent and process technology from Akso in the Netherlands for *fl* 5,000,000 (*fl* is the symbol for Dutch guilders). Payment by Pendleton is due in six months. Explain the various alternatives available to Pendleton to hedge its foreign exchange exposure on this transaction given the following data:

	U.S.	Netherlands
Six-month interest rates, investing	10% per annum	8% per annum
Six-month interest rates, borrowing	13% per annum	11% per annum
Spot rate		fl 1.88/$
Six-month forward rate		fl 1.86/$

Six-month call option on fl 5,000,000 at an exercise price of fl 1.88 and a premium of 3%
Six-month put option on fl 5,000,000 at an exercise price of fl 1.88 and a premium of 1%

Pendleton's cost of capital is 14%. Explain the advantages and disadvantages of each alternative.

◘ 12. Korean Airlines (C08C.WK1)

Korean Airlines (KAL) has just signed a contract with McDonnell Douglas to purchase two new jet aircraft for a total of $60,000,000, with payment in two equal tranches. The first tranche of $30,000,000 has just been paid. The next $30,000,000 is due three months from today. KAL currently has excess cash of 25,000,000,000 won in a Seoul bank, and it is from these funds that KAL plans to make its next payment.

Spot rate:	800 won/$
Three-month forward rate:	795 won/$
Korean three-month interest rate:	5% per annum
U.S. three-month interest rate:	8% per annum

These are the only rates available to KAL for either borrowing or investing. Interest on Korean money market investments is compounded semiannually.

A three-month call option in the over-the-counter (bank) market at a strike price of 790 won/$ sells at a premium of 0.5%, payable at the time the option is purchased.

KAL's foreign exchange advisor forecasts the spot rate in three months to be 792 won/$.

How should KAL plan to make the second payment to McDonnell Douglas if KAL's goal is to maximize the amount of won cash left in the bank at the end of three months? That is, how much in won would be left under each possible alternative? Which alternative do you recommend, and why?

◘ 13. Option Collars: Dayton Once Again (C08D.WK1)

Dayton Manufacturing's Chief Financial Officer (CFO), Herb Hamlin, has just returned from an executive financial seminar in which the lecturer introduced the option collar. From what Herb understands, the firm would hedge its latest export sale (the account receivable for £2,000,000) by simultaneously buying (holding) a put option on British pounds while selling (writing) a call option on British pounds. Both option positions would be for the same amount of British pounds and the same strike price.

Using the following option quotations, you must evaluate whether the option collar would be better or worse than the three-month forward rate of $1.7540/£. Ignore transaction costs. Both options mature in 90 days, and are standard sized options of £31,250 each. Herb wants your report on Monday.

Option	Strike Price	Premium
Put option	$1.7500/£	$0.025/£
Call option	$1.7500/£	$0.035/£

14. Culver Radio, Inc.

The Decision Case at the end of this chapter, Culver Radio, Inc., poses a transaction exposure problem very similar to that of Dayton Manufacturing. Clyde Turner, president and owner of Culver, needs a full evaluation of the best hedging strategy tomorrow over breakfast (7 A.M.) It's going to be a long night.

a) Construct a spreadsheet template like that used for Dayton to analyze Culver's transaction exposure.

b) Write up a summary of what you believe to be the critical issues for Culver, the basic results of your spreadsheet analysis, and your recommendation for the preferred hedging method.

NOTES

1. This quotation is attributed to Daniel Drew, in Bouck White, *The Book of Daniel Drew*, New York: George H. Doran Company, 1910, p. 180.

2. Mark E. Battersby, "Avoiding Risks by Parallel Lending," *Finance Magazine*, September–October 1975, pp. 56–57.

3. Khoury, Sarkis J., and K. Hung Chan, "Hedging Foreign Exchange Risk: Selecting the Optimal Tool," *Midland Corporate Finance Journal*, Winter 1988, pp. 40–52.

BIBLIOGRAPHY

Aubey, R. T., and R. H. Cramer, "Use of International Currency Cocktails in the Reduction of Exchange Rate Risk," *Journal of Economics and Business*, Winter 1977, pp. 128–134.

Babbel, David F., "Determining the Optimum Strategy for Hedging Currency Exposure," *Journal of International Business Studies*, Spring/Summer 1983, pp. 133–139.

Batra, Raveendra N., Shabtai Donnenfeld, and Josef Hadar, "Hedging Behavior by Multinational Firms," *Journal of International Business Studies*, Winter 1982, pp. 59–70.

Beidleman, Carl R., John L. Hillary, and James A. Greenleaf, "Alternatives in Hedging Long-Date Contractual Foreign Exchange Exposure," *Sloan Management Review*, Summer 1983, pp. 45–54.

Booth, Laurence D., "Hedging and Foreign Exchange Exposure," *Management International Review*, vol. 22, no. 1, 1982, pp. 26–42.

Chang, Jack S. K., and Latha Shanker, "A Risk-Return Measure on Hedging Effectiveness: A Comment," *Journal of Financial and Quantitative Analysis*, 22, no. 3, September 1987, pp. 373–376.

Controlling Risk with Foreign Currency Options: Supplement to Euromoney, February 1985.

Dufey, Gunter, and S.I. Srinivasulu, "The Case for Corporate Management of Foreign Exchange Risk," *Financial Management*, Winter 1983, pp. 54–62.

Eaker, Mark R., "Denomination Decision for Multinational Transactions," *Financial Management*, Autumn 1980, pp. 23–29.

——, "The Numeraire Problem and Foreign Exchange Risk," *Journal of Finance*, May 1981, pp. 419–427.

——, and Dwight M. Grant, "Cross-Hedging Foreign Currency Risk," *Journal of International Money and Finance*, March 1987, pp. 85–105.

Evans, Thomas G., William R. Folks, Jr., and Michael Jilling, *The Impact of Statement of Financial Accounting Standards No.8 on the Foreign Exchange Management Practices of American Multinationals: An Economic Impact Study*, Stamford, Conn.: Financial Accounting Standards Board, November 1978.

Folks, William R., Jr., "Decision Analysis for Exchange Risk Management," *Financial Management*, Winter 1972, pp. 101–112.

——, "The Optimal Level of Forward Exchange Transactions," *Journal of Financial and Quantitative Analysis*, January 1973, pp. 105–110.

——, "Optimal Foreign Borrowing Strategies with Operations in the Forward Exchange Markets," *Journal of Financial and Quantitative Analysis*, June 1978, pp. 245–254.

Giddy, Ian H., "Why It Doesn't Pay to Make a Habit of Forward Hedging," *Euromoney*, December 1976, pp. 96–100.

——, "The Foreign Exchange Option as a Hedging Tool," *Midland Corporate Finance Journal*, Fall 1983, pp. 32–42.

Howard, Charles T., and Louis J. D'Antonio, "A Risk-Return Measure of Hedging Effectiveness: A Reply," *Journal of Financial and Quantitative Analysis*, 22, No. 3, September 1987, p. 377.

Jacque, Laurent, "Management of Foreign Exchange Risk: A Review Article," *Journal of International Business Studies*, Spring/Summer 1981, pp. 81–100.

Jones, Eric T., and Donald L. Jones, *Hedging Foreign Exchange: Converting Risk to Profit*, New York: Wiley, 1987.

Kaufold, Howard, and Michael Smirlock, "Managing Corporate Exchange and Interest Rate Exposure," *Financial Management*, Autumn 1986, pp. 64–72.

Kerkvliet, Joe, and Michael H. Moffett, "The Hedging of an Uncertain Future Foreign Currency Cash Flow," *Journal of Financial and Quantitative Analysis*, December 1991 (forthcoming).

Khouri, Sarkis J., and K. Hung Chan, "Hedging Foreign Exchange Risk: Selecting the Optimal Tool," *Midland Corporate Finance Journal*, Winter 1988, pp. 40–52.

Kohlhagen, Steven W., "A Model of Optimal Foreign Exchange Hedging without Exchange Rate Projections," *Journal of International Business Studies*, Fall 1978, pp. 9–19.

Korsvold, Paul, "The Futility of Currency Hedging Models," In Göran Bergendahl, ed., *International Financial Management*, Stockholm: Norstedts, 1982, pp. 104–127.

Lewent, Judy C., and A. John Kearney, "Identifying, Measuring, and Hedging Currency Risk at Merck," *Journal of Applied Corporate Finance*, vol. 2, no. 4, Winter 1990.

Maloney, Peter J., "Managing Currency Exposure: The Case of Western Mining," *Journal of Applied Corporate Finance*, vol. 2, no. 4, Winter 1990.

Park, Yoon S., "Currency Swaps as a Long-Term International Financing Technique," *Journal of International Business Studies*, Winter 1984, pp. 47–54.

Remmers, H.L., *FORAD: International Financial Management Simulation (Players' Manual, Release 2.4)*, Fontainebleau, France: INSEAD, 1990.

Rodriguez, Rita M., "Corporate Exchange Risk Management: Theme and Aberrations," *Journal of Finance*, May 1981, pp. 427–439.

Soenen, Luc A., and E. G. F. van Winkel, "The Real Costs of Hedging in the Forward Exchange Market," *Management International Review*, vol. 22, no. 1, 1982, pp. 53–59.

Swanson, Peggy E., and Stephen C. Caples, "Hedging Foreign Exchange Risk Using Forward Foreign Exchange Markets: An Extension," *Journal of International Business Studies*, Spring 1987, pp. 75–82.

Wheelwright, Steven, "Applying Decision Theory to Improve Corporate Management of Currency-Exchange Risks," *California Management Review*, Summer 1975, pp. 41–49.

Combining Puts and Calls: The Option Collar

The power and flexibility of foreign currency options for transaction exposure management can be demonstrated further through the construction of a "collar." This hedge is created by simultaneously buying a put option and selling a call option, or vice versa. As we will demonstrate for the case of Dayton discussed in this chapter, it results in the creation of a synthetic forward contract for the foreign currency. Dayton's problem is the maximization of U.S. dollar receipts from £1,000,000 to be received in 90 days.

Dayton buys a put option with strike price $1.7500/£. The premium paid for the put option is $0.0015/£. Dayton can write a call option on £ for the same quantity and strike price, £1,000,000 at a strike price of $1.7500/£, earning the premium of $0.0060/£. Since Dayton will be holding the British pounds necessary for fulfilling the call option, this is referred to as a "covered call."

The profit and loss positions for the two options are shown in Exhibit 8A.1.

- Dayton will exercise its put option if the spot exchange rate in 90 days is less than $1.75/£. But if the spot exchange rate is not below $1.75/£, Dayton will not exercise it.

Exhibit 8A.1   The Option "Collar": Simultaneously Buying a Put and Writing a Call

				($/£)			
Ending Spot Rate	1.7300	1.7400	1.7500	1.7600	1.7700	1.7800	1.7900
Buy Put Option:							
Premium cost[1]	−0.0015	−0.0015	−0.0015	−0.0015	−0.0015	−0.0015	−0.0015
Put receipts	1.7500	1.7500	0.0000	0.0000	0.0000	0.0000	0.0000
Spot receipts	0.0000	0.0000	1.7500	1.7600	1.7700	1.7800	1.7900
Total put option	1.7485	1.7485	1.7485	1.7585	1.7685	1.7785	1.7885
Sell Call Option:							
Premium receipts[1]	0.0060	0.0060	0.0060	0.0060	0.0060	0.0060	0.0060
Covering call costs	0.0000	0.0000	0.0000	−1.7600	−1.7700	−1.7800	−1.7900
Spot receipts	0.0000	0.0000	0.0000	1.7500	1.7500	1.7500	1.7500
Total call option	0.0060	0.0060	0.0060	−0.0040	−0.0140	−0.0240	−0.0340
Combined "Collar"	1.7545	1.7545	1.7545	1.7545	1.7545	1.7545	1.7545
Forward rate	1.7540	1.7540	1.7540	1.7540	1.7540	1.7540	1.7540

[1] The total premium cost, at the end of the 90 day period, should also include interest charges on the initial premium paid for the put option, and earned on the call option. These charges are ignored here due to the relatively small values of interest expenses.

- The call option which Dayton wrote will be exercised at spot rates above \$1.75/£; thus the call option will only be exercised (costing Dayton money) when the put option is not exercised (when Dayton earns money).

Since the put and call options are for the same strike price, and because the formation of a collar places Dayton on both sides of the strike price, the final effective rate is merely a result of the difference in the option premiums:

$$
\begin{aligned}
\text{Collar Rate} &= \text{Strike Price} + (\text{Call Premium} - \text{Put Premium}) \\
&= 1.7500 + (0.0060 - 0.0015) \\
&= 1.7500 + 0.0045 \\
&= 1.7545
\end{aligned}
$$

The resulting collar rate is then compared with that of the forward contract. Each is a contractual arrangement, so preference is determined only on the basis of which hedge results in larger U.S. dollar receipts to Dayton. In this case, the option collar is better than the forward rate of \$1.7540/£.

Although it is clearly better than the forward contract, comparing the collar with the put option alone results in the same debate as mentioned previously: whether one wishes to eliminate all exposure (forward contract, money market hedge, option collar), or bound it on the downside (put option alone).

The Characteristics of the Various Currency Hedging Techniques

IMM Futures Market	Forward Interbank Market	Options Market (Listed)	Option Market (Over the Counter)
Trading is conducted in a competitive area by "open outcry."	Trading is done by telephone or telex.	Competitive, auction-like pricing mechanism.	Trading is done by telephone or telex.
Participants are either buyers or sellers of a contract at a single, specified price at any given point in time.	Participants usually make two-sided markets.	Participants are on one side of the market.	Two-sided markets are made by participants.
Non-member participants deal through brokers (Exchange members), who represent them on the IMM floor. Exchange contracts are available to anyone.	Participants deal on a principal-to-principal basis. Access to market is restricted.	Brokered market. Access to everyone.	Principal market.
Market participants usually are unknown to one another.	Participants in each transaction always know who is on the other side of the trade.	Market participants are unknown to one another.	Participants do not necessarily know each other.
The Exchange's Clearing House becomes the opposite side to each cleared transaction: The credit risk for a futures market participant is always the same and there is no need to analyze the credit of other market participants.	Each counter party with whom a dealer does business must be examined individually as a credit risk and credit limits must be set for each. As such, there may be a wide range of credit capabilities of participants.	Exchange Clearing House is used.	Bank is the guarantor.
Price movements have a maximum (adjustable by the Exchange) daily limit.	No daily price limit.	No daily price limit.	No daily price limit.

Money Market Hedge	Matching Maturity and Duration of Exchange Sensitive Assets and Liabilities	Currency Swap	No Hedge
No trading.	Internal market.	Telephone and telex.	No market.
—	Two-sided markets.	Two-sided markets.	No market.
Participants deal on a principal-to-principal basis.	Principal market.	Principal market.	—
Participants in each transaction always know who is on the other side of the trade.	—	Participants do not necessarily know each other.	—
Borrower is assessed individually as to credit risk and credit limits.	No direct external guarantee.	—	—
Price (interest rates) may be adjusted (with or without limits) at regular time intervals if rates are pegged.	—	—	Prices fluctuate without limit.

continued

continued

IMM Futures Market	Forward Interbank Market	Options Market (Listed)	Option Market (Over the Counter)
Margins are required of all participants for both long and short positions. • Initial • Maintenance Variation = one day's change in value of futures position	Margins are not required by banks dealing with other banks, although for smaller, non-bank customers, margins may be required on certain occasions.	100% of the value of the option is paid the second day after the order is executed. *No leverage is possible as compared with forward and futures contract.*	Full cost of option paid at the time of transaction.
Daily marking to market.	No daily marking to market.	No daily marking to market.	No daily marking to market.
No loss on position if prices remain constant.	Prices are "locked in." Any loss is an opportunity loss.	The entire premium is lost if prices remain constant.	The entire premium is lost if prices remain constant.
Represents an obligation.	Represents an obligation.	It is an *option* to do.	Option.
Settlements are made daily via the Exchange's Clearing House. Gains on position values may be withdrawn and losses are collected daily.	Settlement takes place two days after the spot transac-tion (one day for the Canadian Dollar and Mexican Peso). For forward transactions, settlement occurs on the date agreed upon between the bank and its customer.	Settlements are made daily.	Bank arranges the settlement.
Regulated by the Commodities Futures Trading Commission (CTFC).	Self-regulated market	Regulated by CFTC	Regulated by SEC

Source: Khoury, Sarkis J., and K. Hung Chan, "Hedging Foreign Exchange Risk: Selecting the Optimal Tool," *Midland Corporate Finance Journal*, Winter 1988, pp. 44–45. Reprinted with permission.

Money Market Hedge	*Matching Maturity and Duration of Exchange Sensitive Assets and Liabilities*	*Currency Swap*	*No Hedge*
—	All fees paid up front.	All fees paid up front.	—
Marketing to market if rates are floating rates.	No daily marking to market.	Possible daily marking to market.	—
The cost of the hedge is "locked in" $C = a(1 \times f_{us}) - a(1 + f_f)$ where $a = PV$ of foreign currency exposure in \$ (home currency) terms.	No loss if there are major price changes.	Results known in advance.	Cost is unknown.
Represents a debt obligation.	An obligation.	An obligation.	—
Settlement takes place on the date agreed upon between the bank and its customer.	—	Bank arranges settlement.	—
Largely self-regulated. The Federal Reserve System's regulations must be observed across clients.	No direct regulation.	No regulation.	—

CHAPTER 9

Managing Accounting Exposure

Accounting exposure, also called *translation exposure*, results because foreign currency-denominated financial statements of foreign affiliates must be restated (that is, "translated") into the parent's reporting currency so the parent can prepare consolidated financial statements. Translated statements are also used by management to assess the performance of foreign affiliates. While such assessment might also be done in the local currency, translation into a single currency facilitates comparison of affiliates in different countries.

Accounting exposure is the potential for a gain or loss in the parent's net worth and reported net income that arises because exchange rates change. Most foreign affiliates maintain their financial records in the local currency. Hence a change in exchange rates, having its effect through the translation process, usually leads to a change in the parent currency measurement of the affiliate's assets, liabilities, revenues, and expenses.

Three basic conventions for translation have been developed in various countries:

1. The current rate method.
2. The monetary/nonmonetary method.
3. The current/noncurrent method.

A fourth convention, termed the "temporal method," is similar to the monetary/nonmonetary method and is sometimes regarded as a variation of that method. Hybrids among the basic methods have also been used at times.

CURRENT RATE METHOD

Under the current rate method, all assets and liabilities are translated at the current rate of exchange; that is, at the rate of exchange in effect on the balance sheet date. Income statement items, including depreciation and cost of goods sold, are translated at either the actual exchange rate on the dates the various revenues, expenses, gains, and losses are incurred or at an appropriately weighted average exchange rate for the period. Dividends paid are translated at the exchange rate in effect on the date of payment.

Existing equity accounts, such as common stock and paid-in capital, are translated at historical rates. Year-end retained earnings consist of the original year-beginning retained earnings plus or minus any income or loss for the year. However, gains or losses caused by translation adjustments are *not* included in the calculation of net income, and thus the change in retained earnings does not reflect translation gains or losses. Rather, translation gains or losses are reported separately and accumulated in a separate equity account with a title such as "cumulative translation adjustment" (CTA).

When the investment in the foreign affiliate is sold or liquidated, translation gains or losses of past years accumulated in the "cumulative translation adjustment" account are removed from that account and reported as one component of the total gain or loss on sale or liquidation. The total gain or loss is reported as net income or loss for the time period in which the sale or liquidation occurs.

The current rate method became official U.S. practice with the December, 1981, issuance of *Statement of Financial Accounting Standards Number 52* (FAS #52, also referred to as SFAS #52 and FASB #52) by the Financial Accounting Standards Board, the authority in the United States that determines accounting policy for U.S. firms and certified public accountants.

The basic advantage of the current rate method is that the relative proportions of individual balance sheet accounts remain the same. This means that the translation process does not distort such balance sheet ratios as the current ratio or the debt/equity ratio. The main disadvantage of the current rate method is that it violates the accounting principle of carrying balance sheet accounts at historical cost. For example, foreign assets purchased with dollars and then recorded on an affiliate's statements at their foreign currency historical cost are translated back into dollars at a different rate. Thus they are reported in the consolidated statement in dollars at something other than their historical dollar cost.

MONETARY/NONMONETARY METHOD

Under the monetary/nonmonetary method, monetary assets (primarily cash, marketable securities, accounts receivable, and long-term receivables) and monetary liabilities (primarily current liabilities and long-term debt) are translated at current exchange rates, while all other assets and liabilities are translated at historical rates.

Income statement items are translated at the average exchange rate for the period, except for items such as depreciation and cost of goods sold that are directly associated with nonmonetary assets or liabilities. These items are translated at their historical rate.

The basic advantage of the monetary/nonmonetary method is that foreign nonmonetary assets are carried at their original costs in the parent's consolidated statement. In most countries this approach is consistent with the original cost treatment of domestic assets of the parent firm. In practice, however, if some foreign accounts are translated at one exchange rate while others are translated at different rates, the resulting translated balance sheet will not balance! Hence there is a need for a "plug" to remove what has been called the "dangling debit or credit."[1] The true nature of the gain or loss created by use of such a "plug" is open to question.

OTHER TRANSLATION METHODS

Other translation methods have been used from time to time in various countries.

Temporal Method

As mentioned earlier, the temporal method is often regarded as a variation of the monetary/nonmonetary method. If the foreign affiliate keeps all of its accounts on a historical cost basis, the temporal method is in fact identical to the monetary/nonmonetary method. However if the foreign affiliate restates any unexposed assets (such as inventory or net plant and equipment) to market value, the temporal method provides for their translation at the current exchange rate. Such restatement to market value is not uncommon in countries, such as Argentina, experiencing hyperinflation.

The temporal method was required in the United States when *Statement of Financial Accounting Standards Number 8* (FAS #8) was adopted in October 1975, and remained in effect until FAS #52 replaced it in December 1981.

Current/Noncurrent Method

The current/noncurrent method is perhaps the oldest approach. No longer allowable under generally accepted accounting practices in the United States, it was nevertheless widely used prior to the adoption of FAS #8 in 1975. Its popularity gradually waned as other methods were found to give more meaningful results. Under the current/noncurrent method, all current assets and current liabilities of foreign affiliates are translated into the home currency at the current exchange rate, while noncurrent assets and noncurrent liabilities are translated at historical rates.

In the balance sheet, exposure to gains or losses from fluctuating currency values is determined by the net of current assets less current liabilities. Gains or losses on long-term assets and liabilities are not shown currently. Items in the income statement are generally translated at the average exchange rate for the period covered. However, those items that relate to revenue or expense items associated with noncurrent assets (such as depreciation charges) or long-term liabilities (amortization of debt discount) are translated at the same rate as the corresponding balance sheet items.

TECHNICAL ASPECTS OF TRANSLATION

All countries whose businesses have important foreign affiliates have some sort of accounting authority that prescribes whether or not foreign operations must be consolidated and, if so, what translation method must be used. In addition to the basic choice between current rate method and monetary/nonmonetary method, or a hybrid, rules must be established for deciding when and how gains or losses will be recognized in the income statement. Terms, such as "functional" and "reporting," must be defined for the various currencies, and exceptions made for special circumstances, such as when an affiliate operates in a country having an unusually high rate of domestic inflation.

Time of Recognizing Gains or Losses

Translation by any of the methods usually produces a foreign exchange gain or loss when exchange rates change. This translation gain or loss reflects a change in the way values are measured by the accounting process; it does *not* reflect a cash out-of-pocket gain or loss. A remaining accounting question is whether such gain or loss should be recognized in the current income statement, deferred to a later reporting period, or closed directly into retained earnings or an equity reserve account without ever passing through the income statement.

Under FAS #52, translation gains or losses do not influence net income for any given time period but are instead accumulated in a cumulative translation adjustment (CTA) account under consolidated stockholders' equity until substantial or complete liquidation of the assets or the firm occurs. In other words, an unrealized translation gain or loss is held in an equity reserve account until the gain or loss is actually realized. In the case of fixed assets this realization might well be decades into the future. When realized, the gain or loss is reported as net income or loss for that period. Note, however, that *transaction* gains or losses, as distinguished from *translation* gains or losses, are reflected in income for the current period.

When FAS #8 was in effect, gains and losses passed through the quarterly income statement, influencing quarterly as well as annual net income and earnings per share. No reserves were permitted. This "flow through" requirement existed during the late 1970s when the value of the U.S. dollar fluctuated widely. The situation created a whipsaw effect on reported quarterly earnings, which made the provisions of FAS #8 very unpopular with business. In many multinational firms foreign exchange risk management policies were dominated by the desire to manage quarterly earnings so that they appeared to be stable—and rising. Many firms engaged in costly efforts to hedge foreign activities so that quarterly earnings would not fluctuate unduly because of noncash translation gains or losses.

Functional Versus Reporting Currency

FAS #52 differentiates between a foreign affiliate's "functional" and "reporting" currency. *Functional currency* is defined as the currency of the primary economic environment in which the affiliate operates and in which it generates cash flows. The *reporting currency* is the currency in which the parent firm prepares its own financial statement, normally the home country currency.

Management must evaluate the nature and purpose of its foreign operations to decide on the appropriate functional currency. Some of the economic factors that enter into such decisions are listed in Exhibit 9.1.

Exhibit 9.1   Economic Factors to Consider in Determining Functional Currency

	Functional Currency Indicators	
Foreign entity's	*Foreign currency*	*Parent currency*
Cash flows	Primarily in the foreign currency; no direct impact on parent cash flow	Direct impact on parent cash flow; readily available for remittance to parent
Sales price	Determined by local competition; not responsive in short run to exchange rate changes	Determined by worldwide competition or prices; responsive in short run to exchange rate changes
Sales markets	Active local markets for affiliate's products	Sales markets mostly in parent's country or denominated in parent's currency
Expenses	Primarily incurred in local currency	Primarily for components obtained from parent's country
Financing	Primarily in foreign currency, with debt service generated by foreign operations	Primarily from parent or in parent's currency, with parent funds needed for debt service
Intercompany transactions	Few intercompany transactions, with foreign entity quite independent	Many intercompany transactions, with extensive interrelationship with parent's operations

Source: Financial Accounting Standards Board, *Statement of Financial Accounting Standards No.52.* Stamford, Connecticut: Financial Accounting Standards Board, December 1981, derived from material on pp. 26–27.

In general, if the foreign affiliate's operations are relatively self-contained and integrated within a particular country, its functional currency will be the local currency of that country. Thus, for example, the German affiliates of Ford and General Motors, which do most of their manufacturing in Germany and sell most of their output for Deutschemarks, use the Deutschemark as their functional currency. If the foreign affiliate's operations are an extension of the U.S. parent's operations, the functional currency could be the U.S. dollar. An example would be the *maquiladora* assembly plants along the Mexican border across from such cities as San Diego and El Paso. These plants receive all of their raw material from their U.S. parent, and export all of their production back to the U.S. parent.

If the foreign affiliate's functional currency is deemed to be the parent's currency, translation of the affiliate's statements employs the temporal method of FAS #8. Thus many U.S. multinationals continue to use the temporal method for those foreign affiliates that use the dollar as their functional currency, while using the current rate method for their other affiliates. Under FAS #52, if the temporal method is used, translation gains or losses flow through the income statement as they did under FAS #8; they are not charged to the CTA account.

In summary, accounting exposure is the potential for translation losses or gains. Translation is the measurement, in a reporting currency, of assets, liabilities, revenues, and expenses of a foreign operation where the foreign accounts are originally denominated and/or measured in a functional currency that is also a foreign currency. Accounting exposure is thus the possibility that a change in exchange rates will cause a translation loss or gain when the foreign financial statements are restated in the parent's own reporting currency.

Hyperinflation Countries

FAS #52 includes a special provision for translating statements of affiliates of U.S. firms in countries where cumulative inflation has been approximately 100% or more over a three-year period. Financial statements of these affiliates must be translated into the reporting currency using the temporal method of FAS #8.

The rationale for special treatment of hyperinflation countries is to correct the distortion that occurs when depreciation at historical cost is matched against revenue at current prices. Translating depreciation, plant, and equipment at the historical exchange rate yields a higher reporting currency value than would the use of the current (depreciated) exchange rate. This, in turn, leads to a less distorted income statement and balance sheet. If the current rate were used, depreciation would be quite understated relative to replacement costs, profits would be overstated in real terms, and the book value of plant and equipment would eventually nearly disappear from the balance sheet as it becomes worth less and less in reporting currency terms. In effect, FAS #52 declares the functional currency of affiliates in hyperinflation countries to be the reporting currency (U.S. dollars for U.S. firms).

Although the hyperinflation standard is somewhat controversial, it has some precedence in business practice. Russell Taussig has stated it very well:

> When a country is plagued with hyperinflation, it often uses the U.S. dollar or other hard currency as its de facto functional currency for actual transactions regardless of accounting standards. For example, most Israeli retailers in 1982 priced their merchandise in U.S. dollars, not shekels. In the face of triple-digit inflation, they cannot change their prices every other day. The U.S. dollar becomes the unit of account. Also, when an Israeli holds U.S. dollars and the shekel is devalued, his holding in dollars remains the same, whereas if he holds currency in shekels and the shekel is devalued, his holding declines in purchasing power. The U.S. dollar becomes the storehouse of value. Consistent with the mercantile practice of businessmen in highly inflationary economies, the FASB promulgates the accounting standard that the home currency becomes the functional currency when inflation is rampant; otherwise the local currency is the functional currency. Accounting standards-setting simply is patterned after accepted business practice.[2]

CURRENT RATE AND MONETARY/NONMONETARY TRANSLATION EXAMPLE

Use of the current rate method and the monetary/nonmonetary method of translation will be illustrated through continuing the example of Instruments Napoleon, S.A. from Chapter 7. The example in this section deals with balance sheet translation only. The somewhat more complex procedures for translating income statements is described in the appendix to this chapter.

The functional currency of Instruments Napoleon, S.A., is the French franc, and the reporting currency of its parent, Washington Controls, is the U.S. dollar. Assume the following:

1. *Historical exchange rate*: Plant and equipment, long-term debt, and common stock were entered on Instruments Napoleon's books at a time in the past when the exchange rate was FF6.00/$.

2. *Exchange rate during previous quarter*: Inventory currently on hand was purchased or manufactured during the prior quarter when the average exchange rate was FF6.25/$

3. *Exchange rate before devaluation*: On December 31, 1992, the current exchange rate was FF6.40/$.

4. *Exchange rate after devaluation*: By January 2, 1993, the franc is presumed to have dropped 20% in value from the rate two days earlier, to a new exchange rate of FF8.00/$.

The example will also look at the consequences of a strengthening of the franc to a year-end rate of FF5.00/$.

Current Rate Method

The top half of Exhibit 9.2 illustrates translation loss using the current rate method. Assets and liabilities on the pre-devaluation balance sheet are translated at the current rate of FF6.40/$. Capital stock is translated at the historical rate of FF6.00/$, and retained earnings are translated at a composite rate that is equivalent to having the additions to retained earnings of each past year translated at the exchange rate in effect in that year.

As shown in the top half of Exhibit 9.2, the "before depreciation" dollar translation shows an accumulated translation loss from prior periods of $50,000. This balance is the cumulative gain or loss from translating franc statements into dollars in prior years, and is carried separately in the cumulative translation adjustment (CTA) account.

After the 20% depreciation, assets and liabilities are all translated at the new exchange rate of FF8.00/$. The equity accounts, including retained earnings, are translated just as they were before devaluation, and as a result the cumulative translation loss increases to $300,000. The increase of $250,000 in this account (from a cumulative loss of $50,000 to a cumulative loss of $300,000) is this year's expected translation loss measured by the current rate method.

Translation loss is the decrease in value, stated in the parent's reporting currency, of "net exposed foreign assets." "Exposed" means that the value of that asset measured in the reporting currency drops with a devaluation of the functional currency and rises with an appreciation of the functional currency. "Net" exposed assets in this context means exposed assets minus exposed liabilities. Net exposed assets are positive (that is, "long") if exposed assets exceed exposed liabilities, and are negative ("short") if exposed assets are smaller than exposed liabilities.

Exhibit 9.2 Translation Loss Just After a Devaluation of the French Franc.
Instruments Napoleon, S.A.

	French francs	Rate	Just Before Devaluation Dollars	Rate	Just After Devaluation Dollars
Current Rate Method					
Assets					
Cash	1,600,000	6.4	250,000	8.0	200,000
Accounts receivable	3,200,000	6.4	500,000	8.0	400,000
Inventory	2,400,000	6.4	375,000	8.0	300,000
Net plant and equipment	4,800,000	6.4	750,000	8.0	600,000
Total	12,000,000		1,875,000		1,500,000
Liabilities and Net Worth					
Accounts payable	800,000	6.4	125,000	8.0	100,000
Short-term bank debt	1,600,000	6.4	250,000	8.0	200,000
Long-term debt	1,600,000	6.4	250,000	8.0	200,000
Capital stock	1,800,000	6.0	300,000	6.0	300,000
Retained earnings	6,200,000	(a)	1,000,000	(b)	1,000,000
Cumulative translation adjustment (CTA)			<50,000>		<300,000>
Total	12,000,000		1,875,000		1,500,000
Monetary/Nonmonetary Method					
Assets					
Cash	1,600,000	6.4	250,000	8.0	200,000
Accounts receivable	3,200,000	6.4	500,000	8.0	400,000
Inventory	2,400,000	6.25	384,000	6.25	384,000
Net plant and equipment	4,800,000	6.0	800,000	6.0	800,000
Total	12,000,000		1,934,000		1,784,000
Liabilities and Net Worth					
Accounts payable	800,000	6.4	125,000	8.0	100,000
Short-term bank debt	1,600,000	6.4	250,000	8.0	200,000
Long-term debt	1,600,000	6.4	250,000	8.0	200,000
Capital stock	1,800,000	6.0	300,000	6.0	300,000
Retained earnings	6,200,000	(a)	1,009,000	(b)	1,009,000
Translation loss					<25,000>
Total	12,000,000		1,934,000		1,784,000

a Dollar retained earnings before devaluation are the cumulative sum of additions to retained earnings of all prior years, translated at exchange rates in effect in each year.

b Translated into dollars at the same rate as before devaluation. However under the monetary/nonmonetary method the translation loss of $25,000 would be closed into retained earnings, via the income statement, rather than left as a separate line item. Hence under the monetary/nonmonetary method, ending retained earnings would actually be $1,009,000 minus $25,000 = $984,000.

Exhibit 9.3   Calculation of Translation Loss Just After 20% Devaluation of the French Franc, from FF6.40/$ to FF8.00/$. Instruments Napoleon, S.A.

	Current Rate Method	*Monetary/Nonmonetary Method*
Assets		
Cash	$250,000	$250,000
Accounts receivable	500,000	500,000
Inventory	375,000	not exposed
Net plant and equipment	750,000	not exposed
Total exposed assets ("A")	$1,875,000	$750,000
Exposed liabilities		
Accounts payable	$125,000	$125,000
Short-term bank debt	250,000	250,000
Long-term debt	250,000	250,000
Total exposed liabilities ("L")	$625,000	$625,000
Loss if Franc Depreciates 20%		
Net exposed assets ("A"–"L")	$1,250,000	$125,000
times amount of devaluation (as decimal)	x .20	x .20
Translation loss	$250,000	$25,000

Exposure can be measured by creating a "before" and "after" translated balance sheet, as was done in Exhibit 9.2. A simpler method is to multiply "net exposed assets" by the amount of the depreciation, expressed as a decimal. This has been done for the current rate method in the left column of Exhibit 9.3, where it can be seen that a 20% depreciation of the French franc means that net exposed assets of $1,250,000 lose 20% of their value, creating a translation loss of $250,000.

Suppose instead that the franc had appreciated. If, by the end of the year, the French franc had appreciated from FF6.40/$ to FF5.00/$, the appreciation would be 28%. The effect of this is seen in Exhibit 9.4, which starts with the same net exposed assets calculated in Exhibit 9.3. Under the current rate method, the U.S. parent would have a translation gain of $350,000.

Monetary/Nonmonetary Method

Translation of the same accounts under the monetary/nonmonetary method is illustrated in the bottom half of Exhibit 9.2 Under this method, monetary assets and monetary liabilities in the predevaluation French franc balance sheet are translated at the current rate of exchange, while other assets and the equity accounts are translated at their historic rates. For Instruments Napoleon, the historic rate for inventory differs from that for net plant and equipment because inventory was acquired more recently.

Exhibit 9.4 Calculation of Translation Gain After 28% Appreciation of the French Franc, from FF6.40/$ to FF5.00/$ for Instruments Napoleon, S.A.

	Current Rate Method	*Monetary/Nonmonetary Method*
Gain if franc appreciates 28%		
Net exposed assets ("A"–"L")	$1,250,000	$125,000
times amount of		
appreciation (as decimal)	x .28	x .28
Translation gain	$350,000	$35,000

Under the temporal version of the monetary/nonmonetary method used in the United States from 1976 to 1982 (FAS #8), translation losses were not accumulated in a separate equity account but passed directly through each quarter's income statement. Thus in the dollar balance sheet translated before devaluation, retained earnings were the cumulative result of earnings from all prior years translated at historical rates in effect each year, plus translation gains or losses from all prior years. In Exhibit 9.2, no translation loss appears in the predevaluation dollar balance sheet because any losses would have been closed to retained earnings.

The effect of the 20% devaluation is to create an immediate translation loss of $25,000. This amount is shown as a separate line item in Exhibit 9.2 in order to focus attention on it for this textbook example. Under FAS #8, this translation loss of $25,000 would have passed through the income statement, reducing reported net income and reducing retained earnings. In our example, then, ending retained earnings would in fact be $984,000; that is, $1,009,000 minus $25,000. Other countries using the monetary/nonmonetary method do not necessarily require gains and losses to pass through the income statement.

When translation loss is viewed in terms of changes in the value of exposed accounts, the loss of $25,000 under the monetary/nonmonetary method is 20% of net exposure of $125,000, as calculated in the right half of Exhibit 9.3. With a 28% appreciation of the French franc, the translation gain to the U.S. parent would be $35,000, as shown at the bottom of the right column in Exhibit 9.4.

Managerial Implications

Exhibits 9.2 through 9.4 are summarized in Exhibit 9.5. The reason that translation loss or gain is larger under the current rate method is that inventory and net plant and equipment are considered exposed. Hence exposed assets are larger, resulting in larger gains or losses.

The managerial implications of this fact are very important. If management anticipates depreciation of a foreign currency it can minimize accounting exposure by reducing net exposed assets. If management anticipates appreciation of the foreign currency it can increase net exposed assets in order to record a gain.

Exhibit 9.5   Comparison of Losses and Gains Under Two Translation Methods

	Current Rate Method	*Monetary/Nonmonetary Method*
Loss if franc depreciates 20%	$250,000	$25,000
Gain if franc appreciates 28%	$350,000	$35,000

Depending on the accounting method of the moment, management might select different assets and liabilities for reduction or increase. Thus "real" decisions about investments and financing can be dictated by selection of the accounting technique for calculating results, when in fact the method of reporting should be neutral in its influence on operating and financing decisions.

COMPARISON OF ACCOUNTING EXPOSURE WITH OPERATING EXPOSURE

The results of accounting exposure are compared with operating exposure, as calculated in Chapter 7, in Exhibit 9.6. The gains or losses above illustrate that the consequences of operating exposure may differ greatly from the consequences of accounting exposure. A manager guided by accounting measures of loss or gain might, in a situation such as Instruments Napoleon, S.A., avoid France because of the likelihood of a translation loss. Such a manager might fear loss of a bonus tied to reported profits, or possibly loss of a job if the investment in France were made and subsequently the translated income statement reported severe translation losses back to the home office.

Under two of the three assumptions about volume, cost, and price reactions to devaluation, France became a more desirable location for investment precisely because of the operating consequences that followed devaluation. This illustrates the importance of focusing decisions primarily on the operating consequences of changes in exchange rates, and only secondarily on short-run accounting measurements.

Exhibit 9.6   Comparison of Accounting Exposure with Operating Exposure.
Instruments Napoleon, S.A.

Exposure	*Amount of Loss or Gain*
Accounting Exposure (source: Exhibit 9.3)	
Current rate method	$250,000 translation loss
Monetary/nonmonetary method	25,000 translation loss
Operating Exposure (in present value terms; source: Exhibit 7.5, Chapter 7)	
Case 1	$ 104,800 cash loss
Case 2	191,700 cash gain
Case 3	450,300 cash gain

CONSOLIDATION OF ACCOUNTS

Financial statements of Instruments Napoleon, S.A., must be combined with those of its parent and sister affiliates to prepare a consolidated balance sheet and income statement. Translation of statements is necessary not only as an accounting procedure but also as the first step in preparing corporate-wide exposure reports for management use. Balance sheets for Washington Controls, Inc., the U.S. parent, and its two wholly owned affiliates, Instruments Napoleon, S.A., and Canadian Instruments, Ltd., are shown in Exhibit 9.7.

Exhibit 9.7 Nonconsolidated Balance Sheets for Washington Controls, Inc., and its French and Canadian Affiliates, December 31, 1992 (in thousands of currency units)

	Washington Controls (parent only)	Instruments Napoleon	Canadian Instruments
Assets			
Cash	$ 800 [a]	FF 1,600	C$ 600
Accounts receivable	2,400 [b]	3,200	2,000
Inventory	3,000	2,400	1,800
Net plant and equipment	5,000	4,800	3,000
Investment in Instruments Napoleon, S.A.	1,250 [c]		
Investment in Canadian Instruments, Ltd.	3,340 [d]		
	$ 15,790	FF 12,000	C$ 7,400
Liabilities and Net Worth			
Accounts payable	$ 2,000	FF 800	C$ 1,400 [b]
Short-term bank loan	2,000 [e]	1,600	825 [f]
Long-term debt	3,000	1,600	1,000 [g]
Capital stock	4,000	1,800	1,200
Retained earnings	4,790	6,200	2,975
	$ 15,790	FF 12,000	C$ 7,400

a U.S. parent has £100,000 in a London bank, carried on its books as $150,000. This amount is part of the total cash balance of $800,000 shown on the parent's books.

b Canadian Instruments owes the U.S. parent C$600,000, included in accounts payable and carried on the U.S. books at $480,000. Remaining accounts receivable (parent books) and accounts payable (Canadian Instrument's books) are in U.S. and Canadian dollars, respectively.

c The U.S. parent carries its 100% ownership of Instruments Napoleon at $1,250,000, this being the sum of capital stock ($300,000) and retained earnings ($1,000,000), minus translation adjustment ($50,000), before devaluation, as shown in Exhibit 9.2 under the current rate method of translation.

d The U.S. parent carries its 100% ownership of Canadian Instruments at $3,340,000, this being the sum of capital stock (C$1,200,000) and retained earnings (C$2,975,000), the sum times $0.80/C$. (C$4,175,000 x .80 = $3,340,000).

e The U.S. parent has borrowed, on a short-term basis, £200,000 from a London bank, carried on its books as $300,000. Remaining parent short-term bank debt is denominated in U.S. dollars.

f Canadian instruments' short-term bank loan consists of £440,000, carried on Canadian books as C$825,000. (= $660,000.)

g Canadian Instruments' long-term debt consists of FF5,120,000 in Eurofrancs, carried on Canadian books as C$1,000,000.

Exhibit 9.8   Assumed Exchange Rates, December 31, 1992

	Outright Rates	
FF6.40/$	or	$0.15625/FF
C$1.25/$	or	$0.80/C$
£0.6667/$	or	$1.50/£
	Cross Rates	
£0.5333/C$	or	C$1.8750/£
C$0.1953/FF	or	FF5.1200/C$

The nonconsolidated balance sheet of the parent is shown in column 1; column 2 shows the balance sheet of Instruments Napoleon; and column 3 shows the balance sheet of Canadian Instruments. All balance sheets are for December 31, 1992, before any changes in exchange rates. The symbol C$ is used to designate Canadian dollars, while $ by itself means U.S. dollars.

The footnotes to Exhibit 9.7 give details of the financial situation. The U.S. parent has £100,000 on deposit in a London bank; Canadian Instruments owes its U.S. parent C$600,000; the parent carries its investments in Instruments Napoleon and Canadian Instruments at $1,000,000 and $3,340,000, respectively; the U.S. parent has borrowed £200,000 from a London bank; and Canadian Instruments has long-term debt denominated in French francs of FF5,120,000. On December 31, 1992, the various spot exchange rates are as shown in Exhibit 9.8.

The process of creating a consolidated balance sheet is shown in Exhibit 9.9. First, intracompany accounts are canceled. Then remaining foreign currency accounts are translated into U.S. dollars; and the dollar amounts are added horizontally to create, in the right-hand column, the consolidated balance sheet. In this example, translation has been accomplished by the current rate method. Details of the translation for intracompany accounts are given in the notes to Exhibit 9.9.

The net effect of consolidation is to create a worldwide consolidated balance sheet that reports, in U.S. dollar terms, assets of $18,515,000, liabilities of $9,725,000, and shareholders' equity of $8,790,000. As stated earlier, the main purpose of translation is to create such a consolidated balance sheet.

MANAGING ACCOUNTING EXPOSURE

The main technique to manage accounting exposure is called a *balance sheet hedge*. Contractual hedges can also be attempted, but the end result always includes a speculative component.

Balance Sheet Hedge

A balance sheet hedge requires an equal amount of *exposed* foreign currency assets and liabilities on a firm's consolidated balance sheet. If this can be achieved for each foreign

Exhibit 9.9   Consolidated Balance Sheet for Washington Controls, Inc., December 31, 1992 (accounts translated into thousands of U.S. dollars with intracompany accounts removed)

	Washington Controls (parent)	Instruments Napoleon	Canadian Instruments	Consolidated Balance Sheet
Assets				
Cash	$ 800 [a]	$250	$480	$1,530
Accounts receivable	1,920 [b]	500	1,600	4,020
Inventory	3,000	375	1,440	4,815
Net plant and equipment	5,000	750	2,400	8,150
Investment in Instruments Napoleon, S.A.	0 [c]			
Investment in Canadian Instruments, Ltd.	0 [c]			$18,515
Liabilities and Net Worth				
Accounts payable	$ 2,000	$125	$640 [e]	$2,765
Short-term bank loan	2,000 [d]	250	660 [f]	2,910
Long-term debt	3,000	250	800 [g]	4,050
Capital stock	4,000	0 [c]	0 [c]	4,000
Retained earnings	4,790	0 [c]	0 [c]	4,790
				$18,515

a U.S. parent has £100,000 in a London bank, carried on its books as $150,000. This amount is part of the total cash balance of $800,000 shown on the parent's books.

b $2,400,000–$480,000 intracompany debt = $1,920,000.

c Investments in affiliates cancel with the equity of the affiliates in consolidation . If the carrying value on the books of the parent is not equal to the translated equity value of the affiliate, the difference is closed to retained earnings.

d includes £200,000 carried at $300,000.

e Original company balance sheet amount	C$1,4000,000
less intracompany debt	–600,000
	C$800,000
times exchange rate ($0.80/C$)	x.80
U.S.dollar amount	$640,000

f Consists of £440,000 carried as C$825,000. C$825,000 x 0.80 = $660,000. (Alternatively, $440,000 x 1.50 = $660.000.)

g Consists of FF5,120,000 carried as C$1,000,000. C$1,000,000 x 0.80 = $800,000. (Alternatively, FF5,120,000/6.4 = $800,000.)

currency, net accounting exposure will be zero. A change in exchange rates will change the value of exposed assets in an equal but opposite direction to the change in value of exposed liabilities. If a firm translates by the monetary/nonmonetary method, a zero net exposed position is called *monetary balance.*

Because accounting exposure is measured by currency, not by country, equality of exposed assets and liabilities need be achieved only on a worldwide basis and not on the individual balance sheets of each foreign affiliate. Although FAS #52 generally prescribes the current rate method of translation, it should be remembered that the balance sheet of a foreign affiliate whose functional currency is the dollar creates accounting exposure by the monetary/nonmonetary method rather than the current rate method.

The cost of a balance sheet hedge depends on relative borrowing costs. If foreign currency borrowing costs, after adjusting for foreign exchange risk, are higher than parent currency borrowing costs, the balance sheet hedge has a positive cost, and vice versa. Normal operations, however, already involve decisions about the magnitude and currency denomination of specific balance sheet accounts. Thus balance sheet hedges are a compromise in which the denomination of balance sheet accounts is altered, perhaps at a cost in terms of borrowing costs and operating efficiency, to achieve some degree of foreign exchange protection.

To illustrate a balance sheet hedge, let us return again to the accounting exposure previously identified for Instruments Napoleon and its parent, Washington Controls. Data from Exhibits 9.2 and 9.3 are restated in a different format in Exhibit 9.10. The current

Exhibit 9.10   Balance Sheet Exposure (in French francs).
Instruments Napoleon, S.A.

	Balance Sheet Accounts	Current Rate Exposure	Monetary/ Nonmonetary Exposure
Assets			
Cash	1,600,000	1,600,000	1,600,000
Accounts receivable	3,200,000	3,200,000	3,200,000
Inventory	2,400,000	2,400,000	
Net plant and equipment	4,800,000	4,800,000	
Total assets	12,000,000		
Exposed assets		12,000,000	4,800,000
Liabilities and Net Worth			
Accounts payable	800,000	800,000	800,000
Short-term bank debt	1,600,000	1,600,000	1,600,000
Long-term debt	1,600,000	1,600,000	1,600,000
Capital stock	1,800,000		
Retained earnings	6,200,000		
Total liabilities and net worth	12,000,000		
Exposed liabilities		4,000,000	4,000,000
Net exposed assets (FF)		8,000,000	800,000
Divide by exchange rate (FF/$)		6.4	6.4
Net exposed assets ($)		1,250,000	125,000

spot rate is FF6.4/\$, so Instruments Napoleon's contribution to the exposure of Washington Controls in U.S. dollars is:

Current rate method: FF8,000,000/FF6.4 per \$ = \$1,250,000.

Monetary/nonmonetary method: FF 800,000/FF6.4 per \$ = \$ 125,000.

Instruments Napoleon expects the French franc to drop 20% in value from its year-beginning value to a new exchange rate of FF8.00/\$. Under the current rate method, the expected loss is 20% of the exposure of FF8,000,000, or FF1,600,000. At FF6.4/\$, this equals the \$250,000 identified in Exhibit 9.3. Under the monetary/nonmonetary method, the expected loss is 20% of the exposure of FF800,000 or FF160,000. This equals \$25,000.

Although this "loss" is not particularly visible under the current rate method, because it bypasses the income statement and is credited directly to the cumulative translation adjustment account, Washington Controls may nevertheless wish to avoid it, if for no other reason than because the loss reduces the size of total shareholder equity. Under the monetary/nonmonetary method, the loss would pass through the income statement and reduce earnings directly; hence it would be very visible.

To achieve a balance sheet hedge, Washington Controls must either reduce exposed French franc assets without a corresponding reduction in franc liabilities, or increase French franc liabilities without an increase in exposed franc assets. One way to do this would be to exchange French francs for U.S. dollars. If Instruments Napoleon's franc cash balances were too small to reduce, an alternative, two-step approach is possible: (1) French francs could be borrowed by Instruments Napoleon, by Washington Controls, or by any affiliate that Washington Controls also consolidates into its financial statements; and (2) those French francs must be exchanged for nonexposed assets.

Current Rate Method. Under the current rate method, FF8,000,000 should be borrowed. The effect of this first step is to increase *both* an exposed asset (cash) and an exposed liability (notes payable) on the balance sheet of Instruments Napoleon, with no immediate effect on *net* exposed assets. The required follow-up step may take two forms: (1) Instruments Napoleon could exchange the acquired French francs for U.S. dollars, which Instruments Napoleon could continue to hold; or (2) Instruments Napoleon could transfer the borrowed French francs to Washington Controls, perhaps as a French franc dividend or as repayment of intracompany debt. Washington Controls could then exchange the French francs for dollars. In some countries, of course, local monetary authorities will not allow their currency to be so freely exchanged.

French francs could also be borrowed by Washington Controls, or a third affiliate, thus keeping the French franc debt entirely off Instrument Napoleon's books. However, the second step is still essential if worldwide exposure in French francs is to be eliminated; the borrowing entity must exchange the francs for dollars or other nonexposed assets. Any such borrowing should be coordinated by Washington Controls to avoid the possibility that one affiliate is borrowing French francs while another is repaying French franc loans. (Francs can be "borrowed," one should note, by delaying the repayment of existing franc debt; the goal is to increase franc debt, not borrow in a literal sense.)

Monetary/Nonmonetary Method. If translation is by the monetary/nonmonetary method, only FF800,000 need be borrowed. As before, Instruments Napoleon could use the proceeds of the loan to acquire U.S. dollars. However, Instruments Napoleon could also use the proceeds to acquire inventory or fixed assets in France, for under the monetary/nonmonetary method these assets are not regarded as exposed.

Contractual Hedges

One might think accounting exposure could be avoided with a forward market hedge, just as transaction exposure is hedged in the forward market. When applied to accounting exposure, however, this is *not* a hedge. It is an attempt to gain by forward speculation a sum equal to the book loss in translation. Furthermore, the speculative profit would be fully taxable, while the translation loss is not tax deductible.

To illustrate why this is not a hedge, suppose that Instruments Napoleon attempts to hedge its accounting exposure in the forward market by selling the exposed currency forward now, purchasing that currency in the spot market later, and at that later date delivering the purchased currency against the forward contract. The size of the necessary forward contract is determined by the following formula:[3]

$$\text{Forward contract size} = \frac{\text{potential accounting loss in reporting currency.}}{\left(\begin{array}{l}\text{Forward rate in} \\ \text{reporting currency} \\ \text{units per local} \\ \text{currency unit}\end{array}\right) - \left(\begin{array}{l}\text{Expected future spot} \\ \text{rate in reporting} \\ \text{currency units per} \\ \text{local currency unit}\end{array}\right)}$$

The denominator, the difference between the forward rate and the expected future spot rate, gives expected foreign exchange profit per unit of the parent's reporting currency. Dividing this profit per unit into the potential accounting loss gives the amount of foreign currency that must be sold forward.

In the case of Instruments Napoleon, the spot rate one year hence is expected to be FF8.00/$, or $0.1250/FF. Assume that the current one-year forward quote is FF7.5/$, or $0.1333+/FF (the "+" indicates a continuing decimal). Application of the formula to protect against the expected $250,000 loss (from Exhibit 9.3) under the current rate method is:

$$\text{Forward contract size} = \frac{\$250,000}{(\$0.1333) - (\$0.1250)} = \text{FF}30,000,000.$$

If Instruments Napoleon sells French francs forward at $0.1333+/FF and succeeds in buying them back later in the spot market at the (lower) expected spot rate of $0.1250/FF, Instruments Napoleon will earn $0.0083+ on each French franc. Total profit on the hedge, using the contract size of FF30 million, would be as follows:

Proceeds of forward sale of French francs at today's forward quote:

(FF30,000,000 x $0.1333+/FF): $ 4,000,000

Less cost of French francs purchased spot one year hence:

(FF30,000,000 x $0.1250/FF): $3,750,000

Net profit on forward hedge: $ 250,000

This forward hedge provides $250,000 of protection against the $250,000 expected accounting loss *only* if Instruments Napoleon correctly forecasts the future spot exchange rate. If the ending spot rate is *not* FF8.00/$ the firm either loses or gains depending on the direction of the error. Thus an attempted forward market hedge is actually speculation against future spot rates, which could just as easily be done without regard to the existence of accounting exposure. Hence the old bromide: if management is so smart it can consistently profit by speculating in the forward market, it ought to spend its time speculating and get out of its original line of activity.

One should also note that the profit of $250,000 on the forward hedge creates taxable income in most jurisdictions, but the accounting loss is not a taxable loss. Therefore, the required hedge is greater than that above. At a 34% corporate tax rate, the required amount to be sold forward is (FF30,000,000) / (1–0.34) = FF45,454,545!

ACTIVE VERSUS PASSIVE MANAGEMENT OF FOREIGN EXCHANGE EXPOSURE

Should management follow an *active* policy for foreign exchange risk management or *passively* accept the outcome of the marketplace? Chapters 7–9 have shown that the tools exist to protect against most kinds of foreign exchange risk, but they almost always exact a countervailing cost.

A number of theoretical arguments have been made both for and against active management of foreign exchange risk. In general, those in favor of an active strategy believe that international markets for products, factors of production, financial capital, and foreign exchange are characterized by significant imperfections and inefficiencies, and that management can recognize and act upon such imperfections.

Those who favor a passive strategy believe that these markets are reasonably efficient, and that management cannot "outguess" the market. Surveys of managerial attitudes reveal that managers often side with the market imperfections theorists (See Chapter 8, Appendix B).

Operating Exposure

The case for active management of operating exposure hinges on the degree to which purchasing power parity holds. As was shown earlier, purchasing power parity may hold in the long run, but significant deviations can occur in the short run. Furthermore, even if purchasing power parity holds when measured by a particular macroeconomic price index, market prices faced by an individual firm, which probably represent a different mix of goods and services, can create a competitive disequilibrium from that firm's perspective. Since disequilibria situations cannot be predicted accurately, management should pre-position the firm through diversification so it can recognize and take advantage of a disequilibrium situation when it occurs.

Transaction and Accounting Exposure

The case for managing transaction and accounting exposures depends on two factors: (1) the degree to which foreign exchange and money markets are efficient, and (2) management's risk aversion to higher variability in cash flow and reported earnings per share due to foreign exchange gains and losses.

Although some well-designed theoretical studies have shown that the foreign exchange and money markets for some major trading currencies have been efficient for particular time periods, this conclusion cannot be automatically extended to all currencies at all times. Indeed, many theorists and most managers believe that markets for a particular currency at a particular point in time may be inefficient and that the multinational firm is equipped to take advantage of these inefficiencies. They believe this situation exists not only for the very large number of currencies that are pegged but even for some of the widely traded major currencies. Inefficiencies can occur because of speculation, government intervention in the foreign exchange or money markets, political instability, tax law changes, or other government restrictions. If the market is inefficient, mispriced local borrowing, forward contracts, option contracts, or swaps may yield a positive return to those firms equipped to find the loopholes, avoid the restrictions, or just plain speculate.

Even if foreign exchange and money markets are always efficient, however, management is often strongly motivated to protect the firm against *unexpected* changes in future spot rates. The fact that in an efficient market the forward rate may be an *unbiased* predictor of future spot rates does not mean that the forward rate is also an *accurate* predictor of future spot rates. Management wants to ensure that whatever exchange rate may exist in the future, be it the expected rate or an unexpected rate, the variability of reported earnings per share and cash flow will be minimized. Protective techniques may thus be used to guard against the unknown—in effect, to minimize the variance—rather than to respond to a particular belief about the probable future value of a particular currency.

A further benefit of reduced variability in cash flow is the possibility that this will increase the firm's debt capacity because of lower financial risk.

Management's motivation to reduce variability is sometimes reinforced for cosmetic reasons if management believes it will be criticized more severely for incurring foreign exchange losses in its financial statements than for incurring similar or even higher costs in avoiding the foreign exchange loss. Foreign exchange losses appear in the income statement as a highly visible separate line item or as a footnote, but the costs of protection are buried in operating or interest expenses.

This accounting-driven motivation to reduce variability has been strongly attacked by efficient market theorists. They believe that investors can see through the "accounting veil" and therefore have already factored the foreign exchange effect into a firm's market valuation. Furthermore, they believe investors do not value the firm's costly efforts to reduce the foreign exchange effect because investors can do this themselves through diversifying their portfolios internationally.

Choice Between Minimizing Transaction or Accounting Exposure

If management does decide to offset both transaction and accounting exposure, it will find it virtually impossible to offset both exposures at the same time. For example, the easiest way to offset accounting exposure is to require the parent firm and all affiliates to denominate all exposed assets and liabilities in the parent's reporting currency. For U.S. firms and affiliates all assets and liabilities would be held in dollars. Such a firm would have no accounting exposure, but it would have transaction exposure. Each foreign affiliate, which normally prepares its own financial statements in local currency terms before translating into dollars, would experience transaction gains or losses on its local currency financial statements as it settled various dollar-denominated obligations. These "realized" transaction gains or losses would affect taxable income in the country of domicile, and the transaction gains or losses net of tax effect would be translated into dollars as "foreign exchange gain or loss" when the affiliate's income statement was consolidated into that of the parent. The consolidated multinational corporation would thus show some net gain or loss on foreign exchange accounts even though these were transaction gains or losses incurred by affiliates operating in dollars.

To illustrate, assume that a U.S. parent instructs its Japanese affiliate to bill an export to the parent in dollars. The account receivable on the Japanese affiliate's books would be shown in the yen equivalent of the dollar amount and yen profit on the sale would be recorded. If prior to payment for the import by the parent the yen appreciates 5%, the parent will pay only the contracted dollar amount. The Japanese affiliate will receive 5% fewer yen than were expected and booked earlier as profit, and so will have to show a 5% foreign exchange loss on its dollar-denominated accounts receivable. This foreign exchange loss will eventually be translated into dollars when the affiliate's income statement is consolidated with that of the parent. The consolidated U.S.-based multinational firm will show a foreign exchange loss—on dollars!

Similar reasoning will show that if a firm chooses to eliminate transaction exposure, accounting exposure might even be increased. The easiest way to be rid of transaction exposure is to require the parent and all affiliates to denominate all accounts subject to transaction exposure in local currency. Thus each affiliate would avoid any transaction gains or losses when those accounts are settled. However, each affiliate would be creating net accounting exposure by being either long or short in terms of local currency exposed assets or liabilities. The consolidated financial statement of the parent firm would show accounting exposure in each local currency.

Taxes complicate the decision to seek protection against transaction or accounting exposure. Transaction losses are normally considered "realized" losses and are therefore deductible from taxable income. However, accounting losses are only "paper" losses, involve no cash flows, and are not deductible from taxable income. It is highly debatable whether protective techniques that necessitate cash payments, and so reduce net cash flow, should be incurred to avoid noncash losses.

Appalachian Spring Company*

Appalachian Spring Company was founded by Aaron Copland in the late 1930s to manufacture leaf and coil springs for American automobiles. During the 1960s Appalachian Spring opened wholly owned subsidiaries in Germany and Italy to supply automobile springs for the assembly lines of two American automobile manufacturers. Subsequently, European-owned automobile companies became customers as well.

The strengthening of the U.S. dollar relative to other major currencies in the spring of 1991 caused finance manager Len Bernstein to wonder about the accounting and transaction exposure of Appalachian Spring. Mr. Bernstein was particularly worried about the possibility that the dollar would drop to its lower 1990 levels after the Persian Gulf War and economic tensions of the spring had subsided. Although a consolidated balance sheet for 1990 was not yet available, Mr. Bernstein possessed nonconsolidated balance sheets for December 31, 1990, for parent Appalachian Spring (U.S.), as well as for the two European subsidiaries.

	Appalachian Spring, U.S. (000's US$)	German Affiliate (000's DM)	Italian Affiliate (000's Lit)
Assets			
Cash	$ 20,000	DM 40,000	Lit 16,000,000
Accounts receivables	60,000 [a]	80,000 [b]	32,000,000
Inventory	40,000	40,000	32,000,000
Net plant and equipment	120,000	40,000	64,000,000
Investment in affiliates	86,667		
Total assets	$326,667	DM 200,000	Lit 144,000,000
Liabilities and Net Worth			
Accounts payable	$ 40,000	DM 80,000 [a]	Lit 16,000,000
Notes payable	60,000	20,000	64,000,000 [c]
Long-term debt	40,000	20,000	8,000,000
Common stock	60,000	40,000	16,000,000
Retained earnings	126,667	40,000	40,000,000
Total liabilities and net worth	$326,667	DM 200,000	Lit 144,000,000

Notes to financial statements:

a Of the $60,000,000 accounts receivable on the books of Appalachian Spring (U.S.), $40,000,000 is denominated in dollars and due from domestic manufacturers. The remainder consists of DM40,000,000 owed to the U.S. parent by the German affiliate and carried on the U.S. books at $20,000,000.

b The German affiliate has accounts receivable in French francs of FF90,000,000 from Renault, S.A. These are carried on the German books as DM30,000,000 and are included within the total balance of DM 80,000,000.

c The Italian affiliate owes a London Eurobank $20,000,000 (in dollars) and it owes a French bank FF 120,000,000 (in francs). The lire equivalent of these debts, Lit48,000,000,000, is included in the Lit64,000,000,000 of notes payable.

*David K. Eiteman, University of California at Los Angeles, April 1991.

At the present time exchange rates are as follows:

	Spot	*Six-Month Forward*
Germany	DM 2.00/$	DM 1.96/$
France	FF 6.00/$	FF 5.90/$
Italy	Lit 1200/$	Lit 1300/$

Mr. Bernstein decided that he should first prepare a consolidated balance sheet in U.S. dollars for Appalachian Spring Company, using the current rate method of FAS#52 mandated by U.S. generally accepted accounting principles. When this was done he would calculate Appalachian Spring's accounting and transaction foreign exchange exposures.

The ultimate purpose of calculating foreign exchange exposure is to enable Mr. Bernstein to address the steps that might be taken to minimize Appalachian Spring's exposure to changes in foreign exchange rates in the months ahead.

SUMMARY

- Accounting exposure results from translating foreign-currency denominated statements of foreign affiliates into the parent's reporting currency, so that the parent can prepare consolidated financial statements. Accounting exposure is the potential for a translation loss or gain.

- Two basic conventions for translation are used today in most countries: (1) the current rate method, and (2) the monetary/nonmonetary method. Other methods also exist.

- Technical aspects of translation include the question of when to recognize gains or losses in the income statement, the distinction between functional and reporting currency, and the treatment of affiliates in hyperinflation countries.

- The main technique to manage accounting exposure is a balance sheet hedge. This calls for having an equal amount of exposed foreign currency assets and liabilities on a firm's consolidated balance sheet.

- The question is raised of whether management should follow an active policy of foreign exchange risk management or passively accept the outcome of the marketplace. Although hedging tools exist to offset each type of exposure, their use almost always exacts a countervailing cost. The answer to the question for an individual firm depends on its belief about whether or not foreign exchange markets are efficient most of the time. It should be noted that even if management chooses to follow an active policy, it is nearly impossible to offset both transaction and translation exposure simultaneously. If forced to choose, most managers would protect against transaction losses because these are realized cash losses, rather than protect against accounting losses, which are only book losses.

1. Parana Products, S.A.

Parana Products, S.A., is the Brazilian affiliate of a U.S. manufacturing company. Its balance sheet, in thousands of Brazilian cruzeiros (Cr$), for January 1, 1992, is shown below. The January 1, 1992, exchange rate was Cr$150/$.

Parana Products Balance Sheet (thousands of cruzeiros)

Assets		Liabilities and Net Worth	
Cash	Cr$ 60,000	Current liabilities	Cr$ 30,000
Accounts receivable	120,000	Long-term debt	90,000
Inventory	120,000	Capital stock	420,000
Net plant and equipment	240,000		
Total	Cr$540,000	Total	Cr$540,000

a) Determine Parana Products' contribution to the accounting exposure of its parent on January 1, 1992, using the current rate method.

b) Calculate Parana Products' contribution to its parent's accounting loss if the exchange rate on December 31, 1992, is Cr$200/$. Assume all cruzeiro accounts remain as they were at the beginning of the year.

2. Siam Toys, Ltd.

Siam Toys, Ltd. is the Thai affiliate of a U.S. toy manufacturer. Siam Toys uses plastic injection equipment to manufacture toys, which are sold primarily in the United States and Europe. Siam Toys' balance sheet in thousands of Thai bahts (symbol ฿) as of March 31st is as follows:

Assets		Liabilities and Net Worth	
Cash	฿ 3,000	Accounts payable	฿ 1,500
Accounts receivable	4,500	One-year bank loan	1,400
Inventory	4,500	Development loan	3,000
Net plant and equipment	6,000	Capital stock	6,000
		Retained earnings	6,000
Total	฿ 18,000	Total	฿ 18,000

Exchange rates for translating Siam Toys' balance sheet into U.S. dollars are:

฿ 15/$: Historic exchange rate, at which plant and equipment, development loan, and common stock were acquired or issued.

฿ 20/$: March 31st exchange rate, at which inventory was acquired.

฿ 25/$: April 1st exchange rate, after devaluation of 20%.

Assuming no change in balance sheet accounts between March 31st and April 1st, calculate accounting gain or loss by the current rate method (or by monetary-nonmonetary method, if more appropriate). Explain accounting loss in terms of changes in the value of exposed accounts.

3. Croft House Farms, Ltd.

Croft House Farms, Ltd., manufactures orange marmalade in Bradford, West Yorkshire, England. Croft House Farms is the wholly owned subsidiary of Lotts Berry Farm, Inc. of Los Angeles. The functional currency for Croft is the pound sterling, which currently sells at $1.5000/£. The reporting currency for Lotts is the U.S. dollar. Nonconsolidated financial statements for both Croft and Lotts are as follows (in thousands):

Assets	*Lotts, Inc.*	*Croft, Ltd.*
Cash	$ 4,000	£1,000
Accounts receivable	6,000	2,000 [a]
Inventory	4,000	1,000
Net plant and equipment	8,000	3,000
Investment in Croft	4,500	
Total	$26,500	£7,000

Liabilities and Net Worth		
Current liabilities	$10,000 [b]	£2,000
5-year term loan		2,000 [c]
Capital stock	4,000	1,000
Retained earnings	12,500	2,000
Total	$26,500	£7,000

Notes to financial statements:

a Includes £1,000,000 due from Lotts. The amount is denominated in sterling.

b Includes $1,500,000 due to Croft. The amount is denominated in sterling and carried at the exchange rate of $1.50/pound on Lotts' books.

c The entire term loan is for $3,000,000 and is denominated in U.S. dollars. The loan is from a Singapore bank.

a) Prepare a consolidated balance sheet for Lotts and its subsidiary.

b) What is Lotts' accounting exposure in its English subsidiary? Use the current rate method of calculation.

c) Before any business activities take place, the pound sterling depreciates 9% in value relative to the dollar. What is the new spot rate?

d) What is Lotts' accounting loss or gain, if any, by the current rate method?

4. Northwood Company

The Northwood Company of Seattle has a subsidiary in Indonesia, where the currency

NOTES

1. Gerhard G. Mueller, Helen Gernon, and Gary Meek, *Accounting: An International Perspective*, Homewood, Illinois: Richard D. Irwin, 1987. p. 93.

2. Russell A. Taussig, "Impact of SFAS No. 52 on the Translation of Foreign Financial Statements of Companies in Highly Inflationary Economies," *Journal of Accounting, Auditing, and Finance*, Winter 1983, pp. 145–146.

3. This formula ignores taxes for simplicity sake. The tax effect would vary depending on in which tax jurisdiction the forward contact was executed and whether excess tax credits could be utilized.

BIBLIOGRAPHY

Adler, Michael, "Translation Methods and Operational Foreign Exchange Risk Management," in Göran Bergendahl, ed., *International Financial Management*, Stockholm: Norstedt & Soners, 1982, pp. 87–103.

—— and Bernard Dumas, "Should Exposure Management Depend on Translation Accounting Methods?" *Euromoney*, June 1981, pp. 132–138.

Aliber, R. Z., and C. P. Stickney, "Accounting Measures of Foreign Exchange Exposure: The Long and Short of It," *Accounting Review*, January 1975, pp. 44–57.

Arnold, Jerry L., and William W. Holder, *Impact of Statement 52 On Decisions, Financial Reports, and Attitudes*, Morristown, N.J.: Financial Executives Research Foundation, 1986.

Choi, Frederick D. S., Howard D. Lowe, and Reginald G. Worthley, "Accountors, Accountants, and Standard No. 8," *Journal of International Business Studies*, Fall 1978, pp. 81–87.

Eaker, M. R., "The Numeraire Problem and Foreign Exchange Risk," *Journal of Finance*, May 1981, pp. 419–426.

Evans, Thomas G., and Timothy S. Doupnik, *Determining the Functional Currency Under Statement 52*, Stamford, Conn.: Financial Accounting Standards Board, 1986.

——, *Foreign Exchange Risk Management Under Statement 52*, Stamford, Conn. Financial Accounting Standards Board, 1986.

Evans, Thomas G., William R. Folks, Jr., and Michael Jilling, *The Impact of Statement of Financial Accounting Standards No. 8 on the Foreign Exchange Management Practices of American Multinationals: An Economic Impact Study*, Stamford, Conn.: Financial Accounting Standards Board, November 1978.

Financial Accounting Standards Board, *Accounting for the Translation of Foreign Currency Transactions and Foreign Currency Financial Statements*, Statement of Financial Accounting Standards No. 8, October 1975, Stamford, Conn.: Financial Accounting Standards Board, 1975. Reprinted, except for Appendix D, in *Journal of Accountancy*, December 1975, pp. 78–89.

——, *Foreign Currency Translation*, Statement of Financial Accounting Standards No. 52, December 1981, Stamford, Conn.: Financial Accounting Standards Board, 1981.

Garlicki, T. Dessa, Frank J. Fabozzi, and Robert Fonfeder, "The Impact of Earnings Under FASB 52 on Equity Returns," *Financial Management*, Autumn 1987, pp. 36–44.

Houston, Carol Olson, "Translation Exposure Hedging Post SFAS No. 52," *Journal of International Financial Management and Accounting*, 2, nos. 2 and 3, Summer and Autumn 1990, pp. 145–170.

Ijiri, Yuji, "Foreign Currency Accounting and Its Transition," in R. J. Herring, ed., *Management of Foreign Exchange Risk*, Cambridge, England; Cambridge University Press, 1983.

Rayburn, Frank R., and G. Michael Crooch, "Currency Translation and the Funds Statement: A New Approach," *Journal of Accountancy*, October 1983, pp. 51–62.

Ruland, Robert G., and Timothy S. Doupnik, "Foreign Currency Translation and the Behavior of Exchange Rates," *Journal of International Business Studies*, Fall 1988, pp. 461–476.

Rosenfield, Paul, "Accounting for Foreign Operations," *Journal of Accountancy*, August 1987, pp. 103–112.

Sapy-Mazello, Jean-Pierre, Robert M. Woo, and James Czechowicz, *New Directions in Managing Currency Risk: Changing Corporate Strategies and Systems under FAS No. 52*, New York: Business International, 1982.

Taussig, Russell A., "Impact of SFAS No. 52 on the Translation of Foreign Financial Statements of Companies in Highly Inflationary Economies," *Journal of Accounting, Auditing and Finance*, Winter 1983, pp. 142–156.

Accounting Loss Measured During a Year of Operations

The Instruments Napoleon example in this chapter is necessarily simple in order to avoid the complications of translating an income statement. In this appendix, the translation loss created by Instruments Napoleon will be measured at the end of 1993, a year during which it is assumed that the franc depreciates steadily from FF6.40/$ (on December 31, 1992) to FF8.00/$ (on December 31, 1993). The historic exchange rate remains at FF6.00/$.

Translation of an income statement requires calculation of average exchange rates. Instruments Napoleon has an inventory turnover of three months—that is, inventory sold in any quarter was manufactured in the previous quarter. Instruments Napoleon uses first-in, first-out (FIFO) accounting for cost of goods sold. Using average exchange rates for each quarter, we can calculate 1993 average exchange rates for current operating expenses and for cost of goods sold as follows:

Time period	End-of-Quarter Exchange Rate	Quarterly Average Exchange Rate	Average for Sales and Operating Expenses	Average for Cost of Goods Sold
3rd quarter 1992	6.00			
4th quarter 1992	6.40	6.20	—	6.20
1st quarter 1993	6.80	6.60	6.60	6.60
2nd quarter 1993	7.20	7.00	7.00	7.00
3rd quarter 1993	7.60	7.40	7.40	7.40
4th quarter 1993	8.00	7.80	7.80	—
Total			28.80	27.20
Average			FF7.20/$	FF6.80/$

During 1993 the following business activities occur.

- Instruments Napoleon sells 1,000,000 units at the rate of 250,000 units per quarter. Unit sales price is FF12.80, and annual sales revenue is thus FF12,800,000.

- During the year collections from accounts receivable consist of year-beginning receivables (FF3,200,000) and proceeds from sales of the first three quarters (FF9,600,000). Year-end accounts receivable consist of sales of the fourth quarter: 250,000 units at FF12.80 = FF3,200,000.

- Cost of goods sold is FF9.60 per unit. During 1993 year-beginning inventory (250,000 units) is sold. New manufacturing consists of 250,000 units per quarter, and inventory on hand at the end of the year is that manufactured during the fourth quarter: 250,000 units at FF9.60 = FF2,400,000.

- General and administrative expenses of FF1,200,000 are incurred and paid in cash during 1993. Annual depreciation is FF240,000.

- The French corporate income tax rate is 50 percent, and income taxes are paid on a cash basis throughout every year.
- No cash dividends are paid.
- Accounts payable and short-term bank debt are rolled over and renewed, respectively, for the same amount as that at the end of 1992. (For this example, interest on bank debt is ignored.)

As a consequence of the above events, changes in Instruments Napoleon's cash balance during 1993 are as follows.

Year-beginning cash balance (Dec. 31, 1992)	FF1,600,000
Plus:	
Collection of year-beginning accounts receivables	3,200,000
Collection of receivables from sales of first three quarters	9,600,000
Available	14,400,000
Less:	
General and administrative expenses paid	1,200,000
Income taxes paid	880,000
Manufacturing costs for new inventory	9,600,000
Year-end cash balance (Dec. 31, 1993)	FF2,720,000

The income statement for the year ended December 31, 1993, is shown in Exhibit 9A.1, and balance sheets for both December 31, 1992, and December 31, 1993, are shown in Exhibit 9A.2.

In 1993, Instruments Napoleon earned net income of FF880,000. Because no dividends were paid, retained earnings rose from FF6,200,000 to FF7,080,000. This increase is shown both at the bottom of the franc income statement in the surplus reconciliation (Exhibit 9A.1), and also as the increase between the year-beginning and year-ending retained earnings accounts in the franc balance sheet (Exhibit 9A.2).

Current Rate Method

Under the current rate method of translation, all revenue and expense accounts are translated at the *average* exchange rate in effect during the year. This process leads to net income translated into dollars of $122,300 and to year-end retained earnings of $1,122,300. These numbers appear in the current rate translation column of Exhibits 9A.1 and 9A.2.

Under the current rate method, accounting gains and losses are not shown in the income statement, nor are they reflected in the retained earnings account. Rather, any imbalance in the dollar balance sheet from the prior year shows as a change in the cumulative translation adjustment account. Exhibit 9A.2 shows that the cumulative translation adjustment account changes from a credit balance of $50,000 to a credit balance of $312,300. The difference of $262,300 is an accounting loss for the year. It is carried forward to future years in the cumulative translation adjustment account in the equity section of the balance sheet.

Exhibit 9A.1 Income Statements During a Year of Operations: Instruments Napoleon, S.A., Income Statements, Year Ended December 31, 1993 (dollars and francs in thousands)

Item	Income Statement in French Francs	Current Rate Translation		Monetary/ Nonmonetary Translation	
		Rate	Dollars	Rate	Dollars
Sales (@FF12.8/unit)	12,800	7.2[a]	1,777.8	7.2[a]	1,777.8
Direct costs (@FF9.6/unit)	9,600	7.2[a]	1,333.3	6.8[b]	1,411.8
Cash operating expenses	1,200	7.2[a]	166.7	7.2[a]	166.7
Depreciation	240	7.2[a]	33.3	6.0[c]	40.0
Total operating expenses	11,040		1,533.3		1,618.5
Pretax profit	1,760		244.5		159.3
French income tax @50%	880	7.2[a]	122.2	7.2[a]	122.2
Profit after tax	880		122.3		37.1
Foreign exchange gain <loss>	n.a.		n.a.		<38.4>
Net income	880		122.3		<1.3>
Retained earnings, December 31, 1992	6,200		1,000.0		1,009.0
Less dividends paid	0		0.0		0.0
Retained earnings, December 31, 1993	7,080		1,122.3		1,007.7

a Average exchange rate for current year.

b Historic exchange rate for inventory.

c Historic exchange rate for plant and equipment.

n.a. Not applicable. This line would not appear in this statement.

Monetary/Nonmonetary Method

Under the monetary/nonmonetary method of translation, sales and cash operating expenses are translated at the average exchange rate of FF7.20/$. However, cost of goods sold and depreciation are translated at the historical rate of exchange appropriate for each asset category within those groups. A rate of FF6.80/$ was used for cost of goods sold and a rate of FF6.00/$ for depreciation.

Under the monetary/nonmonetary method, pretax operating profit is calculated to be $159,300 (the difference between sales revenue and the various expenses, each translated individually). Income tax expense is translated directly from the franc accounts at the average rate of exchange as $122,200. After-tax profit is calculated to be $37,100. Translation of the balance sheet (Exhibit 9A.2) shows that year-end retained earnings must be $1,007,700, down $1,300 from year-beginning retained earnings of $1,009,000. Since translated earnings were $37,100, an accounting loss of $38,400 was experienced under the monetary/nonmonetary method.

The translation loss of $38,400 is the amount necessary to reconcile the net income figure with the change in retained earnings shown in Exhibit 9A.2. Because this accounting

Exhibit 9A.2 Balance Sheets at Beginning and End of a Year of Operations: Instruments Napoleon, S.A., Balance Sheets, Years Ended December 31, 1992, and December 31, 1993 (dollars and francs in thousands)

Item	Balance Sheet in French Francs	Current Rate Translation		Monetary/ Nonmonetary Translation	
		Rate	Dollars	Rate	Dollars
Balance Sheet, December 31, 1992					
Cash	1,600	6.4	250.0	6.4	250.0
Accounts receivable	3,200	6.4	500.0	6.4	500.0
Inventory	2,400	6.4	375.0	6.25	384.0
Net plant and equipment	4,800	6.4	750.0	6.0	800.0
Total	12,000		1,875.0		1,934.0
Accounts payable	800	6.4	125.0	6.4	125.0
Short-term bank debt	1,600	6.4	250.0	6.4	250.0
Long-term bank debt	1,600	6.4	250.0	6.4	250.0
Capital stock	1,800	6.0	300.0	6.0	300.0
Retained earnings	6,200		1,000.0		1,009.0
Translation adjustment			< 50.0>		
Total	12,000		1,875.0		1,934.0
Balance Sheet, December 31, 1993					
Cash	2,720	8.0	340.0	8.0	340.0
Accounts receivable	3,200	8.0	400.0	8.0	400.0
Inventory	2,400	8.0	300.0	7.8	307.7
Net plant and equipment	4,560	8.0	570.0	6.0	760.0
Total	12,880		1,610.0		1,807.7
Accounts payable	800	8.0	100.0	8.0	100.0
Short-term bank debt	1,600	8.0	200.0	8.0	200.0
Long-term bank debt	1,600	8.0	200.0	8.0	200.0
Capital stock	1,800	6.0	300.0	6.0	300.0
Retained earnings	7,080		1,122.3		1,007.7
Translation adjustment	n.a.		< 312.3>		n.a.
Total	12,800		1,610.0		1,807.7

n.a. Not applicable. This line would not appear in this statement.

loss usually passes through the net income calculation, the loss shows up in Exhibit 9A.1 as a subtraction before the calculation of net income. Note that under the monetary/ nonmonetary method year-end inventory has been translated at FF7.80/$, the historical rate derived from the last quarter of 1993, when that inventory was manufactured.

PART
3

FINANCING FROM A
GLOBAL PERSPECTIVE

One of the three main themes of this book is that although there is a trend toward integration of money and capital markets, which tends to remove market imperfections, excellent opportunities still exist for firms to lower their cost of capital and increase its availability by sourcing funds internationally. Furthermore, investors might increase their return while lowering their risk through international portfolio diversification. Chapter 10 will explain the role banks play as intermediaries in international capital markets. Chapter 11 analyzes the alternative instruments and their costs available to multinationals wishing to source debt internationally. Chapter 12 will describe the state of global equity markets and how firms can source equity internationally. Chapter 13 explains how investors can benefit from international portfolio diversification. This section concludes with Chapter 14's analysis of the cost of capital and financial structure issues for the multinational firm.

CHAPTER 10

International Banking

The growth of multinational business since the end of World War II has been accompanied by a parallel development of international financial centers, with international banks acting as the key financial intermediary in these centers. Although the major focus of this book is on financial management of multinational firms, international banks deserve special attention because they facilitate and support these firms. Furthermore, the banks themselves are usually major multinational enterprises.

International banks facilitate and support multinational firms in the following ways:

- Financing imports and exports (the traditional international banking task).
- Trading foreign exchange and currency options.
- Borrowing and lending in the Eurocurrency market.
- Organizing or participating in international loan syndications.
- Underwriting both Eurobonds and foreign bonds.
- Engaging in project financing.
- Providing international cash management services.
- Soliciting local currency deposits and loans with an intent to operate as a full-service local bank.
- Supplying information and advice to clients, including multinational firms.

Some of the largest world banks attempt to do all of these things. Others have found it advantageous to specialize in a select few of the possible activities. Banks generalize or specialize according to their abilities and size, as well as their perception of what unique services their original home clients need.

In this chapter we first define and identify international financial centers. These are the hubs from which international banks operate. Second, we analyze potential bank strategies under current conditions. Third, we describe the alternative types of banking offices through which international banks implement their strategy. Fourth, we highlight some national differences in the manner that banks offer their services. Fifth, we analyze the risks involved in international lending to developing countries. Sixth, we describe how banks analyze country risk. Seventh, we analyze the various strategies and techniques used by both the developing countries and the banks to manage their international debt problems.

INTERNATIONAL FINANCIAL CENTERS

International banking is concentrated in certain cities that have come to be identified as international financial centers. London, Tokyo, and New York City are the most important, but other locations are also prominent. Four major types of transactions occur in an international financial center that is also an important domestic financial center. These are depicted in Exhibit 10.1.

Exhibit 10.1   Schematic View of Transactions in an International Financial Center

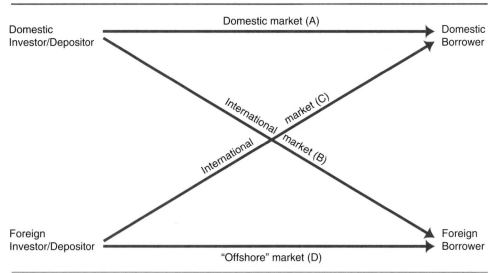

Note: The terms "offshore" and "overseas" are often used in the English language as synonyms for "foreign," presumably because England, the home country of the language, is an island. Describing Luxembourg as an "offshore" financial center seems contrary to a literal meaning of the word, since it is England that is "offshore." However, with the completion of the tunnel under the English Channel (or "Chunnel" as it is sometimes called), it is questionable whether anyone is truly offshore!

Any important national financial center will depend on the presence of a large body of domestic investors or depositors supplying funds to domestic users (Relationship A). Investors supply funds directly to users by purchasing securities such as bonds, commercial paper, or shares of stock, while depositors supply their funds to financial intermediaries (banks, insurance companies, mutual funds, etc.) which pool these receipts and make loans or equity investments from the pool. Most financial intermediaries guarantee the deposit, so the depositor looks to the intermediary rather than to the ultimate borrower for security.

An international financial center exists when domestic funds are supplied to foreign users or when foreign funds are supplied to domestic users. These are the diagonal Relationships B and C. A healthy international financial center will almost always develop business along line D, in which foreign funds are supplied to foreign users.

London, Tokyo, and New York, as the world's most important international financial markets, perform all four of the possible functions. Other cities perform two or three of the four functions quite well and are important regional financial centers. These include Paris, Zurich, Geneva, Amsterdam, Singapore, and Hong Kong.[1]

Still other centers perform only Relationship D. They are usually referred to as "offshore" financial centers. They exist by providing a service for nonresidents while (usually) keeping their international business separate from their domestic business. Typical offshore financial centers are Luxembourg, Cayman Islands, the Bahamas, the Netherlands Antilles, and Bahrain. Jersey, Guernsey, and the Isle of Man function as offshore financial centers for London-based financing.[2]

The major requirements for success as an offshore financial center are the following:[3]

- Economic and political stability, which gives confidence to nonresidents that fund movements will not be restricted.

- An efficient and experienced financial community, able to carry out necessary technical operations with skill.

- Good communication and support services, so that market information can be quickly and efficiently transmitted to participants.

- A regulatory climate that protects investors and depositors but is not unduly restrictive to financial institutions.

Exhibit 10.2 shows how international banking assets were distributed by international financial center at the end of 1989. The most important center was the United Kingdom (London), followed by Japan (Tokyo). The Japanese market has been the fastest-growing segment of the international banking market, especially following the 1986 establishment of a Japanese offshore market. This market is similar in concept to U.S. International Banking Facilities (IBFs) (to be described shortly), in that Japanese banks have a set of segregated accounts that are exempt from certain domestic regulations in order to attract Eurocurrency business. The main depositors and borrowers in this

Exhibit 10.2 International Banking Assets, End-of-Year 1989, by Financial Center (in billions of U.S. dollars)

Positions of Banks in:	External Assets in Domestic Currency	External Assets in Foreign Currency	Local Assets in Foreign Currency
Europe:			
United Kingdom	73.8	850.2	274.5
France	51.0	283.4	74.1
Germany	188.1	80.4	4.4
Luxembourg	3.3	225.7	39.3
Belgium	10.1	151.9	46.8
Netherlands	32.0	118.6	22.9
Switzerland	58.4	65.1	19.4
Sweden	3.4	17.6	47.0
Other European	27.0	163.5	104.1
Total European	447.1	1956.4	632.5
Japan:			
Offshore	183.0	246.0	67.0
Other	189.7	223.3	408.1
United States:			
IBFs[3]	289.6	53.3	0.0
Other	244.6	11.8	0.0
Canada	4.2	46.0	25.3
Asian Centers	4.7 [1]	693.0 [2]	0.0
Carribbean Centers	0.0	438.1	0.0
TOTAL	1362.8	3668.0	1132.9

Source: Bank for International Settlements, *60th Annual Report*, Basle, June 11, 1990, p. 127.

1 Hong Kong only.

2 Including Bahrain.

3 International Banking Facilities.

market are the Japanese banks themselves and their foreign branches. The Euroyen is the currency of denomination. The third most important market is the United States, chiefly because of IBFs.

Exhibit 10.3 shows that the most important currency of denomination is the U.S. dollar, which accounts for about 60% of the international banking market. Other important currencies are the Deutschemark, Swiss franc, Japanese yen, U.K. pound, and the European Currency Unit (ECU).

Exhibit 10.3 The Currency Composition of International Banks' Foreign
Currency Assets (assets at end-of-year 1989, billions of U.S. dollars)

Currency	Cross-Border Positions[1]	Percent of Total	Local Positions in Foreign Currency[1]	Percent of Total
U.S. dollar	1469.9	57.9	753.2	66.5
Deutschemark[2]	341.9	13.5	128.2	11.3
Japanese yen[2]	177.4	7.0	40.4	3.6
Swiss franc[2]	113.8	4.5	57.3	5.1
ECU[2]	104.9	4.1	35.3	3.1
British pound[2]	77.1	3.0	21.9	1.9
Other	251.9	9.9	96.6	8.5
TOTAL	2536.9	100.0	1132.9	100.0

Source: Derived by authors from data contained in The Bank for International Settlements' *60th Annual Report*, Basle, June 11, 1990, p. 134.

1 Positions of banks in industrial reporting countries only. Cross-border positions are claims on nonresidents denominated in all currencies, including the domestic currency. Local positions in foreign currency refers to claims on residents denominated in nondomestic currency.

2 Excluding positions of banks in the United States.

INTERNATIONAL STRATEGIES OF BANKS

International strategies of banks are normally evolutionary, with multinational banking being the final step. Currently, bank strategists are wrestling with the opportunities created by the consequences of the Single European Act (1985) and the strengthening of capital adequacy standards.

Stages of Evolution

Ian Giddy has identified three stages of evolution: arm's-length international banking, offshore banking, and host country banking (multinational banking).[4]

Arm's-length international banking exists when the domestic bank carries on its international banking from within its home country, accepting foreign deposits and making foreign loans. This is usually the first phase of a bank's involvement in international activities. It then evolves naturally into a need to develop relationships with correspondent banks in other countries. The international banking department of the home bank functions primarily as a center for clearing international payments and for financing imports and exports. The main customers are importers, exporters, tourists, and foreign banks.

As the needs of their customers become more sophisticated the next phase for internationalizing the bank's activities is usually to establish an offshore banking presence. In offshore banking, the bank accepts deposits and makes loans and investments in a

Eurocurrency, and books these transactions in an offshore shell branch location. Examples are Eurodollars held in shell branches in the Bahamas or the Cayman Islands or in international banking facilities (IBFs) in the United States. Offshore banks are active in the purchase and placement of short-term funds, in syndicated loans, and in foreign exchange trading. Their depositors and borrowers are usually located in countries other than the home country of the offshore bank. Some offshore banks specialize in taking deposits for relending in their home country.

The ultimate level of international commitment is for a bank to establish itself within other countries. Host-country banking typically involves full-service banking in a foreign country through a branch or subsidiary of the parent bank. Deposits and loans are made in the local currency to residents of the host country, in competition with local banks.

Strategic Consequences of the Single European Market

The Single European Market, to be completed at end-of-year 1992, will have a significant impact on the structure of the banking markets of the EEC. The primary provision of the Single European Act of 1985 on banking is the *Single Banking License*, which will allow banks to operate in all member states without separately licensed and capitalized subsidiaries or branches. These banks would be able to pursue all banking operations allowed by their own home-country license. The single market will create opportunities for previously foreign banks to now be domestic banks.

Although the single banking license will theoretically allow EEC-wide branching, the realities will be considerably more restrictive. Many of the country markets in the EEC are already overbanked, and new branch banking, particularly on the retail level, will not be profitable or likely. The single market will, however, allow many banks to selectively enter foreign niche-markets for specialty banking and financial services.[5] Deutsche Bank's acquisition of Banca d'America d'Italia (Italy) and Morgan Grenfell (United Kingdom) is an example of this selective entry approach, gaining entry into retail and investment banking markets, respectively.

In light of this new, more open single banking market, many banks are entering new markets—and protecting domestic markets—through mergers and strategic alliances. These cooperative ventures allow banks to expand into new higher value-added specialty markets abroad, with the cooperation of a locally based bank, while not threatening that bank, and simultaneously protecting its domestic market. As end-of-year 1992 comes and goes, the final more consolidated and competitive European banking industry will evolve into one of the most sophisticated in the world.

Strategic Consequences of Strengthening Capital Adequacy Standards

The *Basle Accord*, an agreement among the Group of Ten industrial countries and Luxembourg in 1988, established a framework for the measurement of bank capital internationally, and set a standard for minimum capital adequacy. Although the agreement applies only to banks which are internationally active, the same standards are now being adopted by other countries for all their banks.

The Basle Accord divided bank capital into two categories: (1) core capital, which consists of shareholder equity and disclosed reserves; (2) supplementary capital, consisting of a number of hybrid securities (having characteristics of both debt and equity)—mostly subordinated perpetual notes. The capital needs of the bank are determined by a risk-based weighting of both on- and off-balance sheet items. The minimum capital adequacy as stated in the Basle Accord is 4% for each category of bank capital (8% in total) by end-of-year 1992.

The strategic implications of these standards is as yet unclear. The most visible impact to date has been the efforts by banks to increase their core capital levels. Many international banks are purported to be shifting assets to low-risk categories, such as the popular asset-backed securities used by U.S. banks. These have already spread in usage to France, Germany, and the United Kingdom. The standards are definitely altering the decisions banks make regarding the composition of their portfolios, and may have already slowed the expansion of bank balance sheets internationally.

The biggest uncertainty regarding the impacts of the Basle Accord surround the competitiveness of banks with nonbanks. The increased financial intermediation costs from higher minimum capital adequacy standards may result in increased use of securitized assets which previously did not meet the credit standards necessary for market trading. There are also early indications of a slowdown in lending as a result of the higher costs. Time will tell.

TYPES OF BANKING OFFICES

By combining correspondent banking, offshore banking, and host-country banking, a multinational bank can offer a global network to meet the worldwide needs of its client firms. Foreign banking offices of such a global network may be of five types: correspondent banks, representative offices, branch banks, subsidiaries, and affiliates. In addition, U.S. banks now are able to operate International Banking Facilities (IBFs) and Edge Act corporations within the United States. Activities permitted under each form vary somewhat, according to the laws of the various host countries (or, in the case of foreign banks in the United States, according to state laws). The following discussion is necessarily general rather than specific to any single country.

Correspondent Banks

Most major banks of the world maintain correspondent banking relationships with local banks in each of the important foreign cities of the world. The two-way link between banks is essentially one of "correspondence," via fax, cable, and mail, and a mutual deposit relationship. For example, a U.S. bank may have a correspondent bank in Kuala Lumpur, Malaysia, and the U.S. bank will in turn be the correspondent bank for the Malaysian bank. Each will maintain a deposit in the other in local currency.

Correspondent services include accepting drafts, honoring letters of credit, and furnishing credit information. Services are centered around collecting or paying foreign funds, often because of import or export transactions. However, a visiting business person can use the home bank's introduction to meet local bankers.

Under a correspondent banking relationship neither of the correspondent banks maintains its own personnel in the other country. Direct contact between the banks is usually limited to periodic visits between members of the banks' management.

For the business person the main advantage of banking at home with a bank having a large number of foreign correspondent relationships is the ability to handle financial matters in a large number of foreign countries through local bankers whose knowledge of local customs should be extensive. The disadvantages are the lack of ability to deposit in, borrow from, or disburse from a branch of one's own home bank, as well as the possibility that correspondents will put a lower priority on serving the foreign banks' customer than on serving their own permanent customers.

Representative Offices

A bank establishes a representative office in a foreign country primarily to help parent bank clients when they are doing business in that country or in neighboring countries. It also functions as a geographically convenient location from which to visit correspondent banks in its region rather than sending bankers from the parent bank at greater financial and physical cost. A representative office is not a "banking office." It cannot accept deposits, make loans, commit the parent bank to a loan, or deal in drafts, letters of credit, or the Eurocurrency market. Indeed, a tourist cannot even cash a travelers check from the parent bank in the representative office.

The basic function of a representative office is to provide information, advice, and local contacts for the parent bank's business clients and to provide a location where business persons from either country can initiate inquiries about the parent bank's services. Representative offices introduce visiting executives to local banks, and they watch over correspondent banking relationships. They put parent bank customers in contact with local business firms interested in supplying, purchasing, or marketing products or services, and they arrange meetings with government officials if that is needed to obtain permissions, approvals, or government help. They provide credit analysis of local firms and economic and political intelligence about the country.

A representative office is usually small, often one executive, two or three assistants, and clerical help, all of whom work in an office that does not resemble a banking office in the physical sense. The representative and the assistants may have come to the office from the home country, but it is equally likely that they are citizens or permanent residents of the host country. The major advantage of a representative office is that the local representative will have a more precise understanding of the needs of home-country clients than might local correspondents and can thus provide data and advice more suitable to their needs. The local representative will be bilingual, if that is needed, and can advise visitors about local customs and procedures.

If the parent bank eventually decides to open a local general banking office, the existence of a representative office for some prior period usually provides a valuable base of contacts and expertise to facilitate the change. However, representative offices are not necessarily a prelude to a general banking office, nor need an eventual general banking office be the major reason for opening a representative office. In some countries, such as Mexico, foreign banks are precluded from opening new general banking offices. Thus representative offices are the only possible presence in such countries.

The essential disadvantage of the representative office to the business firm is that it cannot conduct general banking activities. Although it can facilitate such transactions with local correspondents, the process may be slower or more cumbersome than a business firm might wish. Because a representative office is usually small, physical limitations do exist on the services that can be supplied to home office clients.

Branch Banks

A foreign branch bank is a legal and operational part of the parent bank, with the full resources of that parent behind the local office. A branch bank does not have its own corporate charter, its own board of directors, or any shares of stock outstanding. Although for managerial and regulatory purposes it will maintain its own set of books, its assets and liabilities are in fact those of the parent bank. However, branch deposits are not subject to reserve requirements or FDIC insurance, in the case of U.S. banks, unless the deposits are reloaned to the U.S. parent bank.

Branch banks are subject to two sets of banking regulations. As part of the parent, they are subject to home-country regulations. However, they are also subject to regulations of the host country, which may provide any of a variety of restrictions on their operations.

The major advantage to a business of using a branch bank is that the branch will conduct a full range of banking services under the name and legal obligation of the parent. A deposit in a branch is a legal obligation of the parent. Services to customers are based on the worldwide value of the client relationship rather than just on the relationship to the local office. Legal loan limits are a function of the size of the parent, not of the branch.

From the point of view of a banker the profits of a foreign branch are subject to immediate taxation at home, and losses of a foreign branch are deductible against taxable income at home. A new office expected to have losses in its early years creates a tax advantage if it is initially organized as a branch, even if eventually the intent is to change it to a separately incorporated subsidiary. From an organizational point of view a foreign branch is usually simpler to create and staff than is a separately incorporated subsidiary.

The major disadvantage of a branch bank is one that accrues to the bank rather than to its customers. The parent bank (not just the branch) may be sued at the local level for debts or other activities of the branch.

Branch banking has been the most important way for U.S. banks to conduct their foreign activities. Foreign branches account for about one-half of all international banking assets held by U.S. banks.[6] Europe is the most important location of U.S. branches with respect to size of assets and historical development. The Caribbean shell branches are also important but their growth has leveled off in recent years. Asia is growing in importance at the same time as Latin America is declining in importance in terms of assets held.[7]

Banking Subsidiaries

A subsidiary bank is a separately incorporated bank, owned entirely or in major part by a foreign parent, which conducts a general banking business. As a separate corporation, the banking subsidiary must comply with all the laws of the host country. Its lending limit is based on its own equity capital rather than that of the parent bank. This limits its ability to service large borrowers, but local incorporation also limits the liability of the parent bank to its equity investment in the subsidiary.

A foreign banking subsidiary often appears as a local bank in the eyes of potential customers in host countries and is thus often able to attract additional local deposits. This will especially be true if the bank was independent prior to being purchased by the foreign parent. Management may well be local, giving the bank greater access to the local business community. A foreign-owned bank subsidiary is more likely to be involved in both domestic and international business than is a foreign branch, which is more likely to appeal to the foreign business community but may well encounter difficulty in attracting banking business from local firms.

Sometimes foreign banks are not allowed to operate branches in a host country but are allowed to operate a locally incorporated subsidiary. Tax laws may favor subsidiaries over branches, both from the local perspective and from the parent country perspective. In the case of U.S. banks, a branch would not be allowed to underwrite corporate securities since this is not allowed in the United States. However, a foreign subsidiary would be allowed to engage in this activity.

Subsidiaries are the second most important organization form for U.S. banks, with about 20% of all international assets held by U.S. banks located in subsidiaries. Over half of the assets of these subsidiaries are located in Europe, particularly in the United Kingdom.[8]

Affiliates

A banking affiliate is a locally incorporated bank owned in part, but not necessarily controlled, by a foreign parent. The remainder of the ownership may be local, or it may be other foreign banks. The affiliated bank itself may be newly formed, or it may be a local bank in which a foreign bank has purchased a part interest.

The major advantage of an affiliated banking relationship is that which springs from any joint venture between parties of different nationalities. The bank acquires the expertise of two or more sets of owners. It maintains its status as a local institution with local ownership and management, but it has continuing and permanent relations with its foreign part owner, including an ability to draw upon the international expertise of that part owner. The major disadvantage is also that common to joint ventures; the several owners may be unable to agree on particular policies important to the viability of the bank.

One special type of affiliate is a *consortium* bank. A consortium bank is a joint venture, incorporated separately and owned by two or more banks, usually of different nationalities. The consortium bank takes customers referred to it by its parent banks and also develops its own business. Banking activities include arranging global syndicates for larger loans or longer-term loans than the parent banks might be willing to handle, underwriting corporate securities, operating in the Eurocurrency market, and arranging international mergers and acquisitions. Some consortium banks now operate as international merchant and investment banks, provide project financing, and give corporate financial advice.

Beginning in 1964, and with increased emphasis after about 1968, a number of multinational consortia of various national parentages were established in Europe. In the early 1980s some of these were restructured as single-parent banks because the bank owners found the consortium bank competing with the shareholding parent bank for their most lucrative customers. Nevertheless, at the same time other consortium banks were being created, often in tax havens such as Luxembourg and the Bahamas.

International Banking Facilities (IBFs)

The Federal Reserve Board of the United States authorized the establishment of U.S.-based international banking facilities (IBFs) in 1981 to help U.S. banks capture a larger proportion of the Eurocurrency business. An IBF is not an institution separate from its parent, but is rather a separate set of asset and liability accounts maintained by the parent but segregated from regular bank books. An IBF is thus an accounting entity rather than a legal entity. The establishing entity may be a U.S.-chartered depository institution, a U.S. branch or agency of a foreign bank, or a U.S. office of an Edge Act corporation. Although physically located in the United States, IBFs are not subject to domestic reserve requirements, FDIC insurance premiums, or interest rate ceilings on deposits.

Federal Reserve concern about the possibility of reserve-free transaction accounts "leaking" into the domestic monetary system led to a number of limitations being imposed on IBFs. The limitations do not apply to foreign branches of U.S.-chartered banks. IBF loan and deposit customers are limited to foreign residents, including banks, other IBFs, and the parent bank. IBF time deposits may be offered to foreign banks and to other IBFs. However, nonbank foreign residents are subject to a minimum maturity requirement of two business days.

Deposits and withdrawals by nonbank customers of IBFs must be at least $100,000 in size, except for transactions to withdraw accumulated interest or close the account. Bank customers, however, are not subject to any minimum transaction amount.

IBFs may not issue negotiable instruments, since such instruments could be transferred to U.S. residents who are not eligible to hold deposits in IBFs. Additionally, IBF loans to foreign nonbank customers are subject to a use-of-proceeds restriction, meaning that such funds may not be used to finance the borrower's operations within the United States.

To attract IBFs, several states, including New York, have agreed to exempt them from state and local taxes. U.S.-owned IBFs are already exempt from federal taxes, but foreign-owned IBFs must pay federal taxes.

IBFs have attracted a significant share of Eurodollar business away from other existing centers, especially those located in the Caribbean shell branches. However, they have not replaced the shell branches because the latter can legally lend to U.S. residents, an activity disallowed the IBFs. During the period 1980–1989, that is, since the establishment of IBFs, the offshore shell branches experienced virtually no growth.[9]

A number of reasons explain the growth of IBFs. From a political risk perspective, U.S. residents and firms would prefer to hold their deposits within the political and legal jurisdiction of the United States rather than offshore in the Caribbean. The same motive attracts some foreign funds seeking political safety. Some Eurodollar business has been attracted to the IBFs from London and other European centers because U.S. firms are able to transact business during the normal working day.

One of the main beneficiaries appears to be foreign banks, particularly Japanese, wishing to maintain a presence in the U.S. market to gain easy access to dollars and to conduct certain types of business they are prohibited from doing at home. In fact, almost all the growth in IBFs since 1982 has been in foreign-owned IBFs, which now hold about three times the assets of U.S.-owned IBFs.[10] However, Japan established its own offshore market at the end of 1986, and had actually surpassed U.S. IBFs in total assets by the end of 1989, totaling more than $496 billion.[11]

Edge Act and Agreement Corporations

Edge Act and Agreement corporations are subsidiaries of U.S. banks, incorporated in the United States under Section 25 of the Federal Reserve Act as amended, to engage in international banking and financing operations. Not only may such subsidiaries engage in general international banking, they may also finance commercial, industrial, or financial projects in foreign countries through long-term loans or equity participation. Such participation, however, is subject to the day-to-day practices and policies of the Federal Reserve System.

Edge Act and Agreement corporations are physically located in the United States. Because U.S. banks cannot have branches outside their own state, Edge Act and Agreement corporations are usually located in other states in order to conduct international banking activities. Growth in Edge Act banking was greatly facilitated in 1979 when the Federal Reserve Board issued new guidelines that permitted interstate branching by Edge Act corporations. Previously an Edge Act corporation had to be separately incorporated in each state. By increasing their interstate penetration through Edge Act corporations, the large money center banks are establishing a physical presence in most of the important regional financial centers in order to prepare for the day when interstate branching will be permitted also for domestic business.

The International Banking Act of 1978 extended the Edge Act privilege to foreign banks operating in the United States. In return, the previous ability of foreign banks to conduct a retail banking business in more than one state was severely limited. They must pick a single state as home base. In that state they can conduct full-service banking. In all other states they must limit their activities to Edge Act banking in the same manner as U.S. banks. In many cases, however, foreign banks already had retail operations in more than one state. These were accorded "grandfather" protection but are not allowed to expand beyond what they had at the time the act was passed.

Origin. Section 25 of the Federal Reserve Act was amended in 1916 to allow national banks and state banks belonging to the Federal Reserve System and having capital and surplus of $1 million (since increased to $2 million) or more to invest up to 10% of that capital and surplus in a subsidiary incorporated under state or federal law to conduct international or foreign banking. A bank forming such a subsidiary would enter into an "agreement" with the Board of Governors of the Federal Reserve System as to the type of activities in which they would engage—hence the name "Agreement corporation."

In 1919 Congress passed an amendment, proposed by Senator Walter E. Edge of New Jersey, that expanded the original provisions of the act to allow such subsidiaries to be chartered "for the purpose of engaging in international or foreign banking or other international or foreign financial operation either directly or through the agency, ownership, or control of local institutions in foreign countries."[12] Subsidiaries chartered under this amendment, known as Edge Act corporations, can make equity investments abroad, an operation barred to domestic banks.

The major operational difference between the two types of organizations is that Agreement corporations must engage primarily in international or foreign banking, while Edge Act corporations may also engage in other foreign financial operations. Edge Act corporations are federally chartered and not subject to the banking laws of the various states. Agreement corporations are normally chartered under state law and operate under state jurisdiction.

Edge Act and Agreement corporations generally engage in two types of activities: direct international banking, including acting as a holding company for the stock of one or more foreign banking subsidiaries, and financing development activities not closely related to traditional banking operations.

International Banking Activities. Edge Act and Agreement corporations may accept demand and time deposits from outside the United States (as well as from within, if such deposits are incidental to or for the purpose of transactions in foreign countries). Each corporation can also make loans, although commitments to any one borrower cannot exceed 10% of capital and surplus. They can issue or confirm letters of credit; make loans or advances to finance foreign trade, including production loans; create bankers' acceptances; receive items for collection; offer such services as remittance of funds abroad, or buying, selling, or holding securities for safekeeping; issue guarantees; act as paying agent for securities issued by foreign governments or foreign corporations; and engage in spot and forward foreign exchange transactions.

Edge Act subsidiaries whose primary activity is international banking may also function as holding companies by owning shares of foreign banking subsidiaries and affiliates. Domestic banks may have branches abroad, but they may not themselves own shares of foreign banking subsidiaries. Thus the Edge Act route permits U.S. banks to own foreign banking subsidiaries, either as wholly owned subsidiaries via an intermediary Edge Act corporation, or as part of a joint venture with foreign or domestic banks or with other nonbanking institutions.

International Financing Activities. Edge Act and Agreement corporations differ from other U.S. banks in their ability to make portfolio-type investments in the equity of foreign commercial and industrial firms, either directly or through the intermediary of official or semiofficial development banks or corporations. Direct investment in a wide variety of local businesses can be made by intermediate-term loans, by purchase of shares of stock, or by a combination of these two methods.

Some longer-term development projects are typically initiated in the foreign country by local business and are referred to the Edge Act corporation by the parent bank. Edge Act corporations engaged only in financing may invest up to 50% of their capital and surplus in a single venture. However, if the Edge Act corporation is also engaged in general banking, the limit is 10% of capital and surplus.

COMPARING BANK SERVICES

In implementing their strategic plan, banks need to be aware of some unusual differences in the way bank services are offered in other countries. Some examples are giro transfer systems, different ways in which banks calculate interest charges, and the range of services available.

Giro Transfer Systems

In the major countries of western Europe, and in parts of Africa and Asia, individuals may make payments through a giro system. The word "giro" itself comes from the Greek gyros, meaning circle or turn. A giro system is a money transfer network, usually operated by the post office, intended to facilitate the transfer of a high volume of transactions involving small sums.

Each individual or business has a giro account number. A person wishing to make a payment completes a giro transfer form with his or her own name and account number and the name and account number of the payee. The form is dropped into a postal collection box, and the giro transfer center in the post office reduces the balance in the payer's account, credits the account of the payee, and mails confirmations to both parties. Account holders may deposit directly into their own account at a post office, by mailing a check, or by having their employer deposit wages or salary directly into the account. Utilities, merchants, or others who normally receive payments from the public may maintain accounts into which their customers pay.

Interest is not paid on giro accounts, and overdrafts or other forms of credit are not a normal part of the system. Postage is free, and the cost of transactions is either free or very nominal.

Several advantages of giro systems over checks are suggested. It is not necessary to verify the presence of sufficient funds since the credit and debit are simultaneous. If the payer's account is short, no transfer can be made. Hence checks cannot bounce, and payers cannot kite against their future deposits. In addition, a giro is not a negotiable instrument and in fact never passes into the hands of the payee. Thus forgeries and alterations are not possible. Lastly, giro transfer systems are easily computerized, providing for great efficiencies of time and cost. The first giro system, it should be noted, was introduced by the Austrian Post Office Savings Bank in 1883, so the concept predates computers by many decades.

Calculating Interest Charges

Local interest charges can be calculated in various ways. In Europe, banks tend to lend on an "overdraft" basis, with borrowers drawing against a previously established line of credit. Although some commissions or service charges may be imposed for establishment of the overdraft privilege, the basic cost is the interest rate levied on the daily overdraft balance. The borrower pays interest only on funds used, since there is no compensating balance requirement, and only for the period in days for which the funds are taken. For this reason, the effective interest cost of an overdraft "loan" is the nominal or stated interest rate paid on the overdraft balance.

By comparison, U.S. banks normally expect or require compensating balances and may at times loan only on the basis of notes with a specific maturity. Thus the effective cost of a U.S. bank loan is above its nominal cost. Of course, the "cost" of the compensating balance depends on whether such balances would in any event be maintained in the bank for operating purposes. Furthermore, it may be possible to arrange a loan from a branch of a U.S. bank in one country by arranging for compensating balances in another currency at a branch in another country. Thus comparison of effective interest cost is difficult.

Range of Services

Local banks generally have better access to informal contacts among local institutions and individuals, especially in countries in which business contacts are very much a matter of long-established social relationships. Local banks may also be better at dealing with local government red tape or at advising one how to handle situations involving bribery or other forms of corruption.

As a general matter, branches of multinational banks try to offer all services available from local banks, although the quality of such services may vary. Multinational banks are likely, however, to be more sophisticated at financing imports and exports and at handling foreign currency transactions, except when local banks are also involved to a considerable extent in the same activities. Banks with a global network of offices can frequently offer help on collection problems, worldwide credit checks, or advice facilities for worldwide clearing of funds with a minimum of float. Multinational banks are usually more interested, experienced, and aggressive in helping business firms with intermediate- and long-term industrial financing, whereas in many parts of the world local banks are more attuned to short-term financing of sales. Banks from various countries also have reputations for basing loans on different criteria. European bankers are often regarded as "asset lenders" who base their assessment of how much to loan on the existence of physical assets. By comparison, U.S. bankers tend to evaluate expected cash flow and to loan on the prospect that budgeted cash flow will be adequate to repay the loan. Japanese bankers have yet another approach. Although loans may be written for 90 days, Japanese banks see themselves as supplying more or less permanent capital, and what appear to be "short-term" loans are repeatedly rolled over.

RISKS IN INTERNATIONAL LENDING TO DEVELOPING COUNTRIES

International bank lending involves a more complex approach to assessing risk than that used in domestic banking, primarily because international banking is conducted in a different legal, social, political, and economic environment. The risks of international bank lending may be classified as *commercial risk* or *country risk*. Since banks often offer their advice to client firms on matters of commercial and country risk, their effectiveness in assessing risk is important beyond the effect on the bank alone.

Commercial Risk

Commercial risk involves assessing the likelihood that a foreign-based client will be unable to repay its debts because of business reasons. Although this risk has a direct domestic counterpart, differences exist. As in the domestic case, a multinational bank will attempt to judge the quality of a foreign client's products, management, and financial condition. Cultural differences and lack of information may inhibit an assessment of the firm's management, while differing accounting standards and disclosure practices may preclude the type of financial analysis common in the home country. The bank may find it difficult to evaluate foreign economic conditions that might affect the client firm, and may need legal advice to determine its position in any bankruptcy proceedings. In many countries, for example, firms cannot easily dismiss workers whose jobs have been rendered obsolete by a change in competition or the introduction of new technology. The magnitude of payments that must be made to redundant workers may have a significant negative impact upon a struggling firm's liquidity, and thus upon its ability to repay any bank loans.

Country Risk

Country risk refers to the possibility that unexpected events within a host country will influence a client firm's or a government's ability to repay a loan. Country risk is usually divided into *sovereign risk* and *currency risk*. This division is useful when the borrower is a private firm, but when the borrower is the government itself, the distinction between sovereign risk and currency risk becomes blurred.

Sovereign risk, also called *political risk*, arises because a host government may exercise its sovereign power to unilaterally repudiate foreign obligations, or may prevent local firms from honoring their foreign obligations. The risk may derive from direct government action or from the indirect consequences of ineffective government, as when a government is unable to maintain law and order.

Currency risk, also called *foreign exchange risk*, arises from the possibility that an unexpected change in exchange rates will alter the home currency value of repayment of loans by foreign clients. If the loan is denominated in the home currency, say, U.S. dollars, the risk is shifted to the borrower. However, the bank still runs the currency risk that the borrower cannot obtain dollars to repay the loan. A bank may partially avoid this possibility by sourcing funds for foreign clients in local currencies. Repayment of principal will not then be subject to a currency risk. However, the profit margin between the lending rate and the local cost of sourcing the funds is of value to the parent bank only in terms of its home currency value. This component remains subject to currency risk.

As described in Chapter 3, the most serious currency risk is that debtor countries will need to reschedule their external hard currency debts and ration access of local firms to hard currencies. Unfortunately the "Debt Crisis" continues to plague both debtor countries and the creditor firms.

Dangers of Lending to Sovereign Nations

With the advantage of hindsight a lively debate also rages over the wisdom of letting the private sector finance developing countries rather than having public sector international institutions, such as the IMF and World Bank, do the financing.

Criticism of bank lending to developing countries runs along the following lines:[13]

1. Evaluation of country risk is extremely complex, because it depends on variables that are not normally analyzed by bankers when making domestic commercial loans. The new variables include unfamiliar political, sociological, macroeconomic, and financial variables.

2. Bankers have a poor track record in anticipating dramatic increases in sovereign risk until it is too late. Unexpected events such as wars (Nigeria, Ethiopia, Iraq/Kuwait, and Lebanon) and social revolutions (Cuba and Iran) are nearly impossible to forecast but are often a prime cause for national default on external debt.

3. Some critics believe that bankers relax international credit standards because of weak domestic and commercial demand for loans.

4. In the event that a nation's foreign debt needs to be restructured, the fact that so many separate banks and international organizations are involved means that coordination is extremely difficult. All creditors must agree for any voluntary restructuring plan to be effective.

5. The concentration of syndicated loans in a relatively few "creditworthy" developing countries, such as Brazil, Argentina, and Mexico, reduces the potential benefit of diversification.

6. Most bank debt is on a variable-interest-rate basis, thus causing the actual burden of interest payments to be uncertain but potentially disastrous to the borrower if interest rates should reach high levels.

7. When countries are unable to service their debt on time, the banks become effectively "locked in" and are forced to reschedule their loans indefinitely to prevent outright

defaults. Such rollovers may disguise loans that should be written off and conceal severe depletions of banks' equity capital. Even if eventually repaid, rollovers impair the ability of banks to make new productive loans elsewhere.

8. Some observers have been suspicious of the stability of the whole Eurocurrency interbank structure. If one major bank should fail, that event might have a domino-effect on other banks because of the "tiering" of Eurocurrency deposits. The ability of banks of lesser stature to raise Eurocurrencies in the short run at reasonable rates to fund their share of "rollovers" to developing countries would be in jeopardy if confidence in the interbank market waned.

9. The ultimate purpose of some loans is to provide financing for balance of payments deficits. This type of loan does not improve the exporting capability of the borrowing country and therefore does not generate the foreign exchange earnings needed to service the debt. Even some of the so-called project loans are substitutes for other foreign loans, which are then used to finance the deficit.

Benefits of Lending to Sovereign Nations

In spite of the negative criticism of commercial bank lending to developing nations, many positive features do exist for this type of lending, from the viewpoint of both the banks and the recipient countries. The benefits can be summarized as follows:

1. International lending has in the past been a very profitable activity for many of the world's largest banks and has, for example, had a major impact on historical earnings of such giants as Citicorp, Chase Manhattan, Bank of America, and Morgan Guaranty.

2. Diversification of foreign lending by country and by type of customer reduces the risk of catastrophic losses to any one bank.

3. Precisely those banks with the most experience and capability in international lending are the ones that are most active in international lending. They are at least relatively better qualified to assess country risk than banks.

4. The reason that loans to developing countries have been concentrated in a relatively few countries is that only those select countries have been able to pass the stringent credit test of international bank lenders. For example, India, Pakistan, and Bangladesh have large foreign debts to international public institutions, such as the World Bank and International Monetary Fund, but virtually no debt to private banks. They have not yet passed the credit test.

5. Developing countries badly need foreign banks to meet even relatively modest development plans. Most of the loans are project loans, which are supposed to generate enough new foreign exchange to service the added foreign debt. If the private banking sector does not respond to the legitimate credit needs of responsible developing countries, an even greater burden will be placed on the international development institutions. Their limited funds will inevitably be diverted away from the poorest developing nations, which have no hope of qualifying for loans from private banks.

6. A number of safeguards exist that reduce the risk on a portion of international loans. These include guarantees by export credit insurance programs in the lenders' own countries, guarantees by a parent on loans to its affiliates, and guarantees by host government agencies on loans to private firms within their country. The latter two do not apply to loans to sovereign states but do serve to reduce overall country risk.

7. Foreign governments and central banks have traditionally given highest priority to preserving their own credit standing, even if private firms within the country must default. Therefore lending to sovereign entities at least ensures first priority on whatever foreign exchange is available to repay external debts.

ANALYSIS OF COUNTRY RISK

Bank managers must develop a better approach to evaluation of both sovereign risk and currency risk of individual countries. Approaches used vary somewhat depending on whether the borrower is the government itself, an industrial firm, or a private commercial bank within the foreign country. The same variables are usually studied for all three client types, but the relative weight given one or another variable may differ substantially. Consideration must also be given to the portfolio effect of loan diversification by country.

Sovereign Risk

Sovereign risk analysis focuses on probable future willingness or ability of a government to honor past obligations or to allow firms and banks within the country to honor their obligations. Variables considered include political stability, since a new government may abrogate obligations incurred by its predecessor. Expected trends in the balance of payments are important because the ability to generate foreign exchange depends on either a favorable current account or a favorable capital account. A third factor is the size of the foreign exchange obligations of the country relative to its GNP and international trade.

All of these seemed to play a part in Argentina's difficulties in honoring its foreign debt obligations in the mid-1980s. The military government, which led the country into the Falklands/Malvinas War with Great Britain, was replaced by a civilian government, which brought its disgraced military predecessors to trial for crimes against the Argentine people. The military government had incurred large foreign debts for projects of dubious economic benefit to the Argentine economy, and foreign exchange earnings were depressed, in part as a result of the world economic situation of the mid-1980s. The debt and balance of payments situation of Argentina was not materially different from that of many other countries. However, the replacement of a disgraced military government after an embarrassing attempt to invade the Falklands/Malvinas Islands was uniquely Argentine.

Currency Risk

Currency risk is judged primarily from projections of a country's balance of payments surplus or deficit on current account, its present and likely future holdings of foreign exchange reserves, which act as a buffer for a limited period of time in the country's ability to repay foreign debt, and the size and maturity structure of its foreign currency debt. These factors, in turn, are influenced by differential rates of domestic and foreign inflation and whether or not the country's exchange rates are allowed to adjust to the differential. In this context, foreign currency debt includes both governmental debt and the debt of private firms and banks within the country.

A Portfolio Approach

In addition to analyzing the "stand-alone risk" of individual countries, banks have analyzed country risk from a *portfolio theory* perspective. International loans can be viewed as a *portfolio* of risky assets whose returns will vary as a result of both commercial and country risks. The total risk of the portfolio will be diminished if the bank successfully diversifies its assets across countries.[14]

International loans are often just part of an ongoing relationship between a bank and its client. The bank may be receiving other compensation from the client, such as fees for foreign exchange transactions or international money management. Denying the loan may bring an end to such fees and may preclude the bank's participation in future loans when the client becomes worthy of credit again. These attributes do not fit neatly into portfolio theory, but they must be remembered in any intuitive application of the concepts of that theory.

Large money center banks cannot easily remove high-risk loans from their portfolios in order to reduce portfolio risk because only a limited secondary market for such loans exists. It is possible to swap a risky loan to one country for a risky loan to another country or for equity. However, when several Latin American governments found themselves unable to repay their debts as scheduled in the 1980s, large money center banks had to increase their risk. They had the choice of extending the maturity of defaulting loans or reporting a loss in earnings for that year. Smaller banks, on the other hand, were able to reduce their risk by refusing to extend the maturities of their Latin American loans. The larger banks were forced to assume the smaller bank's share of the credit to prevent the total loan from going into default.

Portfolio diversification works best if default risk in each country is independent of that in every other country, but often such defaults are closely correlated. For example, default risk for countries in geographical or ideological proximity might be correlated because of a common view of nationalism, as in the case of many Latin American countries; ideologically inspired invasion, as in the case of Kampuchea and Vietnam; drought and starvation, as in the case of East Africa; and civil strife with foreign intervention, as in the case of Nicaragua and El Salvador. International dependency complicates the task of judging risk in an international loan portfolio, but it does not totally negate the advantages of international loan diversification.

In order to guarantee that international loan portfolios are optimally diversified, most banks set "country loan limits" to restrict exposure in any one country.[15] Limits are established by a country limit committee composed of top bank executives. Country managers and staff analysts present recommendations to the country limit committee, of which they may or may not themselves be members.[16] A country limit decision is typically based on two separate pieces of information. One of these is a country risk analysis study, and the other is a marketing plan presented by the bank official in charge of operations in the country being reviewed.

STRATEGIES FOR MANAGING COUNTRY RISK

The country risk associated with the continuing developing country debt crisis is being managed by cooperative efforts between debtor countries and creditor banks.

Debtor Country Strategies

The main strategies used by debtor countries to survive the crisis, besides rescheduling the debts, are austerity, over-devaluation of their currencies, encouraging direct foreign investment, and debt-for-equity swaps.

Austerity. The countries themselves have tried to reduce demand for imports and free up capacity for exports by following tighter monetary and fiscal policies. The result has been a slowing of growth rates and a reduction in per capita consumption. Needless to say, this austerity policy is generally unpopular with the voters even though their governments are able to blame the problem on foreign banks and the IMF. In fact, the IMF has usually taken the lead in suggesting austerity as a condition for further loans from both the public agencies and the private banking sector. Nevertheless, some of the governments are too weak politically to endure austerity policies for a prolonged period. Therefore austerity is not the only solution.

Over-devaluation. Most of the indebted countries have tried to become more competitive in nontraditional exports by over-devaluing their currencies. This means that their real effective exchange rates will lie well below an index value of 100 on purpose. Creditor countries are willing to tolerate what appears to be a "beggar-thy-neighbor" policy in the interest of encouraging debt repayment.

Encouraging Direct Foreign Investment. Many of the debtor countries have taken steps to encourage more incoming direct foreign investment, including encouraging a reversal of the capital flight problem discussed previously in Chapter 3. This means removing barriers such as local ownership requirements, work permits for expatriates, local content requirements, and other interferences with the free market. It also means trying to create a more favorable environment for private enterprise in general and perhaps privatizing many of the inefficient public enterprises.

Debt-for-Equity Swaps. A debt-for-equity swap is a technique to encourage a reversal of capital flight by local citizens and an encouragement to banks to convert from debt to equity claims. As discussed in Chapter 3, creditors are allowed to exchange their loans for equity in local firms. Whether this approach will be successful depends on the terms of the exchange, that is, how much the debt is discounted, and on the desirability of owning local firms. So far the results have been modest relative to the size of external debt. The most successful programs have been run by Brazil, Chile, and Mexico.

Creditor Bank Strategies

The creditor international banks have also taken steps to reduce their own burden of developing country debt. Many of the banks have increased their equity capital base and their loan loss reserves, while greatly reducing any new lending to the debtor countries. Banks have also quietly been selling off some of their exposed loans at big discounts to investors willing to take the risk. For example, in January of 1991 the debt of Brazil was selling for as little as 23 cents on the dollar, while that of Chile had risen to 75 cents on the dollar. A rise in the secondary market price of this debt reflects the secondary market's assessment of the increased likelihood that Chile will service outstanding debt obligations.

Regulatory Authorities Strategies

Regulatory authorities have also stepped in, both to prevent a recurrence of the developing country debt problem and to prevent any massive bank failures. The previously mentioned Basle Agreement requires international banks to maintain at least 4% core equity in their capital structure, but individual country banking authorities have pressured their own banks to have a considerably higher equity ratio. In addition, the pressure is on banks, at least in the United States, to disclose the composition of their international loan portfolios by geographic area and type of loan.

Forfaiting

Most of the attention on the Debt Crisis has focused on Latin American countries since they are causing the most grief for international lenders. Nevertheless the former East Bloc countries have also had their share of grief and rescheduling of external debt. In particular, Poland defaulted seriously in the 1970s and never really recovered.

Eastern European country risk has been a special problem for German, Austrian, and Swiss banks because they have historically been the main lenders in that geographical area. However, these banks have also developed considerable expertise in analyzing Eastern European countries.

Forfaiting Defined.   European banks developed an interesting technique called *forfaiting*, which reduces the risks for multinational firms wishing to export to Eastern European countries. Given the recent political and economic turmoil in Eastern Europe, it is unclear whether *forfaiting* will continue in its traditional role, but it is worth describing as a technique which might be applied elsewhere, such as in Latin America or Africa.

Forfaiting is a technique for arranging medium-term bank financing. Forfaiting denotes the purchase of trade obligations falling due at some future date without recourse to any previous holder of the obligation. The word comes from the French *à forfait*, a term that implies "to forfeit or surrender a right." Under a typical arrangement, an exporter receives immediate cash by discounting promissory notes or trade receivables on a "without-recourse" basis to a specialized finance firm, called a "forfaiter." The forfaiter assesses and subsequently carries all political and commercial risk.

Forfaiting arose because the governments of Eastern Europe and certain other developing nations took an active role in seeking intermediate-term financing to pay for major items of imported capital equipment, including turnkey plants constructed by Western corporations. Such projects require up to a dozen years to complete, so financing was needed for a longer time than could be arranged by traditional bank export departments or even by the export credit guarantee programs of the various exporting countries. Forfaiting firms, most of which are in Switzerland, Austria, or Germany and are affiliated with commercial banks from other European countries, developed the technique of purchasing from the exporter all rights and claims to future cash receipts from the importer without any possibility of recourse to the exporting firm. Although the exporting firm remains responsible for the quality of delivered goods, it receives a clear and unconditional cash payment, while all political and commercial risk of nonpayment by the importer is carried by the forfaiter.

A Typical Forfaiting Transaction. A typical forfaiting transaction involves five parties, as shown in Exhibit 10.4. The steps in the process are as follows:

Step 1. Importer and exporter agree between themselves on a series of imports to be paid for over a lengthy period. Periodic payments are to be made against progress on delivery or completion of the project.

Step 2. The exporter obtains the forfaiter's commitment to finance the transaction at a fixed discount rate, and payments are to be made when the exporter delivers to the forfaiter the appropriate promissory notes or other specified paper. The agreed-upon discount rate is one of the costs to the exporting firm. An additional standby fee of about 0.1% to 0.125% per month is charged by the forfaiter from the date of its commitment to finance until receipt of the actual discount paper issued in accordance with the finance contract. In anticipation of its standby obligation, the forfaiter might borrow the needed funds on a long maturity and reinvest them in short-term maturities, thus ensuring eventual availability of the funds to the exporter.

Step 3. The importer obligates itself to pay for the material by issuing a series of promissory notes, usually maturing every six or twelve months, against progress on delivery or completion of the project. These promissory notes are first delivered to the importer's bank, usually a government-owned bank, where they are endorsed (that is, guaranteed) by that bank. In Europe the guarantee is sometimes referred to as an "aval." At this point the importer's bank becomes the primary obligor in the eyes of all subsequent holders of the notes.

Step 4. The now-endorsed promissory notes are delivered to the exporter.

Step 5. The exporter endorses the notes "without recourse" and discounts them with the

Exhibit 10.4   Typical Forfaiting Transaction

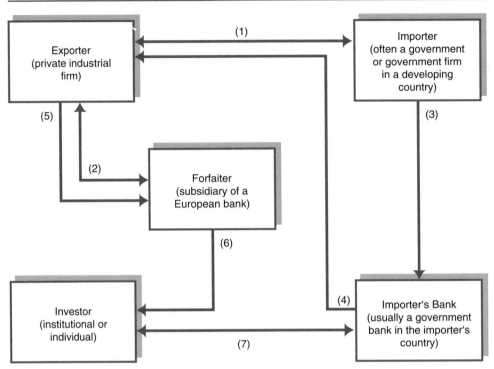

forfaiter, receiving immediately the agreed-upon proceeds, less the amount of the discount taken out by the forfaiter. By endorsing them "without recourse," the exporter assumes no liability for future payment on the notes and thus in effect receives the discounted proceeds free of any further payment difficulties.

Step 6. The forfaiting bank endorses the notes and sells them in the European money market. The notes are now two-name paper (importer's bank and forfaiting firm); although investors can rely on either name, they are in fact attracted to the paper by the endorsement of the forfaiting bank.

Step 7. At maturity the investor holding the notes presents them for collection to the importer or to the importer's bank. If both of these default on repayment, the holder will then present them to the forfaiting bank that guaranteed them.

In effect, the forfaiting bank functions as both a money market firm and a specialist in assessing country risk. As a money market firm, the forfaiter divides the discounted notes into appropriately sized packages and resells them to various investors having different maturity preferences. The forfaiter is supplying its own name as a guarantor of the notes.

As a country risk specialist, the forfaiter assesses and bears the risk that the notes will eventually be paid by the importer or the importer's bank.

Success of the forfaiting technique resides in the belief that the external obligations of a government bank will have a higher priority for payment than will commercial debt, even when incurred by government entities. A government bank's default on an international agreement would destroy the country's credibility. In addition, the endorsing guarantee is perceived to be "off the balance sheet" in that it is a contingent rather than a direct obligation. As an "off balance sheet" obligation, the debt is presumably not considered by other international organizations analyzing the credit risk of the importing country or its banking system.

"Free-For-All: As Global Competition in Banking Heats Up, Europeans Have Edge"*

By Avoiding Excesses of '80s, They Take Fewer Big Hits, Rest on Solid Capital Bases

Innovation Aids the Americans

In the 1990s and beyond, the rough games of high-stakes international banking will probably get even rougher.

"We are in an era of aggressively intensified competition, rapidly shifting definitions of what financial products are, a general slowdown in world economic growth and much, much tougher risk-management demands, " says Robert Dugger, chief economist for the American Bankers Association.

So rough is that looming competition, adds George Vojta, chief of strategic planning at Bankers Trust New York Corp., that of the 40 to 45 banks now aspiring to be global powerhouses, only 6 to 10 will make the grade by the end of the 1990s.

And some specialists predict that most of the winners won't be America's big banks, which dominated world banking from the 1950s through the 1970s, or Japan's, which made a run for the top in the 1980s. Of a dozen banks picked as strong contenders by bankers, regulators and analysts, half are European.

One reason is a bit ironic. "The European banking system is in the good shape it is in because it didn't have the same determination to dominate the world that the U.S. and Japanese did," says Alan Moore, director of corporate banking and treasury at Lloyds Bank PLC. European banks generally have been conservatively managed, treading more carefully in the risky, deregulated free-for-all of international banking. Now, some European giants have a lot going for them, including solid capital bases, strong balance sheets and dominant shares of home markets expected to grow quickly.

Tough Challenges

Yet all the big international banks face difficult problems. Global banking will change "from being a protected industry to a deregulated one," Mr. Vojta says. "Everybody can invade your market; you can invade everybody else's markets. Your survival will be based on your ability to take on all comers and succeed often enough to make sufficient profit to pay shareholders and build capital."

Planning for survival isn't easy, for nobody knows exactly what the future global bank will look like. But in general terms, global banks must be able to serve the financing needs of corporations, big and small, anywhere in the world. They also must be able to garner a commanding share of the increasing flow of capital across national borders and be flexible enough to shift resources to fast-growing areas and high-return businesses.

They must do all this while new technology and new financial products are shaking up the industry, and as corporate clients and investors become ever more global. Already, big banks are battling each other on many fronts: lending, underwriting, financial advice and new financing techniques for corporations, currency and securities trading, leasing, insurance, money management and consumer banking. They are also hurt by overcapacity—too many banks chasing too few customers—and many are struggling to meet international rules requiring them, by early 1993, to have capital equivalent to 8% of assets.

Moreover, the costs of trying to go global and failing will be high. "Mismanaging the process would be confusing to an organization, expensive for the shareholders and unsettling for clients," says Douglas A. Warner III, president of J.P. Morgan & Co. Banks losing out in the scramble could be taken over or become mostly domestic or niche institutions.

Pluses and Minuses

All the contenders enter the race with major handicaps and major advantages. U.S. banks, for example, are plagued with weak capital bases and soured loans to less-developed countries, on real estate and for highly leveraged takeovers. They also keep losing business to nonbank rivals.

But after two decades of competing domestically against insurers, investment banks and money managers, as well as internationally, U.S. banks have developed superior creative skills. "The Americans stand tall," says Lowell Bryan, chief banking consultant at McKinsey & Co. "Europeans and Japanese banks are sitting on top of cartels that are going to have to change. The [global] winners are going to be the ones with the biggest skills. You don't get skills sitting in an oligopoly."

The Japanese giants, backed by a strong economy and powerful corporate customers, are rich in assets. But the world's biggest banks are poor in capital and innovative flair and are learning that size doesn't guarantee performance. In the past year, Japanese banks have been ravaged by soaring interest rates, a plunging stock market and intensifying competition. Now, deregulation threatens many of them by narrowing spreads between borrowing costs and lending income.

"The era of Japanese banks' dominance—if it ever was dominance—is over," declares Daniel J. Kreps, a principal at SRI International, a consulting firm in Menlo Park, California. "They will play a role commensurate with the importance of the Japanese economy, which is considerable. But they won't run" world banking.

Smaller Hits

The well-capitalized European banks have mostly solved their Third World loan problems and are taking much smaller hits from bad real-estate and takeover credits than are U.S. and Japanese banks.

But they have little experience with head-butting competition. Europe's banking sanctuaries—local markets long protected, by law and tradition, from price-cutting competition—will be torn asunder by the planned post-1992 integration of financial markets in the 12-nation European Community. The roughly 300 mergers and partial mergers among Europe's banks in the past two years foreshadow a further competitive shakeout; many analysts predict that today's roster of European banks will be halved, to 800.

However, that attrition could leave the strongest European banks—Germany's Deutsche Bank AG, Union Bank of Switzerland, Crédit Suisse, Swiss Bank Corp. and Britain's Barclays Bank PLC—mightier than ever. All but Barclays are rated triple-A; they are the world's only private-sector banks so designated by each of three major credit agencies. Barclays is rated triple-A by two and double-A by one.

Triple-A status lowers a bank's cost of funds and gives it a competitive edge in earning fees from municipalities and corporations that need backup credit lines. It also attracts wealthy individuals, especially frightened ones. "In a crisis, people just throw money at us; it's almost an embarrassment," says Christopher Roberts, U.S. area head for Credit Suisse.

Leeway in Setting Rates

Each of the five banks, with a dominant position at home, has considerable leeway in setting domestic interest rates and can subsidize forays abroad. In Switzerland, according to Salomon Brothers, four banks hold 53% of the assets; in Britain, 13 banks account for 57% of domestic sterling deposits. By contrast, each of the top 10 U.S. banks has an average of 3% of industry revenues. And foreign banks hold 25% of U.S. banking assets, up from 14% in 1982 and 3.8% in 1973.

In home markets, Europe's banks have long been able to enter businesses, such as investment banking and insurance, denied their U.S. and Japanese rivals. Continental institutions also hold large stakes in industrial companies, and many Japanese banks are in huge interlocking corporate groups, the *keiretsu*. In addition, banks in Europe and Japan can set up branches anywhere in their own countries. U.S. Treasury Department proposals to widen U.S. banks' authority face tough going in Congress.

Relying on the "universal bank" concept, Crédit Suisse and UBS pursue a three-pronged strategy: commercial banking, investment banking and money management. Unlike some British and Japanese banks, none of the Swiss big three pursues consumer banking outside its home turf.

Deutsche Bank and Barclays do. Preparing for 1992, the bank that awestruck competitors call "the Big D" has acquired subsidiaries—mostly retail branch operations—in Italy, Spain, Austria, and the Netherlands. Last year, it shelled out the equivalent of $1.62 billion for Morgan Grenfell Group PLC, a premier British merchant bank. Barclays also has concentrated on Europe, acquiring banks in Germany and opening branches in Spain. It is purchasing Européenne de Banque, once part of the Rothschild interests, to beef up its commercial banking in France.

Targeting Consumers

But nobody matches Citicorp in its lust to be the world's consumer bank. The New York bank's two biggest profit centers are its New York branch system, with 1,200 automated teller machines, and its $30 billion credit-card business, with 27 million cardholders. "It's going to be very unlikely we'll see many other global players in the consumer end of the business," says Richard S. Braddock, Citicorp's president.

In Japan, Citicorp is the only foreign bank competing in the consumer market with the Japanese giants. With designer-finished lobbies and top-of-the-line computer systems, it is targeting wealthy clients. In addition, Citicorp "is better positioned for 1992 on the retail side than many European banks," says Thomas H. Hanley, a Salomon Brothers managing director.

U.S. banks' technological edge enhances their capabilities in trading and in designing and distributing myriad new services—capabilities widely expected to help them seize opportunities as European and Japanese markets are deregulated.

Last year, Bankers Trust sold securities permitting investors to bet on the direction of the Tokyo stock market. Meanwhile, J.P. Morgan and Citicorp arranged for banks around the world to reduce their loan exposure in Argentina by $4.6 billion by taking equity stakes in two newly privatized telephone companies.

"In corporate and investment banking, technology can make up for a lot; you don't have to have a physical presence within each country," Mr. Hanley says.

Heavy Investment

All three banks have invested heavily in servicing corporate clients and constructing sophisticated systems for trading currencies and securities. Bankers Trust, for example, spends about $350 million a year on its computer operations. "The cumulative technology is reaching the point where we've developed barriers to entry, where others don't even want to try to compete," the bank's Mr. Vojta says.

If American banks do get the right to operate without geographic and product constraints at home, McKinsey's Mr. Bryan says, "we have potential winners in [the U.S.]; we don't have to give them advantages [in competing with foreign rivals.] We just have to get out of their way."

That isn't true for most Japanese banks, despite their size. Just a few of them, analysts say, can challenge major U.S. or European banks. Only Industrial Bank of Japan Ltd., Sumitomo Bank Ltd. and Mitsubishi Bank Ltd. have "the experience, technological capability and capital strength necessary to succeed in providing a full range of commercial and investment bank services on an international scale," says Alicia Ogawa, a banking analyst at S.G. Warburg Securities Ltd.

Paradoxically, many banks are retreating to the relative safety of their home markets just when their corporate clients and investors are becoming more global. One reason is that global expansion has caused a lot of disappointment.

In recent years, Chase Manhattan Corp., BankAmerica Corp., Chemical Banking Corp. and other U.S. banks have sold or closed operations abroad to cut losses or meet the new capital standards. One big problem: Many banks venturing abroad never went past the initial move. "Toeholds always look good because they're cheap, but it's sort of, 'Do you want to pay now or want to pay later?'" says Citicorp's Mr. Braddock. "The question is, if you buy the toehold, how do you build it into something substantial? That's a fundamental flaw in a lot of acquisition strategies."

Salomon's Mr. Hanley cites two examples in the U.S. "NatWest doesn't have real critical mass, and Barclays is still looking for market share," he says. NatWest's U.S. units had a 1990 loss of $352.4 million, and other big British banks—Lloyds, Midland Bank PLC, and Standard Chartered Bank PLC—have sold U.S. banks to raise money. Japanese banks, hurt by soured buyout loans and seeking to meet the capital rules, also are selling assets and slowing growth world-wide.

"The banking industry has lost multibillions of dollars in international markets," says Robin Monro-Davies, managing director of IBCA Ltd., a London bank credit-rating agency. "America has been a graveyard for foreign banks."

Barbara Donnely in New York contributed to this article.

SUMMARY

- An international financial center exists when domestic funds are supplied to foreign users or when foreign funds are supplied to domestic users. London, Tokyo, and New York City are, at present, the leading international financial centers.

- International strategies of banks are normally evolutionary. In the first step, arm's-length international banking, domestic banks accept foreign deposits and make foreign loans. In the second stage the domestic bank often establishes an offshore banking presence. This offshore bank accepts deposits and makes loans in foreign currencies, i.e., Eurocurrencies. The final step is for the bank to establish itself within other countries, usually through subsidiaries and affiliates.

- The Single European Market will have a significant impact on the structure of competition in international banking. The primary provision of the 1992 program for banking is the Single Banking License, which will allow banks incorporated within a member country to branch freely throughout the EEC.

- The Basle Accord of 1988 established a framework for measuring bank capital and setting minimum capital adequacy standards. The Accord requires a total capital requirement of 8%, divided between core capital and supplementary capital.

- A number of organizational forms exist for banks to participate in international banking: correspondent banks, representative offices, branch banks, banking subsidiaries, bank affiliates, and international banking facilities (IBFs).

- Country risk is composed of both sovereign (political) risk and currency (foreign exchange) risk.

- Strategies for managing country risk by debtor countries include austerity programs, over-devaluation, different forms of direct foreign investment incentives, and debt-for-equity swaps.

- Forfaiting is a technique to finance Eastern European trade with Western exporters. Under a typical arrangement, an exporter receives immediate cash by discounting promissory notes or trade receivables on a "without recourse" basis to a specialized finance firm, called a "forfaiter." The forfaiter assesses and subsequently carries all political and commercial risk.

1. New International Financial Centers

The following cities seek to become international financial centers. What might the leadership of each city do to establish itself as an international financial center, and what is the likelihood that it will succeed? What advantages and disadvantages exist for each potential center?

- **a)** Anchorage, Alaska
- **b)** Vancouver, British Columbia
- **c)** Bangkok, Thailand
- **d)** Havana, Cuba
- **e)** Berlin, Germany
- **f)** Kuwait City, Kuwait
- **g)** Sydney, Australia

2. Branch Versus Subsidiary

Compare the advantages and disadvantages of a bank conducting its foreign business through a branch versus a wholly owned subsidiary. Under what conditions would each form of organization be appropriate?

3. International Banking Facilities Versus Shell Branches

Many banks have established IBFs, but continue to operate shell branches in the Caribbean. Why do they need both types of organizations? Why have foreign banks been more eager to establish and use IBFs than U.S.-owned banks?

4. Edge Act Corporations

A number of large money center banks have established branch networks of Edge Act Corporations. Why are they doing this? What are the risks, advantages, and disadvantages?

5. Sovereign Lending by Commercial Banks

A Beverly Hills, California, bank advertises for commercial customers by noting that it has no risky foreign loans on its books. Is this marketing approach likely to be successful? Why did so many banks make so many sovereign loans during the 1980s? Should multinational firms avoid banking with commercial banks having large "nonperforming" loans to foreign countries?

6. Banking Competitiveness in the 1990s

The anecdote at the end of this chapter entitled "Free For All" cites a number of reasons why the most competitive banks on world markets in the 1990s may not be either from Japan or the United States. Discuss the major advantages and disadvantages that banks—as grouped by major markets (U.S., Japan, European)—will have in the new more deregulated and competitive banking markets of the 1990s.

7. Forfaiters

Do you believe that forfaiting banks have a future now that the countries of Eastern Europe have repudiated the communist system?

8. Aqua-Slovakia

The new government of Czechoslovakia has decided to make bottled spring water from its eastern provinces a major export. This development will require the construction of several huge bottling plants, which in turn will require items of imported capital equipment. The equipment must be purchased from U.S. companies, which still consider the financing of capital equipment exports to former communist Eastern European countries to be risky.

    a)   How would forfaiting help as a financing scheme?

    b)   Describe the responsibilities of each party involved in a forfaiting transaction.

    c)   What are the two basic functions of a forfaiting firm?

    d)   Trace the commitments and documents involved in a typical forfaiting transaction.

NOTES

1. Excellent overall descriptions of international financial centers can be found in Howard C. Reed, *The Preeminence of International Financial Centers*, New York: Praeger, 1981; and Gunter Dufey and Ian H. Giddy, *The International Money Market*, Engelwood Cliffs, N.J.: Prentice-Hall, 1978. For a more concise discussion of the development of Asian financial centers, see Howard C. Reed, "The Ascent of Tokyo as an International Financial Center," *Journal of International Business Studies*, Winter 1980, pp. 19–35.

2. R. A. Jones, "The British Isles Offshore Financial Centres," *National Westminister Bank Quarterly Review*, November 1982, pp. 53–65.

3. *Op. cit.*, Dufey and Giddy, *The International Money Market*, p. 39.

4. Ian Giddy, "The Theory and Industrial Organization of International Banking," New York: *Columbia University Graduate School of Business Research Working Paper*, no. 343A, June 30, 1980.

5. For a thorough description of the many forms of international banking and financial services see Ingo Walter, *Global Competition in Financial Services: Market Structure, Protection, and Trade Liberalization*, Ballinger Publishing, Cambridge, Mass., 1988.

6. James V. Houpt, "International Trends for U.S. Banks and Banking Markets," *Staff Study of the Board of Governors of the Federal Reserve System*, no. 156. May 1988, p.3.

7. *Ibid*, p. 8.

8. *Ibid*, p. 11.

9. By the end of 1989, IBFs held more than $340 billion in assets, almost entirely Eurodollars; *Federal Reserve Bulletin*, monthly.

10. Moffett, Michael H., and Arthur Stonehill, "International Banking Facilities Revisited," *Journal of International Financial Management and Accounting*, volume 1, no. 1, Spring 1989, pp. 88–103.

11. *Federal Reserve Bulletin*, monthly.

12. Section 25(a) 1, Federal Reserve Act (12 U.S.C. 611–631).

13. The following sources present summaries of the dangers and benefits: Irving S. Friedman, The Emerging Role of Private Banks in the Developing World, New York: Citicorp, 1977; Steven I. Davis, "How Risky Is International Lending?" *Harvard Business Review*, January/February 1977, pp. 135–143; Richard S. Dale and Richard P. Mattione, *Managing Global Debt*, Washington, D.C.: The Brookings Institution, 1983; and Sarkis J. Khoury, "Sovereign Debt: A Critical Look at the Causes and the Nature of the Problem," *Essays in International Business*, University of South Carolina, Center for International Business Studies, July 1985.

14. The reader already familiar with the fundamentals of portfolio theory will recognize this total risk reduction to be composed of both *systematic risk* and *unsystematic risk*. The proper diversification of the portfolio internationally will reduce unsystematic risk. Portfolio theory is explained in-depth in Chapter 13.

15. See Stephen V. O. Clarke, *American Banks in the International Interbank Market*, New York: Salomon Brothers Center for the Study of Financial Institutions, New York University Monograph Series in Finance and Economics, Monograph 1983, no. 4, p. 28, for a listing of the criteria that bank managements should use in setting limits on lending to other banks in foreign countries.

16. Briance Mascarenhas and Ole-Christian Sand, "Country-Risk Assessment Systems in Banks: Patterns and Performance," *Journal of International Business Studies*, Spring 1985, pp. 19–35.

BIBLIOGRAPHY

Ball, Clifford A., and Adrian E. Tschoegl, "The Decision to Establish a Foreign Bank Branch or Subsidiary: An Application of Binary Classification Procedures," *Journal of Financial and Quantitative Analysis*, September 1982, pp. 411–424.

Bank for International Settlements, Sixtieth Annual Report, Basle, Switzerland: B.I.S., June 1990.

Bennett, Paul, "Applying Portfolio Theory to Global Bank Lending," *Journal of Banking and Finance*, June 1984, pp. 153–169.

Bryant, Ralph C., *International Financial Intermediation*, Washington, D.C.: The Brookings Institution, 1987.

Burton, F. N., and H. Inoue, "An Appraisal of the Early-Warning Indicators of Sovereign Loan Default in Country Risk Evaluation Systems," *Management International Review*, 25, no. 1, 1985, pp. 45–56.

Clarke, Stephen V.O., *American Banks in the International Interbank Market*, New York: Salomon Brothers Center, New York University, 1983.

Cline, William R., *Mobilizing Bank Lending to Debtor Countries*, Washington, D.C.: Institute for International Economics, 1987.

Dermine, Jean, ed., *European Banking in the 1990s*, Oxford, UK; Cambridge, MA: Basil Blackwell, 1990.

Doukas, John, "Syndicated Euro-Credit Sovereign Risk Assessments, Market Efficiency and Contagion Effects," *Journal of International Business Studies*, Summer 1989, pp. 255–267.

Fischer, Stanley, "Sharing the Burden of the International Debt Crisis," *American Economic Review*, May 1987, pp. 165–170.

Ganitsky, Joseph, "The Debt Crisis: A New Era for Decision Makers," *Columbia Journal of World Business*, Fall 1986, pp. 73–80.

Garg, Ramesh C., "Loans to LDCs and Massive Defaults," *Intereconomics*, January/February 1981, pp. 19–25.

Goldberg, Ellen S., and Dan Haendel, *On Edge:*

International Banking and Country Risk, New York: Praeger, 1987.

Guild, Ian, and Rhodri Harris, *Forfaiting*, London: Euromoney Publications, 1985.

Haar, Jerry, and William E. Renforth, "Reaction to Economic Crisis: Trade and Finance of U.S. Firms Operating in Latin America," *Columbia Journal of World Business*, Fall 1986, pp. 11–18.

Hay, Richard K., Toby J. Kash, and Michelle J. Walker, "A Tripartite Model of the International Debt Crisis: An Analytical Study," *Columbia Journal of World Business*, Fall 1985, pp. 29–35.

Heller, H. Robert, "The Debt Crisis and the Future of International Bank Lending," *American Economic Review*, May 1987, pp. 171–175.

Houpt, James V., "International Trends for U.S. Banks and Banking Markets," *Staff Study of the Board of Governors of the Federal Reserve System*, No. 156, May 1988.

Hultman, Charles W., and L. Randolph McGee, "International Banking Facilities: The Early Response," *The Bankers Magazine*, May/June 1984, pp. 82–86.

Jain, Arvind K., "International Lending Patterns of U.S. Commercial Banks," *Journal of International Business Studies*, Fall 1986, pp. 73–88.

—— and Douglas Nigh, "Politics and the International Lending Decisions of Banks," *Journal of International Business Studies*, Summer 1989, pp. 349–359.

Johnson, Ronald A., Venkat Srinivasan, and Paul J. Bolster, "Sovereign Debt Ratings: A Judgmental Model Based on the Analytic Hierarchy Process," *Journal of International Business Studies*, First Quarter 1990, pp. 95–117.

Kennedy, Charles R. Jr., *Political Risk Management: International Lending and Investing Under Environmental Uncertainty*, Westport, Conn.: Quorum Books, 1987.

Kettell, Brian, and George A. Magnue, *The International Debt Game: A Study in International Banking Lending*, Cambridge, Mass. Ballinger Publishing, 1986.

Key, Sydney J., "International Banking Facilities,"

Federal Reserve Bulletin, October 1982, pp. 565–577.

Khan, Mohsin S., "Islamic Interest-Free Banking," *IMF Staff Papers*, 33, no. 1, March 1986, pp. 1–27.

Khoury, Sarkis J., *The Deregulation of the World Financial Markets: Myths, Realities, and Impact*, Westport, CT: Quorum Books, 1990.

——, "Sovereign Debt: A Critical Look at the Causes and the Nature of the Problem," *Essays in International Business*, Columbia, S.C.: University of South Carolina, Center for International Business Studies, July 1985.

—— and Alo Ghosh, eds., *Recent Developments in International Banking and Finance*, Lexington, Mass.: Lexington Books, 1987.

Kim, Seung H., and Stephen W. Miller, *Competitive Structure of the International Banking Industry*, Lexington, Mass.: Lexington Books, 1983.

Korth, Christopher M., "Risk Minimization for International Lending in Regional Banks," *Columbia Journal of World Business*, Winter 1981, pp. 21–28.

Lessard, Donald R., "North-South: The Implications for Multinational Banking," *Journal of Banking and Finance*, no. 7, 1983, pp. 521–536.

——, *Capital Flight: The Problem and Policy Responses*, Washington, D.C.: Institute for International Economics, 1987.

——, *Financial Intermediation Beyond the Debt Crisis*, Cambridge, Mass. MIT Press, 1985.

Li, Jane-yu, "Do Commercial Banks Speculate on the Foreign Exchange Market?" *Advances in Financial Planning and Forecasting*, vol. 4, part A, 1990, pp. 151–170.

Mascarenhas, Briance, and Ole C. Sand, "Country-Risk Assessment Systems in Banks: Patterns and Performance," *Journal of International Business Studies*, Spring 1985, pp. 19–35.

——, "Combination of Forecasts in the International Context: Predicting Debt Reschedulings," *Journal of International Business Studies*, Fall 1989, pp. 539–552.

Maxwell, Charles E., and Lawrence J. Gitman, "Risk Transmission in International Banking: An Analysis of 48 Central Banks," *Journal of International Business Studies*, Summer 1989, pp. 268–279.

Moffett, Michael H., and Arthur Stonehill, "International Banking Facilities Revisited," *Journal of International Financial Management and Accounting*, vol. 1, no. 1, Spring 1989, pp. 88–103.

Morgan, John B., "A New Look at Debt Rescheduling Indicators and Models," *Journal of International Business Studies*, Summer 1986, pp. 37–54.

Nigh, Douglas, Kang Rae Cho, and Suresh Krishnan, "The Role of Location-Related Factors in U.S. Banking Involvement Abroad: An Empirical Examination," *Journal of International Business Studies*, Fall 1986, pp. 59–72.

Park, Yoon S., and Jack Zwick, *International Banking in Theory and Practice*, Reading, Mass.: Addison-Wesley, 1985.

Quantock, Paul, ed., *Opportunities in European Financial Services: 1992 and Beyond*, New York: John Wiley, 1990.

Sabi, Manijeh, "An Application of the Theory of Foreign Direct Investment to Multinational Banking in LDCs," *Journal of International Banking Studies*, Fall 1988, pp. 433–447.

Shapiro, Alan C., "Currency Risk and Country Risk in International Banking," *Journal of Finance*, July 1985, pp. 881–891.

——, "International Banking and Country Risk Analysis," *Midland Corporate Finance Journal*, Fall 1986, pp. 56–64.

Smirlock, Michael, and Howard Kaufold, "Bank Foreign Lending, Mandatory Disclosure Rules, and the Reaction of Bank Stock Prices to the Mexican Debt Crisis," *Journal of Business*, July 1987, pp. 347–364.

Smith, Roy C., and Ingo Walter, *Global Financial Services: Strategies for Building Competitive Strengths in International Commercial and Investment Banking*, New York: Harper Business, 1990.

Terrell, Henry S., and Rodney H. Mills, "International Banking Facilities and the Eurodollar Market," *Staff Study of the Board of Governors of the Federal Reserve System*, No. 124, August 1983.

Tschoegl, Adrian E., "International Retail Banking as a Strategy: An Assessment," *Journal of International Business Studies*, Summer 1987, pp. 67–88.

Walter, Ingo, "Competitive Positioning in International Financial Services," *Journal of International Financial Management and Accounting*, volume 1, no. 1, Spring 1989, pp. 15–40.

Wright, Richard W., and Gunter A. Pauli, *The Second Wave: Japan's Global Assault on Financial Services*, New York: St. Martin's Press, 1988.

Zenoff, David B., *International Banking Management and Strategies*, London: Euromoney Publications, 1985.

11 Sourcing Debt Internationally

Cross-border financial markets are an increasingly important source of debt capital for multinational firms. In this chapter we cover cross-border *syndicated bank loans, Euronotes, Eurobonds,* and *swap agreements*. We also demonstrate how foreign-currency denominated debt creates transaction exposure for the issuer.

CROSS-BORDER FINANCIAL MARKETS

Although global capital markets have grown dramatically in recent years, the cross-border share of this market has grown even faster. Exhibit 11.1 shows the total of equities and bonds issued by private and public entities of 11 major countries. Between 1983 and 1988, this version of the global portfolio grew 254%, from $7.6 trillion to $19.3 trillion. However, cross-border holdings by nonresidents grew 306%, from $0.6 trillion in 1983 to $1.8 trillion in 1988. Cross-border holdings represented 9.1% of the global portfolio by the end of 1988. It is this cross-border share of global capital markets which is of prime interest to multinational firms. Their financing needs have become increasingly sophisticated with respect to country source, maturity, interest rate and servicing structures, currency of denomination, collateral, and type of instrument.

The basic conditions necessary for any successful cross-border market are that nonresidents of the country whose currency is used be free to transfer their holdings of that currency at will and that the market have some significant cost advantage over the purely domestic market. The cost advantage is typically derived from its "wholesale" nature and an absence of government interference, such as taxes, reserve requirements, deposit

Exhibit 11.3   Narrow Spread Between Lending and
Deposit Rates in the Eurodollar Market

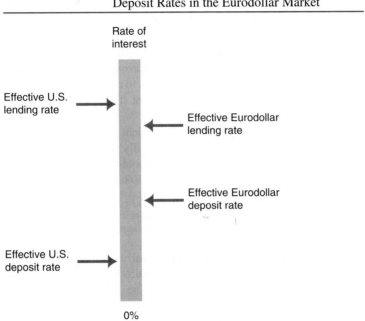

loans within London. In the early 1980s, however, use of this LIBOR base was supplemented by use of a U.S. money market rate base. Consequently both rates serve as the base for different credits. Borrowers usually pay a premium over the base rate determined by their credit worthiness and the terms of the credit.

Eurodollars are lent for both short- and medium-term maturities, with transactions for six months or less regarded as routine. Most Eurodollar loans are for a fixed term with no provision for early repayment.

Standby Eurodollar credits are of two types: a "Eurodollar line of credit" and a "Eurodollar revolving commitment." Under a Eurodollar line of credit, a bank promises to lend Eurodollars up to the credit limit, with the interest rate determined by market conditions when the loan is made. Because the line of credit can be canceled by the bank at any time, the arrangement is essentially one of preparing for borrowing in advance.

Under a Eurodollar revolving commitment, a bank agrees to lend for a period of perhaps three to five years by accepting a series of sequential notes of short maturity. For example, the borrower may renew a series of 180-day notes at each maturity at the interest rate then in effect. Banks charge a fee of about 0.5% per annum on the unused portion of such a revolving, non-revocable commitment.

Structure of a Syndicated Credit

The syndication of loans has enabled banks to spread the risk of very large loans among a number of banks. Syndication has been particularly important because many large multinational firms needed credit in excess of a single bank's loan limit.

A syndicated bank loan or credit is arranged by a lead bank on behalf of its client. Before finalizing the loan agreement, the lead bank seeks the participation of a group of banks, with each participant providing a portion of the total funds needed. The lead manager bank will work with the borrower to determine the amount of the total credit, the floating-rate base and spread over the base rate, maturity, and fee structure for managing the participating banks. The syndicated loan may or may not be totally underwritten by the participating banks. In the case of loans which are under-subscribed, the amount of credit may be altered to reflect market demand. When over-subscribed, allotment is required.

Exhibit 11.4 illustrates a typical syndicated credit. The borrower, Irish Aerospace et.al., faces two sets of expenses: the up-front costs of the initial issuance, and the periodic costs of servicing the debt. The up-front costs are fees paid to the arranging and lead-managing banks for services provided in structuring and marketing the loan, as well as out-of-pocket expenses (legal, printing, etc.). The fees normally range between 0.5 and 2.5 percent of the gross credit. In many cases a portion of this up-front fee will be distributed to participating banks. In this case, Irish Aerospace and its partners must pay a total of 1.5% in up-front fees.

The periodic expenses of the syndicated credit are composed of two elements: (1) the actual interest expense of the loan, normally stated as a spread in basis points over a variable-rate base such as LIBOR; (2) the commitment fees paid on any unused portions of the credit. The spread paid by the borrower is considered the risk premium, reflecting the general business and financial risk applicable to the borrower's repayment capability. Thus Irish Aerospace will pay 93.75 basis points (100 basis points equals 1%) over LIBOR, whereas GPA Airbus will pay only 87.5 basis points over LIBOR. Spreads have typically varied from as little as 1/16 % to over 2 1/2% (paid by the government of Brazil in 1981 and 1982 on what were then termed "Jumbo Loans" of $1 billion or more). The size and nature of the commitment fees paid depends on whether the syndicated loan is a revolving credit or term credit. If a term credit, the borrower has a specified draw-down time schedule for the loan, and there is usually no associated commitment fee. If, however, the credit is in the form of a revolving credit, the participating banks have "theoretically" set aside capital which must be paid for if unused.

Changing Role of the Syndicated Credit

The oil price increases of 1973–1974 and 1979 resulted in increased balance of payments deficits on current account for many oil-importing countries. The deficits were financed partially by syndicated bank loans to such sovereign borrowers as Brazil, Argentina, Chile and many others. As mentioned in Chapter 3, the so-called LDC debt crisis became recognized by mid-1982. As a result, the syndicated loan market volume subsequently dropped from $100 billion in 1982 to $25 billion in 1985 (Exhibit 11.2).

The recent rejuvenation of lending in the syndicated loan market is the result of a new direction in Eurocredit syndication. The primary borrowers in the market today are for securities denominated in foreign currencies and sold within their markets to holders of those foreign currencies. In effect, Eurobond sales fall outside the regulatory domain of any single nation.

Less Stringent Disclosure. Disclosure requirements in the Eurobond market are much less stringent than those of the Securities and Exchange Commission (S.E.C.) for sales within the United States. U.S. firms often find that the registration costs of a Eurobond offering are less than those of a domestic issue and that less time is needed to bring a new issue to market. Non-U.S. firms often prefer Eurodollar bonds over bonds sold within the United States because they do not wish to undergo the costs, and disclosure, needed to register with the S.E.C. For example, top foreign executives resist strongly the idea that their salaries should be public information, or that trading in the shares of their own company should be reported. Preparing foreign financial statements according to U.S. accounting principles is costly and requires more detailed disclosure of operations, such as industry segment breakdown, than is typically required in other countries. However, the S.E.C. has recently relaxed disclosure requirements for certain private placements (Rule #144A), which is expected to improve the attractiveness of the U.S. domestic bond market. Exhibit 11.11 explains the impact of S.E.C. Rule #144A on access to the U.S. private placement market.

Favorable Tax Status. Eurobonds offer tax anonymity and flexibility. Interest paid on Eurobonds is generally not subject to an income withholding tax. As one might suspect, Eurobond interest is not always reported to tax authorities. Prior to June 1984, U.S. corporations issuing Eurobonds were required to withhold up to 30% of each interest payment to foreigners for U.S. income taxes. The rate depended on the foreigner's country of residence and the bilateral tax treaty between that country and the United States. U.S. corporations wishing to issue Eurobonds had to do so through offshore finance affiliates, typically in the Netherlands Antilles, in order to avoid this tax. In 1984, however, the U.S. tax laws were revised to exempt foreign holders of bonds issued by U.S. corporations from any withholding tax. U.S. corporations found it feasible for the first time to sell Eurobonds directly to foreigners. Repeal of the U.S. withholding tax caused other governments, including those of France, West Germany, and Japan, to liberalize their tax rules as a defensive measure to avoid an outflow of capital from their markets.

As stated earlier, Eurobonds are usually issued in bearer form, meaning that the name and country of residence of the owner is not on the certificate. To receive interest, the bearer cuts an interest coupon from the bond and turns it in at a bank. European investors are accustomed to the privacy provided by bearer bonds and are very reluctant to purchase registered bonds, which require holders to reveal their names before they receive interest. Bearer bond status, of course, is also tied to tax avoidance.

Rating of Eurobonds and Other International Issues

Purchasers of Eurobonds do not typically rely on bond-rating services or on detailed analyses of financial statements. General reputation of the issuing corporation and its underwriters has been the major factor in obtaining favorable terms. For this reason, larger

Exhibit 11.11   Private Placements and SEC Rule 144A

A private placement is the sale of a security, debt or equity, to a small set of large institutional investors. The market is dominated by investors who buy and hold for long periods, often to maturity if a debt instrument is involved.

The private placement market in the United States has historically been less active than similar capital markets throughout the world. It has been relatively slow to develop due to the restrictions on security sales arising from the Securities and Exchange Commission Act of 1933. The Act requires securities which are to be sold to be registered. This entails preparing a prospectus containing detailed information about the issuer's financial condition and performance. The cost of the registration process includes out-of-pocket preparation and presentation expenses, time delays, and disclosure of information regarding the firm's private dealings. It has served as a severe damper on the willingness of foreign corporations to borrow in U.S. capital markets.

Although the United States allows private placements, they have previously not been eligible for resale without registration or a rare special exemption. This has caused the private placement market to be largely illiquid in the United States, and has offset the cost advantages of avoiding registration. Securities have therefore sold at significant discounts in the U.S. private placement market.

With the approval of SEC Rule #144A in April 1990, the United States removed several of the major restrictions on the private placement market. Rule #144A provides a "safe harbor" exemption from registration for private placements (and their resale) if certain conditions are met by "qualified institutional buyers." A qualified buyer is an entity holding more than $100 million in securities. The issue may not be of the same class as any other security issued or traded currently in the U.S. markets (the so-called "antifungibility requirement"). In addition, the issuer must provide some basic, although undetailed, current business and financial information. The SEC also simultaneously approved PORTAL, an automated trading system for listing and trading private placements among approved purchasers. Foreign corporations are thought to be the primary group of issuers who will be increasingly attracted to this more open long-term capital source.

---

and better-known multinational firms, state enterprises, and sovereign governments are able to obtain the lowest interest rates. Firms whose names are better known to the general public, possibly because they manufacture consumer goods, are often believed to have an advantage over equally qualified firms whose products are less widely known.

Rating agencies, such as Standard & Poor's (S&P's) provide ratings for selected international bonds for a fee.[2] S&P's ratings for international bonds imply the same credit-worthiness as for domestic bonds of U.S. issuers. S&P's limits its evaluation to the issuer's ability to obtain the necessary currency to repay the issue according to the original terms of the bond, and excludes any assessment of risk to the investor caused by changing exchange rates.

S&P's rates international bonds on request of the issuer. Based on supporting financial statements and other material obtained from the issuer, a preliminary rating is made. The issuer is then informed and given an opportunity to comment. After S&P's determines its final rating, the issuer may decide not to have the rating published. Consequently a disproportionately large number of published international ratings fall into the highest categories, since issuers about to receive a lower rating often decide not to have the rating published.

S&P's review of political risk includes study of the government system, the social environment, and the nation's external relations. Its review of economic risk looks at debt burden, international liquidity, balance of payments flexibility, economic structure, growth performance, economic management, and economic outlook. S&P's also evaluates the bonds of sovereign-supported entities by looking first at their creditworthiness on a stand-alone basis, and then looking at the extent to which sovereign support either enhances or diminishes the borrower's financial strength.

Innovations in the Eurobond Market

The Eurobond market is the most competitive capital market in the world. Each year new innovations in the types of securities are devised to appeal to issuers and investors with particular needs. Three typical innovations are dual currency bonds, currency cocktail bonds, and stripped bonds.

Dual Currency Bonds. The dual currency bond was a relatively popular innovation on the global bond markets in the early- to mid-1980s. A dual currency bond is any debt issue with purchase price and coupons denominated in one currency, and the principal redemption value fixed in a second currency. The instrument is useful for firms wishing to borrow in one currency, pay debt-service in the same currency, but repay the principal at maturity in a second currency to which they expect to have access. The investor is usually attracted by the possibility of an exchange rate change in the investor's favor when the principal is repaid.

Currency Cocktail Bonds. Currency cocktail bonds are denominated in one of several currency baskets, such as SDRs or ECUs. Currency cocktail bonds have been issued from time to time since the mid-1970s. They appeal to investors because interest and principal payments should be more stable than the value of any one of the component currencies because of currency diversification. Such bonds are particularly useful for corporations whose cash receipts from sales are in a variety of currencies. Conceptually some of those currencies will be rising in value while others will be dropping. The net result could parallel the value of the currency cocktail bond.

Stripped Bonds. In 1985 the U.S. Treasury gave serious consideration to issuing U.S. government bonds in bearer form in order to sell them to foreigners. Congressional critics, however, argued that such bonds might be purchased by (or for) U.S. citizens to evade taxes. Eventually the Treasury decided against issuing bearer bonds. Nevertheless, Treasury regulations permit U.S. corporations to sell bearer bonds to foreign residents. In addition, securities firms may buy U.S. Treasury securities, repackage them in trusts, and resell claims on the trust to foreigners in bearer form. These are called "stripped" bonds.

One form of stripped Treasury bonds sold by a syndicate headed by Salomon Brothers, Inc., goes by the acronym of "CATS," which stands for "Certificates of Accrual on Treasury Securities." CATS were first offered in August 1984 as deep discount bonds in bearer form to foreign investors and in registered form to U.S. investors. The two forms are interchangeable, so that bearer bonds resold by foreigners to U.S. residents will be exchanged for registered certificates, and vice versa. Deep discount bonds are sold at a fraction of their maturity value, with the investor's profit derived entirely from recovering the higher maturity value. Such bonds are particularly popular with investors from countries that consider all appreciation as capital gains subject to preferential tax treatment or no tax at all.

In a CATS offering, interest coupons are stripped from the maturity or "corpus" portion of the Treasury bonds. Certificates are then sold against each set of coupons for each interest date as well as against the corpus portion. Hence each CATS is a zero-coupon bond that pays no interest and is sold at a deep discount from maturity value. In its first CATS issue, Salomon Brothers offered $5.3 billion of coupon CATS due semiannually from February 15, 1985, to August 15, 2009; and a corpus CATS consisting of a claim on the $1.7 billion principal, callable August 15, 2009, and maturing August 15, 2014. The corpus portion of the Salomon Brothers issue was offered at $595 for a $1,000 bond, to yield an effective 11 5/8 %.[3]

FOREIGN EXCHANGE RISK AND THE COST OF DEBT

When a multinational firm issues foreign currency-denominated debt, its effective cost equals the after-tax cost of repaying the principal and interest in terms of the parent's own currency. This amount includes the nominal cost of principal and interest in foreign currency terms, adjusted for any foreign exchange gains or losses. For example, if a U.S. multinational firm borrows Deutschemarks for one year at 6% interest, and during the year the mark appreciates by 8% relative to the dollar, the approximate before-tax cost of this debt (k_d) is 14.48%. The calculation is as follows:

cost of debt	equals	interest in DM	times	additional interest due to exchange rate change	plus	additional principal due to exchange rate change	
k_d	=	6%	X	1.08	+	8%	=14.48%.

Another formula that is often used is

cost of debt	equals	principal and interest	times	exchange rate change	minus	principal	times	100
k_d	=	[(1.06	X	1.08)	–	1.00]	X	100.
	=	14.48%.						

Exhibit 11.12   Costs of Borrowing in Foreign Currency Denominated Bonds (percent)

Issuer (parent)	Date of Issue	(A) Cost of Funds at Time of Issue, DM-denominated	(B) Cost of Funds at Time of Issue, US$-denominated	(C) Effective Cost of DM-issue Adjusted for Currency Changes as of Oct. 1973	(D) Effective Cost of DM-issue Adjusted for Currency Changes as of Maturity
National Lead	5-26-67	6.58	7.08	12.38	12.56
General Instrument	5-29-68	7.08	8.33	13.17	14.52
Gulf Oil	9-05-68	6.57	7.51	12.01	12.93
Occidental Petroleum	10-08-68	6.70	7.70	12.20	13.20
Tenneco	12-17-68	6.88	8.13	12.35	13.61
Chrysler	7-10-69	7.14	7.49	13.40	14.50
Studebaker-Worthington	7-31-69	7.65	8.81	14.00	16.60
Int. Standard Electric	9-01-69	7.14	8.40	13.38	14.36
TRW	10-15-69	7.82	8.70	13.17	14.74

Source: Steven M. Dawson, "Eurobond Currency Selection: Hindsight," *Financial Executive*, November 1973, p. 73, updated February 1991. Column A presents expected cost to maturity of issue given coupon, new issue price, maturity, and sinking fund requirements. Column B makes a similar calculation assuming the issue were denominated in U.S. dollars. Columns C and D present costs to maturity after coupons are adjusted by Morgan Guaranty yield for dollar and mark bond issues. Adjustments in columns C and D include the dollar devaluation and mark revaluations subsequent to debt issuance. The yields at maturity (column D) assume that payments of interest, sinking fund, and principal at maturity were made as scheduled at the time of issue. Each principal and coupon payment is adjusted for U.S. bank transfer rate in effect at time of payment.

The added 8.48% cost of this debt in terms of U.S. dollars would be reported as a foreign exchange transaction loss, and it would be deductible for tax purposes. Therefore, the after-tax cost of this debt, when the U.S. income tax rate is 34%, would be:

$$k_d(1 - t) = 14.48\% \times 0.66 = 9.56\%.$$

Multinational firms have discovered that borrowing foreign currency debt on a long-term basis creates considerable exposure to transaction gains or losses. For example, U.S. firms that borrowed long-term Deutschemarks prior to December 1971 rue that day. In an article appropriately titled "Eurobond Currency Selection: Hindsight," Steven Dawson calculated what happened to the nine Deutschemark-denominated bonds that were issued by U.S. firms during the fixed exchange rate period May 1967 to October 1969.[4] Exhibit 11.12, abstracted from his article and updated by Steven Dawson in February 1991, shows that in each case the borrower would have been much better off to have borrowed in dollars. This is despite the fact that the initial nominal interest rate would have been higher for a dollar-denominated issue than for a Deutschemark-denominated one. Exhibit 11.12, column C, shows that most of the damage must have been done during the transition to floating exchange rates (December 1971 to October 1973). Column D shows that the large transaction losses continued right up to maturity.

THE SWAP MARKETS

Although the international debt market has moved the world in the direction of an integrated global capital market, most national capital markets are still partially segmented. Evidence of this is that some firms have a comparative advantage in raising funds—depending on the national capital market, currency of denomination, terms of repayment, size of the firm, credit rating, and other firm-specific characteristics. As a result, the international swap markets have evolved as a way to *arbitrage the comparative advantage* enjoyed by some firms relative to others. (See Chapter 1: Appendix A for a description of comparative advantage).

A financial *swap* is an exchange of financial obligations between two parties, each of whom has incurred a financial obligation in a currency or in a type of interest payment that was not really desired, but was the cheapest alternative. The parties could be two domestic firms resident in the same market, two foreign firms, or a foreign and domestic firm.

Interest Rate Swaps

What is often termed the "plain vanilla" swap is an agreement between two borrowers to exchange fixed-rate for floating-rate financial obligations. This swap normally requires a borrower with relatively cheap access to fixed-rate funds to exchange the debt-service structure with another borrower of slightly lower creditworthiness, who has acquired an obligation at floating rates. Each borrower obtains a payment structure which is "preferred," while still retaining the obligation for the principal repayment. Exhibit 11.13 provides an illustration of how a fixed-for-floating-rate swap works. Although the original interest rate swaps were arranged between two independent parties on their own, in the early 1980s a number of international banks became "arbitragers" in this market. The banks provide the link through which the two parties of the agreement are brought together. It should be noted that the bank is actually accepting some of the financial risk of the transaction. Banks also swap with one another for the same reasons that firms swap.

In addition to the basic "plain vanilla" swap, there are a number of other interest rate swaps, such as the basis swap, in which the variable rate base is exchanged between two parties (for example, LIBOR base with a U.S. rate base). The market for interest rate swaps has continued to grow. The Bank for International Settlements (BIS) estimates that there were over $1 trillion in interest rate swaps outstanding (total notional principal amount) at the end of 1988, with an additional $390 billion in new swaps arranged in the first six months of 1989.[5]

Currency Swaps

Currency swaps enable borrowers to exchange debt service obligations denominated in one currency for the service on similar debt denominated in another currency. By swapping their future cash flow obligations, two parties are able to alter their currency holdings, but do so without incurring increased future currency exposure.

The usual motivation for a currency swap is to replace cash flows scheduled in an "undesired" currency with flows in a "desired" currency. The "desired" currency is

Exhibit 11.13   Structure and Pricing of Interest Rate Swaps

Unilever, U.K., and MIC, U.S., are both in the market for approximately $30 million of debt for a five-year period. Unilever has a AAA credit rating, and therefore has access to both fixed and floating interest rate debt at attractive rates. Unilever would prefer to borrow at floating rates. MIC has an A rating. Although MIC still has access to both fixed and floating rate debt, the fixed rate debt is considered expensive. MIC would prefer to borrow at fixed rates. The firms, through Citibank, could actually borrow in their relatively "advantaged" markets and then swap their debt service payments.

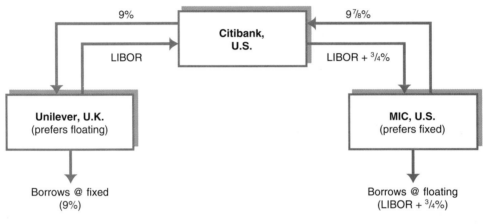

Implementation of the Interest Rate Swap

1.   Unilever borrows at the fixed rate of 9%, and swaps the payments to the bank. The bank then agrees to make the debt service payments of fixed rate 9% on behalf of Unilever.

2.   Unilever agrees in turn to pay the bank a floating rate of LIBOR, enabling it to make debt service payments on a floating rate basis, which it prefers, as well as at a lower interest rate than it could have acquired on its own.

3.   MIC borrows at the floating rate of LIBOR + 3/4%, and then swaps the payments to the bank that agrees to service the floating rate debt payments on behalf of MIC.

4.   MIC agrees in turn to pay the bank a fixed rate of 9 7/8%, enabling MIC to make debt service payments on a fixed rate basis which it prefers. Thus it borrows at lower cost than it could have acquired on its own.

Benefits of the Interest Rate Swap

Each of the borrowers benefits from the interest rate swap by being able to borrow capital in the preferred interest rate structure and at a lower rate than obtainable on their own.

	Unilever, U.K.	*MIC, U.S.*
If borrowing directly:	LIBOR + 1/4%	10.000%
If borrowing through swap:	LIBOR + 0%	9.875%
Savings:	+ 1/4%	+ 0.125%

probably that in which the firm's future operating revenue will be generated. Preferential financial terms in a particular currency arise because of market imperfections caused by such factors as a firm's greater access to borrowing in its home currency, the novelty of a particular debt issue, governmental regulations, and investor preference for buying bonds of domestic firms. Exhibit 11.14 provides a numerical example of a currency swap.

The currency swap market has grown rapidly, doubling in size between 1987 and 1989. Exhibit 11.15 provides a profile of the size and currency composition of the currency swaps arranged by mid-year 1990. The total notional value of currency swaps outstanding at end-of-year 1989 was approximately $494 billion according to Morgan Guaranty and the International Swap Dealers Association (ISDA). Of the $494 billion, $334 billion was with the actual participants (end users) and $115 billion was swap trading between the intermediaries (market makers) who match up end users. The average size and maturity of

---

Exhibit 11.14 Structure and Pricing of Straight Currency Swaps

Assume that Nestle (Switzerland) wishes to obtain the use of NKr15,000,000 for a two-year period. Similarly, Norsk Shipping (Norway) is interested in obtaining Swiss francs for a two-year period, but has been unable to acquire favorable interest rates from Eurobanks for such a loan. The two firms agree to a straight currency swap of NKr15,000,000 for a two-year period, with a specified exchange rate of NKr4.3333/SF. The swap structure would be composed of two major components.

Component 1: Exchange of Currency Principal

Nestle exchanges SF3,461,565 at NKr4.3333/SF with Norsk Shipping for NKr15,000,000. The currency swap is made on October 15, 1991, and will be reversed on October 15, 1993. At the reversal date, the same currency values will apply, with Nestle returning NKr15,000,000 and Norsk Shipping returning SF3,461,565. Because the future rate of exchange is agreed upon at the initial swap date, each firm is able to obtain foreign currency balances without also incurring foreign exchange risk.

Component 2: Compensation for Interest Differentials

In order to compensate the two parties for interest rate differentials between currencies, the firm obtaining the currency with the higher nominal interest yield will compensate the other party for the difference. Swiss and Norwegian government notes of two-year maturities are yielding 3.5% and 8.7% to maturity, respectively, in October of 1991. Since Nestle is obtaining the currency (Norwegian krone) with the relatively higher nominal return, it must compensate Norsk Shipping for the differential, annually, for the two-year period of the straight currency swap by paying Norsk Shipping NKr780,000 per year.

$$\text{Annual Interest Differential Payment} = (0.087 - 0.035) \times NKr15,000,000$$
$$= (0.052) \times Nkr15,000,000$$
$$= NKr780,000$$

It should be noted that it would also be possible to conduct the same transaction by using a future principal reversal exchange rate which would be determined by the differentials in interest rates (international Fisher effect).

Exhibit 11.15   Size and Currency Composition of the Currency Swap Market

Total notional[1] principal of new swaps

	1987	1988	1989	1st half 1990	Outstanding end-1989
Market size (billions of dollars)					
Total[2]	86	124	170	189	449
End user[2]	69	95	123	136	334
Market marker[2]	17	29	47	53	115
Currency (billions of dollars)					
United States dollar	77	104	132	125	354
Japanese yen	27	46	80	85	201
Swiss franc	13	21	17	31	65
German mark	12	17	18	24	54
Australian dollar	14	13	40	33	62
ECU	9	12	13	17	40
British pound	4	10	16	16	33
Other	17	26	39	47	90
Average size (millions of dollars)[3]					
Dollar swaps	26	31	23	24	28
Nondollar swaps	28	32	23	15	29
Average maturity (years)[3]					
Dollar swaps	5.3	5.3	4.9	4.5	4.8
Nondollar swaps	5.1	5.4	5.2	5.0	4.8

Source: From *World Financial Markets*, April 1991, p. 5. Reprinted with permission of Morgan Guaranty Trust Co.

1 Notional principal is the amount that yields the actual two-way interest payments to be exchanged, given the rate formulas in the swap contract. Exchange of principal is not always involved in a currency swap, and is wholly redundant in a single-currency interest rate swap.

2 Adjusted for double-counting due to reporting of the currencies on the two sides of each swap.

3 Swaps with end users, except 1st half of 1990; all swaps at annual rates.

currency swaps has not changed significantly over this rapid growth period, averaging $28 million per swap for an average term of 4.8 years.[6]

The swap market is extremely competitive, with very low profit margins for the financial intermediaries involved. Almost all swaps today involve a major bank as principal in the transaction. Typically, the bank maintains "swap books" in different currencies. For its efforts as principal, a bank will typically earn the present value of from 5 to 12 basis points per year, depending on the currency involved (U.S. dollars and Deutschemarks are lowest). If a swap is brokered by an intermediary which is not a principal, that broker will earn the present value of one basis point per year per counterparty. The partners to the swap typically save from 5 to 50 basis points per year, compared to their next best alternative for raising the same currency and terms without a swap.

Since some commercial risk exists if one of the partners defaults, only firms with quality credit ratings (A or better), or guarantee facilities, can be served by the swap market. Furthermore, a standardized swap contract has been adopted by all players to assure a minimum of legal disputes.

A number of swaps combine an interest rate swap with a currency swap. An actual example is shown in the illustrative case, Security Pacific National Bank and Naturgas Sjaelland, which completes this chapter.

Security Pacific National Bank and Naturgas Sjaelland: Interest Rate/Cross-Currency Swap*

In early April 1989, Gudme Raaschou Investment Bank, Copenhagen, brokered a combined interest rate and cross-currency swap between Security Pacific National Bank (SPNB) and Naturgas Sjaelland I/S (Naturgas). SPNB's London branch wanted DM17,000,000 at a fixed interest rate. Naturgas wanted Swiss francs at a floating interest rate. The terms that were agreed upon can be summarized as follows:

Deutschemark principal amount:	DM17,000,000
Swiss franc principal amount:	SF14,926,000
Effective date:	10 April 1989
Termination date:	10 April 1996
DM fixed rate payer:	SPNB
SF floating rate payer:	Naturgas
Fixed rate payment dates:	10 April and 10 October in each year to and including the termination date, commencing with 10 October 1989.
Floating rate payment dates:	10 April and 10 October in each year to and including the termination date, commencing with 10 October 1989.
DM fixed rate:	6.81 percent per annum; payable semiannually in arrears; interest will be calculated and paid on the basis of a 360-day year of 12 months of 30 days.
SF floating rate:	6-month SF LIBOR will be determined 2 London business days prior to the commencement of each floating rate payment date as the 6-month SF LIBOR quote displayed on Telerate page 3750 at 11:00 A.M. London time.
	LIBOR will be payable semiannually in arrears based on actual days elapsed and a 360-day year.

* This case was summarized from information given to the authors by Aage Jacobsen, Gudme Raaschou Investment Bankers, Ltd. and Security Pacific National Bank, Global Swaps Group. The authors are grateful for receiving permission to publish it.

LIBOR for the first period: SF LIBOR for the period 10 April 1989 through 10 October 1989 has been set at 6.1250 percent.

Initial exchange: For value 10 April 1989, SPNB will pay Naturgas 14,926,000 Swiss francs and Naturgas will pay SPNB DM17,000,000.

Final exchange: For value 10 April 1996, Naturgas will pay SPNB 14,926,000 Swiss francs and SPNB will pay Naturgas DM17,000,000.

Governing law: English.

Because the identical principal values would be exchanged at the termination of the swap as at the beginning, neither party would bear exchange rate risk on the principal. The implied exchange rate from the principal swap was set at the approximate current (April 1989) spot rate of DM1.14/SF.

SUMMARY

- Cross-border financial markets are an increasingly important source of capital for multinational firms, sovereign entities, and international institutions.

- The main components of the international debt markets are bank syndicated loans, Euronotes, and Eurobonds.

- Syndicated loans, known as Eurocredits, are bank loans to business firms, sovereign entities, international institutions, and other banks.

- The basic borrowing rate on syndicated loans is a variable rate of interest based on LIBOR.

- In earlier years, sovereign entities were the main borrowers of syndicated loans, but in recent years corporations have used them to finance leveraged buyouts, mergers, and acquisitions.

- The Euronote market is the collective term used to describe short- to medium-term debt instruments sourced in the Eurocurrency markets.

- Euro-commercial paper is a short-term debt obligation similar to domestic commercial paper but sourced in the Eurocurrency markets.

- Euro-medium-term notes bridge the maturity gap between Euro-commercial paper and Eurobonds. Their terms of repayment are similar to bonds but they have a shorter maturity.

- A Eurobond is underwritten by an international syndicate of financial institutions and is sold exclusively in countries other than the country in whose currency the bond is denominated.

- Eurobonds can be straight fixed-rate issues, floating rate notes, or equity-related issues.

- Eurobonds are attractive because of the absence of regulatory interference, less stringent disclosure requirements, and a favorable tax status due to their bearer form.

- International swap markets have evolved for firms to arbitrage their comparative advantage in accessing certain capital markets relative to other firms.

- Interest rate swaps and currency swaps have become increasingly important as a means for a firm to fund in a desired currency, and with a desired repayment flow, at a lower cost than it could get on its own.

- The cost of foreign-currency-denominated debt includes the nominal cost of principal and interest in foreign currency terms, adjusted for any foreign exchange gains or losses. This creates transaction exposure which can be risky.

1. Federal Republic of Brazil

The Federal Republic of Brazil acquired much of its debt in the late 1970s and early 1980s through large international syndicated loans. By 1980 the Brazilian government had borrowed so frequently from the markets that what was known as "Brazilian pricing" became standard for many such syndicated credits:

Principal	US$500,000,000
Maturity	8.0 years
Base interest rate	LIBOR
Spread	2 1/2%
Syndication fees	1 1/2%

What would be the actual loan proceeds from such a syndicated credit? What would the effective annual cost of funds be for the first year?

2. The BOC Group, plc

The BOC Group, plc, is a multinational manufacturer of carbon-based industrial gas products, healthcare products and services, and specialty graphite industrial products. Although it is incorporated in the United Kingdom, a large portion of its cash flows are in dollars. It now wishes to access the international debt markets for short-term capital which will be hopefully cheaper than bank credit, and acquired at current low interest rates.

If The BOC Group issues a total principal of US$500,000,000 in Euro-commercial Paper (ECP) at a discount, with the following characteristics, what are the total proceeds to BOC of the issues?

Issue	Notional Principal	Yield
90-day ECP	US$300,000,000	8.20%
180-day ECP	US$200,000,000	8.40%

3. Sunshine Products

Sunshine Products of Texas seeks to borrow $800,000 to finance working capital needs. Sunshine finds that it can borrow from a Texas bank for 8% per annum. Because Sunshine has an ongoing subsidiary in Switzerland, it has an established credit position there and so can also borrow Swiss francs at 5% per annum. The Swiss francs would be exchanged for dollars at the spot rate, and dollars would later be used to acquire Swiss francs spot to repay the loan. Sunshine believes that the Swiss franc will appreciate at 4% per annum during the period of the loan.

Where should Sunshine borrow?

4. Spich Corporation (C11A.WK1)

Spich Corporation wishes to raise $2,000,000 in U.S. dollars with debt financing. The funds, needed to finance working capital, will be repaid with interest in one year. Spich's treasurer is considering three sources:

a) Borrow U.S. dollars from Security Pacific Bank at 8%.

b) Borrow British pounds from National Westminster Bank at 14%.

c) Borrow Japanese yen from Sanwa Bank at 5%.

If Spich borrows a foreign currency, it will remain uncovered; that is, it will simply change foreign currency for dollars at today's spot rate and buy foreign currency back one year later at the spot rate then in effect. Spich Corporation has no operations in either the United Kingdom or Japan.

Spich estimates the pound will depreciate 5% relative to the dollar and the yen will appreciate 3% relative to the dollar during the next year. Corporate income tax rates are 34% in the United States, 35% in the United Kingdom, and 40% in Japan.

From which bank should Spich borrow and what is its projected after-tax cost of borrowing (in dollars) from each source?

5. Ford Motor Company (C11B.WK1)

Ford Motor Company wants to borrow $50,000,000 for five years to finance modernization of its Dearborn, Michigan, factories. A five-year bond with a fixed coupon rate of 8% can be sold in the United States at par. Ford can also borrow in the Eurocurrency market, as follows:

a) Borrow Eurodollars for five years at 1% above dollar LIBOR. Dollar LIBOR is currently 7%. The interest rate would be floating, and would be readjusted once each year.

b) Borrow Euromarks for five years at 1% above mark LIBOR. Mark LIBOR is currently 5%. The interest rate would be floating, and would be readjusted annually.

Describe the benefits and risks for Ford of borrowing in the Eurocurrency market instead of in the U.S. domestic market.

6. Security Pacific National Bank and Naturgas Sjaelland Swap

The illustrative case at the end of this chapter described the combined interest rate and currency swap between Security Pacific National Bank (SPNB) and Naturgas Sjaelland (Naturgas) in April 1989. The swap resulted in SPNB acquiring DM17,000,000 for seven years at a fixed interest rate while Naturgas acquired the use of SF14,926,000 for the same period at a floating interest rate.

What is the actual interest payment schedule for each over the seven-year period? Discuss which of the two firms, if either, is accepting more financial risk in the swap.

7. Hakone Corporation

You work for a U.S. investment company that seeks U.S. dollar returns, but which is also quite willing to take foreign exchange risks.

You are negotiating the dollar purchase of a new Euro-yen bond issue of Hakone Corporation. The issue is for one billion yen (¥1,000,000,000), has a maturity of five years, is to be issued at par today, and will pay 80 million yen (¥80,000,000) interest annually starting one year from today.

Your forecasts of the yen/dollar exchange rate are:

Today:	¥135/$.
1 year from today:	130
2 years from today:	125
3 years from today:	120
4 years from today:	110
5 years from today:	100

a) What is the current yield-to-maturity in Japan on yen bonds of this risk and maturity?

b) What dollar price would you be willing to pay for the issue today, if you wanted to obtain an identical yield-to-maturity in dollars, and if you were positive of your foreign exchange forecasts?

c) If the dollar price you would pay today (answer to question (a) above) is not equal to one billion yen at today's exchange rate, explain briefly why you would be willing to pay more or would be able to buy the issue for less than its par value in Japanese yen.

8. Rifkind and O'Brien Corporations

Rifkind and O'Brien corporations both seek funding at the lowest possible cost. They face the following rate structure:

	Rifkind	O'Brien
Credit rating	AA	BB
Cost of fixed rate borrowing	10.0%	13.0%
Cost of floating rate borrowing	LIBOR + 0.5%	LIBOR + 1.0%

a) In what type of borrowing does Rifkind have a comparative advantage? Why?

b) In what type of borrowing does O'Brien have a comparative advantage? Why?

c) If a swap were arranged, what is the maximum savings that could be divided between the two parties?

d) Illustrate a transaction that would generate such a savings divided equally between the two firms.

9. Yorkshire Industries and Huron River Salt Company

Yorkshire Industries, a British industrial firm with a U.S. subsidiary, seeks to refinance some of its existing sterling debt to include floating rate obligations. The best floating rate it can obtain in London is LIBOR + 2.0%. Its current debt is as follows:

$10,000,000 owed to Citibank at 9.3% (fixed) annually.

£5,000,000 owed to Midland Bank at 9.5% (fixed) annually.

Huron River Salt Company wishes to finance exports to Britain with £3,000,000 of pound-denominated fixed-rate debt for six months. Huron River Salt is unable to obtain a fixed interest rate in London for less than 13.5% interest because of its lack of credit history in the United Kingdom. However, Lloyds Bank is willing to extend a floating rate pound sterling loan at LIBOR + 2.0%. Huron River Salt, however, cannot afford to pay more than 12.0%.

How can Yorkshire Industries and Huron River Salt help each other via an interest rate swap? Assume that Yorkshire Industries is in a strong bargaining position and can negotiate the best deal possible, but Huron River Salt won't pay over 12%. Transaction costs are zero, and exchange rates do not change. Show (a) effective post-swap interest rates, and (b) the interest saved by each party over the six-month period of the swap.

10. Yankee Corporation and Kiso Kaido, K.K.

The Yankee Corporation would like to borrow floating rate dollars, which it can do at LIBOR + 0.5%. It can also borrow fixed rate yen at 6%. Kiso Kaido, K.K. has a strong preference for fixed-rate yen debt, which will cost it 7.0%. Kiso Kaido, K.K. could borrow floating dollars at LIBOR + 1.0%.

What is the range of possible cost savings to Yankee Corporation from engaging in a combined interest and currency swap with Kiso Kaido, K.K.?

11. Folks-Adanti, Inc. (C11C.WK1)

Folks-Adanti wants to borrow $50 million or the foreign-currency equivalent for five years. These alternatives are available:

a) *Borrow in U.S. Dollars:* Borrow dollars at 11% per annum with bonds sold at par. Expenses of the issue will be 2.5% of amount borrowed.

b) *Borrow in Deutschemarks:* Borrow Deutschemarks at 8% per annum with bonds sold at 99. Expenses of the issue will be 2.5% of amount borrowed. The current exchange rate is DM1.5557/$, and the mark is expected to appreciate against the dollar by 3% per annum.

c) *Borrow in Japanese Yen:* Borrow yen at 4% per annum, bonds sold at par, and 3.0% off the face value for expenses. The current exchange rate is ¥140.00/$. The yen is expected to appreciate against the dollar by 7% per annum.

Evaluate the cost of each alternative and make a recommendation to the Chief Financial Officer (CFO) regarding the source of capital that is likely to be cheapest for the five year period.

12. Teknekron's Euro-Medium-Term Notes

Teknekron (Belgium) issues US$10,000,000 in Euro-Medium-Term Notes on September 1, 1991. Although the EMTNs are officially "issued" on that date, they are shelf-registered and will be actually sold on continuing dates over the period. All the notes possess 9% per annum coupons paid semiannually.

The first issue is sold on September 1, 1991, and is set to mature on May 1, 1993. What is the market price of this $1,000 EMTN on November 1, 1991, if similar issues are yielding 8% per annum at that time?

NOTES

1. Bank for International Settlements, *60th Annual Report*, Basle, June 11, 1990, p. 136.

2. A detailed description of Standard & Poor's procedure for determining credit ratings for all securities, including international securities, is given in their booklet, *Credit Overview, Corporate and International Ratings*, published by Standard & Poor's Corporation, 25 Broadway, New York, N.Y. 10004.

3. *Wall Street Journal*, January 1, 1985, p. 33.

4. Steven M. Dawson, "Eurobond Currency Selection: Hindsight," *Financial Executive*, November 1973, pp. 72-73, updated by Steven M. Dawson, February 1991.

5. Bank for International Settlements, *60th Annual Report*, Basle, June 11, 1990, p. 149.

6. *Ibid.*, p. 151.

BIBLIOGRAPHY

Areskoug, Kai, "Exchange Rates and the Currency of Denominations in International Bonds," *Economica*, May 1980, pp. 159–163.

Arnold, Tanya S., "How to Do Interest Rate Swaps," *Harvard Business Review*, September/October 1984, pp. 96–101.

Beidleman, Carl R., *Financial Swaps*, Homewood, Ill.: Dow Jones-Irwin, 1985.

Bradley, Finbarr, "An Analysis of Call Strategy in the Eurodollar Bond Market," *Journal of International Financial Management and Accounting*, volume 2, no. 1, Spring 1990, pp. 23–46.

Bullock, Gareth, *Euronotes and Euro-Commercial Paper*, London: Butterworths, 1987.

Chang, Rosita P., Peter E. Koveos, and S. Ghon Rhee, "Financial Planning for International Long-Term Debt Financing," *Advances in Financial Planning and Forecasting*, vol. 4, part B, 1990, pp. 33–58.

Chuppe, Terry M., Hugh R. Haworth, and Marvin G. Watkins, "Public Policy Toward the International Bond Markets in the 1980s," *Advances in Financial Planning and Forecasting*, vol. 4, part B, 1990, pp. 3–32

Debt-Equity Swaps: How to Tap an Emerging Market, New York: Business International, 1987.

de Caires, Bryan, ed., *The Guide to International Capital Markets*, London: Euromoney Publications, 1988.

Doukas, John, "Syndicated Euro-Credit Sovereign Risk Assessments, Market Efficiency and Contagion Effects," *Journal of International Business Studies*, Summer 1989, pp. 255–267.

Fisher III, F. G., *Eurobonds*, London: Euromoney Publications, 1987.

Folks, W.R., Jr., "Analysis of Short-Term, Cross-Border Financing Decisions," *Financial Management*, Autumn 1976, pp. 19–27.

——, "Optimal Foreign Borrowing Strategies with Operations in Forward Exchange Markets," *Journal of Financial and Quantitative Analysis*, June 1978, pp. 245–254.

Heller, Lucy, *Eurocommercial Paper*, London: Euromoney Publications, 1988.

International Capital Markets: Developments and Prospects, Washington, D.C.: IMF, 1990.

Jadlow, Janice Wickstead, "Market Assessment of the Eurodollar Default Risk Premium," *Advances in Financial Planning and Forecasting*, vol. 4, part A, 1990, pp. 105–122.

Jennergren, L. Peter, and Bertil Näslund, "Models for the Valuation of International Convertible Bonds," *Journal of International Financial Management and Accounting*, vol. 2, nos. 2 and 3, Summer and Autumn 1990, pp. 93–110.

Krol, Robert, "The Term Structure of Eurodollar Interest Rates and Its Relationship to the U.S. Treasury-Bill Market," *Journal of International Money and Finance*, 6, No. 3, September 1987, pp. 339–354.

Marr, M. Wayne, Robert W. Rogowski, and John L. Trimble, "The Competitive Effects of U.S. and Japanese Commercial Bank Participation in Eurobond Underwriting," *Financial Management*, Winter 1989, pp. 47–54.

Morgan Guarantee Trust Company, "Swaps: Volatility at Controlled Risk," *World Financial Markets*, April 1991, pp. 1–22.

Remmers, H. Lee,"A Note on Foreign Borrowing Costs," *Journal of International Business Studies*, Fall 1980, pp. 123–134.

Rhee, S. Ghon, Rosita P. Chang, and Peter E. Koveos, "The Currency-of-Denomination Decision for Debt Financing," *Journal of International Business Studies*, Fall 1985, pp. 143–150.

Robichek. Alexander A., and Mark R. Eaker, "Debt Denomination and Exchange Risk in International Capital Markets," *Financial Management*, Autumn 1976, pp. 11–18.

Shapiro, Alan C., "The Impact of Taxation on the Currency-of-Denomination Decision for Long-Term Borrowing and Lending," *Journal of International Business Studies*, Spring/Summer 1984, pp. 15–25.

Smith, Clifford W., Jr., Charles W. Smithson, and Lee MacDonald Wakeman, "The Market for Interest Rate Swaps," *Journal of Financial Management*, Winter 1988, pp. 34–44.

——, "The Evolving Market for Swaps," *Midland Corporate Finance Journal*, Winter 1986, pp. 20–32.

Solnik, Bruno, "Swap Pricing and Default Risk: A Note," *Journal of International Financial Management and Accounting*, volume 2, no. 1, Spring 1990, pp. 79–91.

Stigum, Marcia, *The Money Market*, 3rd edition, Homewood, IL: Dow Jones-Irwin, 1990.

12 Sourcing Equity Internationally

Over the past decade the world's equity markets have grown dramatically in both size and integration. The growth in size has been due to a combination of favorable macroeconomic trends, including good growth prospects in Japan, the United States, and most European countries, more firms going public particularly outside the United States, exchange rate developments, and especially deregulation. The United Kingdom experienced its "Big Bang" of deregulation in October 1986. Immediately thereafter trading volume and market values of listed stocks soared, at least until the big worldwide market break of October 1987. Japan has been rapidly liberalizing its own equity markets with a resulting increase in trading volume, market values, and interest from foreign investors. The EEC countries are also rapidly liberalizing their equity markets, a trend that will culminate in 1992 with the complete elimination of all internal barriers to capital movements. These factors have now made it possible for more firms around the world to access international equity capital for continued growth and international expansion. This chapter describes the state of global equity markets today and the similarities and differences which these markets offer multinational firms choosing to raise equity capital in one or more external markets.

SIZE OF GLOBAL EQUITY MARKETS

Global equity markets have grown dramatically in size and turnover in recent years, but the most dramatic development is the rapid rise and current importance of the Japanese equity market.

345

Exhibit 12.1   Size and Growth of Global Equity Markets (billions of U.S. dollars)

	Market Value of all Listed Issues					Average Annual Growth[a]	
Area or Country	1988	1984	1980	1976	1972	1972–88 %/yr	1980–88 %/yr
North America							
United States	2481	1593	1240	856	864	6.82	9.06
Canada	221	116	113	52	57	8.84	8.75
Total	2702	1709	1353	908	921	6.96	9.03
Europe							
United Kingdom	718	219	190	65	140	10.76	18.08
West Germany	241	78	71	54	43	11.37	16.51
Switzerland	148	43	46	22	17	14.48	15.73
France	224	40	53	28	31	13.16	19.74
Netherlands	86	31	25	17	14	12.01	16.70
Sweden	89	19	12	10	8	16.25	28.46
Italy	135	23	25	9	14	15.22	23.47
Spain	87	12	16	18	22	8.97	23.57
Belgium	58	12	10	9	9	12.35	24.57
Other Countries	74	12	9	6	4	20.00	30.13
Total	1860	489	457	239	303	12.01	19.18
Pacific Area							
Japan	3840	617	357	179	152	22.36	34.57
Australia	134	52	60	20	26	10.79	10.57
Singapore	43	27	24	6	8	11.08	7.56
Hong Kong	74	26	38	12	10	13.33	8.69
Total	4104	722	479	217	195	20.98	30.80
World Total	8680	2945	2289	1371	1423	11.97	18.13

Source: Data abstracted from Bruno Solnik, *International Investments*, second edition, © 1991 Addison-Wesley Publishing Co., Reading, Mass. Reprinted with permission. Original data from Morgan Stanley Capital International.

a Geometric annual average rate of change for the period listed.

Size of Markets

The size and growth of the world's major equity markets is shown in Exhibit 12.1. Although the United States was by far the largest in total capitalization in 1984 at $1593 billion, it was second in size to Japan's equity exchanges by 1988. By end of year 1988, the Japanese equity exchanges totaled $3840 billion, compared to $2481 billion for the United States. The United Kingdom equity markets totaled $718 billion in 1988, with the West German markets a distant fourth at $241 billion. These four country-exchanges dominated world stock exchanges in 1988, with Japan making up 44.2% of all world equity value, the United States 28.6%, the United Kingdom 8.3%, and West Germany 2.8%.

There are a number of reasons why equity markets differ so markedly in size across countries. Traditionally many European firms prefer to remain private, and the legal and institutional structures of their markets actually protect their privacy. For example, in Germany many of the banks, which provide debt financing needed by German firms, also own substantial equity in those firms. This may bias the ownership toward greater use of debt financing as opposed to equity financing. The United States, however, restricts the holding of corporate equities by the commercial banks. U.S. firms have traditionally obtained greater proportions of their capital needs through public equity issues. Finally, the industrial structure of countries may have a large impact on the propensity to go public. That is, many of the same enterprises which are governmentally owned in Asia-Pacific or European countries are private in the United States. Such firms are normally operating in the public service sectors, requiring large capital bases. They are the very ones which provide much of the equity capital base in the United States.

Rise of Japanese Equity Market

The ascendance of Japan to the top of the world equity markets, as measured by total listed values, is the result of two different forces. First, the yen prices of listed stocks on the Japanese exchanges have risen substantially during the 1980s, faster and farther than the other major exchanges as illustrated in Exhibit 12.2. This is a result of the rapid growth of the Japanese economy, the increasing tendency of Japanese firms to list publicly, and the deregulation of the Japanese financial markets. Second, in order to compare international equity market values, domestic currency prices must be translated to a common currency, the U.S. dollar. The Japanese yen appreciated over 100% between 1984 and 1988 versus the U.S. dollar.[1] This caused added appreciation to the value of Japanese stocks when measured in dollars.

An additional indicator of the scale of stock exchange activity on major stock exchanges is the *turnover*, or value of shares traded per year. Exhibit 12.3 illustrates turnover from 1972 to 1988. The dominance of Japan, the United States, the United Kingdom, and West Germany is again clearly established, as these four constituted over 92% of all global equity turnover in 1988. This dominance is understated in the exhibit as only the New York Stock Exchange and the First Section of the Tokyo exchange are included. The turnover on North American, European, and Asian-Pacific exchanges increased roughly by factors of 2, 4, and 9, respectively, in the period between 1984 and 1988 alone.

INSTITUTIONAL DIFFERENCES BETWEEN STOCK MARKETS

U.S. investors might assume that other stock exchanges operate in a style similar to that of the New York Stock Exchange. Nothing could be further from the truth, as can be seen from the institutional arrangements of the world's major stock exchanges listed in Exhibit 12.4. Exchange rules and procedures influence how prices in that market respond to buying and selling pressure.

Exhibit 12.2   Stock Market Price Movements

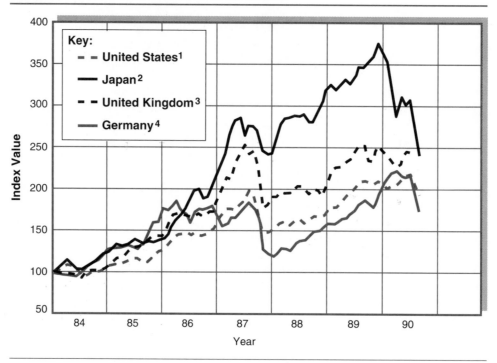

Source: Data abstracted from the *Survey of Current Business*, monthly, and *Business Conditions Digest*, monthly (ending December 1989), U.S. Department of Commerce. All index values set to 1984.01=100.

1 U.S. stock price index is the Standard & Poors 500 (S&P500).

2 Japanese stock price index is the Tokyo Stock Exchange Index (TOPIX).

3 United Kingdom stock price index is the Financial Times ordinary share index (FT100).

4 German stock price index is the Federal Statistical Office general index.

Use of Specialists

One of the most important institutional differences noted in Exhibit 12.4 is the relatively infrequent use of official specialists. It is generally believed that the presence of official specialists, the market-makers sanctioned by the exchanges, increases the volume and continuity of trading, thus increasing a market's liquidity. The United States, Japan, and Germany all employ official specialists, while the United Kingdom does not. Of the 23 country-exchanges listed in Exhibit 12.4, only seven employ official specialists. It remains to be seen if computerized trading will offer the same liquidity and price continuity provided by a specialist system, particularly in times of crisis.

Computerized Trading

A worldwide trend toward computerized trading has developed in recent years. This trend is characterized by computerized execution of orders, as well as computer-directed orders

Exhibit 12.3 Turnover on Major Stock Exchanges (trading volume in billions of dollars)

Area or Country[a]	1988	1984	1980	1976	1972
North America					
United States[b]	1356	756	381	164	160
Canada	68	25	29	7	8
Total	1424	781	410	171	168
Europe					
United Kingdom	166	48	36	13	25
West Germany	174	30	15	10	7
France	69	10	14	6	8
Netherlands	30	12	5	3	3
Sweden	19	9	2	0.5	0.3
Italy	31	4	8	2	3
Spain	28	3	2	3	2
Belgium	11	3	2	1.4	1.1
Denmark	5	0.2	0.1	0.1	0.1
Austria	1	0.1	0.1	0.1	0.1
Total	534	119.3	84.2	39.1	49.6
Pacific Area					
Japan[c]	2181	267	157	76	68
Australia	38	11	10	0.8	1
Singapore	6	7	4	0.5	1
Hong Kong	26	6	19	3	8
Total	2251	291	190	80.3	78
World Total[d]	4211	1190	683	290	295

Source: Data abstracted from Bruno Solnik, *International Investments*, second edition, © 1991 Addison-Wesley Publishing Co., Reading, Mass. Original data from Morgan Stanley Capital International.

a Not available for Switzerland.

b New York Stock Exchange only.

c First Section only.

d World total may not equal sum of column due to rounding.

(program trading). A number of equity markets have adopted quotation systems similar to NASDAQ in the over-the-counter market in the United States. For example, the Stock Exchange trading floor in London has become obsolete. Most trading now occurs "upstairs" directly between offices linked by telephone and facsimile.

Stock trading in Singapore is now conducted through an electronic trading board. Orders are input into a computer, with the highest bid and lowest offer being displayed on a quote board. When a bid and offer are matched the computer automatically executes the trade.

The Paris Bourse purchased the basic computer-trading system used successfully in Toronto, and replaced its "call" system which, although unique, has been considered inefficient.

Exhibit 12.4 Institutional Arrangements of Major Equity Markets

Country	Auction	Official Specialists	Forward Trading on Exchange	Automated Quotations	Computer-Directed Trading	Options/Futures Trading	Price Limits	Transaction Tax (Round-Trip)	Margin Requirements	Trading Off Exchange
Australia	Continuous	No	No	Yes	No	Yes	None	0.6%	None	Infrequent
Austria	Single	Yes	No	No	No	No	5%	0.3%	100%	Frequent
Belgium	Mixed	No	Yes	No	No	No[a]	10%/None[b]	0.375%/0.195%	100%/25%[b]	Occasional
Canada	Continuous	Yes	No	Yes	Yes	Yes	None[c]	0	50%[d]	Prohibited
Denmark	Mixed	No	No	No	No	No	None	1%	None	Frequent
France	Mixed	Yes	Yes	Yes	Yes	Yes	4%/7%[e]	0.3%	100%/20%[f]	Prohibited
Germany	Continuous	Yes	No	No	No	Options	None	0.5%	None	Frequent
Hong Kong	Continuous	No	No	Yes	No	Futures	None[g]	0.6%+	None	Infrequent
Ireland	Continuous	No	No	Yes	No	No	1%	1%	100%	Frequent
Italy	Mixed	No	Yes	No	No	No	10–20%[h]	0.3%	100%	Frequent
Japan	Continuous	Yes	No	Yes	Yes	No[i]	–10%	0.55%	70%[j]	Prohibited
Malaysia	Continuous	No	No	Yes	No	No	None	0.03%	None	Occasional
Mexico	Continuous	No	Yes	No	No	No	10%[k]	0	None	Occasional
Netherlands	Continuous	Yes	No	No	No	Options	Variable[l]	2.4%[m]	None	Prohibited
New Zealand	Continuous	No	No	No	No	Futures	None	0	None	Occasional
Norway	Single	No	No	No	No	No	None	1%	100%	Frequent
Singapore	Continuous	No	No	Yes	No	No[n]	None	0.5%	71%	Occasional
South Africa	Continuous	No	No	Yes	No	Options	None	1.5%	100%	Prohibited
Spain	Mixed[o]	No	No	No	No	No	10%[p]	0.11%	50%[p]	Frequent
Sweden	Mixed	No	No	Yes	No	Yes	None	2%	40%	Frequent
Switzerland	Mixed	No	Yes	Yes	No	Yes	5%[q]	0.9%	None	Infrequent
United Kingdom	Continuous	No	No	Yes	Yes	Yes	None	0.5%	None	Occasional
United States	Continuous	Yes	No	Yes	Yes	Yes	None	0	Yes	Occasional

Source: Richard Roll, "The International Crash of October 1987," *Black Monday and the Future of Financial Markets*, Homewood, IL: Dow-Jones Irwin, 1989. Reprinted with permission.

a. Calls only on just five stocks.
b. Cash/forward.
c. None on stocks; 3–5% on index futures.
d. 10% (5%) for uncovered (covered) futures.
e. Cash/forward, but not always enforced.
f. Cash/forward; 40% if forward collateral is stock rather than cash.
g. "Four Spread Rule": offers not permitted more than four ticks from current bids and asks.

h. Hitting limit suspends auction; auction then tried a second time at end of day.
i. Futures on the Nikkei Index are traded in Singapore.
j. Decreased to 50% on October 21, 1987 "to encourage buyers."
k. Trading suspended for successive periods, 15 and then 30 minutes; effective limit: 30–40%.
l. Authorities have discretion. In October, 2% limits every 15 minutes used frequently.

m. For nondealer transactions only.
n. Only for Nikkei Index (Japan).
o. Groups of stocks are traded continuously for 10 minutes each.
p. Limits raised to 20% and margin to 50% on October 27.
q. Hitting limit causes 15-minute trading suspension. Limits raised to 10–15% in October.

In Zurich, and in the Paris forward market, stocks traditionally were "called" for trading. This was referred to as "open outcry" trading, or "à la criée." All trading in a given stock occurred when its name was called, and stocks could not be traded afterwards. The list of stocks to be traded was called twice a day. This process has now been replaced with the computer.

The Tokyo Stock Exchange recently installed a system similar to the Toronto Stock Exchange's computer-assisted trading system (CATS), which allows traders to execute trades from their offices for certain securities rather than on the trading floor.

The market crash of 1987 raised a number of questions internationally about trading practices, including the use of computer-directed trading and maximum price movement limits. Although these issues have sparked much controversy and study since October of 1987, it is notable that of the four major exchanges, only Japan has a price limit (maximum price fall of 10%). Computer-directed trading is still allowed in New York, Tokyo, and London, but not in Frankfurt. Several major investment banking and brokerage firms in the United States, however, have voluntarily ceased computer-directed trading for their own accounts in recent years.

Transaction Costs

Transaction costs are also quite diverse across equity markets. The United States, Canada, Australia, and most recently the United Kingdom have negotiable commissions. These usually lead to a lower cost for large transactions than the fixed commissions still being used in most of the rest of the world. Furthermore, some countries have specific "stamp" taxes on trades, which further increase the total transaction cost. Exhibit 12.5 provides an overview of the transaction costs across markets.

Listing Requirements

Listing requirements vary greatly. The U.S. Securities and Exchange Commission regulates foreign access to U.S. securities markets. Its requirements are considered fairly costly because of the level and degree of disclosure required, potential legal liabilities, and accounting standards mandated. In addition, listing fees on individual U.S. stock exchanges are not trivial. By contrast, listing requirements for foreign firms in London are fairly liberal, and disclosure requirements, accounting costs, and fees are modest when compared with those in the United States. The Tokyo Stock Exchange has also liberalized listing requirements for foreign firms, but the costs are still high in terms of translation, accounting, and fees. Many other exchanges have very liberal and nearly costless listing requirements but, of course, the payoff for listing in terms of volume of transactions generated is also fairly low.

Taxes

Income and capital gains taxes on securities are handled in a variety of ways too complex to explain here. In general, international tax treaties govern which country gets to tax which kind of income for both corporate and individual investors. The resulting bottom line for international security investors is normally an equalization of tax rates, regardless of where they are paid. Chapter 21 provides a detailed analysis of taxation of foreign source income.

Exhibit 12.5   Estimates of Commissions and Costs, January 1990

Market	Commission Structure			Transaction Taxes (percent)
	Highest rate (percent)	Lowest rate (percent)	Trade size for lower rate (local currency)	
United States	Negotiable (typically: 0.3–1.3)			None
Canada	Negotiable (typically: 0.3-2.0)			None
Japan	1.25	0.15	¥1 billion	0.30 (sell only)
Hong Kong	0.75	0.75		0.355
Singapore	1.0	0.5	S$1 million	0.35 (buy only)
Australia	Negotiable (typically: 0.5–0.75)			0.30
United Kingdom	Negotiable (typically: 0.2–0.5)			0.5 (buy only)
West Germany	0.5	0.5		0.08
Switzerland	1.1	Negotiable (0.2)	SF 500,000	0.09
France	Negotiable (typically: 0.2-0.65)			0.15-0.30
Italy	0.7	0.7		0.1125
Sweden	0.5	0.25	SEK 1 million	1.0

Source: Bruno Solnik, *International Investments*, second edition, © 1991 Addison-Wesley Publishing Co., Reading, Mass. Reprinted with permission.

Other Institutional Differences

The number and nature of differences among exchanges is seemingly endless. For example, in both Frankfurt and Zurich only banks may provide brokerage services. Independent stock brokers and dealers do not exist, and the banks consequently monopolize access to the exchanges. German banks also have a monopoly on investment banking, so that sale of both new and outstanding shares is handled by the same institution. On the other hand, until recently stock trading firms in Paris could not be purchased by banks or foreign investors, a system which was originated by Napoleon. This has been replaced by a more open and deregulated marketplace.

Japanese investors are accustomed to paying much higher price-earnings ratios than U.S. investors. However, the yen price of a Japanese stock is very low, and certificates are issued only in multiples of one thousand shares. One thousand shares is also the unit of trading on the Tokyo Stock Exchange, and odd lots are recorded only on the company's books without issuance of a certificate. Odd lots are sold back to the company at the then current stock price.

GLOBAL MARKET INTEGRATION

There seems to be a universal feeling that equity markets are becoming more *integrated* globally, but the definition of *integrated* is ambiguous. A narrow definition of *integrated* is that equity markets are being linked through *telecommunications* to enable investors to trade worldwide on a 24-hour basis, in both equities and derivative products, and on a computerized or noncomputerized basis. A broader definition of *integrated* would state that stock prices in different national markets are becoming more *closely correlated* with each other. The broadest definition is that firms are able to achieve an *international pricing* of their stock based on unlimited access to all investors worldwide.

Improved Telecommunications

Attempts at linking quotation and trading between exchanges internationally have so far had mixed results. While it is true that investors have greatly increased their use of multiple stock exchanges to execute orders both during and after their normal business hours, fully automated linkages have not yet been widely used.

The Toronto Stock Exchange (TSE) initiated two-way automated trading with the American Stock Exchange (ASE) in 1985, then terminated the link in 1988. The limited trading volume was found to be unidirectional, in this case Canadian investors buying on the ASE. The Toronto Stock Exchange had a similar experience with a two-way link with the Midwestern Stock Exchange in Chicago which has also been terminated.

The international linkages which have been more successful so far have been ones between stocks and derivatives. The Singapore International Monetary Exchange (SIMEX) has had some success with its automated link with the Chicago Mercantile Exchange (CME), although the success is primarily in Eurodollar futures trading. The CME is now pursuing a new 24-hour a day automated trading system using the Reuters network. The American Stock Exchange's link with the European Options Exchange in Amsterdam has been marginally successful to date. The jury is still out on other arrangements internationally such as the Chicago Board of Trade's (CBT) link with the London International Financial Futures Exchange (LIFFE) in U.S. Treasury Bond futures.

Correlation Between Stock Markets

To what extent are stock markets correlated with one another internationally and is there a movement toward closer correlation?

Exhibit 12.6 shows historical correlations of monthly percentage changes in 22 major stock market indices, in local currency terms, for the June 1981 to September 1987 period.[2] Note that this period ends just prior to the worldwide market break of 1987. The exhibit indicates that at least for this period of the 1980s, the major stock markets worldwide were not highly correlated in their movements. Although individual events may cause very high correlations, such as the market breaks of 1987 and 1989 and the initiation of war in the Persian Gulf in 1991, the market indices over time do not indicate consistently high correlations. The highest correlations are between Malaysia and Singapore (.891), Switzerland and Germany (.675), and the United Kingdom and Canada (.590). The vast majority of the market index correlations in Exhibit 12.6, however, indicate stock markets worldwide still show a high degree of independent movement. As we will detail in Chapter 13, this provides opportunities for investors to reduce the risks of portfolios through international diversification.

Exhibit 12.6 Correlation Coefficients of Monthly Percentage Changes in Major Stock Market Indexes (local currencies, June 1981–September 1987)

	Australia	Austria	Belgium	Canada	Denmark	France	Germany	Hong Kong	Ireland	Italy	Japan	Malaysia	Mexico	Netherlands	New Zealand	Norway	Singapore	South Africa	Spain	Sweden	Switzerland	United Kingdom
Austria	.219																					
Belgium	.190	.222																				
Canada	.568	.250	.215																			
Denmark	.217	-.062	.219	.301																		
France	.180	.263	.355	.351	.241																	
Germany	.145	.406	.315	.194	.215	.327																
Hong Kong	.321	.174	.129	.236	.120	.201	.304															
Ireland	.349	.202	.361	.490	.387	.374	.067	.320														
Italy	.209	.224	.307	.321	.150	.459	.257	.374	.216													
Japan	.182	-.025	.223	.294	.186	.361	.147	.150	.067	.275												
Malaysia	.329	-.013	.096	.274	.151	-.0134	-.020	.159	.137	.216	.109											
Mexico	.220	.018	.104	.114	-.174	-.009	.002	.149	.159	.147	.082	.231										
Netherlands	.294	.344	.275	.545	.341	.344	.511	.395	.373	.344	.333	-.021	.038									
New Zealand	.389	.290	.233	.230	.148	.247	.318	.352	.314	.142	-.111	.151	.231	.230								
Norway	.355	.009	.381	.381	.324	.231	.173	.356	.306	.042	.156	.136	.050	.405	.201							
Singapore	.374	.030	.133	.320	.133	-.085	.037	.219	.102	-.038	.066	.262	.202	.196	.212	.280						
South Africa	.279	.159	.143	.385	-.113	.267	.007	-.095	.024	.093	.225	-.013	.058	.058	.038	.156	.156					
Spain	.147	.018	.050	.190	.019	.255	.147	.193	.175	.290	.248	-.071	.059	.170	.095	.075	-.056	-.088				
Sweden	.327	.161	.158	.376	.131	.159	.227	.196	.122	.330	.115	.103	.000	.324	.136	.237	.180	.070	.181			
Switzerland	.334	.401	.276	.551	.283	.307	.675	.379	.290	.287	.130	.099	.026	.570	.397	.331	.157	.112	.192	.334		
United Kingdom	.377	.073	.381	.590	.218	.332	.263	.431	.467	.328	.354	.193	.068	.534	.014	.313	.250	.168	.209	.339	.435	
United States	.328	.138	.250	.720	.351	.390	.209	.114	.380	.224	.326	.347	.063	.473	.083	.356	.377	.218	.214	.279	.500	.513

Source: Richard Roll, "The International Crash of October 1987," *Financial Analysts Journal*, September–October 1988, pp. 20–21.

Exhibit 12.7 Trading-Day Leadership: Correlations Between Daily Percentage Changes in Stock Prices, 1984–1989[a]

Countries and Items	1984–86	1987	1988–89
Overlapping Trading Days[b]			
United Kingdom and Germany	0.127	0.514	0.314
United Kingdom and United States	0.364	0.531	0.405
"Day" Begins in North America[c]			
United States and Japan	0.225	0.492	0.364
United States and Germany	0.335	0.306	0.551
"Day" Begins in Japan[d]			
Japan and Germany	0.123	0.393	0.359
Japan and United Kingdom	0.087	0.473	0.265
Japan and United States	0.106	0.263	0.146
"Day" Begins in Europe[e]			
Germany and United States	0.113	0.394	0.097
United Kingdom and Japan	0.171	0.199	0.270
Germany and Japan	0.083	0.206	0.152

Source: Bank for International Settlements, *59th Annual Report*, June 12, 1989, Basle, p. 79.

a Stock indexes used are: for the United States, Standard & Poors 500 composite index; for Japan the Tokyo TOPIX index; for the United Kingdom the Financial Times 100 index; for West Germany the Commerzbank index.

b To mid-March 1989.

c Correlation between the percentage change in stock prices on the same day.

d Correlation between the percentage change in stock prices in the U.S. and changes in stock prices in Japan and Germany on the following calendar day.

e Correlation between the percentage change in stock prices in Germany and the change in stock prices in the U.S. on the same calendar day, and correlations between the percentage changes in stock prices in the United Kingdom and Germany and the change in stock prices in Japan on the following calendar day.

Trading-Day Leadership

A secondary question to the degree of integration of equity exchange movements is the question of which of the exchanges "leads" the movement of global exchanges. This is something of a quandary in a world in which trading is approaching a 24-hour day. Exhibit 12.7 provides one analysis of this leader-follower question, by determining the correlation between following day trading activity among the four major world exchanges (Tokyo, New York, London, Frankfurt). By altering the defined leader and determining the correlation coefficient between it and the other exchanges, it is possible to determine which market appears to be the one leading the price movements. As seen in Exhibit 12.7, although the values do not seem to be all that correlated in an absolute sense (the highest correlation coefficient is .551), the correlations seem to have risen some in the period following 1987. The coefficients in general seem to indicate that New York has the greater role as leader in world markets, although Tokyo does influence Frankfurt to an appreciable degree.

Exhibit 12.8   Number of Listed Firms on Global Equity Markets in 1983

Country	Stock Exchange	Number of Listed Firms Domestic	Number of Listed Firms Foreign
United States	New York	1500	50
	American	774	48
Japan	Tokyo	1441	11
United Kingdom	London	2217	515
West Germany	Association of German Exchanges	442	173
Switzerland	Zurich	120	164
France	Paris	518	179
Netherlands	Amsterdam	215	256
Sweden	Stockholm	145	5
Italy	Milan	138	0
Belgium	Brussels	204	138
Spain	Madrid	394	0
Denmark	Copenhagen	211	4
Norway	Oslo	113	6
Finland	Helsinki	48	0
Austria	Vienna	62	36

Source: Gabriel Hawawini, *European Markets: Price Behavior and Efficiency*, New York: Salomon Brothers Center for the Study of Financial Institutions and the Graduate School of Business Administration of New York University, Monograph 1984.

International Pricing of Equities

Are stock prices determined primarily by investors in the home market only, or by investors worldwide? Since the answer to this question has a profound influence on a firm's cost of capital, the subject will be treated extensively in Chapter 14. For the moment it is interesting to observe that the shares of many firms are listed on foreign exchanges and traded by means of depository receipts. American Depository Receipts (ADRs) are described later in this chapter.

Extent of Cross-Listing. Exhibit 12.8 shows the extent of cross-listing on major equity exchanges as of the end of 1983. The London Stock Exchange had over 500 foreign listings, of which about 200 were U.S. firms. Shares of 10 U.S. firms were listed on the Tokyo Stock Exchange, and about 50 non-U.S. firms were listed on the New York Stock Exchange. Some 250 foreign stocks were registered with the U.S. Securities and Exchange Commission. Those not listed on any of the organized U.S. exchanges are traded in the U.S. over-the-counter market.

It should be noted that the shares of an individual firm which are trading on more than one market simultaneously should be trading for the same price. Studies which have analyzed these cross-listed shares, and adjusted share prices for transaction costs per exchange and exchange rates, have found that international investor arbitrage does indeed preserve equal prices across exchanges.

Motives for Cross-Listing. A firm may list its stock on foreign stock exchanges for the following reasons:

- as a means of supporting a new equity issue in that market,
- to favorably affect its stock price,
- to facilitate trading for existing foreign shareholders,
- to establish a market for potential stock swaps when acquiring a host country firm,
- to increase the firm's visibility to its customers and employees, and/or
- to satisfy local ownership desires.

Firms domiciled in countries with small, illiquid capital markets have often outgrown that market and are forced to raise new equity and debt abroad. Listing on a stock exchange in the market in which these funds are to be raised is typically required by the underwriters in order to ensure enough post-issue liquidity in the stock. An example of this motivation, the Novo case, is described in detail in Chapter 14.

Even if a new equity issue is not planned and no expectation for a favorable stock price effect exists, firms will still list abroad to facilitate trading for existing stockholders, to establish a market for using their stock for acquisitions in the host country, and for using stock and stock options to compensate local management and employees.

Multinational firms list abroad to build their corporate image, advertise trademarks and products, and become more familiar to host country banks for purposes of raising working capital locally.

Empirical Evidence on Cross-Listing. A recent empirical study of 481 multinational firms by Shahrokh Saudagaran found that the relative size of a firm within its domestic capital market has a significant influence on its decision to list abroad.[3] The larger the firm relative to its domestic capital market, the more likely it is to list abroad. He also found that this tendency was even more pronounced for firms with a relatively large degree of multinationality.

Whether listing on foreign stock exchanges, or for that matter listing on domestic stock exchanges, has a favorable impact on a stock's price is very controversial. Most of the academic studies of the effect on stock price of listing on domestic exchanges in the United States show very marginal impacts, some of which are negative at certain times and some slightly positive.[4] In fact, since the NASDAQ quotation system was introduced, the New York Stock Exchange has had to work harder to convince firms whose stocks trade in the over-the-counter market to list on the New York Stock Exchange. However, whether or not the stock price is influenced, the liquidity benefit of listing on a major exchange still exists.

A recent study of the stock price impacts of overseas listings by John Howe and Kathryn Kelm found generally negative impacts on stock price. They concluded that "corporate managers who are concerned with the financial well-being of their common shareholders should *avoid* foreign listings."[5] It should be noted, however, that their study was limited to U.S. firms that had listed in Basle, Frankfurt and Paris. An obvious omission is London. Furthermore, any favorable effect on stock price is more likely to be experienced by non-U.S. firms listing in New York, London, or Tokyo, as many of them are presently doing.

American Depository Receipts. Cross-listing is usually accomplished by *Depository Receipts*. In the United States, foreign shares are usually traded through American Depository Receipts, or ADRs. These are negotiable certificates issued by a U.S. bank in the United States to represent the underlying shares of stock, which are held in trust at a custodian bank. ADRs are sold, registered, and transferred in the United States in the same manner as any share of stock, with each ADR share representing some multiple of a share of the underlying foreign stock. This permits ADRs to trade in an appropriate price range for the U.S. market even if the price of the foreign share is inappropriate when converted to U.S. dollars.

ADRs can be exchanged for the underlying foreign shares, or vice versa, so arbitrage activities keep foreign and U.S. prices of any given share the same. For example, investor demand in one market will cause a price rise there, which will cause an equivalent price in the other market even when investors there are not as bullish on the stock.

ADRs convey certain technical advantages to U.S. shareholders. Dividends paid by a foreign firm are passed to its custodial bank and then to the bank that issued the ADR. The issuing bank exchanges the foreign currency dividends for U.S. dollars and sends the dollar dividend to the ADR holders. ADRs are in registered form, rather than in bearer form. Transfer of ownership is facilitated because it is done in the United States in accordance with U.S. laws and procedures. In the event of death of a shareholder the estate need not go through probate in a foreign court system.

ADRs are either "sponsored" or "unsponsored." Sponsored ADRs are created at the request of a foreign firm wanting its shares traded in the United States. The firm applies to the Securities and Exchange Commission and a U.S. bank for registration and issuance of ADRs. The foreign firm pays all costs of creating such sponsored ADRs. If a foreign firm does not seek to have its shares traded in the United States but U.S investors are interested, a U.S. securities firm may initiate creation of the ADRs. Such an ADR would be unsponsored.

RECENT INTERNATIONAL EQUITY EVENTS

An overview of the size, nature, and performance of the major stock exchanges around the globe would be incomplete without some discussion of the international stock market crash of October 1987, the crash of 1989, and the Persian Gulf War crisis of 1991.

The Crash of 1987

On Monday, October 19, 1987, the Dow Jones Industrial Average (DJIA) fell by 22.6%. This was the largest single-day drop in history. The DJIA fell an additional 12% the following day. This stock market crash (or what could be termed the largest technical correction in history) seemingly originated in the United States and then spread around the globe. By the end of the crash week, the U.S. Standard & Poors 500 had fallen 12.2%, the Japanese SE "new" index had fallen 12%, the London Financial Times ordinary share index was down 23%, and the Frankfurt FAZ general index was down 11.7%. The Hong Kong market had closed for the week on Tuesday. The Australian, Singapore, and Taiwan markets had fallen 29.3%, 30.8%, and 18.5%, respectively.

Market analysts have concluded that the 1987 crash was the result of three combined factors: a sudden change in expectations regarding the fundamental valuation of equities; a speculative bubble with a temporary market failure; the inability of the markets and the major institutions to cope with the sudden drop in equity values and surge in trading volume. It is also assumed that these forces, arising first in the United States on either the Chicago futures exchanges or on the New York Stock Exchange, were transmitted throughout the globe.[6] The following quotation from Charles Goodhart serves not only as an overview of the October 1987 crash, but also comments on the subject of the preceding section, integration of markets.

> As already noted, the most puzzling aspect of the crash, or so it appeared to us in the FMG [Financial Markets Group at the London School of Economics], was the similarity of decline in stock markets worldwide. This throws doubt on a number of possible explanations. It is hard enough—indeed, generally accepted as impossible—to find "news" that could justify the scale of decline in the NYSE between October 16 and 19, but to seek to find such "news" in every major country, virtually simultaneously, would, indeed, be piling Pilion on Ossa. Again valiant—but not entirely convincing—efforts have been made to identify stock exchanges bubbles developing and breaking simultaneously in New York, London, and Tokyo. I would challenge anyone to find a bubble also in Frankfurt, and yet the stock market there fell in line with the rest in October. Moreover, if it all had been just a bubble breaking, why has the bubble re-inflated so soon in Tokyo, but not elsewhere?
>
> My own personal favorite explanation is that, after an initial decline caused by a "rational" interpretation of worsening fundamentals, the subsequent collapse in U.S. securities markets was the result of a market failure, with a dysfunction between the futures markets, driven down, in part, by portfolio insurance, and the NYSE where the specialists were insufficiently capitalized to absorb the pressures, including the sales arising from programmed trading arbitraging between the two markets.[7]

The Crash of 1989

On Friday, October 13, 1989, the DJIA again suffered a substantial break, this time falling approximately 5% in the final hour of trading. When markets reopened on Monday October 16th, the decline continued and spread worldwide, with the exception of the Tokyo markets. Although the mini-crash of 1989 was less severe for the four major

Exhibit 12.9   Global Equity Market Indexes and Market Performance:
Outbreak of the 1991 Persian Gulf War[a]

Exchange	Index	1/17/91 Close	Net Change	Percent Change
New York	Dow Jones 30 Industrials	2623.51	+114.60	+ 4.57
New York	Standard & Poors 500	327.97	+11.80	+ 3.73
London	Financial Times 30-share	1649.6	+43.3	+ 2.70
London	100-share	2104.6	+49.8	+ 2.42
Tokyo	Nikkei Average	23446.81	+1004.11	+ 4.47
Tokyo	Topix Index	1712.13	+64.57	+ 3.92
Frankfurt	DAX	1422.67	+99.99	+ 7.56
Zurich	Credit Suisse	451.0	+22.3	+ 5.20
Paris	CAC 40	1560.47	+102.70	+ 7.05
Milan	Stock Index	1006	+46.0	+ 4.79
Amsterdam	ANP-CBS General	166.5	+4.2	+ 2.59
Stockholm	Affarsvarlden	884.4	+61.4	+ 7.46
Brussels	Stock Index	4914.47	+249.63	+ 5.35
Australia	All Ordinaries	1237.5	+33.0	+ 2.74
Hong Kong	Hang Seng	3087.83	+103.82	+ 3.48
Singapore	Straits Times	1211.54	+62.46	+ 5.44
Johannesburg	Johannesburg Gold	1179	−164.0	− 12.21
Madrid	General Index	228.59	+14.09	+ 6.57
Toronto	300 Composite	3201.64	+37.15	+ 1.17
Euro-Aust-Far East	MSCI	788.8	+43.4	+ 5.82

Source: From *The Wall Street Journal*, January 18, 1991. Reprinted by permission of *The Wall Street Journal*,
© 1991 Dow Jones & Co., Inc. All rights reserved worldwide.

a Market movements on first full day of trading, January 17, 1991, after outbreak of war.

exchanges, it was large enough and sudden enough to rekindle concerns originating from 1987. This crash is purported to have been sparked by the failure of the United Airlines leveraged buy-out, but studies are as yet inconclusive.

Although it is beyond the scope of this chapter and book, thankfully, to argue the causes of the stock market crashes of 1987 and 1989, it is tempting to lay the blame at someone's doorstep. We will concur with Michael Mussa's rendition of his favorite crash scapegoat.

> I recall a favorite story from the days when I first started teaching at the University of Rochester. I saw a television news report of the suppression of a great riot in the Ohio state prison. The National Guard placed a huge charge of dynamite against a cellblock wall, blew a big hole in the wall, and then rushed in to beat up all the prisoners. Reporters asked the governor after the riot was over who was responsible for the riot. The governor replied with an absolutely straight face that it was the work of outside agitators.[8]

We therefore conclude that the market breaks of 1987 and 1989 were caused by unknown "outside agitators!"

The Persian Gulf War of 1991

The reactions to the Persian Gulf War could also be blamed on "outside agitators" but this time we can identify the villain. As shown on the first full day of stock trading following the initiation of war in the Persian Gulf on January 16, 1991, every stock exchange rose except one. Although the outbreak of armed conflict was not a surprise, and the stock markets had ample time to discount it, it did remove remaining uncertainty. The Johannesburg Gold (South Africa) index was the only one which fell, and that was a result of the historically inverse relation between the price of gold and the price of ordinary equities. The percentage increases per index in Exhibit 12.9 also show a remarkable consistency, ranging from +1.17% in Toronto to +7.56% in Frankfurt. This final point supports those who contend that markets are becoming more closely correlated.

"A New Kind of Arbitrage"

Minneapolis Raider Irwin Jacobs, discovering a new form of global arbitrage, made a nice bundle off Shaklee (*Forbes*, June 12). He noticed that Shaklee's partly owned Japanese subsidiary was trading in Tokyo at a price that made the parent's stake in it worth more than the entire value of the parent on the New York Stock Exchange. Not surprising, given the huge price/earnings multiples Japanese investors are comfortable with.

Jacobs, who made his first money selling distressed merchandise, knows how to turn a dollar. He bought shares in the whole company and induced it to sell its Japanese subsidiary to a Japanese drug company for more than the whole company was worth when he got in. Then he got the Japanese to buy the rest, and doubled his money in five months.

Says William Jacques, a partner at Martingale Asset Management in Boston: "The Shaklee story really emphasized the valuation discrepancies in various markets."

Is there another Shaklee out there? Evidently nothing that juicy, but we have turned up a list of companies with valuable Japanese operations. If a Japanese company's earnings are worth 40 times earnings, why shouldn't an American company's Japanese earnings be worth that much instead of the multiples of 10 to 15 routinely given U.S. stocks?

The *Weekly Toyo Keizai* publishes an annual directory listing the pretax incomes of Japanese subsidiaries of U.S. multinationals. These profit figures are public in Japan, even though the parents generally don't disclose them to their U.S. stockholders.

Next, we assumed a 58% tax rate for the subsidiary, the top rate in Japan, and a multiple for the Japanese operation of 40, which is on the low side. (The average P/E in Tokyo is 55.) We compared the resulting hypothetical valuation of the Japanese operation with the market valuation of the U.S. parent. In the table we list 10 multinationals that have 100%-owned Japanese subsidiaries potentially worth at least 10% of the parent's market value.

What if U.S. Stocks Had Japanese Multiples?

U.S. companies can capitalize on the high P/E multiples of the Tokyo market by taking their Japanese subsidiaries public over there. A handful of U.S. multinationals have done this. Here are some that haven't—yet. They all have Japanese subsidiaries that could be worth a large fraction of their U.S. market capitalizations.

Company	Recent Price	Pretax Profit Japanese Sub at 150 Yen/Dollar	Hypothetical Value of Subsidiary*	Per U.S. Share	Subsidiary Value as % of Parent Co. Value
		($ million)			
Molex	32	$47	$800	31 1/4	98 %
Applied Materials	27 3/4	13	210	13	47
IBM	109 1/2	1,391	23,400	39 1/2	36
Nordson	48	7	120	12 1/2	26
AMP	42 1/4	62	1,040	9 1/2	23
Coca-Cola	56 1/8	270	4,540	12 3/4	23
Mobil	49	179	3,020	7 1/4	15
Digital Equipment	91 3/8	95	1,600	13 1/4	14
Sun Microsystems	16 3/4	10	170	2 1/2	11
Tandem	17 7/8	11	190	2	11

* Assuming an aftertax price/earnings multiple of 40 and a 58% tax rate.

Are these genuinely hidden values? Or is this just amusing arithmetic? Impossible to say. A first step to realizing the values might be a decision by the parent to make a public offering of its Japanese subsidiary. Considering how cheap equity capital is over there, that could become a common tactic over the next decade.

Shinichi Fuki is an associate of New York City-based Jafco America Ventures Inc., an advisory firm to companies considering making public offerings in Japan. He suggests another motivation for a Tokyo offering: In Japan, public companies have prestige that can lead to higher revenues, alliances with better banks and improved recruiting prospects.

Lisle, Ill.-based Molex, a manufacturer of cables and connectors, has a subsidiary potentially worth nearly $800 million, or 98% of the recent value of shares in the U.S. parent traded over the counter. You don't have to bank on a raid by Jacobs to see a buy here. Think of it this way: The non-Japanese operations, which probably earned about $1.30 a share last year, are trading pretty cheap.

Beyond all this lies an intriguing question: Are U.S.-based stocks undervalued? Or is the Tokyo Stock Exchange overvalued? The world seems happy to capitalize Matsushita's substantial U.S. earnings at Japanese multiples, while capitalizing IBM's Japanese earnings at U.S. multiples. To be sure, Matsushita's growth record is better than IBM's; nonetheless, the nearly twofold difference in both price/earnings and price/cash flow multiples is striking. The question arises because the speculative arithmetic above depends entirely on arbitrage between two markets that are very much out of line.

SUMMARY

- Although the United States equity markets have historically been the largest, Japan now constitutes the largest equity market as measured by either market value of listed issues or in annual stock turnover.

- The four largest equity markets, Japan, the United States, the United Kingdom and West Germany dominate world equity trade. In 1988 these four markets represented over 92% of all equity turnover.

- The institutional rules and procedures of the many stock exchanges around the world differ markedly.

- There is some similarity of movement between the major equity markets internationally, particularly when reacting to specific worldwide crises (such as the initiation of war in the Persian Gulf in January 1991). However, more statistically rigorous measures of market integration, such as the correlation coefficients of movements, reveal that the markets remain relatively separated or segmented.

- New York is seemingly the leader of daily movements for the four major markets, although trading occurs 24 hours a day around the globe.

- A multinational firm may list its stock on foreign exchanges for a variety of reasons, the primary goal of which is to reduce the overall cost of capital for the firm. There are, however, a number of nonfinancial reasons, such as building international corporate and product image, advertising, and the desire to avoid domestic regulations.

- Preliminary studies have yielded empirical evidence indicating that listing on a foreign exchange may actually result in a negative stock price movement on the home equity market.

1. Growth of Japanese Equities
What are the factors contributing to the rapid growth of the Japanese equity markets? How has the appreciation of the yen affected this growth in valuation or turnover?

2. Computerized Trading
There has been a definite trend toward computerized trading on world equity markets throughout the 1980s and early 1990s. What are the benefits and costs of this trend? How do they differ between computerized-execution of orders and computerized-direction of orders?

3. Price Limits and Margin Requirements
Limiting price movements (maximum) in a trading session, as well as limiting the amount of borrowed capital in individual security purchases (margin requirements), are both still widely used methods of "stabilizing" market activity.

    a)   What are the arguments for and against these restrictions on market activity?

    b)   Which of the country-exchanges in Exhibit 12.4 are more restrictive and less restrictive in terms of their exchange trading rules?

    c)   What other exchange rules or characteristics would affect market activity?

    d)   How would computerized-trading affect market stability?

4. Equity Market Integration Versus Market Correlation

The terms "integration" and "correlation" are often used interchangeably, although they have very different meanings.

    a)   In reference to stock markets and market activity around the world, differentiate the two terms.

    b)   Would computers and other technological advancements be expected to increase the degree of integration and correlation between markets?

    c)   What evidence exists that the world's markets are increasingly correlated or integrated?

5. Stock Market Crashes and Breaks

What have analysts concluded as being the primary causes of the 1987 and 1989 stock market breaks? Do you believe that these breaks could have been prevented through market restrictions? Do you believe that these breaks were "healthy" for the markets, by bringing world stock prices back down to earth?

NOTES

1. The Japanese yen appreciated from ¥247.96/$ in December of 1984 to ¥123.61 in December of 1988, an appreciation of 100.6% over the four year period.

2. The correlation coefficient between two data series indicates the frequency with which the two series move in the similar direction. The value of the correlation coefficient must fall between −1 and +1. A value of −1 indicates the two series always move in the exact opposite directions, a +1 indicates the series always move together in the same direction. A correlation coefficient of 0 indicates that the two series, statistically speaking, show no detectable relationship.

3. Shahrokh M. Saudagaran, "An Empirical Study of Selected Factors Influencing the Decision to List on Foreign Stock Exchanges," *Journal of International Business Studies*, Spring 1988, pp. 101–127.

4. For example, see G. Sanger and J. McConnell, "Stock Exchange Listings, Firm Value, and Security Market Efficiency: The Impact of NASDAQ," *Journal of Financial and Quantitative Analysis*, March 1986, pp. 1–25. See also L. Ying, W. Lewellen, G. Schlarbaum, and R. Lease, "Stock Exchange Listings and Securities Returns," *Journal of Financial and Quantitative Analysis*, September 1977, pp. 415–432.

5. John S. Howe and Kathryn Kelm, "The Stock Price Impacts of Overseas Listings," *Financial Management*, Autumn 1987, p. 56.

6. For a more in-depth discussion of the events leading up to the stock market crash of 1987 see the Bank for International Settlements, *58th Annual Report*, Basle, June 13, 1988.

7. Charles Goodhart, "The International Transmission of Asset Price Volatility," in *Financial Market*

Volatility, Proceedings of a Symposium Sponsored by the Federal Reserve Bank of Kansas City, Jackson Hole, Wyoming, August 17–19, 1988, p. 83.

8. Michael Mussa, "Commentary on 'The International Transmission of Asset Price Volatility' by

Charles Goodhart, in *Financial Market Volatility*, Proceedings of A Symposium Sponsored by the Federal Reserve Bank of Kansas City, Jackson Hole, Wyoming, August 17–19, 1988, pp. 127–128.

BIBLIOGRAPHY

Agmon, Tamir, "The Relations among Equity Markets: A Study of Share Price Co-Movements in the U.S., U.K., Germany and Japan," *Journal of Finance*, September 1972. pp. 839–855.

——, "Country Risk: the Significance of the Country Factor for Share-Price Movements in the United Kingdom, Germany and Japan," *Journal of Business*, January 1973, pp. 24–32.

Alexander, Gordon J., Cheol S. Eun, and S. Janakiramanan, "International Listings and Stock Returns: Some Empirical Evidence," *Journal of Financial and Quantitative Analysis*, 23, no. 2, June 1988, pp. 135–149.

Alexander, G., C. Eun, and S. Janakiramanan, "Asset Pricing and Dual Listing on Foreign Capital Markets: A Note," *Journal of Finance*, March 1987, pp. 151–158.

——, "International Listings and Stock Returns: Some Empirical Evidence," *Journal of Financial and Quantitative Analysis*, June 1988, pp. 135–151.

Bank for International Settlements, *Annual Report*, annual issues, Basle.

Biddle, Gary C., and Shahrokh M. Saudagaran, "The Effects of Financial Disclosure Levels on Firms' Choices among Alternative Foreign Stock Exchange Listings," *Journal of International Financial Management and Accounting*, 1, no. 1, Spring 1989, pp. 55–87.

Bodurtha, James N., D. Chinhyung Cho, and Lemma W. Senbet, "Economic Forces in the Stock Market: An International Perspective," *Global Finance Journal*, Fall 1989, pp. 21–46.

Choi, Frederick D.S., and Arthur Stonehill, "Foreign Access to U.S. Securities Markets: The Theory, Myth and Reality of Regulatory Barriers," *The*

Investment Analyst, July 1982, pp. 17–26.

Cohen, Kalman, Walter Ness, Robert Schwartz, David Whitcomb, and Hitoshi Okuda, "The Determinants of Common Stock Returns Volatility: An International Comparison," *Journal of Finance*, May 1976, pp. 733–740.

Eun, Cheol S., and S. Jankiramanan, "Bilateral Cross-Listing and the Equilibrium Security Prices," *Advances in Financial Planning and Forecasting*, 4, part B, 1990, pp. 59–74.

Eun, Cheol S., and Bruce G. Resnick, "Estimating the Correlation Structure of International Share Prices," *Journal of Finance*, December 1984, pp. 1311–1324.

Finnerty, Joseph E., and Thomas Schneeweis, "The Co-Movement of International Asset Returns," *Journal of International Business Studies*, Winter 1979, pp. 66–78.

Freund, William C., "Current Issues: International Markets, Electronic Trading and Linkages in International Equity Markets," *Financial Analysts Journal*, May/June 1989, pp. 10–15.

Giovannini, Alberto, and Philippe Jorion, "The Time Variation of Risk and Return in the Foreign Exchange and Stock Markets," *Journal of Finance*, June 1989, pp. 307–326.

Grubel, Herbert G., and Kenneth Fadner, "The Interdependence of International Equity Markets," *Journal of Finance*, March 1971, pp. 89–94.

Gultekin, Mustafa N., N. Bulent Gultekin, and Alessandro Penati, "Capital Controls and International Capital Market Segmentation: The Evidence from the Japanese and American Stock Markets," *Journal of Finance*, September 1989, pp. 849–870.

Hilliard, J., "The Relationship between Equity Indices on World Exchanges," *Journal of Finance*, March 1979, pp. 103–114.

Howe, John S., and Kathryn Kelm, "The Stock Price Impacts of Overseas Listings," *Financial Management*, Autumn 1987, pp. 51–56.

Ibbotson, Roger G., Richard C. Carr, and Anthony W. Robinson, "International Equity and Bond Returns," *Financial Analysts Journal*, July/August 1982, pp. 61–83.

Jaffe, Jeffrey, and Randolph Westerfield, "The Week-End Effect in Common Stock Returns: The International Evidence," *Journal of Finance*, June 1985, pp. 433–454.

Jennergren, L. P., and P. E. Korsvold, "The Non-Random Character of Norwegian and Swedish Stock Market Prices," in E. J. Elton and M. J. Gruber, eds., *International Capital Markets*, Amsterdam: North-Holland, 1975, pp. 37–67.

Jonas, K., and M. Sladkus, "Trends in International Equity Markets: 1975–1986," in C. Beidleman, ed., *The Handbook of International Investing*, Chicago: Probus Publishing Company, 1987.

Larson, John C., and Joel N. Morse, "Intervalling Effects in Hong Kong Stocks," *Journal of Financial Research*, Winter 1987, pp. 353–362.

Maldonado-Bear, Rita, and Anthony Saunders, "International Portfolio Diversification and the Stability of International Stock Market Relationships, 1957–1980," *Financial Management*, Autumn 1981, pp. 54–63.

Meek, G.K., and S.J. Gray, "Globalization of Stock Markets and Foreign Listing Requirements: Voluntary Disclosures By Continental European Companies Listed on the London Stock Exchange," *Journal of International Business Studies*, Summer 1989, pp. 315–336.

Muscarella, Chris, Michael Vetsuypens, "The British Petroleum Stock Offering: An Application of Option Pricing," *Journal of Applied Corporate Finance*, Winter 1989, pp. 74–80.

Philippatos, G.C., A. Christofi, and P. Christofi, "The Inter-Temporal Stability of International Stock Market Relationships: Another View," *Financial Management*, Winter 1983, pp. 63–69.

Reinganum, Marc R., and Alan C. Shapiro, "Taxes and Stock Return Seasonality: Evidence from the London Stock Exchange," *Journal of Business*, April 1987, pp. 281–298.

Roll, Richard, "The International Crash of 1987," *Financial Analysts Journal*, September-October 1988, pp. 19–35.

Saudagaran, Shahrokh M., "An Investigation of Selected Factors Influencing Multiple Listing and the Choice of Foreign Stock Exchanges," *Advances in Financial Planning and Forecasting*, 4, part B, 1990, pp. 75–122.

——, "An Empirical Study of Selected Factors Influencing the Decision to List on Foreign Stock Exchanges," *Journal of International Business Studies*, Spring 1988, pp. 101–128.

Solnik, Bruno H., "Note on the Validity of the Random Walk for European Stock Prices," *Journal of Finance*, December 1973, pp. 1151–1159.

——, "The Distribution of Daily Stock Returns and Settlement Procedures: The Paris Bourse," *Journal of Finance*, December 1990, pp. 1601–1610.

——, *International Investments*, second edition, Reading, Mass.: Addison-Wesley, 1991.

Walter, Ingo, and Roy C. Smith, *Investment Banking in Europe: Restructuring for the 1990s*, Cambridge, Mass.: Basil Blackwell, 1990.

13

International Portfolio Diversification

Cheol S. Eun
College of Business and Management
University of Maryland

In view of the recent trend toward liberalizing domestic capital markets, coupled with the widespread international multiple listings of shares, the hitherto parochial approach to portfolio investment has become outdated. In an integrated world capital market, the investor need not restrict portfolio choice to domestic securities since it is possible to combine foreign with domestic securities in a portfolio. Indeed, increasing integration of international capital markets has been identified earlier as one of the three major trends in today's business world, with far-reaching implications not only for portfolio investment decisions but also for such important issues as capital asset pricing and corporate investment and financing decisions.

International portfolio diversification is not an entirely new idea. In Europe, where each domestic capital market was and still is relatively small, institutional investors have routinely invested internationally. In other developed countries, however, international diversification is still a relatively new concept that has caught on among institutional and individual investors. By the end of 1988 cross-border holdings of equities have been estimated to be $619 billion, or 6.7% of total global equities (see Exhibit 11.1). In what follows, we are going to discuss various arguments for international portfolio diversification, risk/return characteristics of national stock markets, choice of optimal international portfolios, and a few related issues.

GLOBAL RISK DIVERSIFICATION: A CASE FOR INTERNATIONAL INVESTMENT

An internationally diversified portfolio should be substantially less risky than a purely domestic portfolio. A risk-averse investor would hold a well-diversified portfolio, instead of a single or a few securities, in order to reduce risk. The extent to which risk is reduced by portfolio diversification, however, depends critically on how highly the individual securities included in the portfolio are correlated. The less highly correlated the individual securities are, the less risky the portfolio becomes.

To understand this point, consider a portfolio consisting of two stocks. If returns to these stocks are highly positively correlated so that they move up and down together, the possibility of risk reduction by holding these stocks will be minimal. On the other hand, if returns to the two stocks are not correlated with each other, risk reduction will be very substantial and, as a result, the portfolio will be much less risky than either of the two stocks.[1] The preceding analysis suggests that if security returns show lower positive correlation across countries than within a country, gains in terms of risk reduction will result from international diversification.

Exhibit 13.1 provides the average correlation of stock returns within each of eight major countries in the diagonal cells, and the average correlations of stock returns across countries in the off-diagonal cells during the period 1973–1982. It shows that stock returns display much lower positive correlation across countries than within a country. For example, the intra-country average correlation is 0.439 for the United States, 0.653 for Germany, and 0.416 for Japan, whereas the inter-country average correlation of the United States is only 0.170 with Germany and 0.137 with Japan. This correlation structure indicates that the potential for risk reduction via international diversification is indeed substantial. The observed low international correlations may reflect, among other things, independent monetary, fiscal, and exchange rate policies, different endowments of natural resources, divergent industrial bases, and nonsynchronous business cycles among countries.

Exhibit 13.1   Average Correlations of Stock Market Returns, 1973–1982
(all returns converted to U.S. dollars)

Stock Market	AU	FR	GE	JP	NE	SW	UK	US
Australia (AU)	0.586							
France (FR)	0.286	0.576						
Germany (GE)	0.183	0.312	0.653					
Japan (JP)	0.152	0.238	0.300	0.416				
Netherlands (NE)	0.241	0.344	0.509	0.282	0.624			
Switzerland (SW)	0.358	0.368	0.475	0.281	0.517	0.664		
United Kingdom (UK)	0.315	0.378	0.299	0.209	0.393	0.431	0.698	
United States (US)	0.304	0.225	0.170	0.137	0.271	0.272	0.279	0.439

Source: C. Eun and B. Resnick, "Estimating the Correlation Structure of International Share Prices," *Journal of Finance,* December 1984, p. 1314. Reprinted with permission.

Exhibit 13.2 Risk Reduction through Diversification

(a) Risk reduction through domestic diversification

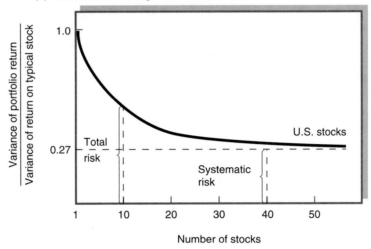

(b) Risk reduction through domestic and international diversification

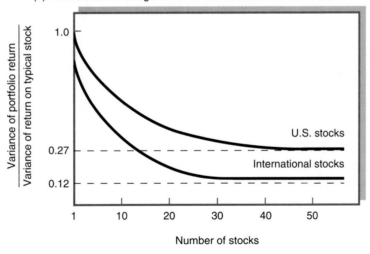

Source: B. Solnik, "Why Not Diversify Internationally Rather Than Domestically?" *Financial Analysts Journal*, July 1974, p. 17. Reprinted with permission.

As an investor increases the number of securities in a portfolio, the portfolio's risk declines rapidly at first and then asymptotically approaches the systematic risk of the market. *Systematic risk* measures the level of nondiversifiable risk in an economy. Exhibit 13.2(a) illustrates this relationship for the United States. It shows that a fully diversified U.S. portfolio is only about 27% as risky as a typical individual stock. This relationship implies that about 73% of the risk associated with investing in a single stock is diversifiable in a fully diversified U.S. portfolio.[2]

Exhibit 13.2(b) shows the same relationship for international diversification as well as U.S. domestic diversification. The most striking fact revealed by Exhibit 13.2(b) is that a fully diversified international portfolio is less than half as risky as a fully diversified U.S. portfolio. Clearly, then, a significant portion of U.S. domestic systematic risk is diversifiable in the context of an international portfolio. Incidentally, a fully diversified international portfolio is found to be only about 12% as risky as a typical individual stock. In view of the well-established fact that security returns are much less highly correlated internationally than domestically, the case for international investment as a means of risk diversification seems to be rather convincing.

RISK AND RETURN IN THE WORLD STOCK MARKETS

In the preceding section, we discussed the gains from international portfolio diversification in terms of risk reduction, without explicitly considering another important aspect of investment, that is, (expected) return. To the extent that investors prefer more wealth to less and are averse to risk, they will try to minimize risk at a given return level, or maximize return at a given risk level. In other words, investors will simultaneously consider both risk and return in making investment decisions. Therefore it would be useful to examine risk/return characteristics of major stock markets of the world.

Exhibit 13.3 shows historical risk/return characteristics of each of fifteen major stock market indices, which represent the fifteen largest stock markets in the world in terms of capitalization value. For each stock market index, it shows the mean return (mean), the standard deviation (S.D.) of return as a measure of total risk, the beta (β), and the Sharpe performance measure (SHP). Betas were calculated using a world index, and they represent the systematic or nondiversifiable risk inherent in each national stock market index. The Sharpe performance measure, which is the mean excess return (above the risk-free rate) per standard deviation, was calculated using the (annualized) risk-free rate of 5 percent. Exhibit 13.3 provides these parameter values from a U.S. dollar investor's perspective, together with the correlation matrix. It was calculated for the ten-year period January 1973–December 1982, a period characterized by flexible exchange rates.

As can be seen from Exhibit 13.3, the pairwise correlation varies widely—from 0.15 for Singapore/Spain and the United States/Spain to 0.78 for the Netherlands/Switzerland. It should be noted that Spain and Italy generally have low correlations with other countries. It should also be noted that the correlations among three European countries, that is, Germany, the Netherlands, and Switzerland are very high, being 0.70 or higher. This result may partly reflect a high degree of economic integration as well as close coordination of economic policies among these countries. As would be expected, the United States and Canada have a high correlation, 0.68.

It can also be seen from Exhibit 13.3 that national stock markets display substantially different risk/return characteristics. Measured in U.S. dollars, for example, the mean

Exhibit 13.3 Summary Statistics of the Monthly Returns for Fifteen Major Stock Markets, 1973–1982 (all returns converted to U.S. dollars)

Stock market	Correlation Coefficient														Mean (%)	S.D. (%)	β	SHP
	AU	BE	CA	FR	GE	HK	IT	JA	NE	SG	SP	SD	SW	UK				
Australia (AU)															0.63	7.97	1.25	0.027
Belgium (BE)	0.36														0.80	5.92	0.84	0.065
Canada (CA)	0.62	0.36													0.78	6.52	1.16	0.056
France (FR)	0.46	0.61	0.46												0.67	8.04	1.16	0.032
Germany (GE)	0.33	0.65	0.31	0.52											0.83	5.44	0.73	0.076
Hong Kong (HK)	0.34	0.36	0.27	0.30	0.33										1.10	14.54	1.52	0.047
Italy (IT)	0.29	0.36	0.28	0.39	0.28	0.21									0.27	8.47	0.74	0.017
Japan (JA)	0.34	0.43	0.29	0.40	0.49	0.45	0.37								0.85	5.77	0.78	0.075
Netherlands (NE)	0.43	0.69	0.53	0.59	0.70	0.45	0.30	0.44							1.01	5.80	1.06	0.102
Singapore (SG)	0.46	0.40	0.41	0.38	0.38	0.48	0.23	0.43	0.54						1.08	10.20	1.54	0.065
Spain (SP)	0.28	0.28	0.24	0.26	0.28	0.20	0.25	0.32	0.31	0.15					-0.46	6.12	0.45	-0.143
Sweden (SD)	0.30	0.44	0.28	0.29	0.42	0.24	0.16	0.35	0.46	0.34	0.23				1.18	5.89	0.66	0.130
Switzerland (SW)	0.48	0.72	0.46	0.60	0.75	0.38	0.38	0.46	0.78	0.53	0.25	0.52			0.77	6.01	1.00	0.059
United Kingdom (UK)	0.46	0.50	0.48	0.53	0.40	0.36	0.38	0.32	0.63	0.58	0.22	0.32	0.54		1.02	9.27	1.47	0.065
United States (US)	0.53	0.37	0.68	0.41	0.32	0.24	0.16	0.27	0.58	0.48	0.15	0.36	0.49	0.46	0.57	4.84	1.03	0.032

Source: C. Eun and B. Resnick, "International Diversification under Estimation Risk: Actual vs. Potential Gains." Reprinted by permission of the publisher, from *Recent Developments in International Banking and Finance*, Vol. 1, edited by Sarkis J. Khoury and Alo Ghosh, Lexington, Mass.: Lexington Books, D.C. Heath & Co. Copyright 1987, D.C. Heath.

monthly return ranges from –0.46% for Spain to 1.18% for Sweden. The standard deviation, on the other hand, ranges from 4.84% for the United States, to 13.54% for Hong Kong, while beta ranges from 0.45 for Spain to 1.54 for Singapore. Roughly speaking, the Hong Kong, Singapore, and U.K. stock markets are characterized by high risk and high return. In contrast, the U.S. market is characterized by low risk and low return. Both the German and the Japanese markets yield medium returns at relatively low risk levels. It is noteworthy that the Swedish market yields the highest return at a very low risk level. Thus it is not surprising that Sweden turns out to be the best performing market with a Sharpe value of 0.130. Other high-performance countries include the Netherlands, Germany, and Japan, followed by Singapore, the United Kingdom, and Belgium. Countries like Spain, Australia, France, and the United States registered rather lackluster performances during the period examined.

CHOICE OF AN OPTIMAL INTERNATIONAL PORTFOLIO

In this section, we discuss choice of an optimal international portfolio, examine its composition, and finally compare the risk/return efficiency of an optimal international portfolio with that of a domestic portfolio. As is well known in portfolio analysis, utility-maximizing investors will strive to identify an "optimal" portfolio—one that has, among all possible portfolios, the greatest ratio of excess return (above the risk-free interest rate) to risk. Once the optimal portfolio is identified, investors will allocate their wealth between the optimal portfolio and the risk-free asset to achieve the desired combination of risk and return.

Exhibit 13.4 presents the composition of an optimal international portfolio, for the holding period 1973–1982, for each of the fifteen national investors. Note that in solving for the optimal international portfolio, the following assumptions were made:

1. Investors can lend or borrow at the annual risk-free interest rate of 5%.

2. Investors use their respective domestic currencies to measure returns.

3. Investors are not allowed to sell stocks short; that is, investors cannot hold stocks in negative amounts.

4. Investors diversify internationally by investing in national stock market indices, rather than individual stocks.

As can be seen from Exhibit 13.4, a U.S. investor's optimal international portfolio consists of the Japan fund, with an investment weight of 11.68%, the Netherlands, with 27.82%, and Sweden, with 60.50%. For the British investor, on the other hand, the optimal international portfolio consists of Belgium (0.73%), Canada (2.63%), Germany (12.03%), Japan (18.44%), the Netherlands (20.62%), Sweden (38.89%), and the United Kingdom (6.65%). Clearly, composition of the optimal international portfolio varies substantially across investors' nationality. This, of course, reflects the fact that investors of different nationalities use different currencies to measure security returns.

Exhibit 13.4 Composition of the Optimal International Portfolio by Country (Holding Period: 1973–1982)

Stock market							From the Currency Perspective of Investors from								
	AU	BE	CA	FR	GE	HK	IT	JA	NE	SG	SP	SD	SW	UK	US
Belgium		0.1122		0.0209			0.0724				0.0347	0.0843		0.0073	0.1168
Canada	0.0916		0.1228				0.0466				0.0182			0.0263	0.2782
Germany		0.0891		0.1318			0.2133				0.0127	0.1553		0.1203	
Hong Kong	0.0130				0.0100	0.0106		0.0268	0.0045	0.0190		0.0111	0.0300		
Italy							0.0157								
Japan	0.2133	0.1803	0.1719	0.1714	0.0030	0.1728	0.1809	0.1491	0.0540	0.0037	0.2306	0.1780		0.1844	
Netherlands	0.2209	0.2169	0.2253	0.2312	0.3105	0.3054	0.1397	0.1740	0.3421	0.2747	0.2967	0.1400	0.1421	0.2062	
Singapore										0.0115			0.0053		
Sweden	0.4612	0.4015	0.4800	0.4447	0.6765	0.5112	0.3314	0.6501	0.5994	0.6912	0.4070	0.4313	0.8226	0.3889	0.6050
United Kingdom														0.0665	
Total	1.0000	1.0000	1.0000	1.0000	1.0000	1.0000	1.0000	1.0000	1.0000	1.0000	1.0000	1.0000	1.0000	1.0000	1.0000

Source: C. Eun and B. Resnick, "Currency Factor in International Portfolio Diversification," *Columbia Journal of World Business,* Summer 1985, p. 48. Reprinted with the permission of the *Columbia Journal of World Business,* copyright 1985.

Note: The risk-free interest rate is assumed to be 5% per annum. Country abbreviations are the same as in Exhibit 13.3.

It is noteworthy in Exhibit 13.4 that Sweden, the Netherlands, and Japan dominate all the other national markets in terms of the investment proportions, regardless of the investor's currency perspective. At a risk-free rate of 5%, the total investment in these three funds ranged from 65.20% (for the Italian investor) to 100% (for the U.S. investor). Moreover, both Sweden and the Netherlands were represented in every national investor's optimal portfolio, and Japan was represented in every portfolio except that of the Swiss investor.

It is also noteworthy that five markets (Australia, France, Spain, Switzerland, and the United States) were not included in any national investor's optimal portfolio. The United States was excluded partly because of its lackluster performance and partly because of its high correlation with Canada, a market with a higher mean return. Switzerland was most probably excluded because of its high correlations with the Netherlands and Germany, both of which had higher mean returns. The United Kingdom and Italy were included in only one portfolio, that of the domestic investor. The reason the U.K. fund was not demanded by foreign investors was probably its high β value. In the case of Italy, the mean return was just too low to be included in an optimal portfolio.[3]

Given the preceding analysis of optimal international portfolio selection, we can now compare the risk/return efficiency of the optimal international portfolio with that of the domestic portfolio and determine the efficiency gains from international diversification, from the viewpoint of each national investor. Let SHP(IP) denote the ratio of excess return to standard deviation of the optimal international portfolio and SHP(DP) the same ratio for the domestic portfolio. In other words,

$$SHP(IP) = \frac{\left(\overline{R}_{IP} - R_f\right)}{\sigma_{IP}}$$

and

$$SHP(DP) = \frac{\left(\overline{R}_{DP} - R_f\right)}{\sigma_{DP}},$$

where

$\overline{R}_{IP}$ = expected return on the international portfolio,

$\overline{R}_{DP}$ = expected return on the domestic portfolio,

R_f = the risk-free interest rate,

σ_{IP} = standard deviation of returns on the international portfolio,

σ_{DP} = standard deviation of returns on the domestic portfolio.

Then the efficiency gains from international diversification can be measured by the SHP differential:

$$\Delta SHP = SHP(IP) - SHP(D)$$

Exhibit 13.5   Gains from International Portfolio Diversification

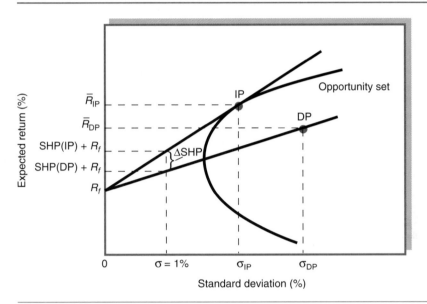

As can be seen from Exhibit 13.5, the SHP differential measures the mean return differential, per unit of standard deviation, that accrues from holding the optimal international portfolio in lieu of the domestic portfolio.

Exhibit 13.6 provides risk, return, and SHP measures of domestic and optimal international portfolios, as well as ΔSHP values, for each national investor. As can be seen from the exhibit, ΔSHP is positive for every national investor and substantial in magnitude for many national investors. This means that every national investor can potentially benefit from international diversification. The gains from international diversification are found to be particularly large for the Australian, French, Italian, Spanish, and U.S. investors. For the Dutch and Swedish investors, on the other hand, the gains are relatively modest.

Considering that the U.S. stock market offers the most extensive diversification opportunity by virtue of its sheer size and well-diversified industry base, it is somewhat surprising that U.S. investors are among those who potentially stand to gain most from international diversification. Exhibit 13.6 shows that U.S. investors can nearly double their portfolio return (from 0.57% per month to 1.09%) at a comparable risk level by holding the optimal international portfolio, as opposed to the U.S. domestic portfolio.

Unlike U.S. investors, who benefit from international diversification mostly in terms of increased portfolio return, Hong Kong investors benefit mostly in terms of reduced portfolio risk. Note that with the standard deviation of 13.48%, Hong Kong is by far the most volatile market in the world. By holding the optimal international portfolio instead of

Exhibit 13.6 Gains from International Diversification by Country
(Monthly Returns: January 1973–December 1982)

Investor's currency	Domestic Portfolio			Optimal International Portfolio			
	$\overline{R}(\%)$	S.D.(%)	SHP	$\overline{R}(\%)$	S.D.(%)	SHP	ΔSHP
Australia	0.76	7.12	0.048	1.24	4.54	0.181	0.133
Belgium	0.82	4.40	0.092	1.08	3.83	0.172	0.080
Canada	0.93	5.94	0.086	1.21	4.40	0.181	0.095
France	0.64	6.62	0.034	1.08	3.93	0.170	0.136
Germany	0.61	3.87	0.024	0.85	4.50	0.096	0.072
Hong Kong	1.11	13.48	0.051	-1.17	4.47	0.168	0.117
Italy	0.92	7.84	0.064	1.68	4.34	0.290	0.226
Japan	0.55	4.10	0.032	0.87	4.64	0.097	0.065
Netherlands	0.76	4.83	0.071	0.88	4.29	0.108	0.037
Singapore	0.80	9.70	0.040	0.86	4.70	0.095	0.055
Spain	0.04	5.26	-0.072	1.61	4.91	0.244	0.316
Sweden	1.52	5.42	0.204	1.34	3.78	0.244	0.040
Switzerland	0.32	4.56	-0.021	0.77	5.07	0.069	0.090
United Kingdom	1.26	8.40	0.100	1.32	4.27	0.212	0.112
United States	0.57	4.84	0.032	1.09	4.87	0.139	0.107

Source: C. Eun and B. Resnick, "Currency Factor in International Portfolio Diversification," *Columbia Journal of World Business,* Summer 1985, p. 51. Reprinted with the permission of the *Columbia Journal of World Business*, copyright 1985.

the domestic portfolio, Hong Kong investors can drastically reduce risk from 13.48% to 4.47% at a comparable level of return. Other national investors, such as those in Australia, Canada, France, and Italy, substantially benefit in terms of both increased return and reduced risk. If the French investors hold their optimal international portfolio instead of the French domestic portfolio, for example, they can increase return from 0.64% per month to 1.08% and, at the same time, reduce risk from 6.62% to 3.93%.

EFFECT OF FLUCTUATING EXCHANGE RATES

When a U.S. investor invests in a foreign stock market, the return on the foreign investment in terms of the U.S. dollar depends not only on the return on the foreign stock market in terms of local currency but also on the change in the exchange rate between the local currency and U.S. dollar. Since the exchange rates among major currencies have been volatile in recent years, exchange rate uncertainty has often been mentioned as one of the potential barriers to international investment.

In examining the effect of fluctuating exchange rates, we take the viewpoint of the U.S. investor investing in six major foreign stock markets, that is, Canada, France, Germany, Japan, Switzerland, and the United Kingdom. The dollar rate of return from investing in the ith foreign stock market, denoted by $R_{i\$}$, is given by

$$R_{i\$} = (1 + R_i)(1 + e_i) - 1,$$

where R_i is the local currency rate of return on the ith stock market and e_i is the rate of appreciation of the local currency against the U.S. dollar. Ignoring the cross-product term of secondary importance, we can well approximate the dollar rate of return by

$$R_{i\$} = R_i + e_i.$$

This equation simply states that the dollar rate of return on the ith foreign stock market is (approximately) equal to the local currency rate of return on the market plus the rate of appreciation of the local currency against the U.S. dollar.

From the above result, the variance of the dollar rate of return, $Var(R_{i\$})$, can be written as

$$Var(R_{i\$}) = Var(R_i) + Var(e_i) + 2\ Cov(R_i, e_i).$$

This equation shows that the exchange rate change contributes to the variance of dollar returns not only through its own variance, $Var(e_i)$, but also through its covariance with the local stock market returns, $Cov(R_i, e_i)$.

Exhibit 13.7 presents the breakdown of the volatility of dollar returns into different components. Contrary to the conventional belief that the exchange market should be substantially less volatile than the stock market, the dollar exchange rates of such major currencies as the German mark and the Japanese yen exhibit nearly as much volatility as their respective stock markets during the sample period of 1980–1985. In the case of Switzerland, the exchange market turns out to be even more volatile than the stock market. For other countries, that is, France, the United Kingdom, and especially Canada, the stock market remains more volatile than its exchange market counterpart. Also note that the covariance between the local stock market returns and the exchange rate changes is positive for each of the six foreign countries. This means that when a foreign currency appreciates against the U.S. dollar, the local stock market return also tends to go up. Exchange rate movements are thus found to reinforce, rather than offset, stock market movements. Exhibit 13.7 also shows that exchange rate changes, through their own variance as well as their covariance with the local stock market returns, account for a significant fraction of the volatility of dollar returns in each country, except Canada. For example, the fraction is 52.35% for Japan, 58.49% for Germany, 69.99% for Switzerland, and 48.77% for the United Kingdom. This figure is calculated by adding columns (7) and (8) in Exhibit 13.7.

As suspected, fluctuating exchange rates were indeed found to reduce potential gains from international investment by rendering foreign investment more risky. This result, however, does not mean that it doesn't pay to diversify internationally. On the contrary, as was shown previously, every national investor can potentially benefit from international

Exhibit 13.7 Decomposition of the Volatility of Stock Market Returns in U.S. Dollars[a]
(Weekly Data: January 1980–December 1985)

Stock Market	(1) $Var(R_i)$	(2) $Var(e_i)$	(3) $Cov(R_i, e_i)$	(4) $Cor(R_i, e_i)$	(5) $Var(R_{iS})$	(6) $\frac{(1)}{(5)} \times 100\%$	(7) $\frac{(2)}{(5)} \times 100\%$	(8) $\frac{2 \times (3)}{(5)} \times 100\%$
Canada	7.37	0.37	0.47	0.281	8.68	84.91	4.26	10.83
France	7.52	3.61	0.52	0.100	12.17	61.79	29.66	8.55
Germany	3.69	3.46	0.87	0.244	8.89	41.51	38.92	19.57
Japan	3.86	2.58	0.83	0.264	8.10	47.65	31.85	20.50
Switzerland	2.35	4.32	0.58	0.180	7.83	30.01	55.17	14.81
United Kingdom	5.21	3.28	0.84	0.205	10.17	51.23	32.25	16.52
United States	5.42	—	—	—	5.42	100.00	—	—

Source: C. Eun and B. Resnick, "Exchange Rate Uncertainty, Forward Contract and International Portfolio Selection," *Journal of Finance*, March 1988, p. 201. Reprinted with permission.
a The variances and covariances of columns (1), (2), (3), and (5) are stated in terms of squared percentages.

diversification in spite of the negative effect of fluctuating exchange rates. The proper conclusion to be drawn is that had the exchange rate uncertainty been absent or had it been controlled effectively, the potential gains from international diversification could have been greater.[4]

PERFORMANCE OF INTERNATIONAL MUTUAL FUNDS

Two different approaches exist for investors seeking international portfolio diversification. First, investors may evaluate risk/return characteristics of foreign securities themselves and invest directly in foreign securities on the basis of their evaluation. In this approach, investors are going to incur substantial information and transaction costs. In addition, they will have to perform security analysis themselves in order to construct optimal international portfolios. The alternative approach is to invest in existing international mutual funds. By investing in international mutual funds, investors can substantially reduce information and transaction costs and, at the same time, benefit from professional management. For the majority of investors, especially individual investors, international mutual funds are about the only practical means of diversifying into foreign securities.

Currently, there exist at least 50 U.S.-based mutual funds that invest a significant portion of their assets in foreign markets. By convention, these funds are classified into three categories: country funds, international funds, and global funds. A country fund is one that invests exclusively in the securities of a single country. A fund that invests at least 25% of its assets in foreign markets is classified as a global fund, whereas a fund investing at least 50% in foreign markets is considered an international fund. Some funds in each of these categories are:

Country Funds:

Japan Fund	Italy Fund
Australia Fund	Canada Fund
Mexico Fund	Korea Fund

Global Funds:

Templeton World	Templeton Growth
New Perspective	Pru-Bache Global
Oppenheimer A.I.M.	Putnam International

International Funds:

Fidelity Overseas	T. Rowe Price International
Scudder International	Merrill Lynch Pacific
Kemper International	Templeton Foreign

It should be noted that most of the previous studies on the gains from international diversification have analyzed "hypothetical" portfolios, such as optimal international

Exhibit 13.8   Performance of International Mutual Funds
(Monthly Returns: 1974–1982)

	Performance Measure	
Fund	*Sharpe*	*Treynor*
ASA Ltd.	0.0906	0.0107
New Perspective	−0.0479	−0.0024
Research Capital	0.1606	0.0119
International Investors	0.1485	0.0128
Keystone International	0.1047	0.0103
Putnam International	0.0111	0.0008
Scudder International	−0.0302	−0.0015
Sogen International	0.0544	0.0037
Templeton Growth	−0.0060	−0.0003
United Continental Growth	0.0415	0.0019
S&P 500 Index	−0.1000	−0.0033

Source: Dennis Proffitt and Neil Seitz, "The Performance of Internationally Diversified Mutual Funds," *Journal of the Midwest Finance Association,* December 1983, p. 45.

portfolios comprising national stock market indices. In reality, investors rarely invest in such a portfolio, but instead invest in international mutual funds. Therefore it is the performance of these funds that determines whether investors can actually reap gains from international diversification.

Proffitt and Seitz evaluated the performance of U.S.-based international mutual funds during the period 1974–1982 as shown in Exhibit 13.8. They used two alternative performance measures, namely, the Sharpe measure (SHP) and the Treynor measure (TRN). These measures are defined as follows:

$$\text{SHP} = \frac{\overline{R}_i - R_f}{\sigma_i}$$

and

$$\text{TRN} = \frac{\overline{R}_i - R_f}{\beta_i},$$

where

$\overline{R}_i$ = mean return on the ith fund,

σ_i = standard deviation of returns to the ith fund,

β_i = systematic risk, or beta risk, of the ith fund,

R_f = risk-free interest rate.

Clearly, both Sharpe and Treynor criteria provide risk-adjusted performance measures. However, the kind of risk considered is different between the two performance criteria. The Sharpe criterion considers the total risk, measured by the standard deviation (σ_i), while the Treynor criterion considers the systematic risk, measured by the beta (β_i). Here, β_i measures the sensitivity of returns on the ith fund to return on the stock market index.[5] In a situation where an investor invests solely or mostly in an international fund, the investor should be concerned with the total risk of the fund. Therefore the Sharpe measure would be relevant in this case. On the other hand, if an international mutual fund is held as a supplement to a well-diversified portfolio, the investor should be concerned with the systematic risk of the fund. Consequently the Treynor measure would be more appropriate.

Exhibit 13.8 presents numerical values for both Sharpe and Treynor performance measures for a selected sample of international mutual funds based in the United States. It shows that by either criterion, every international mutual fund in the sample outperformed the Standard & Poor's 500 Index, which is a broadly based U.S. stock market index. Four of the funds, namely, ASA, International Investors, Research Capital, and Keystone International, registered particularly strong performances. Note also that three international mutual funds and the Standard & Poor's 500 Index had negative performance measures. In other words, the mean returns on these three funds and the Index were less than the (average) risk-free interest rate during the sample period.[6] These empirical results from 1974–1982 offer convincing evidence that U.S. investors have historically been able to capture gains from international diversification via investing in existing international mutual funds.

DO MULTINATIONALS PROVIDE INTERNATIONAL DIVERSIFICATION?

A multinational corporation (MNC) can be viewed as representing a portfolio of internationally diversified cash flows originated in a variety of countries and currencies. Since the cash flows of a MNC are likely to be strongly influenced by foreign factors, it has been suggested that investors may be able to achieve international diversification indirectly by investing in the shares of MNCs.

While this issue is far from complete resolution, Jacquillat and Solnik (1978) found that the share price behavior of MNCs is nearly indistinguishable from that of purely domestic firms. To illustrate this point, they selected MNCs of nine different nationalities and estimated the betas of the MNC shares with regard to both the domestic and the other eight foreign stock market indices. Exhibit 13.9 provides their estimated domestic and foreign beta measures of MNCs by country. The exhibit reveals that the share prices of MNCs act pretty much like those of purely domestic firms, showing far more sensitivity to the index of their home markets than to foreign market indices. It would seem, then, that investing in domestic MNCs is not an effective means of international diversification.[7]

Note that investment in the shares of MNCs was initially proposed as a second-best alternative to direct international portfolio investment in the last decade, when the

Exhibit 13.9 Domestic and Foreign Betas of Multinational Corporations

Nationalities of MNCs	National Stock Market Indices								
	United States	Netherlands	Belgium	West Germany	Italy	Sweden	France	Switzerland	United Kingdom
American	*0.94*	0.12	-0.05	-0.01	-0.04	0.04	0.02	-0.01	-0.07
Dutch	0.31	*0.76*	0.09	0.16	-0.02	-0.28	0.25	-0.21	-0.06
Belgian	-0.27	0.07	*1.04*	0.06	0.03	0.19	0.06	0.08	0.07
German	0.24	0.03	-0.21	*1.18*	-0.02	-0.01	0.10	-0.15	-0.11
Italian	-0.10	0.06	0.10	0.01	*0.83*	0.11	-0.19	-0.16	0.20
Swedish	0.06	-0.15	-0.02	0.08	-0.10	*0.96*	0.01	0.15	0.02
French	-0.10	0.14	0.33	0.18	0.02	-0.16	*0.95*	-0.22	0.03
Swiss	-0.12	-0.23	-0.04	-0.09	-0.02	0.16	-0.11	*1.74*	0.16
British	-0.10	-0.11	0.30	0.09	-0.04	-0.13	-0.09	0.07	*0.84*

Source: B. Jacquillat and B. Solnik, "Multinationals Are Poor Tools for International Diversification," *Journal of Portfolio Management,* Institutional Investor Systems, Inc., Winter 1978, p. 160. Reprinted with permission.

international capital market was much more segmented than it is now. Currently, investors can invest either in the dual-listed foreign shares or in the existing international mutual funds without incurring prohibitive costs; therefore the idea of investing in domestic MNCs as a substitute for international portfolio investment seems to be losing much of its appeal.

A WORD OF CAUTION

Despite the recent trend toward a greater integration of international capital markets, investors in the United States and other countries display a rather strong "home bias" in their portfolio holdings. This may imply that there still exist significant barriers to international investment. These barriers may include:

1. excessive information and transaction costs associated with investing in foreign securities, especially those that are solely listed on the home markets,
2. foreign exchange regulations that make overseas investment costly and, sometimes, impossible,[8]
3. legal restrictions on the ownership of domestic securities by foreigners,[9]
4. double taxation of foreign investment income for certain investors, and, last but not least,
5. the persistence of parochial attitudes on the part of investors.

When investors have to make portfolio decisions subject to investment barriers, they should balance an increased portfolio efficiency accruing from international diversification against extra costs associated with incorporating foreign securities into their portfolios.

Paradoxical as it may sound, increasing integration of capital markets may also cause some of the benefits of international diversification to diminish.[10] For example, since Denmark-based Novo Industri (Chapter 14) was listed on the New York Stock Exchange, its stock price appears to be significantly influenced by overall movements of the U.S. market, rather than those of its Danish home market. As returns on foreign stocks become more closely correlated with returns on the investor's domestic market, the foreign stocks lose some of their diversification appeal.

One answer to this problem is to invest in internationally "nontraded" stocks. This strategy would typically result in higher transaction and information costs, but the payoff in terms of risk reduction may be worth the effort.

SUMMARY

- As international capital markets become more integrated, investors can more easily diversify their investment portfolios internationally, rather than just domestically, and benefit substantially from doing so. The most popular case for international investment is based on global risk diversification. Investors diversify their portfolio holdings in order to reduce risk. To the extent that security returns show lower

positive correlation across countries than within a country, an internationally diversified portfolio will be less risky than a purely domestic portfolio. Empirical evidence
shows that a fully diversified international portfolio could be only half as risky as a
fully diversified U.S. portfolio.

- At a more general level, utility-maximizing investors would hold an "optimal"
  portfolio, one that has the greatest ratio of excess return to risk. The composition of an
  optimal international portfolio for each of fifteen national investors can be examined,
  using different numeraire currencies. The risk/return efficiency of an optimal international portfolio can also be compared with that of a domestic portfolio. The
  comparison reveals that every national investor can potentially benefit from international diversification in terms of extra returns at the domestic-equivalent risk level.

- Investors can benefit from international investment despite the negative effect of
  fluctuating exchange rates. Examination of recent data shows that the exchange rate
  volatility often accounts for 50% or more of the volatility of dollar returns from major
  foreign stock markets. This result implies that controlling exchange rate uncertainty is
  the key to improving the efficiency of international portfolios.

- It has been suggested that investors may be able to benefit from international
  diversification by investing in the shares of multinational firms. While the jury is still
  out on this issue, the share price behavior of multinationals was observed to be very
  similar to that of domestic firms in their home market. This finding casts doubt on the
  argument that investing in multinational firms could be a good substitute for direct
  international portfolio investment. The examination of the performance of U.S.-based
  international mutual funds shows that they often outperformed the U.S. stock market
  in terms of risk/return efficiency. We may, then, infer that despite existing barriers to
  international investment, U.S. investors have successfully captured gains from
  international diversification via investing in international mutual funds. To conclude,
  the case for international, as opposed to purely domestic, diversification seems to be
  rather convincing.

1. Correlations of Security Returns

Exhibit 13.1 shows both the inter-country and intra-country correlations for major countries. Clearly, the inter-country correlations tend to
be substantially lower than the intra-country correlations. Explain
intuitively why this happens. What significance does this fact have for
international investment?

2. Systematic Risk

Exhibit 13.2 shows that the international systematic risk is much less than the U.S.
domestic systematic risk. Discuss what factor is responsible for this result.

3. Security Returns and Currency of Denomination

If you invest in foreign securities, the return measured in your domestic currency would be affected by the change in the exchange rate. How would you measure the exchange risk in this situation? Can you think of a condition under which the exchange rate volatility may actually reduce the risk of foreign investment?

4. Multinational Firms as International Diversification

What are the arguments for and against investing in the domestic multinational companies as a substitute for direct international portfolio investment?

◼ 5. Integrated Markets and Diversification Benefits (C13A.WK1)

An investor is evaluating an equally-weighted two-asset portfolio of the following two securities:

	Return (mean)	Risk (std. dev.)
Boeing (U.S.)	18.6	22.8
Unilever (U.K.)	16.0	24.0

a) What is the expected risk and return for the portfolio if the two securities have a correlation of +0.8?

b) What is the expected risk and return for the portfolio if the two securities have a correlation of +0.2?

c) Some have argued that increasing integration of international capital markets may cause some of the benefits of international portfolio diversification to diminish. Comment on this argument.

6. Sony Shares and Exchange Rate Changes

A U.S. investor just sold a share of Sony, a Japanese firm, for ¥100,000. The share was purchased a year ago for ¥120,000. The exchange rate is ¥140 per dollar now and was ¥190 per dollar a year ago. Compute the rate of return on this investment in dollars as well as in yen. Assume that no dividend payment was received during the holding period. If the U.S. investor had received ¥5,000 as a cash dividend immediately before the share was sold, how would this affect the return calculations?

7. Siemens Shares and Exchange Rate Changes

A U.S. investor is considering investing in the stock of Siemens, a German firm. The estimated standard deviation of the rate of return on Siemens in terms of marks is 20% and that of the rate of change in the dollar–mark exchange rate is 7%. Further, the correlation coefficient between the mark return on Siemens and the rate of change in the exchange rate is estimated at 0.25. Compute the standard deviation of the dollar rate of return on the investment in Siemens.

8. Domestic Portfolio Bias

Despite potential gains from international investment, investors tend to invest heavily in their domestic securities, displaying "home bias" in their portfolio holdings. List possible reasons for this phenomenon.

9. The Capital Asset Pricing Model (CAPM)

Suppose that the international CAPM described in Equation (A.2) in the Appendix is valid. The world market portfolio has an expected return of 15% and a standard deviation of 10%. The U.S. portfolio has a standard deviation of 12% and a world beta of 0.90.

Determine the gains from international diversification in terms of extra returns at the domestic-equivalent risk level from the viewpoint of U.S. investors. (Refer to the chapter Appendix.)

10. Japanese Mutual Fund

An American investor wishes to purchase a mutual fund consisting solely of Japanese stocks. On January 1, 1992, the fund was priced at $60 per share. On December 31, 1992, the fund's market value reached $100 per share. During the year, the yen rose in value from ¥150/$ on January 1 to ¥120/$ on December 31.

a) How much of the fund's market appreciation, in dollar terms, was due to the underlying growth of the Japanese stock portfolio, and how much was the result of the appreciation of the yen?

b) If the American investor requires a 20% annual return, in dollar terms, on the investment during the next year, 1993, what underlying growth (in yen terms) must the mutual fund demonstrate in 1993? Assume that the exchange rate is forecast to fall from ¥120/$ on January 1, 1993, to ¥140/$ on December 31, 1993.

11. Adelaide, Ltd., and AB Lund

Adelaide, Ltd., and AB Lund are publicly held corporations in Australia and Sweden, respectively. Foreign exchange risk and political risk are the same in both countries. Each company would like to issue additional common stock. Assume the following:

	Adelaide, Ltd.	AB Lund
Beta	0.7	0.5
Risk-free rate	5.0%	9.0%
Market return	12.5%	14.5%

a) Compute the cost of equity capital for Adelaide, Ltd., and AB Lund.

b) Does the above calculation indicate whether the capital markets in Australia and Sweden are segmented or integrated? Explain.

NOTES

1. To be precise, as long as the two constituent stocks are less than perfectly positively correlated, it is possible to construct a portfolio that is less risky than either constituent stock. Risk reduction through portfolio diversification is one of the basic tenets of modern portfolio theory, which was pioneered by Harry Markowitz and James Tobin. For a detailed discussion of this topic, refer to any standard investment textbook, such as Robert C. Radcliffe, *Investment: Concepts, Analysis and Strategy*, 2d ed., Glenview, Ill.: Scott, Foresman, 1987.

2. Although risk can be reduced substantially through portfolio diversification, it is not possible to totally eliminate risk. This is so because security returns are affected by a common set of factors.

3. Casual observation of Exhibit 13.4 reveals that most optimal portfolios would be less than fully diversified. This result reflects, in part, the fact that no short sales were allowed in solving for optimal portfolios and, in part, the fact that ex-post rather than ex-ante parameter values were used. If short sales were allowed, investors would take either long or short positions in each country fund, resulting in fully diversified portfolios. Use of ex-ante parameters is also likely to result in more diversified portfolios even if short sales are not allowed.

4. In their recent study, "Exchange Rate Uncertainty, Forward Contract and International Portfolio Selection", *Journal of Finance*, March 1988, pp. 197–215, C. Eun and B. Resnick found that the exchange rate uncertainty is a largely nondiversifiable risk because of the high correlations among the exchange rate changes across currencies, and proposed that two methods of exchange risk reduction, that is, multicurrency diversification and the forward exchange contract on a currency-by-currency basis, should be employed simultaneously. They reported that the simultaneous use of these two methods led to nearly complete elimination of the negative effect of exchange rate uncertainty.

5. Formally, the systematic risk of *i*th fund, β_i, is defined as

$$\beta_i = \text{Cov } (R_i, R_M)/ \text{Var}(R_M),$$

that is, the covariance between the rate of returns to the *i*th fund and the market portfolio, *M*, comprising all securities of the economy, divided by the variance of the market portfolio returns. Unlike the standard deviation, which measures the total risk, the systematic or beta risk measures the contribution of the fund to the risk of the (U.S.) market portfolio.

6. It is rather unusual that the mean returns on the risky portfolios fall short of the risk-free interest rate.

This may be due to the fact that the inflation rate was unusually high during the sample period of 1974–1982. It is well known that the (nominal) interest rate varies directly with the inflation rate, and also that stock returns are negatively correlated with the inflation rate.

7. In contrast to Jacquillat and Solnik (1978), Agmon and Lessard (1977) found in their study of the share price behavior of U.S. multinational firms that as the proportion of international sales increased, the share prices of multinationals exhibited an increasing (decreasing) sensitivity to the world (U.S.) factor. For a detailed discussion of their study, refer to T. Agmon and D. Lessard, "Investor Recognition of Corporate International Diversification," *Journal of Finance*, September 1977, pp. 1049–1055.

8. In many developing countries, which are in need of importing capital, investors are not allowed to acquire foreign exchange for the purpose of foreign portfolio investment. Even in developed countries, overseas portfolio investment can be restricted to a fixed pool of foreign exchange. A historical example is provided by the "investment dollar premium" that existed in the United Kingdom until 1979. Under this system, British portfolio investors often had to purchase dollars at a substantial premium over the regular exchange rate.

9. An example is the restrictions imposed by some governments on the fraction of equities of local firms that can be held by foreigners. Governments in developing as well as developed countries often impose this kind of restriction as a means of safeguarding the domestic control of local firms. In France and Sweden, for instance, foreigners are allowed to purchase at most 20% of the total outstanding shares of a local firm. In countries like India and Mexico, the limit is 49%.

10. I am indebted to Arthur Stonehill for bringing up this point.

BIBLIOGRAPHY

Adler, Michael, and B. Dumas, "International Portfolio Choice and Corporation Finance: A Synthesis," *Journal of Finance*, June 1983, pp. 925–984.

Adler, Michael, and David Simon, "Exchange Risk Surprises in International Portfolios," *Journal of Portfolio Management*, Winter 1986, pp. 44–53.

Agmon, Tamir, "The Relations among Equity Markets: A Study of Share Price Co-Movements in the U.S., U.K., Germany and Japan," *Journal of Finance*, September 1972. pp. 839–855.

——, and D. R. Lessard, "Investor Recognition of Corporate International Diversification," *Journal of Finance*, September 1977, pp. 1049–1056.

Alexander, G., C. Eun, and S. Janakiramanan, "Asset Pricing and Dual Listing on Foreign Capital Markets: A Note," *Journal of Finance*, March 1987, pp. 151–158.

——, "International Listings and Stock Returns: Some Empirical Evidence," *Journal of Financial and Quantitative Analysis*, June 1988, pp. 135–151.

Black, Fischer, "International Capital Market Equilibrium with Investment Barriers," *Journal of Financial Economics*, December 1974, pp. 337–352.

——, "Equilibrium Exchange Rate Hedging," *Journal of Finance*, July 1990, pp. 899–907.

Bonser-Neal, Catherine, Greggory Brauer, Robert Neal, and Simon Wheatley, "International Investment Restrictions and Closed-End Country Fund Prices," *Journal of Finance*, June 1990, pp. 523–548.

Carr, Peter, "The Valuation of Sequential Exchange Opportunities," *Journal of Finance*, December 1988, pp. 1235–1256.

Cho, D., C. Eun, and L. Senbet, "International Arbitrage Pricing Theory: An Empirical Investigation," *Journal of Finance*, June 1986, pp. 313–329.

Christofi, Andreas C., and George C. Philippatos, "An Empirical Investigation of the International Arbitrage Pricing Theory," *Management International Review*, No. 1, 1987, pp. 13–22.

Collins, J. Markham, "A Market Performance Comparison of U.S. Firms Active in Domestic, Developed and Developing Countries," *Journal of International Business Studies*, Second Quarter 1990, pp. 271–287.

Cumby, Robert E., and Jack D. Glen, "Evaluating the Performance of International Mutual Funds," *Journal of Finance*, June 1990, pp. 497–521.

Doukas, John, Nickolaos G. Travlos, "The Effect of Corporate Multinationalism on Shareholders' Wealth: Evidence from International Acquisitions," *Journal of Finance*, December 1988, pp. 1161–1175.

Dufey, Gunter, "Institutional Constraints and Incentives on International Portfolio Investment," *International Portfolio Investment*, U.S. Department of the Treasury OASIA, 1975.

Errunza, Vihang, and Etienne Losq, "How Risky Are Emerging Markets?" *Journal of Portfolio Management*, 14, no. 1, Fall 1987, pp. 62–67.

——, "International Asset Pricing under Mild Segmentation: Theory and Test," *Journal of Finance*, March 1985, pp. 105–124.

——, "Capital Flow Controls, International Asset Pricing, and Investors' Welfare: A Multi-Country Framework," *Journal of Finance*, September 1989, pp. 1025–1037.

Errunza, Vihang R., and Barr Rosenberg, "Investment in Developed and Less Developed Countries," *Journal of Financial and Quantitative Analysis*, December 1982, pp. 741–762.

Errunza, Vihang R., and L. W. Senbet, "The Effects of International Operations on the Market Value of the Firm: Theory and Evidence," *Journal of Finance*, May 1981, pp. 401–418.

Eun, Cheol S., and Bruce G. Resnick, "Estimating the Correlation Structure of International Share Prices," *Journal of Finance*, December 1984, pp. 1311–1324.

——, "Currency Factor in International Portfolio Diversification," *Columbia Journal of World Business*, Summer 1985, pp. 45–53.

——, "International Diversification Under Estimation Risk: Actual vs. Potential Gains," in S. Khoury and A. Gosh, eds., *Recent Developments in International Banking and Finance*, Lexington, Mass.: Heath, 1987, pp. 135–147.

——, "Exchange Rate Uncertainty, Forward Contract and International Portfolio Selection," *Journal of Finance*, March 1988, pp. 197–215.

Fatemi, Ali M., "Shareholder Benefits from Corporate International Diversification," *Journal of Finance*, December 1984, pp. 1325–1344.

Giovannini, Alberto, and Philippe Jorion, "The Time Variation of Risk and Return in the Foreign Exchange and Stock Markets," *Journal of Finance*, June 1989, pp. 307–326.

Grauer, Frederick A., Robert A. Litzenberger, and Richard E. Stehle, "Sharing Rules and Equilibrium in an International Capital Market under Uncertainty," *Journal of Financial Economics*, June 1976, pp. 233–256.

Grauer, Robert R., and Nils H. Hakansson, "Gains from International Diversification: 1968–85 Returns on Portfolios of Stocks and Bonds," *Journal of Finance*, July 1987, pp. 721–741.

Grubel, Herbert G., "Internationally Diversified Portfolios: Welfare Gains and Capital Flows," *American Economic Review*, December 1968, pp. 1299–1314.

——, and Kenneth Fadner, "The Interdependence of International Equity Markets," *Journal of Finance*, March 1971, pp. 89–94.

Gultekin, Mustafa N., N. Bulent Gultekin, and Alessandro Penati, "Capital Controls and International Capital Market Segmentation: The Evidence from the Japanese and American Stock Markets," *Journal of Finance*, September 1989, pp. 849–870.

Hawawini, G, "European Equity Markets: Price Behavior and Efficiency," Monograph 1984, *Salomon Brothers Center*, New York University, 1984.

Hill, Joanne, Thomas Schneeweis, and Jot Yau, "International Multi-Asset Diversification: A Further Analysis," *Advances in Financial Planning and Forecasting*, vol. 4, part A, 1990, pp. 197–214.

Huang, Roger D., and Tsong-Yue Lai, "Financial Asset Substitutability and International Asset Pricing," *Advances in Financial Planning and Forecasting*, vol. 4, part A, 1990, pp. 171–196.

Jacquillat, Bertrand, and Bruno H. Solnik, "Multinationals Are Poor Tools for Diversification," *Journal of Portfolio Management*, Winter 1978, pp. 8–12.

Jaffe, Jeffrey, and Randolph Westerfield, "The Week-End Effect in Common Stock Returns: The International Evidence," *Journal of Finance*, June 1985, pp. 433–454.

Jennergren, L. P., and P. E. Korsvold, "The Non-Random Character of Norwegian and Swedish Stock Market Prices," in E. J. Elton and M. J. Gruber, eds., *International Capital Markets*, Amsterdam: North-Holland, 1975, pp. 37–67.

Jonas, K., and M. Sladkus, "Trends in International Equity Markets: 1975–1986," in C. Beidleman, ed., *The Handbook of International Investing*, Chicago: Probus Publishing Company, 1987.

Jorion, Philippe, "International Portfolio Diversification with Estimated Risk," *Journal of Business*, July 1985, pp. 259–278.

Lee, Adrian F., "International Asset and Currency Allocation," *Journal of Portfolio Management*, 14, no. 1, Fall 1987, pp. 68–73.

Lee, W. Y., and K. S. Sachdeva, "The Role of the Multinational Firm in the Integration of Segmented Capital Markets," *Journal of Finance*, May 1977, pp. 479–492.

Lessard, Donald R., "International Portfolio Diversification: A Multivariate Analysis for a Group of Latin American Countries," *Journal of Finance*, June 1973, pp. 619–633.

——, "World, National, and Industry Factors in Equity Returns," *Journal of Finance*, May 1974, pp. 379–391.

Levy, Hiam, and Marshall Sarnat, "International Diversification of Investment Portfolios," *American Economic Review*, September 1970, pp. 668–675.

Lewellen, Wilbur G., and James S. Ang, "Inflation, Currency Exchange Rates, and the International Securities Markets," *Journal of Business Research*, March 1984, pp. 97–114.

Lewis, Karen K., "The Behavior of Eurocurrency Returns Across Different Holding Periods and Monetary Regimes," *Journal of Finance*, September 1990, pp. 1211–1236.

Maldonado, Rita, and Anthony Saunders, "International Portfolio Diversification and the Inter-

Exhibit 13A.1   Equilibrium Expected Returns on Risky
                        Assets

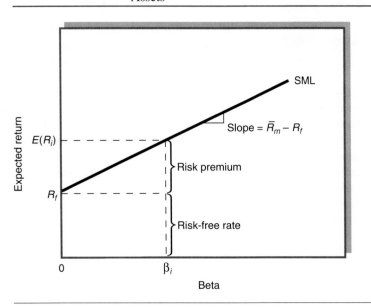

deviation of the ith stock market index, σ_i, and the return is given by the international CAPM, reflecting the world beta of the ith stock market index. In other words,

$$\text{risk: } \sigma_i$$

$$\text{Return: } E(R_i) = R_f + \left[\bar{R}_w - R_f\right]\beta_i^w.$$

We now turn to an alternative to this domestic investment strategy that can potentially yield a higher return at the same risk level. As previously suggested, the investor can combine investment in the world market portfolio, W, with lending or borrowing at the risk-free interest rate to achieve any desired combination of risk and return. This point is illustrated in Exhibit 13A.2.

Exhibit 13A.2 shows that any investor can trade risk for return, or vice versa, along the straight line called the world capital market line (CML). The world CML can be mathematically expressed as follows:

$$\bar{R} = R_f + \left[\frac{\bar{R}_w - R_f}{\sigma_w}\right]\sigma. \tag{A.3}$$

In case the investor's preferred risk level is σ_i, then the expected return on the world CML

Exhibit 13A.2 The World Capital Market Line

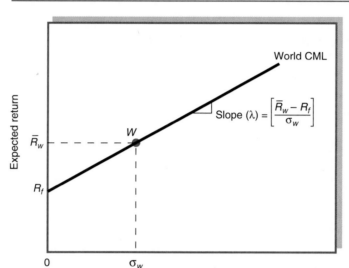

corresponding to this risk level is given by

$$\overline{R}_i = R_f + \left[\frac{\overline{R}_w - R_f}{\sigma_w}\right]\sigma_i. \qquad (A.4)$$

The investor gains from international diversification to the extent that $\overline{R}_i$ exceeds $E(R_i)$. And the magnitude of the gains can be measured by the return differential, $\overline{R}_i - E(R_i)$, at the "domestic-equivalent" risk level, that is, σ_i. From Equations (A.2) and (A.4), the magnitude of gains from international diversification, denoted by ΔR, is given as follows:

$$\Delta R = \overline{R}_i - E(R_i)$$
$$= \left\{R_f + \left[\frac{\overline{R}_w - R_f}{\sigma_w}\right]\sigma_i\right\} - \left\{R_f + \left[\overline{R}_w - R_f\right]\beta_i^w\right\}. \qquad (A.5)$$

Defining the slope of the world CML as

$$\lambda = \left[\frac{\overline{R}_w - R_f}{\sigma_w}\right],$$

and noting that

$$\beta_i^w = \sigma_i \rho_{iw} / \sigma_w, \tag{A.6}$$

we can rewrite Equation (A.5) as

$$\begin{aligned}
\Delta R &= \overline{R}_i - E(R_i) \\
&= (R_f + \lambda \sigma_i) - (R_f + \lambda \rho_{iw} \sigma i). \tag{A.7}
\end{aligned}$$

Rearranging the terms, we finally obtain

$$\Delta R = \lambda \sigma_i (1 - \rho_{iw}).$$

This result indicates that as long as the ith stock market is less than perfectly positively correlated with the world market portfolio, that is, $\rho_{iw} < 1$, there must be positive gains from international diversification, that is, $\Delta R > 0$.

The preceding equilibrium analysis of the gains from international diversification is illustrated in Exhibit 13A.3. Note that the SML is unconventionally illustrated in the mean-standard deviation space, rather than the usual mean-beta space. It can be seen clearly from the exhibit that as long as the correlation ρ_{iw} is less than unity, the SML lies below the world CML, yielding gains from international diversification. The lower the correlation is, the greater will be the gains. In a special case of $\rho_{iw} = 1$, the ith stock market index is a

Exhibit 13A.3   Gains from International Diversification: An Equilibrium Analysis

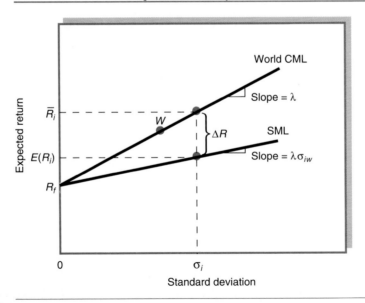

Exhibit 13A.4   Gains from International Diversification

Country	(1) $\sigma_i(\%)$	(2) β_i^w	(3) $\overline{R}_i(\%)$	(4) $E(R_i)(\%)$	(5) $\Delta R(\%)$	(6) $\dfrac{(5)}{(4)} \times 100\%$
Australia	7.97	1.25	8.88	7.44	1.44	19.35
Belgium	5.92	0.84	7.92	6.60	1.32	20.00
Canada	6.52	1.16	8.16	7.32	0.84	11.48
France	8.04	1.16	8.88	7.32	1.56	21.31
Germany	5.44	0.73	7.68	6.48	1.20	18.52
Hong Kong	14.54	1.52	12.00	7.92	4.08	51.52
Italy	8.47	0.74	9.12	6.48	2.64	40.74
Japan	5.77	0.78	7.80	6.54	1.26	19.27
Netherlands	5.80	1.06	7.80	7.08	0.72	10.17
Singapore	10.20	1.54	9.96	8.04	1.92	23.88
Spain	6.12	0.45	7.87	5.88	1.99	33.84
Sweden	5.89	0.66	7.92	6.36	1.56	24.53
Switzerland	6.01	1.00	7.92	6.96	0.96	13.79
United Kingdom	9.27	1.47	9.48	7.92	1.56	19.70
United States	4.84	1.03	7.32	7.02	0.30	4.27
World Market	4.21	1.00	6.96	6.96	N/A	N/A

Note: The risk-free interest rate is assumed to be 5% per annum. Columns (3)-(5) provide annualized returns.

from international diversification.

Let us now apply the concept developed in the preceding analysis to the historical data presented in Exhibit 13A.4 and calculate the gains from international diversification at the "domestic-equivalent" risk level. Note that the world market portfolio, proxied by the Morgan Stanley Capital International Perspective World Index, has the monthly mean return of 0.58% and standard deviation of 4.21% during the period of 1973–1982. The risk-free rate is assumed to be 0.42% per month, or 5% per annum. To show how to calculate the gains, let us assume that the ith country is Australia.

Then

$$E(R_{\mathrm{AU}}) = R_f + (\overline{R}_w - R_f)\beta_{\mathrm{AU}}^w$$
$$= 0.42 + (0.58 - 0.42)(1.25) = 0.62\% \text{ per month } (7.44\% \text{ per annum}),$$

$$\overline{R}_{\mathrm{AU}} = R_f + \left[\frac{\overline{R}_w - R_f}{\sigma_w} \right] \sigma_{\mathrm{AU}}$$

$$= 0.42 + \left[\frac{0.58 - 0.42}{4.21} \right](7.97) = 0.74\% \text{ per month } (8.88\% \text{ per annum}).$$

Thus the gain, ΔR, from international diversification turns out to be 1.44% per annum

Thus the gain, ΔR, from international diversification turns out to be 1.44% per annum for Australia. This represents a 19.35% increase in return over the expected return on the Australian stock market index.

Exhibit 13A.4 presents the annualized gains from international diversification for each country. The numerical results show that national investors can increase returns by roughly 10 to 50% at the domestic-equivalent risk levels. The United States turns out to be the exception, with the least to gain from international diversification. This exception reflects the fact that the U.S. stock market has a higher positive correlation with the world market portfolio than any other market does. The gains are found to be particularly large for such countries as Hong Kong, Italy, and Spain. Finally, a word of caution is in order. The numerical results presented in Exhibit 13A.4 should be interpreted with a grain of salt, since they were obtained under a highly idealized assumption, namely, that the international capital market is essentially an augmented domestic capital market, devoid of additional international dimensions such as exchange rate risk and market imperfections.

14 Cost of Capital and Financial Structure

Since a convincing case has been made for international portfolio diversification in Chapter 13, the purpose of this chapter is to explain how a multinational firm can take advantage of this phenomenon to lower its cost of capital and improve its availability.

The trend toward global integration of capital markets, described in Chapter 12, has made it easier for firms to access new sources of funds not available to them in their domestic capital markets. This greater availability of capital has made it possible to lower a firm's marginal cost of capital. In addition, since market imperfections still exist, it has been possible for some firms to lower their cost of capital still further by obtaining an international pricing of their equity and debt issues rather than being limited to a less favorable pricing in their home capital market.

Our approach in this chapter will be to analyze how market imperfections and other foreign influences are theoretically likely to affect a firm's cost of capital as well as project-specific discount rates. Although the main concepts used to analyze cost of capital in the domestic case provide the foundation for the multinational case, it is necessary to analyze the unique impact of foreign risks and foreign institutional variables. We start by reviewing the domestic cost of capital.

Weighted Average Cost of Capital

A firm's weighted average cost of capital is normally found by combining the cost of equity with the cost of debt in proportion to the relative weight of each in the firm's optimal long-term financial structure. More specifically,

$$K = K_e \frac{E}{V} + K_d(1-t)\frac{D}{V},$$

where

K = weighted average after-tax cost of capital,

K_e = risk-adjusted cost of equity,

K_d = before-tax cost of debt,

t = marginal tax rate,

E = market value of the firm's equity,

D = market value of the firm's debt,

V = total market value of the firm's securities ($E + D$).

Cost of Equity

The cost of equity for a firm can be measured in at least two different ways. The traditional approach, called the dividend capitalization model, measures the cost of equity by the following formula:

$$K_e = \frac{D_1}{P_0} + g,$$

where

K_e = required return on equity,

D_1 = expected dividends per share during year one,

P_0 = market value per share at time zero (beginning of year one),

g = expected growth rate of dividends or market price of a share of stock.

The traditional approach assumes that the required return on equity is determined by the market's preferred tradeoff between risk and return. Risk is typically defined as either the standard deviation, σ, of returns on a share of stock or the coefficient of variation, γ, of returns on a share of stock.

The capital asset pricing model approach is to define the cost of equity for a firm (security) by the following formula:

$$K_e = K_{rf} + \beta(K_m - K_{rf}),$$

where

K_e = expected (required) rate of return on equity,

K_{rf} = rate of interest on risk-free bonds (Treasury bills, for example),

β = coefficient of systematic risk for the firm,

K_m = expected (required) rate of return on the market portfolio of stocks (Standard & Poor's 500 Index, for example).

The main difference between the two approaches to cost of equity is that the dividend capitalization model emphasizes the total risk of expected returns, whereas the capital asset pricing model emphasizes only the systematic risk of expected returns. As detailed in Chapter 13, systematic risk is a function of the total variability of expected returns of the firm relative to the market index and the degree to which the variability of expected returns of the firm is correlated to the expected returns on the market index. Empirical studies show that both approaches to the cost of equity have some validity, depending on the sample and time period tested. In any case, the important point is that the cost of equity is some function of the market's preference for return and risk, however risk is defined.

Cost of Debt

The normal procedure for measuring the cost of debt for a domestic firm requires a forecast of domestic interest rates for the next few years, the proportions of various classes of debt the firm expects to use, and the domestic corporate income tax rate. The interest costs of the different debt components are then averaged according to their proportion in the debt structure. This before-tax average, K_d, is then adjusted for corporate income taxes by multiplying it by the expression [1 – the tax rate], i.e., $K_d(1 - t)$, to find the weighted average after-tax cost of debt.

The weighted average cost of capital is normally used as the risk-adjusted discount rate whenever a firm's new projects are in the same general risk class as its existing projects. On the other hand, a project-specific required rate of return should be used as the discount rate if a new project differs from existing projects in business or financial risk.

MARKET IMPERFECTIONS AND FOREIGN INFLUENCES

The cost of capital for a multinational firm can be influenced by at least eight important variables that arise from its international environment:

1. The *availability of capital* is an important variable in the multinational case, whereas it is typically a given parameter in the domestic case. Does access to international capital markets, as well as access to local capital markets through foreign affiliates, lower the cost of capital for multinational firms relative to domestic firms due to increased *market liquidity*?

2. *Segmented national capital markets* can distort the cost of capital for firms domiciled in these markets. Can firms that happen to reside in such markets lower their cost of capital by sourcing capital in international markets?

3. Are investors willing to pay a premium for shares of multinational firms that serve as proxies to satisfy their *international portfolio diversification motive?* (See Chapter 13.)

4. Should firms adjust their overall cost of capital to reflect *foreign exchange and political risks*? This activity is not the same as adjusting for project-specific risks, since all foreign projects would be analyzed with the same (higher) discount rate.

5. *Taxation policies* of both home and host countries will influence a firm's after-tax cost of capital. How should a firm include tax considerations when sourcing funds and making financial structure decisions?

6. How does the amount of *disclosure* of a firm's financial position affect its access to international equity and debt markets and thus its cost of capital?

7. Multinational operations may change a firm's *optimal financial structure*. How does the added international availability of capital and ability to diversify cash flows internationally affect a firm's optimal debt ratio?

8. What should be the finance structure of affiliates, considering that different lending norms exist in different countries and that a compromise must be struck to reflect affiliate liquidity needs, foreign exchange risk, political risk, legal requirements, and tax minimization?

These issues will be analyzed in the rest of this chapter. It should be noted beforehand, however, that consensus has not yet been reached on many of the issues relating to cost of capital, either domestically or internationally. Therefore we perceive this chapter's role to be to highlight the main arguments for the various conflicting viewpoints rather than to impose a single normative solution on the reader.

AVAILABILITY OF CAPITAL: IMPROVING MARKET LIQUIDITY

In the domestic case an underlying assumption is that total availability of capital to a firm is determined at any time by supply and demand in the domestic capital markets. A firm should always expand its capital budget by raising funds in the same proportion as its optimal financial structure, but as its budget expands in absolute terms, its marginal cost of capital will eventually increase. In other words, a firm can only tap the capital market for some limited amount in the short run before suppliers of capital balk at providing further funds, even if the same optimal financial structure is preserved. In the long run this may not be a limitation, depending on *market liquidity*.

Although no consensus exists about the definition of market liquidity, it can be observed by noting the degree to which a firm can issue a new security without depressing the existing market price, as well as the degree to which a change in price of its securities elicits a substantial order flow. Market liquidity varies greatly from one capital market to another, with the U.S., U.K., Japanese, and Eurocurrency markets being considered the most liquid.

In the multinational case a firm is able to improve market liquidity by raising funds in the Euromarkets, tapping local foreign capital markets, and listing on foreign stock exchanges. Such activity should logically expand the capacity of a multinational firm to raise funds in the short run over what might have been raised if the firm were limited to its

Exhibit 14.1 Availability of Funds and the Cost of Capital

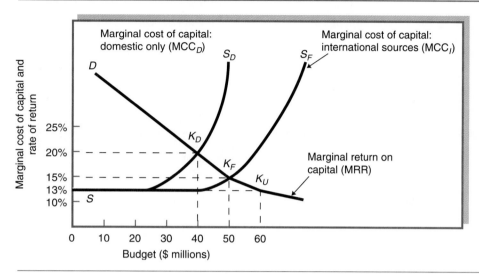

home capital market. This situation still assumes that the firm's optimal financial structure is preserved. Exhibit 14.1 shows how the availability of capital in international markets helps the multinational firm obtain a lower marginal cost of capital and a larger budget than might otherwise have been the case.

Exhibit 14.1 shows that the multinational firm has a given marginal return on capital at different budget levels, represented in the line D. This demand is determined by ranking potential projects according to net present value or internal rate of return. Percentage rate of return to both users and suppliers of capital is shown on the vertical scale. If the firm is limited to raising funds in its domestic market, the line SS_D shows the marginal domestic cost of capital (vertical axis) at various budget levels (horizontal axis). Remember that the firm continues to maintain the same debt ratio as it expands its budget, so that financial risk does not change. The optimal budget in the domestic case is $40 million, where the marginal return on capital (MRR) just equals the marginal cost of capital (MCC$_D$). At this budget the marginal domestic cost of capital, K_D, would be equal to 20%.

If the multinational firm has access to additional sources of capital outside an illiquid domestic capital market, the marginal cost of capital should shift to the right, as shown by line SS_F in Exhibit 14.1. In other words, foreign markets can be tapped for long-term funds at times when the domestic market is saturated because of heavy use by other borrowers or equity issuers, or is unable to absorb another issue of the multinational firm in the short run. Exhibit 14.1 shows that by a tap of foreign capital markets the marginal international cost of capital, K_F, has been reduced to 15%, even while an additional $10 million is raised. This assumes that about $20 million is raised abroad, since only about $30 million could be raised domestically at a 15% cost of capital.

MARKET SEGMENTATION

Segmented capital markets may have an important bearing on a multinational firm's cost of capital. An indirect effect may exist if investors are willing to pay a premium for the stock of multinational firms, as a proxy for an internationally diversified portfolio, if barriers to international investment exist (see Chapter 13).[1] However, a more direct impact may exist if a firm is resident in a segmented market and its stock price is determined only by local investors also resident in that market, rather than by the international investment community.

Definition of Market Segmentation

A national capital market is segmented if the required rate of return on securities in that market differs from the required rate of return on securities of comparable expected return and risk that are traded on other national securities markets (New York and London, for example). On the other hand, if all capital markets are fully integrated, securities of comparable expected return and risk should have the same required rate of return in each national market after adjusting for foreign exchange risk and political risk.

What causes a national capital market to be segmented? Market segmentation is a financial market imperfection caused by government constraints and/or investor perceptions. Government constraints include tax policies, controls on foreign exchange use, restrictions on the free transfer of capital, and interference in the functioning of domestic securities markets. Market segmentation due to investor perceptions is caused by information barriers, such as the quality of corporate disclosure and familiarity with securities markets and institutions. Investors are also influenced by transaction costs, alternative portfolio possibilities, financial risk, foreign exchange risk, and political risk.

Market Efficiency Versus Market Segmentation

A national securities market can be *efficient* in a domestic context and yet *segmented* in an international context. According to finance theory, a market is efficient if security prices in that market reflect all available relevant information and adjust quickly to any new relevant information. Therefore the price of an individual security reflects its "intrinsic value" and any price fluctuations will be "random walks" around this value. This statement assumes that transaction costs are low, that many participants are in the market, and that these participants have sufficient financial strength to move security prices. Empirical tests of market efficiency have been conducted on most of the major European securities markets, Japan, Canada, and, of course, the United States. The results show that many of these markets, and especially the U.S. and U.K. markets, are reasonably efficient.

An efficient national securities market might very well "correctly price" all securities traded in that market on the basis of information available to the investors who participate in that market. However, if that market is segmented, foreign investors would not be participants. Thus securities in the segmented market would be priced on the basis of domestic rather than international standards.

Effect of Market Segmentation on the Cost of Capital

The degree to which capital markets are segmented may have an important influence on a firm's cost of capital. At one extreme, if a firm is sourcing its capital in a fully segmented market, it is likely to have a higher cost of capital than if it had access to other capital markets. However, as will be shown later, a firm may be able to overcome this disadvantage by adopting financial policies that give it access to other capital markets.

From a managerial perspective the difference between sourcing capital in a segmented versus integrated capital market can be shown diagrammatically by using the same example as was used in Exhibit 14.1. Exhibit 14.2 shows how escaping from dependence on a segmented capital market can lower a firm's cost of capital. The line $S'S_U$ represents the decreased marginal cost of capital for a firm that has gained access to other capital markets. As a result of the combined effects of greater availability of capital and international pricing of the firm's securities, the marginal cost of capital, K_U, declines to 13%, and the optimal capital budget climbs to $60 million.

The corporate financial policy implications for firms residing in segmented capital markets were investigated by Stapleton and Subrahmanyan (1977). They concluded:

> In most cases, the effect of segmenting capital markets is to depress security prices and also to produce an incentive for corporations to increase the diversification opportunities available to investors. Three corporate financial policies that effectively reduce the effects of segmented markets are:
>
> **a.**   Foreign portfolio/direct investment by firms.
>
> **b.**   Mergers with foreign firms.
>
> **c.**   Dual listing of the securities of the firm on foreign capital markets.[2]

Exhibit 14.2   Market Segmentation and the Cost of Capital

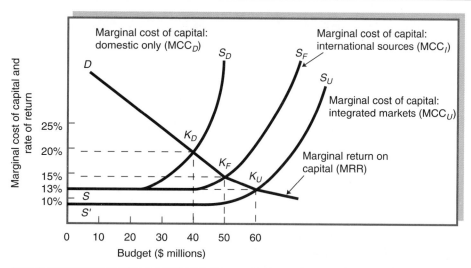

Most of the tests of market segmentation suffer from the usual problem for model builders, namely, the need to abstract from reality in order to have a testable model. In our opinion a realistic test would be to observe what happens to a single security's price when it has been traded only in a domestic market, is "discovered" by foreign investors, and then is traded in a foreign market. Arbitrage should keep the market price equal in both markets. However, if during the transition one observes a significant change in the security's price uncorrelated with price movements in either of the underlying securities markets, one may infer that the domestic market was segmented.

In academic circles tests based on case studies are often considered to be "casual empiricism," since no theory or model exists to explain what is being observed. Nevertheless, something may be learned from such cases, just as scientists learn from observing nature in an uncontrolled environment. Furthermore, case studies that preserve real world complications may illustrate specific kinds of barriers to market integration and ways in which they might be overcome.

Unfortunately, few case studies have been documented where a firm has "escaped" from a segmented capital market. In practice, escape usually means listing on a foreign stock market such as New York or London, and/or selling securities in foreign capital markets. We will illustrate what can be learned from a case study by using the example of Novo Industri A/S, a Danish firm, in the Illustrative Case at the end of this chapter.

TAXATION

A multinational firm is subject to taxation both in the home market and in each host country in which it has affiliates or a commercial presence. Tax planning is the subject of Chapter 21, but for the moment we are interested in how it affects the calculation of cost of capital.

Taxation and the Cost of Retained Earnings and Depreciation

The way in which a parent firm's country of domicile taxes the firm's foreign-source income may have an effect on the cost of equity. Normally the cost of funds from retained earnings and depreciation is considered to be about equal to the cost of equity from new issues of common stock, if we ignore the transactions costs involved in underwriting new issues. In the U.S. multinational case, however, earnings retained in foreign subsidiaries are not subject to U.S. corporate income tax, foreign withholding taxes, or transfer costs until those earnings are repatriated. Walter Ness has pointed out that this tax deferral privilege should therefore reduce the cost of equity for retained earnings of subsidiaries by the value of the tax deferral.[3] (This should also logically include funds retained due to the depreciation tax shield.) Thus Ness feels that the overall cost of equity for a U.S. multinational firm should be adjusted downward to reflect the advantage of tax deferral on retained earnings in subsidiaries.

One can contest this viewpoint on the grounds that U.S. multinational firms have many methods other than dividends of repatriating funds or repositioning them abroad.

These methods, which will be discussed in Chapter 19, include transfer pricing, fees and royalties, intracompany loans, and leads and lags. In most cases they do not involve payment of either the U.S. corporate income tax or foreign withholding tax on dividends. Therefore little difference exists between retained earnings and any other form of equity from the consolidated firm's viewpoint. Investors have already taken the tax deferral advantage into consideration when setting their required return on a multinational firm's equity. What is true, however, is that the U.S. multinational firm may in fact enjoy an effective overall tax rate that is lower than 34% as long as payment of the U.S. corporate income tax is deferred by efficient positioning of funds. Theoretically, of course, these funds might someday be returned to the parent and eventually the stockholders as a "final liquidating dividend," but in the meantime the U.S. Treasury is making an interest-free loan on the deferred taxes.

Taxation and the Cost of Debt

Determining the effective tax impact on the cost of debt for a multinational firm is complicated. First, the tax manager must forecast tax rates in each market in which the firm intends to borrow. Second, the deductibility of interest by each national tax authority must be determined. In some countries, such as the United Kingdom, interest paid to related foreign affiliates is not tax deductible. Third, a determination must be made of which legal entities are most cost effective as borrowers. Fourth, any tax deferral privilege must be considered, although this has the same counterargument as was made for tax deferral on retained earnings.

DISCLOSURE

The worldwide trend toward requiring fuller and more standardized financial disclosure of operating results and balance sheet positions may have the desirable effect of lowering the cost of equity capital. Frederick D. S. Choi has presented a strong theoretical argument for this policy. He concludes:

> Increased firm disclosure tends to improve the subjective probability distributions of a security's expected return streams in the mind of an individual investor by reducing the uncertainty associated with the return stream. For firms which generally outperform the industry average, it is also argued that improved financial disclosure will tend to increase the relative weighting which an investor will place on favorable firm statistics relative to other information vectors which he utilizes in making judgments with respect to the firm. Both of the foregoing effects will entice an individual to pay a larger amount for a given security than otherwise, thus lowering a firm's cost of capital.[4]

The benefit of fuller disclosure was particularly important to firms desiring to raise debt in the Eurocurrency or Eurobond markets, according to empirical findings by Choi reported in later studies.[5] A study of European firms, mostly multinationals, which were preparing to float bond issues on the Eurobond market, revealed that the majority preceded their flotation by increasing their volume and quality of financial disclosure. The inference is that this action was taken on the advice of their investment bankers in hopes of lowering the cost of debt and increasing the chance that the issue would be a successful sellout.

Another piece of evidence supporting the idea that executives believe fuller disclosure may reduce the cost of debt is a recent trend for European and Japanese firms to request bond ratings by Moody's and Standard & Poor's. Previously few non-U.S. firms asked for ratings because of the cost and degree of disclosure required. Now such firms feel they should follow the U.S. bond-rating practice if they expect to compete for funds successfully with U.S. firms in the Eurobond and U.S. bond markets. Bond-rating services have become quite cognizant of the variety of institutional, accounting, and legal differences that make fair comparisons of financial strength across national boundaries a very difficult task.[6] Nevertheless, Moody's and Standard & Poor's attempt to maintain the same quality of standards for non-U.S. bond issues as for U.S. issues.

OPTIMAL FINANCIAL STRUCTURE

The theory of optimal financial structure must be modified considerably to encompass the multinational firm. A number of new variables must be considered:

1. How does international availability of capital affect the optimal debt ratio of a multinational firm?

2. Can financial risk for a multinational firm be reduced through international diversification of cash flows?

3. What should be the finance structures of foreign affiliates, taking into consideration varying country norms, availability of funds, foreign exchange risk, political risk, and tax minimization?

After a brief review of the domestic theory of optimal financial structure, each of these questions will be treated in order.

Theory of Optimal Financial Structure

After many years of debate, finance theorists are still in disagreement on whether or not an optimal financial structure exists for a firm, and if so, how it can be determined. The great debate between the so-called traditionalists and the Modigliani and Miller school of thought has apparently ended in a compromise theory. When taxes and bankruptcy costs are considered, a firm has an optimal financial structure determined by that particular mix of debt and equity that minimizes the firm's cost of capital for a given level of business risk. If the business risk of new projects differs from the risk of existing projects, the optimal mix of debt and equity would change to recognize tradeoffs between business and financial risks.

Exhibit 14.3 illustrates how the cost of capital varies with the amount of debt employed. As the debt ratio, defined as total debt divided by total assets, increases, the overall cost of capital (K) decreases because of the heavier weight of low-cost debt

Exhibit 14.3   Cost of Capital and Financial Structure

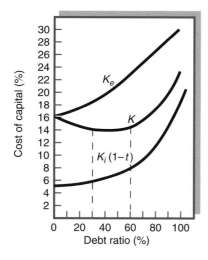

Key: debt ratio = $\dfrac{\text{total debt}}{\text{total assets}}$

K = weighed average after-tax cost of capital

K_e = cost of equity

$K_i(1-t)$ = after-tax cost of debt

$30\% - 60\%$ = minimum cost of capital range

$[K_i(1-t)]$ compared to high-cost equity (K_e). The low cost of debt is, of course, due to the tax deductibility of interest shown by the term $(1-t)$.

Partly offsetting the favorable effect of more debt is an increase in the cost of equity (K_e), because investors perceive greater financial risk. Nevertheless, the overall weighted average after-tax cost of capital (K) continues to decline as the debt ratio increases, until financial risk becomes so serious that investors and management alike perceive a real danger of *insolvency*. This result causes a sharp increase in the cost of new debt and equity, thus increasing the weighted average cost of capital. The low point on the resulting U-shaped cost of capital curve, which is at 14% in Exhibit 14.3, defines the debt ratio range in which the cost of capital is minimized.

Most theorists believe that the low point is actually a rather broad flat area encompassing a wide range of debt ratios, 30% to 60% in Exhibit 14.3, where little difference exists in the cost of capital. They also believe that, at least in the United States, the range of the flat area and the location of a particular firm's debt ratio within that range are determined by a variety of noncost variables. Two such variables have an important effect on the financial structure of multinational firms, namely, availability of capital and financial risk. These are discussed in the next two sections.

Availability of Capital

It was shown earlier in this chapter that international availability of capital to a multinational firm may allow it to lower its cost of equity and debt compared with most domestic firms. In addition, international availability permits a multinational firm to maintain its desired debt ratio, even when significant amounts of new funds must be raised. In other words, a *multinational firm's marginal cost of capital is constant for considerable ranges of its capital budget*. This statement is not true for most small domestic firms because they do not have access to the national equity or debt markets. They must either rely on internally generated funds or borrow short- and medium-term from commercial banks.

Multinational firms domiciled in countries that have illiquid equity markets are in almost the same situation as small domestic firms. They must rely on internally generated funds and bank borrowing, although the larger non-U.S. multinationals also have access to Eurobond and foreign bond markets. If they need to raise significant amounts of new funds to finance growth opportunities, they may need to borrow more than would be optimal from the viewpoint of minimizing their cost of capital. This is equivalent to saying that *their marginal cost of capital is increasing at higher budget levels*.

As an illustration of the effect of availability of capital on optimal financial structure and the marginal cost of capital, Exhibit 14.4 presents a graphical comparison between a U.S. multinational firm and either a non-U.S. multinational firm that faces an illiquid equity market at home or a small domestic U.S. firm.

In Exhibit 14.4(a) a U.S. multinational firm is depicted as enjoying a constant marginal cost of capital at all levels of its likely capital budget. Thus it is able to raise funds in the proportion desired for minimizing its cost of capital (K). In this example it can minimize its cost of capital by choosing any debt ratio between 30% and 60%, which is the lowest (flat) part of its cost of capital curve. If it chooses 45%, for example, it can raise all the funds it needs in the proportion of 45% debt and 55% equity without raising the cost of these funds. Even if internally generated funds are insufficient to maintain this proportion, it can sell new equity at about the same price as its existing equity. The optimal capital budget for the U.S. multinational firm in this example happens to be $90 million (Exhibit 14.4a). This is the point where its marginal return on capital just equals its marginal cost of capital. In other words, if it ranks all capital budgeting projects according to their internal rate of return (IRR), the last project to be accepted would be the one whose IRR just equals the firm's 14% marginal weighted average after-tax cost of capital (K).

Neither the non-U.S. multinational firm, which is assumed not to have access to a liquid national equity market, nor the small U.S. domestic firm can raise funds in the proportions desired to minimize their cost of capital (K). Yet they are assumed to have the same relationship between their cost of capital (K) and their debt ratios as the U.S. multinational firm. In other words, the left-hand graphs are identical (Exhibits 14.4a and 14.4b). Furthermore, all three firms are assumed to face the same opportunities, represented by the marginal return on capital curves (MRR). The difference is that the non-U.S. multinational firm and small U.S. domestic firm can maintain their optimal debt ratio range (30% to 60%) only for capital budgets up to $40 million (Exhibit 14.4b, right side). At that

Exhibit 14.4 Cost of Capital and Financial Structure: Constant Versus Rising Marginal Cost of Capital

(a) U.S. Multinational Firm

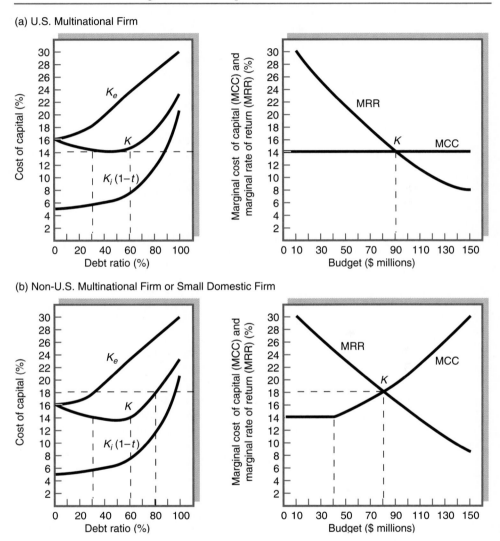

(b) Non-U.S. Multinational Firm or Small Domestic Firm

point they have committed all their internally generated funds plus the optimal proportion of additional debt. If they wish to reach their optimal budget, which is $80 million, they must borrow all the remaining $40 million. Neither firm can raise $40 million in its national equity markets, except perhaps at exorbitant rates or with unacceptable loss of control. Nevertheless, despite increasing their debt ratios to 80%, and thus their cost of capital (K) to 18%, both firms should borrow the additional $40 million in order to realize their profit potential. Their profit potential is maximized at the point in the capital budget where the marginal return on capital (MRR) equals the marginal cost of capital (MCC) (Exhibit 14.4b, right side).

It should be noted that not only do the non-U.S. multinational firm and the U.S. domestic firm have a higher cost of capital, which is 18% compared to 14% for the U.S. multinational firm, but their optimal capital budget is lower, $80 million compared to $90 million for the U.S. multinational firm. Thus it is not surprising that financial market imperfections have been cited frequently in this book as factors that give U.S. multinational corporations an advantage over U.S. domestic firms or non-U.S. multinationals that do not have access to liquid equity markets. It should also be noted, however, that a number of large non-U.S. multinational firms do indeed have access to U.S. equity markets for new issues and are also listed on U.S. stock markets. Furthermore, the equity markets in the United Kingdom are considered to be fairly liquid, and equity markets in the EEC and Japan are rapidly improving.

Financial Risk Reduction Through International Diversification of Cash Flows

The theoretical possibility exists that multinational firms are in a better position than domestic firms to support higher debt ratios because their cash flows are diversified internationally. The probability of a firm covering fixed charges under varying conditions in product, financial, and foreign exchange markets should improve if the variability of its cash flows is minimized.

By diversifying cash flows internationally, the multinational firm might be able to achieve the same kind of reduction in cash flow variability as portfolio investors receive from diversifying their security holdings internationally. The same argument applies, namely, that returns are not perfectly correlated between countries. For example, in 1980–1985 the economies of Germany and Japan were growing slowly, but the United States was experiencing comparatively healthy growth. Therefore one might have expected returns, on either a cash flow or an earnings basis, to be depressed in Germany and Japan while being favorable in the United States. A multinational firm with operations located in all three of these countries could rely on its strong U.S. cash inflow to cover debt obligations, even if the German and Japanese affiliates produced weak net cash inflows.

In contrast, a domestic German or Japanese firm would not enjoy the benefit of cash flow international diversification but would have to rely entirely on its own depressed net cash inflow from domestic operations. Perceived financial risk for the German firm would have been greater than for a multinational firm because the variability of its German domestic cash flows could not be offset by positive cash flows elsewhere in the world.

Despite the theoretical elegance of these arguments a study by Kwang Lee and Chuck Kwok came to the opposite conclusion.[7] They found that, after adjusting for size, multinational firms actually have a lower debt ratio than their domestic equivalents.[8] Despite international diversification of cash flows, bankruptcy risk was about the same for multinational and domestic firms. However, agency costs of debt were higher for the multinational firms as a result of political risks, market imperfections, and the complexity of international operations. These costs led to a lower debt ratio for multinational firms.

FINANCIAL STRUCTURE OF FOREIGN AFFILIATES

If one accepts the theory that minimizing the cost of capital for a given level of business risk and capital budget is an objective that should be implemented from the perspective of the consolidated multinational firm, then the financial structure of each affiliate is relevant only to the extent that it affects this overall goal. In other words, an individual affiliate does not really have an independent cost of capital, and therefore its finance structure should not be based on an objective of minimizing its own independent cost of capital.

On the other hand, market imperfections and national institutional constraints dictate that *variables other than minimizing the cost of capital* are often major determinants of debt ratios for firms outside the United States. A question is thus raised about whether a multinational firm should consider these country norms that are not related to cost when it establishes finance structures for its foreign affiliates. In order to answer this question, we will present some empirical findings that describe financial structure norms in representative countries. Then we will analyze whether a multinational firm should attempt to conform to these country norms within the broader constraint of minimizing their cost of capital on a consolidated worldwide basis.

Country Debt Ratio Norms

Financial structure norms for firms vary widely from one country to another but cluster together for firms domiciled in the same country. This is the conclusion of a long line of empirical studies which have investigated this question from 1969 to the present time.[9]

In our opinion the most definitive study has been by William Sekely and J. Markham Collins.[10] They compared debt ratios for 677 firms in nine industries in 23 countries. Their results are presented in Exhibit 14.5. These results confirm most previous studies, which also concluded that cultural factors, related to each host country's political, legal, social, institutional, and tax environments, cause debt ratios to cluster by country rather than by industry or size. Sekely and Collins have gone a step further, however, and identified seven "cultural realms." These are groupings of countries with similarities in financial structure norms. The realms and countries grouped in each one are as follows.[11]

Anglo-American:	Australia, Canada, South Africa, United Kingdom, and United States
Latin American:	Argentina, Brazil, Chile, and Mexico
West Central Europe:	Benelux, Switzerland, and West Germany
Mediterranean Europe:	France, Italy, and Spain
Scandinavia:	Denmark, Finland, Norway, and Sweden
Indian Peninsula:	India and Pakistan
Southeast Asia:	Malaysia and Singapore

Exhibit 14.5 Debt Ratio for Selected Industries and Countries (arranged in order of increasing use of debt)[1]

	Alcoholic Beverages	Automobiles	Chemicals	Electrical	Foods	Iron & Steel	Nonferrous Metals	Paper	Textiles	Country Mean
Singapore	0.20	0.22		0.57	0.28	0.28	0.38			0.34
Malaysia		0.60	0.41		0.30	0.38	0.30	0.77	0.69	0.37
Argentina	0.29	0.42		0.44	0.35	0.32				0.38
Australia		0.50	0.52	0.51	0.45	0.53	0.34	0.48	0.54	0.46
Chile			0.33	0.28	0.70	0.48	0.50	0.47		0.46
Mexico	0.18		0.47	0.57	0.59	0.53	0.47	0.47		0.47
South Africa	0.59	0.50	0.51		0.46	0.53	0.32	0.42	0.69	0.50
Brazil		0.66	0.48	0.53	0.57	0.61		0.37		0.54
United Kingdom	0.45	0.73	0.50	0.60	0.55	0.51	0.57	0.56	0.52	0.55
United States	0.51	0.58	0.55	0.54	0.56	0.54	0.58	0.58	0.50	0.55
Benelux	0.41	0.62	0.60	0.51	0.64	0.61	0.49	0.65	0.54	0.56
Canada	0.55		0.45	0.52		0.69	0.61	0.68		0.58
India	0.08	0.75	0.55			0.49	0.69	0.74	0.48	0.60
Switzerland				0.63	0.54	0.64				0.60
West Germany		0.57	0.56	0.66	0.49	0.60	0.70	0.70	0.65	0.62
Denmark	0.66		0.47	0.74	0.69	0.52	0.61	0.74		0.63
Spain	0.79	0.59	0.64	0.45	0.66	0.82	0.70	0.85	0.43	0.64
Sweden		0.75	0.67	0.67	0.63	0.67	0.64	0.61	0.60	0.68
France	0.56	0.67	0.72	0.72	0.78	0.73	0.67	0.74	0.74	0.71
Finland	0.40	0.82	0.71	0.73	0.77	0.73	0.72	0.76	0.82	0.72
Pakistan		0.87	0.87				0.71	0.66	0.70	0.72
Norway			0.76	0.67	0.79	0.62		0.82	0.75	0.74
Italy		0.49	0.65	0.79	0.85	0.87	0.86	0.77	0.83	0.76
Industry Mean	0.49	0.58	0.56	0.59	0.62	0.61	0.58	0.63	0.70	

Source: William S. Sekely and J. Markham Collins, "Cultural Influences on International Capital Structure," *Journal of International Business Studies,* Spring 1988, p. 91. Reprinted with permission.

1 Debt ratios are defined as total debt divided by total assets at book value. Data are for the period 1979–1980. Data were obtained from *Moody's Industrial Manual* for the U.S. and *Moody's International Manual* for all other firms. Data represent 677 firms in nine industries in 23 countries.

Low debt ratios were typical of the Southeast Asian, Latin American, and Anglo-American groups. High debt ratios were found in the Scandinavian, Mediterranean, and Indian Peninsula groups. The West Central Europe group had debt ratios in the middle of the seven groups.

Within a country neither industry nor size were important determinants of debt ratios. This finding was also true for earlier international studies, but contradicts the U.S.-based theory that industry is a determinant.

Other comparative international studies also concluded that country-specific environmental variables are key determinants of debt ratios. Janette Rutterford studied debt ratios in the United States, United Kingdom, France, Germany, and Japan. She concluded as follows:

> Accounting variations across countries appear to exaggerate the differences in debt-equity ratios between countries but, if these variations are allowed for, the essential differences still remain.
>
> Tax factors, whether assuming a Modigliani and Miller model or an investor clientele model such as that proposed by Miller, do not appear to be able to explain cross-sectional differences. A relatively high tax advantage to debt or likely demand for debt in a particular country is not related to a high aggregate leverage ratio.
>
> Agency costs of debt, on the other hand, do seem to be able to explain why Japanese, French and German corporations continue to rely heavily on debt finance, a dependence which dates in most cases from post-World War II reorganization and central government encouragement. The close relationships established between the banks and their client firms reduce both moral hazard risk and the cost associated with information asymmetry. Firms in these countries have therefore not needed to rely heavily on the more expensive (in agency cost terms) external finance.
>
> U.S. and U.K. corporations have had lower agency costs of equity relative to those for debt, since banks, at least in the U.K., appear to have restricted their lending and the agency costs of debt securities are higher than for bank finance. As a result, both countries have well-developed equity markets, with efficient information dissemination, stringent auditing and monitoring procedures and low issue costs which keep the agency costs of equity to a minimum.[12]

Carl Kester compared a large sample of U.S. and Japanese manufacturing firms. He concluded as follows:

> After adjusting for accounting reserves and liquid assets, Japanese manufacturing is not as highly leveraged as it might first appear. Indeed, on a market value basis there is no significant country difference in leverage between U.S. and Japanese manufacturing after controlling for characteristics such as growth, profitability, risk, size and industry classification.
>
> While a significant country difference exists when leverage is measured on a book value basis, this result is concentrated among the mature, capital-intensive industries. It does not appear to be a general characteristic common to all Japanese manufacturing.
>
> The foregoing notwithstanding, it must still be recognized that the *composition* of Japanese capital and ownership structure is quite different from that commonly observed in the United States. Moreover, it is different in ways that could result in a competitive

advantage for Japanese corporations even if the overall degree of leverage is not significantly different. By blunting incentives to engage in asset substitution or to underinvest, the rolling over of short-term bank loans and the substantial ownership of equity by major lenders are effective means of promoting optimal investment while funding heavily with debt.[13]

An earlier study by an international consortium of researchers conducted interviews with financial executives of 87 firms in four industries in five countries (France, Japan, the Netherlands, Norway, and the United States).[14] These executives responded that in determining the optimal financial structure for their firms the following factors were more important than minimizing the cost of capital:

1. risk: defined as the degree of cash flow coverage of fixed charges under varying market conditions,

2. availability of capital, and

3. international factors related to financing foreign operations, and reacting to foreign exchange and political risks. A number of institutional, cultural, and historical reasons explain why these noncost factors are important debt ratio determinants for both U.S. and non-U.S. firms.

Localized Financial Structures for Foreign Affiliates

Within the given constraint of minimizing its consolidated worldwide cost of capital, should a multinational firm take differing country debt ratio norms into consideration when determining its desired debt ratio for foreign affiliates?

For definition purposes the debt considered here should be only that which is borrowed from sources outside the multinational firm. This debt would include local and foreign currency loans as well as Eurocurrency loans. The reason for this definition is that parent loans to foreign affiliates are often regarded as equivalent to equity investment both by host countries and by investing firms. A parent loan is usually subordinated to other debt and does not create the same threat of insolvency as an external loan. Furthermore, the choice of debt or equity investment is often arbitrary and subject to negotiation between host country and parent firm.

The main advantages of a finance structure for foreign affiliates that conforms to local debt norms are as follows:

1. A localized financial structure reduces criticism of foreign affiliates that have been operating with too high a proportion of debt (judged by local standards), often resulting in the accusation that they are not contributing a fair share of risk capital to the host country. At the other end of the spectrum, it would improve the image of foreign affiliates that have been operating with too little debt and thus appear to be insensitive to local monetary policy.

2. A localized financial structure helps management evaluate return on equity investment relative to local competitors in the same industry. In economies where interest rates are relatively high as an offset to inflation, the penalty paid reminds management of the need to consider price level changes when evaluating investment performance.

3. In economies where interest rates are relatively high because of a scarcity of capital, the penalty paid for borrowing local funds reminds management that unless return on assets is greater than the local price of capital—that is, negative leverage—they are probably misallocating scarce domestic resources. This factor may not appear to be relevant to management decisions, but it will certainly be considered by the host country in making decisions with respect to the firm.

The main disadvantages of localized financial structures are as follows:

1. A multinational firm is expected to have a comparative advantage over local firms in overcoming imperfections in national capital markets through better availability of capital and the ability to diversify risk. Why should it throw away these important competitive advantages to conform to local norms that are established in response to imperfect local capital markets, historical precedent, and institutional constraints that do not apply to the multinational firm?

2. If each foreign affiliate of a multinational firm localizes its financial structure, the resulting consolidated balance sheet might show a financial structure that does not conform to any particular country's norm. The debt ratio would be a simple weighted average of the corresponding ratio of each country in which the firm happened to operate. This feature could increase perceived financial risk and thus the cost of capital for the multinational firm, but only if two additional conditions are present:

   a) The consolidated debt ratio must be pushed completely out of the discretionary range of acceptable debt ratios in the flat area of the cost of capital curve, shown previously in Exhibit 14.3.

   b) The multinational firm must be unable to offset high debt in one foreign affiliate with low debt in other foreign or domestic affiliates at the same cost. If the International Fisher Effect is working, replacement of debt should be possible at an equal after-tax cost after adjusting for foreign exchange risk. On the other hand, if market imperfections preclude this type of replacement, the possibility exists that the overall cost of debt, and thus the cost of capital, could increase for the multinational firm if it attempts to conform to local norms.

3. The debt ratio of a foreign affiliate is in reality only cosmetic, since lenders ultimately look to the parent and its consolidated worldwide cash flow as the source of repayment. In many cases, debt of affiliates must be guaranteed by the parent firm. Even if no formal guarantee exists, an implied guarantee usually exists since almost no parent firm would dare to allow an affiliate to default on a loan. If it did, repercussions would surely be felt with respect to the parent's own financial standing, with a resulting increase in its cost of capital.

In our opinion a compromise position is possible. Both multinational and domestic firms should try to minimize their overall weighted average cost of capital for a given level of business risk and capital budget, as finance theory suggests. However, if debt is available to a foreign affiliate at equal cost to that which could be raised elsewhere, after adjusting for foreign exchange risk, then localizing the foreign affiliate's financial structure should incur no cost penalty and yet would also enjoy the advantages listed above.

Naturally, if a particular foreign affiliate has access to local debt at a lower cost, after adjusting for foreign exchange risk, than other sources of debt available to the multinational firm, the multinational firm should borrow all it can through that foreign affiliate. The reverse would be true if the foreign affiliate only had access to higher-cost debt than available elsewhere. Nothing should be borrowed externally through that foreign affiliate.

These disequilibrium situations for a foreign affiliate can only occur in imperfect or segmented markets because otherwise the International Fisher Effect should eliminate any such opportunities. The fact that opportunities to lower the cost of debt do exist is simply evidence of market imperfections or segmentation.

In summary, a multinational firm should probably follow a policy of borrowing at lowest cost, after adjusting for foreign exchange risk, anywhere in the world without regard to the cosmetic impact on any particular affiliate's financial structure. This policy assumes that local regulations permit this practice. The objective for a multinational firm is the same as that for a domestic firm, namely, to minimize its consolidated cost of capital for a given level of business risk and capital budget. On the other hand, if conforming to host country debt norms does not require a cost penalty, but merely replaces debt in one affiliate by debt in another, worthwhile advantages can be realized. These advantages include better public relations with host country monetary authorities and more realistic evaluation of performance of foreign affiliates relative to competition with host country firms.

CHOOSING AMONG SOURCES OF FUNDS TO FINANCE FOREIGN AFFILIATES

In addition to resolving the issue of choosing an appropriate financial structure for foreign affiliates, financial managers of multinational firms need to choose among alternative sources of funds to finance foreign affiliates.

Potential Sources of Funds

Sources of funds available to foreign affiliates can be classified as shown in Exhibit 14.6. In general terms they include the following:

- Funds generated internally by the foreign affiliates.
- Funds from within the corporate family.
- Funds from sources external to the corporate family.

The choice among the sources of funds ideally involves simultaneously *minimizing the cost* of external funds after adjusting for *foreign exchange risk*, choosing internal sources in order to *minimize worldwide taxes* and *political risk*, and ensuring that *managerial motivation* in the foreign affiliates is geared toward minimizing the firm's consolidated worldwide cost of capital, rather than the foreign affiliate's cost of capital.

Exhibit 14.6   Potential Sources of Capital for Financing a Foreign Affiliate

| Funds generated internally by the foreign affiliate | Depreciation and other noncash charges |
| | Retained earnings |

Funds from within the corporate family	Funds from parent corporation	Equity investment	Cash
			Real goods
		Cash loans	
		Leads and lags in paying intracompany accounts	
	Funds from sister affiliates	Cash loans	
		Leads and lags in paying intracompany accounts	
	Affiliate borrowing with parent guarantee		

Funds from sources external to corporate family	Borrowing from sources in parent country	Banks and other financial institutions
		Securities markets or money markets
	Borrowing outside of parent country	Local currency debt
		Third-country currency debt
		Eurocurrency debt
	Local equity	Individual local shareholders
		Joint-venture partners

Needless to say, this task is almost impossible, and the tendency is to place more emphasis on one of the variables at the expense of others. Some notable theoretical attempts have been made to solve the problem, but all of these have had to ignore one or more of the variables in order to optimize a specific model.[15]

Minimizing the cost of new long-term external funds, after adjusting for foreign exchange risk, has already been analyzed earlier from the viewpoint of minimizing the cost of debt and equity to the consolidated worldwide firm. This is a more appropriate perspective than analyzing external funds from the viewpoint of a foreign affiliate.

The political risk implications of various strategies for financing foreign affiliates will be treated in Chapter 16. Political risk needs to be integrated with other considerations of cost, taxes, foreign exchange risk, and managerial motivation, but so far this integration has not been accomplished in theory or practice.

At least a portion of the financing problem is to provide short-term financing when and where it is needed by the affiliates. This problem can best be analyzed as an exercise in optimal positioning of funds within the multinational family group; that is the subject of Chapter 19. However, one issue that often arises in connection with short-term financing—and is not related to optimal positioning—is the question of parent guarantees of bank borrowing by foreign affiliates.

Parent Guarantees of Bank Loans to Foreign Affiliates

A large portion of bank lending to foreign affiliates is based on formal or informal guarantees by the parent firm. Parent guarantees can take a variety of forms. The strongest type is an "unlimited guarantee" in which the lender is protected on all loans to the affiliate without regard to amount or time limit. Other guarantees are limited to a single loan agreement between a lender and an affiliate and constitute only part of the specific loan agreement.

Yet another type of guarantee is a purchase agreement under which the parent commits itself to purchase the affiliate's promissory note from the lender in case the affiliate defaults. A weaker version of this is a "collection guarantee" in which the parent guarantees only that the lender will be able to collect the note. The lender must first try to collect the note from the affiliate before turning to the guarantor-parent. An even weaker arrangement, which is not a true guarantee, is for the parent to subordinate its own claims on the affiliate to those of the lender.

Robbins and Stobaugh note that some parents that will not provide a legal guarantee will nevertheless supply a "moral" guarantee, also referred to as a "monkey" or "Oklahoma" letter.[16] Such a letter indicates the willingness of the parent to stand behind its subsidiary to protect the reputation of the entire corporate system. Robbins and Stobaugh quote one such letter: "It is as inconceivable to us as it would be to you that we would change our ownership or draw out our investment without first notifying you and honoring our proportion of all debts."[17] Under a moral guarantee the parent might decide not to honor its obligation if the affiliate's difficulties were caused by political harassment rather than by adverse business fortunes.

When a parent is willing to guarantee a loan, that parent will often want the guarantee effective only under the home country legal jurisdiction. This policy ensures that any litigation will take place under a known set of laws and that the parent will not become a political whipping boy in a foreign court system.

If a direct parent guarantee to a bank is involved, that guarantee will often be to an entity in the home country. For example, the Italian affiliate of a U.S. manufacturing firm borrows in Italy with a parent guarantee. If the loan is from the Milan branch of a U.S. bank, the guarantee will be made to the U.S. parent bank. If the loan is from the parent office of an Italian bank, the guarantee will be made to the U.S. branch of that Italian bank.

Parents are not the only source of guarantees. A given affiliate's loans may also be guaranteed by sister affiliates, perhaps for reasons of legal jurisdiction or perhaps to put a smaller limit on the effective amount of the guarantee.

Novo Industri A/S (Novo)*

Novo is a Danish multinational firm that produces industrial enzymes and pharmaceuticals (mostly insulin). In 1977 Novo's management decided to internationalize its capital structure and sources of funds. This decision was based on the observation that the Danish securities market was both illiquid and segmented from international markets. In particular, the lack of availability and the high cost of equity capital in Denmark resulted in Novo having a higher cost of capital than its main multinational competitors, Eli Lilly (United States), Miles Laboratories (United States, owned by Bayer, Germany), and Gist Brocades (the Netherlands).

Apart from the cost of capital, Novo's projected growth opportunities signaled an eventual need to raise new long-term capital beyond what could be raised in the limited Danish market. Since Novo is a world technology leader in its specialties, planned capital investments in plant, equipment, and research could not be postponed until internal financing from cash flow became available. Novo's competitors would preempt any markets not served by Novo.

Even if an equity issue of the size required could have been raised in Denmark, the required rate of return would have been unacceptably high. For example, Novo's price/earnings ratio was typically around 5, while that of its foreign competitors was well over 10. Yet Novo's business and financial risk appeared to be about equal to that of its competitors. A price/earnings ratio of 5 appeared appropriate for Novo only within a domestic Danish context when Novo was compared with other domestic firms of comparable business and financial risk.

If Denmark's securities market were integrated with world markets, one would normally expect foreign investors to rush in and buy "undervalued" Danish securities. In

---

* The Novo case material is a condensed version of Arthur Stonehill and Kåre B. Dullum, *Internationalizing the Cost of Capital in Theory and Practice: The Novo Experience and National Policy Implications*, Copenhagen: Nyt Nordisk Forlag Arnold Busck, 1982; and New York: Wiley, 1983. Novo Industri A/S acquired Nordisk Insulin after this case was written. The name was changed to Novo-Nordisk, which was described in the Illustrative Case at the end of Chapter 7.

that case firms like Novo would enjoy an international cost of capital comparable to that of their foreign competitors. Strangely enough, no Danish government restrictions existed that would have prevented foreign investors from holding Danish securities. Therefore one must look for investor perception as the main cause of market segmentation in Denmark at that time.

At least six characteristics of the Danish securities market were responsible for market segmentation:

1. Disparity in the information base of Danish and foreign investors.
2. Taxation.
3. Alternative sets of feasible portfolios.
4. Financial risk.
5. Foreign exchange risk.
6. Political risk.

Disparity in the Information Base
Certain Danish institutional characteristics caused Danish and foreign investors to be uninformed about each other's equity securities. The most important information barrier was the Danish regulation that prohibited Danish investors from holding foreign private sector securities.[18] Therefore Danish investors had no incentive to follow developments in foreign securities markets nor to factor such information into their evaluation of Danish securities. As a result, Danish securities might have been priced correctly in the efficient market sense relative to each other, considering the Danish information base, but priced incorrectly considering the combined foreign and Danish information base. Another detrimental effect of this regulation was that foreign securities firms did not locate offices or personnel in Denmark, since they had no product to sell. Lack of a physical presence in Denmark reduced the ability of foreign securities analysts to follow Danish securities.

A second information barrier was lack of enough Danish security analysts who followed Danish securities. Only one professional securities analysis service was published (Børsinformationen), and that was in the Danish language. A few Danish institutional investors employed in-house analysts, but their findings were not available to the public.

Other information barriers include language and accounting principles. Naturally financial information is normally published in Danish, using Danish accounting principles. A few firms, such as Novo, publish English versions, but almost none use U.S. or British accounting principles or attempt to show any reconciliation with such principles.

Taxation
Danish taxation policy had all but eliminated investment in common stock by individuals. Until a tax law change in July 1981, capital gains on shares held for over two years were taxed at a 50% rate. Shares held for less than two years, or for "speculative" purposes, were taxed at personal income tax rates, with the top marginal rate being 75%. In contrast, capital gains on bonds were tax-free. This situation resulted in bonds being issued at deep

discounts, because the redemption at par at maturity was considered a capital gain. Thus most individual investors held bonds rather than stocks. This factor reduced the liquidity of the stock market and increased the required rate of return on stocks if they were to compete with bonds.

Feasible Set of Portfolios

Because of the prohibition on foreign security ownership at the time, Danish investors had a very limited set of securities from which to choose a portfolio. In practice, Danish institutional portfolios were composed of Danish stocks, government bonds, and mortgage bonds. Since Danish stock price movements are closely correlated with each other, Danish portfolios possessed a rather high level of systematic risk. In addition, government policy had been to provide a relatively high real rate of return on government bonds after adjusting for inflation. The net result of taxation policies on individuals and attractive real yields on government bonds was that required rates of returns on stocks were relatively high by international standards.

From a portfolio perspective Danish stocks provide an opportunity for foreign investors to diversify internationally. If Danish stock price movements are not closely correlated with world stock price movements, inclusion of Danish stocks in foreign portfolios should reduce their systematic rise. Furthermore, foreign investors are not subject to the high Danish income tax rates, since they are normally protected by tax treaties, which typically limit their taxes to 15% on dividends and capital gains. As a result of the international diversification potential, foreign investors might require a lower rate of return on Danish stocks than Danish investors, other things being equal. However, other things may not be equal, because foreign investors may perceive Danish stocks to carry more financial, foreign exchange, and political risk than their own domestic securities.

Financial, Foreign Exchange, and Political Risks

Financial leverage utilized by Danish firms is relatively high by U.S. and U.K. standards but not abnormal for Scandinavia, Germany, Italy, and Japan. In addition, most of the debt is short-term, with variable interest rates. Just how foreign investors would view financial risk in Danish firms depends on what norms they follow in their home countries. We know from Novo's experience in tapping the Eurobond market in 1978 that Morgan Grenfell, their British investment bankers, were eager for Novo to maintain a debt ratio (debt/total capitalization) closer to 50% rather than the traditional Danish 65–70%.

Foreign investors in Danish securities are subject to foreign exchange risk. Whether this is a plus or a minus factor depends on the investor's home currency, perception about the future strength of the krone, and its impact on a firm's economic exposure. Through personal contacts with foreign investors and bankers, Novo's management did not believe foreign exchange risk was a factor in Novo's stock price, because their operations were perceived as being well diversified internationally.

From the same interviews, with respect to political risk, Denmark is perceived as a stable Western democracy but with the potential to cause periodic problems for foreign investors. In particular, Denmark's national debt is regarded as too high for comfort, although this judgment has not yet shown up in the form of risk premiums on Denmark's

Eurocurrency syndicated loans. The other threat perceived by foreign investors is that Denmark will move toward implementing "economic democracy" in a more substantial manner. Economic democracy would result in a mandatory profit-sharing plan whereby a central fund, governed by labor unions, would eventually become a major shareholder in private sector firms. Despite these general concerns about Denmark's political situation, investors in Novo in particular indicated that their evaluation of Novo's prospects was not influenced by political risk.

Barriers to Internationalization

Although Novo's management in 1977 wished to escape from the shackles of Denmark's segmented and illiquid capital market, many barriers had to be overcome. It is worthwhile to describe some of these, since they typify the barriers faced by other firms from segmented markets who wish to internationalize their capital structure.

Novo had been a family-owned firm, from its founding in the 1920s by the two Petersen brothers until 1974, when it went public and listed its "B" shares on the Copenhagen Stock Exchange. (The "A" shares were held by the Novo Foundation; the "A" shares were sufficient to maintain voting control.) However, Novo was essentially unknown in investment circles outside Denmark. To overcome this *disparity in the information base*, Novo increased the level of its financial and technical disclosure in both Danish and English versions. This procedure was aided in late 1977 by Grieveson, Grant and Company, a British stock brokerage firm, which had started to follow Novo's stock and issued the first professional securities analysis report about Novo in English.

The information gap was further closed when Morgan Guaranty Trust Company of New York, Novo's main foreign commercial banker, was consulted about alternative strategies to tap international capital markets. Its advice was to try a Eurobond issue. It then introduced Novo to Morgan Grenfell, a leading U.K. investment bank, which confirmed the recommended strategy. In 1978 Morgan Grenfell successfully organized a syndicate to underwrite and sell a $20 million convertible Eurobond issue for Novo. In connection with this offering Novo listed its shares on the London Stock Exchange to facilitate conversion and to gain visibility. These twin actions were the keys to dissolving the information barrier, and, of course, they also raised a large amount of long-term capital on favorable terms, which would have been unavailable in Denmark.

Despite the favorable impact of the Eurobond issue on availability of capital, Novo's cost of capital actually increased when Danish investors reacted negatively to the potential dilution effect of the conversion right. During 1979 Novo's stock price declined from around DKr300 per share to around DKr200-225 per share.

During 1979 a fortuitous event occurred. Biotechnology began to attract the interest of the U.S. investment community, with several sensationally oversubscribed stock issues by such start-up firms as Genentech and Cetus. Thanks to the aforementioned information gap, Danish investors were unaware of these events and continued to value Novo at a low price/earnings ratio of 5, compared with over 10 for its established competitors and 30 or more for these new potential competitors.

At this point Novo felt that it had to position itself with its customers in the U.S. market as a firm that had a proven track record in biotechnology, in contrast to the "blue sky" promises of the recent start-up firms. A failure to do so could lead to the faulty conclusion that Novo was not at the forefront in technology. Therefore, to protect its customer base, Novo organized a seminar in New York City on April 30, 1980. About 40 journalists and financial analysts attended the seminar. Soon after the seminar a few sophisticated individual U.S. investors began buying Novo's stock and convertibles through the London Stock Exchange. Danish investors were only too happy to supply this foreign demand. Therefore, despite relatively strong demand from U.S. and British investors, Novo's share price increased only gradually, reaching back to the DKr300 level by midsummer. However, during the following months foreign interest began to snowball, and by the end of 1980 Novo's stock price had reached the DKr600 level. Moreover, foreign investors had increased their proportion of share ownership from virtually nothing to around 30%. Novo's price/earnings ratio had risen to around 16, which was now in line with those of its international competitors but not with those of the Danish market. At this point one must conclude that Novo had succeeded in internationalizing its cost of capital. Other Danish securities remained locked in a segmented capital market. Exhibit 14.7 shows that the movement in the Danish stock market in general did not parallel the rise in Novo's share price, nor could it be explained by movement in the U.S. or U.K. stock markets as a whole.

To improve the liquidity of its shares held by U.S. investors and to increase the availability of capital by tapping the U.S. new-issues market, Novo decided to sponsor an American depositary receipts (ADR) system in the United States, have its shares quoted on the over-the-counter market (NASDAQ), and retain a U.S. investment banker to advise it about a U.S. stock issue. Goldman Sachs was selected for this purpose. Morgan Guaranty Trust Company of New York established the ADR system in April 1981. Novo's shares were split five for one in the U.S. market by issuing five times as many American depositary shares as there were underlying Danish krone shares held in the bank.

During the first half of 1981, under the guidance of Goldman Sachs and with the assistance of Morgan Grenfell and Copenhagen Handelsbank, Novo prepared a prospectus for SEC registration of a U.S. stock offering and eventual listing on the New York Stock Exchange. The main barriers encountered in this effort, which would have general applicability, were connected with preparing financial statements that could be reconciled with U.S. accounting principles and the higher level of disclosure required by the SEC. In particular, industry segment reporting was a problem both from a disclosure perspective and an accounting perspective because the accounting data were not available internally in that format. As it turned out, the investment barriers in the United States were relatively tractable, although expensive and time-consuming to overcome.

The more serious barriers were caused by a variety of institutional and government regulations in Denmark. The latter were never designed so that firms could issue stock at market value, since Danish firms typically issue stock at par value with preemptive rights. Even Novo's own stockholders had to be educated about the value of giving up their preemptive rights, but by this time Novo's stock price, driven by continued foreign buying, was so high that virtually nobody in Denmark thought it was worth the price foreigners were willing to pay. In fact, prior to the time of the share issue in July 1981, Novo's stock

Exhibit 14.7   Novo B's Share Prices Compared to Stock Market Indices

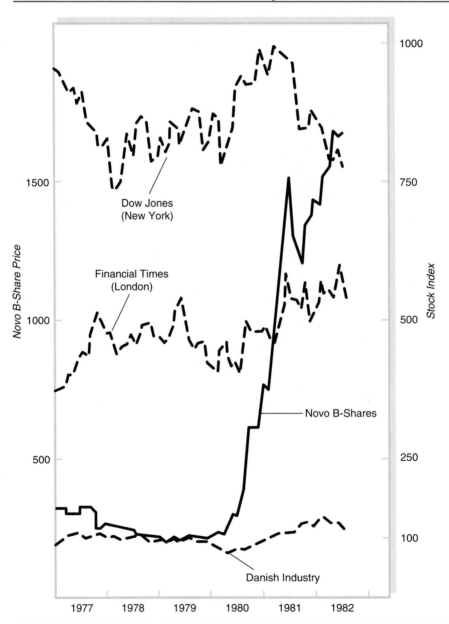

Source: Arthur I. Stonehill and Kåre B. Dullum, *Internationalizing the Cost of Capital: The Novo Experience and National Policy Implications*, John Wiley: New York, 1982, p. 73.

price had risen to over DKr1500, before settling down to a level around DKr1400. Foreign ownership had increased to over 50% of the shares outstanding.

Market segmentation was very apparent during the first half of 1981. Published and unpublished reports by Danish security analysts, bankers, and the popular press consistently claimed that Novo was seriously overvalued, while their foreign counterparts were consistently touting Novo as undervalued. The difference in views was based partly on investor perceptions of the importance of biotechnology and Novo's role in this field.

One final piece of evidence on market segmentation can be gleaned from the way Danish and foreign investors reacted to the announcement of the proposed new U.S. share issue on May 29, 1981. Novo's share price dropped 156 points in Copenhagen, equal to about 10% of its market value. As soon as trading started in New York six hours later, the share price immediately recovered all its loss. The Copenhagen reaction was typical for an illiquid market. Investors worried about the dilution effect of the new share issue since it would increase the number of shares outstanding by about 8%. They did not believe that Novo could invest the new funds at a rate of return that would not dilute future earnings per share. They also feared that the U.S. shares would eventually flow back to Copenhagen if biotechnology lost its glitter.

The U.S. reaction to the announcement of the new stock issue was consistent with what one would expect in a liquid and efficient market. U.S. investors viewed the new issue as creating additional demand for the stock as Novo became more visible because of the selling efforts of a large, aggressive syndicate. Furthermore, the marketing effort was directed at institutional investors who were previously underrepresented among Novo's U.S. investors. They had been underrepresented because U.S. institutional investors want to be ensured of a liquid market in a stock so that they may get out, if desired, without depressing the stock price. The wide distribution effected by the new issue, plus SEC registration and a New York Stock Exchange listing, all added up to more liquidity.

SUMMARY

- Minimizing the cost of capital for a multinational firm is complicated by a number of environmental factors that distinguish multinational firms from domestic firms, as well as multinational firms headquartered in one country from those headquartered in another country.

- Access to international sources of both debt and equity increases the short-term availability of capital to multinational firms, thus allowing them to enjoy a constant marginal cost of capital over large variations in capital budgets.

- Firms that must source their long-term funds in segmented national capital markets are likely to have a higher cost of capital than firms that can source funds in integrated capital markets.

- Taxation policies of both home and host countries will influence a firm's after-tax cost of capital and the manner in which it finances its affiliates.

- Full disclosure of operating results appears to have a favorable influence on the cost of capital of non-U.S. multinational firms that have raised capital in international markets. A difference in opinion exists about the effect on cost of capital of taxes on earnings retained abroad.

- The optimal financial structure of multinational firms could differ from that of domestic firms because of the greater availability of capital to multinational firms as well as their ability to diversify their cash flows internationally.

- The optimal financial structure should be determined from the viewpoint of the consolidated worldwide multinational firm. Within this broad guideline the financial structure of a foreign affiliate might be determined in part by its host country norms. This assumes no increase in cost of capital to the multinational firm as a whole but rather substitution of debt in one country for debt in another.

- To choose among the large variety of sources of funds available to finance foreign affiliates, the financial manager of a multinational firm must consider tradeoffs among cost, foreign exchange risk, political risk, taxes, and managerial motivation.

1. Wilson Corporation

Wilson Corporation, a large U.S. manufacturing firm, wants to finance an $80 million expansion. Wilson wants a capital structure that is 50% debt and 50% equity. Its corporate combined federal and state income tax rate is 40%.

Wilson finds that it can finance in the U.S. domestic market at the following rates. Both debt and equity would have to be sold in multiples of $10 million, and these cost figures show the component costs in increments of $5 million, raised half by equity and half by debt.

	Cost of Domestic Equity (percent)	Cost of Domestic Debt (percent)
Up to $20 million of new capital:	12	8
$21 to $40 million of new capital:	16	12
$41 to $60 million of new capital:	22	16

A London bank advises Wilson that funds could be raised in London in the Eurodollar market at the following costs, also in multiples of $5 million with the 50/50 capital structure preserved.

	Cost of Euro-equity (percent)	Cost of Euro-debt (percent)
Up to $20 million of new capital:	14	6
$21 to $40 million of new capital:	14	10
$41 to $60 million of new capital:	24	18

Each increment of cost would be influenced by the total amount of capital raised. That is, if Wilson first borrowed $10 million in the Eurodollar market at 6% and matched this with an additional $10 million of equity, additional debt would cost 12% in the United States and 10% in Europe. The same relationship holds for equity financing.

    a) Calculate the lowest average cost of capital for each increment of $20 million of new capital, where Wilson raises $10 million in the equity market and an additional $10 million in the debt market at the same time.

    b) If Wilson plans an expansion of $40 million, how should that expansion be financed? What will be the weighted average cost of capital for the expansion?

2. Ex-Post Cost of a Foreign-Currency Bond

Find a bond denominated in a foreign currency that has been issued by a U.S. firm and has been outstanding at least five years. Track the annual interest cost of servicing this bond after considering exchange rate changes but not considering taxes. Compare this cost to what the cost would have been if the U.S. firm had issued a dollar-denominated bond at the time it issued the foreign-currency-denominated bond. Assume that the bond is retired at the end of this year so that the gain or loss on principal will be counted in your calculations. Assume no further changes in exchange rates before the end of this year and that the interest is paid at the end of each year.

3. Optimal Financial Structure

U.S.-based multinational Beaver products, Inc. has a wholly owned subsidiary in Milan, Italy. It is considering the proper debt ratio for the Italian subsidiary. Beaver's optimal debt ratio is 45%. What are the possible considerations in determining the Italian subsidiary's capital structure?

4. Liaoning Products

Liaoning Products of Dalian, People's Republic of China, wants to borrow $400,000 for one year to finance dollar-denominated export sales to the United States. An American bank will lend $400,000 at 10% per annum.

A Japanese bank will lend ¥50,000,000 to Liaoning Products at 6% per annum. The current exchange rate is ¥125/$, so Liaoning Products can exchange the yen for $400,000. Liaoning Products will use its dollar earnings to buy yen next year to repay the Japanese bank.

The Japanese yen is expected to appreciate 4% against the U.S. dollar during the next year. Should Liaoning Products add dollar debt or yen debt to its capital structure?

5. Valdivia Vineyards

Valdivia Vineyards of Chile was recently acquired by Sauvignon Winery of Napa, California. As assistant financial manager of Sauvignon Winery in charge of the Latin Beverage Division, you wonder if you should finance Valdivia's Chilean peso debt into dollars. At present Valdivia is paying 50% p.a. interest on Ps 100 million of five-year maturity peso debt, but you could refinance into dollar debt costing on 10% p.a, saving some 40 percentage points on the cost of debt. All Valdivia's wine is exported to the United States, where it is sold for dollars.

The current exchange rate is Ps 32/$, and both Chile and the United States have a 34% corporate income tax. Because of Chile's high inflation, you expect the exchange rate to drop to Ps 48/$ one year from now, and to continue to deteriorate thereafter at the same rate.

6. Segmented Capital Markets

Pick a country that you believe has a segmented capital market. Explain why you believe this market is segmented. Are there any firms within this country that have a chance to internationalize their cost of capital by raising capital outside of this country? If so, how should they proceed?

NOTES

1. For a summary of empirical work on the multinational firm as a proxy for internationally diversified portfolios, see Marjorie T. Stanley, "Capital Structure and Cost of Capital for the Multinational Firm," *Journal of International Business Studies*, Spring/Summer 1981, pp. 103–120. Important tests of this hypothesis have been undertaken by John S. Hughes, Dennis E. Logue, and Richard J. Sweeney, "Corporate International Diversification and Market Assigned Measures of Risk and Diversification," *Journal of Financial and Quantitative Analysis*, November 1975, pp. 627–637; Tamir Agmon and Donald R. Lessard, "Investor Recognition of Corporate International Diversification," *Journal of Finance*, September 1977, pp. 1049–1055; Wayne Y. Lee and Kanwal S. Sachdeva, "The Role of the Multinational Firm in the Integration of Segmented Markets," *Journal of Finance*, May 1977, pp. 479–492; Alan M. Rugman, "Risk Reduction by International Diversification," *Journal of International Business Studies*, Fall 1976, pp. 75–80; Bertrand Jacquillat and Bruno H. Solnik, "Multinationals Are Poor Tools for Diversification," *Journal of Portfolio Management*, Winter 1978, pp. 8–12; Vihang Errunza and Lemma W. Senbet, "The Effects of International Operations on the Market Value of the Firm: Theory and Evidence," *Journal of Finance*, May 1981, pp. 401–417.

2. Richard C. Stapleton and Marti G. Subrahmanyam, "Market Imperfections, Capital Market Equilibrium, and Corporation Finance," *Journal of Finance*, May 1977, p. 317.

3. Walter L. Ness, Jr., "U.S. Corporate Income Taxation and the Dividend Remittance Policy of Multinational Corporations," *Journal of International Business Studies*, Spring 1975, pp. 67–77.

4. Frederick D. S. Choi, "Financial Disclosure in Relation to a Firm's Capital Costs," *Accounting and Business Research*, Autumn 1973, p. 279.

5. Frederick D. S. Choi, "European Disclosure: the Competitive Disclosure Hypothesis," *Journal of International Business Studies*, Fall 1974, pp. 15–23. Also see Frederick D. S. Choi, "Financial Disclosure and Entry to the European Capital Market," *Journal of Accounting Research*, Autumn 1973, pp. 159–175.

6. For a good description of how the ratings are done on non-U.S. firms, see Keith Wheelock, "An Aaa or a Baa—How Moody's Provides Its Ratings," *Euromoney*, June 1975, pp. 28–32.

7. Kwang Chul Lee and Chuck C. Y. Kwok, "Multinational Corporations vs. Domestic Corporations: International Environmental Factors and Determinants of Capital Structure," *Journal of International Business Studies*, Summer 1988, pp. 195–217. This article summarizes Lee's doctoral dissertation, which was supervised by Kwok at the University of South Carolina and won the Academy of International Business's outstanding dissertation award for 1986.

8. The fact that multinational firms have a lower debt ratio than equivalent domestic firms was also a conclusion of an article by Allen Michel and Israel Shaked, "Multinational Corporations vs. Domestic

Corporations: Financial Performance and Characteristics," *Journal of International Business Studies*, Fall 1986, pp. 89–100.

9. See the following references in the bibliography at the end of this chapter: Stonehill and Stitzel (1969), Remmers et al. (1974), Toy et al. (1974), Stonehill et al. (1975), Shapiro (1978), Errunza (1979), Aggarwal (1981), Stanley (1981), Collins and Sekely (1983), Sarathy and Chatterjee (1984), Wright and Suzuki (1985), Kester (1986), Sekely and Collins (1988), Lee and Kwok (1988), and Hodder (1990).

10. William S. Sekely and J. Markham Collins, "Cultural Influences on International Capital Structure," *Journal of International Business Studies*, Spring 1988, pp. 87–100.

11. *Ibid.*, pp. 92 and 95.

12. Janette Rutterford, "An International Perspective on the Capital Structure Puzzle," *Midland Corporate Finance Journal*, Fall 1985, p. 72.

13. W. Carl Kester, "Capital and Ownership Structure: A Comparison of United States and Japanese Manufacturing Corporations," *Financial Management*, Spring 1986, p. 15.

14. Arthur Stonehill, Theo Beekhuisen, Richard Wright, Lee Remmers, Norman Toy, Antonio Parés,

Alan Shapiro, Douglas Egan, and Thomas Bates, "Financial Goals and Debt Ratio Determinants: A Survey of Practice in Five Countries," *Financial Management*, Autumn 1975, pp. 27–41. Since this survey was conducted in 1973, it is likely that some of the results no longer apply. However, the survey is still illustrative of the noncost factors that are important to financial executives in choosing a financial structure.

15. See Alan C. Shapiro, "Evaluating Financing Costs for Multinational Subsidiaries," *Journal of International Business Studies*, Fall 1975, pp. 25–32; Clovis de Faro and James V. Jucker, "The Impact of Inflation and Devaluation on the Selection of an International Borrowing Source," *Journal of International Business Studies*, Fall 1973, pp. 97–104; William R. Folks, Jr., "The Analysis of Short-Term Cross-Border Financing Decisions," *Financial Management*, Autumn 1976, pp. 19–27.

16. Sidney M. Robbins and Robert B. Stobaugh, *Money in the Multinational Enterprise*, New York: Basic Books, 1973, p. 68.

17. *Ibid.*, p. 68.

18. This prohibition has since been dropped with a corresponding reversal of its negative effects on Danish valuation of domestic securities.

BIBLIOGRAPHY

Adler, Michael, "The Cost of Capital and Valuation of a Two-Country Firm," *Journal of Finance*, March 1974, pp. 119–132.

——, and Bernard Dumas, "Optimal International Acquisitions," *Journal of Finance*, March 1975, pp. 1–19.

——, "International Portfolio Choice and Corporation Finance: A Synthesis," *Journal of Finance*, June 1983, pp. 925–984.

Aggarwal, Raj, "Investment Performance of U.S.-Based Multinational Companies: Comments and a Perspective of International Diversification of Real Assets," *Journal of International Business Studies*, Spring/Summer 1980, pp. 98–104.

——, "International Differences in Capital Structure

Norms: An Empirical Study of Large European Companies," *Management International Review*, 1981/1, pp. 75–88.

Agmon, Tamir, and Donald Lessard, "Investor Recognition of Corporate International Diversification," *Journal of Finance*, September 1977, pp. 1049–1055.

Allan, Iain, "Return and Risk in International Capital Markets," *Columbia Journal of World Business*, Summer 1982, pp. 3–23.

Baldwin, Carliss Y., "Competing for Capital in a Global Environment," *Midland Corporate Finance Journal*, Spring 1987, pp. 43–64.

Bonser-Neal, Catherine, Greggory Brauer, Robert Neal, and Simon Wheatley, "International

Investment Restrictions and Closed-End Country Fund Prices," *Journal of Finance*, June 1990, pp. 523–548.

Booth, Laurence David, "Taxes, Funds Positioning, and the Cost of Capital for Multinationals," *Advances in Financial Planning and Forecasting*, vol. 4, part B, 1990, pp. 245–270.

Boris, C. E. V., "Leverage and Financing of Non-Financial Companies: An International Perspective," *BIS Economic Papers*, no. 27, May 1990.

Brown, Betty C., and Jay T. Brandi, "Security Price Reactions to Changes in Foreign Currency Translation Standards," *Journal of Accounting, Auditing and Finance*, Summer 1986, pp. 185–205.

Choi, Frederick D. S., "Financial Disclosure and Entry to the European Capital Market," *Journal of Accounting Research*, Autumn 1973, pp. 159–175.

——, "Financial Disclosure in Relation to a Firm's Capital Costs," *Accounting and Business Research*, Autumn 1973, pp. 272–282.

——, "European Disclosure: The Competitive Disclosure Hypothesis," *Journal of International Business Studies*, Fall 1974, pp. 15–23.

Choi, Frederick D. S., and Arthur Stonehill, "Foreign Access to U.S. Securities Markets: The Theory, Myth and Reality of Regulatory Barriers," *The Investment Analyst*, July 1982, pp. 17–26.

Choi, Jongmoo Jay, "Diversification, Exchange Risk, and Corporate International Investment," *Journal of International Business Studies*, Spring 1989, pp. 145–155.

——, "A Model of Firm Valuation with Exchange Exposure," *Journal of International Business Studies*, Summer 1986, pp. 145–152.

Cohn, Richard A., and John J. Pringle, "Imperfections in International Financial Markets: Implications for Risk Premia and the Cost of Capital to Firms," *Journal of Finance*, March 1973, pp. 59–66.

Collins, J. Markham, "A Market Performance Comparison of U.S. Firms Active in Domestic, Developed and Developing Countries," *Journal of International Business Studies*, Second Quarter 1990, pp. 271–287.

——, and William S. Sekely, "The Relationship of Headquarters, Country, and Industry Classification to Financial Structure," *Financial Management*, Autumn 1983, pp. 45–51.

Dawson, Steven M., "Eurobond Currency Selection: Hindsight," *Financial Executive*, November 1973, pp. 72–73.

Dodd, Mikel T., and James A. Millar, "Financial Structure in Japanese and American Firms: An Indirect Test of Agency Relationships," *Journal of International Financial Management and Accounting*, vol. 2, nos. 2 and 3, Summer and Autumn 1990, pp. 131–144.

Doukas, John, and Nickolaos G. Travlos, "The Effect of Corporate Multinationalism on Shareholders' Wealth: Evidence from International Acquisitions," *Journal of Finance*, December 1988, pp. 1161–1175.

Dufey, Gunter, "Institutional Constraints and Incentives on International Portfolio Investment," *International Portfolio Investment*, U.S. Department of the Treasury OASIA, 1975.

——, and Ian H. Giddy, "International Financial Planning: The Use of Market-Based Forecasts," *California Management Review*, Fall 1978, pp. 69–81.

Eaker, Mark R., "Denomination Decisions for Multinational Transactions," *Financial Management*, Autumn 1980, pp. 23–29.

Errunza, Vihang R., "Determinants of Financial Structure in the Central American Common Market," *Financial Management*, Autumn 1979, pp. 72–77.

—— "Financing MNC Subsidiaries in Central America," *Journal of International Business Studies*, Fall 1979, pp. 88–93.

——, and Lemma W. Senbet, "The Effects of International Operations on the Market Value of the Firm: Theory and Evidence," *Journal of Finance*, May 1981, pp. 401–417.

——, "International Corporate Diversification, Market Valuation, and Size-Adjusted Evidence," *Journal of Finance*, July 1984, pp. 727–743.

Fatemi, Ali M., "The Effect of International Diversification on Corporate Financing Policy," *Journal of*

Business Records, 16, no. 1, January 1988, pp. 17–30.

Friend, Irwin, and Ichiro Tokutsu, "The Cost of Capital to Corporations in Japan and the U.S.A.," *Journal of Banking and Finance*, 11, no. 2, June 1987, pp. 313–328.

Gultekin, Mustafa N., N. Bulent Gultekin, and Alessandro Penati, "Capital Controls and International Capital Market Segmentation: The Evidence from the Japanese and American Stock Markets," *Journal of Finance*, September 1989, pp. 849–870.

Hodder, James E., and Lemma W. Senbet, "International Capital Structure Equilibrium," *Journal of Finance*, December 1990, pp. 1495–1516.

Hughes, John S., Dennis E. Logue, and Richard J. Sweeney, "Corporate International Diversification and Market Assigned Measures of Risk and Diversification," *Journal of Financial and Quantitative Analysis*, November 1975, pp. 627–637.

Kester, W. Carl, "Capital and Ownership Structure: A Comparison of United States and Japanese Manufacturing Corporations," *Financial Management*, Spring 1986, pp. 5–16.

Lee, Kwang Chul, and Chuck C. Y. Kwok, "Multinational Corporations vs. Domestic Corporations: International Environmental Factors and Determinants of Capital Structure," *Journal of International Business Studies*, Summer 1988, pp. 195–217.

Lee, W. Y., and K. S. Sachdeva, "The Role of the Multinational Firm in the Integration of Segmented Capital Markets," *Journal of Finance*, May 1977, pp. 479–492.

Lessard, Donald R., "Finance and Global Competition: Exploiting Financial Scope and Coping with Volatile Exchange Rates," *Midland Corporate Finance Journal*, Fall 1986, pp. 6–29.

McCauley, R. N., and S. A. Zimmer, "Explaining International Differences in the Cost of Capital," *Federal Reserve Bank of New York Quarterly Review*, Summer 1989, pp. 7–28.

Remmers, Lee, Arthur Stonehill, Richard Wright, and Theo Beekhuisen, "Industry and Size as Debt Ratio Determinants for Manufacturing Internationally," *Financial Management*, Summer 1974, pp. 24–32.

Remolona, E. M., "Why International Trends in Leverage Have Been So Different," New York: Federal Reserve Bank of New York (Working Paper No. 9002), February, 1990.

Rugman, Alan M., *International Diversification and the Multinational Enterprise*, Lexington, Mass.: Lexington Books, 1979.

Sarathy, Ravi, and Sangit Chatterjee, "The Divergence of Japanese and U.S. Corporate Financial Structure," *Journal of International Business Studies*, Winter 1984, pp. 75–89.

Sekely, William S., and J. Markham Collins, "Cultural Influences on International Capital Structure," *Journal of International Business Studies*, Spring 1988, pp. 87–100.

Senbet, Lemma W., "International Capital Market Equilibrium and the Multinational Firm Financing and Investment Policies," *Journal of Financial and Quantitative Analysis*, September 1979, pp. 455–480.

Shapiro, Alan C., "Evaluating Financing Costs for Multinational Subsidiaries," *Journal of International Business Studies*, Fall 1975, pp. 25–32.

——, "Financial Structure and Cost of Capital in the Multinational Corporation," *Journal of Financial and Quantitative Analysis*, June 1978, pp. 211–226.

Stanley, Marjorie T., "Capital Structure and Cost of Capital for the Multinational Firm," *Journal of International Business Studies*, Spring/Summer 1981, pp. 103–120.

Stapleton, Richard C., and Marti Subrahmanyam, "Market Imperfections, Capital and Market Equilibrium, and Corporation Finance," *Journal of Finance*, May 1977, pp. 307–319.

Stonehill, Arthur, and Kåre Dullum, *Internationalizing the Cost of Capital*, New York: Wiley, 1982.

Stonehill, Arthur, Theo Beekhuisen, Richard Wright, Lee Remmers, Norman Toy, Antonio Parés, Alan Shapiro, Douglas Egan, and Thomas Bates, "Financial Goals and Debt Ratio Determinants: A Survey of Practice in Five Countries," *Financial Management*, Autumn 1975, pp. 27–41.

Stonehill, Arthur, and Thomas Stitzel, "Financial

Structure and Multinational Corporations," *California Management Review*, Fall 1969, pp. 91–96.

Stulz, Rene M., "On the Effects of Barriers to International Investment," *Journal of Finance*, September 1981, pp. 923–933.

Toy, Norman, Arthur Stonehill, Lee Remmers, Richard Wright, and Theo Beekhuisen, "A Comparative International Study of Growth, Profitability and Risk as Determinants of Corporate Debt Ratios in the Manufacturing Sector," *Journal of Financial and Quantitative Analysis*, November 1974, pp. 875–886.

Wright, Richard, and Sadahiko Suzuki, "Financial Structure and Bankruptcy Risk in Japanese Companies," *Journal of International Business Studies*, Spring 1985, pp. 97–110.

PART 4

DIRECT FOREIGN INVESTMENT DECISIONS

The decision to become multinational is probably a strategic necessity for firms operating in industries which are typified by worldwide competitors. A firm can no longer hide behind a strong competitive position in its domestic market because sooner or later it may be out-competed by more profitable foreign multinationals locating in that domestic market, or by competition from imports.

Our definition of a multinational firm is one which has *located production and service facilities abroad through the process of direct foreign investment*. In addition to 100%-owned direct foreign investments, this definition would include joint ventures, and acquisitions or mergers. It would not include firms that only export, license, or perform management contracts abroad. *Strategic alliances* are a gray area depending on the extent of cooperation and degree of ownership involved.

Chapter 15 analyzes the strategic mo-

tives for direct foreign investment and alternative modes of foreign entry. Since nonfinancial considerations dominate purely financial ones, the relevant literature that is cited is in the domain of corporate strategy and international economics rather than in corporate finance. International financial managers must know and understand this related body of thought.

Chapter 16 covers the management of political risk incurred when a firm locates facilities abroad. Once again the relevant literature is not in corporate finance but rather in the social sciences, particularly political science.

Chapter 17 analyzes the capital budgeting decision for investing in a foreign project. At last the corporate finance literature is relevant! However, the normal domestic capital budgeting model must be modified to take into account foreign exchange risks, political risks, and differing tax environments.

15 Corporate Strategy and Direct Foreign Investment

The foreign investment decision results from a complex process that differs in many respects from that governing the domestic investment decision. Foreign investments are usually motivated by a wider and more complicated set of strategic, behavioral, and economic considerations. The investigation process is often longer, more costly, and yields less information on which to evaluate opportunities. Financial evaluations of initial foreign investments using traditional discounted cash flow techniques are not relied on as heavily as they are in domestic investments because of greater perceived business, political, and foreign exchange risks. In this chapter we first examine the strategic motives for direct foreign investments. We then analyze the mode of foreign entry.

STRATEGIC MOTIVES FOR DIRECT FOREIGN INVESTMENT

An immense body of literature has emerged in the last 30 years to explain the rapid growth of direct foreign investment. Many theories have been proposed and tested. Each theory typically explains why direct foreign investment occurs in certain industries or in particular types of firms. No one theory has been able to explain direct foreign investment for all types of industries, firms, and countries. Nevertheless, in the last 15 years significant attempts have been made to synthesize the various theories into one grand theory. Our approach in this chapter is to summarize these various theories and attempts at synthesis, because in combination they constitute a good explanation of most direct foreign investment.

To place the theories in perspective, we note that they have one theme in common. They all attempt to explain why a firm resorts to direct foreign investment rather than relying on exporting, licensing, or management contracts. The original classical theory of international trade was based only on exporting and importing as determined by comparative advantage and the law of factor proportions. Since direct foreign investment, licensing, and management contracts were not part of the classical theory, why have they become so important in recent years? More specifically, why does a firm establish direct foreign investments rather than license foreign firms or operate abroad under a management contract? To answer these questions, we will now examine the various strategic, behavioral, and economic theories that have been proposed and tested during the last 30 years.

Empirical Studies

Surveys and case studies of multinational firms indicate that their motivations for making direct foreign investments are based on five main types of strategic considerations. Firms may be classed as:

1. market seekers,
2. raw material seekers,
3. production efficiency seekers,
4. knowledge seekers, and/or
5. political safety seekers.[1]

Market seekers produce in foreign markets either to satisfy local demand or to export to markets other than their home market. U.S. automobile firms manufacturing in Europe for local consumption are an example of market-seeking motivation.

Raw material seekers extract raw materials wherever they can be found, either for export or for further processing and sale in the host country. Firms in the oil, mining, plantation, and forest industries fall into this category.

Production efficiency seekers produce in countries where one or more of the factors of production are underpriced relative to their productivity. Labor-intensive production of electronic components in Taiwan, Malaysia, and Mexico is an example of this motivation.

Knowledge seekers operate in foreign countries to gain access to technology or managerial expertise. For example, German, Dutch and Japanese firms have purchased U.S.-located electronics firms for their technology.

Political safety seekers acquire or establish new operations in countries that are considered unlikely to expropriate or interfere with private enterprise. For example, Hong Kong firms have invested heavily in manufacturing, services, and real estate in the United States, Canada, and Australia in anticipation of the consequences of China's takeover of the British colony in 1997.

The five types of strategic considerations just described are not mutually exclusive. For example, forest products firms seeking wood fiber in Brazil would also find a large Brazilian market for a portion of their output.

Strategic Versus Financial Considerations. Why do strategic rather than financial considerations seem to be very important motivations for direct foreign investment? Perceived political and foreign exchange risks often cloud the determination of an appropriate risk-adjusted required rate of return for a foreign project. As a result, the range of expected outcomes may be so large as to reduce the credibility of any financial discounted cash flow analysis that attempts to find a single-valued expected net present value. Therefore, although discounted cash flow analysis is still used appropriately to analyze specific projects, it is not usually the deciding factor in choosing the original countries in which a multinational firm will invest. Empirical studies of large samples of multinational firms lend support to this conclusion.

Based on a sample of 100 detailed questionnaires and 50 in-depth interviews, a study of multinational firms undertaken by the Conference Board concluded the following:

> Even in discussions of the technical application of various financial criteria the ever-present main point proved to be that considerations of market position dominate the decision-making process. They determine the need, the urgency, and the desirability of an investment, while financial evaluations are used mainly to test the validity of marketing assumptions and to determine both the financial requirements and the financial means for attaining marketing goals. Thus, for the most part, financial considerations are pertinent to the how to rather than to the whether to finance a foreign investment.[2]

A second, independent study surveyed 92 U.S. and 18 non-U.S. multinational corporations. The results showed the following:

> Financial investment criteria were used most often in evaluating relatively small cost-saving projects, replacement projects, and other projects which would fall under the purview of local managers. For relatively large or strategic investments, however, financial investment criteria were used only as a rough screening device to prevent obviously unprofitable projects from wasting the time of the board of directors.[3]

Behavioral Considerations. Yair Aharoni's study of the strategic aspects of the foreign investment decision process found two sets of behavioral motives. One set arose from a stimulus from the external environment and the other from within an organization on the basis of personal biases, needs, and commitments of individuals and groups.[4] His study of 38 primarily market-seeking U.S. firms that had considered investing in Israel found the following important external stimuli.

1. An outside proposal, provided it comes from a source that cannot be easily ignored. The most frequent sources of such proposals are foreign governments, the distributors of the company's products, and its clients.

2. Fear of losing a market.

3. The "bandwagon" effect: very successful activities abroad of a competing firm in the same line of business, or a general belief that investment in some area is "a must."

4. Strong competition from abroad in the home market.[5]

In addition to these four motives, Aharoni found some auxiliary motives:

When some unutilized resources exist in the company, or when fixed costs can be spread over additional areas, these facts can be used as a "point of sale" by a proposer or by an executive interested in foreign investments. The existence of such factors will not by itself cause a decision to look abroad, but it may work as a catalyst toward such a decision. These factors augment the impact of the initiating force and may therefore be regarded as auxiliary forces.

The auxiliary forces uncovered in the field research were:

1. Creation of a market for components and other products.
2. Utilization of old machinery.
3. Capitalization of know-how; spreading of research and development and other fixed costs.
4. Indirect return to a lost market through investment in a country that has commercial agreements with these lost territories.[6]

Aharoni's study is a good example of the behavioral theory of a firm, first articulated by Herbert Simon (1947) and improved by Richard Cyert and James March (1963).[7] As was true for the domestic case, the behavioral approach to the foreign investment decision is usually a specific decision on a specific opportunity evaluated sequentially in response to a specific motivating force. It is not, typically, a program to search for all possible foreign investment opportunities, gather all the relevant data for each, compare and rank them, and choose those which rank highest. Of course, there can be numerous alternatives involved in one opportunity, or perhaps several foreign and domestic opportunities are evaluated at the same time. Thus there is a need for ranking, but the constraint is more likely to be lack of management time and ability than lack of funds. In this case the ranking process may really be decided by the choice of which alternatives to investigate. *The sequence and intensity of investigation, including the strength of the motivating force, thus becomes the major determinant of the foreign investment decision.*

Although survey and case studies of the foreign investment decision emphasize strategic motives, these may very well be consistent with rational, profit-seeking, economic motives. According to modern extensions of international economic theory, executives of multinational firms may be operating in a manner that is consistent with maximizing long-run profit (net earnings or cash flow) and market value of common stock, often under conditions of worldwide oligopolistic competition.

Product and Factor Market Imperfections: Sources of Competitive Advantage

The modern theory of direct foreign investment can be traced to Stephen Hymer's doctoral dissertation at the Massachusetts Institute of Technology in 1960.[8] Hymer was the first person to identify imperfections in national and international markets for products and factors of production as sources of competitive advantage which lead to direct foreign investment. His work was later extended by Charles Kindleberger (1969) and became the basis for numerous other theories based on product and factor market imperfections.[9] The more notable of these theories are associated with Harvard economists Richard Caves (1971) and Raymond Vernon (1966).[10]

The most recent extensions of the market imperfections theory have been developed by economists in the United Kingdom, namely, Peter Buckley and Mark Casson (1976) and John Dunning (1977).[11] In addition to theories based on imperfections in product and factor markets, complementary theories based on financial market imperfections have been developed by a number of scholars, no one of whom has emerged as the dominant spokesperson.

According to the Hymer–Kindleberger theory, product and factor market imperfections open the door to direct foreign investment. Market imperfections may occur naturally, but they are usually caused by policies of firms and governments. For example, firms in oligopolistic industries seek to create unique competitive advantages through product differentiation and/or preemptive investments to capture foreign raw material sources. Governments create market imperfections through tariff and nontariff barriers to trade, preferential purchasing policies, tax incentives, capital market controls, and similar policies.

One of the most important market imperfections created by governments was the original formation of the EEC in 1957 and the European Free Trade Area (EFTA) in 1958. These trade blocs motivated a large influx of direct foreign investment from nonmember countries during the later 1950s, continuing throughout the 1960s. A second wave is now being motivated by the prospect of the final realization of the *European Internal Market* after 1992 by an expanded 12-member EEC.

Opportunities have also been created by governments in less developed countries that have potentially large, protected markets, such as Brazil, Indonesia, Nigeria, and India. It should be noted, however, that government policies to create protected markets can attract direct foreign investment only if the market is sufficiently large, or protected, to overcome diseconomies of scale from production units of less than optimal size.

Although government policies, oligopolistic competition, or natural barriers may create potentially large, protected markets, foreign firms operating manufacturing plants in these markets must enjoy some competitive advantages not possessed by local firms in order to be compensated for such inherent disadvantages as lack of knowledge about local customs, differing local tastes, and unfamiliar legal systems, as well as greater communication and control costs. Furthermore, the competitive advantages must allow the firm to earn a higher rate of return from direct foreign investment than would be earned by similar projects of comparable risk in the home market. If these conditions are not met, the firm will prefer to cover foreign markets through exporting, licensing, or management contracts.

The most important competitive advantages enjoyed by multinational firms are (1) economies of scale and scope arising from their large size; (2) managerial and marketing expertise; (3) superior technology owing to their heavy emphasis on research; (4) financial strength; and (5) differentiated products. We will discuss each of these in turn.

Economies of Scale and Scope. Economies of scale and scope can be developed in production, marketing, finance, research and development, transportation, and purchasing.

In each of these areas there are significant competitive advantages to being *large*, whether because of international or just domestic operations. Production economies can come from the use of large-scale, automated plant and equipment or from an ability to rationalize production through worldwide specialization. For example, some automobile manufacturers, such as Ford, produce engines in one country, transmissions in another, bodies in another, and assemble still elsewhere, with the location often being dictated by *comparative advantage*. Marketing economies occur when firms are large enough to use the most efficient advertising media to create worldwide brand identification, as well as to establish worldwide distribution, warehousing, and servicing systems. Financial economies derive from access to the full range of financial instruments and sources of funds, such as the Eurocurrency and Eurobond markets. In-house research and development programs are typically restricted to large firms because of the minimum-size threshold for establishing a laboratory and scientific staff. Transportation economies accrue to firms that can ship in carload or shipload lots. Purchasing economies come from quantity discounts and market power.

Empirical studies lend some support to the hypothesis that multinationals must be large to succeed. In comparing U.S. manufacturing multinationals with U.S. domestic firms in the same industry, Horst found that the only statistically significant variable was firm size.[12] Wolf found size linked with profitability for a large sample of U.S. multinationals when using 1962 data but not 1966 data.[13] The problem with such studies is the difficulty of determining causality. Are multinationals larger and more profitable than domestic firms because they are multinational, or are they multinational because they are larger and more profitable?

Managerial and Marketing Expertise. Managerial expertise includes skill in managing large industrial organizations from both a human and technical viewpoint. It also encompasses knowledge of modern analytical techniques and their application in functional areas of business. Virtually no empirical studies exist to test whether managerial expertise leads to success in large, protected, worldwide oligopolistic markets. Servan-Schreiber popularized the managerial expertise (and technology) thesis in *The American Challenge*, but this book was based on case studies and intuitive reasoning.[14] For example, he cited the great depth of management in U.S. firms due to the U.S educational opportunities to study business administration (management) at both the undergraduate and graduate levels. This situation contrasted with the elitist approach to management education in Europe at the time the book was written (1968).

Managerial expertise can be developed through prior experience in foreign markets. In almost all empirical studies multinational firms have been observed to export to a market before establishing a production facility there. Likewise, they have prior experience sourcing raw materials and human capital in other foreign countries either through imports, licensing, or direct foreign investments. In this manner the multinational firms can partially overcome the supposed superior local knowledge of host country firms.

Technology. Technology includes both scientific and engineering skills. It is not limited to multinationals, but U.S. firms in general have had an advantage in terms of access to continuing new technology spin-offs from the military and space programs. Empirical studies have supported the importance of technology as a characteristic of multinational firms. Raymond Vernon's product cycle theory, which is discussed later, is based on the fact that multinational firms are the originators of much of the new technology because of research and development activities on new products initially launched in their home markets.[15] Empirical tests of this theory seem to confirm the relationship between research and development and direct foreign investment.[16]

Financial Strength. Financial strength includes not only economies of scale but the ability to reduce risk through diversification of operations and borrowing sources. Typically multinationals have had both lower cost and better availability of capital than foreign and domestic competitors, as explained in Chapter 14.

Differentiated Products. An important extension of the market imperfections theory was made by Richard Caves (1971), who studied direct foreign investment from the perspective of the economics of industrial organizations.[17] Caves noted that multinational firms are typically in industries characterized by research or marketing intensity or both. These firms create their own firm-specific advantages by producing and marketing *differentiated products.* Such products originate from research-based innovations or heavy marketing expenditures to gain brand identification. Furthermore, the research and marketing process continues to produce a steady stream of new differentiated products. It is difficult and costly for competitors to copy such products, and they always face a time lag if they try. Having developed differentiated products for the domestic home market, the firm may decide to market them worldwide, a decision consistent with the desire to maximize return on heavy research and marketing expenditures.

Product differentiation does not necessarily mean that worldwide markets must always be serviced by direct foreign investment. Caves classifies differentiated products into three groups. If the costs of a product benefit from economies of scale in production and the product can be marketed without significant adaptation to local market conditions, Caves predicts that exports will be the preferred method of selling. If the product does not enjoy economies of scale, or if the product involves a proprietary process, licensing of foreign firms may occur. However, if the firm's main competitive advantage is embodied in research, marketing, and managerial expertise, rather than in any specific existing differentiated products, then expansion may take the form of direct foreign investment.

Product Cycle Theory

Differentiation with a time lag is the basis for the *product cycle theory* which was first proposed by Raymond Vernon and his colleagues at Harvard Business School.[18] It suggests that direct foreign investment is a natural stage in the life cycle of a new product from its inception to its maturity and eventual decline. The socioeconomic development, economies of scale, and oligopolistic competition that are found in the most advanced industrial countries lead firms in these countries to undertake intensive research and development efforts. New technologically advanced, or differentiable, products are discovered.

The new products are first introduced in the home market. Close coordination of production and sales is required while the product is improved and the production process standardized. After a short time lag the product is exported. As the new product reaches maturity, competition from nearly similar products narrows profit margins and threatens both export and the home markets.

At this stage foreign manufacturing locations are sought where market imperfections in the cost of factors of production create a chance for lower unit production costs. Thus the foreign investment is essentially a *defensive* investment designed to preserve profit margins in both export and home markets.

Examples of defensive investments can be found in many labor-intensive less developed countries. For example, the price of labor in Mexico, Puerto Rico, Hong Kong, Korea, Indonesia, Malaysia, Taiwan, and Thailand is low for its productivity. This feature has attracted direct foreign investment in labor-intensive industries. If laborers in these countries earn the local currency equivalent of $2.50 per hour and are as productive as their U.S. counterparts, who earn $5 per hour, a firm can cut its per-unit labor cost in half. Of course, other factors of production, such as shipping, tariffs, equipment, plant, and land, may cost much more in these countries, thereby offsetting the labor differential. Furthermore, over time labor costs may increase more rapidly in these countries than in the United States because of foreign demand for their services. In the meantime, however, a temporary market imperfection for labor exists and attracts direct foreign investment.

Richard Moxon has studied the motivation for U.S. investment in offshore electronics plants, which is an example of investment based on product cycle theory.[19] The bulk of the offshore electronic plants in the study were owned by 20 U.S. parent firms and located primarily in Mexico and Taiwan, with a smaller number in Hong Kong, Korea, and Singapore. They were exporting their output to their U.S. parents under Items 806.30 and 807.00 of the U.S. Tariff Schedules, under which U.S. duties are assessed only on their foreign value added. In most cases the parent exported materials to the subsidiary, which then conducted the labor-intensive operations and shipped the assemblies back to the parent.

On the basis of interviews with executives of the parent firms, confirmed by regression studies of the characteristics of the imports and the electronics industry, Moxon found the following.

- The offshore investments were defensive in nature, being a response to strong price competition in the U.S. market from low-priced imports from foreign producers, especially from Japan. Without the offshore investment the U.S. market might have been entirely lost to imports.

- Labor-intensive products not requiring too much skill were selected for offshore production. Not only were the foreign wages lower than U.S. wages, but the workers had a more acceptable attitude toward tedious assembly work. Their productivity was higher, their turnover was lower, and their quality standards were better on standardized tasks than for their U.S. counterparts.

- Shipping costs were an important determinant of which products and operations were conducted offshore. Small, lightweight assemblies were feasible. Products that were heavy, bulky, easily damaged in shipping, or required rapid delivery were not manufactured offshore.

- Tariffs were not an important consideration because of the low overall U.S. tariffs on electronics and the favorable provisions on imports under Items 806.30 and 807.00. Sales growth in the United States encouraged offshore production since it permitted U.S. facilities to remain in production and not put U.S. workers out of work.

- Products that were simple, standardized, and in high-volume production were produced offshore. These were products where automation had gone as far as it could in the United States. Custom-made and highly engineered products were produced in the United States.

- Political and economic risks were offset by use of multiple sourcing both offshore and in the United States, despite loss of economies of scale.

- Subcontracting to foreign producers occurred only when the product's volume was too low for the parent to gain the inherent economies of scale, or when fluctuations in the parent's production required peak load backup. Only the simplest products, with minimum technology transfer, were subcontracted. The foreign subcontractors could realize economies of scale and reduce fluctuation by producing for several firms as well as themselves.

- As U.S. firms gained favorable experience in offshore production, more complex offshore production operations were undertaken, such as full assembly and testing.

Defensive Investments

Although the product cycle theory initiated the idea of defensive investments, many other theories of defensive investments followed.

Follow the Leader. Knickerbocker (1973) developed a *follow the leader theory* of defensive direct foreign investment.[20] He noted that in oligopolistic industries when one competitor undertakes a direct foreign investment, other competitors follow very quickly with defensive direct investments into that market. He hypothesized that the followers were motivated by a desire to deny any competitive advantages, such as the benefits of economies of scale, to the others.

Knickerbocker's theory does not explain why the leader initiates the original direct foreign investment, but presumably the reason springs from the opposite side of the same coin. For example, firms are observed entering potentially large markets prematurely with direct foreign investments in an attempt to gain economies of scale and preempt economies of scale from the other competitors. Some of the manufacturing investments in large, growing, less developed countries fall into this category. Even in countries where the size and growth potential of the market are permanently limited, multinationals will make direct investments or acquisitions of firms that are riskier and less profitable than themselves because of the favorable impact on their economies of scale and diversification of risk for the firms as a whole, and denial of these advantages to other oligopolistic competitors. Multinationals sometimes make direct investments of a defensive nature in the home markets of competitors even though such investments appear in accounting statements to be unprofitable. The purpose is to disrupt the easy market share of competitors in their home market in order to reduce their economies of scale and thereby their competitiveness in other markets. U.S., European, and Japanese automobile manufacturing firms have sometimes considered defensive investments in each other's markets in this light.

Defensive investments are even more apparent in the raw-material-producing industries, such as in oil, tin, copper, bauxite, rubber, and forest products. Control over sources of raw material, and conversely denial of these sources to competitors, causes a number of preemptive, defensive-type investments, similar to those of market-seeking oligopolists.

Another characteristic that is an important motivation for direct investments in raw materials is the need to develop economies of scale through both horizontal and vertical integration. The raw materials are typically just one stage in a multistage production process reaching all the way from raw materials to final consumers. The independents who perform only one stage in the process are often in a poor bargaining position. The fully integrated producers have alternative sources of supply and control the final markets. Thus, although an investment in raw materials may not be profitable in itself, it creates the opportunity for downstream profits that are not available to the independents.

Credibility. Defensive investments also occur when *credibility* with an existing customer base becomes important. For example, this factor motivated Novo Industri, A/S to establish a plant to manufacture industrial enzymes in North Carolina in the United States.[21] Novo enjoyed a large export market for industrial enzymes in the United States. However, enzymes are intermediate products that are used in the production of such end products as detergents and fructose. Quality control and guaranteed availability are critical in the continuous processes employed in such industries. Therefore despite the loss of economies of scale in Denmark, and suboptimal economies of scale in the United States, Novo felt obligated to establish a manufacturing presence in the United States to maintain its credibility in the marketplace.

Growth to Survive. Another version of defensive investments suggests that firms invest abroad because they have saturated the domestic market and any further expansion domestically would lead to destructive retaliation by the other oligopolists or antitrust action (in the United States).[22] Growth abroad, either through new investments or acquisitions, is the natural reaction of firms that have a "grow to survive" attitude. In these firms, however, there could also be an intuitive understanding that growth leads to improving economies of scale relative to competitors and therefore ultimately to superior financial performance.

Knowledge Seekers. Multinational firms that have been identified as *knowledge seekers* provide still another example of defensive investments. These are firms trying to maintain or acquire a better position in one or more of the key competitive variables. In particular, they are trying to improve managerial expertise, technology, or knowledge of product and factor markets. This goal is accomplished most efficiently by acquisition of foreign firms that already possess some of these attributes. There may also be an element of improving economies of scale and financial strength in these types of acquisitions. Philips (the Netherlands), Siemens (Germany), and NEC (Japan) have all made important acquisitions of U.S. firms in the integrated circuit and semiconductor business. Most acquisitions were located near San Francisco in the area known popularly as "Silicon Valley." This area is one of several centers of excellence in the electronics field.

Follow the Customer. The growing presence abroad of service firms is a final example of defensive investments. Banking, advertising, legal, consulting, and accounting firms have typically followed their clients abroad. Their motivation is to counter efforts by other international and local service firms to steal their clients. They are forced to invest in facilities and staff in key foreign locations both for credibility and for convenience.

Internalization

The theory of *internalization* is an attempt to synthesize and extend those theories of direct foreign investment that are based on market imperfections. Peter Buckley and Mark Casson (1976) and John Dunning (1977) hypothesize that the mere existence of imperfect markets and competitive advantages for oligopolistic firms is not sufficient to guarantee direct foreign investment.[23] As was pointed out earlier, Caves claims that the advantaged firms could cover foreign markets through exports, licensed production, or management contracts. Thus for direct foreign investment to occur, competitive advantages must be firm-specific, not easily copied, and in a form that allows them to be transferred to foreign affiliates. For example, economies of scale and financial strength are not necessarily firm-specific because they can be and are achieved by many firms throughout the world. Certain kinds of technology can be purchased, licensed, or copied. Even differentiated products can lose their advantage to slightly altered versions given enough marketing effort and the right price.

According to the theory of internalization, the key ingredient for maintaining a firm-specific competitive advantage is possession of proprietary information and control of the human capital that can generate new information through expertise in research, management, marketing, and technology. Needless to say, once again large research-intensive firms are most likely to fit this description.

Why does possession of information lead to direct foreign investment? In the words of Alan Rugman, one of the theory's proponents:

> Information is an intermediate product par excellence. It is the oil which lubricates the engine of the MNE [multinational enterprise]. There is no proper market for the sale of information created by the MNE and therefore no price for it. There are surrogate prices; for example, those found by evaluating the opportunity cost of factor inputs expended in the production and processing of a new research discovery or by an ex post evaluation of the extra profits generated by that discovery, assuming all other costs to remain the same. Yet there is no simple interaction of supply and demand to set a market price. Instead the MNE is driven to create an internal market of its own in order to overcome the failure of an external market to emerge for the sale of information. This internal market of the MNE is an efficient response to the given exogenous market imperfection in the determination of the price of information. Internalization allows the MNE to solve the appropriability problem by assigning property rights in knowledge to the MNE organization.
>
> The creation of an internal market by the MNE permits it to transform an intangible piece of research into a valuable property specific to the firm. The MNE will exploit its advantage in all available markets and will keep the use of information internal to the firm in order to recoup its initial expenditures on research and knowledge generation. Production by subsidiaries is preferable to licensing or joint ventures since the latter two arrangements cannot benefit from the internal market of an MNE. They would therefore dissipate the information monopoly of the MNE, unless foreign markets were segmented by effective international patent laws or other protective devices.[24]

Although the theory of internalization is appealing as a high-level synthesis of market imperfections theories, it lacks empirical verification. Testing such a theory is difficult where no observable market exists external to the firm. Furthermore, we do observe cases where multinational firms have been willing to license information in one market at the same time as they are exploiting it through export or direct foreign investment in other markets. Therefore, John Dunning has proposed an *eclectic theory* of international production in which location-specific factors explain why a firm might serve a particular market by direct foreign investment or export or management contract or licensing.[25]

MODE OF FOREIGN ENTRY

Having decided on direct foreign investment, a multinational firm must then decide on a mode of foreign entry. The main choices are:

1. A *joint venture* with one or more local partners.
2. A 100%-owned *greenfield* (newly established) foreign subsidiary.
3. A *merger* with or *acquisition* of an existing local firm.
4. A *strategic alliance* with one or more partners.

Joint Venture Versus 100%-Owned Greenfield Foreign Subsidiary

A joint venture between a multinational firm and a host country partner is a viable strategy if, and only if, one finds the right local partner. Some of the obvious advantages of having a compatible local partner are:

1. The local partner understands the customs, mores, and institutions of the local environment. This might take years for a multinational firm to acquire on its own with a 100%-owned greenfield subsidiary.

2. A key attribute is whether the local partner can provide competent management, not just at the top but also with respect to middle management.

3. Some host countries require, or certainly prefer, that foreign firms share ownership with local firms or investors. In such a case, 100% foreign ownership is not a realistic alternative to a joint venture.

4. Access to the host country's capital markets may be enhanced by the local partner's contacts and reputation.

5. In some cases a local partner may possess technology which is appropriate for the local environment, or maybe can be used worldwide.

6. If the purpose of the investment is to serve the local market, the public image of a firm which is partially locally-owned may improve its sales possibilities.

Despite this impressive list of advantages, joint ventures are not as common as 100%-owned foreign subsidiaries because multinational firms fear interference by the local partner in certain critical decision areas. Indeed, what is optimal from the viewpoint of the local venture may be suboptimal for the multinational operation as a whole. The most important potential conflicts are:

1. If the wrong partner is chosen, political risk is increased rather than reduced. Imagine the standing of joint ventures undertaken with the family or associates of General Noriega in Panama or Ferdinand Marcos in the Philippines just before their overthrow. The local partner must be credible and ethical or the venture is worse off for being a joint venture.

2. Local and foreign partners may have divergent views about the need for cash dividends, or about the desirability of growth financed from retained earnings versus new financing.

3. Transfer pricing on products or components bought from or sold to related companies creates a potential for conflict of interest.

4. Control of financing is another problem area. A multinational firm cannot justify its use of cheap or available funds raised in one country to finance joint venture operations in another country.

5. Ability of a firm to rationalize production on a worldwide basis can be jeopardized. This was the reason that Ford Motor Company bought out the 45% minority interest

in British Ford in 1960 despite very unfavorable reaction in both the United States and United Kingdom.

6. In some cases financial disclosure of local results is made necessary by having locally traded shares, whereas if the firm is wholly owned from abroad such disclosure is not needed. Disclosure gives nondisclosing competitors an advantage in setting strategy.

7. The problem of valuation of equity shares is difficult. How much should the local partner pay for its share? What is the value of contributed technology, or of contributed land in a country like China where all land is state owned? It is highly unlikely that foreign and host country partners have similar opportunity costs of capital, expectations about the required rate of return, or similar perceptions of appropriate premiums for business risk. Insofar as the venture is a component of the portfolio of each investor, its contribution to portfolio return and variance may be quite different between them.

Mergers and Acquisitions

The 1980s was characterized by a spate of mergers and acquisitions both with domestic and with foreign partners. Cross-border mergers have played an important role in this activity. A recent study by McKinsey, the international consulting firm, estimated that in 1989 alone, cross-border mergers valued at $112 billion were consummated within the global *triad* (EEC, Japan, and the United States).[26] The impending 1992 completion of the EEC Internal Market stimulated many of these investments, as European, Japanese, and U.S. firms jockeyed for stronger market positions within the EEC. However, the weak value of the U.S. dollar, long-run U.S. growth prospects, and political safety in the United States motivated more takeovers of U.S. firms by foreign firms, particularly from the United Kingdom and Japan, than vice versa. This was a reversal of historical trends when U.S. firms were net buyers of foreign firms rather than net sellers to foreign firms.

Advantages and Disadvantages. As opposed to a greenfield investment, a cross-border merger has the following advantages:

1. It is a much quicker way to establish an operating presence in a host country, or a whole geographic market such as the EEC.

2. It may be a cost-effective way to capture valuable technology rather than developing it internally.

3. It may be a necessity to be "grandfathered" in with "insider" status in the EEC before the 1992 Internal Market becomes a reality.

4. Economies of scale can be gained with a larger base whether the merger is cross-border or domestic.

5. Foreign exchange operating exposure can be reduced by servicing a market with local manufacturing rather than through imports. This is an implementation of the diversification strategy recommended in Chapter 7.

6. According to internalization theory, cross-border mergers are another way for a firm to exploit its proprietary knowledge and products internally when an efficient external market does not exist.

7. In the case of foreign takeovers in the United States, the price and timing may be right considering the weakness of the dollar and the presence of a recession.

As in the domestic merger case, cross-border mergers have some potential pitfalls:

1. Cultural differences may inhibit the melding of two organizations of different nationality, customs, and values.

2. The price paid by the acquirer may be too high and the method of financing too costly.

3. Unfavorable host country political reactions may occur when a takeover is by a foreign firm.

4. Labor troubles can arise because of unequal union contracts, seniority, favoritism, or a host of other potential grievances.

5. Contractual agreements, license fees, transfer prices, and other commercial relationships between the parties will be more closely scrutinized than when they were independent.

Unfriendly Takeovers. Whereas successful takeovers within the Continental EEC countries and Japan have almost always been friendly, such has not been the case in the United Kingdom and the United States. This relates to some basic differences in corporate and investor philosophies between the Anglo-American equity markets and those in the rest of the world.

The Anglo-American equity markets are characterized by a philosophy that a corporation's objective should be to *maximize stockholder wealth*. Whether all firms behave in this manner is open to debate, but if management deviates too much from this objective they can be removed through the discipline of the marketplace, that is, a takeover by others. This discipline is made possible by the "one-share-one-vote" rule which dominates the Anglo-American markets.

In contrast, the Continental European and Japanese equity markets are characterized by a philosophy that a corporation's objective should be to *maximize corporate wealth*.[27] This means that a firm should treat stockholders on a par with other corporate interest groups, such as management, labor, the local community, suppliers, creditors, and even the government. The goal is to earn as much as possible in the long run but to retain enough to increase the corporate wealth for the benefit of all the interest groups.

One might wonder why stockholders do not enforce their own objectives when management does *not* act as their *agent*. The answer is that the non-Anglo-American countries are not characterized by the corporate "one-share-one-vote" rule. Furthermore, many other antitakeover defenses exist which make it virtually impossible to force an unfriendly merger.

Exhibit 15.1 presents a recent survey of takeover defenses in seven non-Anglo-American countries. It shows that dual classes of voting stock are prevalent in six of the seven countries. The controlling class of stock is usually held by the founders, a foundation, or investors friendly to existing management. Nine other takeover defenses are listed along with the countries in which they are used. Note in particular the importance of strategic alliances (number 8) and close personal relationships (number 9). For example, it was the Belgian and European "Establishment" which defeated Carlo de Benedetti's unsuccessful bid to takeover Société Generale de Belgique, Belgium's largest company, in 1988.

Strategic Alliances

Strategic alliances are currently in vogue in the world of international business. The definition of strategic alliance is unclear because it connotes different meanings to different observers. One form of cross-border strategic alliance is where two firms exchange a share of ownership with each other. As pointed out in Exhibit 15.1, this can be a takeover defense if the prime purpose is for a firm to place some of its stock in stable and friendly hands. If that is all that occurs, it is just another form of portfolio investment, not direct foreign investment.

Exhibit 15.1   A Survey of Takeover Defenses in Seven Non-Anglo-American Countries

Type of Takeover Defenses	Countries in the Survey in Which the Defense Is Used[a]
1. Dual classes of voting stock	Denmark, France, the Netherlands, Norway, West Germany, and Switzerland
2. Restrictions on the number of shares which can be voted	West Germany and Switzerland
3. Restrictions on foreign ownerships of shares	France, Japan, Norway, and Switzerland
4. Provisions in the corporate charter which might require a super-majority vote on a takeover bid	Japan, Switzerland, and West Germany
5. Selling a special issue of voting shares or convertible preferred to "stable" or "friendly" investors	France, Japan, the Netherlands, Norway, Switzerland, and West Germany
6. Finding a "white knight"	France, the Netherlands, Norway, and Switzerland
7. Control by a foundation	Denmark, the Netherlands, and Switzerland
8. Forming a strategic alliance and/or having interlocking boards of directors	France, Japan, the Netherlands, Norway, and West Germany
9. Relying on a network of close personal relationships, i.e., belonging to "the establishment"	Denmark, France, Japan, the Netherlands, Norway, Switzerland, and West Germany
10. Government regulations controlling competition and monopolies	France, the Netherlands, and West Germany

Source: Arthur Stonehill and Kåre Dullum, "Corporate Wealth Maximization, Takeovers, and the Market for Corporate Control," *Nationaløkonomisk Tidsskrift* (Denmark), Number 1, 1990, p. 87. Reprinted with permission.

a The seven countries which were included in the survey are Denmark, France, Japan, the Netherlands, Norway, Switzerland, and West Germany (prior to reunification with East Germany).

A more comprehensive strategic alliance is where, in addition to exchanging stock, the partners establish a separate joint-venture to develop and manufacture a product or service. Numerous examples of such strategic alliances can be found in the automotive, electronics, telecommunications, and aircraft industries. Such alliances are particularly suited to high tech products where the cost of research and development is high and timely introduction of improvements is important.

A third level of cooperation might involve joint marketing and servicing agreements where each partner represents the other in certain markets. Some observers believe such arrangements begin to resemble the *cartels* which were prevalent in the 1920s and 1930s. Because they reduce competition, cartels have been banned by international agreements and many national laws.

Strategic alliances involving joint ventures and marketing agreements are quasi-direct foreign investment. They enjoy the same advantages and disadvantages as previously identified for other types of joint ventures. The main difference here is that strategic alliances often also involve an exchange of stock between the parent firms.

It remains to be seen if the current wave of strategic alliances with and between partners in the EEC are stable and durable. It seems as if most firms feel they should be treating the Internal Market as if it were a "United States of Europe." Strategic alliances are a quick way to get EEC-wide coverage before it is too late. This is particularly attractive to firms which have historically served the EEC markets through exports, licensing, or minor direct investment in assembly and service facilities. Specifically, firms located in Austria, Sweden, Norway, Finland, and Switzerland are feeling the pressure to become "insiders." Strategic alliances with EEC partners have also been popular with firms from the United States, Japan, Canada, and Australia. After the euphoria associated with 1992 wears off it is possible many of these hurried strategic alliances will be dissolved and be replaced in a more deliberate manner by traditional types of direct foreign investment.

Licensing and Management Contracts as Alternatives to Direct Foreign Investment

In recent years a number of host countries have demanded that multinational firms sell their services in "unbundled form" rather than only through direct investment. For instance, they would like to purchase managerial expertise and knowledge of product and factor markets through *management contracts*, and technology through *licensing agreements*.

Licensing is a popular method for nonmultinational firms to profit from foreign markets without the need to commit sizable funds. Since the foreign producer is typically 100% locally owned, political risk is minimized.

The main disadvantage of licensing is that license fees are likely to be lower than direct investment profits, although the return on the marginal investment might be higher. Other disadvantages include possible loss of quality control, establishment of a potential competitor in third-country markets, possible improvement of the technology by the local licensee, which then enters the original firm's home market, and possible loss of opportunity to enter the licensee's market with a direct investment later on. Yet another disadvantage is the risk the technology will be stolen.

Multinational firms have not typically used licensing of independent firms. On the contrary, most licensing arrangements have been with their own foreign affiliates or joint ventures. License fees have been a way to spread the corporate research and development cost among all operating units and a means of repatriating profits in a form typically more acceptable to some host countries than dividends.

Management contracts are similar to licensing insofar as they provide for some cash flow from a foreign source without significant foreign investment or exposure. Management contracts probably lessen political risk because it is easy to repatriate the managers. International consulting and engineering firms have traditionally conducted their foreign business on the basis of a management contract.

Whether licensing and management contracts are cost effective compared to direct foreign investment depends on the price host countries are willing to pay for the unbundled services. If the price were high enough, many firms would prefer to take advantage of market imperfections in an unbundled way, particularly in view of the *lower political, foreign exchange, and business risks*. Since we observe multinationals continuing to prefer direct investments, we must assume that the price for selling unbundled services is still too low.

Why is the price of unbundled services too low? The answer may lie in the synergy created when services are bundled as direct investments in the first place. Managerial expertise is often dependent on a delicate mix of organizational support factors that cannot be transferred abroad efficiently. Technology is a continuous process, but licensing usually captures only the technology at a particular point in time. Most important of all, however, economies of scale cannot be sold or transferred in small bundles. By definition they require large-scale operations. How can even a relatively large operation in a small market achieve the same economies of scale as a large operation in a large market?

Despite the handicaps, some multinationals have successfully sold unbundled services. An example would be sales of managerial expertise and technology to the OPEC countries. In this case, however, the OPEC countries are both willing and able to pay a price high enough to approach the returns on direct foreign investment (bundled services) while only receiving the lesser benefits of the unbundled services.

Silica Glass, Inc.*

The sparkle, color, and artistry were mesmerizing. Mike Harrelson was amazed as he held the crystalline Christmas tree ornament up to the firelight. It was May 15, 1991, and the ornament was the product of the world-renowned glass artistry of the Thüringen region of Germany, until recently East Germany. Mike Harrelson is president of Silica Glass, Inc., a firm which had just made an offer for one of the glass manufacturing firms of this Thüringen region. The Treuhandanstalt, the German government

---

* Michael H. Moffett, Oregon State University, May 1991. Reprinted with permission.

agency in charge of the privatization effort for enterprises formerly of East Germany, had not really rejected the offer, but made a counterproposal. The crystal ornament was elegantly simplistic; this acquisition was not. Mike wished to reevaluate his strategy.

Background

Silica Glass, Incorporated (U.S.), is a worldwide leader in the production of glass fiber. Silica fiber is a synthetic fiber of proprietary glass composition. The glass fiber is in turn used in many different industrial applications, some of which were in other divisions of the same company.

Silica's products had grown steadily in quality and sales for a number of years; however, the firm itself had undergone a number of significant ownership and strategy changes. The primary product lines had been developed under Silica Products in the early 1980s. The firm was taken over in 1984 by a takeover specialist who used it as a "cash cow," milking the enterprise for cash flows but reinvesting little. Two years later, operations were sold to Primavera, a southeastern U.S. holding company which had new plans for Silica.

Primavera saw more long-term growth potential for the series of products manufactured by Silica. Primavera's strategy was to expand sales and acquire additional operations which would increase the overall value of the total Silica operation, that is, grow the firm. Although several of the Silica divisions showed healthy profitability, the product lines were very narrow and market expansion limited. Rapid growth would likely be obtained through merger and acquisition, rather than direct sales growth. Moreover, sales, particularly in the domestic market, were being squeezed by new competitive products.

Silica's Markets

The glass fiber market is a highly specialized one. Silica's sales were currently split both between intradivisional sales (50%) and external sales (50%). External sales were in turn divided between the United States (75%), Western Europe (20%), and the Pacific Rim (5%). Silica had grossed nearly $25 million in sales in 1989, and held approximately 25% market share worldwide in these specialized glass fiber products. World markets in general were expected to grow at a 10–15% per year rate in the coming decade.

The problem was intrafirm sales. While outside sales were expected to grow at nearly 30% per year for the next five years, the internal sales to other corporate divisions were expected to decline nearly 25% annually over the same period. Mike's division was looking at a substantial squeeze. The internal sales decline was fairly certain, as new nonglass synthetics were coming onto the market which would make the products of several other corporate divisions obsolete. Hence, Mike's division needed new sales outside the firm. The solution was fairly clear (or at least Mike had thought so initially): focus on external sales growth through increased market share.

Silica's major competitor, both in the United States and worldwide, is GlassPro, a major midwestern U.S. corporation. GlassPro is a firm of substantially larger size and product scope, but presently has only one glass fiber production facility, located in Ohio. GlassPro often experienced excess capacity in short periods of sluggish sales. GlassPro would therefore probably not be expanding into European production in the foreseeable future. A third but relatively minor competitor was Sonnenberg Glaswerks GmbH, located in Sonnenberg, East Germany. Although Sonnenberg produced glass fiber, sales were limited to the Eastern Bloc prior to German unification. With unification, however, Sonnenberg could constitute new competition for both U.S. firms throughout Western Europe.

European Production and 1992

Mike Harrelson had concluded that the rapid sales growth Silica was experiencing, both in the United States and Europe, required immediate manufacturing expansion. Initiating production in Europe was a strong possibility.

Silica believed it should locate new production capability in Europe for a number of reasons. First, the recent growth in the European market represented new opportunities which would be better served by producing within the region. Second, the possibility of a single-Europe, the 1992 program, also created increasing debate over a possible "Fortress Europe." Although the protectionism debate was not considered significant in many industries, Silica had reason to believe it was real. Silica was aware of tentative discussions between the European Commission (EC) in Brussels and a French glass-fiber producer. The French producer is currently a world leader in glass-fiber production, but does not produce the technologically complex fibers of the two U.S.-based firms. The EEC's concern was clear: it was interested in fostering European production of high quality (and high value-added) glass fiber. Mike had a suspicion that once European production of glass fiber began, new protectionist legislation might come forward against foreign firms exporting into Europe.

With the support of Primavera Corporation, Mike Harrelson started exploring possibilities for European manufacturing in the spring of 1990. The question was where to produce in Europe, and how to enter. Mike initially explored greenfield investment possibilities, searching first in the United Kingdom, France, western Germany, and Luxembourg, for affordable property for plant construction. What Mike found was costly, and not encouraging. A second alternative was then explored: the acquisition of an existing facility—one with a glass furnace in place which might allow a cheaper production start-up.

Mike focused on Sonnenberg Glaswerks in the Thüringen region of former East Germany. Sonnenberg, or what was left of it, was known to have had some of the most advanced technology in the world in glass manufacturing for over four centuries. The fame and product development had stopped with the inception of the communist government in East Germany in 1945. The following 45 years resulted in little advancement. There had been no new capital investment. The facilities at Sonnenberg were a mix of the technology of different eras. The two 15-ton furnaces in place were of a technology over 50 years out of date.

By the spring of 1990 Sonnenberg was producing a mediocre glass fiber and was badly in need of new capital, technology, and marketing skills if it was to survive the transition to a capitalist market economy. The unification of Germany now provided Mike Harrelson with the opportunity to salvage something of Sonnenberg's history and productive capability while getting Silica's foot in the door of European production.

Privatization and the Treuhandanstalt

Whereas the opening of Eastern Europe produced massive drives for reindustrialization and privatization for some countries (for example, Poland, Czechoslovakia, Hungary, and Bulgaria), it was different for the former West and East Germanies. Because western Germany was already one of the world's true industrial giants, its economy could provide a jump-start to the revitalization of the east. The east, however, could be absorbed into the whole rather than independently reindustrialized like other Eastern European economies. West Germany approached much of the redevelopment with triage analysis, quietly separating the previous East German enterprises into: (1) those that would not be competitive; (2) those that were well-positioned and prepared for competing with western businesses; (3) those that might survive if provided with infusions of capital, technology, and expertise. The major problem and motivation for selection and action was maintenance of employment. Eastern Germany was rapidly falling into a depression.

To orchestrate the privatization process, a government-constructed holding company was set up—the Treuhandanstalt. The Treuhandanstalt was charged with winding-up over 8,000 firms. The process required the formation of Western-style balance sheets and operating statements for every firm. It was also necessary to quickly assess which firms required immediate cash injections in order to stay afloat until they could be sold or closed.

Sonnenberg Glaswerk GmbH was held by a regional holding company known as Glasring Thüringen AG. Sonnenberg was one of 17 different enterprises for which Glasring Thüringen was responsible (see Exhibit 15.2). Thüringen's role was to follow the directives of the Treuhandanstalt and wind-up the 18 firms while doing everything possible to ensure employment.

Exhibit 15.2 East German Privatization: Glasring Thüringen AG

TREUHANDANSTALT
(German government organization for privatization, owner of regional holding companies including Glasring Thüringen)

Glasring Thüringen AG
(regional holding company for privatization of the following firms)

- Sühl[ER] Glaswerke GmbH*
- Rudolstadt[ER] Thermometerwerk GmbH
- Sühl[ER] Glasmachinenbau GmbH
- Saalfeld[ER] Glaswerke GmbH
- Zella-Mehlisglas GmbH
- Deutsche Schaumglas GmbH
- Sonnenberg[ER] Christbaumschmuck GmbH
- Thüringer Glasschmuck GmbH
- Zella-Mehlis[ER] Metallchristbaumschmuck GmbH
- Staaken[ER] Quarzschmelze GmbH
- Schmalkalden Pharmaglas GmbH
- Haselbach[ER] Glaswerk GmbH
- Naumburg[ER] Glasfaser GmbH
- Sonnenberg[ER] Glaswerk GmbH
- Langewiesen[ER] Thermos GmgH
- Gotha[ER] Rhonglas GmbH
- Sühl[ER] Ilmkristall GmbH

* GmbH is the German reference for corporation, the corporate entity with limited liability.

Proposed Acquisition

After initial exploratory meetings in the spring of 1990, a second visit in September resulted in a tentative arrangement. Silica proposed the acquisition of Sonnenberg Glaswerks, with 75% ownership by Silica, and the remaining 25% remaining with Sonnenberg (actually its present management). The 75% ownership level was necessary in order to obtain tax benefits under EEC law. Although no one had actually owned Sonnenberg in the recent past (under a communist system), Glasring Thüringen AG would hold the 25% minority ownership under the proposal. Silica would be guaranteed first-refusal on the sale of this 25% share (Silica had wanted 100% ownership, but this was unacceptable to Glasring Thüringen). Since Glasring Thüringen was really only a privatization agency, Mike suspected that its 25% ownership would be "given" to the present management of Sonnenberg. Sonnenberg management still saw itself as owners although they had no equity investment or legal standing. In fact, in the preliminary discussions with management, the chief operating officer of Sonnenberg had wished to discuss a joint venture with Silica in which he would be the other equity holder, albeit with no capital investment.

Silica's offer was to invest approximately DM1,500,000 ($1,000,000 at the present exchange rate of DM1.5000/$) in new capital and technology, and provide all marketing and sales expertise. One-fourth of this capital would be required for new plant and equipment, along with an additional 30% subsidy package provided by the German government for specific health, safety, environmental, and machinery needs. The remaining DM1,125,000 would provide working capital for expanded operations. Present contracts such as one with Naumburg Glasfaser would continue. These would provide some minimal cash flows during the transition.

Mike Harrelson returned to the United States to await the completion of balance sheet analysis, but feeling positive about the feasibility of the project. Mike waited for financial information throughout October, November, and into December. The process, which had moved so quickly and smoothly, had ground to a halt. Communication was difficult, and there seemed to be no response to queries for additional information.

Glasring Thüringen AG's Counter-proposal

Mike Harrelson returned to Sonnenberg in mid-December to investigate the problems first-hand. The problems of the Treuhandanstalt and Glasring Thüringen had intensified as unemployment had continued to increase.* Glasring Thüringen now proposed an alternative arrangement: Silica would not only acquire Sonnenberg Glaswerks GmbH, but also acquire a second facility 50 kilometers away, Sühl Glaswerke, GmbH. The two were to be sold together, and not singly. This was different. Silica would now be expected to split production between the two different facilities, thus adding to direct and indirect operating

---

* The difficulties which the Treuhandanstalt had been having in finding suitable joint venture partners were severe. For example, the offer by the West German firm BASF for Synthesewerk Schwarzheide, an East German polyeurethane maker, had been low to say the least: BASF would pay nothing for Synthesewerk Schwarzheide; BASF would not be liable for any environmental liabilities resulting from Synthesewerk Schwarzheide's operations prior to purchase (1945–1990); BASF would be granted ownership by the end of September 1990. The offer was made in August 1990.

costs as well as overhead expenses. Mike explored the possibility of consolidating the two operations at one facility, Sühl, but Glasring Thüringen's interests were firmly in the maintenance of regional employment without worker dislocation. In exchange for the acquisition of the second facility, Glasring Thüringen agreed to the same purchase price; two firms for one! This would increase operating costs substantially, but since there were still no balance sheets or operating statements available, the amount of the cost increase could not be identified.

By late January 1991 there was still no response on the requests for financial information on Sonnenberg. Without some estimates of production costs, material costs, and particularly energy costs, the competitiveness of the existing glaswerks could not be determined. There was also no word on the acquisition approval process.*

Mike Harrelson decided to try and force the process. A fax to Glasring Thüringen explained that without positive movement on approval, financial documentation, and price negotiation by mid-March, the acquisition offer by Silica would be terminated. The fax went without response until early March when a hastily called meeting in Berlin once again brought Mike into negotiations, this time with an expanded cast: the director of Glasring Thüringen, the assistant chief administrator of the Treuhandanstalt, and the president of Deutsche Bank, Berlin. Mike was astounded to find out that the acquisition had only been brought to the attention of the directors of the Treuhandanstalt and Glasring Thüringen in the past two weeks. The offer and negotiation process had evidently been mired in the lower levels of the bureaucracy. In addition, the previous counter-proposal was now expanded to include a third firm in the Glasring, Sonnenberg Christbaumschmuck GmbH, the actual producer of the famous crystal Christmas ornaments. Although small, the additional component would require some attention and capitalization by Silica. The meeting ended on a positive note with assurances of rapid progress, but no financial discussions or documents yet put forward.

The Netherlands Alternative

Upon Mike Harrelson's return to the United States back in December of 1990 he had decided to reopen consideration of greenfield investment within the EEC. Mike had instructed Silica's representatives in the Netherlands to search out potential properties for use in a greenfield investment. The timing was fortunate.

Philips, one of the largest firms in Europe, had been forced to announce major plant closures and literally thousands of layoffs. The restructuring resulted from its own continuing problems and the recession in the United States and United Kingdom beginning in the third quarter of 1990. There was an abundance of available facilities and skilled employees, all in a region of extremely well-developed transportation and communication infrastructure. The city of Haarlem, according to Silica's representative, had two different

---

* The April first assassination of Detlev Rohwedder, the director of the Treuhandanstalt, did not aid the process either. The murder of Mr. Rohwedder at his Düsseldorf villa by the German Red Army faction known as the Baader-Meinhof gang, was a terrorist action intended to slow the restructuring of former East Germany. The Baader-Meinhof gang is thought to have had ties to the former East German secret police, the Stasi. Ironically, Mr. Rohwedder was born in the Thüringia region of East Germany.

properties which might be developed to the company's needs. Silica also had existing sales in the Netherlands, and an increasing number of clients in the bordering countries of Belgium, France, and Germany. It did constitute a relatively central location for servicing Western Europe.

The Netherlands Foreign Investment Agency office in San Mateo, California, responded quickly with information regarding labor costs and benefit guidelines, estimates of electricity costs, and other needed material and facility cost information. Of particular note was that for major electrical power users like Silica, the Netherlands provided extremely cheap block-rate packages, which were even less than those in the Pacific Northwest of the United States. Mike now believed that the Netherlands—if they could provide investment subsidies that were competitive with those of Germany—could be a legitimate alternative to the Sonnenberg acquisition.

Entry Preference

Mike Harrelson now had serious doubts about the rapidly expanding acquisition in Germany. He had been negotiating with the German parties—and there seemed to be an ever-increasing number of interested parties—for over a year and still had little to show for it. Much of what he was now reading indicated a worsening business environment in the former East Germany. On the other hand, the recession-induced events in the Netherlands as well as the rapid movement of the Dutch authorities had resulted in the Netherlands being a legitimate alternative. The two avenues to EEC entrance were, however, inherently different.

As Mike Harrelson held the crystal Christmas tree ornament up to the light (a memento of the last meeting in Berlin when he was offered its maker, Sonnenberg Christbaumschmuck), he knew he must decide soon. December 31st of 1992 was no longer such a distant date.

SUMMARY

- The direct foreign investment decision results from a complex process motivated by strategic, behavioral, and economic considerations. Surveys and case studies of multinational firms indicate that their strategic motivations classify them into five main types: market seekers; raw material seekers; production efficiency seekers; knowledge seekers; and political safety seekers.

- Behavioral studies show that the foreign investment decision is often motivated by a strong stimulus from the external environment, or from within an organization on the basis of personal biases, needs, and commitments of individuals and groups. The investigation process itself, particularly the choice of projects to be investigated, is a major determinant of the foreign investment decision.

- The economic rationale for direct foreign investment is based on a theory of imperfections in individual national markets for products, factors of production, and financial assets. Product and factor market imperfections provide an opportunity for multinational firms to outcompete local firms, particularly in industries characterized by worldwide oligopolistic competition, because the multinational firms have superiority in economies of scale, managerial expertise, technology, differentiated products, and financial strength.

- Oligopolistic competition also motivates firms to make defensive investments abroad to save both export and home markets from foreign competition.

- The product cycle theory suggests that new products are first developed in the most advanced countries by large firms that have the ability to undertake research and development. The new products are introduced into the home market and later exported. As the product matures and the production process becomes standardized, foreign competition reduces profit margins and threatens the home market. Part of the production process is then defensively relocated abroad to take advantage of lower unit costs of labor or other factors of production.

- Defensive direct foreign investments may also be motivated by "follow-the-leader" behavior; a desire to establish credibility with local customers; a "grow-to-survive" philosophy; a desire to gain knowledge by acquiring firms with valuable expertise; and a need to follow the customer in the case of service firms.

- The theory of internalization holds that firms having a competitive advantage because of their ability to generate valuable proprietary information can only capture the full benefits of innovation through direct foreign investment.

- Once a multinational firm has decided on direct foreign investment, it must choose between four major modes of entry: a joint venture with a local partner(s); a 100%-owned greenfield subsidiary; a merger or acquisition of an existing local firm; a strategic alliance with a partner(s).

- The success of a joint venture depends primarily on the right choice of a partner. For this reason and a number of issues related to possible conflicts in decision making between a joint venture and a multinational parent, the 100%-owned foreign subsidiary approach is more common.

- The surge in merger and acquisition activity in the 1980s focused attention on the distinction between the Anglo-American stockholder wealth maximization model, and the Continental European corporate wealth maximization model. The Anglo-American philosophy has led to much of the merger and acquisition activity in which a firm is taken over by others through the discipline of the marketplace. The Continental European philosophy, however, treats stockholders on par with other corporate interest groups. Takeover defenses effectively stifle hostile takeovers.

- The impending completion of the European Internal Market at end-of-year 1992 has induced a surge in cross-border entry through strategic alliances. Although some forms of strategic alliances share the same characteristics as joint ventures, they often also include an exchange of stock.

1. Direct Foreign Investment in the EEC after 1992

The EEC plans to eliminate all internal barriers to the movement of capital by the end of 1992. What impact do you think this will have on direct foreign investment within the EEC? Which theories of direct foreign investment do you think will apply?

2. Japanese Direct Foreign Investment in the United States

Several Japanese firms have recently launched direct foreign investments in the United States, particularly in the automobile and electronics industries. What theories, if any, best explain the Japanese motives for these investments?

3. Japanese Direct Foreign Investment in Korea

Japanese firms have recently started new direct foreign investments in Korea. What do you think is the motivation behind these investments? What theories apply?

4. Management Contracts Versus Direct Foreign Investment

What are the relative merits of management contracts compared to direct foreign investments? Answer this question both from the perspective of a host country as well as from the perspective of a firm that has the management contract.

5. Direct Foreign Investment and the International Debt Problem

Some have suggested that one of the solutions to the international debt problem is for the debtor countries to encourage more direct foreign investment within their borders. How do you think such a policy would affect the host country's debt problem? What would be the best ways for a country to encourage direct foreign investment? What are the advantages and disadvantages of such a policy?

6. Direct Foreign Investment in the Service Industries

Most of the service industries, such as accounting, law, advertising, and banking, have become multinational. What motivates these industries to establish offices abroad? What theories apply?

7. One-Share-One-Vote Versus Dual Classes of Stock

The Securities and Exchange Commission has recently reaffirmed the desirability of U.S. firms pursuing a "one-share-one-vote" policy. On the other hand, many European companies have two types of share capital, A and B shares, with differential voting rights. Compare the desirability of these two different policies. Why do you believe the Europeans allow differential voting rights?

8. Joint Ventures

What are the advantages and disadvantages of joint ventures from the viewpoint of:
- **a)**   the multinational firm?
- **b)**   the local joint venture partners?
- **c)**   the host country?

9. Licensing Versus Direct Foreign Investment
Compare licensing to direct foreign investment from the viewpoint of:
  a) the licensor (multinational firm).
  b) the licensee (host country firm).
  c) the host country.

NOTES

1. The first four classifications were suggested in W. Dickerson Hogue, "The Foreign Investment Decision Making Process," *Association for Education in International Business Proceedings*, December 29, 1967, pp. 1–2. They were also contained in Lee Nehrt and W. Dickerson Hogue, "The Foreign Investment Decision Process," *Quarterly Journal of AISEC International*, February/April 1968, pp. 43–48.

2. *U.S. Production Abroad and the Balance of Payments*, New York: The Conference Board, 1966, p. 63.

3. Arthur Stonehill and Leonard Nathanson, "Capital Budgeting and the Multinational Corporation," *California Management Review*, Summer 1968, p. 40.

4. Yair Aharoni, *The Foreign Investment Decision Process*, Boston: Harvard Graduate School of Business Administration, Division of Research, 1966.

5. *Ibid.*, pp. 54–55.

6. *Ibid.*, pp. 70–71.

7. Herbert Simon, *Administrative Behavior*, New York: Macmillan, 1947; and Richard Cyert and James March, *A Behavioral Theory of the Firm*, Englewood Cliffs, N.J.: Prentice-Hall, 1963.

8. Stephen Hymer, Ph.D. dissertation, Massachusetts Institute of Technology, 1960. This study was later published as *The International Operations of National Firms: A Study of Direct Foreign Investment*, Cambridge, Mass.: MIT Press, 1976.

9. Charles P. Kindleberger, *American Business Abroad: Six Lectures on Direct Investment*, New Haven: Yale University Press, 1969.

10. Richard E. Caves, "International Corporations: The Industrial Economics of Foreign Investment," *Economica*, February 1971, pp. 1–27; and Raymond Vernon, "International Investment and International Trade in the Product Cycle," *Quarterly Journal of Economics*, May 1966, pp. 190–207.

11. Peter J. Buckley and Mark Casson, *The Future of the Multinational Enterprise*, London: Macmillan, 1976; and John H. Dunning, "Trade Location of Economic Activity and the MNE: A Search for an Eclectic Approach," in Bertil Ohlin, Per-Ove Hesselborn, and Per Magnus Wijkman, eds., *The International Allocation of Economic Activity*, New York: Holmes and Meier, 1977, pp. 395–418.

12. Thomas Horst, "Firm and Industry Determinants of the Decision to Invest Abroad: An Empirical Study," *Review of Economics and Statistics*, August 1972, pp. 258–266.

13. Bernard N. Wolf, "Size and Profitability among U.S. Manufacturing Firms: Multinational versus Primarily Domestic Firms," *Journal of Economics and Business*, Fall 1975, pp. 15–22.

14. J. J. Servan-Schreiber, *The American Challenge*, London: Hamish Hamilton, 1968.

15. Raymond Vernon, International Investment and International Trade in the Product Cycle," *Quarterly Journal of Economics*, May 1966, pp. 190–207.

16. W. Gruber, D. Mehta, and R. Vernon, "The R & D Factor in International Trade and International Investment of United States Industries," *Journal of Political Economy*, February 1967, pp. 20–37. Also see Se'ev Hirsch, *Location of Industry and International Competitiveness*, Oxford: Oxford University Press, 1967; S. Hirsch, "Multinationals: How Different Are They?" in G. Y. Bertin, ed., *The Growth of*

the Large Multinational Corporation, Paris: Centre Nationale de la Recherche Scientifique, 1973.

17. *Op cit.*, Caves, "International Corporations."

18. *Op cit.*, Vernon, "International Investment"; Gruber, Mehta, and Vernon, "R & D Factor in International Trade."

19. Richard W. Moxon, "The Motivation for Investment in Offshore Plants: The Case of the U.S. Electronics Industry," *Journal of International Business Studies*, Spring 1975, pp. 51–66. Also see Richard W. Moxon, "Offshore Production in the Less-Developed Countries: A Case Study of Multinationality in the Electronics Industry," *The Bulletin*, nos. 98 and 99, New York University, July 1974, pp. 1–90.

20. A good synthesis of oligopoly theory and its relation to multinational firms can be found in Fred T. Knickerbocker, *Oligopolistic Reaction and the Multinational Enterprise*, Boston: Harvard Graduate School of Business Administration, 1973.

21. This information came from a close working relationship between one of the authors and officials of the firm.

22. For studies of the "growth" version of international oligopoly theory, see Bela Belassa, "American

Direct Investment in the Common Market," Banca Nazionale del Lavoro, *Quarterly Review*, June 1966, pp. 121–146. Also see Stephen Hymer and Robert Rowthorn, "Multinational Corporations and International Oligopoly: The Non-American Challenge," in Charles P. Kindleberger, ed., *The International Corporation: A Symposium*, Cambridge, Mass.: MIT Press, 1970, pp. 57–91.

23. *Op cit.*, Buckley and Casson, *Future of the Multinational Enterprise*; and Dunning, "Trade Location."

24. Alan Rugman, "Internalization as a General Theory of Foreign Direct Investment: A Re-Appraisal of the Literature," *Weltwirtschaftliches Archiv*, vol. 116, no. 2, June 1980, pp. 368–369.

25. See all of the John Dunning bibliographical citations.

26. Joel A Bleeke, James Isono, David Ernst, and Douglas D. Weinberg, "The Shape of Cross-Border M & A," *The McKinsey Quarterly*, Spring 1990, pp. 15–26.

27. The best description of the *corporate wealth maximization model* from a financial perspective can be found in: Gordon Donaldson, *Managing Corporate Wealth: The Operation of a Comprehensive Financial Goal System*, New York: Praeger, 1984.

BIBLIOGRAPHY

Aharoni, Yair, *The Foreign Investment Decision Process*, Boston: Harvard Graduate School of Business Administration, Division of Research, 1966.

Akhter, Seyed H., and Robert F. Lusch, "Environmental Determinants of U.S. Foreign Direct Investment in Developed and Developing Countries: A Structural Analysis," *The International Trade Journal*, vol. V, no. 3, Spring 1991, pp. 329–360.

Anderson, Erin, and Hubert Gatignon, "Modes of Foreign Entry: A Transaction Cost Analysis and Propositions," *Journal of International Business Studies*, Fall 1986, pp. 1–26.

Arpan, Jeffrey S., and David A. Ricks, "Foreign Direct Investment in the U.S., 1974–1984,"

Journal of International Business Studies, Fall 1986, pp. 149–154.

Beamish, Paul W., and John C. Banks, "Equity Joint Ventures and the Theory of the Multinational Enterprise," *Journal of International Business Studies*, Summer 1987, pp. 1–16.

BenDaniel, David J., and Arthur H. Rosenbloom, *The Handbook of International Mergers & Acquisitions*, Englewood Cliffs, NJ: Prentice-Hall, 1990.

Bleeke, Joel A., James Isono, David Ernst, and Douglas D. Weinberg, "The Shape of Cross-Border M&A," *The McKinsey Quarterly*, Spring 1990, pp. 15–26.

Buckley, Peter J., "The Limits of Explanation: Testing the Internalization Theory of the Multinational

Enterprise," *Journal of International Business Studies*, Summer 1988, pp. 181–193.

Casson, Mark, *The Firm and the Market: Studies on Multinational Enterprises and the Scope of the Firm*, Cambridge, Mass.: MIT Press, 1987.

Choi, Jongmoo Jay, "Diversification, Exchange Risk, and Corporate International Investment," *Journal of International Business Studies*, Spring 1989, pp. 145–155.

Contractor, Farok J., "Ownership Patterns of U.S. Joint Ventures Abroad and the Liberalization of Foreign Government Regulations in the 1980s: Evidence from the Benchmark Surveys," *Journal of International Business Studies*, First Quarter 1990, pp. 55–73.

Davidson, William H., "The Location of Foreign Direct Investment Activity: Country Characteristics and Experience Effects," *Journal of International Business Studies*, Fall 1980, pp. 9–22.

Doukas, John, and Nicholas G. Travlos, "The Effect of Corporate Multinationalism on Shareholders' Wealth: Evidence from International Acquisitions," *Journal of Finance*, December 1988, pp. 1161–1175.

Dunning, John H., *Explaining International Production*, Winchester, Mass.: Unwin Hyman, 1988.

——, "The Eclectic Paradigm of International Production: A Restatement and Some Possible Extensions," *Journal of International Business Studies*, Spring 1988, pp. 1–32.

——, ed., *Multinational Enterprises, Economic Structure, and International Competitiveness*, New York: Wiley, 1985.

——, and Alan M. Rugman, "The Influence of Hymer's Dissertation on the Theory of Foreign Direct Investment," *American Economic Review*, May 1985, pp. 228–232.

Ehrman, Chaim Meyer, and Morris Hamburg, "Information Search for Foreign Direct Investment Using Two-Stage Country Selection Procedures: A New Procedure," *Journal of International Business Studies*, Summer 1986, pp. 93–116.

Franko, Lawrence G., "Use of Minority and 50-50 Joint Ventures by United States Multinationals

During the 1970s: The Interaction of Host Country Policies and Corporate Strategies," *Journal of International Business Studies*, Spring 1989, pp. 19–40.

Geringer, J. Michael, and Louis Hebert, "Control and Performance of International Joint Ventures," *Journal of International Business Studies*, Summer 1989, pp. 235–254.

Ghertman, Michel, "Foreign Subsidiary and Parents' Roles During Strategic Investment and Divestment Decisions," *Journal of International Business Studies*, Spring 1988, pp. 47–68.

Giddy, Ian H., "The Demise of the Product Cycle Model in International Business Theory," *Columbia Journal of World Business*, Spring 1978, pp. 90–97.

Gomes-Casseres, Benjamin, "Firm Ownership Preferences and Host Government Restrictions: An Integrated Approach," *Journal of International Business Studies*, First Quarter 1990, pp. 1–22.

Gordon, Sara L., and Francis A. Lees, *Foreign Multinational Investment in the United States: Struggle for Industrial Supremacy*, Westport, Conn.: Quorum Books, 1986.

Grosse, Robert, "The Theory of Foreign Direct Investment," *Essays in International Business*, Columbia: University of South Carolina, Center for International Business Studies, December 1981.

Guisinger, Stephen, "Total Protection: A New Measure of the Impact of Government Intervention on Investment Profitability," *Journal of International Business Studies*, Summer 1989, pp. 280–295.

Hanink, Dean M., "A Mean-Variance Model of MNF Location Strategy," *Journal of International Business Studies*, Spring 1985, pp. 165–170.

Hennart, Jean-Francois, "Internalization in Practice: Early Foreign Direct Investment in Malaysian Tin Mining," *Journal of International Business Studies*, Summer 1986, pp. 131–144.

——, "Can the 'New Forms of Investment' Substitute for the 'Old Forms?' A Transaction Costs Perspective," *Journal of International Business Studies*, Summer 1989, pp. 211–234.

Hisey, Karen B., and Richard E. Caves, "Diversification Strategy and Choice of Country: Diversifying Acquisitions Abroad by U.S. Multinationals, 1978–1980," *Journal of International Business Studies*, Summer 1985, pp. 51–64.

Horaguchi, Haruo, and Brian Toyne, "Setting the Record Straight: Hymer, Internalization Theory and Transaction Cost Economics," *Journal of International Business Studies*, Third Quarter 1990, pp. 487–494.

Hymer, Stephen H., *The International Operations of National Firms: A Study of Direct Foreign Investment*, Cambridge, Mass.: MIT Press, 1976.

Kim, Wi Saeng, and Esmeralda O. Lyn, "Foreign Direct Investment Theories, Entry Barriers, and Reverse Investments in U.S. Manufacturing Industries," *Journal of International Business Studies*, Summer 1987, pp. 53–66.

——, "FDI Theories and the Performance of Foreign Multinationals Operating in the U.S.," *Journal of International Business Studies*, First Quarter 1990, pp. 41–54.

Kimura, Yui, "Firm-Specific Strategic Advantages and Foreign Direct Investment Behavior of Firms: The Case of Japanese Semiconductor Firms," *Journal of International Business Studies*, Summer 1989, pp. 296–314.

Kobrin, Stephen J., and Donald R. Lessard, "Large Scale Direct OPEC Investment in Industrialized Countries and the Theory of Foreign Direct Investment—A Contradiction," *Weltwirtschaftliches Archiv*, December 1976, pp. 660–673.

Kogut, Bruce, and Harbir Singh, "The Effect of National Culture on the Choice of Entry Mode," *Journal of International Business Studies*, Fall 1988, pp. 411–432.

Mascarenhas, Briance, "International Strategies of Non-Dominant Firms," *Journal of International Business Studies*, Spring 1986, pp. 1–26.

Moxon, Richard W., "The Motivation for Investment in Offshore Plants: The Case of the U.S. Electronic Industry," *Journal of International Business Studies*, Spring 1975, pp. 51–66.

Murray, Alan I. and Carne Siehl, *Joint Ventures and Other Alliances: Creating a Successful Cooperative Linkage*, New York: Financial Executive Research Foundation, 1989.

Nigh, Douglas, "The Effect of Political Events on United States Direct Foreign Investment: A Pooled Time-Series Cross-Sectional Analysis," *Journal of International Business Studies*, Spring 1985, pp. 1–17.

Ravichandran, R., and J. Michael Pinegar, "Risk Shifting in International Licensing Agreements: A Note," *Journal of International Financial Management and Accounting*, vol. 2, nos. 2 and 3, Summer and Autumn 1990, pp. 181–195.

Robinson, Richard D., ed., *Direct Foreign Investment: Costs and Beneftis*, New York: Praeger Publishers, 1987.

Rugman, Alan M., "Internalization as a General Theory of Foreign Direct Investment: A Re-Appraisal of the Literature," *Weltwirtschaftliches Archiv*, 116, no. 2, 1980, pp. 365–379.

——, "Internalizational Theory and Corporate International Finance," *California Management Review*, Winter 1980, pp. 73–79.

——, "Internalization Is Still a General Theory of Foreign Direct Investment," *Weltwirtschaftliches Archiv*, September 1985.

Salehizadeh, Mehdi, "Regulation of Foreign Direct Investment by Host Countries," *Essays in International Business*, Columbia: University of South Carolina, Center for International Business Studies, May 1983.

Sleuwaegen, Leo, "Monopolistic Advantages and the International Operations of Firms: Disaggregated Evidence from U.S. Based Multinationals," *Journal of International Business Studies*, Fall 1985, pp. 125–134.

Swamidass, Paul M., "A Comparison of the Plant Location Strategies of Foreign and Domestic Manufacturers in the U.S.," *Journal of International Business Studies*, Second Quarter 1990, pp. 301–317.

Tallman, Stephen B., "Home Country Political Risk and Foreign Direct Investment in the United States," *Journal of International Business Studies*, Summer 1988, pp. 219–234.

Terpstra, Vern, and Chwo-Ming Yu, "Determinants of Foreign Investment of U.S. Advertising Agencies," *Journal of International Business Studies*, Spring 1988, pp. 33–46.

Vernon, Raymond, "International Investment and International Trade in the Product Cycle," *Quarterly Journal of Economics*, May 1966, pp. 190–207.

——, "The Product Cycle Hypothesis in a New International Environment," *Oxford Bulletin of Economics and Statistics*, 41, 1979, pp. 255–267.

Wilson, Brent D., "The Propensity of Multinational Companies to Expand Through Acquisitions," *Journal of International Business Studies*, Spring–Summer 1980, pp. 59–65.

Wright, Mike, and Ken Robbie, "Corporate Restructuring, Buy-Outs, and Managerial Equity: The European Dimension," *Journal of Applied Corporate Finance*, vol. 3, no. 4, Winter 1991, pp. 46–58.

Yang, Ho C., James W. Wansley, and William R. Lane, "A Direct Test of the Diversification Service Hypothesis of Foreign Direct Investment," *Advances in Financial Planning and Forecasting*, vol. 4, part A, 1990, pp. 215–238.

Yu, Chwo-Ming J., and Kiyohiko Ito, "Oligopolistic Reaction and Foreign Direct Investment: The Case of the U.S. Tire and Textiles Industries," *Journal of International Business Studies*, Fall 1988, pp. 449–460.

16 Political Risk Management

Multinational firms are influenced by political events within host countries and by changes in political relationship between host countries, home countries, and even third countries. The possibility of such events occurring and having an influence on the economic well-being of the parent firm is called *political risk*. Conceptually the effect on the parent firm can be either positive or negative, although in practice managerial attention usually focuses on possible negative events.

Political risk management refers to steps taken by firms to assess the likelihood of unexpected political events, to anticipate how such events might influence corporate well-being, and to protect against loss (or to attempt to gain) from such events.

Stephen Kobrin points out that multinational firms face a broad range of political and economic risks that can usefully be viewed along two dimensions. The first dimension distinguishes between *country-specific*, or macro, risks which affect all foreign firms in a country without regard to how they are organized; and *firm-specific*, or micro, risks which are specific to an industry, a firm, or a project.[1] Country-specific risk is of most concern to international bankers, who often set overall loan limits to specific countries based on their perception of country risk.[2] Firm-specific risk is of greater concern for multinational firms.

Kobrin's second dimension distinguishes between those political events that affect *ownership of assets*, such as requiring full or partial divestment; and those that affect the *operations of a firm* and thus its cash flows and returns.

Kobrin argues that most political risk problems of multinational firms involve firm specific risks, and involve operations rather than ownership. Consequently political risk seldom leads to violence or a major discontinuity in the firm's operations. Most often politically inspired changes involve constraints, such as restrictions on the free setting of prices, limitations on the use of expatriate executives or workers, or local content regulations for manufactured goods.[3]

GOAL CONFLICT AS THE ROOT CAUSE OF POLITICAL RISK

To the casual observer old enough to remember the post World War II era, "political risk" brings to mind the abrupt expropriations of both domestic and foreign private businesses in Eastern Europe and China as those territories came under Communist control. Similar expropriations occurred in Cuba in 1960 after Fidel Castro imposed a Communist government, and in Iran following the 1979 ouster of the Shah by the Ayatollah Khomeini. Other examples also date from decades ago: Chile expropriated a number of U.S. companies, including several U.S. copper companies in 1971. Peru took over a subsidiary of Exxon in 1968. Libya expropriated Occidental Petroleum's oil fields in 1969.

Expropriation is defined as official government seizure of private property. It is recognized by international law as the right of any sovereign state, provided the expropriated owners are given *prompt* compensation at *fair market value* in *convertible currencies*. Therein lies the rub, for promptness is usually delayed by extensive negotiations and appeals. Fair market value is in the eyes of the beholder, with firms arguing for "going concern" value and governments arguing for depreciated historical book value. Convertible currencies are often in short supply to the government.

Expropriation is a macro risk as defined earlier, and has not been a major problem for multinational businesses in recent decades.

Contemporary political risk is more often micro, and arises from a conflict of bona fide objectives between governments and private firms. Governments that are good, informed, and honest try to serve a constituency consisting of their citizens. Firms acting ethically are responsible to a constituency consisting of their owners, employees, suppliers, creditors, customers, and potential customers. The valid needs of these two separate sets of constituents need not be the same, but it is governments that set the rules. Consequently, governments impose constraints on the activities of private firms as part of their normal administrative and legislative functioning.

A separate type of political risk arises when governments are unsure of their status or survival. This is the situation in the Soviet Union and the former Communist countries of Eastern Europe at the present time. It is also present in post-Tiananmen China. When the basic nature of governance is changing rapidly, a firm cannot be sure which governmental representative speaks (or will be speaking next year) for the host country. The conflict reduces to goal conflicts between domestic political forces, with the multinational firm being a bystander to the process. This present type of risk in ex-Communist (and "reformed Communist") countries will be discussed later.

GOAL CONFLICTS BETWEEN MULTINATIONAL FIRMS AND HOST GOVERNMENTS

Historically, conflicts between objectives of multinational firms and host governments have arisen over such issues as the firm's impact on economic development, perceived infringement on national sovereignty, foreign control of key industries, sharing or nonsharing of ownership and control with local interests, impact on a host country's balance of payments, influence on the foreign exchange value of its currency, control over export markets, use of domestic versus foreign executives and workers, and "exploitation" of natural resources. Attitudes about conflicts are often colored by views toward free enterprise versus state socialism, the degree of nationalism or internationalism present, or the place of religious views in determining appropriate economic and financial behavior.

From the viewpoint of the multinational firm, all national economic, political, social, cultural, and ideological goals—as well as the policy instruments to accomplish them—are parameters that circumscribe the firm's activities. It is unfortunate for the multinational firm that often government policies are unclear, or that two or more policies seem to be contradictory. Such ambiguity exists because ordering and implementing national priorities is not a science. Multinational firms must learn to live with such ambiguity. The important thing to remember is that they must be able to *anticipate* and *adapt* to changing national priorities and the resulting changes in the policy instruments.

Even when multinational firms succeed in adapting to host-country priorities, host-country governments may still feel ambivalent toward them. There is no consensus as to what constitutes favorable or unfavorable performance by multinational firms with respect to national goals. Some economically oriented studies, for example, show a favorable quantitative impact of foreign-owned firms on such host-country economic goals as growth, employment, price stability, and balance of payments. Such views may also be popular, as they are at the present time in countries recently freed from Communism. Or they may be unpopular, as befits contrary economic ideologies, a view which is also supported by other economic studies. No complete methodology has been developed which quantifies the impact foreign-owned firms have on a host country's less tangible political, social, cultural, and ideological goals.

An attempt at understanding can be obtained by looking first at potential goal conflicts between the multinational firm and government economic policies and then at the multinational firm's impact on government non-economic policies.

Goal Conflicts with Government Economic Policies

Although national economic priorities vary, most countries wish to have a sustainable rate of growth in per capita GNP and income, full employment, price stability, balance in their external accounts, and a fair distribution of income. Operations of multinational firms sometimes interfere with the smooth functioning of policy instruments chosen by the government to attain these ends. Major areas where conflict may arise include the following:

1. Monetary policy.
2. Fiscal policy.
3. Balance of payments and exchange rate policy.
4. Economic protectionism.
5. Economic development policies.

Monetary Policy. Most governments attempt to control the cost and availability of domestic credit and long-term capital as a means of achieving the national economic priorities listed above. Affiliates of multinational firms in such a country are subject to these same monetary and credit constraints. However, they can often circumvent the spirit of such financial constraints, even when complying with the letter of the law. For example, if local credit becomes too expensive or unavailable because of purposeful national monetary policy, the affiliate may turn to its parent or to sister affiliates for additional capital. Thus the affiliate is able to implement its spending plans while local, often smaller, competitors are restricted because of a lack of access to external capital.

National monetary policy is also frustrated when multinational firms suddenly convert large amounts of foreign exchange into local currency to buy out a local company or carry out a large new investment. Multinationals may also hold excess working capital or speculative funds temporarily while riding out a foreign exchange crisis in one or more other countries (so called hot money flows.) These activities create an instant increase in the local money supply, which has to be offset by central bank open market or other operations. Hence multinational firm activities may be viewed as frustrating national monetary policy.

Fiscal Policy. Operations of multinational firms may influence government revenues and government expenses. On the revenue side, tax concessions used to lure the firm to that country mean that the government fails to receive revenue which it might later need. Recognizing that such a concession is the fault of the government which granted it, a succeeding administration may regret the actions of its predecessors and invalidate previous agreements. On the expenditure side, greenfield investments by multinational firms may create a need for governmental spending on new roads or railroads, public utilities, housing, schools, and health facilities. The government may lack the revenue to provide these. When a multinational firm provides them a dependency relationship is established, and the foreign firm may be accused of paternalism or economic imperialism.

Balance of Payments and Exchange Rate Policies. Because of balance of payment or exchange-rate problems, governments often promulgate regulations which hamper the operations of all firms. Latin American countries, in particular, have resorted to frequent devaluations, use of multiple exchange rates for different categories of imports and exports, licensing of imports, import deposit requirements, demands for extended credit terms to finance imports, and refinancing outstanding debt with loans from foreign lenders where possible. Exchange control, including inconvertibility of currency, can be particularly damaging to multinational firms because local inflation typically diminishes the value of blocked funds. Nevertheless, multinational firms must understand both the causes and likely policy responses to a host country's balance of payments deficit or strong pressure on its currency.

Economic Protectionism. National economic policy constraints are often motivated by protectionism, sometimes under the guise of balance of payments policies and sometimes under the guise of economic development. Negotiations under the General Agreement on Tariffs and Trade (GATT) have reduced the general level of tariffs during the past three decades, but nontariff barriers remain. Nontariff barriers, which restrict imports by something other than a financial cost, are often difficult to identify because they are promulgated as health, safety, or sanitation requirements. A list of the major types of nontariff barriers is shown in Exhibit 16.1.

Specific examples of nontariff barriers include Japan's ruling that certain imports of canned goods were unacceptable because the figures for the day, month, and year of canning were spaced too far apart on the labels. The French regard their ban on whiskey advertisements as a social regulation, not a deterrent to sales of imports. The United States has long excluded fresh Argentine beef because of hoof-and-mouth disease in that country, although most European countries have not found a similar exclusion necessary. However, in January 1989 the EEC banned imports of meat produced with the aid of growth hormones, a move that excluded U.S. meat imports.

The GATT agreements have generally been ineffective in dealing with nonmerchandise trade, such as patents, copyrights, consulting, legal services, and accounting. These are areas in which the United States may have a comparative advantage.

Examples of nontariff barriers used by the U.S. government include "persuasion" of foreign countries to "voluntarily" impose quotas on their exports to the United States of such items as cotton shirts, steel, television sets, shoes, and automobiles. The same types of quotas exist in Western Europe.

Economic Development Policies. Protection of "infant industries" has often been advanced as a defensible argument for a protective tariff or restriction on foreign investment, even though many industries are protected long after they have matured. Examples include requirements in India, Mexico, Brazil, and Argentina that multinational firms manufacture an increasing proportion of components locally rather than assemble imported components with a minimum of local manufacture. Automobile firms are particularly vulnerable to such rules. Other restrictive rules require local ownership in joint ventures rather than 100% foreign ownership. Similar requirements specify mostly local rather than expatriate managers. While such requirements have some merit in the context of goal-driven governmental policies, they often inhibit a multinational firm from rationalizing production on a worldwide basis, and thus from lowering costs and sales prices to consumers.

Exhibit 16.1   Types of Nontariff Barriers

1. Specific limitations on trade, which either limit the amount of imports directly or establish import procedures that make importing more difficult.

    a) Quotas, which limit the quantity or value allowed for specific imported products for specific time periods.
    b) Licensing requirements that must be met before trading.
    c) Proportion restrictions of foreign to domestic goods or content.
    d) Minimum import price limits set equal to or above domestic prices.
    e) Embargoes prohibiting products originating in specific countries.

2. Customs and administrative entry procedures, which include inconsistent procedures for valuation, classification of documents, or assessing fees.

    a) Valuation of imports on an arbitrary basis at the discretion of customs officials.
    b) Antidumping countermeasures against imported goods sold below prices in the home market of the exporter.
    c) Tariff classifications that are inconsistent.
    d) Documentation requirements that are overburdensome.
    e) Fees charged to cover costs of entry procedures.

3. Unduly stringent or discriminating standards imposed in the name of protecting health, safety, and quality.

    a) Disparities between quality standards required by different countries.
    b) Differing intergovernmental acceptance standards or testing methods.
    c) Application of packaging and labeling standards in unduly stringent or discriminating ways.

4. Governmental participation in trade.

    a) Government procurement policies that favor domestic over imported products without regard to relative price and quality.
    b) Export subsidies, either directly or via taxes or export credit terms, provided by government.
    c) Countervailing duties charged by importing country to offset export subsidies granted by exporting country.
    d) Domestic assistance programs granted all domestic producers, both exporters and those producing for domestic consumption.

5. Charges on imports.

    a) Prior import deposit requirements, requiring a non-interest-bearing deposit equal to some percentage of import value (sometimes up to 100%) to be deposited prior to time of import and refunded at a later date. The "cost" is equal to the cost of capital on the funds so tied up.
    b) Border tax adjustments, in which border taxes are levied on imports to tax them in the same manner as domestic goods and are rebated on exports. Countries relying on indirect taxes (such as the value-added taxes used in Europe) are given an advantage over countries relying on direct taxes (such as corporate income taxes), since indirect taxes can be rebated but direct taxes cannot be rebated.
    c) Administrative fees levied.
    d) Special supplementary duties levied.
    e) Import credit discrimination.
    f) Variable levies.

6. Other nontariff barriers.

    a) Voluntary export restraints by exporting country, often at the request (with or without political pressure) of the importing country.
    b) Orderly marketing agreements, wherein countries agree formally to restrict trade.

Source: Adapted from material in A.D. Cao, "Non-tariff Barriers to U.S. Manufactured Exports," *Columbia Journal of World Business,* Summer 1980, pp. 93–102.

Although direct foreign investment has often been heralded as contributing to economic development and is eagerly sought by many developing countries, the very fulfillment of its promise has often unintentionally created a "dual economy." Local citizens associated with the foreign firms, either as employees or suppliers, have prospered and advanced economically to become an elite class. Other citizens, untouched by the foreign firms or industry sector being developed, are left in their original state of poverty. Thus a two-class society is created, causing its own problems of internal dissension, jealousy, greed, and graft. The early plantation, oil, and mining investments were often the inadvertent victims of their own success, having been blamed for creating these dual economies.

Goal Conflicts with Government Noneconomic Policies

Even when all political groups within a host country agree that direct foreign investment is good for the country, some may oppose it on non-economic grounds. The most common non-economic arguments against multinational firms are the following:

1. Economic imperialism.
2. National security and foreign policy.
3. Private enterprise inconsistent with a social transition.
4. Incompatibility with host-country religion or cultural heritage.

Economic Imperialism. In many ex-colonial countries a widespread suspicion exists that multinational firms represent a new and invidious form of imperialism, albeit economic rather than political or military. These countries often fail to differentiate between profit-motivated private foreign enterprises and the home governments of such firms—a failure helped greatly when home governments seek a ban on foreign investments in politically unpopular countries. U.S. Congressional pressure against investment in China after the Tiananmen Square massacre in June, 1989, gave credence to ideas that private firms are, after all, under the thumb of their home governments. It is not yet clear in the ideology of free enterprise at what point, short of war, a government should override the economic independence of its own multinational businesses.

It seems obvious to most U.S. citizens that the U.S. government and business do not cooperate closely on direct foreign investments. In fact, much U.S. political activity seems predicated on government and popular distrust of business and so suggests the opposite. However other governments, such as Japan, actively support and encourage their own multinational firms, seeing such policies as necessary for a strong economy.

National Security and Foreign Policy. Host countries sometimes become alarmed that foreign control of key industry sectors will impair national security or an independent foreign policy. One need only read Servan-Schreiber, *The American Challenge*, to perceive the French attitude of a quarter century ago toward U.S. dominance of the French computer, electronics, and other defense-related industries.[4] Canada screens and controls new direct foreign investments because of its concern that more than half of

Canadian manufacturing and mining is U.S.-owned, including most of the growth sectors and those related to national security. Japan excludes foreign rice and certain other foodstuffs as part of a policy of remaining self-sufficient in food, even though at an inordinately high cost to consumers. The United States blocked the Japanese purchase of Fairchild Industries in 1987 on grounds of national security.

Social Transition. The most dramatic conflicts between foreign investors and host governments have occurred during periods of social transition in the host country. Examples are Russia after World War I, the Eastern European countries and China after World War II, Cuba in 1959, Libya in 1969, Chile in 1971, and Iran in 1979. At these times private enterprises, including many large ones that were foreign owned, were expropriated.

The years 1989 and 1990 marked the beginning of another major social transition, the recognized failure of Communism as an economic system within the Soviet Union, the overthrow of Communist leaders in the Eastern European countries, and the use of force in China to preserve Communist Party power. The unique risks and opportunities associated with this social transition will be discussed later.

Religious and Cultural Heritage. In some cases the Judeo-Christian religious and cultural heritages of many multinational firms conflict with the traditions of the host countries. In the Middle East, for example, oil company executives and technicians bring with them a liberal outlook toward women in business and toward consumption of alcohol that is in direct contrast to the teaching of Islam. Western acceptance of women as executives, and their assignment to positions of responsibility involving negotiations and decision making in the Middle East, Asia, and Africa, often conflict with established local mores. Therefore these countries fear close contact with Western ideas. The presence in 1991 of large numbers of U.S. and other Western troops in the Persian Gulf area, including women military personnel, compounded local concern that contact with the West will undermine the area's cultural heritage.

Religion and culture also create personal risks for business executives. During the 1980s foreign business executives in Argentina and other Latin American countries were kidnapped and held for ransom. The decade began, in fact, with Iran's holding of U.S. diplomats as hostages for over one year. On a larger scale, Saddam Hussein held thousands of foreigners, both ordinary workers and executives, from countries as diverse as the United States and Sri Lanka, as human shield hostages in Iraq in 1990. This will cast a shadow on the political risk of doing business in that part of the world in the future.

EVENTS IN EASTERN EUROPE, THE SOVIET UNION, AND CHINA

During the 1980s it became evident that Communism was an economic failure. Even though generally imprisoned within their own national borders, residents of the Communist countries realized ever more clearly that they were poor and were getting poorer relative to the non-Communist world. Pressure for reform mounted.

Reform evolved in several ways. China began first, late in the 1970s, allowing economic freedom for agriculture and small business entities. By the mid-1980s it had opened its borders for foreign businesses and tourists alike, and had started sending thousands of students to the United States and other Western countries. China's approach was primarily economic, with minimal change in the centralized political system and no intention by Communist party leaders of relinquishing their absolute authority or perquisites. Major economic improvements followed, but they led, inevitably, to demands for freedom of press and the political right to debate changes in national policy. Large demonstrations in Tiananmen Square, Beijing, and smaller demonstrations in other cities led eventually to the Beijing massacre of June 1989, in which the People's Liberation Army brutally reasserted the absolute power of Communist rulers. It is generally believed that thousands were killed. These events, witnessed by bystanders and through worldwide television coverage, further damaged the credibility of the government. China became a less attractive place in which to invest when compared with other countries.

Tiananmen was followed, within a few months, by a rush of people escaping from Eastern Europe, and shortly thereafter by the fall of the Communist governments of Poland, East Germany, Czechoslovakia, Bulgaria, Romania, and Hungary. The wall dividing East and West Berlin, long a symbol of Communist repression, was torn down block by block. In October 1990, the former East German Democratic People's Republic was incorporated into West Germany. These Eastern European countries adopted policies of actively seeking direct foreign investment by multinational firms. Unlike China, economic reform followed the political liberation achieved by ousting Communist regimes installed and supported by the Soviet Union.

During these same years, the Soviet Union moved strongly toward political reform under the *glasnost* (political reform) policies of President Mikhail S. Gorbachev. Political reform preceded most economic reform (*perestroika*). The various republics that make up the Soviet Union began to demand independence or a greater degree of self-determination. By 1990 it was evident that the economy of the Soviet Union was in ruins. Within the Soviet Union a debate raged over the speed with which the economy should move to free markets as a way to restore economic health. Western direct foreign investment was actively sought.

In all three areas, economic opportunities now exist for multinational firms. The abusive rhetoric of the prior 40 years died almost overnight. Investment by multinational firms and increased trade with the West are now seen as the preferred route to economic improvement. The attitude of Western firms ranges from euphoria over the possibilities for new markets to culture shock at the dismal state of existing manufacturing practices in Eastern Europe.[5]

Unfortunately, the people of these countries desire almost instantaneous prosperity. However, four and a half decades of lagging behind the West cannot be overcome quickly. The tide of rising expectations in China, Eastern Europe, and the Soviet Union may well outrun any realistic rate of economic improvement. This is not dissimilar to what has happened in the poorer countries of Africa and Latin America.

In possession of new-but-inexperienced political freedom, the people of these countries may not allow any government sufficient time or power to effect genuine reform. Thus a risk exists that these countries will suddenly revert to dictatorial governments of the left or right because the pace of economic development under democracy is perceived as being too slow.

Rather than goal conflict in the traditional sense, then, a new type of political risk arises because political governance of these areas is in turmoil. Democratic institutions are immature and inexperienced. Many new leaders still have questionable backgrounds. Any agreement reached with a particular set of leaders may turn out to have been negotiated with the wrong group.

For example, should one negotiate an agreement with the central government of the Soviet Union, as in times past, or with the separate governments of the 15 individual republics, such as Russia, Ukraine, Azerbaijan, Lithuania, Estonia, or Tadjikstan? Some companies, such as Chevron, are reported to be conducting parallel negotiations with local authorities to ensure they at least have the permission of the correct entity.[6] Moscow's two Pizza Huts were shut down for 18 hours while local officials argued over whether the U.S. franchise should report to the Moscow city council or some other governmental body.[7]

In Eastern Europe, will agreements of the present governments of, say, Poland or Czechoslovakia be honored by succeeding governments if democratic political systems become more functional, political leaders more experienced, and consumers more patient? In short, the new political risk is of political instability internal to countries which as a matter of national policy and general consensus now actively seek Western investment. The risk is now of being caught in the middle of groups contesting who has authority.

CORRUPTION

Although most political risk falls under the heading of goal conflict between multinational firm and host government, political corruption and blackmail is also a risk contributor.

A 1989 political scandal in Venezuela arose because foreign corporations had legally transmitted funds out of the country through a government agency, Recadi, created to administer Venezuela's complex foreign exchange regulations. The agency was abolished early in 1989 by the new Venezuelan president, and an investigation started over alleged corruption. At the beginning of the investigation, arrest warrants were issued for some 47 foreign executives, and 60 others were ordered not to leave the country. About 100 top executives from major multinational firms were reported to have fled the country, not because they considered themselves guilty, but because they could end up in prison, without bail, for a very long time, while claims against their firm were investigated.[8]

Firestone Tire and Rubber Company was reported to have sold all but 19% of its 70% interest in a Kenya factory after experiencing a prolonged period of delays in obtaining licenses to import critical raw materials, nonapproval of work permits for expatriate technicians, nonapproval of requests for price increases, and delays in approval of plans for plant expansion. The sale was to a holding company with ties to Kenya's president, after which the company's problems disappeared. Almost half of U.S.-owned companies in Kenya are reported to have reduced their equities to as little as 14% by selling out to Kenyans with powerful political connections.[9]

GOVERNMENT REGULATIONS THAT MAY CONFLICT WITH THE OPERATIONS OF MULTINATIONAL FIRMS

In the pursuit of national goals, host governments often adopt laws and administrative rules which restrict operations of business firms in their jurisdictions. Sometimes inadvertently and sometimes by intent such rules may be particularly burdensome to multinational firms. Regulations with the most potential for conflict can be classified as nondiscriminatory, discriminatory, and wealth depriving.

Nondiscriminatory Regulation

Nondiscriminatory regulations are usually mild and not particularly directed against foreign-controlled operations. Often they have an equal impact on foreign subsidiaries, joint ventures, local firms with management or licensing agreements with foreign firms, and purely domestic firms. Some examples of nondiscriminatory regulations are the following:

- Requiring that local nationals hold top management positions or seats on boards of directors.
- Establishing rules for transfer pricing that favor the host country's tax base.
- Requiring export industries to sell in the home market at a breakeven price in order to subsidize local consumption of the particular product. (A common example is pharmaceutical firms.)
- Requiring construction of social overhead facilities (schools, workers' housing and health care facilities, roads) by the investing firm.
- Requiring a given percentage of local content in manufactured goods.
- Allocating all foreign exchange to purchases deemed in the national interest, and consequently restricting the availability of foreign exchange for such "nonessential" purposes as dividends or royalty fee payments.

Discriminatory Regulation

Discriminatory regulations give local firms or national groups specific advantages over foreign firms. Often the intent is to protect weaker local firms from local-based foreign competition, much in the way that tariffs protect local firms from import competition. Some examples are:

- Nationalizing an industry dominated by foreigners. In 1988, Brazil's Congress approved a constitutional provision that "exploration and mining of mineral resources and deposits may be carried out only by Brazilians or national companies" with government authorization.[10] The vote, 343 to 126, was reportedly followed by cheers of "Brazil, Brazil, Brazil," and singing of the national anthem by congressmen. Opposing congressmen pointed out that Brazilian businesses did not have the capital required for successful mining and that the provision was "xenophobic" and detrimental to Brazil's development.[11]

- Allowing only joint ventures, with the foreign firms limited to less than 50% ownership. Local control may be required directly, or as a criteria for access to credit from local banks or the right to sell to the local government.

- Requiring special taxes or fees for a foreign firm to operate locally. Foreign firms, for example, may have to pay very high visa fees for expatriate managers, or very high income taxes on expatriates' salaries, which are based on salary levels back home.

- Requiring foreign firms to source labor through a host government agency, and to pay wages and social charges set by the government at a higher level than those required for local firms.

- Encouraging a national boycott of a firm's goods, or encouraging a strike of its workers. The Falklands/Malvinas war between the United Kingdom and Argentina in 1982 led not only to such pressures against British firms in Argentina, but also to pressure against U.S. firms. This example illustrates how firms from a neutral third country (the United States) may experience politically inspired penalties because of their home country's historic ties to one of the belligerents.

Wealth Deprivation by Host Governments

Wealth deprivation involves host government regulations which cause economic loss for foreign firms. That loss may be partial, as when the result is to weaken a foreign firm, or total, as in cases of expropriation. Wealth deprivation may take the form of nationalization of an entire industry or expropriation of a single firm.

Cases of wealth deprivation include the following:

- Enforcing price controls with threats. In 1988 a Brazilian court suspended price controls imposed on Autolatina, a holding company for Ford Motor Company and Volkswagen. The suspension was for the period that the courts were to consider Autolatina's claim that such controls were illegal under Brazilian law. When Ford and Volkswagen raised prices on the day after the price controls were suspended, the Brazilian Ministry of Finance ordered official bank credit cut off to the company, called in tax inspectors to examine Autolatina's books, and threatened to arrest Autolatina officials.[12] The Brazilian court subsequently ordered the government to stop punitive measures against Autolatina, but also rescinded its order suspending the price controls.

- Restricting distribution of products. In late 1986 and in 1987 the Singaporean government imposed severe circulation restrictions on *The Asian Wall Street Journal*, *Time Magazine*, *Asia Week*, and the *Far Eastern Economic Review*. The restrictions were punishment for unfavorable press coverage of the mid-1987 "detentions" (that is, imprisonments) without trial of 22 persons alleged to have organized a Marxist plot to overthrow the government. The government claimed it did not need to prove the allegations in a court of law.[13] Lee Hsien Loong, Singapore's Minister for Trade and Industry, son of the prime minister, and a person widely regarded as the prime minister's eventual successor, stated that "In some cases, restricting the circulation of the journal is a sufficient countermeasure" because it "hurts its sales and advertising revenues, but does not deprive Singaporeans of access to information."[14] In 1990 the *Asian Wall Street Journal* stopped all circulation in Singapore because of the pressure.

- Imposing restrictions on dividends and mandating reinvestment. In 1985, Peruvian police armed with submachine guns seized U.S.-owned Belco Petroleum Company's Lima headquarters. This followed nationalization of the company, taking control of its assets, and freezing of its bank accounts. Peruvian president Alan Garcia claimed that Belco had refused to accept new conditions for required reinvestment of its profits in new exploration and production.[15]

Home-Country Attempts at Wealth Deprivation

Not all attempts at wealth deprivation come from foreign governments. Home-country political action groups, as well as home-country governments, sometimes try to put their own companies in a bind. The United States, in particular, tends toward rules that hurt the international competitiveness of its firms in the interest of emotional politics. Attempts to force U.S. multinationals out of the People's Republic of China after the Tiananmen massacre in 1989 is one example. The key issue is whether U.S. business should be allowed to deal with governments that the United States would like to censor, as compared to the view that a continued presence by U.S. business is likely to be advantageous in the long run.

In 1990 Vietnam Airlines was prevented from buying two European Airbus A310's to upgrade its international services. The purchase was blocked by the United States on the grounds that the engines were manufactured in the United States. Political risk was imposed by the United States on its allies, France and the United Kingdom. Vietnam Airlines subsequently purchased six used Soviet-built Tupulov TU134's.[16]

In 1988 a U.S. grand jury indicted Manuel Noriega, then dictator of Panama, for drug dealings. The U.S. Internal Revenue Service then issued regulations instructing U.S. corporations in Panama that they would receive credit against their U.S. taxes for Panamanian taxes paid only if those taxes were paid to deposed Panamanian President Eric A. Delvalle. The goal was to deny cash to the Noriega regime, but one effect was to put U.S. corporations into the middle of a political squabble.

In 1986 a conservative U.S. political action group spearheaded a drive to force Chevron and Gulf Oil out of Angola. Posters and leaflets were distributed at gasoline stations, carrying such headings as "Wanted, for Supplying $2 Billion-Plus of Aid and Comfort Annually to America's Soviet Enemy in Cuban-Occupied Angola," along with a picture of the chairman of the board of Chevron Corporation. Their intent was to spur U.S.

efforts to overthrow the Angolan government. Their activities coincided with the visit to Washington of Angolan UNITA rebel guerrilla leader Jonas Savimbi.[17]

Chevron's response pointed out that withdrawal from Angola would simply lead to the transfer of Angolan oil production to a non-U.S. oil company, and that the U.S. Government's Export-Import Bank was continuing to advance funds to Chevron and other companies operating in Angola. Earlier the U.S. State Department had justified Chevron's continued operations in Angola on the basis that Angola's long-term economic interests lie with the West and that U.S. business could serve a key role in resolving the Angolan problem.

ASSESSING POLITICAL RISK

How can multinational firms anticipate government regulations which, from the firm's perspective, are discriminatory or wealth depriving? Normally a twofold approach is utilized.

At the macro level, firms attempt to assess a host country's political stability and attitude toward foreign investors. At the micro level, firms analyze whether their firm-specific activities are likely to conflict with host-country goals as evidenced by existing regulations. The most difficult task, however, is to anticipate changes in host-country goal priorities, new regulations to implement reordered priorities, and the likely impact of such changes on the firm's operations.

Predicting Political Stability

Macro political risk analysis is still an emerging field of study. Political scientists in academia, industry, and government study country risk for the benefit of multinational firms, government foreign policy decision makers, and defense planners.

Political risk studies usually include an analysis of the historical stability of the country in question, evidence of present turmoil or dissatisfaction, indications of economic stability, and trends in cultural and religious activities. Data is usually assembled by reading local newspapers, monitoring radio and television broadcasts, reading publications from diplomatic sources, tapping the knowledge of outstanding expert consultants, contacting other business persons who have had recent experience in the host country, and finally conducting on-site visits.

Despite this impressive list of activities, the prediction track record of business firms, the diplomatic service, and the military have been spotty at best. When one analyzes trends, whether in politics or economics, one tends to predict an extension of the same trends. It is rare that a forecaster is able to predict a cataclysmic change in direction. For example, who predicted the overthrow of the Shah of Iran and the ascent of a dogmatic theocratic government there? Who predicted the overthrow of Ferdinand Marcos in the Philippines and the emergence of Corazon Aquino to power in 1986? Who predicted the collapse of Communism in Eastern Europe and the turmoil in the Soviet Union in 1990? Finally, who predicted the invasion of Kuwait by Iraq in 1990?

Predicting Firm-Specific Risk

From the viewpoint of a multinational firm, assessing the political stability of a host country is only the first step, since the real objective is to anticipate the effect of political changes on activities of a specific firm. Indeed, different foreign firms operating within the same country may have very different degrees of vulnerability to changes in host-country policy or regulations. One does not expect a Kentucky Fried Chicken franchise to experience the same risk as a Ford manufacturing plant.

The need for firm-specific analyses of political risk has led to a demand for "tailor-made" studies undertaken in-house by professional political risk analysts. This demand is heightened by the observation that outside professional risk analysts rarely even agree on the degree of macro-political risk which exists in any set of countries. For example, *Business Week* compared Businesses International's *Country Assessment Service*, which surveys some 70 countries twice a year, with Frost and Sullivan's *World Political Risk Forecasts*, which surveys about 60 countries every month. These two services were selected because they are among the better known political risk services in the United States. The listings of the ten best political risks and the ten worst political risks in 1980 are shown in Exhibit 16.2. Only five countries (West Germany, Japan, Malaysia, Singapore, and the Netherlands) appear in both lists of the ten best, and only three countries (Iran, Nicaragua, and the Philippines) appear in both lists of the ten worst.

The rankings in Exhibit 16.2 make interesting reading a decade after publication because current readers have the benefit of hindsight in judging their accuracy. In 1980 the Shah of Iran had just been deposed. Fighting in Nicaragua had hardly started. Ferdinand Marcos appeared fully in control of the Philippines. The students who in 1987 were

Exhibit 16.2   Ten Best and Ten Worst Political Risk Countries, 1980, as Ranked by Frost and Sullivan and Business International

Ten Best Political Risks		Ten Worst Political Risks	
Frost and Sullivan	*Business International*	*Frost and Sullivan*	*Business International*
United States	Singapore	El Salvador	Iran
Denmark	Netherlands	Iran	Yugoslavia
Singapore	Norway	Nicaragua	South Korea
Finland	Kuwait	Zaire	Algeria
West Germany	Saudi Arabia	Zambia	Brazil
Austria	Switzerland	Libya	Nicaragua
Canada	West Germany	Bolivia	India
Japan	Britain	Turkey	China
Malaysia	Malaysia	Pakistan	Thailand
Netherlands	Japan	Philippines	Philippines

Source: Business Week, December 1, 1980, p. 69.

demonstrating for democracy in Korea were but little children. Note that *Business International* placed Kuwait on its "Ten Best"!

In-house political risk analysts relate the macro risk attributes of specific countries to the particular characteristics and vulnerabilities of their client firms. Dan Haendel notes that the framework for such analysis depends on such attributes as the ratio of a firm's foreign to domestic investments, the political sensitivity of the particular industry, and the degree of diversification.[18] Mineral extractive firms, manufacturing firms, multinational banks, private insurance carriers, and worldwide hotel chains are all exposed in fundamentally different ways to politically inspired restrictions.

Even with the best possible firm-specific analysis, multinational firms can not be assured that the political or economic situation will not change. Thus it is necessary to plan protective steps in advance to minimize the risk of damage from such potential change.

Possible protective steps can be divided into three categories:

1. Negotiating the environment prior to foreign investment.

2. Establishing operating strategies after the investment is made.

3. Preparing a crisis plan in case the situation deteriorates.

NEGOTIATING THE ENVIRONMENT PRIOR TO INVESTMENT

The best approach to political risk management is to anticipate problems and negotiate understandings beforehand. Different cultures apply different ethics to the question of honoring prior "contracts," especially when they were negotiated with a previous administration. Nevertheless, prenegotiation of all conceivable areas of conflict provides a better basis for a successful economic future for both parties than does overlooking the possibility that divergent objectives will evolve over time.

Negotiating Investment Agreements

An investment agreement spells out specific rights and responsibilities of both the foreign firm and the host government. In the colonial and immediate post-colonial period, such agreements were often called "concession agreements." As the word "concession" suggests, such agreements were often negotiated from unequal bargaining positions. Today the presence of multinational firms is as often sought by development-seeking host governments as a foreign location is sought by a multinational firm. All parties have alternatives and so bargaining is appropriate.

An investment agreement should spell out policies on financial and managerial issues, including the following:

- The basis on which fund flows, such as dividends, management fees, royalties, patent fees, and loan repayments, may be remitted.

- The basis for setting transfer prices.

- The right to export to third-country markets.

- Obligations to build, or fund, social and economic overhead projects, such as schools, hospitals, and retirement systems.

- Methods of taxation, including the rate, the type of taxation, and how the rate base is determined.

- Access to host-country capital markets, particularly for long-term borrowing.

- Permission for 100% foreign ownership versus required local ownership (joint venture) participation.

- Price controls, if any, applicable to sales in the host-country markets.

- Requirements for local sourcing versus import of raw materials and components.

- Permission to use expatriate managerial and technical personnel, and to bring them and their personal possessions into the country free of exorbitant visa charges or import duties.

- Provision for arbitration of disputes.

- Provisions for planned divestment, should such be required, indicating how the going concern will be valued and to whom it will be sold.

Investment Insurance and Guarantees: OPIC

Multinational firms can sometimes transfer political risk to a public agency through an investment insurance and guarantee program. Many developed countries have such programs to protect investments by their nationals in developing countries.

The U.S. investment insurance and guarantee program is managed by the government-owned Overseas Private Investment Corporation (OPIC), organized in 1969 to replace earlier programs. OPIC's stated purpose is to mobilize and facilitate the participation of U.S. private capital and skills in the economic and social progress of less developed friendly countries and areas, thereby complementing the developmental assistance of the United States. However, OPIC is also charged with conducting its operations on a self-sustaining basis, as well as with protecting the interests of U.S. firms abroad.

OPIC operates two main programs: project financing, and insurance of U.S. private investments in less developed countries. Project financing consists of assisting U.S. lenders and business firms in searching out and financing worthwhile projects. OPIC provides: (1) protection against loss from political and commercial risks by arranging for repayment of principal and interest on loans made to eligible borrowers; (2) a direct investment fund that offers dollar financing from OPIC's own resources; and (3) a feasibility study program that assists in the financing of studies to determine the viability of new projects in developing nations. OPIC offers insurance coverage for four separate types of political risk:

- *Inconvertibility* is the risk that the investor will not be able to convert profits, royalties, fees, or other income, as well as the original capital invested, into dollars.

- *Expropriation* is the risk that the host government takes a specific step that for one year prevents the investor or the foreign affiliate from exercising effective control over use of the property.

- *War, revolution, insurrection, and civil strife* coverage applies primarily to the damage of physical property of the insured, although in some cases inability of a foreign affiliate to repay a loan because of a war may be covered.
- *Business income* coverage provides compensation for loss of business income resulting from events of political violence that directly cause damage to the assets of a foreign enterprise.

OPERATING STRATEGIES AFTER THE INVESTMENT DECISION

Although an investment agreement creates obligations on the part of both foreign investor and host government, conditions change and agreements are often revised in the light of such changes. The changed conditions may be economic, or they may be the result of political changes within the host government. The firm that sticks rigidly to the legal interpretation of its original agreement may well find that the host government first applies pressure in areas not covered by the agreement and then possibly reinterprets the agreement to conform to the political reality of that country. Most multinational firms, therefore, follow a policy of adaptation to changing host-country priorities whenever possible, if for no other reason than out of their own self-interest.

The essence of such adaptation is anticipating host-country priorities and making the activities of the firm of continued value to the host country. This assumes the host government acts rationally in seeking its country's self-interest. While large latitude may exist between different views of the country's self-interest, if the government itself is exploiting the country, as did Ferdinand Marcos in the Philippines, then the future of the firm's activities are in doubt no matter how accommodating it tries to be.

Future bargaining position can be enhanced by careful consideration of policies in production and logistics, marketing, finance, organization, and personnel.

Production and Logistic Strategies

Production and logistics policies to enhance bargaining position include local sourcing, location of facilities, control of transportation, and control of technology.

Local Sourcing. Host governments may require foreign firms to purchase raw material and components locally as a way to maximize value added and increase local employment. From the viewpoint of the foreign firm trying to adapt to host-country goals, local sourcing reduces political risk, albeit at a tradeoff with other factors. Local strikes or other turmoil may shut down the operation; and such issues as quality control, high local prices because of lack of economies of scale, and unreliable delivery schedules become important. Often the foreign firm acquires lower political risk only by increasing financial and commercial risk.

Facility Location. Production facilities may be located so as to minimize risk. The natural location of different stages of production may be resource-oriented, footloose, or market-oriented. Oil, for instance, is drilled in and around the Persian Gulf, Venezuela, and Indonesia. No choice exists for where this activity takes place. Refining is footloose. Whenever possible, oil companies have built refineries in politically safe countries, such as Western Europe or small islands (such as Singapore or Curacao), even though costs might be reduced by refining nearer the oil fields. They have traded off reduced political risk and financial exposure for possibly higher transportation and refining costs.

Control of Transportation. Control of transportation has been an important means to reduce political risk. For many years the United Fruit Company and the Standard Steamship Company had a powerful lever on those Latin American countries which were dependent on banana exports. The companies owned the refrigerator ships and controlled market outlets. Control of oil pipelines that cross national frontiers, oil tankers, ore carriers, and railroads have all been used at times to influence the bargaining power of both nations and companies.

Control of Technology. Control of key patents and processes is a viable way to reduce political risk. If a host country cannot operate a plant because it does not have technicians capable of running the process, or of keeping up with changed technology, abrogation of an investment agreement with a foreign firm is unlikely. This works best when the foreign firm is steadily improving the technology, and it ceases to work once the rate of technological advancement ceases.

Marketing Strategies

Marketing techniques to enhance a firm's bargaining position include control of markets, brand names, and trademarks.

Control of Markets. Control of markets is a common strategy to enhance a firm's bargaining position. As effective as the OPEC cartel was in raising the price received for crude oil by its member countries in the 1970s, marketing was still controlled by the international oil companies. OPEC's need of the oil companies limited the degree to which its members could dictate terms.

Control of export markets for manufactured goods is also a source of leverage in dealings between foreign-owned firms and host governments. The multinational firm would prefer to serve world markets from sources of its own choosing, basing the decision on considerations of production cost, transportation, tariff barriers, political risk exposure, and competition. The selling pattern that maximizes long-run profits from the overall viewpoint of the worldwide firm rarely maximizes exports, or value added, from the perspective of the host countries. Some will argue that if the same plants were owned by local nationals and were not part of a worldwide integrated system, more goods would be exported by the host country. The contrary argument is that self-standing local firms might never obtain foreign market share because they lack economies of scale on the production side and are unable to market in foreign countries.

Brand Name and Trademark Control. Control of a brand name or trademark can have an effect almost identical to that of controlling technology. It gives the multinational firm a monopoly on something that may or may not have substantive value but quite likely represents value in the eyes of consumers. Ability to produce for and market under a world brand name is valuable for local firms, and thus represents an important bargaining attribute for maintaining an investment position.

Financial Strategies

Financial strategies can be adopted to enhance the continued bargaining position of a multinational firm. Many of these are covered elsewhere in this book, so for the moment it is sufficient to list some of the more popular techniques.

Thin Equity Base. Foreign affiliates can be financed with a thin equity base and a large proportion of local debt. If the debt is borrowed from locally owned banks, host-government actions which weaken the financial viability of the firm also endanger local creditors.

Multiple-source Borrowing. If the firm must finance with foreign source debt, it may borrow from banks in a number of countries rather than just from home country banks. If, for example, debt is owed to banks in Tokyo, Frankfurt, London, and New York, nationals in a number of foreign countries have a vested interest in keeping the borrowing affiliate financially strong. If the multinational is U.S.-owned, a fallout between the United States and the host government is less likely to cause the local government to move against the firm if it also owes funds to these other countries.

Shared Ownership. Local ownership, either directly via local shareholders or institutionally through a joint venture, means that local investors have a vested interest in the economic health of the firm.

Contractual Devices. Contractual devices such as hedging, swaps, linked financing, and export credit insurance reduce the risk to the firm.

Organizational Strategies

Organization ownership strategies which are designed to minimize political risk have previously been discussed in Chapter 15. These include:

- Finding the right local joint venture partner
- Licensing a local firm to produce products or services
- Managing a local business via a management contract

One other organizational strategy worth discussing is the location of regional headquarters in safe places. For example, many U.S. and European firms have found it advantageous to locate their Latin American regional headquarters in Coral Gables,

Florida, rather than in Latin America itself. Nearness to the Miami International Airport, cost savings such as avoiding cost-of-living allowances and school tuition for executives and families, lack of vulnerability to pressure for bribes and payoffs, and an efficient telephone system are some of the advantages cited. However, it is equally important to avoid offending countries that would not have the regional headquarters. Because of jealousies between the various Latin American countries, individual political leaders have less objection to a regional headquarters in Florida than in a neighboring nation. In addition, the regional headquarters does not become a hostage to local politics and never has to be moved. If the political climate in any individual country deteriorates, the firm can simply hold back on local operations or pull out with a minimum of disturbance to other Latin American affiliates.

CRISIS PLANNING[19]

Firms should plan in advance what they will do if or when the general uncertainty in a foreign environment turns to chaos. Anticipatory planning is essential because it forces management to think about its vulnerabilities. The major objective is to develop either company-wide contingency plans or plans for parts of the firm that are vulnerable. Questions to ask include whether standard operating procedures cover perceived risks; what can be done to protect physical property; which executives or employees are likely to be in personal danger; and which records are so vital that their protection should be attempted.

Three years before the February 1986 revolution in the Philippines many firms doubted the Marcos administration could last up to the scheduled 1987 elections. To monitor developments firms employed a wide array of channels of information. They used their respective embassies in Manila, trade associations, and the expatriate community. For example, Japanese business persons in Manila met regularly and exchanged information, as did business persons from the United States. Firms used different methods to assess the situation, including attending seminars held by local research centers, informal discussion with counterparts from other firms, and regular meetings of senior management. Some firms utilized the political risk analysis conducted by their head office, although the major responsibility for assessing the situation rested on the head of the local affiliate.

Suggestions derived from the Philippines experience included maintaining a low profile before any trouble starts. A foreign firm should keep itself neutral and employees should avoid activities that attract media attention.

A deteriorating political situation and a weak economy go hand in hand. This was particularly true in the Philippines in the last years of the Marcos administration. Firms sought to keep operations at a level that enabled them to retain the major portion of their trained staff. It was suggested that local nationals should be used to staff positions whenever possible, and their knowledge of the situation should be used as inputs in planning. Use of the greatly increased number of non-U.S. nationals who had received MBA or other equivalent training in the United States was recommended.

Specific planning in anticipation of disruption should be made if the situation calls for it. One firm dusted off its standard operating procedures manual, reviewed those parts that addressed the potential disruptions they anticipated, and made sure that all concerned knew what was required of them. A firm with operations in a rebel-infested island in the Philippines instructed expatriate staff on procedures to take as a response to reports of kidnap threats, making sure to keep the procedures simple enough not to hamper the expatriates' day-to-day activities. Another firm instructed its expatriate staff to limit their evening activities to certain areas of the city to avoid exposure to random acts of kidnapping. As a rule, foreign employees should be sure they are registered with their local embassy so that they can receive information on official evacuation plans. As a crisis actually unfolds, as it did during the February 1986 revolution and the August 1987 coup attempt in the Philippines, they should stay home to await instructions.

In the Philippines a few firms had even more elaborate plans. One firm was reported to have assigned radios to key executives and to have laid out a schedule of emergency meetings well in advance of anticipated trouble. Employees were briefed on what their firm would do to protect their lives and property, and emergency stores of food, water, and medical supplies were set aside. Some U.S. firms created "safe houses" in Manila from which employees could be evacuated to Clark Air Force Base (a U.S. facility) or U.S. naval ships.

These plans were not needed in the Philippines in February 1986 or August 1987 as the violence was confined to certain areas of Metro-Manila and was not directed at multinationals. However political situations can deteriorate quickly and in directions that are difficult to anticipate. Having prepared plans and knowing what should be done is inexpensive insurance.

SUMMARY

- Political risk is the possibility that a multinational firm may be adversely influenced by political events within a host country, or by a change of political relationships between that host country and another country.

- Political risk arises because of a conflict in goals between host governments and firms. It arises when the normal functioning of governmental administrative and legislative processes leads to regulations which influence the well-being of the firm. Occasionally these political events constitute "expropriation," but far more frequently they are simply regulatory constraints imposed on the activities of private business firms.

- Most political risk events are micro and project specific, affecting only certain firms in certain industries, rather than all foreign firms. Government regulation of foreign firms may be classified as nondiscriminatory, discriminatory, or wealth depriving.

- To minimize their vulnerability to political risk, multinational firms must constantly position themselves to be in a good bargaining position with their host governments.

Before an investment is undertaken an investment agreement is often negotiated in which all areas of possible future contention are discussed. Most multinational firms can also turn to a home-country political risk insuring agency. In the United States this is OPIC, the Overseas Private Investment Corporation.

■ Once an investment is undertaken, the parent firm should establish and maintain policies that will enhance the firm's continual value to the host country. A variety of risk-reducing policies can be undertaken in the areas of production and logistics, marketing, finance, organization, and personnel. Last, the firm should have a well designed plan to deal with major crises should they occur.

1. Goal Conflict—Indonesia/General Motors

Assume that General Motors Corporation is considering establishing an automobile manufacturing plant in Indonesia. Prepare an analysis of all the potential areas of goal conflict between General Motors and Indonesia.

2. Political Risk Forecast—Indonesia

Considering your answers to Question 1, prepare a political risk forecast for a General Motors plant in Indonesia. Consider both the potential for political unrest in Indonesia and whether General Motors would be affected by such unrest. Use current periodicals and newspapers to gather your data.

3. Operating Strategies—Indonesia

Assume General Motors decides to build the automobile plant in Indonesia. Recommend to General Motors operating strategies that should reduce their political risk in Indonesia. Include strategies for marketing, production, finance, and organization.

4. Crisis Plan—Indonesia

Prepare a crisis plan for General Motors in Indonesia in case political conditions should deteriorate.

5. Divestment—the Philippines

Assume that Federated Department Stores owns a chain of retail clothing stores in the Philippines. Given the current situation in the Philippines, prepare a plan for Federated Department Stores that will enable them to divest their stores in the Philippines with maximum gain or minimum loss.

6. Iowa Foods, Inc.

Keith Smith, manager of Iowa Foods, Inc., is determining whether or not to purchase insurance through OPIC for a new capital investment in the Philippines. The government of President Corazon Aquino appears to be drifting, several coups d'état have been attempted, and it is not clear she will survive until the next scheduled election in 1992.

Communists on the political left and former military officers on the political right are creating instability. The original analysis of the project assumed no overthrow of the Aquino government, but a coup d'état now appears to be an even toss-up.

After reading various political risk assessments, Smith concludes that if the government falls the odds are one in ten that the Communists will prevail. If that happens, the probability of expropriation is 70%. If expropriated, the best that can be hoped for is a 70% chance of 40% compensation for the equity two years after the situation has stabilized. The other possibility is a 30% probability of no compensation.

Should a military government take over, Smith judges the probability of expropriation at only 10%. In that case, there exists a probability of 30% for full compensation immediately, 60% for full compensation in one year, and 10% for no compensation.

Iowa Foods' equity in the Philippines is $1.5 million. Its weighted average cost of capital is 16%, and OPIC charges $0.80 per $100 of coverage. OPIC would pay immediately on any expropriation. Should Smith purchase OPIC insurance?

7. Japanese Financial Goals

It is widely believed that the goal of most large Japanese companies is to "maximize corporate wealth" in the long run. The survival of the firm is paramount rather than maximizing shareholders' wealth. What are the characteristics of the Japanese society and business system that make corporate wealth maximization a more desirable goal than shareholder wealth maximization?

8. Political and Economic Barriers Facing the United States

Most Americans believe that many political and economic barriers exist in other countries that inhibit exports to those markets from the United States. Explain some typical barriers and why they exclude U.S. goods and services.

9. U.S. Political and Economic Barriers Facing Other Countries

Citizens of other countries believe the United States has its own set of barriers that deny them equal access to the U.S. market. What are some of these barriers? Are the foreign complaints justified? Why?

10. Antibribery Law

The United States has passed a law prohibiting U.S. firms to bribe foreign officials and business persons even in countries where bribery is a common practice. Some U.S. firms claim this has placed the United States at a disadvantage compared to host-country firms and other foreign firms that are not hampered by such a law. Discuss the ethics and practicality of the U.S. bribery law.

11. Colonial Legacy and Economic Imperialism

Some independent countries that were formerly colonies claim that their economic development is still hampered by the colonial legacy and its aftermath, economic imperialism. Explain whether these arguments are justified or whether they are just excuses for poor performance because of other factors.

NOTES

1. Stephen J. Kobrin, *Managing Political Risk Assessment: Strategic Response to Environmental Change*, Berkeley: University of California Press, 1982, p. 35.

2. See, for example, Swiss Bank Corporation's detailed explanation of its own country risk assessment approach in its *Economic & Financial Prospects: Supplement*, February/March, 1988.

3. *Op cit*, Kobrin, 1982.

4. J. J. Servan-Schreiber, *The American Challenge*, London: Hamish Hamilton, 1968.

5. "To Western Industry, East Block Auto Market is Losing Some Luster," *Wall Street Journal*, November 14, 1990, p. 1.

6. Paul Hofheinz, "The New Russian Revolution," *Fortune*, November 19, 1990, p. 130.

7. Robert W. Gibson, "Reform Makes It Harder to Do a Soviet Deal," *Los Angeles Times*, December 2, 1990, p. D1.

8. "A Crackdown in Caracas Sends Foreign Executives Fleeing," *Business Week*, July 31, 1989, p. 46; and "Many Executives Flee Venezuela in Scandal Over Dollar Reserves—Even Multinational Officials Who Aren't Implicated Fear Jail and Slow Justice," *Wall Street Journal*, August 24, 1989, p. 1.

9. "Kenya Corruption Overwhelms Investors," *Los Angeles Times*, Part I, June 25, 1989, p. 4.

10. "Brazil Plans to Bar Foreign Firms from Mining,"

Los Angeles Times, April 30, 1988.

11. *Ibid.*

12. "Brazilian Court Sanctions Ford, VW Price Increase," *Wall Street Journal*, November 11, 1987.

13. "Gov't Cuts Review's Sales to 500 Copies," *Straits Times* (overseas edition), January 2, 1988, p. 1.

14. "When the Press Misinforms," Address by Brig-Gen (Res) Lee Hsien Loong, Minister for Trade and Industry and 2nd Minister for Defense (Services), Singapore, at the 40th World Congress of Newspaper Publishers on May 26, 1987, at Helsinki, Finland. Singapore Government Press Release no. 40/May 15–1/87/05/26, p. 13.

15. "Peru Seizes Assets of U.S. Oil Company," *Los Angeles Times*, December 29, 1985. Also see "Occidental Petroleum Avoids Seizure in Peru; Belco's Status Unclear," *Los Angeles Times*, December 28, 1985.

16. "Vietnam Opens Up to the West," *Far Eastern Economic Review*, November 29, 1990, p. 50.

17. "Chevron in Angola Flap," *Los Angeles Times Business*, January 30, 1986.

18. Dan Haendel, *Foreign Investment and the Management of Risk*, Boulder, Colo.: Westview Press, 1979, p. 5.

19. This section has benefitted greatly from the ideas of Manolete Gonzales, who has been conducting an ongoing study of crisis planning in the Philippines.

BIBLIOGRAPHY

Beaty, David, and Oren Harari, "Divestment and Disinvestment From South Africa: A Reappraisal," *California Management Review*, Summer 1987, pp. 31–50.

Blitzer, Charles R., Panos E. Cavoulacos, and Donald R. Lessard, "Contract Efficiency and Natural Resource Investment in Developing Countries," *Columbia Journal of World Business*, Spring 1984, pp. 10–18.

Boddewyn, J. J., "Foreign and Domestic Divestment and Investment Decision: Like or Unlike?" *Journal of International Business Studies*, Winter 1983, pp. 23–35.

Brewer, Thomas L., *Political Risks in International Business*, New York: Praeger, 1985.

——, "The Instability of Governments and the Instability for Controls on Funds Transfers by Multinational Enterprises: Implications for Political

Risk Analysis," *Journal of International Business Studies*, Winter 1983, pp. 147–157.

Bulcke, D. Vanden, and J. J. Boddewyn, *Investment and Divestment Policies in Multinational Corporations in Europe*, London: Saxon/Teakfield; New York: Praeger, 1979.

Chase, Carmen D., James L. Kuhle, and Carl H. Walther, "The Relevance of Political Risk in Direct Foreign Investment," *Management International Review*, 28, no. 3, 1988, pp. 31–38.

Cosset, Jean-Claude, and Bruno Doutriaux de la Rianderie, "Political Risk and Foreign Exchange Rates: An Efficient-Markets Approach," *Journal of International Business Studies*, Fall 1985, pp. 21–56.

Doz, Yves L., Christopher A. Barlett, and C. K. Prahalad, "Global Competitive Pressures and Host Country Demands," *California Management Review*, Spring 1981, pp. 63–74.

——, and C. K. Prahalad, "How MNCs Cope with Host Government Demands," *Harvard Business Review*, March/April 1980, pp. 149–160.

Eiteman, David K., "A Model for Expropriation Settlement: The Peruvian-IPC Controversy," *Business Horizons*, April 1970, pp. 85–91.

Encarnation, Dennis J., and Sushil Vachani, "Foreign Ownership: When Hosts Change the Rules," *Harvard Business Review*, September/October 1985, pp. 152–160.

Fayerweather, John, ed., *Host National Attitudes toward Multinational Corporations*, New York: Praeger, 1982.

Ghadar, Fariborz, Stephen J. Kobrin, and Theodore H. Moran, eds., *Managing International Political Risk: Strategies and Techniques*, Washington, D.C.: Ghadar and Associates, 1983.

Gladwin, Thomas N., and Ingo Walter, *Multinationals under Fire*, New York: Wiley, 1980.

Green, Robert T., and Christopher M. Korth, "Political Instability and the Foreign Investor," *California Management Review*, Fall 1974, pp. 23–31.

Haendel, Dan, *Foreign Investment and the Management of Political Risk*, Boulder, Colo.: Westview Press, 1979.

Hawkins, Robert G., Norman Mintz, and Michael Provissiero, "Government Takeovers of U.S Foreign Affiliates," *Journal of International Business Studies*, Spring 1976, pp. 3–15.

Kim, W. Chan, "Competition and the Management of Host Government Intervention," *Sloan Management Review*, Spring 1987, p. 33–39.

Kobrin, Stephen J., "The Environmental Determinants of Foreign Direct Manufacturing Investment: An Ex-Post Empirical Analysis," *Journal of International Business Studies*, Fall/Winter 1976, pp. 29–42.

——, "Political Risk: A Review and Reconsideration," *Journal of International Business Studies*, Spring/Summer 1979, pp. 67–80.

——, "Political Assessment by International Firms: Models or Methodologies?" *Journal of Policy Modeling*, May 1981, pp. 251–270.

——, *Managing Political Risk Assessment: Strategic Response to Environmental Change*, Berkeley: University of California Press, 1982.

Knudsen, Harald, "Explaining the National Propensity to Expropriate: An Ecological Approach," *Journal of International Business Studies*, Spring 1974, pp. 51–71.

Mandel, Robert, "The Overseas Private Investment Corporation and International Investment," *Columbia Journal of World Business*, Spring 1984, pp. 89–95.

Minor, Michael, "Changes in Developing Country Regimes for Foreign Direct Investment: The Raw Materials Sector, 1968–1985," *Essays in International Business*, no. 8, September 1990.

Nigh, Douglas, "The Effect of Political Events on United States Direct Foreign Investment: A Pooled Time Series Cross-Sectional Analysis," *Journal of International Business Studies*, Spring 1985, pp. 1–17.

Phillips-Patrick, Frederick J., "Ownership, Asset Structure, and Political Risk," *Advances in Financial Planning and Forecasting*, vol. 4, part A, 1990, p. 239.

Poynter, Thomas A., "Government Intervention in Less Developed Countries: The Experience of Multinational Companies," *Journal of International Business Studies*, Spring/Summer 1982, pp. 9–25.

Rogers, Jerry, ed., *Global Risk Assessments: Issues, Concepts and Applications,* Riverside, Calif.: Global Risk Assessments, Inc., 1988.

Root, Franklin R., "U.S. Business Abroad and Political Risks," *MSU Business Topics*, Winter 1968, pp. 73–80.

Rummel, R. J., and David A. Heenan, "How Multinationals Analyze Political Risk," *Harvard Business Review*, January/February 1978, pp. 67–76.

Ryans, J. K., and J. C. Baker, "The International Centre for Settlement of Investment Disputes," *Journal of World Trade Law*, January/February 1976, pp. 65–79.

Salehizadeh, Mehdi, *Regulation of Foreign Direct Investment by Host Country, Essays in International Business*, no. 4, Columbia: University of South Carolina, 1983.

Sethi, S. Prakash, and K. A. N. Luther, "Political Risk Analysis and Direct Foreign Investment: Some Problems of Definition and Measurement," *California Management Review*, Winter 1986, pp. 57–68.

Stoever, William A., "LDC Governments: Takeovers and Renegotiations of Foreign Investments," *California Management Review*, Winter 1979, pp. 5–14.

Tallman, Stephen B., "Home Country Political Risk and Foreign Direct Investment in the United States," *Journal of International Business Studies*, Summer 1988, pp. 219–234.

Tipgus, Manuel A., "Compliance with the Foreign Corrupt Practices Act," *Financial Executive*, August 1981, pp. 38–48.

Wilson, Brent D., *Disinvestment of Foreign Subsidiaries*, Ann Arbor, Mich.: UMI Research Press, 1980.

Yonah, Alexander, and Robert A. Kilmarx, *Political Terrorism and Business: The Threat and Response*, New York: Praeger, 1979.

Although the original decision to undertake an investment in a particular foreign country may be determined by a mix of strategic, behavioral, and economic decisions, the specific project, as well as all reinvestment decisions, should be justified by traditional financial analysis. For example, a production efficiency opportunity may exist for a U.S. firm to invest abroad, but the type of plant, mix of labor and capital, kinds of equipment, method of financing, and other project variables must be analyzed within the traditional financial framework of discounted cash flows. Consideration must also be given to the impact of the proposed foreign project on consolidated net earnings and on the market value of the parent firm.

FOREIGN COMPLEXITIES

Capital budgeting for a foreign project uses the same theoretical framework as domestic capital budgeting. Project cash flows are discounted at the firm's weighted average cost of capital, or the project's required rate of return, to determine net present value; or, alternatively, the internal rate of return that equates project cash flows to the cost of the project is sought. However, capital budgeting analysis for a foreign project is considerably more complex than the domestic case for a number of reasons:

- Parent cash flows must be distinguished from project cash flows. Each of these two types of flows contributes to a different view of value.

- Parent cash flows often depend on the form of financing. Thus cash flows cannot be clearly separated from financing decisions, as is done in domestic capital budgeting.

493

- Remittance of funds to the parent must be explicitly recognized because of differing tax systems, legal and political constraints on the movement of funds, local business norms, and differences in how financial markets and institutions function.

- Cash flows from affiliates to parent can be generated by an array of nonfinancial payments, including payment of license fees and payments for imports from the parent.

- Differing rates of national inflation must be anticipated because of their importance in causing changes in competitive position, and thus in cash flows over a period of time.

- The possibility of unanticipated foreign exchange rate changes must be remembered because of possible direct effects on the value to the parent of local cash flows, as well as an indirect effect on the competitive position of the foreign affiliate.

- Use of segmented national capital markets may create an opportunity for financial gains or may lead to additional financial costs.

- Use of host-government subsidized loans complicates both capital structure and the ability to determine an appropriate weighted average cost of capital for discounting purposes.

- Political risk must be evaluated because political events can drastically reduce the value or availability of expected cash flows.

- Terminal value is more difficult to estimate because potential purchasers from the host, parent, or third countries, or from the private or public sector, may have widely divergent perspectives on the value to them of acquiring the project.

Since the same theoretical capital budgeting framework is used to choose among competing foreign and domestic projects, a common standard is critical. Thus all foreign complexities must be quantified as modifications to either expected cash flow or the rate of discount. Although in practice many firms make such modifications arbitrarily, readily available information, theoretical deduction, or just plain common sense can be used to make less arbitrary and more reasonable choices.

PROJECT VERSUS PARENT VALUATION

A strong theoretical argument exists in favor of analyzing any foreign project from the viewpoint of the parent. Cash flows to the parent are ultimately the basis for dividends to stockholders, reinvestment elsewhere in the world, repayment of corporate-wide debt, and other purposes that affect the firm's many interest groups. However, since most of a project's cash flows to its parent, or to sister affiliates, are financial cash flows rather than operating cash flows, the parent viewpoint usually violates a cardinal concept of capital budgeting, namely, that financial cash flows should not be mixed with operating cash flows. Often the difference is not important because the two are almost identical, but in some instances a sharp divergence in these cash flows will exist. For example, funds that are permanently blocked from repatriation, or "forcibly reinvested," are not available for dividends to the stockholders or for repayment of corporate debt. Therefore shareholders will not perceive the blocked earnings as contributing to the value of the firm, and creditors will not count on them in calculating interest coverage ratios and other evidence of ability to service debt.

Evaluation of a project from the local viewpoint serves some useful purposes, but should be subordinated to evaluation from the parent's viewpoint. In evaluating a foreign project's performance relative to the potential of a competing project in the same host country, one must pay attention to the project's local return. Almost any project should at least be able to earn a cash return equal to the yield available on host government bonds with a maturity the same as the project's economic life, if a free market exists for such bonds. Host government bonds ordinarily reflect the local risk-free rate of return, including a premium equal to the expected rate of inflation. If a project cannot earn more than such a bond yield, the parent firm should buy host government bonds rather than invest in a riskier project—or, better yet, invest somewhere else!

If the theory of direct foreign investment is correct, multinational firms should invest only if they can earn on a project a risk-adjusted return greater than local-based competitors can earn on the same project. If they are unable to earn superior returns on foreign projects, their stockholders would be better off buying shares in local firms, where possible, and letting those companies carry out the local projects.

Apart from these theoretical arguments, surveys over the last 23 years show that in practice multinational firms continue to evaluate foreign investments from both the parent and project viewpoint. Responses of multinational firms to surveys by Stonehill and Nathanson (1968), Baker and Beardsley (1973), Oblak and Helm (1980), Bavishi (1981), Kelly and Philippatos (1982), and Stanley and Block (1983) reveal that firms calculate and evaluate rates of return by using cash flows to and from the parent alone, as well as to and from the foreign project alone.[1] In a 1978–1979 study of 156 U.S. multinationals, Bavishi reported that in appraising foreign projects, 42% of the firms use cash flow from the foreign project's viewpoint, 21% use cash flow from the parent's viewpoint, and 37% use both.[2] In their study of 121 U.S. multinational firms, conducted in the early 1980s, Stanley and Block found that 48% of their 121 respondents evaluate foreign projects on the basis of the project's cash flows, 36% on the basis of parent cash flows, and 16% on both.[3]

The attention paid to project returns in the various survey results probably reflects emphasis on maximizing reported consolidated net earnings per share as a corporate financial goal. As long as foreign earnings are not blocked, they can be consolidated with the earnings of both the remaining affiliates and the parent.[4] Even in the case of temporarily blocked funds, some of the most mature multinational firms do not necessarily eliminate a project. They take a very long-run view of world markets.

If reinvestment opportunities in the country where funds are blocked are at least equal to the parent firm's required rate of return (after adjusting for anticipated exchange rate changes), temporary blockage of transfer may have little practical effect on the capital budgeting outcome because future project cash flows will be increased by the returns on forced reinvestment. Since large multinationals hold a portfolio of domestic and foreign projects, corporate liquidity is not impaired if a few projects have blocked funds; alternate sources of funds are available to meet all planned uses of funds. Furthermore, a long-run historical perspective on blocked funds does indeed lend support to the belief that funds are almost never permanently blocked. However, waiting for the release of such funds can be frustrating, and sometimes the blocked funds lose value because of inflation or unexpected exchange rate deterioration while blocked, even though they have been reinvested in the host country to protect at least part of their value in real terms.

In conclusion, most firms appear to evaluate foreign projects from both parent and project viewpoints. The parent's viewpoint gives results closer to the traditional meaning of net present value in capital budgeting. Project valuation provides a closer approximation of the effect on consolidated earnings per share, which all surveys indicate is of major concern to practicing managers.

Adjusting for Risk—Parent Viewpoint

In analyzing a foreign project from the parent's point of view, the additional risk that stems from its "foreign" location can be handled in at least two ways. The first method is to treat all foreign risk as a single problem by increasing the discount rate applicable to foreign projects relative to the rate used for domestic projects to reflect the greater foreign exchange risk, political risk, and other uncertainties perceived in foreign operations.

In the second method, which we prefer, all foreign risks are incorporated in adjustments to forecasted cash flows of the project. The discount rate for the foreign project is risk-adjusted only for overall business and financial risk, in the same manner as that for domestic projects.

Adjusting the Discount Rate. Adjusting the discount rate applied to a foreign project's cash flow to reflect political and foreign exchange uncertainties does not penalize net present value in proportion either to the actual amount at risk or to possible variations in the nature of that risk over time. Combining all risks into a single discount rate discards much information about the uncertainties of the future.

For example, political uncertainties are a threat to the entire investment, not just to annual cash flows. Potential loss depends partly on the terminal value of the unrecovered parent investment, which will vary depending on how the project was financed and whether political risk insurance was obtained. Furthermore, if the political climate were expected to be unfavorable in the near future, any investment would probably be unacceptable. Political uncertainty usually relates to possible adverse events that might occur in the more distant future, but that cannot be foreseen at the present. Adjusting the discount rate for political risk thus penalizes early cash flows too heavily while not penalizing distant cash flows enough.

In the case of foreign exchange risk, changes in exchange rates have a potential effect on future cash flows because of economic exposure. The direction of the effect, however, can either decrease or increase net cash inflows, depending on where the products are sold and where inputs are sourced. The variety of outcomes under economic exposure was explained in the Instruments Napoleon example in Chapter 7. To increase the discount rate applicable to a foreign project, on the assumption that the foreign currency might depreciate more than expected, ignores the possible favorable effect of a foreign currency depreciation on the project's competitive position. Increased sales volume might more than offset a lower value of the local currency. Such an increase in the discount rate also ignores the possibility the foreign currency may appreciate. That is, foreign exchange risk is two-sided.

Apart from anticipated political and foreign exchange risks, multinational firms sometimes worry that taking on foreign projects may increase the firm's overall cost of capital because of investors' perceptions of foreign risk. This worry seems reasonable if the firm was investing in Libya, Iran, Lebanon, or Angola in the 1980s, especially if the firm's operations are heavily centered in one such unreliable country, and if that country is in the news frequently in a context of rampant xenophobia. However, the argument loses persuasiveness when applied to diversified foreign investments with a heavy balance in the industrial countries of Canada, Western Europe, Australia, and Asia, where in fact the bulk of direct foreign investment is located. These countries have a reputation for treating foreign investments by consistent standards, and empirical evidence confirms that a foreign presence in these countries may not increase the cost of capital. In fact, some studies indicate that required returns on foreign projects may even be lower than those for domestic projects.

Adjusting Cash Flows. In the rest of this chapter we will use the method that adjusts cash flows rather than the discount rate in treating risk. Cash flows to the parent will be discounted by the rate of return appropriate for the business and financial risks of comparable domestic projects. Any risk unique to the foreign location of the project will be incorporated into project cash flows.

It should be noted that many multinational firms do adjust the discount rate for foreign projects despite the theoretical limits of this method. The aforementioned Baker and Beardsley survey found that 49% of the responding multinationals add a premium percentage for risk to their required rate of return on foreign investments.[5] The authors remark that these tended to be firms with a relatively small percentage of foreign sales. Firms with a larger foreign commitment did not typically change the discount rate, but instead presumably adjusted cash flows. The Oblak and Helm survey also reported that slightly more than half of the responding firms varied the discount rate for foreign projects, but the other half did not.[6] Of those that varied the discount rate, 40% subjectively varied their weighted average cost of capital, while 44% used the local (that is, foreign) weighted average cost of capital.

In their 1983 study, Stanley and Block found that 62% of their respondents used some risk-adjustment technique, but that risk-adjusted discount rates and risk-adjusted cash flows were used with similar frequency. They also found that the use of risk adjustment techniques is independent of the percentage of foreign sales to total sales.[7]

Adjusting for Risk—Project Viewpoint

From the project point of view, "foreign" risks also exist. A foreign affiliate has foreign exchange exposure on both its imports and exports. Since the prime purpose of finding a project rate of return is to compare it with alternative opportunities to invest funds locally, the appropriate discount rate should be the one required by *local* investors for projects of the same business and financial risk class. This approach forces the parent to remember that local inflation and risk must be reflected in the required rate of return for local projects.

For comparisons within the host country, a project's actual financing or parent-influenced debt capacity should be overlooked, since these would probably be different for local investors than they are for a multinational owner. In addition, the risks of the project to local investors might differ from those perceived by a foreign multinational owner because of the opportunities a multinational firm has to take advantage of market imperfections. Moreover, the local project may be only one out of an internationally diversified portfolio of projects for the multinational owner, whereas it might have to stand alone, without international diversification, if undertaken by local investors. Since diversification reduces risk, the multinational firm can require a lower rate of return than is required by local investors.

Thus the discount rate used locally must be a hypothetical rate based on a judgment as to what independent local investors would probably demand were they to own the business. Consequently, application of the local discount rate to local cash flows provides only a rough measure of the value of the project as a stand-alone local venture, rather than an absolute valuation.

Kim Electronics (Kimtron)

To illustrate some of the foreign complexities of multinational capital budgeting, we will analyze a hypothetical "market seeking" investment by a U.S. manufacturing firm in Korea. A project analysis team has collected the following facts.

Product. Kim Electronics (Kimtron) is the wholly owned Korean affiliate of Fairtel, a U.S. electronic component manufacturer. Fairtel manufactures customized integrated circuits (ICs) for use in computers, automobiles, and robots. Kimtron has been Fairtel's distribution affiliate in Korea, but consideration is now being given to making Kimtron a manufacturing affiliate. Kimtron's products would be sold primarily in Korea, and all sales would be denominated in Korean won.

Sales. Sales in the first year are forecasted to be Won 22,000 million. The physical volume of sales is expected to grow at 8% per annum for the foreseeable future.

Working capital. Kimtron needs gross working capital (that is, cash, receivables, and inventory) equal to 20% of sales. Half of gross working capital can be financed by local accruals and accounts payable, but the other half must be financed by Kimtron or Fairtel.

Inflation. Prices are expected to increase as follows.

Korean general price level:	+6% per annum
Kimtron average sales price:	+6% per annum
Korean raw material costs:	+2% per annum
Korean labor costs:	+8% per annum
U.S. general price level:	+3% per annum

Parent-supplied components. Components sold to Kimtron by Fairtel have a direct cost to Fairtel equal to 96% of their sales price.

Depreciation. Plant and equipment will be depreciated on a straight-line basis for both accounting and tax purposes over an expected life of eight years. No salvage value is anticipated.

License fees. Kimtron will pay a license fee of 2% of sales revenue to Fairtel. This fee is tax-deductible in Korea but provides taxable income to Fairtel.

Taxes. The Korean corporate income tax rate is 30%, and the U.S. rate is 34%. Korea has no withholding tax on dividends, interest, or fees paid to foreign residents.

Cost of capital. The weighted average cost of capital used in Korea by companies of comparable risk is 22%. Fairtel also uses 22% for its investments.

Exchange rates. In the year in which the initial investment takes place, the exchange rate is Won 800 to the dollar. Fairtel forecasts the won to depreciate relative to the dollar at 3% per annum. Consequently, year-end exchange rates are forecasted to be as follows.

Year	Calculation	Won/dollar
0	(given)	800.00
1	800.00 x 1.03 =	824.00
2	824.00 x 1.03 =	848.72
3	848.72 x 1.03 =	874.18
4	874.18 x 1.03 =	900.40
5	900.40 x 1.03 =	927.42

Dividend policy. Kimtron will pay 65% of accounting net income to Fairtel as an annual cash dividend. Kimtron and Fairtel estimate that over a five-year period the other 35% of net income must be reinvested to finance working capital growth.

Financing. Kimtron will be financed by Fairtel with a $9,000,000 purchase of Won 7,200,000,000 common stock, all to be owned by Fairtel.

    In order to prepare the normal cash flow projections, the project team has made the following assumptions.

1. *Sales revenue* in the first year of operations is expected to be Won 22,000 million. Won sales revenue will increase annually at 8% because of physical growth and at an additional 6% because of price increases. Consequently, sales revenue will grow at $(1.08)(1.06) = 1.1448$, or 14.48% per annum.

2. *Korean raw material* costs in the first year are budgeted at Won 3,000 million. Korean raw material costs are expected to increase at 8% per annum because of physical growth and at an additional 2% because of price increases. Consequently raw material costs will grow at $(1.08)(1.02) = 1.1016$, or 10.16% per annum.

3. *Parent-supplied component costs* in the first year are budgeted at Won 8,000 million. Parent-supplied component costs are expected to increase annually at 8% because of physical growth, plus an additional 3% because of U.S. inflation, plus another 3% in won terms because of the expected deterioration of the won relative to the dollar.

Consequently the won cost of parent-supplied imports will increase at (1.08) (1.03) (1.03) = 1.1458, or 14.58% per annum.

4. *Direct labor costs* in the first year are budgeted at Won 4,000 million. Korean direct labor costs are expected to increase at 8% per annum because of physical growth, and at an additional 8% because of increases in Korean wage rates. Consequently Korean direct labor will increase at (1.08) (1.08) = 1.1664, or 16.64% per annum.

5. *General and administrative expenses* are budgeted at Won 5,000 million in the first year. Although largely fixed, G&A expenses are nevertheless expected to rise 1% annually as Kimtron expands production and sales.

6. *Liquidation value.* At the end of five years, the project (including working capital) is expected to be sold on a going-concern basis to Korean investors for Won 8,000 million, equal to $8,626,081 at the expected exchange rate of Won 927.42/$. This sales price is free of all Korean and U.S. taxes, and will be used as a terminal value for capital budgeting purposes.

Given the facts and stated assumptions, the beginning balance sheet is presented in Exhibit 17.1; Exhibit 17.2 shows revenue and cost projections for Kimtron over the expected five-year life of the project.

Exhibit 17.3 shows how the annual increase in working capital investment is calculated. According to the facts, half of gross working capital must be financed by Kimtron or Fairtel. Therefore half of any annual increase in working capital would represent an additional required capital investment.

Exhibit 17.4 forecasts project cash flows from the viewpoint of Kimtron. Thanks to a healthy liquidation value, the project has a positive net present value and an IRR greater than the 22% local (Korean) cost of capital for projects of similar risk. Therefore Kimtron passes the first of the two tests of required rate of return.

Exhibit 17.1   Beginning Balance Sheet, Kimtron (year 0)

	Millions of Won	Thousands of Dollars
Assets		
1. Cash balance	720	900
2. Accounts receivable	0	0
3. Inventory	1,280	1,600
4. Net plant and equipment	6,000	7,500
5. Total	8,000	10,000
Liabilities and Net Worth		
6. Accounts payable	800	1,000
7. Common stock equity	7,200	9,000
8. Total	8,000	10,000

Exhibit 17.2   Revenue and Cost Data for Kimtron (millions of won)

			Year		
Item	1	2	3	4	5
1. Total sales revenue	22,000	25,186	28,832	33,007	37,787
2. Korean raw material	3,000	3,305	3,641	4,010	4,418
3. Components purchased from parent	8,000	9,166	10,502	12,033	13,787
4. Korean labor	4,000	4,666	5,442	6,347	7,404
5. Total variable costs [(2) + (3) + (4)]	15,000	17,137	19,585	22,391	25,609
6. Gross profit [(1) − (5)]	7,000	8,049	9,248	10,616	12,178
7. License fee [2% of (1)]	440	504	577	660	756
8. General & administrative	5,000	5,050	5,101	5,152	5,203
9. Depreciation	750	750	750	750	750
10. EBIT [(6) − {(7) + (8) + (9)}]	810	1,745	2,820	4,055	5,469
11. Korean income taxes (30%)	243	524	846	1,216	1,641
12. Net income [(10) - (11)]	567	1,222	1,974	2,838	3,828
13. Cash dividend [65% of (12)]	369	794	1,283	1,845	2,488

Does Kimtron also pass the second test? That is, does it show at least a 22% required rate of return from the viewpoint of Fairtel?

Exhibit 17.5 shows the calculation for expected after-tax dividends from Kimtron to be received by Fairtel. The manner in which dividends from abroad are taxed by the United States is explained in more detail in Chapter 21. For purposes of this example, note that Fairtel must pay regular U.S. corporate income taxes (34% rate) on dividends received from Kimtron. However, the U.S. tax law allows Fairtel to claim a tax credit for income taxes paid to Korea on the Korean income that generated the dividend. The process of

Exhibit 17.3   Working Capital Calculation for Kimtron (millions of won)

			Year		
Item	1	2	3	4	5
1. Total revenue	22,000	25,186	28,832	33,007	37,787
2. Net working capital needs at year-end [20% of (1)]	4,400	5,037	5,766	6,601	7,557
3. Less year-beginning working capital	2,000	4,400	5,037	5,766	6,601
4. Required addition to working capital	2,400	637	729	835	956
5. Less working capital financed in Korea by accruals and accounts payable	1,200	319	365	417	478
6. Net new investment in working capital	1,200	319	365	418	478

Exhibit 17.4   Project Cash Flows for Kimtron, All-Equity Basis (millions of won)

Item	0	1	2	3	4	5
				Year		
1. EBIT [Ex. 17.2, (10)]		810	1,745	2,820	4,055	5,469
2. Korean income taxes (30%)		<243>	<524>	<846>	<1,216>	<1,641>
3. Net income, all equity basis[a]		567	1,222	1,974	2,838	3,828
4. Depreciation		750	750	750	750	750
5. Liquidation value						8,000
6. Half of addition to working capital		<1,200>	<319>	<365>	<417>	<478>
7. Cost of project	<7,200>					
8. Net cash flow	<7,200>	117	1,653	2,360	3,171	12,100
9. PV factor (22%)	1.000	0.820	0.672	0.551	0.451	0.370
10. PV each year	<7,200>	96	1,111	1,299	1,431	4,477
11. Cumulative NPV	<7,200>	<7,104>	<5,993>	<4,694>	<3,263>	1,214
12. IRR = 26.78%						

Conclusion: The project is viable from a project point of view, because net present value is a positive won 1,214 million and IRR is 26.78%, which is greater than the 22% local (Korean) cost of capital for projects of similar risk.

---

a Because Kimtron has no long-term debt, and thus no interest expense, line (3) in this exhibit equals line (12) of Exhibit 17.2. If Kimtron had interest expense, line (12) of Exhibit 17.2 would have been calculated after deducting interest, whereas line (3) here would have been before interest expenses.

calculating the original income in Korea is called "grossing up" and is illustrated in Exhibit 17.5, lines (1), (2), and (3). This imputed Korean won income is converted from won to dollars in lines (4) and (5). Then the U.S. income tax is calculated at 34% in line (6). A tax credit is given for the Korean income taxes paid, as calculated in line (7). Line (8) then shows the net additional U.S. tax due, and line (10) shows the net dividend received by Fairtel after the additional U.S. tax is paid.

Finally, Exhibit 17.6 calculates the rate of return on cash flows from Kimtron from the viewpoint of Fairtel. Unfortunately, in this case Kimtron does not pass the test because it has a slightly negative net present value and an IRR of 21.26%, not quite enough for the 22% rate of return required by Fairtel.

Sensitivity Analysis

So far the project investigation team has used a set of "most likely" assumptions to forecast rates of return. It is now time to subject the most likely outcome to sensitivity analyses. The same probabilistic techniques are available to test the sensitivity of results to political and foreign exchange risks as are used to test sensitivity to business and financial risks. Popular techniques include the use of decision tree analysis, reducing cash flows to certainty equivalents, adjusting the discount rate to reflect the degree of riskiness of the project, and measuring the statistical dispersion of expected returns. Many decision

Exhibit 17.5 After-Tax Dividend Received by Fairtel from Kimtron

Item			Year			
	0	1	2	3	4	5
In Millions of Won						
1. Cash dividend paid [Ex. 17.2, (13)]		369	794	1,283	1,845	2,488
2. 65% of Korean income tax [Ex. 17.2, (11)}		158	340	550	791	1,066
3. Grossed-up dividend [(1) + (2)]		527	1,134	1,833	2,635	3,555
4. Exchange-rate (won/$)	800.00	824.00	848.27	874.18	900.40	927.42
In Thousands of Dollars						
5. Grossed-up dividend [(3)/(4) x 1000]		639.0	1.336.7	2,097.2	2,926.9	3,833.1
6. U.S. tax (34%)		217.2	454.5	713.0	995.2	1303.3
7. Credit for Korean taxes [(2)/(4) x 1000]		191.7	401.0	629.1	878.1	1149.9
8. Additional U.S. tax due [(6) − (7), if (6) is larger]		25.6	53.5	83.9	117.1	153.3
9. Excess U.S. tax credit [(7) − (6), if (7) is larger]		-0-	-0-	-0-	-0-	-0-
10. Dividend received by Fairtel, after all taxes[a] [(1)/(4) x 1000 − (8)]		421.7	882.2	1,384.1	1,981.8	2,529.9

[a] Exact values may appear not to sum due to rounding error. Precise values shown here are generated from spreadsheet C17A.WK1.

makers feel more uncomfortable about the necessity to guess probabilities for unfamiliar political and foreign exchange events than they do about guessing their own more familiar business or financial risks. Therefore it is more common to test sensitivity to political and foreign exchange risk by simulating what would happen to net present value and earnings under a variety of "what if" scenarios.

Exhibit 17.7 illustrates the results of a possible sensitivity analysis on the rate of depreciation of the Korean won. The Net Present Value (NPV) Profile of the project from the parent's viewpoint is constructed from the net after-tax cash flows received by Fairtel, discounted over a range of discount rates. If the Korean won were to depreciate at a 6% annual rate as opposed to the 3% rate initially assumed, the project's value worsens (NPV profile shifts downward).

Political Risk

What if Korea should impose controls on the payment of dividends or license fees to Fairtel? The impact of blocked funds on the rate of return from Fairtel's perspective would depend on when the blockage occurs, what reinvestment opportunities exist for the blocked funds in Korea, and when the blocked funds would eventually be released to Fairtel. One could simulate various scenarios for blocked funds and rerun the cash flow analysis in Exhibit 17.6 to estimate the effect on Fairtel's rate of return.

Exhibit 17.6   Net Present Value to Fairtel of Cash Flows from Kimtron

Item	0	1	2	3	4	5
In Millions of Won						
1. License fee from Kimtron (2%) [Ex. 17.2, (7)]		440	504	577	660	756
2. Margin on exports to Kimtron [4% of (3) in Ex. 17.2]		320	367	420	481	551
3. Total receipts		760	870	997	1,141	1,307
4. Exchange rate (won/$)	800.0	824.0	848.72	874.18	900.41	927.42
In Thousands of Dollars						
5. Pre-tax receipts [(3)/(4) x 1000]		922.3	1,05.5	1,140.2	1,267.7	1,409.5
6. U.S. taxes (34%)		<313.6>	<348.7>	<387.7>	<431.0>	<479.2>
7. License fees and export profits, after tax		608.7	676.8	752.5	836.7	930.3
8. After-tax dividend [Ex. 17.5, (10)]		421.7	882.2	1,384.1	1,931.8	2,529.9
9. Project cost	<9,000.0>					
10. Liquidation value						8,626.1
11. Net cash flow	<9,000.0>	1,030.4	1,559.0	2,136.7	2,768.5	12,086.3
12. PV factor (22%)	1.000	0.820	0.672	0.551	0.451	0.370
13. PV each year	<9,000.0>	844.6	1,047.5	1,176.7	1,249.7	4,471.9
14. Cumulative NPV	<9,000.0>	<8,155.4>	<7,107.9>	<5,931.2>	<4,681.6>	<209.6>
15. IRR = 21.26%						

Conclusion: The project as designed is not viable from a parent point of view because its net present value is negative $209,600, and its IRR is 21.26%, slightly less than the parent's 22% required rate of return.

What if Korea should expropriate Kimtron? The effect of expropriation would depend on the following four factors.

1. How much compensation will the Korean government pay and how long after expropriation will this occur?

2. How much debt is still outstanding to Korean lenders and has the parent, Fairtel, guaranteed this debt?

3. What are the tax consequences of the expropriation?

4. What are the future cash flows forgone?

Many expropriations eventually result in some form of compensation to the former owners. This compensation can come from a negotiated settlement with the host government or from payment of political risk insurance by the parent government. Negotiating a settlement takes time, and the eventual compensation is sometimes paid in installments over a further period of time. Thus the present value of the compensation is

Exhibit 17.7 Kimtron's Net Present Value Profile and Exchange Rate Sensitivity Analysis[a]

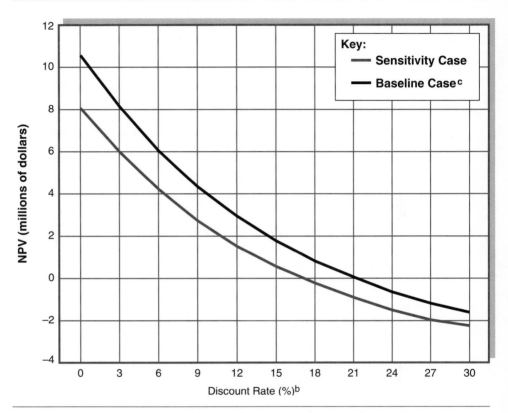

a Net present value profile shown is Kimtron's value from Fairtel's point of view. Net cash flows are from line 11 in Exhibit 17.6.

b The internal rate of return (IRR) is that discount rate which causes the project from the parent's point of view to have a net present value of zero.

c Baseline NPV profile is the result of the assumptions discussed in the case. Sensitivity NPV profile is the result of assuming the Korean won to depreciate 6% per year rather than the baseline assumption of 3% per year.

often much lower than its nominal value. Furthermore, most settlements are based on book value of the firm at the time of expropriation rather than the firm's market value.

Repayment of local debt would usually receive first claim on any compensation funds paid. Thus the debt remaining to Korean lenders would be paid before Fairtel could receive the balance of settlement funds. If no compensation agreement can be negotiated, it might be possible for Fairtel to default on Korean debt. In the more general case, however, local debt might be supplied by a subsidiary of a U.S. bank in the host country. The parent bank would probably expect to be repaid by the parent firm from funds outside the expropriating country if necessary.

The tax consequences of expropriation would depend on the timing and amount of capital loss recognized by the U.S. government. This loss would usually be based on the uncompensated book value of the Korean investment. The problem is that there is often some doubt as to when a write-off is appropriate for tax purposes, particularly if negotiations for a settlement drag on. In some ways a nice clear expropriation without hope of compensation, such as occurred in Cuba in the early 1960s, is preferred to a slow "bleeding to death" in protracted negotiations. The former leads to an earlier use of the tax shield and a one-shot write-off against earnings, whereas the latter tends to depress earnings for years, as legal and other costs continue and no tax shelter is achieved.

The value of future cash inflows forgone is really the key to the effect of expropriation on project rate of return in capital budgeting. According to Exhibit 17.6, if expropriation comes after the fourth year, the project will have a $1,249,700 negative cumulative net present value. The project would have a breakeven net present value of zero only if its terminal value is high enough to compensate for cash inflows forgone. In this case terminal value is composed of net compensation plus any tax shield. Therefore net compensation plus tax shield would need to have a net present value of $1,249,700 for Fairtel to realize the required 22% rate of return on Kimtron. The same type of analysis can be used to find a breakeven year or terminal value if funds are permanently blocked. Blocked funds reduce net present value in the same manner as expropriation, but without the benefit of a tax shield or compensation.

Foreign Exchange Risk

The project team assumed that the Korean won would depreciate versus the U.S. dollar at 3% per year. What if the rate of depreciation were 10% per year? Although this would make the assumed cash flows to Fairtel worth less in dollars, economic exposure analysis would be necessary to determine whether the cheaper won made Kimtron more competitive. Since all of Kimtron's sales are in Korea, and they import components priced in dollars from Fairtel, it would seem that Kimtron's profitability would be worse rather than better. However, if Kimtron were exporting product, the lower value for the won should have a favorable impact on profits.

What if the won should appreciate by 10% per year against the dollar? The same kind of economic exposure analysis is needed. In this particular case we might guess that the effect would be positive on both local sales in Korea and the value in dollars of dividends and license fees paid to Fairtel by Kimtron.

Other Sensitivity Variables

With reference to Exhibits 17.4 and 17.6, project rate of return to Fairtel would also be sensitive to a change in the assumed liquidation value, the margin percentage on exports to Kimtron, the size of the license fee paid by Kimtron, the size of the initial project cost, the amount of working capital financed locally, and the tax rates in Korea and the United States. Since some of these variables are within control of Fairtel it is still possible that the Kimtron project would qualify at the 22% required rate of return, particularly if the initial investment could be reduced, license fees raised, and the margin increased on exports to Kimtron from Fairtel.

SUMMARY

- Capital budgeting for foreign projects involves many complexities that do not exist in domestic projects.

- A foreign project should be judged on its net present value from the viewpoint of funds that can be freely remitted to the parent.

- Comparison of a project's net present value to similar projects in the host country is useful for evaluating expected performance relative to potential.

- Risks that are peculiar to foreign operations, such as political risk and foreign exchange risk, can be best accommodated by adjusting project cash flows rather than adjusting the project's risk-adjusted discount rate.

- An illustrative example, Kimtron, was analyzed in some detail. Rates of return were calculated from both the project's viewpoint and the parent's viewpoint.

- Once the most likely outcome is determined, a sensitivity analysis is normally undertaken. Foreign project returns are particularly sensitive to changes in assumptions about exchange-rate developments, political risk, and how the repatriation of funds is structured.

■ 1. Kimtron (C17A.WK1)

Kimtron, the proposed Korean subsidiary of the U.S. parent corporation, Fairtel, was analyzed in the chapter on the basis of the baseline assumptions regarding sales, costs, interest rates, and exchange rates.

The chief financial officer at Fairtel wishes you to conduct a number of sensitivity studies on the impact of other assumed values for these critical factors.

a) What is the net present value of Kimtron from the parent's viewpoint if the Korean won were to depreciate at an annual rate of 6% against the dollar?

b) What is the net present value of Kimtron from the project's and parent's viewpoint, if the sales price were to increase only 4% per year rather than 6% per year?

c) What is the impact on both the project's and parent's potential returns from Kimtron if the proposed license fee paid by Kimtron to Fairtel was increased to 3.5% from the original 2%.

■ 2. Strawberry Computers (C17B.WK1)

Strawberry Computers, a rapidly growing personal computer manufacturer, wants to expand its operations in Europe by establishing one subsidiary on the Continent in 1992. Analysis has narrowed the choice to two possibilities: Deutsche Erdbeere GmbH, in

Germany, and Fraise La France, S.A., in France. At the moment, only the following summary of expected cash flows (in thousands of currency units) is available:

Deutsche Erdbeere, GmbH	1992	1993	1994	1995	1996	1997
Total cash inflows (DM)		5,000	3,600	4,000	5,000	10,000
Total cash outflows (DM)	13,000	1,000	200	300	400	1,000
Additional cash outflows ($)		100	120	150	150	none

Fraise La France, S.A.	1992	1993	1994	1995	1996	1997
Total cash inflows (FF)		20,000	19,000	21,500	22,400	25,800
Total cash outflows (FF)	56,000	1,000	1,000	1,500	1,400	5,800
Additional cash outflows ($)		none	100	200	300	400

The forecasted exchange rates for 1992 are DM1.5000/$ and FF5.0000/$. Strawberry's currency advisor expects the French franc to remain unchanged over the 1992 to 1997 period, but the German mark to depreciate 4% per year. If the weighted average cost of capital for Strawberry Computers and either project is 15%, which prospect looks most promising?

3. Belgian Billiard Balls

The Belgian owner of a Brussels billiard ball manufacturing firm wants to manufacture in the United States to supply the U.S. market. The original investment will amount to BF12 million ($400,000 at the current spot rate of BF30/$), all in fixed assets, which may be depreciated over five years by the straight-line method. An additional BF3 million ($100,000) will be needed for working capital.

The Belgian entrepreneur expects to sell her ownership interest in the U.S. subsidiary (i.e., sell it as a going concern) at the end of three years for $100,000, clear of all income taxes in both countries, at which time she will purchase a country villa in the Ardennes mountains in Belgium and retire. Hence she wants to repatriate all funds to Belgium as fast as possible.

In evaluating the venture, the following forecasts are used:

End of Year	Unit Demand in U.S.	Unit Sales Price	Exchange Rate (BF/$)	Fixed Cash Operating Expenses	Depreciation
0			30		
1	700,000	$1.00	30	$100,000	$80,000
2	900,000	1.03	25	103,000	80,000
3	1,000,000	1.06	25	106,000	80,000

Variable manufacturing costs are expected to be 50% of sales. No additional funds need to be invested in the U.S. subsidiary during the first five years.

The United States imposes no restrictions on repatriation of any funds of any sort. The U.S. corporate tax rate is 40% and the Belgian rate is 50%. Both countries allow a tax credit for taxes paid in the other country.

The Belgian entrepreneur's weighted average cost of capital is 18% per annum, and her objective is to maximize her present wealth.

a) Is the investment attractive to the Belgian owner if she remains a Belgian resident?

b) Supposing the Belgian entrepreneur decided to emigrate to the United States at the beginning of the investment period, with the intention to retire in the Adirondack Mountains instead of the Ardennes after three years. Would this change her decision?

4. Solid Steel Corporation

Solid Steel Corporation of the United States is considering a capital investment in Egypt. The project would import raw steel bars and beams and fabricate them into forms suitable for local construction. Under current law, 100% of foreign investor cash flow from depreciation and 50% of annual accounting income must be retained within Egypt until the investment is five years old. Blocked funds may be invested in treasury deposits at 6% per annum, tax free, and compounded annually.

For analytical purposes, all cash flows will be valued as if they occur on December 31st. The investment outlay will occur on December 31, 1991, and earnings will be available for local currency dividend payments on December 31st, 1992 though 1996. All blocked funds may be exchanged for dollars on December 31, 1996. The exchange rate between Egyptian pounds and U.S. dollars is forecast to be:

(Dec. 31)	1991	1992	1993	1994	1995	1996
£E/$	3.0	3.2	3.4	3.6	3.8	4.0

Other information:

1. Investment outlay: $5,000,000 (£E 15,000,000) for plant and equipment. $3,000,000 (£E 9,000,000) is required for working capital.

2. Recovery: Building and equipment will be depreciated on a straight-line basis over five years. Working capital will be recovered in full at the end of five years.

3. Sales are expected to be £E 15,000,000 per year with no growth. Variable cash costs will be 40% of sales, and fixed cash costs are £E 1,000,000/year.

4. Income taxes are 40% in both Egypt and the United States.

5. Solid Steel's weighted average cost of capital for projects of this type is 15%. In Egypt similar projects would be expected to earn 25%.

From the dollar viewpoint of parent Solid Steel:

a) What is the present value of the expected dividend stream?

b) What is the present value of the blocked funds to be received at the end of the fifth year?

c) What is the present value of any other cash inflows? (Explain what they are.)

d) What is the net present value of the project?

e) List techniques Solid Steel might use to increase the net present value of the project.

5. Hofflander Ink Company (C17C.WK1)

Hofflander Ink Company currently exports U.S. ink to Mexico. Export sales revenue is expected to be $1,000,000 next year (year 1), and sales are expected to grow at the rate of 10% per annum for the next five years. After five years a locally owned Mexican competitor will be operational and all imports of U.S. ink will be banned. Hofflander's pre-U.S. income tax profit on exports to Mexico is 10% of gross export revenue.

To reduce the foreign exchange cost of ink over the next five years, Mexico has asked Hofflander to manufacture ink locally for a limited time. An investment of $1,800,000 for capital assets would be expended this year (year 0). These capital assets will be depreciated on a straight-line basis over five years, at the end of which time Mexico will assume full ownership of the operations by paying Hofflander $200,000 for all production rights and the fully depreciated plant. This terminal payment would be fully taxable in both Mexico and the United States.

If Hofflander decides to invest in Mexico, ink sales will jump initially because of government protection against other imports, and will be $2,200,000 in year 1. Thereafter sales would increase at the rate of only 8% per year until the end of the fifth year. Direct costs of manufacturing will equal 50% of sales. Bulk chemicals supplied from the United States by Hofflander will constitute 30% of these direct costs of manufacturing, while the other 70% of direct costs of manufacturing will be for expenses incurred locally within Mexico. On bulk chemicals sold to the affiliate, Hofflander will make a 50% pretax profit margin. Local fixed cash costs will be equivalent to $200,000 per year.

The rate of exchange between the U.S. dollar and the Mexican peso is Ps 3,000/$, and is expected to remain at that rate for the foreseeable future. Consequently, Hofflander is doing all of its analysis in dollar terms.

Corporate taxes are 30% in Mexico and 40% in the United States. The appropriate discount rate for the project is 15%. All accounting profits from the subsidiary, as well as the terminal $200,000 may be repatriated to the United States at the end of each year. The terminal value is taxable to the extent that it is greater than the remaining net book value of plant and equipment.

a) Is the proposal, as given, worthwhile from a project point of view? What is its net present value?

b) Is the proposal, as given, worthwhile from the parent's point of view? What is its net present value?

c) Suppose that Hofflander Ink were told by Mexico that if it did not make the investment, Mexico would give exclusive rights to a German competitor. How would such a policy influence the investment decision? What is the new parent net present value?

6. Pasadena Electronics, Inc.

Pasadena Electronics, Inc., of California currently exports 24,000 low-density light bulbs per year to Thailand under an import agreement that expires in five years. In Thailand, the bulbs are sold for the baht equivalent of $60 per set. Direct manufacturing costs and shipping together amount to $40 per set, and there are no other costs. The market for this type of bulb in Thailand is stable, neither growing nor shrinking. Pasadena holds the major portion of the market.

The Thai government has invited Pasadena to open an assembly plant so that imported bulbs can be replaced by local production. If Pasadena makes the investment, it will operate the plant for five years and then sell the building and equipment to Thai investors at net book value at the time of sale, plus the current amount of any working capital. Pasadena will be allowed to repatriate all net income and depreciation funds to the United States at the end of each year.

Pasadena's anticipated outlay in 1992 would be:

Building and equipment	$1,000,000
Working capital	1,000,000
Total outlay	$2,000,000

Depreciation and investment recovery. Building and equipment will be depreciated over five years on a straight-line basis. Funds equal to annual depreciation charges may be returned to the United States annually. At the end of the fifth year, the $1,000,000 of working capital may also be repatriated to the United States.

Sales price. Locally assembled switches will be sold for the Thai baht equivalent of $60 each.

Operating expenses.

Materials purchased in Thailand (dollar amount of baht cost)	$20 per set
Raw materials imported from U.S. parent	10 per set
Total variable costs	$30 per set

The $10 transfer price for components sold by Pasadena to its Thai subsidiary consists of $5.00 of direct costs incurred in the United States and $5.00 of pretax profit to Pasadena. There are no other operating costs in either Thailand or the United States.

Taxes. Both Thailand and the United States have a corporate income tax rate of 40%.

Cost of capital. Pasadena uses a 15% discount rate to evaluate all domestic and foreign projects.

Assume the investment is made at the end of 1992, and all operating cash flows occur at the end of 1993 through 1997. The baht/dollar exchange rate is expected to remain constant over the next five years.

a) Do you recommend that Pasadena make the investment?

b) Pasadena learns that if it decides not to invest in Thailand, Matsushita Electronics will probably make an investment similar to that being considered by Pasadena. Matsushita would be protected by the Thai government against imports. How would this information affect your analysis and recommendations?

c) After the analysis in part b above, you discover the following: The anticipated investment of $1,000,000 in building and equipment includes the book value of some surplus equipment now in the United States which Pasadena intended to ship to Thailand and factor in at its book value of $400,000. However, that plant and equipment could have been sold in the United States for $800,000 after all taxes; that is, it is worth $800,000 rather than $400,000. How would this information affect your analysis and recommendations?

d) Assume the conditions of question b above. Thailand reduces income tax charged to foreign firms from 50% to 20% in order to attract foreign investors. How would this information affect your analysis and recommendation?

e) How would your analysis and recommendation for d, above, differ if Pasadena expected to have a permanent presence in Thailand, and if it expected long-run growth opportunities in Thailand?

f) Assume the conditions of question b above. Imports from the United States are paid for at once. However, Thailand blocks all other cash remittances to the United States until the end of the fifth year, at which time all free cash may be repatriated. Funds invested in Thailand earn 3% per annum, compounded annually. How would this information affect your analysis and recommendation?

g) Assume the conditions of question f above. Pasadena is able to enter into an arrangement to use operating cash (depreciation and earnings) to purchase canned tum yum soup for shipment to and eventual sale in the United States. The Thai cost of tum yum soup is charged against Thai earnings at full cost. The supply of tum yum is unlimited, but U.S. tastes are such that it can be sold only at 80% of its Thai purchase price. How would this opportunity affect your analysis and recommendation?

NOTES

1. Arthur Stonehill and Leonard Nathanson, "Capital Budgeting and the Multinational Corporation," *California Management Review*, Summer 1968, pp. 39–54. James C. Baker and Laurence J. Beardsley, "Multinational Companies' Use of Risk Evaluation and Profit Measurement for Capital Budgeting Decisions," *Journal of Business Finance*, Spring 1973, pp. 38–43. David J. Oblak and Roy J. Helm, Jr., "Survey and Analysis of Capital Budgeting Methods Used by Multinationals," *Financial Management*, Winter 1980, pp. 37–41. Vinod B. Bavishi, "Capital Budgeting Practices at Multinationals," *Management Accounting*, August 1981, pp. 32–35. Marie E. Wicks Kelly and George C. Philippatos, "Comparative Analysis of the Foreign Investment Evaluation Practices by U.S.-Based Manufacturing Multinational Corporations," *Journal of International Business Studies*, Winter 1982, pp. 19–42. Marjorie Stanley and Stanley Block, "An Empirical Study of Management and Financial Variables

Influencing Capital Budgeting Decisions for Multinational Corporations in the 1980s," *Management International Review*, vol. 23, no. 3, 1983, pp. 61–71.

2. *Op cit.,* Bavishi, "Capital Budgeting Practices," p. 34.

3. *Op Cit.,* Stanley and Block, "Management and Financial Variables."

4. U.S. firms must consolidate foreign affiliates that are over 50% owned. If an affiliate is between 20% and 50% owned, it is usually consolidated on a pro-rata basis. Affiliates less than 20% owned are normally carried as unconsolidated investments.

5. *Op cit.,* Baker and Beardsley, "Risk Evaluation and Profit Measurement," p. 39.

6. *Op cit.,* Oblak and Helm, "Capital Budgeting Methods," p. 39.

7. *Op cit.,* Stanley and Block, "Management and Financial Variables," pp. 66–67.

BIBLIOGRAPHY

Agmon, Tamir, "Capital Budgeting and Unanticipated Changes in the Exchange Rate," *Advances in Financial Planning and Forecasting,* 4, part B, 1990, pp. 295–314.

Baker, James C., and Laurence J. Beardsley, "Multinational Companies' Use of Risk Evaluation and Profit Measurement for Capital Budgeting Decisions," *Journal of Business Finance*, Spring 1973, pp. 38–43.

Bavishi, Vinod B., "Capital Budgeting Practices at Multinationals," *Management Accounting*, August 1981, pp. 32–35.

Booth, Laurence D., "Capital Budgeting Frameworks for the Multinational Corporation," *Journal of International Business Studies*, Fall 1982, pp. 113–123.

Dinwiddy, Caroline, and Francis Teal, "Project Appraisal Procedures and the Evaluation of Foreign Exchange," *Economics*, February 1986, pp. 97–107.

Dotan, Amihud, and Arie Ovadia, "A Capital-Budgeting Decision—The Case of a Multinational Corporation Operating in High-Inflation Countries," *Journal of Business Research*, October 1986, pp. 403–410.

Freitas, Lewis P., "Investment Decision Making in Japan," *Journal of Accounting, Auditing & Finance*, Summer 1981, pp. 378–382.

Gordon, Sara L., and Francis A. Lees, "Multinational Capital Budgeting: Foreign Investment under Subsidy," *California Management Review*, Fall 1982, pp. 22–32.

Hodder, James E., "Evaluation of Manufacturing Investments: A Comparison of U.S. and Japanese Practices," *Financial Management*, Spring 1986, pp. 17–24.

Kelly, Marie E. Wicks, *Foreign Investment Evaluation Practices of U.S. Multinational Corporations*, Ann Arbor: UMI Research Press, 1983.

——, and George C. Philippatos, "Comparative Analysis of the Foreign Investment Evaluation Practices by U.S.-based Manufacturing Multinational Corporations," *Journal of International Business Studies*, Winter 1982, pp. 19–42.

Lessard, Donald R., "Evaluating International Projects: An Adjusted Present Value Approach," in Donald R. Lessard, ed., *International Financial Management: Theory and Application*, New York: Wiley, 1985, pp. 570–584.

Mehta, Dileep R., "Capital Budgeting Procedures for a Multinational," in P. Sethi and R. Holton, eds., *Management of Multinationals*, New York: Free Press, 1974, pp. 271–291.

Oblak, David J., and Roy J. Helm, Jr., "Survey and Analysis of Capital Budgeting Methods Used by Multinationals," *Financial Management*, Winter 1980, pp. 37–41.

Shapiro, Alan C., "Capital Budgeting for the Multinational Corporation," *Financial Management*, Spring 1978, pp. 7–16.

——, "International Capital Budgeting," *Midland Corporate Finance Journal*, Spring 1983, pp. 26–45.

Stanley, Marjorie, and Stanley Block, "An Empirical Study of Management and Financial Variables Influencing Capital Budgeting Decisions for Multinational Corporations in the 1980s", *Management International Review*, no. 3, 1983.

Stonehill, Arthur, and Leonard Nathanson, "Capital Budgeting and the Multinational Corporation," *California Management Review*, Summer 1968, pp. 39–54.

Adjusted Present Value (APV)

A project that is financed differently than that of the parent firm could be evaluated with an alternative analysis called Adjusted Present Value (APV). For example, consider a parent firm whose capital structure is 60% equity and 40% debt, but is evaluating the financial feasibility of a potential foreign subsidiary that would be only 40% equity and 60% debt. Discounting the potential subsidiary's estimated net operating cash flows by the parent's weighted average cost of capital (based on its own capital structure) could be inappropriate.

APV divides the present value analysis into two components: (1) the net operating cash flows which are customarily considered the only relevant cash flows; (2) the interest expense tax shields resulting from the use of debt in the financing of the project. Each component cash flow is discounted by its appropriate cost of all-equity and all-debt discount rates, respectively.

Net Present Value

For example, assume Kimtron was capitalized with 40% equity capital from Fairtel and the remaining 60% debt, the Fairtel's capital structure was 40% debt and 60% equity, the cost of debt 12%, the cost of equity 18%, and U.S. taxes 34%, the weighted average cost of capital would be:

$$WACC = (0.40)\ (12\%)\ (1 - 0.34) + (0.60)\ (18\%) = 14.98\%.$$

The normal net present value approach demonstrated in the chapter would discount net operating cash flows as follows:

$$NPV = (\$9,000.0) + \frac{\$1,030.4}{(1+0.1498)^1} + \frac{\$1,559.0}{(1+0.1498)^2} + \frac{\$2,136.7}{(1+0.1498)^3} + \frac{\$2,768.5}{(1+0.1498)^4} + \frac{\$12,086.3}{(1+0.1498)^5}$$
$$= \$2,079.3.$$

The NPV of the project is then evaluated with one cost of capital, the weighted average.

Adjusted Present Value

APV would decompose the valuation into the above net operating cash flows and the tax shields arising from the use of debt in the foreign subsidiary. The net operating cash flows (NOCF) from above would then be discounted by the cost of equity for a similar project undertaken with 100% equity. For illustration purposes here, we use the firm's current cost of equity:

$$NPV\ (NOCF) = (\$9,000.0) + \frac{\$1,030.8}{(1+0.18)^1} + \frac{\$1,560.0}{(1+0.18)^2} + \frac{\$2,136.6}{(1+0.18)^3} + \frac{\$2,767.9}{(1+0.18)^4} + \frac{\$12,085.5}{(1+0.18)^5}$$
$$= \$1,004.3.$$

The tax shields resulting from the use of debt in Kimtron are found by estimating the annual interest expense $720,000 ($6,000,000 in debt at 12% per year), and the Korean tax savings resulting from interest expense deductions of $216,000 (30% Korean income tax on $720,000) over the life of the project.

$$\text{NPV (tax shield)} = \frac{\$216}{(1+0.12)^1} + \frac{\$216}{(1+0.12)^2} + \frac{\$216}{(1+0.12)^3} + \frac{\$216}{(1+0.12)^4} + \frac{\$216}{(1+0.12)^5}$$
$$= \$778.6.$$

The total APV for Kimtron would be:

$$\text{APV} = \$1,004.3 + \$778.6 = \$1,783.0.$$

The resulting APV could be a more appropriate valuation of the cash flows when the project is financed differently from that of the parent firm. Although the net operating cash flows are valued lower (higher discount rate of straight equity applied to them), the tax shields resulting from the increased used of debt in the subsidiary (discounted at the cost of debt) offset the loss in equity-financed cash flows. Although APV is a viable method of analysis it is not nearly as widely used in practice as the traditional method using a weighted average cost of capital.

PART

5

MANAGEMENT OF ONGOING OPERATIONS

Although not as glamorous as the topics already covered, management of ongoing operations occupies most of the working time of international financial executives.

Chapter 18 covers the traditional topic of import/export financing. Emphasis is on the need for specialized trade-oriented instruments, documentation requirements, and various government programs to stimulate exports.

Chapter 19 analyzes selected aspects of working capital management. It describes the strategy of unbundling international fund transfers such as dividends, royalties, fees, and home office overhead. Transfer pricing is one of the most time-consuming and ambiguous activities performed by financial executives. Also covered is the problem of dealing with blocked funds. The chapter concludes with the manage-

ment of cash, accounts receivable, and inventory.

Chapter 20 analyzes how the performance of foreign subsidiaries can be evaluated by the parent firm. In particular, exchange rate changes can seriously impact this performance measurement. Also covered are some differences in international accounting standards and the possible misuse of ratio analysis when making international corporate comparisons.

Chapter 21 describes the influence of taxation on multinational firms. Emphasis is on differences in national tax environments and how countries tax foreign source income of their own multinational firms. An appendix provides a detailed description of how the United States taxes foreign source income of U.S. firms.

preference is as follows:

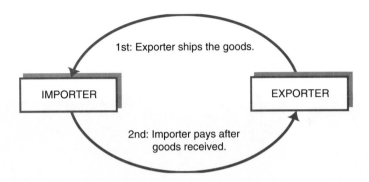

The exporter has an opposite set of preferences:

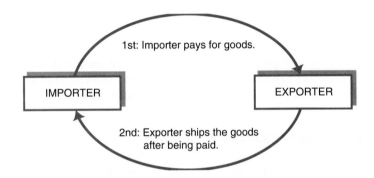

The dilemma of not trusting a stranger in a foreign land is solved by using a bank as an intermediary. A greatly simplified view is the following:

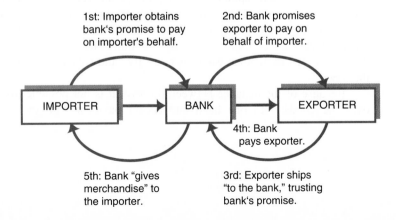

In this simplified view, the importer obtains the bank's promise to pay on its behalf, knowing that the exporter will trust the bank. The bank's promise to pay is called a *letter of credit*.

The exporter ships the merchandise to the importer's country. Title to the merchandise is given, in due course, to the bank on a document called an *order bill of lading*. The exporter requests the bank to pay for the goods, which the bank does. The document to request payment is a *sight draft*. The bank, having paid for the goods, now passes title to the importer, whom the bank trusts. At that time or later, depending on their agreement, the importer reimburses the bank.

The three key documents and their interaction will be described in the following pages. They constitute a system which evolved over centuries to protect both importer and exporter from (1) the risk of noncompletion, (2) foreign exchange risk, and (3) to provide a means of financing.

Risk of Noncompletion

Once importer and exporter agree on terms, the seller usually wants to maintain legal title to the goods until paid, or at least until assured of payment. The buyer, however, is reluctant to pay before receiving the goods, or at least before receiving title to them. Each wants assurance that the other party will complete its portion of the transaction. The three key documents that we will be examining—the letter of credit, the draft, and the bill of lading—are part of a carefully constructed system to determine who will bear the financial loss if one of the parties defaults at any time.

Protection Against Foreign Exchange Risk

In international trade, foreign exchange risk arises from transaction exposure. If the transaction requires payment in the exporter's currency, the importer carries the foreign exchange risk. If the transaction calls for payment in the importer's currency, the exporter has the foreign exchange risk.

Transaction exposure can be hedged by the techniques described in Chapter 8, but to do this the exposed party must be certain that payment of a specified amount will be made on a particular date. The three key documents described in this chapter assure both amount and time of payment, and thus lay the groundwork for effective hedging.

Financing the Trade

Most international trade involves a time lag because funds are tied up while the merchandise is in transit. Once the risks of noncompletion and of exchange rate changes are disposed of, banks are willing to finance goods in transit. A bank can deal with the financial aspects of a trade, as evidenced by the key documents, without exposing itself to questions about the quality of the merchandise or other physical aspects of the shipment.

Traditional Trade Versus Multinational Sourcing

The risk of noncompletion and foreign exchange risk are most important when the international trade is episodic, with no outstanding agreement for recurring shipments and no sustained relationship between buyer and seller. When the import/export relationship is of a recurring nature, as in the case of manufactured goods shipped weekly or monthly to a final assembly or retail outlet in another country, and when it is between countries whose currencies are considered strong, the exports may well be billed on open account after a normal credit check. Banks provide credit information and collection services outside of the system of processing drafts drawn against letters of credit.

In the remainder of this chapter we will examine the letter of credit, the draft, the bill of lading, and a few additional documents that support these key documents. We will also discuss countertrade, which is a nonfinancial system to carry out international trade. Forfaiting, which is related to international trade, was discussed in Chapter 10 on banking.

LETTER OF CREDIT

A letter of credit, abbreviated L/C, is an instrument issued by a bank at the request of an importer, in which the bank promises to pay a beneficiary upon presentation of documents specified in the letter of credit. A letter of credit reduces the risk of noncompletion, since the bank agrees to pay against documents rather than actual merchandise. The relationship between the three parties can be seen in Exhibit 18.1.

In international trade a letter of credit is sometimes referred to as a *commercial letter of credit*, a *documentary letter of credit*, or simply a *credit*. A commercial letter of credit

Exhibit 18.1   Parties to a Letter of Credit

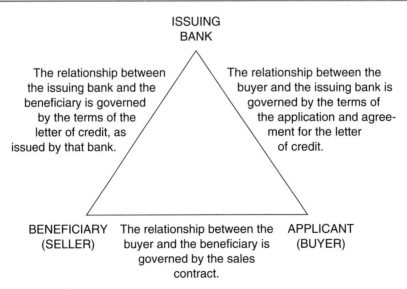

Source: First National Bank of Chicago, *Financing U.S. Exports,* compiled by Patricia A. Ferris, January 1975, p. 21.

is somewhat different from a *traveler's letter of credit*, since the latter is normally used for noncommercial transactions. Traveler's letters of credit usually call for clean (nondocumentary) drafts—a distinction that will be explained later in this chapter. Payment under a commercial letter of credit is usually by documentary drafts.

Normally a commercial letter of credit is used as part of the financing of a commercial transaction. Although details vary, depending on the type of letter of credit and its provisions, the following transaction is typical. An importer (buyer) and exporter (seller) agree on a transaction. The importer applies to its local bank for the issuance of a letter of credit on a form such as shown in Exhibit 18.2. In Exhibit 18.2 a U.S. importer, XYZ, Inc., of Torrance, California, is applying to Security Pacific National Bank for a letter of credit good up to the amount of $7,690.20, to be issued to Japanese exporter, ABC Co., Ltd., of Tokyo.

The importer's bank, Security Pacific in Exhibit 18.2, will issue the letter of credit according to its assessment of the importer's creditworthiness, or the bank might require a cash deposit or other collateral from the importer in advance. The importer's bank will want to know the type of transaction, the amount of money involved, and what documents must accompany the draft that will be drawn against the letter of credit. The application in Exhibit 18.2 is for the importation of PVC blue discharge hose, and the draft is to be payable 90 days after sight.

If the importer's bank is satisfied with the credit standing of the applicant, it will issue a letter of credit guaranteeing to pay for the merchandise if shipped in accordance with the instructions and conditions contained in the credit. Exhibit 18.3 shows the letter of credit issued by Security Pacific National Bank for the import of PVC blue discharge hose. The credit specifies exactly what documents must accompany the draft drawn against the credit: commercial invoice, customs invoice, packing list, insurance policy or certificate, and a clean-on-board ocean bill of lading.

At this point the credit of the bank has been substituted for that of the importer, and the letter of credit becomes a financial contract between the issuing bank and the designated beneficiary, ABC Co., Ltd., of Tokyo. This financial contract is a separate transaction from the sale of the merchandise. If the terms of the letter of credit are met, any payment problems that develop at a later date are of concern only to the importer and the issuing bank. All other parties to the transaction may rely on the bank's credit without concern about the financial status of the importer.

The importer's bank issuing the letter of credit sends the document to a correspondent in the exporter's country, or to the exporter's bank, which advises the exporter (the beneficiary) of the establishment of a letter of credit in its name.

After shipping the merchandise, the exporter draws a draft against the issuing bank in accordance with the terms of the letter of credit, attaches the required documents, and presents the draft to its own bank for payment. At this point different combinations of events are possible. Let us assume that the exporter's bank has not itself confirmed the credit. That is, the exporter's bank has not added its own promise to pay to the promise of the issuing bank. In this case the exporter's bank will receive the draft and accompanying documents and forward them to the bank of the importer, which issued the credit. If all the

Exhibit 18.2   Application for Letter of Credit

TO: **SECURITY PACIFIC NATIONAL BANK** **S**   LETTER OF CREDIT APPLICATION AND SECURITY AGREEMENT
INTERNATIONAL BANKING GROUP

PLEASE ISSUE YOUR IRREVOCABLE LETTER AND ADVISE THE BENEFICIARY BY [X] AIRMAIL [ ] CABLE SHORT DETAILS [ ] CABLE FULL OF DETAILS

IN FAVOR OF **ABC Co., Ltd.   No. 10 Mori Bldg 1-81-1, Toranomon, Minator-Ku, Tokyo, 105, Japan**
(NAME & ADDRESS)
FOR ACCOUNT OF **XYZ, Inc. 55555 Hawthorne Blvd., Suite 400-14 Torrance, California 90503**
(NAME & ADDRESS)

UP TO THE   AVAILABLE BY DRAFTS   OF INVOICE VALUE
AGGREGATE SUM OF **US$7,690.20**   ON YOU OR YOUR   ACCOMPANIED BY THE FOLLOWING
CORRESPONDENT AT **90** SIGHT FOR **100** % DOCUMENTS INDICATED BY X 1
(USANCE)

[X] SIGNED COMMERCIAL
INVOICE (S) **3**   [X] SPECIAL CUSTOMS INVOICE (S) **3**   [X] PACKING LIST **3**
(INDICATE NUMBER OF COPIES)

[X] NEGOTIABLE MARINE & WAR RISK INSURANCE POLICY CERTIFICATE FOR **110** %
OF CIF VALUE WITH CLAIMS PAYABLE IN THE UNITED STATES

[ ] OTHER DOCUMENTS

[X] FULL SET OF CLEAN ON BOARD
OCEAN BILLS OF LADING   [X] TO ORDER OF SHIPPER BLANK ENDORSED   [ ] TO ORDER   SPECIMEN

[ ] AIRWAY BILL AIR CONSGNMENT
NOTE CONSIGNED TO

[ ] RAILROAD/TRUCK BILL OF
LADING CONSIGNED TO

SHOWING   FREIGHT PREPAID   FREIGHT COLLECT   MARKED NOTIFY **XYZ, Inc. 55555 Hawthorne Blvd., Suite 400-14 Torrance, California 90503**

EVIDENCE
SHIPMENT OF **PVC Blue Discharge Hose**
(SPECIFY COMMODITY ONLY OMITTING DETAILS AS TO GRADE, QUALITY, PRICE, ETC.)

FROM **Nagoya, Japan**   TO **CIF, Los Angeles, Calif.**   SHIPMENT TERMS (CHECK ONE [X]) [ ]   [ ] FOB [X] CIF [ ] C&F
(PORT OF SHIPMENT)   (DESTINATION)   (OTHER)

LATEST SHIPMENT DATE IS **Oct. 30, 19xx**   PARTIAL SHPMENTS PERMITTED [ ] YES [X] NO   TRANSHIPMENT PERMITTED [ ] YES [X] NO

LATEST NEGOTIATION DATE IS **Nov. 10, 19xx**   INSURANCE TO BE EFFECTED BY **Seller**
(BUYER OR SELLER)

SPECIAL INSTRUCTIONS   (INDICATE HERE ANY SPECIAL INTRUCTIONS YOU WISH INCLUDED IN THE LETTE OF CREDIT)

[X] COMMERCIAL INVOISED MUST CONTAIN SHIPPER'S SIGNED
CERTIFICATON THAT GOODS ARE IN ACCORDANCE WITH BUYER'S PURCHASE ORDER NO. **2944** PROFORMA INVOICE NO ____ DATED ____

[ ]

ADVISE CREDIT THROUGH BENEFICIARY'S BANK NAMED HERE **Security Pacific National Bank, Tokyo, Japan**
(IF BENEFICIARY IS UNKNOWN WE WILL USE OUR CORRESPONDENT BANK)

DEBIT OFFICE   ACCOUNT   MAIL SHIPPING
TO: NAME ____   NUMBER ____   DOCUMENTS TO **DEF Co, Customs Broker, San Pedro**

<table>
<tr><td rowspan="5">FOR BANK USE ONLY</td><td>EXTENSION OF THIS CREDIT UNDER CUSTOMER'S LIABILITY HAS BEEN APPROVED BY AN AUTHORIZED LOAN OFFICER OF SECURITY PACIFIC NATIONAL BANK.

OFFICE: ____</td><td>DIRECT INQUIRIES   PHONE
TO OUR MR __J. Smith__   NUMBER ____

WE AND EACH OF US AGREE THAT THE TERMS AND CONDITIONS SET FORTH ON THIS AND THE REVERSE HEREOF ARE HEREBY MADE A PART OF THIS APPLICATION AND ARE ACCEPTED AND AGREED TO BY US</td></tr>
<tr><td>APPROVING OFFICER'S
SIGNATURE AND TITLE ____</td><td>FIRM
NAME **XYZ Inc. 55555Hawthorne Blvd., Torrance**</td></tr>
<tr><td>HEAD OFFICE
I.B.G.
L/C NO **308,590**   APPROVAL ____</td><td>AUTHORIZED
SIGNATURE (S) ____</td></tr>
</table>

02331-7 2-76* 50 10Y   TITLE ____

Source: Security Pacific National Bank.

Exhibit 18.3 Letter of Credit

IRREVOCABLE
DOCUMENTARY
LETTER OF CREDIT

CABLE ADDRESS
SEPACBANK

SECURITY PACIFIC NATIONAL BANK
INTERNATIONAL BANKING GROUP

☐ Post Office Box 7637
San Francisco, California 94120

☒ Head Office - Post Office Box 92890
Los Angeles, California 90009

☐ Post Office Box 1971
San Diego, California 92112

¥ ABC Co., Ltd.
¥ No. 10 Mori Bldg 1-18-1 Toramon, Minato-Ku
¥ Tokyo, 105, Japan
¥

Advised by AIRMAIL/CABLE through

¥ Security Pacific National Bank
¥ International Banking Office
¥ Tokyo, Japan

WE ESTABLISH OUR IRREVOCABLE LETTER OF CREDIT NUMBER L/C 308,590 DATE 9-22-xx IN YOUR FAVOR

FOR THE ACCOUNT OF XYZ, Inc., 55555 Hawthorne Blvd., Suite 400-14 Torrance, California 90503

UP TO THE AGGREGATE SUM OF SEVEN THOUSAND SIX HUNDRED NINETY AND 20/100 UNITED STATES DOLLARS*
*   *   *   *($7,690.20)
AVAILABLE BY YOU DRAFT (S) AT 90 days SIGHT FOR 100 % INVOICE DRAWN ON US

AND ACCOMPANIED BY THE FOLLOWING DOCUMENTS:

1. Signed Commercial Invoices in triplicate, certifying that goods are in accordance with buyer's purchase order No. 2944.
2. Special Customs Invoices in triplicate.
3. Packing List in triplicate.
4. Negotiable Marine & War Risk Insurance Policy/Certificate for 110% of CIF value with claims payable in the United States.
5. Full set of clean on board Ocean Bills of Lading to the order of shipper, blank endorsed, showing "Freight Prepaid", marked Notify: XYZ, Inc., 55555 Hawthorne Blvd., Suite 400-14 Torrance, California 90503.

SPECIMEN

EVIDENCE SHIPMENT OF PVC Blue Discharge Hose

FROM Nagoya, Japan

To CIF, Los Angeles, California

PARTIAL SHIPMENTS ARE not PERMITTED
TRANSHIPMENT IS not PERMITTED. INSURANCE IS TO BE EFFECTED BY Seller

LATEST NEGOTIATION DATE OF THIS LETTER OF CREDIT IS November 10, 19xx

DRAFTS DRAWN AND NEGOTIATED UNDER THIS LETTER OF CREDIT MUST BE ENDORSED HEREON AND MUST BEAR THE CLAUSE:
"DRAWN UNDER SECURITY PACIFIC NATIONAL BANK LETTER OF CREDIT NUMBER 308,590   DATED 9-22-xx
WE HEREBY ENGAGE WITH THE BONA FIDE HOLDERS THAT DRAFTS DRAWN STRICTLY IN COMPLIANCE WITH THE TERMS OF THIS CREDIT
AND AMMENDMENTS SHALL MEET WITH DUE HONOR UPON PRESENTATION XXXXXXXXXXXXXXXXXXXXXXXXXXXXXX
THIS CREDIT IS SUBJECT TO THE UNIFORM CUSTOMS AND PRACTICE FOR DOCUMENTARY CREDITS (1974 REVISION), INTERNATIONAL
CHAMBER OF COMMERCE PUBLICATION NUMBER 290.

*TO THE DRAWEE BANK

Authorized Signature

WHEN OPENED BY CABLE. THIS CREDIT IS ONLY AVAILABLE IF
ATTACHED TO OUR CORRESPONDENT'S ADVICE OF CABLED
CREDIT. THE TWO CONSTITUTING EVIDENCE OF THE OUTSTAND-
ING AMOUNT OF THIS CREDIT.

051821 1-77 PS

Source: Security Pacific National Bank.

terms and conditions expressed on the letter of credit have been complied with and the required documents are attached, the importer's bank will honor the draft. In this instance it will pay the exporter's bank. When the exporter's bank receives the funds, it pays the exporter.

The importer's bank, in turn, collects from the importer in accordance with the terms agreed upon at the time the letter of credit was opened. The importer might have to pay at once in order to obtain the documents, including the order bill of lading that is needed to obtain the physical possession of the merchandise. Alternatively, the bank may release the documents to the importer and the importer may promise to pay at some later date, usually under a trust receipt arrangement.

In the previous example the importer's bank decided to pay after inspecting the documents, and the exporter's bank functioned only as a collection organization. An alternative procedure would have been for the exporter's bank to *confirm* the letter of credit. The exporter's bank would then itself honor drafts drawn against the credit when first presented and obtain reimbursement from the importer's bank. The distinction between confirmed and unconfirmed letters of credit will be explained more fully later in this section.

We emphasize here that a letter of credit is a promise to pay *against specified documents*, which must accompany any draft drawn against the credit. The letter of credit is not a guarantee of the underlying commercial transaction. To constitute a true letter of credit transaction, the following five elements must all be present with respect to the issuing bank:

1. The issuing bank must receive a fee or other valid business consideration for the letter of credit.

2. The bank's letter of credit must contain a specified expiration date or be for a definite term.

3. The bank's commitment must have a stated maximum.

4. The bank's obligation to pay must arise only on the presentation of specific documents, and the bank must not be called on to determine disputed questions of fact or law.

5. The bank's customer must have an unqualified obligation to reimburse the bank on the same condition as the bank has paid.

Types of Letters of Credit

Most commercial letters of credit are *documentary*, meaning that certain documents must be included with any drafts drawn under the terms of the credit. Documents required usually include an order bill of lading, a commercial invoice, and any of the following: consular invoice, insurance certificate or policy, certificate of origin, weight list, certificate of analysis, packing list. Commercial letters of credit are also classified as follows.

Irrevocable Versus Revocable. An irrevocable letter of credit obligates the issuing bank to honor drafts drawn in compliance with the credit and can be neither canceled nor modified without the consent of all parties, including in particular the beneficiary (exporter). A revocable letter of credit can be canceled or amended at any time before payment; it is intended to serve as a means of arranging payment but not as a guarantee of payment.

Confirmed Versus Unconfirmed. A letter of credit issued by one bank can be confirmed by another, in which case both banks are obligated to honor drafts drawn in compliance with the credit. An unconfirmed letter of credit is the obligation only of the issuing bank. An exporter is likely to want a foreign bank's letter of credit confirmed by a domestic bank when the exporter has doubts about the foreign bank's ability to pay. Such doubts may arise if the exporter is unsure of the financial standing of the foreign bank, or if political or economical conditions in the foreign country are unstable.

The desirability of confirmation was apparent from an event in 1975. The Bank of Nigeria, that country's central bank, refused to pay on irrevocable letters of credit that it had issued for the import of material ordered for Nigeria's development. Flush with income earned as a member of OPEC and desirous of furthering its economic development, Nigeria ordered more cement and other items than could be unloaded by available port facilities. By October 1975, some 400 ships were backed up in Lagos harbor, and the estimated delay for a newly arriving ship was 450 days. The governor of the Bank of Nigeria lamented (*Business Week*, November 3, 1975): "It is the exporters and shipowners who are making things difficult." The bank refused to honor its supposedly irrevocable letters of credit. Bankers termed the event virtually unprecedented in international trade. Exporters to Nigeria suffered major losses. Had the exporters insisted that their own banks confirm the Bank of Nigeria's "irrevocable" letters of credit, the losses would have been borne by the confirming bank rather than the exporters. An underlying assumption is that a confirming bank is better able to judge the credibility of a bank issuing a letter of credit than is a merchant.

Revolving Versus Nonrevolving. Most letters of credit are nonrevolving; they are valid for one transaction only. Under some circumstances, a revolving credit is issued. A $10,000 revolving weekly credit means that the beneficiary is authorized to draw drafts up to $10,000 each week until the credit expires. The period of a revolving credit might be daily, weekly, or monthly. Because the maximum exposure under an irrevocable revolving credit is very great (the buyer cannot stop its obligation to pay for future shipments even if it is dissatisfied with the merchandise), most revolving credits are issued in revocable form. A revolving credit may be *noncumulative*, in which case any amount not used by the beneficiary during the specified period may not be drawn against in a later period; or it may be *cumulative*, in which case undrawn amounts carry over to future periods. Under a cumulative revolving credit of, say, $10,000 per week, a beneficiary who drew only $7,000 in one week could draw up to $13,000 the following week.

Issuers of Letters of Credit

From an exporter's point of view a documentary letter of credit is one of the following:

1. An irrevocable letter of credit issued by a foreign bank and confirmed irrevocably by a domestic bank. (On occasion the credit may be confirmed by a third-country foreign bank. For example, a U.S. exporter might receive a letter of credit from an African bank confirmed by a French or English bank.)

2. An irrevocable letter of credit issued by a domestic bank.

3. An irrevocable letter of credit issued by a foreign bank without the responsibility or endorsement of a domestic bank. In this situation the domestic bank transmits information (when the letter is opened) and forwards drafts for collection but does not lend its guarantee.

4. A revocable letter of credit established to arrange for payment.

Exporters generally prefer types 1 and 2 above, since they need look no further than a bank in their own country for compliance with the terms of the letter of credit. Although a letter of credit issued by a foreign bank alone (type 3) might well be of the highest esteem, most exporters are not in a position to evaluate or deal with foreign banks directly should difficulties arise.

Every irrevocable letter of credit must indicate an expiration date beyond which documents for payment or acceptance will not be accepted. Documents, such as drafts or bills of lading, must be presented within a reasonable time after issue, for if there is undue delay, the bank may refuse to accept them.

Advantages and Disadvantages of Letters of Credit

The primary advantage of a letter of credit is that it facilitates international trade. The exporter gains because it can sell against the promise to pay of a bank rather than of a commercial firm. The exporter is also in a more secure position as to the availability of foreign exchange to pay for its sale. If the letter of credit is confirmed by a bank in the exporter's country, the problem of blocked foreign exchange is eliminated. Even if the letter of credit is not confirmed, the issuing foreign bank is more likely to be aware of foreign exchange conditions and rules than is the importing firm itself. Last, should the importing country change its foreign exchange rules, it is likely to allow already outstanding bank letters of credit to be honored for fear of throwing its own domestic banks into international disrepute.

An exporter may find that an order backed by an irrevocable letter of credit will facilitate obtaining domestic pre-export financing. If the exporter's reputation for delivery is good, a local bank may lend funds to process and prepare the merchandise for shipment. Once the merchandise is shipped in compliance with the terms and conditions of the credit, payment for the business transaction is made and funds will be generated to repay the pre-export loan.

The major advantage to the importing firm of a letter of credit is that the firm need not pay out funds until the documents have arrived and unless all conditions stated in the credit have been fulfilled. The main disadvantages are the fee charged by the importer's bank for issuing its letter of credit, and the likelihood that the letter of credit reduces the importer's borrowing line of credit from the importer's bank.

Liabilities of Banks under Letters of Credit

When banks issue letters of credit they incur certain obligations that are specified in detail in *Uniform Customs and Practices for Documentary Credits*, published by the United States Council of the International Chamber of Commerce.[1]

The basic nature of a letter of credit is that the bank is obligated to pay against documents, not actual goods. Thus banks must carefully examine all documents to be sure that they are in accordance with the original terms and conditions of the letter of credit. However, banks are not liable for defects in the documents themselves, as long as any defect was not apparent on the face of the document. Thus, for example, the bank is not responsible for detecting false documents; for verifying that the quantities, quality, weights, or condition of the goods is other than what is stated on the documents; or for validating the good faith and performance of any of the parties to the underlying transaction. The bank is not responsible if messages are delayed or lost, or mistranslated; and it is not responsible for the consequences of such events as strikes, lockouts, riots, or war.

DRAFT

A *draft*, sometimes called a *bill of exchange* (B/E), is the instrument normally used in international commerce to effect payment. A draft is simply an order written by an exporter (seller) instructing an importer (buyer) or its agent to pay a specified amount of money at a specified time. (A personal check is another type of draft; the drawer writes an order to a bank to pay a specified amount of money on demand to the order of a designated beneficiary.)

The person or business initiating the draft is known as the *maker*, *drawer*, or *originator*. Normally this is the exporter who sells and ships the merchandise. The party to whom the draft is addressed is the *drawee*. The drawee is asked to *honor* the draft, that is, to pay the amount requested according to the stated terms. In commercial transactions the drawee is either the buyer, in which case the draft is called a *trade draft*, or the buyer's bank, in which case the draft is called a *bank draft*. Bank drafts are usually drawn according to the terms of a letter of credit. A draft may be drawn as a bearer instrument, or it may designate a person to whom payment is to be made. This person, known as the *payee*, may be the drawer itself or it may be some other party such as the drawer's bank.

International practice is to use drafts to settle trade transactions. This differs from domestic custom in which sellers usually ship merchandise on open account, followed by a commercial invoice indicating the amount due and terms for payment. In domestic practice the buyer usually obtains possession of the merchandise without signing a formal document directly indicating its obligation to pay. International practice, in contrast, often requires payment or a formal promise to pay before the buyer can obtain the merchandise.

Negotiable Instruments

Because drafts can become *negotiable instruments*, they provide a convenient instrument for financing the international movement of the merchandise. To become a negotiable instrument, a draft or bill of exchange must conform to the following requirements:[2]

- It must be in writing and signed by the maker or drawer.
- It must contain an unconditional promise or order to pay a definite sum of money.

- It must be payable on demand or at a fixed or determinable future date.
- It must be payable to order or to bearer.

If the draft is drawn in conformity with the above requirements so as to be a negotiable instrument, a person receiving it is a *holder in due course*. This is a privileged legal status that enables the holder to receive payment despite any personal disagreements between drawee and maker because of controversy over the underlying commercial transaction. If the drawee dishonors the draft, payment must be made to any holder in due course by any prior endorser or by the maker. This clear definition of the rights of parties who hold a negotiable instrument as a holder in due course has contributed significantly to the widespread acceptance of various forms of drafts, including personal checks.

Types of Drafts

Drafts are of two types: *sight drafts* and *time drafts*. A sight draft is payable on presentation to the drawee; the drawee must pay at once or dishonor the draft. A time draft, also called a *usance draft*, allows a delay in payment. It is presented to the drawee, who accepts it by writing or stamping a notice of acceptance on its face. Once accepted, the time draft becomes a promise to pay by the accepting party. When a time draft is drawn on and accepted by a bank, it becomes a *banker's acceptance*. When a time draft is drawn on and accepted by a business firm, it becomes a *trade acceptance*.

A time draft drawn by ABC Co., Ltd., of Tokyo for its export of PVC blue discharge hose against the letter of credit shown earlier is illustrated in Exhibit 18.4. ABC Co., Ltd., is instructing Security Pacific National Bank to pay to the Commercial Bank, Ltd. (ABC's bank), the sum of $7,690.20 ninety days after the draft is first presented to Security Pacific. When the draft is presented to Security Pacific, that bank will check to see that all terms of the letter of credit have been complied with and will then stamp the face of the draft with the acceptance inscription shown with the draft in Exhibit 18.4. A bank officer will sign, and the draft becomes a bankers' acceptance maturing in 90 days. Because the draft in Exhibit 18.4 was accepted on October 11, it will mature on January 9.

Because payment on an acceptance is not made at the time of presentation, the acceptance serves as a device to finance merchandise in transit or held in inventory prior to sale. In practice, most time drafts are made payable 30, 60, 90, or some other specified number of days after (1) the date of the draft, or (2) the date of acceptance. Bankers' acceptances are usually sold in the short-term money market at a discount from face amount, thus providing a short-term liquid security for investors. The investor relies on the bank's promise to pay.

Depending on the quality of drawee, trade acceptances may not be as marketable as bankers' acceptances. However, they do constitute a written promise by the drawee to pay on a specific date. On due date the holder (usually the exporter) can present the trade acceptance for collection through the accepting firm's bank. The bank itself is not obligated to pay, but when the drawee is asked for payment by its own bank, the pressure to pay is great. A trade acceptance can be viewed as a documented, written account receivable, as compared with an open-book account receivable.

Exhibit 18.4   Time Draft and Stamp Including Acceptance by Bank

SECURITY PACIFIC NATIONAL BANK	NO. TKT61037 Tokyo, Japan October 4, 19 xx

NO. TKT61037   Tokyo, Japan (City & State)   October 4, 19. xx

AT 90 days _____ SIGHT OF THIS   **FIRST BILL OF EXCHANGE** (SECOND UNPAID)

PAY TO THE ORDER OF The Commercial Bank, Ltd   SPECIMEN $ 7,690.20

Seven Thousand Six Hundred Ninety and 20/100--------------------------------- DOLLARS (U.S.)
VALUE RECEIVED AND CHARGE TO ACCOUNT OF

XYZ, Inc. California, U.S.A. Drawn under Security Pacific National Bank
Letter of Credit # 308590 dated September 22, 19xx

To Security Pacific National Bank

    International Banking Group

    Los Angeles, California

                                                Managing Director
                                                ABC CO., LTD

05228-2 11-73 P.S.

The transaction which gives rise to
this instrument is the
                IMPORTATION
of PVC BLUE DISCHARGE HOSE
from   NAGOYA, JAPAN
to   LOS ANGELES, CALIFORNIA
No. _____ $ _____ 7,690.20
SPECIMEN CCEPTED
        October 11,19xx
        PAYABLE AT
INTERNATIONAL BANKING GROUP
SECURITY PACIFIC NATIONAL BANK
    LOS ANGELES, CALIFORNIA

By _____
        Authorized Signature

Source: Security Pacific National Bank.

The time period of a draft is referred to as its *tenor* or *usance*. To qualify as a negotiable instrument, and so be attractive to a holder in due course, a draft must be payable on a fixed or determinable future date. For example, 60 days after sight is a determinable date, such a maturity being established precisely at the time the draft is accepted. However, payment "on arrival of goods" is not determinable since the date of arrival cannot be known in advance. Indeed, there is no assurance that the goods will arrive at all. Third parties would have no interest in investing in it because they could not be certain they would ever be paid. However, even a nonnegotiable acceptance can function as a device to obtain payment, since it is a legal obligation to pay unless there is some defect in the underlying commercial transaction.

Drafts are also classified as *clean* or *documentary*. A clean draft is an order to pay unaccompanied by any other documents. When it is used in trade, the seller has usually sent the shipping documents directly to the buyer, who thus obtains possession of the merchandise independent of its payment (on a clean sight draft) or acceptance (on a clean time draft). Clean drafts are often used by multinational firms shipping to their own affiliates, because matters of trust and credit are not involved. Clean drafts are also used for nontrade remittances, for example, when collection of an outstanding debt is sought. Use of a clean draft puts pressure on a recalcitrant debtor by forcing it to convert an open-account obligation into documentary form. Failure to pay or accept such a draft when presented through a local bank can damage the drawee's reputation.

Most trade drafts are documentary, which means that various shipping documents are attached to the draft. Payment (for sight drafts) or acceptance (for time drafts) is required to obtain possession of the documents, which are in turn needed to obtain the goods involved in the transaction. If documents are to be delivered to the buyer on payment of the draft, it is known as a "D/P draft"; if the documents are delivered on acceptance, the draft is called a "D/A draft."

If no letter of credit exists but the exporter wants to control the merchandise until payment is made, the exporter will use a documentary sight draft drawn directly on the importer. However, this instrument does not eliminate all risk. An irresponsible buyer may refuse to accept the shipment for such reasons as a drop in prices or a loss of the market in which the buyer intended to resell. Then the exporter will have to find another buyer or pay to have the merchandise shipped back to the exporter's plant.

Bankers' Acceptances

When a draft is accepted by a bank, it becomes a *bankers' acceptance*. As such it is the unconditional promise of that bank to make payment on the draft when it matures. In quality the bankers' acceptance is practically identical to a marketable bank certificate of deposit (CD). The holder of a bankers' acceptance need not wait until maturity to liquidate the investment, but it may sell the acceptance in the money market, where constant trading in such instruments occurs.

The first owner of the bankers' acceptance created from an international trade transaction will be the exporter, who receives the accepted draft back after the bank has stamped it "accepted." The exporter may hold the acceptance until maturity and then collect. On an acceptance of, say, $100,000 for six months the exporter would receive the face amount less the bank's acceptance commission of 1.5% per annum:

Face amount of the acceptance	$100,000
Less 1.5% per annum commission for 6 months	– 750
Amount received by exporter in 6 months	$ 99,250

Alternatively, the exporter may "discount"—that is, sell at a reduced price—the acceptance to its bank in order to receive funds at once. The exporter will then receive the face amount of the acceptance less both the acceptance fee and the going market rate of discount for bankers' acceptances. If the discount rate were 7% per annum, the exporter would receive the following:

Face amount of the acceptance	$100,000
Less 1.5% per annum commission for 6 months	−750
Less 7% per annum discount rate for 6 months	−3,500
Amount received by exporter at once	$ 95,750

The discounting bank may hold the acceptance in its own portfolio, thus earning for itself the 7% per annum discount rate, or the acceptance may be resold in the acceptance market. At present 10 to 15 acceptance dealers in New York City buy and sell acceptances at a spread (between buying and selling price) of 1/8% to 1/4%. The dealers may hold the acceptances themselves, but more frequently they resell them to investors.

BILL OF LADING

The third key document for financing international trade is the *bill of lading*, or B/L. The bill of lading is issued to the exporter by a common carrier transporting the merchandise. It serves three purposes: a receipt, a contract, and a document of title.

As a receipt, the bill of lading indicates that the carrier has received the merchandise described on the face of the document. Exhibit 18.5 shows a bill of lading issued by Mitsui O.S.K. Lines, Ltd., for shipment on the vessel America Maru of 90 rolls of PVC blue discharge hose from Nagoya, Japan, to Los Angeles, California. The carrier is not responsible for ascertaining that the containers hold what is alleged to be their contents, so descriptions of merchandise on bills of lading are usually short and simple. If shipping charges are paid in advance, the bill of lading will usually be stamped "freight paid" or "freight prepaid." If merchandise is shipped collect—a less common procedure internationally than domestically—the carrier maintains a lien on the goods until freight is paid.

As a contract, the bill of lading indicates the obligation of the carrier to provide certain transportation in return for certain charges. Common carriers cannot disclaim responsibility for their negligence through inserting special clauses in a bill of lading. The bill of lading, as a contract, may specify alternative ports in the event that delivery cannot be made to the designated port, or it may specify that the goods will be returned to the exporter at the exporter's expense.

As a document of title, the bill of lading can be used to obtain payment or a written promise of payment before the merchandise is released to the importer. The bill of lading can also function as collateral against which funds may be advanced to the exporter by its local bank prior to or during shipment and before final payment by the importer.

Characteristics of the Bill of Lading

Bills of lading are either *straight* or *to order*. A straight bill of lading provides that the carrier deliver the merchandise to the designated consignee. A straight bill of lading is *not*

Exhibit 18.5   Bill of Lading

Shipper ABC Co., Ltd No. 10 Mori Bldg 1-18-1 Toranomon, Minato-ku Tokyo, 105, Japan	(Forwarding Agent:) B/L No. HO33-23758

Mitsui O.S.K. Lines. Ltd.

BILL OF LADING

Consignee

TO ORDER OF SHIPPER

Received by the Carrier from the shipper in apparent good order and condition unless otherwise indicated herein the Goods or the container (s) or package (s) said to contain the cargo herin mentioned, to be carried subject to all the terms and conditions appearing on the face and back of this Bill of Lading by the vessel named herein or any substitute at the Carrier's option and/or other means of transport, from the place of delivery shown herein and there to be delivered unto order or assigns. If required by the Carrier, this Bill of Lading duly endorsed must be surrendered in exchange for the Goods or delivery order.

In accepting this Bill of Lading, the Merchant agrees to be bound by all the stipulations, exceptions, terms and conditions on the face and back hereof, whether written, typed, stamped or printed, as fully as if signed by the Merchant, any local custom or privilege to the contrary notwithstanding, and agrees that all agreements or freight engagements for and in connection with the carriage of the Goods are superseded by this Bill of Lading.

In witness to hereof, the undersigned, on behalf of Mitsui O.S.K. Lines, Ltd. the Master and the owner of the Vessel, has signed the number of Bill (s) of Lading stated below all of this tenor and date, one of which being accomplished, the others to stand void.

Notify Party

XYZ, Inc.
55555 Hawthorne Boulevard
Suite 400-14
Torrance, California 90503

(Terms of Bill of Lading continued on the back hereof)

Pre-carriage by I.C.T.	Place of receipt NAGOYA C.F.S.
Ocean vessel AMERICA MARU	Port of loading NAGOYA, JAPAN

Part of discharge LOS ANGELES, CALIFORNIA, U.S.A.	Place of delivery	Final destination for the Merchant's reference LOS ANGELES C.F.S.

Container No. Seal No. Marks and Numbers	No. of Con- tainers or packages	Kind of packages: description of goods	Gross weight	Measurment
MOLU2850842 41013509 CT1U2565602 MOL35097 No. 1-90 MADE IN JAPAN Remark: L/C No. 308,590	 90 ROLLS	 PVC BLUE DISCHARGE HOSE SPECIMEN	 4980 KGS	 6.836 CBM

(left margin rotated text: Particulars furnished by Shipper)

• Total number of Container or other packages or units received by the Carrier (in words)	NINETY (90) ROLLS ONLY			

Freight and charges	Received tons	Rate per	Prepaid	Collect
6.836 M3 C.A.F. C.F.S. CHARGE	 FREIGHT PREPAID	$77.00/M3 6% ·12,650/M3	US$525.60 US$31.54 US$557.14 ·86,475	

Exchange rate @·267.75	Prepaid at TOKYO, JAPAN	Payable at	Place and date of issue TOKYO, JAPAN
	Prepaid at ·167,263	No. of original B(s)/l. THREE (3)	MITSUI O.S.K. LINES, LTD.
	LADEN ON BOARD THE VESSEL		by
Date	Signature		

Source: Security Pacific National Bank and Mitsui O.S.K. Lines, Ltd.

title to the goods and is not required for the consignee to obtain possession. Because a straight bill of lading is not title, it is not good collateral for loans. Therefore, a straight bill of lading is used when the merchandise has been paid for in advance, when the transaction is being financed by the exporter, or when the shipment is to an affiliate.

An order bill of lading directs the carrier to deliver the goods to the order of a designated party. An additional inscription may request the carrier to notify someone else of the arrival. The order bill of lading grants title to the merchandise only to the person to whom the document is addressed, and surrender of the order bill of lading is required to obtain the shipment.

The order bill of lading is typically made payable to the order of the exporter, who thus retains title to the goods after they have been handed to the carrier. Title to the merchandise remains with the exporter until payment is received, at which time the exporter endorses the order bill of lading (which is negotiable) in blank or to the party making the payment, usually a bank. The most common procedure would be for payment to be advanced against a documentary draft accompanied by the endorsed order bill of lading. After paying the draft, the exporter's bank forwards the documents through bank clearing channels to the bank of the importer. The importer's bank, in turn, releases the documents to the importer after payment (sight drafts), after acceptance (time drafts addressed to the importer and marked D/A), or after payment terms have been agreed (drafts drawn on the importer's bank under provisions of a letter of credit).

Variations in the Bill of Lading

A *clean* bill of lading indicates that the goods were received by the carrier in apparently good condition. The carrier is not obligated to check the condition of the merchandise beyond external visual appearance. A *foul* bill of lading indicates that the merchandise appeared to have suffered some damage before being received for shipment. A foul bill of lading lacks complete negotiability.

An *on-board* bill of lading indicates that the merchandise has been placed on board the vessel whose name is designated on the document. This form is preferred to a *received-for-shipment* bill of lading, which allows for the possibility that the goods are sitting on the dock and might remain there for some time. A received-for-shipment bill of lading is not an acceptable document unless it has been specifically authorized in the letter of credit. Similarly, unless authorized otherwise by the letter of credit, banks will refuse to accept *on-deck* bills of lading, indicating that the goods have been stowed on deck. Received-for-shipment bills of lading may be issued when goods are first received on the carrier's premises; they can be converted to an on-board form by an appropriate stamp showing the name of the vessel, the date, and the signature of an official of the carrier.

ADDITIONAL DOCUMENTS

The draft, the bill of lading, and the letter of credit are the major documents required in most international transactions. However, additional documents may be needed as a condition of the letter of credit for honoring a draft. The more common additional documents include those described below.

A signed *commercial invoice* is issued by the seller and contains a precise description of the merchandise. Unit prices, financial terms of sale, and amount due from the buyer are indicated, as are shipping conditions related to charges, such as "FOB" (free on board), "FAS" (free alongside), "C & F" (cost and freight), or "CIF" (cost, insurance, freight).

Insurance documents must be as specified in the letter of credit and must be issued by insurance companies or their agents. The insurance may be issued to the exporter, who must then endorse the policy to the importer, or it may be issued in the name of the importer. The document must be expressed in the same currency as the credit and must not be dated later than the date of shipment carried on the face of the shipping documents. Insurance must be of types and for risks specified in the letter of credit.

Consular invoices are issued by the consulate of the importing country to provide customs information and statistics for that country and to help prevent false declarations of value. The consular invoice may be combined with a certificate of origin of the goods.

Certificates of analysis may be required to ascertain that certain specifications of weight, purity, sanitation, etc., have been met. These conditions may be required by health or other officials of the importing country—especially in the case of foods and drugs—or they may be insisted on by the importer as assurance that it is receiving what it ordered. The certificates may be issued by government or private organizations, as specified in the letter of credit.

Packing lists may be required so that the contents of containers can be identified, either for customs purposes or for importer identification of the contents of separate containers.

An *export declaration* is a document prepared by the exporter to assist the government to prepare export statistics.

DOCUMENTATION IN A TYPICAL TRADE TRANSACTION

A trade transaction could conceivably be handled in many ways. The transaction that would best illustrate the interactions of the various documents would be an export financed under a documentary commercial letter of credit, requiring an order bill of lading, with the exporter collecting via a time draft accepted by the importer's bank. Such a transaction is illustrated in Exhibit 18.6:

1. Importer places an order for the goods with Exporter, inquiring if Exporter would be willing to ship under a letter of credit.

2. Exporter agrees to ship under a letter of credit and specifies relevant information such as prices, terms, etc.

3. Importer applies to its bank, Bank I, for a letter of credit to be issued in favor of Exporter for the merchandise Importer wishes to buy.

4. Bank I issues the letter of credit in favor of Exporter and sends it to Bank X, Exporter's bank, or to a correspondent bank in the country of export.

5. Bank X advises Exporter of the opening of a letter of credit in the Exporter's favor. Bank X may or may not confirm the letter of credit to add its own guarantee to the document.

6. Exporter ships the goods to Importer.

7. Exporter presents a 90-day time draft to Bank X, drawn on Bank I in accordance with Bank I's letter of credit and accompanied by such other documents as required, including the order bill of lading. Exporter endorses the order bill of lading in blank so that title to the goods goes with the holder of the documents—Bank X at this point in the transaction.

8. Bank X presents the draft and documents to Bank I. Bank I accepts the draft, taking possession of the documents and promising to pay the now-accepted draft in 90 days.

Exhibit 18.6 Typical Trade Transaction

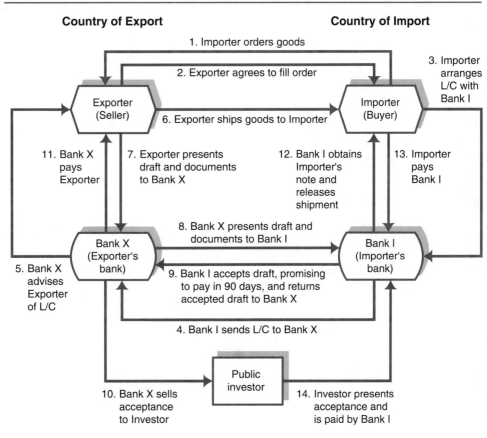

9. Bank I returns the accepted draft to Bank X. Alternatively, Bank X could have asked Bank I to accept and discount the draft; then Bank I would have returned cash less a discount fee rather than the accepted draft to Bank X.

10. Bank X, having received back the accepted draft, now a bankers' acceptance, must choose between several alternatives. Bank X may sell the acceptance in the open market at a discount to a public investor. The investor will typically be a corporation or financial institution with excess cash it wants to invest for a short period of time. Bank X may also hold the acceptance in its own portfolio.

11. If Bank X has discounted the acceptance with Bank I (mentioned in step 8 above) or has discounted it in the local money market, Bank X will transfer the proceeds less any fees and discount to Exporter. Another possibility would be for Exporter itself to take possession of the acceptance, hold it for 90 days, and present it for collection. Normally, however, exporters prefer to receive the discounted cash value of the acceptance at once rather than wait for the acceptance to mature and receive a slightly greater amount of cash.

12. Bank I notifies Importer of the arrival of the documents. Importer signs a note or makes some other agreed plan to pay the bank for the merchandise in 90 days, and Bank I releases the underlying documents so that Importer can obtain physical possession of the shipment.

13. In 90 days Bank I receives from Importer funds to pay the maturing draft.

14. On the same day—the 90th day after acceptance—the holder of the matured acceptance presents it for payment and receives its face value. The holder may present it directly to Bank I, as in the diagram, or return it to Bank X and have Bank X collect it through normal banking channels.

EXPORT CREDIT INSURANCE

The exporter who insists on cash or letter of credit payment for foreign shipments is likely to lose orders to competitors from other countries that provide more favorable credit terms. Better credit terms are often made possible by means of export credit insurance, which provides assurance to the exporter or the exporter's bank that, should the foreign customer default on payment, the insurance company will pay for a major portion of the loss. Because of the availability of export credit insurance, commercial banks are willing to provide medium- to long-term financing (five to seven years) for exports.

Since credit has become an increasingly competitive component of the terms of export selling, governments of at least 35 countries have established entities that insure credit risks for exports. Details of these systems appear in the various editions of the World's Principal Export Credit Insurance Systems published by the International Export Credits Institute, New York.

Competition between nations to increase exports by lengthening the period for which credit transactions can be insured could lead to a credit war and to unsound credit decisions. To prevent such an unhealthy development, a number of leading trading nations joined together in 1934 to create the Berne Union (officially, the Union d'Assureurs des Crédits Internationaux) for the purpose of establishing a voluntary international understanding on export credit terms. The Berne Union recommends maximum credit terms for many items including, for example, heavy capital goods (five years), light capital goods (three years), and consumer durable goods (one year).

Export Credit Insurance in the United States

In the United States, export credit insurance is provided by the Foreign Credit Insurance Association (FCIA). This is an unincorporated association of private commercial insurance companies operating in cooperation with the Export-Import Bank, an independent agency of the U.S. government.

The FCIA provides policies protecting U.S. exporters against the risk of nonpayment by foreign debtors as a result of commercial and political risks. Losses due to commercial risk are those that result from the insolvency or protracted payment default of the buyer. Political losses arise from actions of governments beyond the control of buyer or seller. FCIA political coverage generally protects against the following events.

- A buyer's inability to legally obtain U.S. dollars or other approved currencies and to transfer those funds to the insured.

- Loss of transportation or insurance charges incurred after shipment because of the politically-caused interruption of a voyage outside the United States, when it is not practical to recover the charges from the buyer.

- The occurrence after shipment of any of the following, when it is not the fault of the buyer, issuing bank, or the insured or its agents:

    1. Cancellation or nonrenewal of an export license, or the imposition of restrictions on the export of products that were not subject to license or restriction prior to shipment.
    2. Cancellation of authority to import the products of the buyer's country.
    3. Imposition of laws that prevent import of the products into the buyer's country, or that prevent exchange of local currency into U.S. dollars or some other approved currency.

- The occurrence of any of the following after shipment but on or before the date of default:

    1. War, hostilities, civil war, rebellion, revolution, insurrection, civil commotion, or similar disturbances.
    2. Governmentally authorized requisition, expropriation, confiscation of, or intervention in, the specific business of the buyer, issuing bank, or guarantors.

FCIA Policies

The FCIA offers short-term policies, involving payment terms up to 180 days, and medium-term policies, with payment terms from 181 days to five years. Coverage up to seven years may be arranged on a case-by-case basis for aircraft, marine, and other sales, if necessary to meet government-supported foreign competition. Coverage is for U.S. goods produced and shipped from the United States during the policy period, and applies to credit sales to a foreign buyer or to export letters of credit opened by a foreign issuing bank.

Generally, commercial coverage ranges from 90% to 95% and political coverage ranges from 95% to 100%, depending on the type of policy and options chosen by the exporter. Premiums depend on a number of variables, including the length of credit terms being offered, the exporter's previous experience with export sales, the risk associated with the countries to which goods are shipped or services are rendered, and the spread of risk covered by the policy. Details of the provisions of various types of policies can be obtained from the Foreign Credit Insurance Association at 40 Rector Street, 11th Floor, New York, New York 10006.

GOVERNMENT PROGRAMS TO HELP FINANCE EXPORTS

Governments of most export-oriented industrialized countries have special financial institutions that provide some form of subsidized credit to their own national exporters. These export finance institutions offer terms that are better than those generally available from the competitive private sector. Thus domestic taxpayers are subsidizing lower financial costs for foreign buyers in order to create employment and maintain a technological edge.

In the United States the chief government agency is the Export-Import Bank of the United States, headquartered in Washington, D.C. Other organizations include the Overseas Private Investment Corporation (OPIC) and the Private Export Funding Corporation (PEFCO).

Export-Import Bank

The Export-Import Bank (also called Eximbank) is an independent agency of the U.S. government, established in 1934 to stimulate and facilitate the foreign trade of the United States. Interestingly, the Eximbank was originally created primarily to facilitate exports to the Soviet Union.

In 1945 the Eximbank was rechartered "to aid in financing and to facilitate exports and imports and the exchange of commodities between the United States and any foreign country or the agencies or nationals thereof." The bank has $1 billion of nonvoting stock paid in by the U.S. Treasury and has the option of borrowing an additional $6 billion from the Treasury if and when needed.

The Eximbank facilitates the financing of U.S. exports through various loan guarantee and insurance programs. The Eximbank guarantees repayment of medium-term (181 days to five years) and long-term (five years to ten years) export loans extended by U.S. banks to foreign borrowers.

The Eximbank's medium- and long-term, direct-lending operation is based on participation with private sources of funds. Essentially the Eximbank lends dollars to borrowers outside the United States for the purchase of U.S. goods and services. Proceeds of such loans are paid to U.S. suppliers. The loans themselves are repaid with interest in dollars to the Eximbank. The Eximbank requires private participation in these direct loans in order to: (1) ensure that it complements rather than competes with private sources of export financing; (2) spread its resources more broadly; and (3) ensure that private financial institutions will continue to provide export credit.

The Eximbank also guarantees lease transactions, finances the costs involved in the preparation by U.S. firms of engineering, planning, and feasibility studies for non-U.S. clients on large capital projects, and supplies counseling for exporters, banks, or others needing help in finding financing for U.S. goods.

Private Export Funding Corporation (PEFCO)

The Private Export Funding Corporation, or PEFCO, is a private corporation formed in 1970 to help finance U.S. exports by making U.S. dollar loans to foreign purchasers of goods or services manufactured or originated in the United States. PEFCO was established, with the support of the U.S. Department of the Treasury and of Eximbank, to mobilize private capital to supplement financing already available through Eximbank, commercial banks, and other lending institutions. PEFCO's loans are repayable in U.S. dollars and are unconditionally guaranteed by Eximbank. The attorney general of the United States, in turn, has ruled that all obligations of Eximbank are general obligations of the United States, backed by the government's full faith and credit. Because all PEFCO's loans are guaranteed by Eximbank, PEFCO itself does not evaluate credit risks, appraise economic conditions in foreign countries, or review other factors that might affect the collectibility of its loans.

Impetus for the formation of PEFCO came from the Bankers' Association for Foreign Trade. PEFCO's stockholders are 49 U.S. commercial banks from all regions of the country, one investment banking firm, and seven manufacturing companies. The manufacturing firms are major U.S. exporters, with aircraft manufacturers and suppliers playing a prominent part.

PEFCO's capital comes primarily from long-term secured notes sold in the open market, short-term notes payable sold in the open market, and shareholders' equity.

COUNTERTRADE

The word *countertrade* refers to a variety of international trade arrangements "in which the sale of goods and services by a producer is linked to an import purchase of other goods and services."[3] In other words, an export sale is tied by contract to an import. The countertrade may take place at the same time as the original export, in which case credit is not an issue; or the countertrade may take place later, in which case financing becomes important.

Countertrade became popular in the 1960s and 1970s as a way for the Soviet Union and the Eastern European communist countries to manage foreign exchange risk by ensuring that imports today would be matched by present or future exports. In the last decade the technique has been used by noncommunist less developed nations for much the same reason.

Jean-François Hennart, who classified countertrade practices according to the diagram in Exhibit 18.7, points out that there are two broad categories, each of which has three subcategories:[4]

1. Transactions which avoid the use of money:

   a) Simple barter.
   b) Clearing arrangements.
   c) Switch trading.

2. Transactions which use money or credit but impose reciprocal commitments.

   a) Buyback.
   b) Counterpurchase.
   c) Offset.

Simple Barter

Simple barter is a direct exchange of physical goods between two parties. It is a one-time transaction carried out under a single contract that specifies both the goods to be delivered and the goods to be received. The two parts of the transaction occur at the same time, and no money is exchanged. Money may be used as the numeraire by which the two values are established and the quantities of each good are determined.

A famous example of classical barter was an 18-year agreement whereby Pepsico sent Pepsi syrup to 37 bottling plants in the Soviet Union in return for Stolichnaya vodka which Pepsi then marketed in the United States. In a recent extension of that agreement involving Pepsico's Pizza Hut subsidiary, Moscow agreed to compensate Pepsico with ten Soviet-made freighters to sell on the international market.[5]

A more complicated deal involves Philip Morris shipping cigarettes to the Russian Republic, for which it receives urea for use in making fertilizer. Philip Morris ships the urea to China, and China in turn ships glassware to North America for retail sale by Philip Morris.[6]

Clearing Arrangements

In a clearing arrangement, each party agrees to purchase a specified (usually equal) value of goods and service from the other, with the cost of the transactions debited to a special account. At the end of the trading period any residual imbalances may be cleared by shipping additional goods or by a hard currency payment. In effect, the addition of a clearing agreement to a barter scheme allows for a time lag between barter components. Thus credit facilitates eventual matching of the transactions.

Switch Trading

Switch trade involves transferring use of bilateral clearing balances from one country to another. For example, an original export from Canada to Romania is paid for with a balance deposited in a clearing account in Romania. Although the clearing account may be *measured* in Canadian dollars (or in any other currency), the balance can be used only to purchase goods from Romania.

Exhibit 18.7   Classification of Forms of Countertrade

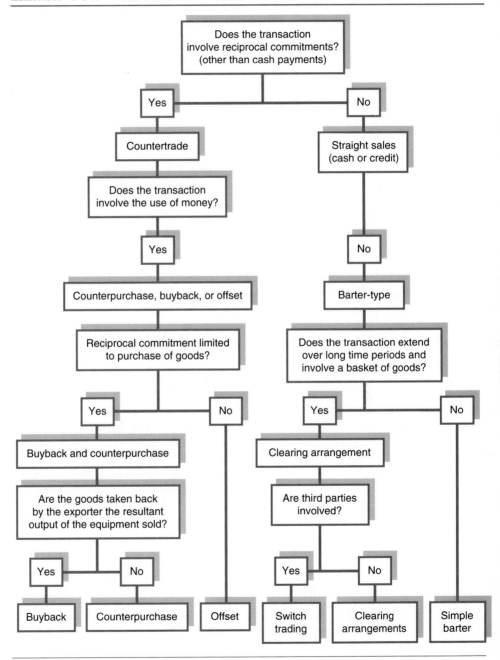

Source: Jean-Francois Hennart, "Some Empirical Dimensions of Countertrade," *Journal of International Business Studies,* Second Quarter 1990, p. 245. Reprinted with permission.

The original exporter from Canada might buy unrelated goods from Romania or it might sell the clearing balance at a substantial discount to a "switch trader," often located in Vienna, who in turn purchases goods from Romania for sale elsewhere. The Canadian exporter in effect exchanges the blocked clearing balance for hard currency at a substantial discount with a specialist firm equipped to export merchandise from Romania. The Romanian goods themselves are quite cheap, given the discount, so the switch trader can resell the merchandise at a low price in world markets. Those who oppose this practice note that it is in effect dumping below true cost, which hurts competing manufacturers in other countries. However, because the "dumping" is not done by the original country of manufacture it escapes international agreements on dumping.

An example of a switch trade is a Polish/Greek clearing agreement that existed before Greece joined the EEC. Poland had sold Greece more goods than it had purchased, and so ended up with a dollar-denominated clearing balance in Greece. A switch trader bought the right to 250,000 clearing dollars from Poland for $225,000 and then resold them for $235,000 to a European sultana merchant, who in turn used them to purchase Greek sultanas through the Greek Foreign Trade Bank.[7] (A sultana is a small white seedless grape used for both raisins and wine making.)

Buyback, or Compensation Agreement

A compensation agreement or buyback transaction is an agreement by an exporter of plant or equipment to take compensation in the form of future output from that plant. A buyback contract is essentially two parallel money transactions, and the seller is fully compensated by receipts of output from the plant and equipment. Such an arrangement has attributes that make it, in effect, an alternative form of direct investment. The value of the buyback usually exceeds the value of the original sale, as would be appropriate to reflect the time value of money.

An example of a buyback is the agreement by several Western European countries to provide steel pipe and compressors for a gas pipeline from the Soviet Union to Europe, with compensation from gas delivered through that pipeline. Another example is an agreement between Occidental Petroleum and the Soviet Union under which Occidental supplies the Soviet Union with one million tons of U.S. superphosphoric acid per year for 20 years and in turn receives 4 million tons of Soviet ammonia, urea, and potash. Occidental helped construct the extra ammonia production and pipeline capacity in the Soviet Union.

Production sharing is the term used for a similar arrangement involving natural resources or energy projects.

Counterpurchase

A counterpurchase transaction involves an initial export, but with the exporter receiving back merchandise that is unrelated to items the exporter manufactures. The importer provides a "shopping list" for the exporter. One example of counterpurchase is an agreement between McDonnell Douglas and Yugoslavia in 1966 under which McDonnell

Douglas sold DC-9's to Yugoslovenski Aerotransport for $199 million cash and $26 million in Yugoslav goods. The Yugoslav products, imported into the United States over the subsequent decades, have included Zagreb hams, wines, dehydrated vegetables, and even some power transmission towers that were retransferred to the Los Angeles Department of Water and Power.[8] McDonnell Douglas reportedly houses a Yugoslav trading firm at one of its aircraft plants to deal with the goods acquired in countertrade.

Other counterpurchase examples are the pre-German reunification purchase by West Germany's Volkswagenwerk of coal, oil, and machinery from then East Germany in return for selling 10,000 automobiles to East Germany; and Rolls Royce's sales of jet parts to Finland in return for Rolls Royce's marketing Finnish TV sets and other consumer durables in the United Kingdom.

Offset

Offset refers to the requirement of importing countries that their purchase price be offset in some way by the seller. Offset is common in the purchase of weapons and other large-ticket items. Reciprocal concessions may involve agreement to source some of the production locally, to increase imports from the buying country, or to transfer technology.

Reasons for the Growth of Countertrade

In theory, countertrade is a movement away from free multilateral trade. It is a slow, expensive, and convoluted way of conducting trade that often forces firms (such as McDonnell Douglas) to set up operations to deal in products very remote from their expertise. The basic problem is that the agreement to take back goods in some form of barter suggests that these goods cannot be sold in the open market for as high a price as is being locked into the countertrade agreement.

Nevertheless, several reasons are advanced in support of countertrade. First, from the perspective of a centrally planned economy, countertrade reduces the risk of fluctuations in export receipts by assuring that future exports will provide foreign exchange roughly equivalent to the cost of the original import.[9] Centrally planned economies have never been competent at marketing their products in foreign countries, perhaps because marketing was not needed at home. In these countries, production plans are made by a central authority, and the production system does not respond well to sudden changes in export demand. Countertrade provides an assured market for a period of time, and can be negotiated by governmental officials who set economic production quotas, rather than by the managers of individual plants who do not control the availability of resources.

Second, countertrade exports avoid domestic price controls and base prices set by international cartels or commodity agreements. In the case of barter, goods change hands without the explicit use of prices. Consequently any domestic price controls are passed over. Goods can be "sold" abroad at "prices" that are substantially below those charged local customers. Nigeria, Iran, Libya, Indonesia, Iraq, Qatar, and Abu Dhabi are reported to have used barter deals to sell oil below the OPEC cartel agreed-upon price.[10]

Third, because foreign exchange is not created, it need not be turned over to a central bank. Yet the entity that pays for its original imports with mandated countertrade exports in effect earns foreign exchange which it is able to keep to itself to pay for the import.

Fourth, countertrade enables a country to export merchandise of poor design or quality. The merchandise is often sold at a major discount in world markets. Whether or not this constitutes a discount on the original sale, or even dumping, depends on how that original sale was priced. To the extent that communist and former communist countries have a reputation for poor quality, the fact that the goods are marketed in foreign countries by reputable firms gives buyers some assurance of quality and after-sale service.

Donald Lecraw found that countertrade was most successful for large firms experienced in exporting large, complex products; for firms vertically integrated or that could accommodate countertrade take backs; and for firms that traded with countries having inappropriate exchange rates, rationed foreign exchange, and import restrictions. Importers who were relatively inexperienced in assessing technology or in export marketing also enjoyed greater success.[11]

SUMMARY

- Over many years, established procedures have arisen to finance international trade. The basic procedure rests on the interrelationship between three key documents, the letter of credit, the draft, and the bill of lading. Variations in each of these three key documents provide a variety of ways to accommodate any type of transaction.

- In the simplest transaction, in which all three documents are used and in which financing is desirable, an importer applies for and receives a letter of credit from its bank. In the letter of credit, the bank substitutes its credit for that of the importer and promises to pay if certain documents are submitted to the bank. The exporter may now rely on the promise of the bank rather than on the promise of the importer.

- The exporter typically ships on an order bill of lading, attaches the order bill of lading to a draft ordering payment from the importer's bank, and presents these documents, plus any of a number of additional documents, through its own bank to the importer's bank. If the documents are in order, the importer's bank either pays the draft (a sight draft) or accepts the draft (a time draft). In the latter case the bank promises to pay in the future. At this step the importer's bank acquires title to the merchandise through the bill of lading, and it then releases the merchandise to the importer against payment or promise of future payment.

- If a sight draft is used, the exporter is paid at once. If a time draft is used, the exporter receives the accepted draft, now a bankers' acceptance, back from the bank. The exporter may hold the bankers' acceptance until maturity or sell it at a discount in the money market.

- The process of international trade is facilitated by various national programs to provide export credit insurance and direct financial support.

- Countertrade provides an alternative to traditional importing and exporting. In countertrade, a seller provides a buyer with goods or services and promises in return to take back (barter) or purchase (other forms of countertrade) goods or services in partial or full payment.

1. Basic Needs
Explain the basic needs of import-export financing and the main instruments used to deal with those needs.

2. Baltimore Pump Company
Baltimore Pump Company has received an order for merchandise to be exported to Kuwait under the terms of a letter of credit issued by Swiss Bank Corporation on behalf of the Kuwaiti importer. The letter of credit specifies that the face value of the shipment, $8,000,000, will be paid nine months after Swiss Bank Corporation accepts a draft drawn by Baltimore Pump in accordance with the terms of the letter of credit.

The current discount rate on nine-month acceptances is 12% per annum, and Baltimore Pump judges its weighted average cost of capital to be 20%. The commission for selling in the discount market is 1.5% of the face amount.

Baltimore Pump wonders how much cash it can expect from the sale if it holds the acceptance until maturity. Alternatively, it wonders if it should sell the acceptance at once at a discount in the U.S. money market.

3. Documenting an Export
Explain and diagram the steps involved in an export of canned peas from California to Japan, using a confirmed letter of credit, payment to be made 90 days from sight.

4. Confirmed letter of Credit
Explain why an exporter might want a confirmed letter of credit rather than an unconfirmed one. What are its advantages and disadvantages?

5. Bankers' Acceptances
Explain the advantages and disadvantages of using bankers' acceptances for financing an export. Compare its cost to that of alternative methods of financing, using data from current sources.

6. Letter of Credit Versus Export Credit Insurance
An alternative to using a letter of credit is to use export credit insurance. What are the advantages and disadvantages of using export credit insurance compared to a letter of credit for an export of a yacht from Florida to Canada?

7. Eximbank and PEFCO
The Eximbank and PEFCO both provide supplementary long-term financing of U.S. exports. Why are these institutions necessary? How do they function?

8. Countertrade

Using current sources of information, such as indexes to either the *Wall Street Journal* or the *New York Times*, find an example of countertrade and explain how it is working.

NOTES

1. The address of the International Chamber of Commerce is 1212 Avenue of the Americas, New York, New York 10036.

2. *Uniform Commercial Code*, Section 3104(1).

3. Donald J. Lecraw, "The Management of Countertrade: Factors Influencing Success." *Journal of International Business Studies*, Spring 1989, p. 43.

4. Jean-Francois Hennart, "Some Empirical Dimensions of Countertrade," *Journal of International Business Studies,* second quarter 1990, pp. 243–270.

5. Robert W. Gibson, "Reform Makes It Harder to Do a Soviet Deal, *Los Angeles Times,* December 2,

1990, p. D10.

6. *Ibid.*

7. Rupert Birley, "Can't Pay? Will Pay, but in Sultanas," *Euromoney*, May 1983, p. 187.

8. Chris MacKenzie, "How Many Canned Hams Buy a Jet?" *The Travel Agent*, January 28, 1982, pp. 90–92.

9. Hennart, *op cit.* p. 247.

10. *Ibid.,* p. 249, quoting *Petroleum Economist*, May 1984.

11. *Ibid.,* p. 57.

BIBLIOGRAPHY

Banks, Gary, "The Economics and Politics of Countertrade," *The World Economy*, June 1983, pp. 159–182.

Birley, Rupert, "Can't Pay? Will Pay, but in Sultanas," *Euromoney*, May 1983, pp. 187–189.

Celi, Louis J., and I. James Czechowicz, *Export Financing, A Handbook of Sources and Techniques*, Morristown, N.J.: Financial Executives Research Foundation, 1985.

Cohen, Stephen S., and John Zysman, "Countertrade, Offsets, Barter and Buybacks," *California Management Review*, Winter 1986, pp. 41–56.

Dizard, John W., "The Explosion of International Barter," *Fortune*, February 7, 1983, pp. 88–95.

Export Credit Financing Systems in OECD Member Countries, Paris: OECD, 1987.

Export-Import Bank of the United States, "EXIMBANK Program Summary," February 1984, pp.1–12.

Francis, Dick, *The Countertrade Handbook*, Westport, Conn.: Quorum Books, 1987.

The Guide to Export Finance 1988, London: Euromoney Publications, 1988.

A Handbook on Financing U.S. Exports, 5th edition, Washington, D.C.: Machinery and Allied Products Institute (MAPI), 1988.

Hennart, Jean-François, "Some Empirical Dimensions of Countertrade," *Journal of International Business Studies*, Second Quarter 1990, pp. 243–270.

Huszagh, Sandra M., and Fredrick W. Huszagh, "International Barter and Countertrade," *International Marketing Review*, Summer 1986, pp. 7–19.

Khoury, Sarkis J., "Countertrade: Forms, Motives, Pitfalls, and Negotiation Requirements," *Journal of Business Research*, June 1984, pp. 257–270.

Korth, Christopher M., ed., *International Countertrade*, Westport, Conn.: Quorum Books, 1987.

Lecraw, Donald J., "The Management of Countertrade: Factors Influencing Success." *Journal of International Business Studies*, Spring 1989, pp. 41–59.

Loeber, Dietrich Andre, and Ann Porter Friedland, "Soviet Imports of Industrial Installations under Compensation Agreements: West Europe's Siberian Pipeline Revisited," *Columbia Journal of World Business*, Winter 1983, pp. 51–62.

Mirus, Rolf, and Bernard Yeung, "Economic Incentives for Countertrade," *Journal of International Business Studies*, Fall 1986, pp. 27–40.

Rodriguez, Rita M., ed., *The Export-Import Bank at Fifty: The International Environment and the Institution's Role*, Lexington, Mass.: Lexington Books, 1987.

Ryder, Frank R., "Challenges to the Use of the Documentary Credit in International Trade Transactions," *Columbia Journal of World Business*, Winter 1981, pp. 36–47.

Uniform Customs and Practices for Documentary Credits, New York: United States Council of the International Chamber of Commerce, 1974.

A Summary of U.S. Export Administration Regulations, Washington, D.C.: U.S. Department of Commerce, 1985.

Venedikian, Harry M., and Gerald A. Warfield, *Export-Import Financing*, 2nd ed., New York: Wiley, 1986.

Verzariu, Pompiliu, *Countertrade, Barter, and Offsets: New Strategies for Profit in International Trade*, New York: McGraw-Hill, 1984.

19 CHAPTER

Working Capital Management

Management of working capital assets requires both a *flow* and a *stock* perspective. From a flow perspective, managing the location of liquid funds is most important. *Location* means both the currency in which liquid funds are held and the country where such holdings are placed. From a stock perspective, managing the appropriate levels and composition of cash balances, accounts receivable, inventories, and short-term debt is the main task.

The first part of this chapter deals with positioning: techniques to move liquid funds from one location to another, including dividend remittances, royalties and other fees, transfer pricing, and blocked funds. The second part deals with determining and maintaining appropriate international balances of cash, accounts receivable, and inventory.

CONSTRAINTS ON POSITIONING FUNDS

In domestic business, fund flows among units of a large company are generally unimpeded, and decisions about where to locate working cash balances or excess liquidity are usually based on marginal rates of return and gains from operating with minimal cash. With possibly minor exceptions all funds are denominated in the currency of the home country.

If a firm operates multinationally, political, tax, foreign exchange, and liquidity considerations impose significant restrictions on the idea that funds may easily and without cost be moved anywhere in the world. These constraints create the environment for special consideration of the problem of positioning funds multinationally.

Political constraints can block the transfer of funds either overtly or covertly. Overt blockage occurs when a currency becomes inconvertible or subject to other exchange controls that prevent its transfer at reasonable exchange rates. Covert blockage occurs when dividends or other forms of fund remittances are severely limited, heavily taxed, or prevented by other means.

Tax constraints arise because of the complex and possibly contradictory tax structures of various national governments through whose jurisdictions funds might pass.

Foreign exchange transaction costs are incurred when funds are moved from one currency to another. These costs, in the form of fees and the difference between bid and offer prices, are profit for the commercial banks and dealers that operate the foreign exchange market. Although usually a small percentage of the amount of money exchanged, such costs become quite significant for large sums or frequent transfers.

Liquidity constraints must be satisfied for each affiliate while maintaining good banking relationships locally and worldwide. This local interface is easily forgotten when trying to optimize worldwide corporate liquidity.

UNBUNDLING INTERNATIONAL FUND TRANSFERS

Multinational firms sometimes "unbundle" their transfer of funds into separate flows for each purpose. Host countries are then more likely to perceive that a part of what might otherwise be called "remittance of profits" constitutes an essential purchase of specific benefits that command worldwide values and benefit the host country. Unbundling allows a multinational firm to recover funds from its affiliates without piquing host country sensitivities with large "dividend drains." An item-by-item matching of remittance to input, in the form of royalties for patents, fees for services, etc., is equitable to host country and foreign investor alike. If all investment inputs are unbundled, part of what might appear to be residual profits may turn out to be tax-deductible expenses related to a specific purchased benefit. Unbundling also facilitates allocation of overhead from a parent's international division to each operating affiliate in accordance with a predetermined formula. Finally, unbundling facilitates the entry of local capital into joint-venture projects, because *total* remuneration to different owners can be in proportion to the value of their different types of contribution rather than only in proportion to the ownership interest.

In the following sections we consider fund transfer techniques to pay for the bundle of contributions a parent might make to an affiliate and vice versa. Specifically we examine dividend policy, royalties, fees, contributions to overhead, transfer pricing, and reactions to blocked funds.

INTERNATIONAL DIVIDEND REMITTANCES

Payment of dividends is the most common method by which firms transfer funds from affiliate to parent. Determinants of dividend policy include tax considerations, political risk, foreign exchange risk, and several less important factors.

Taxes

Host country tax laws influence the dividend decision. Countries such as Germany tax retained earnings at one rate while taxing distributed earnings at a lower rate. Most countries levy withholding taxes on dividends paid to foreign parent firms. Parent country taxes also influence the decision. Tax influences on decision making, including dividends, will be discussed in detail in Chapter 21.

Political Risk

Political risk can motivate parent firms to require foreign affiliates to remit all locally generated funds in excess of stipulated working capital requirements and planned capital expansions. Such policies, however, are not universal. To enhance the financial self-reliance of affiliates, some parent firms do not demand remittances. In many cases neither of these extremes is followed. Instead, the normal managerial response to potential government restrictions is to maintain a constant dividend payout ratio so as to demonstrate that an established policy is being consistently carried out. Host governments are more likely to accept the idea of regular dividend payments because they provide a framework based on precedent against which to judge whether a particular dividend is "normal," or is an attempt to flee from the currency to the detriment of host country foreign exchange reserves.

Foreign Exchange Risk

If a foreign exchange loss is anticipated, affiliates may speed up the transfer of funds to their parent through dividends. This "lead" is usually part of a larger strategy of moving from weak currencies to strong currencies. However, decisions to accelerate dividend payments ahead of what might be normal must take into account interest rate differences and the negative impact on host country relations. Leads and lags were discussed in Chapter 8.

Other Factors

Among other factors that influence dividend policy are the age and size of the foreign affiliate. Older affiliates often provide a greater share of their earnings to their parent, presumably because as the affiliate matures it has fewer reinvestment opportunities. With regard to size, large firms tend to use rule-of-thumb guidelines to set policy, while small firms have few set policies but "play it by ear." Medium-sized firms often use dividend policy as one of several techniques for positioning funds throughout the system.[1]

Existence of joint-venture partners or of local stockholders is also a factor influencing dividend policy. Optimal positioning of funds internationally cannot dominate the valid claims of partners or local stockholders for dividends. The latter do not necessarily benefit from the world perspective of the multinational parent. Robbins and Stobaugh found evidence that local stock ownership leads to more stable dividend payments regardless of earnings. Firms hesitate to reduce dividends when earnings falter; but they also hesitate to increase dividends following a spurt in earnings because it might be difficult to reduce dividends later, should earnings be lower.[2]

ROYALTIES, FEES, AND HOME OFFICE OVERHEAD

Royalties represent remuneration paid to the owners of technology, patents, or trade names for the use of the technology or the right to manufacture or sell under the patents or trade names. A royalty rate may be expressed as a fixed monetary amount per unit or as a percentage of gross revenue.

A fee is compensation for professional services and expertise supplied to an affiliate by a parent or another affiliate. Fees are sometimes differentiated into management fees for general expertise and advice, and technical assistance fees for guidance in technical matters. Fees are usually paid for identifiable benefits received by the affiliate, in contrast to overhead charges, to be discussed below, which are for more general benefits. Fees are usually a fixed charge, either in total for supplying the services for a stated period of time, or on a time-rate basis varying with the number of man-hours devoted to the affiliate. Fee provisions usually require an affiliate to pay travel and per diem expenses of the individuals involved.

A home office overhead allocation is a charge to compensate the parent for costs incurred in the general management of international operations and for other corporate overhead that must be recovered by the operating units. Overhead may be charged for regional cash management, research and development, corporate public relations, legal and accounting costs for the entire enterprise, or a share of the salaries and other costs of top management. Home office overhead is often levied throughout an entire company as a predetermined percentage of sales. In other instances the charge may be based on a pro rata sharing of specific costs, which can be matched to the various units.

Financial Management Implications

Payment of royalties and fees is especially suitable when unbundling of remuneration is desired. In joint ventures the resources contributed by one of the partners may include technology and know-how, while the other partner may be the primary supplier of monetary capital. The supplier of technology can readily accept royalty or fee compensation for that input and then accept a smaller proportion of net income as return on its investment of monetary capital.

Not all companies desire unbundling. Some parent firms do not want to impair the competitiveness of affiliates with charges for services that could be regarded as remote.

Sometimes royalty and fee payments are allowed by the host country, even when dividend payments are restricted. A company might organize the contractual part of its investment agreements so that if the free movement of funds via dividends is limited, options for repositioning funds via royalties and fees remain open.

Income Tax Aspects

Royalties and fees have certain tax advantages over dividends, especially when the host country income tax rate is above the parent rate. Royalties and fees are usually deductible locally. If the affiliate compensates the parent by dividends, local income taxes are paid before the dividend distribution and withholding taxes are paid on the dividend itself. The

Exhibit 19.1   Tax Effect, Bundled Versus Unbundled Compensation to Parent

	Case 1: Bundled $4,000 Dividend	Case 2: Unbundled Royalty + $1,600 Dividend	Case 3: Unbundled Royalty + $2,416 Dividend
Affiliate Statement			
Net income before taxes and compensation to parent	$10,000	$10,000	$10,000
Less royalties and fees	—	2,400	2,400
Taxable income in host country	10,000	7,600	7,600
Less host country tax @ 50%	5,000	3,800	3,800
Available for dividends	5,000	3,800	3,800
Cash dividend to parent	4,000	1,600	2,416
Reinvested locally	$ 1,000	$ 2,200	$ 1,384
Parent Statement			
Dividends received	$ 4,000	$ 1,600	$ 2,416
Add back foreign income tax	4,000	1,600	2,416
Grossed-up dividend in U.S.	8,000	3,200	4,832
Tentative U.S. tax at 34%	2,720	1,088	1,643
Less credit for foreign taxes	4,000	1,600	2,416
Additional U.S. tax on dividends	—	—	—
Royalty received	$ —	$ 2,400	$ 2,400
Less U.S. tax on royalty @ 34%	—	816	816
Royalty received after U.S. tax	—	1,584	1,584
Net dividend after all taxes	$ 4,000	$ 1,600	$ 2,416
Net royalty after all taxes	—	1,584	1,584
Total cash received in the U.S.	$ 4,000	$ 3,184	$ 4,000
Total Taxes Paid			
Taxes paid to host government	$ 5,000	$ 3,800	$ 3,800
Taxes paid to U.S. government	—	816	816
Total taxes paid	$ 5,000	$ 4,616	$ 4,616
Contribution to Worldwide Income			
Original income before any taxes	$10,000	$10,000	$10,000
Less total taxes paid	5,000	4,616	4,616
Contribution to consolidated income	$ 5,000	$ 5,384	$ 5,384

a Dividends of $4,000 are 80% of available income of $5,000. Hence 80% of taxes of $5,000, or $4,000, is added back.

b Dividends of $1,600 are 42.1% of available income of $3,800. Hence 42.1% of taxes of $3,800, or $1,600, is added back.

c Dividends of $2,416 are 63.6% of available income of $3,800. Hence 63.6% of taxes of $3,800, or $2,416, is added back.

$1,000 under both combinations. If each affiliate has the same income tax rate and if other expenses are constant, net income on a consolidated basis is $400.

The low-markup policy, in which the manufacturing affiliate "charges" the distribution affiliate $1,400 for the goods, results in a cash transfer of $1,400 from the distribution country to the manufacturing country. The high-markup policy, where the goods are "sold" at $1,700, causes an additional $300 of cash to move from distribution to manufacturing country. If it were desirable to transfer funds out of the distribution country, the high-markup policy would achieve this end.

Income Tax Effect

A major consideration in setting a transfer price is the income tax effect. Worldwide corporate profits may be influenced by setting transfer prices to minimize taxable income in a country with a high income tax rate and maximize income in a country with a low income tax rate.

The income tax effect is illustrated in Exhibit 19.3, which is identical to Exhibit 19.2 except that the manufacturing affiliate pays income taxes of 25% while the distribution affiliate pays income taxes of 50%. Under the low-markup policy the manufacturing

Exhibit 19.3   Tax Effect of Low Versus High Transfer Price on Net Income

Assumption: Manufacturing affiliate pays income taxes at 25%. Distribution affiliate pays income taxes at 50%.

	Manufacturing Affiliate	Distribution Affiliate	Consolidated Company
Low-Markup Policy			
Sales	$ 1,400	$ 2,000	$ 2,000
Less cost of goods sold[a]	1,000	1,400	1,000
Gross profit	$ 400	$ 600	$ 1,000
Less operating expenses	100	100	200
Taxable income	$ 300	$ 500	$ 800
Less income taxes (25%/50%)	75	250	325
Net income	$ 225	$ 250	$ 475
High-Markup Policy			
Sales	$ 1,700	$ 2,000	$ 2,000
Less cost of goods sold[a]	1,000	1,700	1,000
Gross profit	$ 700	$ 300	$ 1,000
Less operating expenses	100	100	200
Taxable income	$ 600	$ 200	$ 800
Less income taxes (25%/50%)	150	100	250
Net income	$ 450	$ 100	$ 550

a Cost of goods sold for the Distribution affiliate is the amount of sales of the Manufacturing affiliate.

affiliate pays $75 of taxes and the distribution affiliate pays $250, for a total tax bill of $325 and consolidated net income of $475.

If the firm adopts a high-markup policy, so that the merchandise is transferred at an intracompany sales price of $1,700, the same $800 of pre-tax consolidated income is allocated more heavily to the manufacturing affiliate and less heavily to the distribution affiliate. As a consequence, total taxes drop by $75 and consolidated net income increases by $75.

In the absence of government interference, the firm would prefer the high-markup policy. Needless to say, government tax authorities are aware of the potential income distortion from transfer price manipulation. A variety of regulations and court cases exist on the reasonableness of transfer prices, including fees and royalties as well as prices set for merchandise. If a government taxing authority does not accept a transfer price, taxable income will be deemed larger than was calculated by the firm, and taxes will be increased. An even greater danger, from the corporate point of view, is that two or more governments will try to protect their respective tax bases by contradictory policies that subject the business to double taxation on the same income.

Typical of laws circumscribing freedom to set transfer prices is Section 482 of the U.S. Internal Revenue Code. Under this authority the Internal Revenue Service (IRS) can reallocate gross income, deductions, credits, or allowances between related corporations in order to prevent tax evasion or to reflect more clearly a proper allocation of income. Under the IRS guidelines and subsequent judicial interpretation, the burden of proof is on the taxpayer to show that the IRS has been arbitrary or unreasonable in reallocating income. The "correct price" according to the guidelines is the one that reflects an *arm's length price*, that is, a sale of the same goods or service to an unrelated customer.

IRS regulations provide three methods to establish arm's length prices: comparable uncontrolled prices, resale prices, and cost-plus. A comparable uncontrolled price is regarded as the best evidence of arm's length pricing. Such prices arise when transactions in the same goods or services occur between the multinational firm and unrelated customers, or between two unrelated firms. The second-best approach to arm's length pricing starts with the final selling price to customers and subtracts an appropriate profit for the distribution affiliate to determine the allowable selling price for the manufacturing affiliate. The third method is to add an appropriate markup for profit to total costs of the manufacturing affiliate. The same three methods are recommended for use in member countries by the Organization for Economic Cooperation and Development (OECD) Committee on Fiscal Affairs.[3]

Although all governments have an interest in monitoring transfer pricing by multinational firms, not all governments use these powers to regulate transfer prices to the detriment of multinational firms. In particular, transfer pricing has some political advantages over other techniques of transferring funds. Although the recorded transfer price is known to the governments of both the exporting and importing countries, the underlying cost data are not available to the importing country. Thus the importing country finds it difficult to judge how reasonable the transfer price is, especially for nonstandard items such as manufactured components. Additionally, even if cost data could be obtained, some of the more sophisticated governments might continue to ignore the transfer pricing leak. They recognize that the foreign investors must be able to repatriate a reasonable profit by their own standards, even if this profit seems unreasonable locally. An unknown or unproven transfer price leak makes it more difficult for local critics to blame their government for allowing the country to be "exploited" by foreign investors. On the other hand, if the host government has soured on foreign investment, transfer price leaks are less likely to be overlooked. Thus within the *potential* and *actual* constraints established by governments, opportunities may exist for multinational firms to alter transfer prices away from an arm's length market price.

Managerial Incentives and Evaluation

When a firm is organized with decentralized profit centers, transfer pricing between centers can disrupt evaluations of managerial performance. This problem is not unique to multinational firms but has been a controversial issue in the "centralization versus decentralization" debate in domestic circles. In the domestic case, however, a modicum of coordination at the corporate level can alleviate some of the distortion that occurs when any profit center suboptimizes its profit for the corporate good. This statement might also be true in the multinational case, but coordination is often hindered by longer and less-efficient channels of communication and the need to consider the unique variables that influence international pricing. Even with the best of intent, a manager in one country finds it difficult to know what is best for the firm as a whole when buying at a negotiated price from an affiliate in another country. If corporate headquarters establishes transfer prices and sourcing alternatives, managerial disincentives arise if the prices seem arbitrary or unreasonable. Furthermore, if corporate headquarters makes more decisions, one of the main advantages of a decentralized profit center system disappears. Local management loses the incentive to act for its own benefit.

Tariff and Quota Effect

Transfer pricing may have an influence on the amount of import duties paid. If the importing affiliate pays ad valorem import duties, and if those duties are levied on the invoice (transfer) price, duties will rise under the high-markup policy.

The incidence of import duties is usually opposite to the incidence of income taxes in transfer pricing, but income taxes are usually a heavier burden than import duties. Therefore transfer prices are more often viewed from an income tax perspective. In some instances, however, import duties are actually levied against internationally posted prices, if such exist, rather than against the stated invoice price. If so, duties will not be influenced by the transfer price policy. Income taxes will still be affected by both the residual location of operating profit and the deductibility of the assessed import duties.

Related to the tariff effect is the ability to lower transfer prices to offset the volume effect of foreign exchange quotas. Should a host government allocate a limited amount of foreign exchange for importing a particular type of good, a lower transfer price on the import allows the firm to bring in a greater quantity. If, for example, the imported item is a component for a locally manufactured product, a lower transfer price may allow production volume to be sustained or expanded, albeit at the expense of profits in the supply affiliate.

Effect on Joint-Venture Partners

Joint ventures pose a special problem in transfer pricing, because serving the interest of local stockholders by maximizing local profit may be suboptimal from the overall viewpoint of the multinational firm. Often the conflicting interests are irreconcilable. When Ford Motor Company decided to rationalize production on a worldwide basis so that each division could specialize in certain products or components, it was forced to abandon its policy of working with joint ventures partly because of the transfer pricing problem. It had to purchase the large British minority interest in Ford, Ltd., in 1961, despite the well-publicized and ill-timed drain on the U.S. balance of payments. For identical reasons, General Motors has seldom worked with joint ventures despite its recent arrangement with Toyota.

Transfer Pricing in Practice

Given the potential for conflicting objectives, what transfer pricing policies do multinational firms utilize in practice? A recent empirical study of 164 U.S. multinational firms by Al-Eryani, Alam, and Akhter sheds considerable light on this question.[4] Their findings are presented in Exhibit 19.4.

Although Section 482 of the U.S. Internal Revenue Code requires use of "arms length" pricing, only 35% of the responding firms indicated that they used "market based" methods to set the "arms length" transfer price (bottom of Exhibit 19.4). Almost all of the other firms used either some version of a "cost plus" price or a "negotiated" price. This split presumably reflects the relative proportion of products which had a recognized external market price compared to products or components that had no external market price.

The authors of Exhibit 19.4 used the response data to test various hypotheses about the determinants motivating a firm's choice of a particular transfer pricing policy. They found that "legal" and "size" variables were statistically significant determinants of market-based transfer pricing. Legal considerations include compliance with tax rules (Section 482), customs regulations, antidumping laws, antitrust laws, and the accounting norms of host countries. Large-size firms with multiple products and locations were also likely to use market-based transfer pricing whenever possible. This was probably because they are highly visible and it would be difficult to customize transfer pricing given the complexities of their sales networks.

Another interesting finding of the study was that "economic restrictions (such as exchange controls, price controls, and restrictions on imports), political-social conditions, and the extent of economic development in host countries are either unimportant or are secondary determinants of a market-based transfer pricing strategy."[5] Furthermore, they found no statistical support for assuming that these variables influenced nonmarket-based

Exhibit 19.4   Frequency of Use of International Transfer Pricing Methods

	MDCs[a]		LDCs[b]		TOTAL	
	#	%	#	%	#	%
Nonmarket-Based Methods						
Actual unit full cost	4	4	4	5	8	5
Actual unit full cost plus fixed markup	15	15	11	15	26	15
Actual unit variable cost	0	0	0	0	0	0
Actual unit variable cost plus fixed markup	3	3	2	3	5	3
Standard unit full cost plus fixed markup	15	16	10	13	25	15
Standard unit full cost	5	5	0	0	5	3
Standard unit variable cost	1	1	0	0	1	0
Standard unit variable cost plus fixed markup	5	5	4	5	9	5
Marginal cost	0	0	0	0	0	0
Opportunity cost	2	2	0	0	2	1
Negotiated price	13	13	12	16	25	15
Mathematical programming	1	1	3	4	4	2
Dual pricing	1	1	1	1	2	1
Total nonmarket based	65	66	47	62	112	65
Market-Based Methods						
Prevailing market price	17	18	12	16	29	17
Adjusted market price	15	16	16	22	31	18
Total market based	32	34	28	38	60	35
Total number of firms[c]	97	100	75	100	172	100

Source: Mohammad F. Al-Eryani, Pervaiz Alam, and Syed Akhter, "Transfer Pricing Determinants of U.S. Multinationals," *Journal of International Business Studies,* Third Quarter, 1990, p. 420.

a MDCs = more developed countries

b LDCs = less developed countries

c Total number of responses exceeds 76 firms in the MDC group because some firms identified the use of more than one transfer pricing method. On the other hand, the total number of responses for the LDC group is less than 88 because some firms did not identify the transfer pricing method they used for multinational transfers.

transfer pricing policies. These findings suggest that transfer pricing policies are not very sensitive to the positioning of funds considerations which were described earlier in this chapter.

The study also found that internal considerations, such as performance evaluation of subsidiaries and their management, were not statistically significant determinants of transfer pricing policies. Presumably multinational firms prefer to maintain separate sets of books for that purpose.

In a much earlier study of 60 non-U.S. multinational firms and their U.S. affiliates, Jeffrey S. Arpan found distinct national differences with respect to the weight accorded host country environmental variables and internal company parameters. Canadian, French, Italian, and U.S. parent firms judged that the tax effect of transfer pricing was the most important consideration.[6] British parent firms emphasized the strong financial appearance of their U.S. affiliates. Inflation was an important consideration by all parent firms except those in Scandinavia; these firms considered acceptability to the host government to be the most important determinant of their transfer pricing policies. German firms appeared to be least concerned about transfer pricing policies. Non-U.S. firms, in contrast to U.S. firms, did not consider the evaluation of managerial performance to be important because, contrary to the practice of many U.S. firms, they did not usually operate their foreign affiliates on a profit center basis.

BLOCKED FUNDS

When a government runs short of foreign exchange and cannot obtain additional funds through borrowing or attracting new foreign investment, it usually limits transfers of foreign exchange out of the country. In theory this does not discriminate against foreign-owned firms because it applies to everyone; in practice foreign firms have more at stake. Depending on the degree of shortage, the host government might simply require approval of all transfers of funds abroad, thus reserving the right to set a priority on the use of scarce foreign exchange in favor of necessities rather than luxuries. In very severe cases the government might make its currency nonconvertible into other currencies, thereby fully blocking transfers of funds abroad. In between these positions are policies that restrict the size and timing of dividends, debt amortization, royalties, and service fees.

Multinational firms can react to the potential for blocked funds at three stages.

1. Prior to making an investment, they can analyze the effect of blocked funds on expected return on investment, the desired local financial structure, and optimal links with affiliates.

2. During operations they can attempt to move funds through a variety of positioning techniques.

3. Funds that cannot be moved must be reinvested in the local country in a manner that avoids deterioration in their real value because of inflation and/or exchange depreciation.

Preinvestment Strategy

Management can consider blocked funds in their capital budgeting analysis, as was done in the example in Chapter 17. Temporary blockage of funds normally reduces the expected net present value and internal rate of return on a proposed investment. Whether the investment should nevertheless be undertaken depends on whether the expected rate of return, even with blocked funds, exceeds the required rate of return on investments of the same risk class. Preinvestment analysis also includes the potential to minimize the effect of blocked funds by means of heavy local borrowing, swap agreements, and other techniques to reduce local currency exposure and thus the need to repatriate funds. Sourcing and sales links with affiliates can be predetermined so as to maximize the potential for moving blocked funds.

Moving Blocked Funds

What can a multinational firm do to transfer funds out of countries having exchange or remittance restrictions? Three popular approaches have already been discussed:

1. Unbundling services, described earlier in this chapter.
2. Transfer pricing, also described earlier in this chapter.
3. Leading and lagging payments, described in Chapter 8.

Three additional approaches are:

1. Using fronting loans.
2. Creating unrelated exports.
3. Obtaining special dispensation.

Fronting Loans. A *fronting loan* is a parent-to-affiliate loan channeled through a financial intermediary, usually a large international bank. Fronting loans differ from "parallel" or "back-to-back" loans, discussed in Chapter 8, in that the latter involve offsetting loans between commercial businesses arranged outside the banking system. Fronting loans are sometimes referred to as *link financing*.

In a direct intracompany loan the parent or an affiliate loans directly to the borrowing affiliate, and at a later date the borrowing affiliate repays the principal and interest. In a fronting loan, by contrast, the "lending" U.S. parent deposits funds in, say, a London bank, and that bank loans the same amount to the borrowing affiliate in a third (host) country. From the bank's point of view the loan is risk-free, because the bank has 100% collateral in the form of the parent's deposit. In effect the bank "fronts" for the parent—hence the name. Interest paid by the borrowing affiliate to the bank is usually slightly higher than the rate paid by the bank to the parent, allowing the bank a margin for expenses and profit.

Use of fronting loans increases chances for repayment should political turmoil occur between the home and host countries. Government authorities are more likely to allow the local affiliate to repay a loan to a large international bank in a neutral country than to allow the same affiliate to repay a loan directly to its parent. To stop payment to the international bank would hurt the international credit image of the country, whereas to stop payment to the parent corporation would have minimal impact on that image and might even provide some domestic political advantage.

A fronting loan may have a tax advantage. Assume, as depicted in Exhibit 19.5, that a finance affiliate, wholly owned by the parent and located in a tax haven country, deposits $1,000,000 in an intermediary commercial bank at 8% interest, and the bank in turn lends $1,000,000 to an operating affiliate at 9%. The operating affiliate is located in a country where the income tax rate is 50%. Interest payments net of income tax effect will be as follows:

1. The operating affiliate pays $90,000 interest to the intermediary bank. Deduction of interest from taxable income results in a net after-tax cost of $45,000.

Exhibit 19.5   Tax Aspects of a Fronting Loan

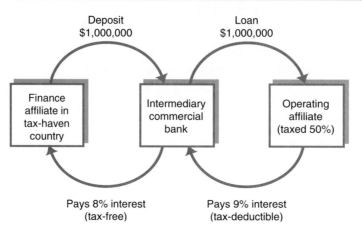

2.   The intermediary bank receives $90,000, retains $10,000 for its services, and pays $80,000 interest on the deposit of the finance affiliate.

3.   The finance affiliate receives $80,000 interest on deposit, tax free.

The net result is that $80,000 of cash is moved from the operating affiliate to the finance affiliate. Since the after-tax cost to the borrowing affiliate is only $45,000, the system has been able to move an additional $35,000 out of the country by virtue of the tax shield. If the finance affiliate had made a direct loan to the operating affiliate, the host government of the operating affiliate would be in a position to disallow the interest charge as a tax-deductible expense by ruling that it was a substantive dividend to the parent disguised as interest. Note that the fronting loan, as a device, provides no protection against changes in exchange rates.

Creating Unrelated Exports.   One approach to blocked funds that benefits both affiliate and host country is the creation of unrelated exports. Because the main reason for stringent exchange controls is usually a country's persistent inability to earn hard currencies, anything a multinational firm can do to create new exports from the host country helps the situation and provides a potential means to transfer funds out.

Some new exports can often be created from present productive capacity with little or no additional investment, especially if they are in product lines related to existing operations. Other new exports may require reinvestment or new funds, although if the funds reinvested consist of those already blocked, little is lost in the way of opportunity costs. A multinational firm already in Brazil, for example, might locate research and development laboratories there and pay for them with blocked cruzeiros. Key research personnel could be transferred to Brazil to supplement local talent, their salaries and expenses being picked up on the local payroll. A Brazilian architectural and engineering firm might be hired to provide services for the worldwide enterprise, being paid in cruzeiros to design plants in France or Florida.

Export equivalents can also be created with little investment in certain service activities. The Brazilian affiliate, for example, could host conventions or other business meetings in Rio de Janeiro for its multinational parent. Employees of the firm might be sent on company-sponsored vacations to Brazil, and employees of the parent flying anywhere in the world might be asked to use Varig, the Brazilian national airline, wherever possible, flying on tickets purchased in Brazil by the Brazilian affiliate and paid for with cruzeiros.

All such activities benefit Brazil because they provide export-oriented jobs and earnings. They benefit the multinational firm because they provide a way to use effectively funds that would otherwise remain tied up in the Brazilian money market.

Another approach for a parent dealing with blocked currency is to arrange barter agreements. A country such as Brazil would probably not allow barter deals involving coffee or other commodities already sold on world markets for hard currencies, but it might permit a barter for exports of goods or services not normally exported. For example, Brazilian textiles might be bought from the Brazilian affiliate by the parent in exchange for imports into Brazil of the parent's products or equipment. The parent (not in the textile business) arranges for the sale of the textiles in the parent country. Countertrade, of which barter is one form, was discussed in Chapter 18.

Special Dispensation. If all else fails and the multinational firm is investing in an industry that is important to the economic development of the host country, the firm may bargain for special dispensation to repatriate some portion of the funds that otherwise would be blocked. Firms in "desirable" industries such as telecommunications, semiconductor manufacturing, instrumentation, pharmaceuticals, or other research and high-technology industries, may receive preference over firms in mature industries. The amount of preference received depends on bargaining among informed parties, the government and the business firm, either of which is free to back away from the proposed investment if unsatisfied with the terms.

Self-fulfilling Prophecies. In seeking "escape routes" for blocked funds—or for that matter in trying to position funds through any of the techniques discussed in this chapter—the multinational firm may increase political risk and cause a change from partial blockage to full blockage. The possibility of such a self-fulfilling cycle exists any time a firm takes action that, no matter how legal, thwarts the underlying intent of politically authored controls. In the statehouses of the world, as in the editorial offices of the local press and TV, multinational firms and their affiliates are always a potential scapegoat.

Forced Reinvestment

If funds are indeed blocked from transfer into foreign exchange, they are by definition "reinvested." Under such a situation the firm must find local opportunities that will maximize rate of return for a given acceptable level of risk.

If blockage is expected to be temporary, the most obvious alternative is to invest in local money market instruments. Unfortunately, in many countries such instruments are not available in sufficient quantity or with adequate liquidity. In some cases government treasury bills, bank deposits, and other short-term instruments have yields that are kept artificially low relative to local rates of inflation or probable changes in exchange rates. Thus the firm often loses real value during the period of blockage.

Forced reinvestment may take the form of direct loans. The back-to-back or parallel loan discussed in Chapter 8 is one type, as is the fronting loan discussed earlier in this chapter.

If short- or intermediate-term portfolio investments, such as bonds, bank time deposits, or direct loans to other companies, are not possible, direct investment in additional production facilities may be the only alternative. Often this investment is what the host country is seeking by its exchange controls, even if the fact of exchange controls is by itself counterproductive to the idea of additional foreign investment. Examples of forced direct reinvestment can be cited for Peru, where an airline invested in hotels and in maintenance facilities for other airlines; for Turkey, where a fish canning company constructed a plant to manufacture cans needed for packing the catch; and for Argentina, where an automobile company integrated vertically by acquiring an automobile transmission manufacturing plant previously owned by a supplier.

If investment opportunities in additional production facilities are not available, funds may simply be used to acquire other assets expected to increase in value with local inflation. Typical purchases might be land, office buildings, or commodities that are exported to global markets. Even inventory stockpiling might be a reasonable investment, given the low opportunity cost of the blocked funds.

MANAGING INTERNATIONAL CASH BALANCES

Cash balances, including marketable securities, are held partly in anticipation of day-to-day cash disbursements and partly as protection against unanticipated variations from budgeted cash flows. These two motives are commonly called the transaction motive and the precautionary motive. Cash may also be held for speculative purposes; however, this aspect is beyond our consideration in this chapter because it does not involve normal day-to-day operations. Cash management in a multinational firm can benefit from both centralized depositories and multilateral netting.

Centralized Depositories

Operational benefits can be gained by centralizing cash management in any business with widely dispersed operating affiliates. Internationally the procedure calls for each affiliate to hold only a minimum cash balance for transaction purposes. No cash for precautionary purposes is held locally—unless management of the central pool issues specific instructions to override the general rule. All excess funds are remitted to a central cash depository, where a single authority has responsibility for placing the funds in such currencies and money market instruments as will best serve the firm as a whole.

The central depository has advantages of size and information. It is located where information can be collected and decisions made about the relative strengths and weaknesses of various currencies. Interest rate information on alternative investments for each currency is also available, as is experience with the mechanical functioning of the various money markets. Although in theory such information might be available to the treasurer of each affiliate, in practice that individual can seldom specialize in money market management alone.

Funds held in the central pool can quickly be returned to a local affiliate that is short of cash. This return is achieved either by wire transfer or by creating a worldwide bank credit line. The bank would instruct its branch office in the particular country to advance emergency funds to the local affiliate.

Another reason for holding all precautionary balances in a central pool is that the total pool, if centralized, can be reduced in size without any loss in the level of protection. For example, assume a firm possesses three affiliate operations: Italy, Germany, and France. Each affiliate maintains a precautionary cash balance equal to the expected cash needs plus a safety margin of three standard deviations of the expected balance. Cash needs are assumed to be normally distributed in each country, and the needs are independent from one country to another. Three standard deviations means there exists a 99.87% chance that actual cash needs will be met.

The cash needs of the individual affiliates, and the total precautionary cash balances held, are shown in Exhibit 19.6 and diagrammed in Exhibit 19.7. The total precautionary cash balances of the three affiliates is $46,000,000. This total includes $28,000,000 in expected cash needs, and $18,000,000 in idle cash balances (the three standard deviations of the individual expected cash balances) held as the safety margin.

What would happen if the firm maintained all precautionary balances in a single account in one European financial center? Because variances are additive when probability distributions are independent, the equivalent standard deviation for the single account would be the following:

$$\text{Std. Dev. of Centralized Depository} = \sqrt{(1,000,000)^2 + (2,000,000)^2 + (3,000,000)^2}$$
$$= \sqrt{14,000,000}$$
$$= \$3,741,657.$$

Therefore, a firm using a centralized depository would hold a centralized cash balance of the following:

Centralized cash balance	=	Sum of expected cash needs	+	Three standard deviations of expected sum
	=	$28,000,000	+	(3 x $3,741,657)
	=	$39,224,972		

Exhibit 19.6   Decentralized Cash Budgeting versus a Centralized Depository

Decentralized Cash Budgeting

Country	Expected Cash Need (A)	One Standard Deviation (B)	Cash Balance Budgeted for Adequate Protection[a] (A + 3B)
Italy	$10,000,000	$1,000,000	$13,000,000
Germany	6,000,000	2,000,000	12,000,000
France	12,000,000	3,000,000	21,000,000
Total	$28,000,000	$6,000,000	$46,000,000

Centralized Depository

Country	Expected Cash Need (A)	One Standard Deviation (B)	Cash Balance Budgeted for Adequate Protection[a] (A + 3B)
Italy	$10,000,000		
Germany	6,000,000	$3,741,657	$11,224,972
France	12,000,000		
Total	$28,000,000	$3,741,657[b]	$39,224,972

a Adequate protection is defined as the expected cash balance plus three standard deviations, assuming that the cash flows of all three individual affiliates are normally distributed.

b The standard deviation of the expected cash balance of the centralized depository is calculated as follows:

$$\sqrt{(1,000,000)^2 + (2,000,000)^2 + (3,000,000)^2} = \$3,741,657.$$

A budgeted cash balance three standard deviations above the aggregate expected cash need would require only $11,224,972 in potentially idle cash, as opposed to the previous total idle cash balance of $18,000,000. Budgeted investment in cash balances is reduced by $6,775,028.

Central money pools are usually maintained in major money centers such as London, New York, Zurich, and Tokyo. Additional popular locations for money pools include Liechtenstein, Luxembourg, the Bahamas, and Bermuda. Although these countries do not have strong diversified economies, they offer most of the other prerequisites for a corporate financial center: freely convertible currency, political and economic stability, access to international communications, and clearly defined legal procedures. Their additional advantage as a so-called tax haven is also desirable.

A second advantage of centralized cash management is that one affiliate will not borrow at high rates while another holds surplus funds idle or invests them at low rates. Managers of the central pool can locate the least expensive sources of funds, worldwide, as well as the most advantageous returns to be earned on excess funds. If additional cash

Exhibit 19.7 Precautionary Balances (in thousands of dollars)

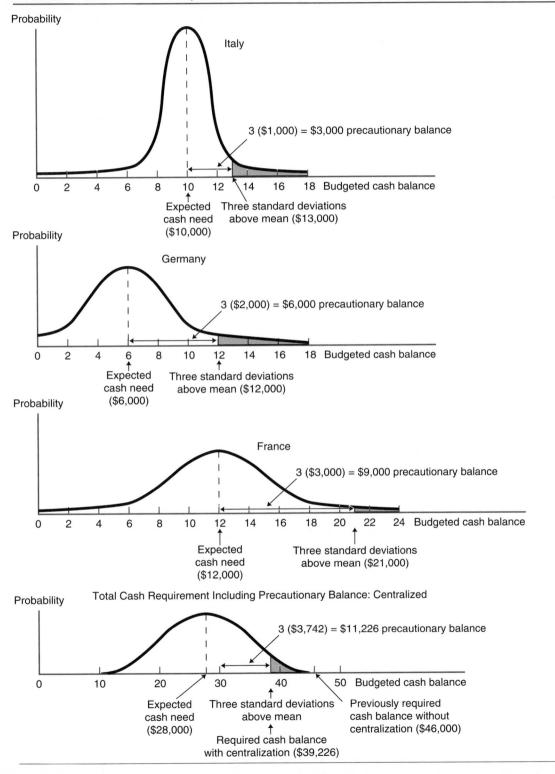

is desired, the central pool manager can determine the location of such borrowing. A local affiliate manager would never borrow at a rate above the minimum available to the pool manager. If the firm has a worldwide cash surplus, the central pool manager can evaluate comparative rates of return in various markets, transaction costs, exchange risks, and tax effects.

Use of a centralized depository system does not necessarily imply use of a single bank, for the essence of the centralized depository is centralized information and decisions. Actual funds may be placed in as many banks as are desired.

Near-term Cash Planning

Moving funds from country to country, as is required for the operation of a centralized depository, has a cash cost in terms of exchange rate spreads and a managerial cost in terms of loss of local affiliate control of its resources. These costs are particularly burdensome if such funds are mislocated, that is, denominated in the wrong currency from the viewpoint of near-term cash needs. Mislocated funds can be minimized by the use of a multinational cash forecasting system.

To illustrate, assume that the European headquarters of a multinational firm operates a central cash pool in Belgium, and that the firm has operating affiliates in the United Kingdom, Sweden, Germany, and France. At the close of daily banking hours in each country, the four affiliates report to Brussels by wire or FAX their end-of-day cash balances in cleared funds. As is true for netting systems, the daily report will be in a designated reporting currency, with actual local currency cash balances translated at an exchange rate specified by the corporate treasurer. Assume that the reporting currency is the U.S. dollar.

The daily cash report for each unit might appear as in Exhibit 19.8. According to the reports in Exhibit 19.8, the British affiliate has an end-of-day cash balance in pounds sterling equivalent to $150,000. In other words, the British affiliate could have disbursed an additional $150,000 (in sterling) that day without creating a negative cash balance or exceeding intended overdraft privileges. Similarly, the Swedish affiliate has an end-of-day balances of $250,000, and the German and French affiliates have end-of-day balances equal to $600,000 and $500,000.

At the end of each day the central pool manager compiles a report in the form shown in Exhibit 19.9. This daily cash ledger shows the end-of-day cash balances at each affiliate and the previously agreed upon minimum operating balance to be maintained there for day-to-day operations. In the example, the British affiliate ended the day with a cash balance of $150,000, but it needed $200,000. At the end of the day it was $50,000 short of normal operating funds. Similarly the Swedish affiliate was short $375,000, while the German and French affiliates had cash balances above their operating needs. For Europe as a whole, the company had a surplus cash of $225,000.

The essence of effective cash planning is to use the information in the daily cash ledger to cover any deficits, decide upon any borrowing, and put any excess cash into the currency and/or money market instruments most appropriate in light of expectations about future cash needs, interest rates, and possible changes in exchange rates.

Exhibit 19.8 European Cash Management Pool—Daily Cash Reports (thousands of dollars)

DAILY CASH REPORT

Date _____ March 7, 19XX _____

Location _____ United Kingdom _____

End-of-day cash balance _____ +150 _____

Five-day forecast:

	receipt	disburse	net
+1	300	400	−100
+2	400	350	+50
+3	300	250	+50
+4	250	650	−400
+5	200	250	−50
Net for period			−450

DAILY CASH REPORT

Date _____ March 7, 19XX _____

Location _____ Sweden _____

End-of-day cash balance _____ −250 _____

Five-day forecast:

	receipt	disburse	net
+1	100	200	−100
+2	100	150	−50
+3	50	zero	+50
+4	200	75	+125
+5	200	200	zero
Net for period			+25

DAILY CASH REPORT

Date _____ March 7, 19XX _____

Location _____ Germany _____

End-of-day cash balance _____ +600 _____

Five-day forecast:

	receipt	disburse	net
+1	400	100	+300
+2	350	100	+250
+3	300	150	+150
+4	300	400	−100
+5	200	100	+100
Net for period			+700

DAILY CASH REPORT

Date _____ March 7, 19XX _____

Location _____ France _____

End-of-day cash balance _____ +500 _____

Five-day forecast:

	receipt	disburse	net
+1	100	400	−300
+2	300	100	+200
+3	500	200	+300
+4	100	100	zero
+5	150	225	−50
Net for period			+150

For example, if an imminent drop in value of the British pound were anticipated, the required minimum cash balance for the United Kingdom could be reduced from $200,000 to some lower level. If local overdrafts were possible, the required "minimum" might be a negative number.

As seen in Exhibit 19.8, one additional item of information is usually requested in each daily cash report. This is a forecast of expected cash receipts and disbursements for

Exhibit 19.9   European Cash Management Pool—Central Office Compilation

CASH LEDGER (March 7, 19XX)
(thousand-dollar equivalents of local currency)

Location	End-of-day cash balance	Required minimum	Excess local cash balance
United Kingdom	+150	200	−50
Sweden	−250	125	−375
Germany	+600	250	+350
France	+500	200	+300
Europe-wide cash gain (or loss)			+225

each of the following five days. Only local affiliate managers have the detailed knowledge for such near-term cash forecasting. This forecast, which moves forward day to day, serves at least three purposes: First, each affiliate is forced to revise its operating cash budget daily, and the actual cash result can be measured against the accuracy of the forecasts of each of the previous five days. Second, information that assists in the decision to transfer funds to or from the central pool is given. For example, although France currently has a cash surplus of $300,000 (Exhibit 19.9), the following day a deficit of $300,000 is expected. Depending on interest rates and the cost of exchange transactions, the central pool might instruct the French affiliate to invest its surplus funds overnight in France against the following day's deficit, rather than transmit the funds to Belgium and then have Belgium cover the next day's deficit with a remittance back to France.

Third, an estimate of future net cash flows for all of Europe is needed to determine the appropriate maturities for any investing or borrowing by the central pool. Should the Europe-wide net cash gain of $225,000 on March 7 (Exhibit 19.9) or any portion of it be put into longer maturities, or should it be put into the short-term money market because of cash needs the following day or week?

Information received and tabulated in the cash ledger, Exhibit 19.9, is used for decisions about where to direct cash movements. Given the needs (United Kingdom and Sweden) and excess cash balances (Germany and France) one possible set of routings that would clear balances for the day and leave the daily surplus of $225,000 in the central pool would be as shown in Exhibit 19.10. Many other combinations are possible, but both responsibility and supporting information are concentrated in one location—the European cash manager in Belgium.

Information from the individual affiliate five-day forecasts is also compiled into a Europe-wide forecast, as shown in Exhibit 19.11. The sum of columns for each day shows the Europe-wide cash gain or loss, and that figure is used for deciding whether or not daily excess funds should be sent to the pool or allowed to accumulate at the local level. It is also used to decide what investment maturities, if any, should be sought by the central pool, for

Exhibit 19.10 European Cash Management Pool—Possible Cash Routing Instructions (thousands of dollars)

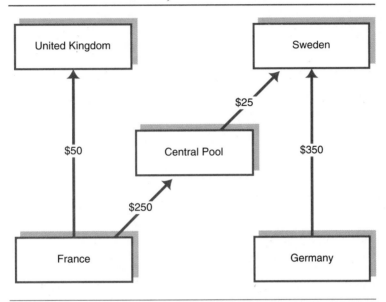

decisions to approach the company's banks to borrow more funds, for deciding what currencies to borrow or invest, and for decisions to repay bank loans. In this example, the company is going to gain $425,000 over the week, as shown in the lower right corner, but will be short of cash on the first and fourth day that follow.

Exhibit 19.11 European Cash Management Pool—Five-Day Cash Forecast (thousands of dollars)

Location	Days from the Present +1	+2	+3	+4	+5	Five-Day Total
United Kingdom	−100	+50	+50	−400	−50	−450
Sweden	−100	−50	+50	+125	zero	+25
Germany	+300	+250	+150	−100	+100	+700
France	−300	+200	+300	zero	−50	+150
European cash gain by day, forecast	−200	+450	+550	−375	zero	+425

Multilateral Netting

Multilateral netting of payments is useful primarily when a large number of separate foreign exchange transactions occur between affiliates in the normal course of business. Netting reduces the settlement cost of what would otherwise be a large number of crossing spot transactions.

Multilateral netting is an extension of bilateral netting. If a Belgian affiliate owes an Italian affiliate $5,000,000, while the Italian affiliate simultaneously owes the Belgian affiliate $3,000,000, a bilateral settlement calls for a single payment of $2,000,000 from Belgium to Italy and the cancellation, via offset, of the remainder of the debt.

A multilateral system is an expanded version of this simple bilateral concept. Assume that payments are due between European affiliates of the same multinational firm at the end of a month of operations. Each obligation reflects the accumulated transactions of the prior month. These obligations are shown in the top third of Exhibit 19.12.

Without netting, Belgium, for example, must make three separate payments and will receive three separate receipts. If Belgium paid each individual invoice, rather than accumulated balances at the end of the month, it would generate a multitude of costly small bank transactions every day. The daily totals would add up to the monthly accumulated balances shown in the diagram.

In order to reduce bank transaction costs, such as the spread between foreign exchange bid and ask quotations and transfer fees, many multinational firms have established their own multilateral netting centers. Others have contracted with banks to manage their netting activities. With netting, the affiliates transmit information about their obligations to a single center, which combines them in the form shown in Exhibit 19.12.

Note that total payments add up to $43,000,000. If the cost of foreign exchange transactions and transfer fees were 0.5%, the total cost of settlement would be $215,000. Using information from the netting matrix in the middle of Exhibit 19.12, the netting center can order three payments which settle the entire set of obligations. The United Kingdom can be instructed to remit $3,000,000 to Italy, and Belgium can be instructed to remit $1,000,000 each to France and Italy. Total foreign exchange transfers are reduced to $5,000,000, and transaction costs are reduced to $25,000.

Some countries, such as France and Italy, limit or prohibit netting, and some permit netting on a "gross settlements" basis only. For a single settlement period all receipts may be combined into a single receipt and all payments into a single payment. However, these two may not be netted. Thus two large payments must pass through the local banking system. The reason for such a requirement is usually a desire to subsidize local banks by forcing firms to pay for transactions that are not necessary, although this real reason may be concealed behind a statement that certain types of data are needed.

Permission to net payments is granted by individual permit in some countries such as France and Spain. Firms that manufacture locally are often given permission, while those that only sell are often denied. A survey of 194 multinational firms by Business International reported that 33% of the European and 28% of the U.S. firms used multilateral netting.[7] Some firms reported savings of several million dollars.[8]

Exhibit 19.12 Multilateral Netting Matrix (thousands of dollars)

CASH FLOWS BEFORE MULTILATERAL NETTING

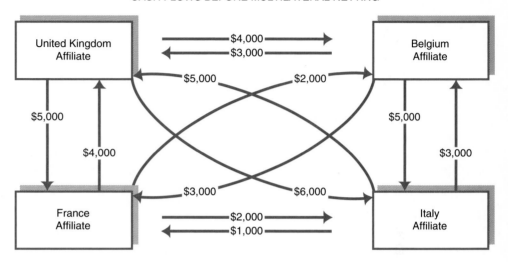

Calculation of Net Obligation

| | Paying Affiliate | | | | | |
Receiving affiliate	U.K.	Belgium	France	Italy	Total receipts	Net receipts (payments)
United Kingdom	—	$3,000	$4,000	$5,000	$12,000	($3,000)
Belgium	4,000	—	2,000	3,000	9,000	($2,000)
France	5,000	3,000	—	1,000	9,000	$1,000
Italy	6,000	5,000	2,000	—	13,000	$4,000
Total payments	$15,000	$11,000	$ 8,000	$ 9,000	$43,000	—

CASH FLOWS AFTER MULTILATERAL NETTING

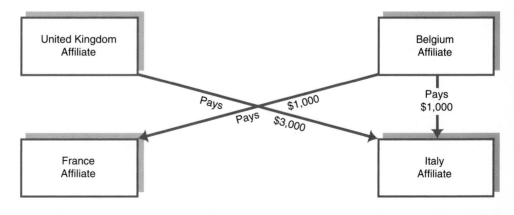

MANAGING RECEIVABLES

Multinational accounts receivable are created by two separate types of transactions: sales to related affiliates and sales to independent buyers having no ownership relationship with the selling firm. Within-family accounts receivable are usually managed by leads and lags and through reinvoicing centers, topics that were discussed in Chapter 8.

Independent Customers

Management of accounts receivable from independent customers involves two types of decisions: In what currency should the transaction be denominated, and what should be the terms of payment? Domestic sales are almost always denominated in the local currency. At issue is whether export sales should be denominated in the currency of the exporter, the currency of the buyer, or a third-country currency. Competition or custom will often dictate the answer, but if negotiating room exists, the seller should prefer to price and to invoice in the strongest currency. Since the buyer would prefer to pay in the weakest currency, and since both parties are likely to be equally well informed about the risk involved, the usual result is a tradeoff in which a price or a terms-of-payment concession is granted by the seller in order to obtain the sale in a hard currency. Alternatively, the buyer pays more or pays sooner if payment in a soft currency is desired.

Parties to the transaction are likely to deviate from this straightforward bargaining position only if they have different opinions about the relative strengths of the currencies involved or if their own financial situation is strong enough to absorb the weak currency position. For example, a seller is more willing to price and invoice in a weak currency if that seller already has debts in that currency, for the sales proceeds can be used to retire the debt without any obvious loss. From the point of view of opportunity cost, that seller nevertheless forgoes an exchange gain. The buyer may be willing to pay in a hard currency if the buyer intends to resell the merchandise in a hard currency.

Payment Terms

Another factor is terms of payment. Considered by themselves, receivables from sales in weak currencies should be collected as soon as possible to minimize loss of exchange value between sales date and collection date. Accounts receivable resulting from sales in hard currencies may be allowed to remain outstanding longer. In fact, if the seller is expecting an imminent devaluation of its home currency, it might want to encourage slow payment of its hard currency receivables, especially if the home government requires immediate exchange of foreign currency receipts into the home currency. An alternative, if legal, would be for the seller to accept the proceeds abroad and keep them on deposit abroad rather than return them to the home country.

In some economies accounts receivable are used as a basis for short-term financing in preference to inventory financing. This situation occurs most often in inflationary economies and in economies in which the banking system is institutionally oriented toward discounting paper rather than financing merchandise.

In inflationary economies the demand for credit usually exceeds the supply. Often, however, a large business (be it multinational or a large local concern) has better access to the limited, cheaper credit that is available locally than do smaller domestic businesses, such as local distributors, retail merchants, or smaller manufacturers. Assume, for example, that the cost of local credit to a large multinational manufacturer/seller is 30% per annum, while the cost of credit to a potential retailer/buyer in the same economy is 50% per annum. Both manufacturer and retailer will benefit by maximizing sales volume to the ultimate customer if the manufacturer finances the transactions as long as possible and adds the financing costs (at 30%) to the sales price. In other words, it is better for the seller to finance the buyer's inventory at 30% per annum in the form of long-term receivables than for the buyer to finance the inventory directly for 50% per annum.

Self-liquidating Bills

Some banking systems, often for reasons of tradition, have a predilection toward self-liquidating, discountable bills. In many European countries it is easier to borrow from a bank on the security of bills (receivables in negotiable form) generated from sales than on the security of physical inventory. Napoleon is alleged to have had a philosophy that no good French merchant should be required to wait for funds if good merchandise has been sold to good people, provided a document exists showing sales of the items. The document must have the signature of the buyer and the endorsement of the seller and the rediscounting bank. Thus in France it is often possible to reduce net investment in receivables to zero by selling entirely on trade acceptances that can be discounted at the bank.

The European predilection for discountable bills has a very real rationale behind it. According to European commercial law, which is based on the "Code Napoléon," the claim certified by the signature of the buyer on the bill is separated from the claim based on the underlying transaction. For example, a bill is easily negotiable because objections about the quality of the merchandise by the buyer do not affect the claim of the bill holder. In addition, defaulted bills can be collected through a particularly speedy judicial process that is much faster than the collection of normal receivables. Thus there is nothing mystical about the preference of European countries for commercial bills, and retail buyers often finance their entire inventory with receivable financing from the manufacturer/seller.

Other Terms

In many countries government bodies facilitate inventory financing in the guise of receivable financing by extending export credit or by guaranteeing export credit from banks at advantageous interest rates. When the term of the special export financing can be extended to match the payment of the foreign purchaser, the foreign purchaser is in effect able to finance its inventory through the courtesy of the exporter's government.

In some environments credit terms extended by manufacturers to retailers are of such long maturities as to constitute "purchase" of the retailer, such "purchase" being necessary to build an operational distribution system between manufacturer and ultimate customer.

In Japan, for example, customer payment terms of 120 days are fairly common, and a manufacturer's sales effort is not competitive unless sufficient financial aid is provided to retailers to make it possible or beneficial for them to buy the manufacturer's product. Financial aid is reported to take the form of outright purchase of the retailer's capital stock, working capital loans, equipment purchase, subsidy or loan, and consideration of payment terms. Yet this is a normal way of doing business in the Japanese environment.

In summary, a multinational firm often manufactures or sells a product in a credit-short or inflationary economy, in a country where the banking system is oriented toward self-liquidating bills, or in locations where competition causes suppliers to finance their commercial customers. Longer collection periods have implications not only for the amount of financing that must be budgeted for a venture but also for the criteria by which the performance of local managers is evaluated.

INVENTORY MANAGEMENT

Operations in inflationary, devaluation-prone economies sometimes force management to modify its normal approach to inventory management. In some cases management may choose to maintain inventory and reorder levels far in excess of what would be called for in an economic order quantity model.

Under conditions where local currency devaluation is likely, management must decide whether to build up inventory of imported items in anticipation of the expected devaluation. After the devaluation imported inventory will cost more in local currency terms. One trade off is a higher holding cost because of the bloated level of inventory and high local interest rates which normally reflect the expected devaluation. A less obvious trade-off is the possibility that local government will enforce a price freeze following devaluation. This freeze would prevent the imported inventory from being sold for an appropriate markup above its now-higher replacement value. Still worse, the devaluation may not occur as anticipated, leaving management holding an excessive level of inventory until it can be worked down. Disposing of excessive inventory will be particularly painful if competitors have followed the same strategy of speculating on imported inventory.

Anticipating Price Freezes

To circumvent an anticipated price freeze, management can establish the local currency price of an imported item at a high level, with actual sales being made at a discount from this posted price. In the event of a devaluation, sales continue at the posted prices but discounts are withdrawn. This technique circumvents the price freeze only if that freeze is expressed in terms of posted rather than effective price. In any event it provides no protection against competitive price squeezes. An alternative is to sell at the posted price but increase selling, promotion, or other marketing mix activities, which can later be reduced.

If imported inventory is a commodity, another strategy is to purchase the commodity in the forward market. Then if local prices are frozen, the forward contract can be sold abroad for the same currency in which it is denominated. On the other hand, if local price controls are based on a fixed markup over cost, the forward contract can be exercised and the commodity imported at the now-higher local currency cost, which becomes the basis for the markup. If options on the commodity are available, the same benefit can be achieved. The certain cost of the option should be compared with the uncertain trading gain or loss on the forward contract.

Free-Trade Zones

A free-trade zone is a combination of the old idea of duty-free ports and new legislation that gives breaks on customs duties to manufacturers who structure their operations to benefit from the technique. The old duty-free ports were typically in the dock area of major seaports. Modern free-trade zones, by comparison, are often located away from a port area. For example, the Italian firm of Olivetti has such a zone in Harrisburg, Pennsylvania.

Free-trade zones increasingly are locations for assembly or manufacturing activity. Retailers use the zones to sort, label, or store imported clothing and appliances until the date of final sale. Manufacturers often complete work on partially assembled imports within the zone. When work is performed in a free-trade zone, import duties are usually assessed only on the lower import cost and not on the higher value created by work performed within the zone. Additionally, the time of payment of duties is usually delayed. An item imported into the United States in January for, say, three months of additional finishing and storage before an April sale will be charged duty in January. The same item left in a free-trade zone until April will be assessed the same amount of duty, but payment will not be made until April. Free financing of the duty charges for three months is obtained!

A free-trade zone can also be used to circumvent a price freeze because merchandise in the zone has not yet been formally imported. Often a price freeze will not apply to items not yet imported into the country. Alternatively, the importer retains an option to sell the merchandise elsewhere at world market prices without the loss of import duties and transactions costs that would have already been paid if the merchandise had been formally imported.

Tektronix B*

In late December 1983 Barbara Block, Assistant Treasurer-International, Tektronix, Inc., was reviewing one more time various alternative approaches to managing Tektronix's foreign exchange exposure and working capital management practices. During the period 1981–1983 the increasing strength of the U.S. dollar had led to mounting foreign exchange transaction losses totaling nearly $9 million. These were primarily incurred by the foreign manufacturing and sales affiliates. In addition, Tektronix was suffering from adverse economic exposure due to producing equipment in

---

*Doug Schafer and Barbara Block of Tektronix, and Arthur Stonehill, Oregon State University, 1988. Reprinted with permission.

Oregon, U.S.A., for export to the foreign affiliates. These exports were invoiced in U.S. dollars to the affiliates but sold to customers who were billed in local currency by the affiliates. The increasing strength of the U.S. dollar made it difficult for the affiliates to maintain their operating margins when pricing larger custom orders which would not be delivered and billed for several months. It also complicated routine updating of catalogs and price lists for more standardized products.

Background

Tektronix is a U.S. corporation, headquartered in Beaverton, Oregon, that develops, manufactures, sells, and services electronic measurement, display and control instruments and systems throughout the industrialized world and in certain developing countries. The financial results of these activities are measured in U.S. dollars.

Almost since the company's beginning in 1946, Tektronix has had product sales outside of the United States. In 1948 Tektronix established its first foreign distribution agreement in Sweden. During the early 1950s Tektronix established other distribution networks in Belgium, Germany, Austria, and Canada. In 1958 Tektronix commenced manufacturing operations on the Isle of Guernsey, followed by other manufacturing affiliates located in the Netherlands and the United Kingdom. A major manufacturing joint venture in Japan was also established with Sony. By late 1983 Tektronix had 21 foreign operating subsidiaries and joint ventures (see Exhibit 19.13).

During the late 1970s and early 1980s Tektronix established subsidiaries in Austria, Finland, Germany, Italy, Norway, and Spain. Since Tektronix follows a policy of establishing subsidiaries with a minimum of equity capital, the majority of each subsidiary's capital came from intercompany U.S. dollar loans, lagged intercompany payables, and local bank credit. The capital mix decision for each subsidiary is made by the corporate finance department in Beaverton, Oregon.

In the case of Finland, Italy, Norway, and Spain there were credit restrictions in each country that resulted in inadequate availability of local credit facilities. The decision was made to finance the start-up of these subsidiaries with mostly intercompany U.S. dollar loans and lagged intercompany payables to supplement the local credit facilities.

For several years, as these subsidiaries became established in their local market they experienced operational difficulties and losses requiring additional working capital funds. Again these requirements were funded by further lagging the subsidiaries' intercompany payables. Some additional share capital increases were also made. Since all of the intercompany loans and payables were denominated in U.S. dollars the company experienced large exposures to changes in the value of the dollar.

Exchange Rates

In late 1980, the U.S. dollar began strengthening and this trend continued, with vigor, for several more years. Many competitors sourced from European factories and pricing competition became very fierce. Tektronix's marketing affiliates tried to minimize price increases as the dollar soared in order to hold market share. In 1981 the DM traded from 1.80 to a low of 2.55 against the dollar, and the French franc declined from 4.45 to 6.00. Tektronix's prices to most European customers had increased as much as 30%. During the

Exhibit 19.13 Tektronix—International (1983)

Americas-Pacific Operations:

  Tektronix, Inc., Beaverton, Oregon

European Operations:

  Tektronix Europe B. V., Amstelveen, The Netherlands

  Tektronix Limited, Guernsey, Channel Islands

International Manufacturing:

  Sony/Tektronix Corporation*, Tokyo and Gotemba, Japan

  Tektronix Guernsey Limited, Guernsey, Channel Islands

  Tektronix Holland N. V., Heerenveen, The Netherlands

  Tektronix U.K. Limited, Hoddesdon, United Kingdom

International Sales and Service:

  Australia-Tektronix Australia Pty. Limited, Sydney, Adelaide, Brisbane, Canberra, Melbourne and Perth

  Austria-Tektronix Ges.mbH, Vienna

  Belgium-Tektronix S. A., Brussels

  Brazil-Tektronix Industria e Comercio Ltda., Sao Paulo and Rio de Janeiro

  Canada-Tektronix Canada, Inc., Barrie, Calgary, Edmonton, Halifax, Montreal, Ottawa, Toronto, Vancouver
    and Winnipeg

  Denmark-Tektronix A/S, Copenhagen

  Finland-Tektronix Oy, Helsinki

  France-Tektronix, Paris, Aix-Les-Milles, Lyon, Nanterre, Rennes, Strasbourg and Toulouse

  Germany-Tektronix GmbH, Cologne, Berlin, Hamburg, Karlsruhe, Munich, Nuremberg

  Ireland-Tektronix U.K. Limited, Dublin

  Italy-Tektronix S.p.A., Milan, Rome and Turin

  Japan-*Sony/Tektronix Corporation, Tokyo, Fukuoka, Nagoya, Osaka, Sendai and Tsuchiura

  Mexico-*Tektronix S. A. de C. V., Mexico City

  The Netherlands-Tektronix Holland N. V., Badhoevedorp

  Norway-Tektronix Norge A/S, Oslo

  Spain-Tektronix Espanola S. A., Madrid and Barcelona

  Sweden-Tektronix A. B., Stockholm and Gothenburg

  Switzerland-Tektronix International A. G., Zug and Geneva

  United Kingdom-Tektronix U.K. Limited, London, Harpenden, Livingston, Maidenhead and
    Manchester

* Joint Venture Companies

three-year period 1981–1983 the dollar continued to strengthen with the DM hitting a low of almost 2.80 and the French franc weakening to almost 8.50.

Pricing Procedures

Tektronix's products are not stocked at the local sales affiliates, so orders take an average of three months between order and shipment. Terms range from 30 days to 180 days after shipment with the majority being under 90 days. The sales affiliates bill their customers in their local currency and pay the factories for the products in dollars. They price the products by applying a profit margin to the dollar cost and then use an estimated future exchange rate to convert the quote to local currency. However, in actual practice the competition does not allow very much discretion in anticipatory pricing.

The affiliates' cost of sales varied as the exchange rates changed and they had to buy U.S. dollars to pay the factories. Their sales prices in local currency, however, were generally fixed. In some countries the affiliates had the ability to use currency clauses which allowed them to share the currency fluctuations, from the time of the quote until the goods were received, with the customer. This practice was used to varying degrees from 90–100% in Scandinavia to almost 0% in Germany. The affiliates could only use this practice where competition allowed.

Foreign Exchange Exposure Management

The affiliates were in a losing battle for the past three years. They were taking fewer and fewer orders at higher and higher prices. Many times their markup in local currency was not enough to cover the cost of their intercompany purchases due to the local currency weakening beyond their anticipated price list rate. Tektronix's policies forbid the use of forward currency contracts for backlog hedges. Forward currency contracts were used by the parent company in Beaverton for transaction exposures (intercompany payables that were already on the affiliates books). This was a policy that had been in place since the inception of the overseas affiliates.

Many of the sales affiliates had limited or no ability to do forward currency contracts, at the time, due to foreign exchange controls. A change in company policy that would allow Tektronix's subsidiaries to hedge backlog would therefore be of little or no benefit to them. The Operations Managers of the subsidiaries were crying for help. Their margins were shrinking, or disappearing altogether, and they were losing market share due to the frequent price list changes and requests for currency clauses (see Exhibit 19.14).

Tektronix's main concern about letting the affiliates use forward contracts was one of control. The company's treasury functions are very centralized and therefore the affiliates' finance departments are staffed with accounting and administrative personnel. They did not have the necessary knowledge and experience to manage a backlog exposure management program.

At the same time backlog exposures originally became a major issue, Tektronix undertook a study to evaluate all of its various types of exposures and the hedging alternatives (strategic and tactical) available to best manage those exposures. The study covered reinvoicing, netting, finance companies, and traditional hedging tools such as leads, lags, and forward currency contracts.

Exhibit 19.14   Selected Financial Data for Tektronix's Foreign Affiliates and Joint Ventures (thousands of dollars)

Foreign Affiliates

Tektronix has 18 foreign operating subsidiaries located in Australia, Belgium, Brazil, Canada, Denmark, Finland, France, Germany, Guernsey, Italy, the Netherlands, Norway, Spain, Sweden, Switzerland, and the United Kingdom with a branch in Ireland. The assets, liabilities, sales, and income of foreign subsidiaries are included in the consolidated financial statements in these amounts:

	1983	1982	1981	1980	1979	1978
Current assets	$233,030	$218,375	$208,864	$169,051	$141,446	$106,098
Current liabilities	69,334	68,528	68,207	55,483	39,090	32,105
Facilities	29,727	34,787	28,938	22,185	18,585	15,337
Other assets	95	603	410	907	1,118	889
Other liabilities	7,598	9,449	8,228	7,857	6,732	2,222
Net sales	$367,215	$377,167	$364,785	$321,741	$252,597	$185,472
Gross profit	106,268	109,479	105,403	97,367	77,878	57,352
Operating income	34,760	30,808	34,285	37,446	29,941	22,281
Income before taxes	34,916	34,326	33,301	39,781	31,809	23,632
Earnings	21,787	23,426	19,401	29,882	22,583	16,714

Joint Ventures

Tektronix also has investments in three joint venture companies located in Austria, Japan, and Mexico. The Company's share of the assets, liabilities, sales, and income of these unconsolidated affiliates consisted of:

	1983	1982	1981	1980	1979	1978
Current assets	$31,166	$33,429	$32,173	$24,873	$21,713	$12,991
Current liabilities	15,149	16,166	16,892	12,903	10,936	7,359
Facilities	13,023	9,114	8,686	5,477	3,939	3,577
Other assets	4,213	3,895	4,236	3,063	3,202	3,662
Other liabilities	1,560	1,237	1,417	1,558	1,145	1,772
Net sales	$57,368	$61,520	$59,660	$46,064	$40,551	$25,457
Gross profit	18,668	21,613	23,728	16,107	16,740	10,118
Operating income	7,761	11,161	14,181	8,859	10,385	6,017
Income before taxes	7,966	10,419	15,575	8,041	10,618	7,235
Earnings	3,636	4,023	7,597	2,930	5,222	4,249

When the study was completed and presented to management in late 1982, the company was experiencing a slowdown in growth (see Exhibits 19.15 and 19.16) and expense-cutting procedures were being evaluated. Another factor impacting the choice of alternative currency management techniques was that approximately 30% of all international orders from affiliates were naturally hedged with currency clauses with varying percentages in each country.

As of December 1983 recommendations made by the study had not yet been accepted. However, Barbara Block continued to be concerned about the potential for further

Exhibit 19.15   Tektronix Consolidated Financial Statement (thousands of dollars)

	1983	1982	1981	1980	1979	1978
Current assets	$639,680	$621,981	$573,791	$540,917	$428,787	$357,704
Cash	96,867	73,331	47,862	57,145	41,788	66,208
Accounts receivable	210,843	230,573	204,952	198,069	153,568	115,100
Inventories	292,885	290,268	293,705	263,563	214,533	163,523
Prepaid expenses	39,085	27,809	27,272	22,140	18,898	12,873
Current liabilities	$197,428	$233,267	$214,527	$193,831	$153,135	$107,556
Short-term debt	33,675	66,334	50,175	45,809	28,997	10,351
Accounts payable	78,569	63,856	60,405	49,034	42,033	33,108
Income taxes payable	15,280	23,118	28,778	27,404	20,444	18,458
Accrued compensation	69,904	79,959	75,159	71,584	61,661	45,639
Working capital	$442,252	$388,714	$359,264	$347,086	$257,652	$250,148
Facilities	397,290	379,122	304,912	276,771	194,454	119,533
Other Assets	50,444	41,184	30,050	24,005	19,666	13,893
Long-term debt	152,342	132,060	146,143	136,196	62,094	37,086
Deferred tax liability	43,691	441,124	30,765	23,974	19,150	16,029
Other liabilities	32,258	5,387	4,774	4,354	5,728	3,763
Shareowners' equity	$661,695	$630,449	$557,544	$483,338	$402,800	$326,696
Share capital	78,097	64,277	52,515	41,884	31,950	24,332
Reinvested earnings	595,957	566,172	505,029	441,494	370,850	302,364
Currency adjustment	(12,359)					
Common shares (thousands)	19,059	18,807	18,574	18,372	18,143	17,913

exchange losses. The most recent foreign exchange exposure report had just been compiled and is shown in Exhibit 19.17.

Cash Management

Another related concern facing Barbara Block was in the area of cash management. As the number of Tektronix's international affiliates increased in the 1970s and early 1980s the problems and complexities of managing cash within the intercompany payment network increased to the point that the system was almost unmanageable (see Exhibit 19.18).

Each sales affiliate sourced products from up to four different factories. Therefore, each factory received payments from as many as eighteen different affiliates. The payment procedure had each affiliate paying on a fixed day each month, theoretically, but this system did not always work since an affiliate could decide at the last moment not to pay.

When making intercompany payments the procedure stated that the sending affiliate was to telex the receiving affiliate details of the payment (i.e., amount of transfer, date of transfer, sending bank, and receiving bank) before the transfer was sent, so that the receiving affiliate could manage its cash in a more efficient manner. This procedure

Exhibit 19.16 Consolidated Income and Reinvested Earnings (thousands of dollars)

	1983	1982	1981	1980	1979	1978
Net sales	$1,191,380	$1,195,748	$1,061,834	$971,306	$786,936	$598,886
Cost of sales	615,941	595,340	513,145	485,464	359,740	266,474
Gross income	$575,439	$600,408	$548,689	$512,842	$427,196	$332,412
Engineering expense	125,393	109,086	91,147	77,797	60,561	49,832
Selling expense	185,355	180,631	157,105	135,405	113,461	86,850
Administrative expense	120,920	108,977	100,715	88,343	68,044	53,063
Profit sharing	29,316	55,267	61,686	63,448	63,682	48,528
Operating income	$114,455	$146,447	$138,036	$147,849	$121,448	$94,139
Interest expense	25,832	29,537	25,274	15,956	6,428	4,246
Nonoperating income	(25,509)	9,493	19,360	5,029	11,631	6,068
Income before taxes	$63,114	$126,403	$132,392	$136,922	$126,651	$95,961
Income taxes	14,400	49,950	52,225	51,850	49,500	39,115
Earnings	$48,714	$79,453	$80,167	$85,072	$44,152	$56,846
Nonoperating income (Expense) from currency gains (losses)	($3,035)	($2,679)	($3,039)	$1,729	$435	($15)

encountered problems such as the sending affiliate forgetting to send a notification telex and also lost telexes. These problems made it very difficult for the person responsible for managing the cash in each factory.

Another problem with the current intercompany payment procedure was the loss of value on float that occurred between the paying affiliate and the receiving affiliate. It was not uncommon for the paying affiliate's bank to charge its account one or two days before the receiving affiliate's bank credited its account. With over $300 million flowing between the sales affiliates and the factories on an annual basis, this situation was very expensive.

Buying the necessary U.S. dollars to pay their intercompany purchases also caused problems for the sales affiliates. Some of them had relatively small intercompany payables each month. Commissions as a percent of the dollars purchased are substantially higher for smaller foreign exchange transactions. Therefore, they were paying relatively large commissions to purchase their U.S. dollars.

The final major concern regarding the current intercompany payment procedure was the large transfer costs that some of the international banks charged. With the large amount of money being transferred and the large number of transfers, bank transfer charges were becoming substantial for the consolidated company.

Recommendation
The desire to minimize the effect of currency fluctuations at the subsidiary level, the limited flexibility to hedge backlog exposures in certain countries, the lack of timely

Exhibit 19.17   Exposures, December 1983 (thousands of dollars)[a]

	Equity	Earnings	Backlog
EMS Exposures			
Belgian franc	426	394	1,835
Danish krone	128	1,387	2,471
Deutsche mark	105	5,365	10,538
Dutch guilder	5,275	25,391[b]	12,393
Irish punt		429	1,491
Italian lira	3,710	1,847	3,634
Total EMS	$9,644	$34,813	$32,362
Other European Exposures			
Austrian schilling	122	1,115	2,237
British pound	20,375	(9,846)[c]	23,783
Finnish markka	199	590	1,254
Norwegian krone	235	1,350	3,125
Spanish peseta	175	2,340	4,528
Swedish krona	2,035	5,248	1,349
Swiss franc	32,890	398	1,532
Total Other	$56,031	$1,195	$37,808
Am/Pac Exposures			
Australian dollar	5,378	458	2,548
Brazilian cruzado	0	400	2,103
Canadian dollar	10,745	2,583	6,381
Japanese yen	45,958	3,169	7,436
Mexican peso	0	142	283
Total Am/Pac	$62,081	$6,752	$18,751
Exposure Summary			
EMS	9,644	34,813	32,362
Other European	56,031	1,195	37,808
Am/Pac	62,081	6,752	18,751
Total Exposures	$127,756	$42,760	$88,921

a Not actual numbers

b Includes: $25,990 translation, ($525) transaction.

c Includes: ($5,428) translation, ($4,418) transaction.

transaction exposure information, and the numerous problems with effectively managing cash with the current system, contributed to Tektronix's desire to review alternative approaches to currency management. Barbara Block knew that she needed to develop a comprehensive set of tools to address these concerns and she wondered what she should recommend in light of the current internal and external financial environments.

Exhibit 19.18 Tektronix's Current Settlement System

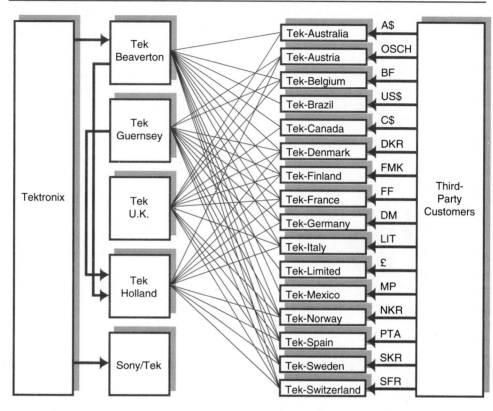

Note: All cash payments occur from right to left. All intracompany payables are denominated in U.S. dollars.

SUMMARY

- Financial managers of multinational firms must control international liquid assets in order to maintain adequate liquidity in a variety of currencies while also minimizing political and foreign exchange risk.

- The first half of this chapter looked at ways that funds can be positioned in a multinational firm. The concept of unbundling remittances was described. Determinants of dividend policy were explained, and the use of royalties, fees, and home office overhead was discussed.

- Transfer pricing was considered in terms of possible conflicting goals of fund positioning, tax and tariff minimization, and fair treatment of managers and joint-venture partners.

- Techniques for moving blocked funds, such as fronting loans, creating unrelated exports, and obtaining special dispensating were discussed, and the deployment of funds under forcible reinvestment was examined.

- The second half of the chapter looked at uniquely international aspects of managing cash, accounts receivable, and inventories. Cash balances are held to provide planned disbursements and to protect the firm against unanticipated variations from budgeted cash flows in an array of currencies. Techniques of cash management include the use of centralized depositories and multilateral netting.

- Accounts receivable management was discussed in terms of receivables from independent customers. Inventory management was viewed in terms of ways to protect inventory values in the face of adverse exchange rate changes and anticipated price freezes.

■ 1. Torino Lock, S.A. (C19A.WK1)

Miller Lock Company has manufactured standardized door locks in Connecticut for many years. Each lock has per unit direct labor costs of $10, direct material costs of $5, and overhead of $2. A portion of production is sold (transferred) to Torino Lock, S.A., Miller's wholly owned distribution affiliate in Italy, for $22 per unit. Torino Lock incurs an additional $3 per lock of direct costs and resells to European builders for $30 per lock. No other costs are involved, except for income taxes, which until 1986 were 46% in both countries.

Comprehensive tax reform legislation passed by the U.S. Congress in 1986 lowered U.S. corporate income taxes to 34%, effective in 1987, but at that time Miller made no change in its transfer price to Torino. In 1991, Sarah Lodge, Miller's new director of international operations, was reviewing current transfer price policy. She judged that Miller could raise or lower its export sales price to Torino by up to 10% without causing a tax challenge from either Italian or U.S. tax authorities. She wondered if Miller should change the transfer price applied to exports to Italy.

   a) In 1991, what was Miller's consolidated after-tax profit per unit sold to Italy?

   b) What do you recommend for a transfer price in 1992?

   c) If your recommendation were adopted, what will be Miller's consolidated after-tax profit per unit sold to Torino?

   d) Miller becomes concerned that the Italian lire might devalue. How would this information influence your recommendation in question b above?

2. Cuzco, S.A.

Cuzco, S.A., of Peru is 100% owned by Berkeley Manufacturing Company of the United States. Net escudo sales of Cuzco this past year were equal to $80,000,000, when measured in U.S. dollars, and net income before taxes and before any royalty payments was $10,000,000. The corporate income tax rate in Peru is 50% and the corporate income tax rate in the United States is 34%.

Cuzco is allowed to distribute 80% of its after-tax Peruvian income to Berkeley Manufacturing Company as a dividend. Alternatively Cuzco may remit royalties of 2% of net sales revenue. Royalty fees would be paid out of Peruvian pretax income, and if paid the Peruvian affiliate could still pay dividends up to 70% of after-tax income.

Royalties and dividends received in the United States are subject to the U.S. tax rate of 34%, grossed up in the case of dividends for the proportion of income taxes paid in Peru and with a U.S. tax credit for Peruvian taxes.

a) What distribution policy should Berkeley apply to Cuzco to maximize parent cash flow?

b) If Berkeley wanted to maximize consolidated net income, and did not care about dividends, should it adopt a different policy?

3. Eurowide Corporation (C19B.WK1)

Eurowide Corporation has subsidiaries in Italy, France, Germany, and Denmark. It does its accounting in Deutschemarks. Historically Eurowide has maintained separate precautionary cash balances for each of these countries at a level equal to three standard deviations above the expected cash need in each country.

a) What could Eurowide save by maintaining all precautionary balances in a single concentrated account in one European financial center? (Assume cash needs in each country are normally distributed and are independent of each other.)

	Expected Cash Need	One Standard Deviation
Italy	DM 50,000,000	DM 10,000,000
France	45,000,000	5,000,000
Germany	30,000,000	3,000,000
Denmark	40,000,000	7,000,000

b) What other advantages might accrue to Eurowide from centralizing its European cash holdings? Are these advantages realistic?

4. Hietaniemi Brewery

Hietaniemi's VII-A Lager beer has a world reputation. It is brewed and sold in Hong Kong and the United States as well as in the home country of Finland. At the end of September 1992, unsettled intracompany debts in U.S. dollars are as follows:

Hong Kong unit: owes $7,000,000 to U.S. affiliate.

owes $9,000,000 to Finnish parent.

U.S. unit: owes $3,000,000 to Finnish parent.

owes $4,000,000 to Hong Kong affiliate.

Finnish parent: owes $3,000,000 to U.S. affiliate.

owes $5,000,000 to Hong Kong affiliate.

Foreign exchange transaction spreads average 0.5% of funds transferred.

a) How should Hietaniemi Brewery settle these intracompany obligations? What would be the savings in transaction expenses over the no-netting alternative?

b) Before settling the above accounts, Hietaniemi Brewery decides to invest US$6,000,000 in Australia to build a new brewery in Adelaide. Can this type of decision be incorporated into the settlement process? How, and what would be the total bank charges? Explain.

NOTES

1. Sidney M. Robbins and Robert B. Stobaugh, *Money in the Multinational Enterprise*, New York: Basic Books, 1973, p. 85.

2. *Ibid.*

3. "Transfer Pricing and Multinational Enterprises," Report of the Organization for Economic Cooperation and Development Committee on Fiscal Affairs, Paris: OECD, 1979.

4. Mohammad F. Al-Eryani, Pervaiz Alam, and Syed Akhter, "Transfer Pricing Determinants of U.S. Multinationals," *Journal of International Business Studies*, Third Quarter, 1990, pp. 409–425.

5. *Ibid.*, p. 422.

6. Jeffrey S. Arpan, "International Intracorporate Pricing: Non-American Systems and Views," *Journal of International Business Studies*, Spring 1972, p. 9.

7. Business International, *New Techniques in International Exposure and Cash Management, Volume I: The State of the Art*, New York: Business International Corporation, 1977, p. 237.

8. Business International, *Solving International Financial and Currency Problems*, New York: Business International Corporation, 1976, p. 27.

BIBLIOGRAPHY

Al-Eryani, Mohammad F., Pervaiz Alam, and Syed H. Akhter, "Transfer Pricing Determinants of U.S. Multinationals," *Journal of International Business Studies*, Third Quarter 1990, pp. 409–425.

Anvari, M., "Efficient Scheduling of Cross-Border Cash Transfers," *Financial Management*, Summer 1986, pp. 40–49.

Arpan, Jeffrey S., "International Intracorporate Pricing: Non-American Systems and Views," *Journal of International Business Studies*, Spring 1972, pp. 1–18.

Barrett, M. Edgar, "Case of the Tangled Transfer Price," *Harvard Business Review*, May/June 1977, pp. 20–36, 176–178.

Benvignati, A. M., "An Empirical Investigation of International Transfer Pricing by U.S. Manufacturing Firms," in A. M. Rugman, and L. Eden, eds., *Multinationals and Transfer Pricing*, New York: St. Martin's Press, 1985.

Bergendahl, Göran, "Multi-Currency Netting in a Multi-National Firm," in Göran Bergendahl, ed., *International Financial Management*, Stockholm: Norstedts, 1982, pp. 149–173.

Burns, Jane O., "Transfer Pricing Decisions in U.S. Multinational Corporations," *Journal of International Business Studies*, Fall 1980, pp. 23–39.

Business International, *Automating Global Financial Management*, Morristown, N.J.: Financial Executives Research Foundation, 1988.

Business International Corporation (BIC), *Solving International Pricing Problems*, New York: BIC, 1965.

Crum, Roy L., and Lee A. Tavis, "Allocating Multinational Resources When Objectives Conflict: A

Problem of Overlapping Systems," *Advances in Financial Planning and Forecasting*, vol. 4, part B, 1990, pp. 271–294.

Fowler, D. J., "Transfer Prices and Profit Maximization in Multinational Enterprise Operations," *Journal of International Business Studies*, Winter 1978, pp. 9–26.

Gentry, James A., Dileep R. Mehta, S. K. Bhattacharya, Robert Cobbaut, and Jean-Louis Scaringella, "An International Study of Management Perceptions of the Working Capital Process," *Journal of International Business Studies*, Spring-Summer 1979, pp. 28–38.

Granick, David, "National Differences in the Use of Internal Transfer Prices," *California Management Review*, Summer 1975, pp. 28–40.

Greene, J., and M. G. Duerr, *Intercompany Transactions in the Multinational Firm*, New York: Conference Board, 1970.

Greenhill, C.R., and E. O. Herbolzheimer, "Control of Transfer Prices in International Transactions: The Restrictive Business Practices Approach," in R. Murray, ed., *Multinationals Beyond the Market*, New York: John Wiley, 1981, pp. 185–194.

Keegan, Warren J., "Multinational Pricing: How Far Is Arm's Length?" *Columbia Journal of World Business*, May-June 1969, pp. 57–66.

Kim, Seung, H., and Stephen W. Miller, "Constituents of the International Transfer Pricing Decision," *Columbia Journal of World Business*, Spring 1979, pp. 69–77.

Kopits, George F., "Intra-Firm Royalties Crossing Frontiers and Transfer-Pricing Behaviour," *Economic Journal*, December 1976, pp. 791–805.

Lecraw, D. J., "Some Evidence on Transfer Pricing by Multinational Corporations," in A. M. Rugman and L. Eden, eds., *Multinationals and Transfer Pricing*, New York: St. Martin's Press, 1985.

Masson, Dubos J., "Planning and Forecasting of Cash Flows for the Multinational Firm: International Cash Management," *Advances in Financial Planning and Forecasting*, vol. 4, part B, 1990, pp. 195–228.

Mirus, Rolf, and Bernard Yeung, "The Relevance of the Invoicing Currency in Intra-Firm Trade Transactions," *Journal of International Money and Finance*, 6, No. 4, December 1987, pp. 449–464.

Ness, Walter L., Jr., "U.S. Corporate Income Taxation and the Dividend Remittance Policy of Multinational Corporations," *Journal of International Business Studies*, Spring 1975, pp. 67–77.

Plasschaert, S. R. F., "Transfer Pricing Problems in Developing Countries," in A. M. Rugman and L. Eden, eds., *Multinationals and Transfer Pricing*, New York: St. Martin's Press, 1985, pp. 247–266.

Pugel, Thomas, and Judith L. Ugelow, "Transfer Pricing and Profit Maximization in Multinational Enterprise Operations," *Journal of International Business Studies*, Spring/Summer 1982, pp. 115–119.

Rutenberg, David P., "Maneuvering Liquid Assets in a Multinational Company: Formulation and Deterministic Solution Procedures," *Management Science*, June 1970, pp. B-671–684.

Shapiro, Alan C., "Optimal Inventory and Credit-Granting Strategies under Inflation and Devaluation," *Journal of Financial and Quantitative Analysis*, January 1973, pp. 37–46.

——, "Payments Netting in International Cash Management," *Journal of International Business Studies*, Fall 1978, pp. 51–58.

Shulman, James, "When the Price Is Wrong by Design," *Columbia Journal of World Business*, May–June 1967, pp. 69–76.

Soenen, L. A., "International Cash Management: A Study of Practices of U.K.-Based Companies," *Journal of Business Research*, August 1986, pp. 345–354.

Soenen, L. A., and Raj Aggarwal, "Corporate Foreign Exchange and Cash Management Practices," *Journal of Cash Management*, March–April 1987, pp. 62–64.

Srinivasan, VenKat, and Yong H. Kim, "Payments Netting in International Cash Management: A Network Optimization Approach," *Journal of International Business Studies*, Summer 1986, pp. 1–20.

———, Susan E. Moeller and Yong H. Kim, "International Cash Management: State-of-the-Art and Research Directions," *Advances in Financial Planning and Forecasting*, vol. 4, part B, 1990, pp. 161–194.

Tang, R. Y. W., *Transfer Pricing Practices in the United States and Japan*, New York: Praeger Publishers, 1979.

Tansuhaj, Patriya S., and James W. Gentry, "Foreign Trade Zones in Global Marketing and Logistics," *Journal of International Business Studies*, Spring 1987, pp. 19–34.

Transfer Pricing and Multinational Enterprises, Report of the OECD Committee on Fiscal Affairs, Paris: Organization for Economic Co-Operation and Development, 1979.

UNCTAD (United Nations Commission on Trade and Development), *Dominant Positions of Market Power of Transnational Corporations: Use of the Transfer Pricing Mechanisms*, Geneva: UNCTAD/ST/MD/6, 1977.

Yunker, Penelope J., "A Survey of Subsidiary Autonomy, Performance Evaluation and Transfer Pricing in Multinational Corporations," *Columbia Journal of World Business*, Fall 1983, pp. 51–64.

———, *Transfer Pricing and Performance Evaluation in Multinational Corporations: A Survey Study*, New York: Praeger Publishers, 1982.

20 Performance Evaluation and Control

A multinational firm must be able to relate actual results to predetermined and acceptable goals. It must be able to measure the performance of each of its affiliates on a consistent basis, and managers of affiliates must be given unambiguous objectives against which they will be judged. The criteria for internal evaluation and control should be designed for that purpose, and not be the byproduct of reports initially designed and prepared for financial accounting or for local statutory and tax purposes.

Evaluation is carried on not only by internal management for planning and control purposes, but also by outsiders. Outside evaluation centers around analysis of a firm's official financial statements. Comparing a firm's financial statements with those of its competitors helps managers evaluate their own performance or find how policies of their firms differ from those of other firms. Bankers and rating agencies use financial statements to assess relative strengths and weaknesses of applicants for credit. Security analysts, portfolio managers, and investors use them to help select among competing securities. Government officials use them for a variety of regulatory purposes.

This chapter discusses the following topics, which are relevant for both internal and external evaluation of performance and control purposes.

- What are the purposes of multinational evaluation and control systems?
- What evaluation criteria are commonly used?
- How do fluctuations in exchange rates impact a firm's budget control system?
- How do firms organize internally for international financial decision-making?
- For purposes of comparative financial statement analysis, how do national differences in accounting systems, specific accounting principles, levels of disclosure, and auditing bias the results?

- An illustrative case comparing matched Japanese, Korean, and U.S. firms reinforces how the complexities can distort any comparative international evaluation of performance.

PURPOSES OF MULTINATIONAL CONTROL SYSTEMS

If a multinational enterprise is to function in a coordinated fashion, it must set goals for and then monitor the performance of its affiliates. Specific standards must be set, ways to measure performance against those standards devised, and managerial behavior directed toward fulfilling those standards. All of this must be done in the context of the unique problems that arise from operating in foreign environments.

Managers of foreign affiliates must be able to run their own operations efficiently according to achievable objectives. Higher management should evaluate their personal success according to criteria that are both clear in a quantitative sense and equitable in considering the nonquantifiable factors of operating in a foreign environment. Furthermore, the criteria by which managers are to be judged must be congruent with the goals of the firm so that managerial action furthers the best long-run interests of the firm.

In a survey of 125 multinational firms, William Persen and Van Lessig found that almost all firms expand and modify their domestic profitability measures when applying them to foreign affiliates.[1] In addition, some firms establish foreign affiliates for objectives not related to normal corporate profit-oriented goals. Such exceptions include ensuring sources of supply, maintaining a presence in a given market, and conforming with government regulations. Although these goals have some very long-run focus on profits, performance measurement in the short run is not meaningful.

Respondents to the Persen and Lessig survey identified four important purposes of an internal evaluation system.[2] In order of importance they are as follows.

1. *To ensure adequate profitability.* By choosing this criterion as the most important, respondents indicated that all other purposes are secondary to the basic corporate goal of profitability.

2. *To have an early warning system if something is wrong.* Although intuitively appealing, this goal is difficult to implement in practice because failure to meet targeted results may be due to valid and nonrecurring problems unique to international operations or to the fact that the original target was unrealistic.

3. *To have a basis for allocating resources.* This goal arises primarily in the context of requests from foreign affiliates for new funds that total more than the parent has available. Top management needs a fair and equitable means of rationing limited resources while serving overall corporate goals.

4. *To evaluate individual managers.* Respondents indicated that managers are often evaluated by criteria in addition to profit contribution, such as their success in developing organizations or in expanding product lines.

COMPLEXITIES OF INTERNATIONAL PERFORMANCE EVALUATION

Internal financial evaluation of foreign affiliates is both unique and difficult. Use of one foreign exchange translation method, in an attempt to measure results in the home currency, will present a different measure of success or of compliance with predetermined goals than use of some other translation method. Even though an internal control system stands independent of such accounting rules as FAS #52, evidence suggests that most firms start with the translation system used for financial reporting. Such a starting point is probably inappropriate when the goal is an effective control system, but it does lessen the cost of an entirely separate reporting procedure.

The results of any control system must be judged against distortions of performance caused by widely differing national business environments. Because many direct foreign investments are made to enhance strategic interaction with the rest of the worldwide system, one cannot evaluate such investments as if they stand alone.

Costs often not attributed to affiliates in a formal measurement system include implied costs to the parent of guaranteeing affiliate loans or holding safety inventory in the home country to serve foreign affiliates. Benefits to the worldwide system include profits to the parent or related affiliates from additional exports, royalties and management fees, keeping the parent abreast of technological developments in other countries, preempting markets, enlarging economies of scale, and denying such benefits to competing firms.

International measurement systems are distorted by decisions to benefit the world system at the expense of a specific local affiliate. For example, an affiliate in a low-interest country may finance another affiliate in a high-interest country. Although the system benefits, the first affiliate will have excess interest charges and the second will save on interest. Positioning of funds sometimes requires artificial transfer prices between related affiliates for tax, foreign exchange, or liquidity reasons. Management must devise a fair and consistent method of adjusting the basic reports to reflect the "self-sacrifice" of one affiliate for another.

Additional variables that may invalidate comparisons of reports from affiliates in separate countries include nationally imposed barriers on fund remittances, differential rates of inflation, requirements for certain levels of legal reserves financed via earnings retention, customs that call for profit sharing with workers, differing standards between countries over primary corporate goals, and variations in the work ethic and/or labor productivity. By and large, these variables are not significant in differentiating among domestic affiliates, but a company that seeks to extend a domestic control system abroad must ponder the significance of the financial data obtained.

CRITERIA FOR PERFORMANCE EVALUATION

Multinational firms almost invariably use more than one criterion when evaluating the results of their foreign affiliates. The reason for multiple criteria springs from complications that are uniquely foreign: changing currency values, financial reporting rules (FAS #52),

Exhibit 20.1   Financial Criteria Used to Evaluate Performance of Overseas Unit and Subsidiary Manager

Items	U.S. MNCs N=64 Avg.[a]		Non-U.S. MNCs N=24 Avg.[a]		Total Responses N=88 Avg.[a]	
	Unit	Mgr	Unit	Mgr	Unit	Mgr
Return on investment	1.8	2.2	2.1	2.2	1.9	2.2
Return on equity	3.0	3.0	2.9	3.0	3.0	3.0
Return on assets	2.3	2.3	2.2	2.4	2.3	2.3
Return on sales	2.2	2.1	1.9	2.1	2.1	2.1
Contribution to earnings per share	2.8	3.2	3.5	3.4	3.0	3.2
Operating cash flow to subsidiary	2.5	2.7	2.2	2.5	2.4	2.7
Operating cash flow to parent	2.3	2.8	2.5	2.6	2.3	2.7
Residual income	3.4	3.3	3.4	3.2	3.4	3.3
Budget compared to actual sale	2.0	1.6	1.9	1.8	1.9	1.7
Budget compared to actual profit	1.5	1.4	1.4	1.3	1.5	1.3
Budget compared to actual ROI[b]	2.3	2.4	2.4	2.5	2.3	2.4
Budget compared to actual ROA[c]	2.6	2.7	2.7	2.2	2.7	2.5
Budget compared to actual ROE[d]	3.1	2.9	3.2	3.1	3.1	3.0

Source: F.D.S. Choi and I.J. Czechowicz, "Assessing Foreign Subsidiary Performance: A Multinational Comparison," *Management International Review,* 4–83, p. 16.

a 1 = most important; 2 = important; 3 = less important; 4 = not used.

b ROI = return on investment

c ROA = return on assets

d ROE = return on equity

different nominal and real interest rates, and organizational uncertainty about what these differences mean or who should be responsible for them.

Choi and Czechowicz Survey

In a research study conducted for Business International, Fred Choi and James Czechowicz found that multiple criteria are used to evaluate foreign performance.[3] Financial criteria dominate performance evaluation systems. Budget compared to actual is the single most important criterion both for 64 U.S. multinational firms and for 24 non-U.S. multinational firms. Return on investment is second in importance. Choi and Czechowicz's rankings of financial criteria are shown in Exhibit 20.1.

Performance of the affiliate as a unit and performance of the manager tended to be judged by similar criteria. Of interest in the survey is that U.S. multinationals rate cash flow to the parent as more important than cash flow to the affiliate, whereas non-U.S. multinationals reverse the order of ranking.

Exhibit 20.2 Nonfinancial Criteria Used to Evaluate Performance of Overseas Unit and Subsidiary Manager

Items	U.S. MNCs N=64 Avg.[a]		Non-U.S. MNCs N=24 Avg.[a]		Total Responses N=88 Avg.[a]	
	Unit	Mgr	Unit	Mgr	Unit	Mgr
Increasing market share	1.8	1.5	1.7	1.6	1.8	1.5
Quality control	2.2	1.9	2.4	2.0	2.3	1.9
Cooperation with parent company and affiliates	2.4	2.0	2.5	2.1	2.4	2.0
Relationship with host country government	2.1	1.8	2.4	1.9	2.1	1.9
Environment compliance	2.4	2.3	2.5	2.4	2.4	2.3
Employee development	2.4	2.0	2.4	2.2	2.4	2.0
Labor turnover	2.7	2.5	2.8	2.7	2.8	2.6
Research and development in foreign unit	3.1	3.2	2.8	2.7	3.0	3.1
Productivity improvement	2.2	2.1	1.7	1.6	2.0	2.0
Employee safety	2.4	2.2	2.2	2.3	2.4	2.2
Community service	2.9	2.8	2.8	2.5	2.9	2.7

Source: F.D.S. Choi and I.J. Czechowicz, "Assessing Foreign Subsidiary Performance: A Multinational Comparison," *Management International Review*, 4–83, p. 17.

a 1 = most important; 2 = important; 3 = less important; 4 = not used.

Choi and Czechowicz found strong evidence for the importance of nonfinancial criteria in the evaluation process. As shown in Exhibit 20.2, increasing share of the market is the single most important nonfinancial criterion for U.S. multinationals. Non-U.S. multinationals rank productivity improvement equal in importance to increasing market share.

Performance Relative to a Budget

Performance relative to a budget was the most important criterion, according to the survey, for measuring affiliate performance. It is also implicit in the four major objectives of foreign affiliate evaluation discussed earlier. Budget analysis involves comparing actual sales revenue and operating expenses at the end of a time period with an earlier budget in which both sales and expenses were forecast. The essence of such a system is that any difference between actual and budget be explained in terms of price and/or volume variances. Variances are traced to the person or unit responsible. Variances are also part of the accumulated experience used to make a better budget in the ensuing time period.

The underlying principle of such a budget and variance analysis system is that operating management be held responsible for those variables affecting the performance which they can control, and that they not be judged over variations in performance that they cannot influence.

THE IMPACT OF EXCHANGE RATE CHANGES ON PERFORMANCE EVALUATION

Foreign exchange rates enter a multinational control system at two points: in the drafting of an initial operating budget for a foreign affiliate at the beginning of a time period, and in the measurement or tracking of realized performance at the end of that time period.

Any foreign affiliate may prepare its operating budget in local currency units. However, control over a multinational network necessitates intercountry comparisons. This means that the basic operating budget must also be expressed in parent currency terms. Any change in exchange rates will cause a variance between budget and performance. Although the variance is a price variance, it differs in implications from other price variances caused by unanticipated deviations in sales prices or factor costs. Design of the control system will determine where, within the corporate structure, responsibility for exchange rate variance lies.

Lessard–Lorange Model

A detailed explanation of the impact of exchange rates on a control system has been developed by Donald Lessard and Peter Lorange.[4] They point out that three possible rates might be used in either the budget process or the tracking process. Hence nine combinations are theoretically possible. Of these nine, five are reasonable while four are inherently illogical. The full range of combinations is shown in Exhibit 20.3.

Exhibit 20.3   Possible Combinations of Exchange Rates in the Control Process

	Rate used to track performance relative to budget		
	Initial	Projected	Ending
Initial	A–1 Budget on initial Track on initial	A–2 Budget on initial Track on projected	A–3 Budget on initial Track on ending
Projected	P–1 Budget on projected Track on initial	P–2 Budget on projected Track on projected	P–3 Budget on projected Track on ending
Ending	E–1 Budget on ending Track on initial	E–2 Budget on ending Track on projected	E–3 Budget on ending Track on ending

Rate used for determining budget

Source: Donald R. Lessard and Peter Lorange, "Currency Changes and Management Control: Resolving the Centralization/Decentralization Dilemma," *Accounting Review,* July 1977, p. 630.

At the time the actual budget is created (that is, before the period of operations) two exchange rates can be used: (1) the spot rate at that time (the "initial" rate), or (2) a rate that is forecast to be in effect at the end of the budget period. This latter rate might well be the forward exchange rate since the forward rate may be the best unbiased predictor of future spot rates. A third possibility is to have a budget that is continually updated as exchange rates change. At the beginning of the time period this budget would be identical to a budget based on an initial rate; however, it would be revised with the passage of time, so that an end-of-period rate would be used in the last iteration. For tracking purposes performance may be measured at the end of the period by any of the same three rates.

Of the nine combinations shown in Exhibit 20.3, four are illogical on their face and so have been shaded out. Combinations P-1, E-1, and E-2 involve forecast or ending exchange rates for creating the budget but ignore these data in the tracking step. Combination A-2 involves tracking at a rate projected at the time the budget is prepared but does not use this rate in preparation of the budget. The remaining five combinations are reasonable alternatives that involve variations in assigning the responsibility for minimizing exchange rate risk.

The three variations on the diagonal, A-1, P-2, and E-3, track at the same rate as used in the budget. Under these three combinations the operating manager has no responsibility for variations caused by changes in exchange rates. In the remaining two combinations, A-3 and P-3, some degree of exchange rate responsibility is given to the operating manager. The differences between these five combinations will be explained with a hypothetical example.

Assume that a foreign affiliate may invest in a project that will generate local currency (LC) incomes as follows:

Sales	LC100,000
Cost of sales	75,000
Operating expenses	10,000
Operating income	LC 15,000

For simplicity, assume no income taxes. Assume further that the contemplated venture necessitates a net investment in exposed assets of LC50,000, that the initial exchange rate at the time the budget is drawn is LC20 = $1, that there is an equal likelihood that the end-of-period exchange rate will be either LC20 = $1 or LC30 = $1, and that as a consequence the projected future exchange rate is the weighted average, or LC25 = $1. Last, assume that any change in the exchange rate will not have an effect on the local currency operating results.

Using the format of Exhibit 20.3 the reasonable combinations of budget and performance measurement are as shown in Exhibit 20.4. Under the diagonal combinations of A-1, P-2, and E-3, budget and performance will be the same. Variance will be zero. As we indicated earlier, measurements of performance in these three combinations are free of any influence of exchange rate changes. The operating manager is not responsible for adjusting operations to incorporate beliefs about future exchange rates. The manager may still be charged with forwarding opinions and information to the corporate treasurer's

Exhibit 20.4   Performance Versus Budget under Alternate Control Systems (amounts in dollars)

	A-1				A-3		
	Budget initial (LC20=$1)	Track at initial (LC20=$1)			Budget at initial (LC20=$1)	Track at ending rate (50% chance LC20=$1)	(50% chance LC30=$1)
Sales	5,000	5,000			5,000	5,000	3,333
Cost of sales	3,750	3,750			3,750	3,750	2,500
Operating expense	500	500			500	500	333
Loss on exposed assets[a]	0	0			0	0	833
Operating income (loss)	750	750			750	750	(333)
Variance from budget		0				0	−1,083

			P-2		P-3		
			Budget at projected (LC25=$1)	Track at projected (LC25=$1)	Budget at projected (LC25=$1)	Track at ending rate (50% chance LC20=$1)	(50% chance LC30=$1)
Sales			4,000	4,000	4,000	5,000	3,333
Cost of sales			3,000	3,000	3,000	3,750	2,500
Operating expense			400	400	400	500	333
Loss on exposed assets[a]			500	500	500	0	833
Operating income (loss)			100	100	100	750	(333)
Variance from budget				0		650	−433

					E-3		
					Budget at ending (LC30=$1)	Track at ending (LC30=$1)	See footnote b
Sales					3,333	3,333	
Cost of sales					2,500	2,500	
Operating expense					333	333	
Loss on exposed assets[a]					833	833	
Operating income (loss)					(333)	(333)	
Variance from budget						0	

a Loss on exposed assets: beginning exposed assets = LC50,000 ÷ 20 = $2,500. If ending rate is LC25 = $1, ending exposed assets = LC50,000 + 25 = $2,000; loss = $500. If ending rate is LC30 = $1, ending exposed assets = LC50,000 ÷ 30 = $1,667; loss = $833.

b Re combination E-3: if the ending rate were LC20 = $1, both budget and tracking would reflect this fact, with an ending variance of zero.

office that will be useful in forecasting future exchange rates, but this responsibility is an advisory rather than an operating one.

A-1: Budget at Initial; Track at Initial. If budget and tracking are at the initial rate (combination A-1), the project appears profitable both before and after the fact. The assumption in this instance is that exchange rates will not change, or perhaps that any attempt to predict future rates is useless. In either instance opinions about future exchange rates do not enter either budget or tracking process.

P-2: Budget at Projected; Track at Projected. In combination P-2 a projection of future exchange rates is required. Budgeted profits are $100, rather than the $750 in combination A-1. The desirability of the project is influenced by the corporate treasurer's forecast of future exchange rates, and responsibility for judging the impact of exchange rate changes is placed on the corporate treasurer. The operating manager is free of such responsibility, and a change in exchange rates does not create a variance.

E-3: Budget at Ending: Track at Ending. Combination E-3 involves revising the budget during the operating period as exchange rates change. Thus performance at the end of the time period will be measured in terms of the actual ending rate, and the budget will have been revised to incorporate that actual ending rate. In the example in Exhibit 20.4 this rate might be the possible ending rate of LC30 = $1 (shown in the exhibit), or it might be the equally possible ending rate of LC20 = $1. The latter combination is not shown, since in either instance variance of performance relative to budget will be zero. In combination E-3 the operating manager has no direct concern with changes in the exchange rate; and because the budget in E-3 is revised with the passage of time, it does not require a forecast at the time of preparation. Although the ending budget shows a 50% chance of loss of $333, derived in large part from a translation loss on exposed assets of $833, this information was not available and did not enter into plans at the beginning of the budget period.

A-3: Budget at Initial; Track at Ending. The remaining two combinations, A-3 and P-3, place some degree of responsibility for foreign exchange risk on the operating manager. In combination A-3 performance is tracked at the ending rate and compared with a budget prepared at the initial rate. In the example used in the illustration, ending exchange rates have an equal probability of remaining at LC20 = $1 or of changing to LC30 = $1. If they remain the same, budgeted profit will remain the same ($750) and variance will be zero. However, if the local currency drops in value to LC30 = $1, a loss of $333 will result, with a variance from budget of minus $1083. Combination A-3 throws full responsibility for exchange rate risk on the operating manager, who may or may not have the ability to forecast future rates and the ability to adjust operations to achieve desired protection. Furthermore, such foreign exchange protection as might be acquired is not coordinated with exchange protection decisions in the parent or other affiliates. At the extreme, one might imagine an operating manager in France buying pounds forward at the same time that the operating manager in the United Kingdom is buying francs forward. As each minimizes risk for the local affiliate, the firm as a whole pays for two transactions that net each other out and provide no additional corporate-wide protection!

P-3: Budget at Projected; Track at Ending. Combination P-3 judges the operating manager against a budget based on projected exchange rates. Variations in performance that result because actual exchange rates differ from projected rates are the responsibility of the operating manager. In Exhibit 20.4 operating income was either significantly above or below budget. A risk-averse operating manager might well make decisions to protect against this type of risk. Combination P-3 is perhaps useful if operating plans can be changed during the operating cycle in response to exchange rate shifts; in fact, it is designed to encourage such a response by the operating manager. However, if operating plans cannot be changed, minimization of the variance caused by actual rates deviating from projected may in fact be either difficult or expensive. Combination P-3 makes the manager responsible for "errors" in the original projection of future exchange rates, since an "error" in the original projection will influence the ending variance. Yet the manager is not responsible for the original projection against which results are judged.

Comparisons. Of the various combinations, Lessard and Lorange support combination P-2, in which projected exchange rates are incorporated into both the budget and the tracking process. By using what they term "internal forward rates," Lessard and Lorange show that two major criteria for good management control systems are satisfied. Goal congruence exists because a corporate-wide point of view will prevail in making decisions in which exchange rate changes might have an impact. Furthermore, operating managers are treated fairly in that they receive neither blame nor credit for variations in performance caused by exchange rate changes that are anticipated.

In using the term "internal forward rates" to characterize combination P-2, Lessard and Lorange note that the corporate treasurer is acting in a manner analogous to an internal banker by "buying forward" receipts in foreign currencies at a guaranteed rate. The operating unit is "guaranteed" that its profits will be measured at the internal forward rate. In the meantime any actual forward protection can be coordinated on a company-wide basis. Lessard and Lorange note that the use of internal forward rates necessitates exchange rate forecasting, a difficult task at best and one that may be fruitless in the light of evidence that some exchange markets are efficient and exchange rate changes random. Nevertheless, they observe that if future exchange rates are in fact random and unpredictable, even more importance attaches to the need to shield the operating manager from being judged by changes in operating performance caused by such variation.

Hyperinflation and Economic Exposure

The Lessard–Lorange model has been extended to incorporate distortions in performance evaluation caused by hyperinflation and economic exposure. Laurent Jacque and Peter Lorange have shown that use of the Lessard–Lorange model recommendations to evaluate affiliates located in countries experiencing hyperinflation and rapid exchange rate devaluation can yield distorted results.[5] Deviations from purchasing power parity can be expected under conditions of hyperinflation because countries vary in how they respond. Some countries prevent their exchange rate from adjusting freely, with a consequent currency overvaluation, while other countries allow free adjustment of their exchange rate. Jacque and Lorange suggest that management "environmentalize" their performance evaluation systems to take into account these different national reactions. Variances in an affiliate's operating results due to economic exposure, which is of course beyond their control, should be removed. A variance smoothing model is proposed as a means to accomplish this task.

Lessard and Sharp have also recognized the need to deal with realized variances in the operating budget of an affiliate caused by economic exposure.[6] Their analysis is valid for countries with or without hyperinflation, as long as they are experiencing exchange rate deviations from purchasing power parity. They suggest adjusting the budget performance standard based on realized exchange rates and a predetermined agreement on how operating performance is likely to be affected by changes in real effective exchange rates.

The Stewart PPP-Normalized Approach

G. Bennett Stewart suggests measuring performance by use of a "normalized" exchange rate, derived by calculating what the exchange rate would be if the market properly adjusted for purchasing power parity (PPP) over the short run.[7] His logic is that actual exchange rates fluctuate around an "intrinsic value," being at times overvalued and at times undervalued. Actual year-end exchange rates fail to adjust in the short run because of such nonmarket factors as government policies to spur economic growth, cushion the immediate domestic shock of recent exchange rate changes, or correct for prior but misguided economic policies. In the long run, however, both exchange rates and local profitability return to purchasing power parity conditions. If performance is measured by intrinsic-value, or normalized, exchange rates, firms can avoid the whipsaw effect of having some years reported as more profitable than they really are and other years reported as less profitable.

Stewart's proposal is treated in depth in his work cited above. The essence of his suggestion can be illustrated with a two-period hypothetical model, using Mexico as an example:

	Period 1	Period 2
Mexican price index	100	130
U.S. price index	100	105
Ratio, Mexico to United States		1.283
Actual exchange rate	Ps1,000/$	Ps1,100/$
PPP-normalized exchange rate	Ps1,000/$	Ps1,238/$

Both asset values and net operating profit should be measured in the reporting currency in accordance with the PPP-normalized exchange rate, and then rates of return on investment recalculated to measure performance efficiency. One must note that the approach assumes that exchange rates are in equilibrium in Period 1.

Exchange Rates in Performance Evaluation—Practice

Because the dominant method of performance evaluation is the degree of adherence to budgets, actual practice in relationship to the model set up by Lessard and Lorange is important. A survey by Business International found that 66% of the sample firms budgeted at projected and tracked at ending.[8] This is combination P-3 in the Lessard–Lorange model. It makes the local manager responsible for deviations from the projected rate.

Opinions differ as to whether local affiliates should or should not be held responsible for variance caused by exchange rate changes, or whether the responsibility should somehow be a joint responsibility. Those who believe local management should not be held responsible argue that local managers have no control over exchange rate changes, or that over the longer run exchange rate fluctuations will offset each other and that real performance in the local market will, over time, produce adequate dollar results. Another reason advanced is that local managers lack ability or time to make sophisticated exchange rate forecasts.[9]

Those who argue that the local manager should have full or partial responsibility for exchange rate induced variance believe that this policy is essential to keep affiliate management aware of the need to think about possible exchange rate changes and that ultimately home currency profitability is the firm's goal. These firms usually expect the local manager to undertake whatever action seems appropriate to minimize exchange rate losses. Nevertheless, many of these firms treat exchange rate variance as a separate item in a variance report and remain very flexible about how much responsibility after the fact is charged to the local manager.

ORGANIZING FOR INTERNATIONAL FINANCIAL CONTROL

How should the financial staff of a multinational firm organize itself to carry out tasks requiring specialized international expertise? Should international financial policy and/or decisions be made at corporate headquarters or at the local affiliate level, or perhaps at an intermediate regional headquarters? In short, who is responsible and where should that person be located? How a business firm answers these questions determines what type of evaluation and control system is needed.

In their pioneering survey of 187 U.S. multinational firms, Sidney Robbins and Robert Stobaugh identified three phases that multinational companies pass through as their foreign business becomes increasingly important.[10]

When a firm is just starting its overseas expansion, headquarters knows little about the unique financial problems of multinational business and does not believe any special attention is required. This phase, which Robbins and Stobaugh label "Ignoring the System's Potential," was found to occur primarily in "small" multinational enterprises. At this level international financial management at headquarters is characterized by a very small staff, or perhaps only a single person, with neither the time nor the experience to make decisions. This small central staff essentially monitors foreign affiliates, which in turn tend to operate very much on their own without parental supervision. At the local level managers strive to improve affiliate performance but not necessarily total system performance.

As the international business of multinational firms expands, Robbins and Stobaugh found, companies enter Phase 2, "Exploiting the System's Potential." Firms at this level tend to centralize most important international financial decisions in a central staff having the requisite expertise and desire to optimize the system. Evolution into Phase 2 occurs as parent management becomes aware that international financial decisions require a different expertise from domestic financial management. This awareness is brought on by experience, increased profit importance of foreign operations, and the need to consolidate foreign affiliates into parent financial statements.

Robbins and Stobaugh found that as a firm's foreign sales continue to expand, organization for financial management evolves into Phase 3, "Compromising with Complexity." At this point parent management finds itself facing a dilemma in which accumulated experience, the scale of foreign operations, and the relative importance of foreign operations all combine to suggest maintenance of tight central controls. However, the increased number of relationships among an increased number of affiliates makes centralized decision making too complex to be effective. This dilemma is resolved by having a relatively large central international finance staff, which delegates responsibility to the various affiliates in the form of specific guidelines prescribed in a "rule book" issued by headquarters. In effect, the central staff determines policy, issues appropriate directives, and then monitors the affiliates for their compliance with the directives. Actual decisions, however, are made at the local level. Robbins and Stobaugh observed that rule books or "bibles" are often in the form of several volumes of standardized procedures.

COMPARATIVE ANALYSIS OF FINANCIAL STATEMENTS

Financial statements are as useful as the underlying accounting data and degree of disclosure. Unfortunately, uniform worldwide standards of accounting, disclosure, and auditing do not exist. Each country has its own norms. Therefore comparison of financial statements of firms based in different countries can be very misleading without a thorough understanding of comparative accounting.

Lack of uniform standards also creates information barriers for the investment community. Unfamiliar foreign accounting principles, lack of disclosure, and distrust of auditing standards can prevent investors from diversifying their portfolios internationally in an optimal manner. As was mentioned earlier in this book, barriers to the free flow of information can create market inefficiencies affecting firms seeking to lower their cost of capital by tapping international capital markets.

The purpose of this section is to highlight some of the principal international differences in accounting standards, disclosure practices, and auditing requirements.[11] Even with such an understanding, however, it is easy to misinterpret the underlying economic situation being reported in financial statements. In particular, international comparisons using traditional ratio analysis can lead to unwarranted conclusions about risk, return, liquidity, and efficiency. One must also understand the economic, cultural, and political environment of the country in which the reporting firm is located. In the next section we will analyze the use and misuse of international ratio analysis using an illustrative case.

Classification of Different Accounting Systems

Choi and Mueller have classified world accounting systems into four basic types, based on the philosophies behind each approach.[12] Their four frameworks are: (1) macroeconomic, (2) microeconomic, (3) independent discipline, and (4) uniform accounting system.

Macroeconomic Framework. A macroeconomic approach to accounting has been adopted by some countries, of which Sweden is perhaps the prototype. The underlying hypothesis is that the accounting system should facilitate government administrative direction of the economy, based on the following postulates.

- The firm is the essential unit in the economic fabric of a nation.
- The firm best accomplishes its goals through close coordination of its activities with the national economic policies of its environment.
- Public interest is best served if enterprise accounting interrelates with national economic policies.

On this basis the function of accounting is primarily to measure in monetary terms economic transactions and business events of business firms, so that economic planners are better equipped with the data needed to monitor and direct economic activities in desired directions.

Microeconomic Framework. A second set of countries, including the Netherlands, has adopted a microeconomic approach to accounting. Under this philosophy the major thrust of accounting thought evolves from traditional Western microeconomic theory. Major postulates for a microeconomic-oriented accounting system are the following.

- Individual firms provide focal points for business activities.
- The main policy of a business firm is to ensure its continued existence.
- Optimization, in an economic sense, is a firm's best policy for survival.
- Accounting is a branch of business economics.

From these postulates springs the most important concept of microeconomic-oriented accounting: The accounting process must focus on maintaining constant, in real terms, the monetary capital of a business entity. Measurement of income centers on determining that increment in the value of the firm which, if it were removed, would nevertheless leave the firm with constant invested capital in real terms. Especially as developed in the Netherlands, the microeconomic approach to accounting has therefore focused quite heavily on adjusting for inflation.

Independent Discipline Approach. The third type of system is based on accounting as an independent and professional discipline. The accounting systems of the United States, Canada, and the United Kingdom are of this type. This approach to accounting assumes that business is basically an art and that factors of judgment and estimation cannot be eliminated from business processes. Accounting is therefore a matter of independent judgment, and inductive reasoning from existing business practices is the foundation for creation of accounting concepts. From this pragmatic approach to accounting concepts and practices are developed "generally accepted accounting principles." Such principles are not clearly listed and defined, nor set by government statute; rather they are a set of conventions that have evolved through years of practice and through voluntary acceptance by the business community.

Under the independent discipline approach to accounting, accounts for a particular firm should be consistent from year to year, but no theoretical or practical reason exists for the reports of one firm to be maintained in a manner consistent with those of another, similar firm. One firm may transfer inventory costs on a LIFO (last-in, first-out) basis, while its competitor may use FIFO (first-in, first-out). An asset may be depreciated over ten years by one firm, while another business depreciates identical assets over some other lifetime. Each firm seeks to report its financial position and income in a manner that, in its subjective opinion, is an accurate portrayal of what has transpired.

Uniform Accounting Systems. A uniform accounting system, involving identical terminology and account classifications for all firms, constitutes the fourth approach. Some of its attractions are that it appears to make accounting more scientific, that it supplies a rational and consistent method for controlling the commercial sector of the economy, and that it affords a relatively simple way to achieve uniformity among firms. Training of personnel to operate the system is simplified since education consists primarily of "how-to-do-it" information. Accountants working for one firm can easily transfer to other firms. Uniform accounting also facilitates equitable collection of taxes and easier tabulation of national economic statistics.

Uniform accounting systems have several disadvantages, however. Such an approach is alleged to run counter to the actual nature of business because it seeks to treat alike what are in fact basic differences. Comparative analysis, although facilitated on a mechanical basis, may in fact suffer because the system provides less meaningful information for widespread public use. Uniform accounting is also alleged to conflict with modern concepts of managerially oriented accounting systems using statistical and economic concepts within a management information system. Uniformity, it is also charged, tends to restrict the development of new accounting theories and practices and to hinder the process of improving an existing system.

Uniform accounting systems in various forms have been adopted in France, Germany, and Argentina. In Sweden uniform systems are used in some economic sectors such as the metal working industry but not in other sectors.

Specific Differences in Accounting Principles

A helpful checklist of specific differences in accounting principles has been developed by Bavishi, Choi, Shawky, and Sapy-Mazella in a study for Business International Corporation.[13] They analyzed 32 accounting variables in financial statements over a three-year period (1978–1980) for 1,000 leading firms distributed among 20 industries, and based in

24 different countries. Seven variables that were most frequently treated differently were identified. Six of these remain relevant today: (1) consolidation, (2) goodwill, (3) deferred taxes, (4) long-term leases, (5) discretionary reserves, and (6) inflation adjustment. (The seventh, foreign exchange translation, is no longer relevant because the U.S. adopted the current rate method of translation in 1981, as described in Chapter 9.)

Consolidation of Accounts. The Business International study found that firms in 19 of the 24 countries surveyed consolidate both domestic and foreign subsidiaries more than 50% owned. The exceptions are Finland and Italy, where consolidation is a minority practice, India, and South Korea. German companies consolidate domestic but not foreign subsidiaries. Unconsolidated (minority owned) subsidiaries are carried at cost in Germany, Norway, and Sweden; and about half of the time in Australia, Denmark, and South Africa. Most other countries appear to use the equity method of carrying unconsolidated subsidiaries.

In the United States consolidation is generally required if the parent owns 50% or more of the affiliate, although exceptions exist when the affiliate is engaged in an entirely different line of business (for example, when a manufacturing firm owns a finance company) or is in the process of liquidation or expropriation. Affiliates that are between 20% and 50% owned are usually carried on an "equity" basis, meaning that the parent carries them at the original cost of the investment plus the parent's share of all reinvested earnings since the time of purchase. If the affiliate has earnings in excess of cash dividends, the carrying value on the parent's books is gradually increased. Affiliates that are less than 20% owned are usually carried at cost. If a market value exists for their shares, this separate market value may be shown in a footnote.

Whenever a parent has a nonconsolidated foreign affiliate, an opportunity exists for manipulation of reported earnings. If the foreign affiliate is carried at cost alone, the parent does not recognize the affiliate's earnings until received as a dividend. In such instances, when domestic earnings need bolstering, the parent can funnel foreign profits into parent earnings via larger-than-usual dividend declarations from abroad. Similarly, earnings reported by the parent can be held down, if that is deemed desirable, by reducing the dividend flow from nonconsolidated affiliates.

Goodwill. Goodwill is not amortized in Germany and Malaysia, and is amortized by only a minority of companies in the United Kingdom, Switzerland, Ireland, Finland, Norway, Italy, and South Africa. Practice in the Netherlands is about evenly mixed, and no data were found for Brazil, Austria, or India. In the remaining countries goodwill is amortized.

Deferred Taxes. Accounting for deferred taxes when accounting income is not equal to taxable income is done in all countries except Belgium, Switzerland, Austria, Sweden, Finland, Norway, Italy, Spain, India, and South Korea.

Long-term Leases. Long-term leases are capitalized on the balance sheet in only three countries—the United States, Canada, and Mexico. A minority of companies in Belgium also capitalize long-term leases.

Discretionary Reserves. Unlike U.S. practice, in which earnings are regarded as automatically reinvested unless distributed as dividends, in many countries all earnings are disposed of in the form of specific appropriations to designated reserves, as cash dividends, as special bonuses to directors or officers, or as specific and permanent reinvestment. Unallocated retained earnings do not exist, except possibly for a small, unallocated residual balance that is carried over to the following year.

General purpose, purely discretionary reserves are used to "smooth" income by charging a hypothetical nonrealized expense to the income statement in good years. This lowers income in the good year, but provides a "reserve" for arbitrarily increasing net income in an adverse year by reversing the charge. Obviously, use of such a reserve severely distorts any ratio based on net income or on the equity section of the statement. The authors observed the use of reserves that impacted the income statement before calculation of net income in many countries. Countries where discretionary reserves were not allowed were the United States, Canada, Mexico, the United Kingdom, Ireland, Austria, Australia, South Korea, and South Africa.

In some countries allocations of the year's earnings must be approved by stockholders at an annual meeting, which takes place after publication of the annual report. Thus the annual report as such does not reveal the disposition of earnings. In these countries supplemental memoranda issued separately from the annual report are necessary to obtain a full perspective on disposition of earnings.

Inflation Adjustment. Historical cost is reported as the basic valuation approach in only five countries, the United States, Canada, Germany, Japan, and Australia, and as a minority practice in the Netherlands. Of these six countries, only firms in the United States provide supplementary inflation-adjusted financial statements on a consistent basis. Such supplementary statements are a minority practice in Canada, Australia, and the Netherlands. Additionally, statements from the United Kingdom and Ireland (neither of which adheres completely to a historical cost basis for its basic reports) include supplementary inflation-adjusted statements.

Disclosure

The degree of disclosure in financial statements varies significantly by country. The main reason for such differences can be traced to differing assumptions about the purpose of published financial statements. In some countries, including the United States, the income statement is regarded as the financial statement of prime interest. Income statements usually reveal sales, various categories of expenses, and profits for an interval of time. Current trends within the United States are toward making income statements even more revealing. For example, major U.S. firms are required to disclose operating results by product or division lines. The balance sheet is relegated to secondary importance.

United States focus on the income statement derives from the fact that most large U.S. corporations are publicly owned, with stockholder wealth dependent primarily on stock market prices, which, in turn, are influenced to a large extent by reported and expected earnings per share. Because of U.S. tax laws and a general level of affluence in living standards, U.S. stockholders prefer increased wealth, as measured both by rising stock prices and/or increased dividends.

In most European and Latin American countries, the balance sheet is the most important statement, reflecting major concern in these countries over the ownership of existing wealth (as distinct from the creation of new income) and the strength of the firm relative to claims of creditors. Income statements provide a paucity of information from a public stockholder's point of view; and stockholders, in turn, are usually more concerned with dividends than with stock price appreciation. For example, European firms tend to hide earnings and to reveal less about how assets are valued than is common in the United States. Income statements often start with "gross trading profit" (that is, gross profit) without any disclosure of sales or cost of goods sold. Trends in sales and in gross profit margins cannot be discerned, with the result that judgments about the competitive strength of a company are difficult to make.

Methods by which asset values and depreciation expenses are determined are often not explained. Indeed, notes to financial statements do not appear in the profusion to which the U.S. stockholder is accustomed. As a result, a comparison between firms of both asset position and depreciation impact on earnings is not possible. Furthermore, the degree of consolidation included in a published set of statements is often not revealed, with the result that the earnings of nonconsolidated subsidiaries are concealed. At times, nonrecurring income from the sale of assets is mixed with operating profit, further hindering the ability of an outsider to judge true earnings potential.

In some countries various forms of accelerated depreciation are permitted. However, in contrast with the United States, many foreign countries require "flow-through" accounting, with the result that the greater depreciation used for tax purposes must also be shown on public reports and so used to reduce reported earnings. By comparison, most U.S. firms use straight-line depreciation in reporting to their shareholders, even when using accelerated depreciation to reduce income taxes.

European secrecy is founded in part on tradition. However, the weight of custom is buttressed by the absence of significant legal requirements forcing disclosure of financial results for publicly owned firms; by lack of market pressures from creditors, such as banks and stockholders; and, at least until recently, by the lack of any great pressure for new public equity financing. Recently, the need to tap new sources of capital has forced some firms to reveal more information. An added reason often advanced for traditional European understatement of earnings is a fear by corporate officers and directors that, if higher earnings are reported, stockholders will demand higher dividends or trade unions seek pay increases. Tax avoidance is a third possibility, although in general tax collectors have access to greater internal data.

Auditing

Because of the great diversity of accounting practices in various countries, the opinion of a competent, professional, and independent auditor is indispensable if dependence is to be placed on foreign financial statements. Most of the large public accounting firms have gone international with their clients, so that subsidiaries in Lima and Dusseldorf are audited by the same firm that audits parent books in New York or Chicago. Financial reports of local independent firms are often audited by a variety of parties with some official status, not all of whom have the professional qualifications of independence necessary to render a reliable opinion.

Variations in the auditor's function were explained in a comparison of legislation governing corporation audits in Latin countries with auditing practiced in what the author, a former vice-rector of the University of Buenos Aires, termed the "Anglo-Saxon" system. The Latin countries all had statutes similar to the Italian Civil Code, which established that a *sindaco* should supervise the company's administration, take care that the requirements of the law and the bylaws were duly met, and check the company's accounts and records. However, in general the statutes prescribed no particular qualifications for becoming a *sindaco*. In English-speaking countries and in Scandinavian countries, on the other hand, financial reports were deemed to be a reporting to the owners as to how well management had fulfilled its trust. Because stockholders must base their evaluation of the efficiency of management on meaningful, full, and fair disclosure, it was the function of an independent auditor to determine that the financial statements accurately portrayed the data. However, auditing standards differ by country. For example, it has been reported that in Japan the "lowly" auditor would not dare cause loss of face on the part of the "senior" accounting manager by seeking to verify independently such accounts as accounts receivable and inventories.

Auditing procedures in various countries also differ in some respects. In many European and Latin American countries canceled checks become the property of the bank and are not returned with the bank statement. Therefore verification of disbursements is more difficult. European auditing standards do not normally require physical inventory taking or confirmation of accounts receivable. In some countries sampling and statistical approaches may be used to verify amounts, while in others detailed counts are required. In some countries auditors may have varying degrees of business relationships with the firms they audit. At the other extreme, an auditor in Denmark may not participate in any business enterprise because of the possible development of a conflict of interest.

Use and Misuse of International Ratio Analysis: Japan, Korea, and the United States*

Given the differences in accounting practices, a cross-country comparison of firms using traditional ratio analysis could easily yield misleading conclusions. Frederick Choi and five colleagues illustrated this point in a study that undertook a comparison of firms from Japan, Korea, and the United States using ratio analysis.[14] The "Choi study" first compared aggregate financial ratios for a large sample of manufacturing

---

* This case was written by Arthur Stonehill based on the study cited in footnote 14 ("Choi Study") in which he was a co-author.

firms in the three countries, as shown in Exhibit 20.5. A close look at these ratios would suggest that Japanese and Korean firms are less profitable and efficient, and suffer higher financial risk, than their U.S. counterparts.

In order to remove the effects on aggregate ratios of size, industry, and other extraneous variables, a paired comparison was made between ten Japanese firms and ten U.S. counterparts. Likewise, eight Korean firms were compared to eight similar U.S. firms. With exception of the efficiency ratios, the same relative differences in ratios were observed as in Exhibit 20.5.

Since differences due to accounting principles might explain most of the observed ratio differences, the Choi study restated the ten Japanese and eight Korean statements to conform to U.S. generally accepted accounting principles (U.S. GAAP). Although accounting restatement made some difference, most of the same relative differences in ratios remained.

Despite the results of the ratio analysis, the Choi study concluded that it would be a misuse of ratio analysis to infer that Japanese and Korean firms are less profitable, less efficient, and riskier than their U.S. counterparts. One must delve more deeply into the underlying political, economic, and historical environment of Japan and Korea to explain each ratio.

Leverage

Two of the main measures of financial risk traditionally used in ratio analysis are the debt ratio (total debt at book value divided by total assets at book value) and times interest earned (EBIT divided by interest charges). The large sample of unadjusted ratios presented in Exhibit 20.5 shows Japanese debt ratios averaged 84%, Korean 78%, and U.S. only 47%. In the adjusted matched pairs comparison the Japanese firms averaged 64%, Korean firms 79%, and U.S. firms 49%. As shown in Exhibit 20.5, times interest earned for both Japanese and Korean firms was 1.60, compared with 6.50 for U.S. firms. Thus ratio analysis alone would suggest that Japanese and Korean firms are excessively leveraged by U.S. standards.

The financial risk of Japanese firms is not nearly as high as the ratios would indicate. Enterprise groupings called *keiretsu* ensure that high levels of interdependence exist between banks and their related industrial borrowers. Consequently, a bank hesitates to impose financial penalties on delinquent borrowers, but would rather postpone interest and principal or even refinance the loan. If necessary, a bank will install one of its officials in the management of a borrowing firm in trouble. Other firms in the *keiretsu* group may prepay receivables owed to the troubled firm or slow down on their collections from it. In effect, the family holds together and the lending bank need not view itself as an outsider in the sense that a U.S. bank would. The bank's risk is reduced by assured backing from the central bank. It can also demand additional collateral from a firm if needed. In Japan, the cost of equity is substantially higher than the cost of debt because of a traditional system of issuing new shares at par, rather than higher market prices. Companies that have issued shares at market have had to return the premiums to shareholders in the form of higher dividend rates or stock dividends because of pressure from securities companies.

Exhibit 20.5 Mean Differences in Aggregate Financial Ratios, 1976–1978, for Japan, Korea, and the United States (unadjusted)

Enterprise Category (number of firms)	Current Ratio	Quick Ratio	Debt Ratio	Times Interest Earned	Inventory Turnover	Collection Period	Fixed Assets Turnover	Total Assets Turnover	Profit Margin	Return on Total Assets	Return on Net Worth
All Manufacturing											
Japan (976)	1.15	0.80	0.84	1.60	5.00	86	3.10	0.93	0.013	0.012	0.071
Korea (354)	1.13	0.46	0.78	1.80	6.60	33	2.80	1.20	0.023	0.028	0.131
U.S. (902)	1.94	1.10	0.47	6.50	6.80	43	3.90	1.40	0.054	0.074	0.139
Chemicals											
Japan (129)	1.30	0.99	0.79	1.80	7.10	88	2.80	0.90	0.015	0.014	0.065
Korea (54)	1.40	0.70	0.59	2.40	7.10	33	1.60	0.90	0.044	0.040	0.100
U.S. (n.a.)	2.20	1.30	0.45	6.50	6.50	50	2.80	1.10	0.073	0.081	0.148
Textiles											
Japan (81)	1.00	0.77	0.81	1.10	6.20	66	3.50	0.92	0.003	0.003	0.017
Korea (34)	1.00	0.37	0.83	1.30	4.90	30	2.20	1.00	0.010	0.011	0.064
U.S. (n.a.)	2.30	1.20	0.48	4.30	6.50	48	5.80	1.80	0.027	0.049	0.094
Transportation											
Japan (85)	1.20	0.86	0.83	1.90	3.90	116	4.50	0.90	0.017	0.015	0.092
Korea (14)	0.95	0.40	0.91	1.90	18.60	18	1.10	0.80	0.026	0.021	0.221
U.S.	1.60	0.74	0.52	8.70	5.60	31	6.50	1.60	0.049	0.078	0.161

Source: Adapted from Frederick D.S. Choi, Hisaaki Hino, Sang Kee Min, Sang Oh Nam, Junichi Ujiie, and Arthur I. Stonehill, "Analyzing Foreign Financial Statements: The Use and Misuse of International Ratio Analysis," *Journal of International Business Studies*, Spring/Summer 1983, p. 116.

Note: Data on Japan from the Bank of Japan, data on Korea from the Bank of Korea, and data on the United States from the U.S. Federal Trade Commission. n.a. Not applicable.

Not every feature of the Japanese system reduces financial risk. Lewis Freitas has identified some offsetting features.[15] Lifetime employment means that labor costs are fixed rather than variable as in the United States. Dividends are normally considered fixed on a per share basis, so that they in fact constitute a more or less obligatory cash outflow. Trade receivables are often discounted on a full recourse basis with local banks, at which time they are taken off the balance sheet. Were these receivables financed directly, additional debt would appear on the balance sheet. Additionally, because of close ties within groupings of firms, any given firm is likely to have fully guaranteed the debts of affiliates, unconsolidated subsidiaries, and possibly subcontractors whose relation to the firm is exclusive even though they are not legally defined affiliates.

The high leverage of Korean firms can be explained by environmental factors. Korean firms face an extremely thin equity market that has only been in operation since 1973. In contrast, interest rates on borrowing from government-dominated commercial banks are subsidized, making the cost of bank debt cheap for major companies in comparison to the free market rates charged in Korea's unregulated curb market.

Additional help for Korean firms comes directly from the government, which grants tax and trade privileges and special financing to firms whose activities are deemed beneficial to the nation. The government can be counted upon to come to the help of these companies if they are in trouble, so a Korean firm with very large debt is viewed favorably, rather than unfavorably, because the debt is evidence of a close association with the government.

Liquidity

The average Japanese current ratio in Exhibit 20.5 was 1.15, and for Korea the ratio was 1.13. U.S. firms, by contrast, had an average ratio of 1.94. Patterns for the quick ratio were similar: 0.80, 0.46, and 1.10 respectively. In Japan, lenders prefer to make short-term loans because interest rates can be adjusted to market more frequently. Borrowers find short-term rates lower than long-term rates, and since the short-term debt is easy to renew, it becomes long-term in nature.

The Korean long-term market is not developed. Thus Korean firms find it necessary to rely on short-term debt, rolled over, to finance both working capital and long-term needs. Consequently, much of the short-term debt in the denominator of the current and quick ratio is in fact long-term in nature.

Efficiency

The greatest difference in efficiency ratios is between collection periods. The average collection period for Japan was 86 days, for Korea 33 days, and for the United States 43 days. In both Japan and Korea, a purchaser seldom pays cash on being invoiced, but instead takes another 20 to 30 days to pay. In Korea a note for an additional 60 to 120 days may be given, a practice which appears to spring from a need to accommodate the working capital shortage of important customers. The low Korean collection period is attributable to the fact that these notes are not included in the numerator of the ratio; if the Korean ratio is adjusted for notes receivable it averages between 105 and 110 days. In Japan the long collection period often stems from a desire to avoid putting a buyer in a financial bind, especially during a recession, so that its stable employment base will not be threatened. Such mutual support in difficult times helps assure future patronage.

The second efficiency ratio is fixed asset turnover. In Japan, sales were 3.10 times fixed assets, in Korea they were 2.80, and in the United States they were 3.90. The Japanese/U.S. difference is not significant. The reason for the lower turnover for Korean firms appears to rise from the fact that Korean development has been spurred by enormous investments in fixed plant and equipment. Much of this investment has been in heavy industries, such as chemicals, which need large fixed assets. The tendency to build well in advance of anticipated sales leads to a lower turnover. The ratio is further lowered because Korean price controls keep the numerator (sales) down for domestic goods as part of a policy of resisting inflation.

Profitability

Profitability was measured by both profit margins (return on sales) and return on total assets. Profit margins were 1.3% for Japan, 2.3% for Korea, and 5.4% for the United States. Since these were not offset by the turnover ratio, return on total assets was 1.2% for Japan, 2.8% for Korea, and 7.4% for the United States. Return on net worth was 7.1%, 13.1%, and 13.9%, respectively, for the three countries. As can be seen, the ratios indicate that U.S. firms are significantly more profitable than their Japanese or Korean counterparts.

One reason appears to be that Japanese managers are not as concerned with short-run profits as their U.S. counterparts. Management jobs are more secure, and a greater proportion of shares is held by related banks, suppliers, and corporate customers. All of these parties are more interested in strong long-run basic business ties than in maximizing market price, especially in the short run. Additionally, price competition in export markets is very intense among Japanese companies, lowering margins and rates of return.

Profits are more important for Korean companies. However, export pricing policies and government controls keep prices and margins low.

SUMMARY

- Multinational firms must design and install control systems that produce information in a form valid for internal evaluation and control of individual affiliates. In addition, managers of those units must be given clear directives and know that they will be judged accordingly. These directives must motivate managers to behave in a manner consistent with corporate goals.

- Comparison of actual results with operating budgets is the dominant criterion for performance evaluation of foreign affiliates. Performance relative to budget in an international context involves decisions about which exchange rate to use in the budgeting process and which exchange rate to use in the assessment of results. Although a variety of combinations are possible, use of a projected exchange rate in budgeting and the end-of-period actual rate in assessment is most common.

- Financial statements provide the information for evaluation by a wide variety of outsiders. Comparability of statements internationally is hindered, however, by lack of uniform accounting, disclosure, and auditing standards. Six major areas of worldwide diversity are: (1) consolidation, (2) goodwill, (3) deferred taxes, (4) long-term leases, (5) discretionary reserves, and (6) inflation adjustment.

- Disclosure practices vary significantly depending partly on the assumed purpose of published financial statements. U.S. firms focus on perfecting the income statement because of the belief that market value is influenced by reported earnings. Most European and Latin American firms concentrate on the balance sheet because of a concern over the ownership of wealth and the strength of a firm relative to claims of creditors.

- Auditing standards vary widely with respect to the function and procedures of the audit and qualifications necessary to be an auditor.

- International ratio analysis can result in misleading conclusions. Ratios may be distorted by accounting differences. More importantly, ratio analysis needs to be interpreted in the context of a country's political, economic, and historical environment.

1. Centralization of Foreign Exchange Management
Surveys of financial executives of MNCs show that foreign exchange management is usually centralized rather than decentralized under the control of subsidiaries. What is the rationale for centralizing the foreign exchange function?

2. Criteria to Evaluate Performance—Brazil Versus Germany
Assume that IBM has manufacturing subsidiaries in both Brazil and Germany. Recommend which criteria should be used to evaluate the performance of each subsidiary. What adjustments need to be made to make a fair comparison of performance between these two subsidiaries?

3. Exchange Rates in the Control Process
Using the Lessard–Lorange model (Exhibit 20.3), recommend which system of budgeting and tracking would be appropriate for the IBM subsidiary in Germany and for the IBM subsidiary in Brazil. Explain the reasons for your selections.

4. Acquisition of Short-term Funds
What are the advantages and disadvantages of centralizing the responsibility for short-term borrowing at the corporate level rather than with the subsidiaries?

5. Harmonization of Accounting Systems
By 1992 the EEC Commission would like to harmonize corporate accounting systems as much as possible as part of the move toward one internal market. Given the diversity of existing accounting systems, why is harmonization desirable? What would be easy to harmonize and what would be more difficult?

6. Consolidation

In some countries, such as Korea and India, most firms do not consolidate majority-owned subsidiaries. What are the advantages and disadvantages of this policy?

7. Specific Differences in Accounting

Find a West European firm's annual report as well as an annual report from a U.S.-based firm. Explain the specific differences in accounting principles that are evident in the two annual reports. Be sure to look at footnotes for clues to the differences.

8. Balance Sheet Versus Income Statement

It has been often stated that U.S. firms focus on presenting their income statement in a favorable light, whereas European firms concentrate on presenting a favorable balance sheet. Why do you think these differences exist? In which ways are these differences apparent in the two annual reports you analyzed in Question 7?

9. Ratio Analysis

Using the same two annual reports as in Question 7, compare the two firms based on their main financial ratios as was done for the Japan/Korea/United States sample in Exhibit 20.5. Interpret your results with respect to relative leverage, liquidity, efficiency, and profitability. Are there characteristics of the environment of your two countries that might invalidate your ratio comparison?

10. Copacabana, S.A.

Copacabana, S.A., is the Brazilian affiliate of Beach, Inc., of Miami, USA. Beach, Inc., invested US$4 million in Brazil on January 2, 1992, at a time when the Brazilian cruzeiro was Cr$100/US$. This was also the exchange rate when the 1992 budget was prepared. Beach, Inc., sees no need for further capital investment in Brazil.

Beach, Inc., forecasts that the exchange rate on December 31, 1992, will be Cr$200/US$, based on an assessment of an equal likelihood that the exchange rate will be Cr$150/US$ or Cr$250/US$. Copacabana assures Beach, Inc., that any change in exchange rates will not have an effect on local currency operating results. The actual exchange rate, at the end of the year, was in fact Cr$250/US$.

Copacabana's operating budget for 1992 was:

Sales	Cr$120,000,000
Operating Expenses	− 80,000,000
Earnings before interest and taxes (EBIT)	Cr$ 40,000,000

a) Prepare a tabular presentation, in dollars, showing budget and actual under the five approaches shown in Exhibit 20.3. Which one is best in your opinion? Why?

b) How, if at all, would you change the control system used for Copacabana if the Brazilian manager were solely responsible for both transaction and translation gains and losses? Why?

NOTES

1. William Persen and Van Lessig, *Evaluating the Financial Performance of Overseas Operations*. New York: Financial Executives Research Foundation of the Financial Executives Institute, 1979, pp. 11–12.

2. *Ibid.*, p. 16.

3. Frederick D. S. Choi and I. J. Czechowicz, "Assessing Foreign Subsidiary Performance: A Multinational Comparison," *Management International Review*, 4–83, 1983, pp. 14–25.

4. Donald R. Lessard and Peter Lorange, "Currency Changes and Management Control: Resolving the Centralization/Decentralization Dilemma," *Accounting Review*, July 1977, pp. 628–637.

5. Laurent L. Jacque and Peter Lorange, "The International Control Conundrum: The Case of Hyperinflationary Subsidiaries, *Journal of International Business Studies*, Fall 1984, pp. 185–201.

6. Donald R. Lessard and David Sharp, "Measuring the Performance of Operations Subject to Fluctuating Exchange Rates," *Midland Corporate Finance Journal*, Fall 1984, pp. 18–30.

7. G. Bennett Stewart, "A Proposal for Measuring International Performance," *Midland Corporate Finance Journal*, Summer 1983, pp. 56–71.

8. Jean-Pierre Sapy-Mazella, Robert M. Woo, and James Czechowicz, *New Directions in Managing Risk: Changing Corporate Strategies and Systems under FAS No. 52*, New York: Business International Corporation, 1982, p. 195.

9. Persen and Lessig, *Op cit.,* p. 95.

10. Sidney M. Robbins and Robert B. Stobaugh, "Evolution of the Finance Function," *Money in the Multinational Enterprise*, New York: Basic Books, 1973. This chapter was reprinted in substantially the same form as "Growth of the Financial Function," *Financial Executive*, July 1973, pp. 24–31.

11. For a more in-depth discussion of differences between accounting methodologies in various countries, see David K. Eiteman, "Foreign Investment Analysis," in Frederick D. S. Choi, ed., *Handbook of International Accounting*, New York: John Wiley, 1991, Chapter 20.

12. Frederick D. S. Choi and Gerhard G. Mueller, *International Accounting*, Englewood Cliffs, N.J.: Prentice-Hall, 1984, pp. 45–52.

13. Vinod B. Bavishi, Frederick D. S. Choi, Hany A. Shawky, and Jean-Pierre Sapy-Mazella, *Analyzing Financial Ratios of the World's 1000 Leading Industrial Corporations*, New York: Business International Corporation, 1981.

14. Frederick D. S. Choi, Hisaaki Hino, Sang Kee Min, San Oh Nam, Junichi Ujiie, and Arthur I. Stonehill, "Analyzing Foreign Financial Statements: The Use and Misuse of International Ratio Analysis," *Journal of International Business Studies*, Spring/Summer 1983, pp. 113–131.

15. Lewis Freitas, "Views from Abroad: Japan," *Journal of Accounting, Auditing, and Finance*, Fall 1980, pp. 269–274.

BIBLIOGRAPHY

Aggarwal, Raj, and James C. Baker, "Using Foreign Subsidiary Accounting Data: A Dilemma for Multinational Corporations," *Columbia Journal of World Business*, Fall 1975, pp. 83–92.

Arnold, Jerry L., and William Holder, *Impact of Statement 52 on Decisions, Financial Reports, and Attitudes*, Morristown, N.J.: Financial Executives Research Foundation, 1986.

Arpan, Jeffrey, and Dhia D. Al Hashim, *International*

Dimensions of Accounting, Boston: Kent Publishing Company, 1984.

Arpan, Jeffrey S., and Lee H. Radebaugh, *International Accounting and Multinational Enterprises*, New York: John Wiley & Sons, 1985.

Balhaoui, Ahmed, *International Accounting: Issues and Solutions*, Westport, Conn.: Greenwood Press, 1985.

Bavishi, Vinod B., Frederick D. S. Choi, Hany A. Shawky, and Jean-Pierre Sapy-Mazella,

Analyzing Financial Ratios of the World's 1,000 Leading Industrial Corporations, New York: Business International Corporation, 1981.

Chang, Lucia S., Kenneth S. Most, and Carlos W. Brain, "The Utility of Annual Reports: An International Study," *Journal of International Business Studies*, Spring/Summer 1983, pp. 63–84.

Choi Frederick D. S., "Resolving the Inflation/Currency Translation Dilemma," *Management International Review* 27, no. 2, 1987, pp. 26–34.

Choi, Frederick D. S., and Sungbin Chun Hong, "The Feasability and Decision Utility of Restating Accounting Information Sets: Korea," *Advances in Financial Planning and Forecasting*, vol. 4, part B, 1990, pp. 123–144.

Choi, Frederick D. S., and Vinod B. Bavishi, "Diversity in Multinational Accounting," *Financial Executive*, August 1982, pp. 45–49.

Choi, Frederick D. S., and I. J. Czechowicz, "Assessing Foreign Subsidiary Performance: A Multinational Comparison," *Management International Review*, 4–83, 1983, pp. 14–25.

Choi, Frederick D. S., Hisaaki Hino, Sang Kee Min, Sang Oh Nam, Junichi Ujiie, and Arthur I. Stonehill, "Analyzing Foreign Financial Statements: The Use and Misuse of International Ratio Analysis," *Journal of International Business Studies*, Spring/Summer 1983, pp. 113–131.

Choi, Frederick D. S., and Gerhard G. Mueller, *International Accounting*, Englewood Cliffs, N.J.: Prentice-Hall, 1984.

——, *Frontiers of International Accounting: An Anthology*, Ann Arbor, Mich.: UMI Research Press, 1985.

Czechowicz, James, Frederick Choi, and Vinod Bavishi, *Assessing Foreign Subsidiary Performance, Systems and Practices of Leading Multinational Companies*, New York: Business International, 1982.

Daley, Lane, James Jiambalvo, Gary Sundem, and Yasumasa Kondo, "Attitudes Toward Financial Control Systems in the United States and Japan," *Journal of International Business Studies*, Fall 1985, pp. 91–110.

Demirag, Istemi S, "Assessing Foreign Subsidiary Performance: The Currency Choice of U.K.

MNCs, *Journal of International Business Studies*, Summer 1988, pp. 257–275.

Enthoven, Aldophe J. H., "International Management Accounting: Its Scope and Standards," *International Journal of Accounting*, Spring 1982, pp. 59–74.

Fox, Samuel, and Norlin G. Rueschhoff, *Principles of International Accounting*, Austin, Tex.: Austin Press, 1986.

Freitas, Lewis P., "Views from Abroad: Japan." *Journal of Accounting, Auditing, and Finance*, Fall 1980, pp. 269–274.

Geringer, J. Michael, and Louis Hebert, "Control and Performance of International Joint Ventures," *Journal of International Business Studies*, Summer 1989, pp. 235–254.

Gernon, Helen, "The Effect of Translation on Multinational Corporations' Internal Performance Evaluation," *Journal of International Business Studies*, Spring/Summer 1983, pp. 103–112.

Grant, Robert M., "Multinationality and Performance Among British Manufacturing Companies," *Journal of International Business Studies*, Fall 1987, pp. 79–90.

Gray, Dahli, "Corporate Preferences for Foreign Currency Accounting Standards," *Journal of Accounting Research*, Autumn 1984, pp. 760–764.

Gray, Sidney J., L. B. McSweeney, and J. C. Shaw, *Information Disclosure and the Multinational Corporation*, New York: Wiley, 1984.

Graziano, Loretta, *Currency Fluctuations and the Perception of Corporate Performance*, Westport, Conn.: Quorum Books, 1986.

Holzer, H. Peter, et al., *International Accounting*, New York: Harper and Row, 1984.

Holzer, H. Peter, and Hanns-Martin W. Schoenfeld, eds., *Managerial Accounting and Analysis in Multinational Enterprises*, Berlin and New York: Walter de Gruyter, 1986.

Hosseini, Ahmad, and Raj Aggarwal, "Evaluating Foreign Affiliates: The Impact of Alternative Foreign Currency Translation Methods," *International Journal of Accounting*, Fall 1983, pp. 65–87.

With tax planning so complex, this chapter cannot aim to create tax experts. Rather it sets out to acquaint the reader with the overall international tax environment. At least a minimum of sophisticated knowledge of tax structures is needed by every international financial executive because many decisions require consideration of such factors. As shown earlier, taxes have a major impact on corporate net income and cash flow through their influence on foreign investment decisions, financial structure, determination of the cost of capital, foreign exchange management, working capital management, and financial control. The sections that follow explain the most important aspects of the international tax environments and specific features that affect multinational operations.

NATIONAL TAX ENVIRONMENTS

Every country possesses its own bewildering array of taxes, making it imperative that the multinational corporation seek local tax counsel in each host country in which it operates. International accounting firms publish summaries, which are frequently updated.

Role of Corporate Income Taxes

The United States is almost unique in its heavy reliance on corporate and individual income taxes as a main source of federal tax revenue. Other countries rely proportionately more on indirect taxes, such as the value-added tax, turnover (sales) taxes, excise taxes, and border taxes.

Nominally, domestic corporate income tax rates do not vary too widely among the main industrial countries. Typical national tax rates, as well as dividend-withholding rates, on the earnings of large corporations are shown in Exhibit 21.1.

As seen in Exhibit 21.1, Germany and Japan differentiate between retained earnings and distributed earnings by charging a lower tax rate on distributed earnings. The dividend recipient pays some or all of the difference as personal income tax. The purpose of this provision is to eliminate part of the double taxation of dividends.

The mid-section of Exhibit 21.1 illustrates tax rates for a group of less industrialized countries which have relatively moderate corporate income tax rates as incentives to encourage local private investment by both domestic and foreign firms.

Certain countries assess extremely low corporate income tax rates either to stimulate local business enterprises or to attract tax haven affiliates of multinational firms. Examples of very-low-tax countries are shown in the bottom-section of Exhibit 21.1.

In a number of countries, corporate income taxes are also assessed at the local (state, provincial, canton, city, etc.) level. This increases the overall effective tax rate, even though local income taxes are usually deductible from taxable income at the national level. Local income taxes are relatively important in Germany, Sweden, Switzerland, and the United States.

Certain countries, notably the Netherlands, Belgium, Luxembourg, Switzerland, and Italy, will grant very attractive tax breaks to firms which locate in high priority areas or bring other designated benefits to the country.

Some developing countries give "tax holidays" to investing foreign firms as an incentive to invest. The tax holiday typically guarantees no income taxes for the first few

Exhibit 21.1   National Tax Rates and Withholding Rates for Selected Industrial Countries, Less Industrialized Countries, and Low-Tax Countries

Main Industrial Countries

	Maximum corporate tax		Nonresident, nontreaty withholding tax on dividends[a]
Germany	50%	(36% on profits distributed to stockholders)	25%
Japan	40%	(35% on income earmarked for dividends)	20%
Canada	38%	(34.5% on Canadian manufacturing & processing)	25%
United Kingdom	35%		None
France	34%	(42% on profits distributed to stockholders)	25%
United States	34%		30%
Sweden	30%		30%

Less Industrialized Countries

	Maximum corporate tax		Nonresident, nontreaty withholding tax on dividends[a]
Philippines	35%		35%
Spain	35%		25%
Indonesia	35%		20%
Thailand	35%	(30% if firm registered on securities exchange)	20%
Mexico	35%		None
Korea	34%		25%
Singapore	31%		None
Brazil	30%		25%
Argentina	20%		20%

Low-Tax Countries

	Maximum corporate tax		Nonresident, nontreaty withholding tax on dividends[a]
Channel Islands (Guernsey, Jersey)	20%		None
Hong Kong	16.5%		None
Liechtenstein	7.5 to 15%		4%
Switzerland	3.63 to 9.8%	(plus cantonal taxes raising average rates to 22 to 35%)	35%
Bahamas	None		None
Bermuda	None		None
Cayman Islands	None		None
Vanuatu	None		None
Bahrain	None		None

Source: Compiled from data in Price Waterhouse, *Corporate Taxes: A Worldwide Summary*, 1991, Price Waterhouse, 1285 Avenue of the Americas, New York, NY 10019, USA.

[a] Withholding taxes on dividends paid to foreign stockholders are usually reduced because of the presence of international tax treaties, and rates in the 5% to 15% range are common when such treaties exist.

years while the firm is being established. Another benefit is to allow accelerated depreciation, which in itself reduces the tax base toward zero.

Various definitions of taxable corporate income create greater disparities between countries than do differences in nominal corporate tax rates. An expense that may be tax-deductible in one country, such as housing for corporate executives or school allowances for their children, may not be deductible in another. Brazil, Mexico, and some other countries plagued by inflation allow assets to be revalued in keeping with the rise in prices, thus permitting correspondingly greater depreciation and inventory costs for tax purposes. Even without such "indexing," depreciation rates for tax purposes vary significantly among countries. In Sweden, Norway, Italy, and undoubtedly elsewhere, earnings can be set aside tax-free for use at a later date for investment in underdeveloped parts of the country, or in some cases to be spent in a countercyclical manner when the country is in recession.

For many years corporate income tax rates in less developed countries slowly increased, although this trend now seems to be reversing. In the 1970s and earlier, U.S. tax rates were 52% and the United States taxed foreign-source income but reduced that tax by the amount of foreign income taxes paid. An incentive existed for host countries to raise their tax rate to the point where the foreign tax credit just equaled parent-country tax liability on income earned in the host country. Insofar as the tax was going to be paid anyway, and corporate behavior was probably influenced only by the total tax paid in both countries, host countries reasoned (quite logically) that the tax might as well be paid to them rather than to the United States or other wealthier countries from which foreign investments came.

The apparent reversal in this trend has come as the United States and other industrial countries have lowered their own corporate tax rates in an effort to stimulate business expansion. As a result, tax rates worldwide are gradually becoming more equal.

Value-Added Tax

One type of tax that has achieved great prominence is the value-added tax. It has been adopted as the main source of revenue from indirect taxation by all members of the EEC, most other countries in Western Europe, a number of Latin American countries, and scattered other countries.[1] One of the present goals of the EEC Commission is to achieve some measure of harmonization of value-added tax programs in the member countries. However, considerable resistance has been encountered. In prior decades the U.S. Treasury, and several task forces recommended that the United States adopt a version of the value-added tax. However this was not done and such an event appears unlikely at present. Value-added tax rates for various countries are shown in Exhibit 21.2.

The value-added tax is a type of national sales tax collected at each stage of production or sale of consumption goods in proportion to the value added during that stage. In general, production goods such as plant and equipment have not been subject to the value-added tax. Certain basic necessities such as medicines and other health-related expenses, education and religious activities, and the postal service are usually exempt or taxed at lower rates.

Exhibit 21.2   Value-Added Tax Rates

Europe

Denmark	22%
Norway	20%
Sweden	20%
Belgium	19% (25% on luxury goods, 6% on basic necessities)
France	18.6%
United Kingdom	15%
Germany	14%
Spain	12% (33% on luxury goods, 6% on basic necessities)

Latin and South America

Argentina	15.6%
Mexico	15%
Brazil	Normally 8–10%, but up to 300% in certain cases

Asian Pacific

Korea	10%
Philippines	10%
Indonesia	10%
Hong Kong	None
Singapore	None

Source: Compiled from data in Price Waterhouse, *Corporate Taxes, A Worldwide Summary,* 1991 edition.

Exhibit 21.3 presents an example of how a wooden fence post would be assessed for value-added taxes in the course of its production and subsequent sale. A value-added tax of 10% is assumed. The original tree owner sells to the lumber mill, for $0.20, that part of a tree that ultimately becomes the fence post. The grower has added $0.20 in value up to this point by planting and raising the tree. While collecting $0.20 from the lumber mill, the grower must set aside $0.02 to pay the value-added tax to the government. The lumber mill processes the tree into fence posts and sells each post for $0.40 to the lumber wholesaler. The lumber mill has added $0.20 in value ($0.40 less $0.20) through its processing

Exhibit 21.3   Value-Added Tax Applied to the Sale of a Wooden Fence Post

Stage of Production	Sales Price	Value Added	Value-Added Tax at 10%	Cumulative Value-Added Tax
Tree owner	$0.20	$0.20	$0.02	$0.02
Lumber mill	$0.40	$0.20	$0.02	$0.04
Lumber wholesaler	$0.50	$0.10	$0.01	$0.05
Lumber retailer	$0.80	$0.30	$0.03	$0.08

activities. Therefore the lumber mill owner must set aside $0.02 to pay the mill's value-added tax to the government. In practice, the owner would probably calculate the mill's tax liability as 10% of $0.40, or $0.04, with a tax credit of $0.02 for the value-added tax already paid by the tree owner. The lumber wholesaler and retailer also add value to the fence post through their selling and distribution activities. They are assessed $0.01 and $0.03 respectively, making the cumulative value-added tax collected by the government $0.08, or 10% of the final sales price.

The value-added tax has several advantages, which led to its adoption in Europe.[2]

1. Under GATT rules, an indirect tax such as the value-added tax can be rebated on exports and levied on imports as a kind of border or excise tax. Thus the effective after-tax cost of goods that are exported is lower by the amount of the value-added tax than the cost of the same goods sold domestically. Whether exports become more profitable depends on how demand varies with the foreign import price, but at least there is more leeway to reduce prices competitively on exports than on domestic sales. GATT regulations do not allow direct taxes, such as the income tax on which the United States relies, to be rebated on export sales.

2. The value-added tax has been politically more acceptable in Western Europe than a number of alternative sources of tax revenue. For example, the value-added tax does not cause the same kind of economic distortions as some of the indirect taxes it replaced. In Germany the turnover tax required that a tax be assessed and collected every time a product changed hands. In the example in Exhibit 21.3 a 10% turnover tax would be collected from the tree owner. If the lumber mill was owned by someone else, that person, too, would pay a 10% turnover tax when selling the fence post to the wholesaler, etc. Since at no step is credit received for turnover taxes paid previously, the final tax bill includes taxes assessed on previously paid taxes. To avoid the compounding of taxes, many German firms were forced to integrate vertically, even when this integration was undesirable from an economic or social point of view. Because it is not assessed on the basis of a change in ownership, the value-added tax avoids distortion due to compounding.

3. The value-added tax may have some advantages compared to the corporate income tax. Since the value-added tax is usually assessed on all consumption goods produced, it cannot be avoided by book write-offs, accelerated depreciation, loss carry-forwards, loose expense account practices, interest on debt, artificial transfer prices, etc. Profitable and unprofitable firms, no matter how much levered by debt, are taxed alike. Therefore it forces the unprofitable firm to improve or go out of business faster than it might otherwise, thus reallocating scarce economic resources in a more optimal manner from the national economic viewpoint.

4. The value-added tax has also been proposed as a substitute for property taxes, local sales taxes, payroll taxes, and miscellaneous indirect taxes. In each case there would be some political support for a value-added tax from groups believing that one of these other taxes is even more onerous.

have on private economic behavior. For example, the U.S. government's policy on taxation of foreign-source income does not have as its sole objective the raising of revenue but has multiple objectives. These include the following:

- The desire to neutralize tax incentives that might favor (or disfavor) U.S. private investment in developed countries.
- Provision of an incentive for U.S. private investment in developing countries.
- Improvement of the U.S. balance of payments by removing the advantages of artificial tax havens and encouraging repatriation of funds.
- Raising of revenue.

The ideal tax should not only raise revenue efficiently but also have as few negative effects on economic behavior as possible. Some theorists argue that the ideal tax should be completely neutral in its effect on private decisions and completely equitable among taxpayers. However, other theorists claim that national policy objectives—such as balance of payments or investment in developing countries—should be encouraged through an active tax incentive policy rather than require taxes to be neutral and equitable. Most tax systems compromise between these two viewpoints.

In the case of U.S. taxation of foreign investment income, there is considerable theoretical debate about its impact on U.S. multinational firms. In particular, the concept of neutrality needs to be defined. One way to view neutrality is to require that the burden of taxation on each dollar of profit earned in U.S. operations by a U.S. multinational firm be equal to the burden of taxation on each dollar-equivalent of profit earned by the same firm in its foreign operations. This situation is called *domestic neutrality*. A second way to view neutrality is to require that the tax burden on each foreign affiliate of a U.S. firm be equal to the tax burden on its competitors in the same country. This situation is called *foreign neutrality*. The U.S. Treasury tends to favor the domestic neutrality viewpoint, whereas U.S. multinational firms tend to favor foreign neutrality.

In practice, it is difficult to measure domestic or foreign tax neutrality. How should different definitions of taxable income be taken into account? Should indirect taxes, such as turnover or value-added taxes, be considered part of the total tax burden? Since taxes purchase government services, how should the varying quantity and quality of these services be recognized?

The issue of tax equity is also difficult to define and measure. In theory, an equitable tax is one that imposes the same total tax burden on all taxpayers who are similarly situated and located in the same tax jurisdiction. In the case of foreign investment income, the U.S. Treasury argues that since the United States uses the nationality principle to claim tax jurisdiction, U.S.-owned foreign affiliates are in the same tax jurisdiction as U.S. domestic affiliates. Therefore a dollar earned in foreign operations should be taxed at the same rate and paid at the same time as a dollar earned in domestic operations.

Tax Deferral

If the nationality principle of tax jurisdiction is upheld, it would end the tax-deferral privilege for many multinational firms. Foreign affiliates of multinational firms pay host-country corporate income taxes, but many parent countries defer claiming additional income taxes on that foreign-source income until it is remitted to the parent firm. For example, U.S. corporate income taxes on some types of foreign-source income of U.S.-owned affiliates incorporated abroad are deferred until the earnings are remitted to the United States. In the case of earnings of unincorporated foreign branches of U.S. firms, however, no deferral privilege exists. Foreign earnings are immediately subject to U.S. income taxes, but the parent also receives an immediate foreign tax credit for income taxes paid to the host country. Many of the industrialized countries treat the foreign-source income deferral privilege in about the same manner as does the United States, but it is impossible to generalize about this point. In fact, some countries do not tax foreign-source income at all.

Foreign Tax Credit

To prevent double taxation of the same income, most countries grant a foreign tax credit for income taxes paid to the host country. For example, if a Japanese affiliate of a U.S. firm earns the yen equivalent of $1,000,000 and pays $400,000 in income taxes (40% rate) to Japan, the U.S. firm can claim a credit against taxes due to the United States of $400,000 when it remits the earnings to the United States. Normally foreign tax credits are also available for withholding taxes paid to other countries on dividends, royalties, interest, and other income remitted to the parent. The value-added tax and other sales taxes are not eligible for a foreign tax credit but are typically deductible from pre-tax income as an expense.

Countries differ on how they calculate the foreign tax credit and what kinds of limitations they place on the total amount claimed. The U.S. method of calculating the foreign tax credit and limitations on its use are explained in the appendix of this chapter.

Tax Treaties

A network of bilateral tax treaties, many of which are modeled after one proposed by the Organization for Economic Cooperation and Development (OECD), provides another means of reducing double taxation. Tax treaties normally define how certain kinds of joint income should be allocated between national taxing jurisdictions. This issue is particularly important for firms that are primarily exporting to another country rather than doing business there through a "permanent establishment." The latter would be the case for manufacturing operations. A firm that only exports would not want any of its other worldwide income taxed by the importing country. Tax treaties define what is a "permanent establishment" and what constitutes a limited presence for tax purposes.

Tax treaties also typically result in reduced withholding tax rates between the two signatory countries. This practice is important to both multinational firms operating through foreign affiliates and individual portfolio investors receiving income from dividends, interest, or royalties.

Intercompany Transactions

The problem of intercompany transactions, particularly transfer pricing, has been discussed earlier in a broader framework than just its tax aspects. Nevertheless, the transfer price implications of Section 482 of the U.S. tax code, as well as similar provisions in other countries, are worthy of a more detailed analysis from the tax viewpoint. This subject is highly technical and one that often changes because of tax court rulings. Therefore we cannot do it justice in this book but suggest that the reader refer to articles cited in the bibliography.

ORGANIZING FOR FOREIGN OPERATIONS

A thorough knowledge of foreign tax environments and the manner in which the parent country taxes foreign source income is indispensable background for planning the way in which a multinational firm should organize its foreign operations.

Branch Versus Locally Incorporated Affiliate

A multinational firm normally has a choice of whether to organize a foreign affiliate as a branch of the parent or as a local corporation. Both tax and nontax consequences must be considered. Nontax factors include the locus of legal liability, public image in the host country, managerial incentive considerations, and local legal and political requirements. Although important, nontax considerations are really outside the scope of this chapter on tax planning.

One major tax consideration is whether the foreign affiliate is expected to run at a loss for several years after start-up. If so, it might be preferable to organize originally as a branch operation to permit these anticipated losses to be consolidated in the parent's income statement for tax purposes. For example, tax laws in the United States and many other countries do not permit a foreign corporation to be consolidated for tax purposes, even though it is consolidated for reporting purposes, but do permit consolidation of foreign branches for tax purposes.

A second tax consideration is the net tax burden after paying withholding taxes on dividends. Most countries charge a withholding tax on dividends paid to foreign residents in lieu of requiring them to file an income tax return. The actual amount of withholding tax varies from country to country but is usually modified by numerous bilateral tax treaties. For example, the rate charged by the United States varies. It is 30% for residents of countries with no tax treaty with the United States (such as Hong Kong). It is 5% for residents of 18 countries (including, for example, the United Kingdom, France, and Switzerland). It is 10% for seven countries (including Canada, People's Republic of China, and Japan). A non-U.S. multinational firm with a U.S.-incorporated affiliate would first pay the 34% corporate income tax on U.S. earnings and then an additional withholding tax on dividends remitted to the parent. If the U.S. affiliate is a branch, the withholding tax would be avoided. Thus a multinational firm must weigh the benefit of tax deferral of home country taxes on foreign-source income, which could be achieved by incorporation of the foreign affiliate, against the possible extra tax burden paid to the host government in the form of withholding taxes on dividends.

A third tax consideration is important for firms engaged in natural resource exploration and development. Some countries allow exploration costs, and possibly part of development costs, to be written off as a current expense rather than require them to be capitalized and amortized over succeeding years. Therefore many of the multinational oil and mining firms choose to operate these activities overseas as branches rather than subsidiaries. U.S. firms have an additional incentive to use the branch form of organization overseas, because this practice permits their use of the special depletion allowances permitted under the U.S. tax laws.

Further complicating the choice of structure are the various special-purpose organization forms permitted or encouraged by some countries. These are normally motivated by a country's desire to increase its exports or to promote development of less developed countries. For example, a U.S. firm can reduce the effective tax on foreign income by establishing a so-called possessions corporation in a U.S. possession such as Puerto Rico, Guam, or Samoa.

Tax-Haven Affiliates

Many multinational firms have foreign affiliates that act as tax havens for corporate funds awaiting reinvestment or repatriation. Tax-haven affiliates are partially a result of tax-deferral features on earned foreign income allowed by some of the parent countries to their multinational firms. Tax-haven affiliates are typically established in a country that can meet the following requirements.

- It must have a low tax on foreign investment or sales income earned by resident corporations and a low dividend withholding tax on dividends paid to the parent firm.

- It must have a stable currency to permit easy conversion of funds into and out of the local currency. This requirement can be met by permitting and facilitating the use of Eurocurrencies.

- It must have the facilities to support financial services—for example, good communications, professional qualified office workers, and reputable banking services.

- It must have a stable government that encourages the establishment of foreign-owned financial and service facilities within its borders.

Switzerland is a typical location for a European tax-haven affiliate by virtue of its excellent qualifications on all four points above. The Cayman Islands, the Bahamas, Liechtenstein, and Malta have established themselves as alternative tax havens. In some cases the financial overhead facilities were not available but have been set up by multinational corporations seeking the ideal combination of location, communications, currency stability, and low taxes.

The typical tax-haven affiliate owns the common stock of its related operating foreign affiliates. (There might be several tax-haven affiliates spotted around the world.) The tax-haven affiliate's equity is typically 100% owned by the parent firm. All transfers of funds might go through the tax-haven affiliates, including dividends and equity financing. Thus the parent country's tax on foreign-source income, which might normally be paid when a dividend is declared by a foreign affiliate, could continue to be deferred until the tax-haven affiliate itself pays a dividend to the parent firm. This event can be postponed indefinitely if foreign operations continue to grow and require new internal financing from the tax-haven affiliate. Thus multinational firms are able to operate a corporate pool of funds for foreign operations without having to repatriate foreign earnings through the parent country's tax machine.

For U.S. multinational firms the tax-deferral privilege operating through a foreign affiliate was not originally a tax loophole. On the contrary, it was granted by the U.S. government to allow U.S. firms to expand overseas and place them on a par with foreign competitors, which also enjoy similar types of tax deferral and export subsidies of one type or another.

Unfortunately, some U.S. firms distorted the original intent of tax deferral into tax avoidance. Transfer prices on goods and services bought from or sold to related affiliates were artificially rigged to leave all the income from the transaction in the tax-haven affiliate. This manipulation could be done by routing the legal title to the goods or services through the tax-haven affiliate, even though physically the goods or services never entered the tax-haven country. This maneuver left no residual tax base for either exporting or importing affiliates located outside the tax-haven country. Needless to say, tax authorities of both exporting and importing countries were dismayed by the lack of taxable income in such transactions.

One purpose of the U.S. Internal Revenue Act of 1962 was to eliminate the tax advantages of these "paper" foreign corporations without destroying the tax-deferral privilege for those foreign manufacturing and sales affiliates that were established for business and economic motives rather than tax motives. Nevertheless, in some cases U.S. firms may have found loopholes in the law, permitting them to continue to use their tax havens as originally intended. Others do not benefit from tax deferral but have found these affiliates useful as finance control centers for foreign operations.

SUMMARY

- Tax planning for multinational operations is a complex technical subject that requires the inputs of experienced tax and legal counsel in both parent and host countries. Nevertheless, the financial manager of a multinational firm should be acquainted with the national tax environments in the host countries in which the firm operates. This environment includes the role of local income taxes, value-added taxes, and other indirect taxes, and the less tangible aspects of local tax morality.

- The financial executive must also understand how the parent country taxes foreign-source income in order to organize efficiently for foreign operations. Important considerations include how the parent's country views tax neutrality as well as how it treats tax deferral, foreign tax credits, and intercompany transactions. Bilateral tax treaties may also influence the way foreign operations are structured.

- Finally, the financial manager must choose the specific organization form that would be optimal for each foreign location as well as for the group as a whole. This activity typically involves choosing the branch or corporate form of organization. It also might require use of one or more special-purpose corporations or tax-haven affiliates.

1. Cuenca, S.A.

Cuenca, S.A., of Ecuador is the only foreign subsidiary of a U.S. company. The U.S. parent anticipates Cuenca will earn S/.100,000,000 (S/. stands for sucres, the Ecuadorian currency) next year, before any royalties are paid to the parent and before Ecuadorian corporate income taxes of 25%. The U.S. parent wants to remit and retain the maximum amount of cash from Ecuador. It is free to remit all after-tax Ecuadorian income in the form of a dividend, or if it wishes, it may remit 40% of pretax Ecuadorian income in the form of a royalty, deductible before calculating Ecuadorian taxes, and then remit the available after-tax Ecuadorian income as a dividend.

Dividends and royalties received in the United States are both subject to the U.S. 34% corporate income tax. The U.S. tax on dividends would be calculated on grossed-up Ecuadorian income, with a credit for Ecuadorian taxes paid. Royalties are fully taxed in the United States, and any unused tax credit from dividends cannot be used to reduce taxes on royalties.

The current exchange rate between Ecuador and the United States is S/.1,000 = $1.00, and this rate is not expected to change.

What would be the after-all-tax amount received in the United States under both policies? Which policy would you recommend?

2. Schweinfurt Ball Bearings, GmbH (C21A.WK1)

Schweinfurt Ball Bearings, GmbH., is the German subsidiary of a U.S. ball bearing company. German corporate taxes are 50% and U.S. corporate taxes are 34%. The current exchange rate is DM1.50/$. Schweinfurt Ball Bearing has no debt, and its earnings before taxes (EBT) are DM2,200,000, which it distributes as follows:

EBT	DM 2,200,000
Less German taxes (50%)	−1,100,000
Net income	1,100,000
Less dividends (80% payout)	DM 880,000
Retained in Germany	DM 220,000

a) How would imposing a 5% royalty charge on Schweinfurt alter cash flows received in the United States, total worldwide taxes paid, and consolidated world income?

b) How would a combined 5% royalty charge and a reduced dividend payment rate, from 80% to 50%, alter U.S. cash flows, worldwide tax payments, and consolidated income?

3. Tableware, Inc., in Korea (C21B.WK1)

Tableware, Inc., of the United States manufactures and distributes both sterling silver and stainless steel flatware throughout the United States. In recent years Tableware has manufactured its stainless steel flatware in Korea.

This past year Korean earnings, expressed in U.S dollar terms were $10,000,000. Korean income taxes are 20%, and U.S. income taxes are 34%. If Tableware, Inc., wants to receive 40% of its Korean after-tax earnings as a dividend in the United States, what will be post-tax retained earnings in Korea and in the United States? What contribution does the Korean subsidiary make to its parent's pre-tax earnings and to its retained earnings, given this dividend policy and ignoring the effect of any other subsidiaries?

4. Tableware, Inc., in Denmark

Tableware, Inc., has its top quality sterling silver flatware manufactured by its subsidiary in Denmark. This past year Danish earnings, expressed in U.S. dollar terms, were $10,000,000. Danish income taxes are 50%, and U.S. income taxes are 34%. If Tableware, Inc., wants to receive 40% of its Danish after-tax earnings as a dividend in the United States, what will be after-tax retained earnings in Denmark and in the United States? What contribution does the Danish subsidiary make to its parent's pre-tax earnings and to its retained earnings, given this dividend policy and ignoring the effect on worldwide retained earnings?

5. Tableware, Inc., in Korea and Denmark, Part (A)

Tableware, Inc., decides to integrate dividend policy from its Korean and Danish subsidiaries. It is able to combine dividends and tax credits from the two subsidiaries when calculating its U.S. tax liability. Assuming dividends from both countries remain at 40% of local after-tax net income, what is the combined effect on worldwide retained earnings?

6. Tableware, Inc., in Korea and Denmark, Part (B)

Tableware, Inc., now decides to change its dividend policy in order to minimize worldwide taxes and maximize consolidated retained earnings. However total dividends received from the two subsidiaries will be held constant at $5,200. What should be the resulting dividend policy?

NOTES

1. An excellent summary of the experience of various countries with value-added taxes, as well as information on each country's system, can be found in Price Waterhouse, *Value-Added Tax*, November 1979.

2. Dan Throop Smith, "Value-Added Tax: The Case For," *Harvard Business Review*. November/December 1970, pp. 77–85.

3. Stanley S. Surrey, "Value-Added Tax: The Case Against," *Harvard Business Review*, November/December 1970, pp. 86–94.

BIBLIOGRAPHY

Bannock, Graham, *VAT and Small Business: European Experience and Implications for North America*, Washington, D.C.: Canadian Federation of Independent Business Research and Education Foundation, 1986.

Brecher, Stephen M., Donald W. Moore, Michael M. Hoyle, and Peter G. B. Trasker, *The Economic Impact of the Introduction of VAT*, Morristown, N.J.: Financial Executives Research Foundation, 1982.

Chown, John F., "Tax Treatment of Foreign Exchange Fluctuations in the United States and United Kingdom," *Journal of International Law and Economics*, George Washington University, no. 2, 1982, pp. 201–237.

Christian, Ernest S., Jr., *State Taxation of Foreign Source Income*, New York: Financial Executives Research Foundation, 1981.

"DISC/FSC Legislation: The Case of the Phantom Profits," *Journal of Accountancy*, January 1985, pp. 83–97.

Dolan, D. Kevin, "Intercompany Transfer Pricing for the Layman," *Tax Notes*, October 8, 1990, pp. 211–228.

Frisch, Daniel J., "The Economics of International Tax Policy: Some Old and New Approaches," *Tax Notes*, April 30, 1990, pp. 581–591.

Gelinas, A. J. A., "Tax Considerations for U.S. Corporations Using Finance Subsidiaries to Borrow Funds Abroad," *Journal of Corporate Taxation*, Autumn 1980, pp. 230–263.

Goldberg, Honey L., "Conventions for the Elimination of International Double Taxation: Toward a Developing Country Model," *Law and Policy in International Business*, No. 3, 1983, pp. 833–909.

Hartman, David G., "Tax Policy and Foreign Direct Investment in the United States," *National Tax Journal*, December 1984, pp. 475–487.

Hemelt, James T., and Cynthia Spencer, "United States: Tax Effective Management of Foreign Exchange Risks," *European Taxation*, 30, no. 3, 1990, pp. 67–71.

Kaplan, Wayne S., "Foreign Sales Corporations: Politics and Pragmatics," *Tax Executive*, April 1985, pp. 203–220.

OECD, *Taxation in Developed Countries*, Paris: OECD, 1987.

Peat, Marwick, Mitchell & Co., *Foreign Sales Corporations*, New York: Peat, Marwick, Mitchell & Co., 1984.

Prest, A. R., *Value Added Taxation*, Washington, D.C.: American Enterprise Institute, 1980.

Price Waterhouse, *Corporate Taxes—A Worldwide Summary*, New York: Price Waterhouse, 1991, updated periodically.

Schiff, Michael, *Business Experience with Value Added Taxation*, New York: Financial Executives Research Foundation, 1974.

Sharp, William M., Betty K. Steele, and Richard A. Jacobson, "Foreign Sales Corporations: Export Analysis and Planning," *Taxes, the Tax Magazine*, March 1985, pp. 163–200.

Sherman, H. Arnold, "Managing Taxes in the Multinational Corporation," *The Tax Executive*, Winter 1987, pp. 171–181.

U.S. Taxation of Foreign-Source Income

An overall understanding of parent country taxation of foreign-source income is important for non–tax-specializing executives, if for no other reason than it prepares them to understand the advice of tax specialists. This appendix deals with U.S. government taxation of foreign-source income earned by U.S. multinational firms, including certain key provisions of the U.S. tax code as revised in 1986.

U.S. corporations are taxed within the United States on their worldwide income. The timing and amount of U.S. taxation, however, depends on how that income is classified, how taxes already paid in a foreign country are treated in calculating additional U.S. tax liability, and whether the particular foreign-source income falls under one of a number of exceptions to the overall general principles. We will treat each of these three dependencies in the sections that follow.

CLASSIFICATIONS OF FOREIGN-SOURCE INCOME

Income earned by the foreign affiliates of U.S. shareholders, including parent firms of multinational enterprises, can be classified as shown in Exhibit 21A.1.

Classification by Income Type and Country of Origin

Any home country could decide to tax separately income from each separate foreign country by each separate type of income. In other words, each individual cell in Exhibit 21A.1 could require a separate tax calculation and payment by the parent firm.

Alternatively, all types of income for each foreign country could be pooled, and a tax levied only on the sum of foreign income from each country. In Exhibit 21A.1, all types of income from the United Kingdom would be pooled and taxed at one time. A separate calculation would be required for Mexican-source income, and so on.

A third alternative would be to tax by type of income, with the parent allowed to pool income from many countries as long as it was of the same type. In Exhibit 21A.1, all overall income from the United Kingdom, Mexico, Korea, and so on, would be pooled and taxed as overall income. Similarly, all passive income from all countries would be pooled and taxed one time.

Finally, of course, all foreign-source income from all countries and by all types could be put into one grand international pool and taxed once.

As a *general* matter, the United States uses the third alternative. Under the Tax Reform Act of 1986, effective January 1, 1987, foreign-source income must be classified by type, or "basket," and separate taxes calculated and paid on the sum within that basket. However, within each basket, income from various countries may be pooled. Nevertheless, certain exceptions exist to this general principle. These will be explained as they arise.

Classification by Earned Versus Distributed Income

Another classification is also possible. Within each cell, that is, for each type of income from each country, home country taxes could be levied on income (1) at the time earned

Exhibit 21A.1   Classification of Foreign-Source Income

By type of income:	By country where earned:			
	United Kingdom	Mexico	Korea	Other Countries…
Overall, or residual, basket	Earned	Earned	Earned	Earned
	Paid out	Paid out	Paid out	Paid out
Passive income basket	Earned	Earned	Earned	Earned
	Paid out	Paid out	Paid out	Paid out
High-withholding-tax interest basket	Earned	Earned	Earned	Earned
	Paid out	Paid out	Paid out	Paid out
Other baskets	Earned	Earned	Earned	Earned
	Paid out	Paid out	Paid out	Paid out

abroad, or (2) only when that foreign-source income is paid out to the home country as a dividend. With some important exceptions, the United States taxes foreign-source income of separately incorporated subsidiaries only at the time that income is paid out to the United States as a dividend. However, earnings of unincorporated branches are taxed at the time earned. The most important exception to this principle is Subpart F income received from controlled foreign corporations (CFCs), a topic that will be discussed separately later in this appendix.

In earlier chapters of this book we have sometimes used the generic term "affiliate" to refer generally to all forms of foreign operation. In this section on taxation it is essential to differentiate between foreign-incorporated subsidiaries and other forms such as branches.

"BASKETS": CLASSIFYING INCOME BY TYPE

A major change in the U.S. tax laws in 1986 was the creation of a large number of "baskets" for separate categories or streams of foreign income. The changes eliminated a number of the tax advantages available when taxes on income taxed in a foreign country at a high rate are used to reduce U.S. income taxes on income taxed in foreign countries at lower rates.

The number and type of baskets used by any U.S.-based multinational firm depends in part on the foreign activities it is engaged in and in part on how its foreign operations are owned. In general the basket classification is as follows.

1. An *overall* basket receives all residual income not allocated to any of the remaining specialized baskets. Dividends paid from the active conduct of a foreign trade or business fall into the overall basket.

2. A *passive income* basket receives dividends from less-than-10% owned companies; rents and royalties not derived from the active conduct of trade or business; interest received from unrelated parties; Subpart F inclusions to the extent attributable to passive income of controlled foreign corporations (CFCs); interest from 50%-or-less owned subsidiaries; foreign personal holding company income; gains from the sale or exchange of property that generate passive income; dividends, interest, rents, and royalties from a CFC to the extent attributable to passive income of that CFC; commodities transactions gains; and foreign currency gains. However, high-withholding-tax interest; financial service income, and interest from export financing are not regarded as passive income but are included in another basket.

3. A *high-withholding-tax* interest basket includes interest received that has been subject to a foreign gross withholding tax of 5% or more. However, export financing interest is excluded from this basket.

4. An *export financing interest* basket includes interest derived from financing the sale for use or consumption outside the United States of property manufactured or otherwise produced in the United States for which not more than 50% of the market value is attributable to products imported into the United States.

5. A *financial service income* basket includes income derived from the active conduct of banking, financing, insurance, or similar businesses, including service fee income, earnings from interest rate and currency-swap businesses, management fees, income from fiduciary services and charge and credit services, and premium and other insurance company income. Financial service income does not include high-withholding-tax interest.

6. A *shipping income* basket includes income earned from foreign-based shipping operations.

7. Additional baskets may exist for distributions from CFCs. Income from CFCs is treated as a separate basket for the parent if it is attributable to or allocable to separate basket income at the CFC level. Hence CFCs must themselves keep track of overall, passive, high-withholding-tax, financial service, shipping, and dividend income from their own 10% to 50% owned subsidiaries.

8. A separate basket exists for distributions from 10% to 50% owned, noncontrolled corporations. Separate rules allocate dividends, interest, rents and royalties from such corporations to other baskets, including the parent's passive basket.

9. A foreign sales corporation (FSC) and a domestic international sales corporation (DISC) basket may be created if the firm has income from these sources. FSCs and DISCs are described later in this appendix.

FOREIGN TAX CREDITS

U.S. corporations are taxed within the United States on their worldwide income, under a system that allows U.S. tax credit for taxes *deemed paid* to foreign host governments.

"Worldwide income" includes dividends and other distributions received from foreign-incorporated subsidiaries plus all profits (and minus all losses) from branches. We will first explain the basic concept and reason behind the allowance of foreign tax credits and then look at the particulars of how they are calculated under various circumstances.

Basic Concept of Foreign Tax Credits (FTCs)

A *tax credit* is a direct reduction of taxes that would otherwise be due and payable. It differs from a *deductible expense*, which is an expense used to reduce taxable income before the tax rate is applied. A $100 tax credit reduces taxes payable by the full $100, whereas a $100 deductible expense reduces taxable income by $100 and taxes payable by $100(t), where t is the tax rate. Tax credits are more valuable on a dollar-for-dollar basis than are deductible expenses.

Without credits for foreign taxes paid, sequential taxation by the host government and then by the United States would result in a very high cumulative tax rate. To illustrate, assume the wholly owned foreign subsidiary of a U.S. parent earns $10,000 before local income taxes and pays a dividend equal to all of its after-tax income. The host country income tax rate is 30%, and the U.S. tax rate is 34%. For simplicity we will assume no withholding taxes. Total taxation with and without allowances for tax credits would be as follows.

	Without Tax Credits	With Tax Credits
Before-tax foreign income	$10,000	$10,000
Less foreign tax @ 30%	−3,000	−3,000
Available to U.S. parent and paid as dividend	7,000	7,000
Less additional U.S. tax at 34%	−2,380	
Less incremental tax (after credits)		− 400
Profit after all taxes	$ 4,620	$ 6,600
Total taxes, both jurisdictions	5,380	3,400
Effective overall tax rate	53.8%	34.0%

If tax credits are not allowed, sequential levying of both a 30% host country tax and then a 34% U.S. tax on the income that remains results in an effective 53.8% tax, a cumulative rate that would render many U.S. firms noncompetitive with single-country local firms. The effect of allowing tax credits is to limit total taxation on the *original* before-tax income to no more than the highest single rate in the jurisdictions where the flow of income might be taxed.

The $400 of additional U.S. tax under the tax credit system, above, is the amount needed in this example to bring total taxation ($3,000 already paid plus the additional $400) up to but not beyond 34% of the original $10,000 of before-tax foreign income. The technique of this calculation will be explained next.

Calculating the Direct Foreign Tax Credit (FTC)

A *direct* tax is a tax imposed directly on the income of a taxpayer. Direct taxes include income taxes, dividend withholding taxes, and war profit taxes. *Indirect* taxes are, as the name suggests, imposed indirectly. They include value-added taxes, sales taxes, excise taxes, and property taxes.

Within each basket category, dividends received from U.S. corporate subsidiaries are fully taxable in the United States at U.S. tax rates but with tax credits allowed for direct taxes paid on income in a foreign country. Exceptions to this general principle exist, especially for income that falls into some of the baskets listed earlier. Indirect taxes are deductible as an expense, but do not serve as the base for tax credits.

The amount of foreign tax allowed as a credit depends on (1) foreign income before host-country taxes, (2) tax rates in the host country and the United States, and (3) the proportion of foreign after-tax income paid as a cash dividend to the U.S. parent. Other complicating factors are the basket classification and situations where the dividend exceeds that year's income. For the moment these complications will be ignored.

The following examples are based on a foreign subsidiary that earns $10,000 before local taxes, with a foreign income tax rate of 30%, a foreign dividend withholding rate of 8%, and a U.S. tax rate of 34%.

Example 1: Foreign Subsidiary with a 100% Payout. Assume that the foreign subsidiary earns $10,000 before local taxes in its overall tax basket, and pays taxes and dividends as follows:

Foreign subsidiary income before local taxes	$10,000
Foreign income tax at 30%	−3,000
Available and declared as dividend	7,000
Less foreign dividend withholding tax at 8%	− 560
Cash dividend amount received in the U.S.	$6,440

The U.S. parent takes the *full* before-tax foreign income into its taxable income. This is called *grossing up*. The parent then calculates a tentative U.S. tax against the grossed-up income, but reduces payment of this liability by taking a *deemed-paid credit* for taxes already paid on the same original income in the host country. The calculations are as follows:

Included in U.S. taxable income		$10,000
U.S. (tentative) tax thereon at 34%	$ 3,400	
Less credit for		
Foreign income taxes paid	−3,000	
Foreign withholding taxes	− 560	
Additional U.S. taxes due	None	
Total taxes paid ($3,000 + $560)		$3,560
Re maining in U.S. after all taxes		$6,440

In this instance the $3,560 sum of foreign income and withholding taxes exceeds the tentative U.S. tax charge of $3,400, so no additional taxes are due in the United States. The original $10,000 of before-tax income is subject to the highest rate of the two countries. If the combined foreign income and withholding taxes had totaled less than 34% of the original $10,000 of foreign income, additional U.S. taxes would have been paid.

If the amount of foreign tax deemed paid exceeds what would have been paid under U.S. tax rates, an *excess tax credit* is created. In this example foreign tax payments ($3,560) are $160 larger than what the U.S. parent would have paid on the same income ($3,400). The

$160 difference is an excess tax credit. It can be carried back two years and forward five years. However, if it cannot be fully used in this manner, tax planners try to find other ways to use the excess tax credit, but tax legislation is designed to limit use of such excess tax credits. The creation of an array of baskets in 1986 was designed to limit using of excess tax credits from one type of foreign income to reduce taxes on other types of income.

Example 2: Foreign Subsidiary with a 40% Payout. Assume that the foreign subsidiary is the same as before except that after paying local taxes it declares a cash dividend to its U.S. parent of $2,800, equal to 40% of its $7,000 after-tax income.

Foreign subsidiary income before local taxes	$10,000
Foreign income tax at 30%	−3,000
Available for dividends	7,000
Declared as a dividend (40% of $7,000)	$ 2,800
Less foreign dividend withholding tax at 8%	− 224
Cash dividend amount received in the U.S.	$ 2,576

If the dividend declared is $2,800, some $224 is retained by the host country as a withholding tax, and only $2,576 is actually received in the United States. The dividend withholding tax acts as a substitute for local personal income taxes, which are of course not paid by nonresident foreigners.

In calculating the amount of foreign tax credit allowed, the U.S. parent can take all of the withholding tax plus that portion of foreign income taxes paid that is equal to the proportion of net income available for dividends that is paid out as a dividend. The formula for determining the amount of creditable deemed paid tax is:

$$\text{Deemed-paid credit} = \frac{\begin{array}{c}\text{dividends received}\\ \text{(including witholding tax)}\end{array}}{\begin{array}{c}\text{after-tax net earnings and profits}\\ \text{of foreign corporation}\end{array}} \times \text{creditable foreign taxes}$$

$$= \frac{\$2,800}{\$7,000} \times \$3,000$$

$$= \$1,200.$$

Consequently the tax credit calculation would be as follows.

Dividend received (before withholding tax)		$ 2,800
Plus foreign deemed-paid tax		1,200
Gross dividend included in U.S. taxable income		4,000
U.S. (tentative) tax thereon at 34%	$ 1,360	
Less credit for		
Foreign income taxes paid	−1,200	
Foreign withholding taxes paid	− 224	
Additional U.S. taxes due	None	
Total taxes actually paid ($1,200 + $224)		1,424
Remaining in U.S. after all taxes		$ 2,576

Again, no additional U.S. taxes are due because the combined foreign income and withholding tax rate exceeds the U.S. tax rate.

Example 3: Foreign Branch. Branches differ from incorporated subsidiaries in that all profits are taxed in the United States regardless of whether any profits are remitted to the U.S. parent. Additionally, losses of a branch are immediately deductible against U.S. taxable income. (Losses of a foreign incorporated subsidiary are not deductible.) Assume that circumstances are similar to Example 1 above, but that the foreign affiliate is a branch.

Foreign branch income before local taxes		$ 10,000
Foreign income tax at 30%		−3,000
Profits attributable to the foreign branch		7,000
Included in U.S. taxable income		$ 10,000
U.S. (tentative) tax thereon at 34%	$ 3,400	
Less credit for foreign income taxes paid	−3,000	
Additional U.S. taxes due	400	
Total taxes paid ($3,000 + $400)		$ 3,400
Remaining in U.S. after all taxes		$ 6,600

In this instance dividends are not relevant. Because the host country tax rate of 30% is below the U.S. rate of 34%, an additional tax of $400 is due in the United States. Total taxes on the original $10,000 of income are $3,400, or 34%, the higher of the two country's income tax rates.

Management Aspects of Using Foreign Tax Credits

If income is received from a foreign country that imposes higher corporate income taxes than the United States, total creditable taxes will exceed U.S. taxes on that foreign income. The amount of credit a taxpayer can use in any year, however, is limited to the U.S. tax on that foreign income. Foreign tax credits cannot be used to reduce taxes levied on income that year from U.S. sources.

Nevertheless, excess foreign tax credits that cannot be used in a particular year can be carried back for two years and forward for five years and can be treated like foreign creditable taxes for those carry-over years.

The total foreign tax creditable in any one year is limited according to the following formula:

$$\text{Creditable tax limitation} = \frac{\text{total foreign taxable income}}{\text{total taxable income}} \times \text{U.S. tax (on total income)}.$$

As noted, creditable taxes are foreign income taxes paid on earnings by a foreign corporation that has paid a dividend to a qualifying U.S. corporation. In order to qualify, the U.S. corporation must own at least 10% of the voting power of the distributing foreign corporation. Furthermore, if the 10% owned (first-tier) foreign corporation itself owns

10% or more of another (second-tier) foreign corporation, and the second-tier corporation owns 10% or more of a third-tier corporation, a portion of the second- and third-tier corporations' foreign income taxes will also be creditable to the U.S. taxpayer to the extent that earnings are distributed to the first- and second-tier corporations. However, there must be a minimum indirect ownership of 5% in the second- and third-tier corporations.

The preceding examples assumed that dividends equal 100% or some lesser percent of the earnings and profits of the foreign subsidiary. If dividends in any year *exceed* the earnings and profits of that year, the calculation is based on an accumulated pool of all post-December 31, 1986, undistributed earnings and foreign taxes.

Pooling Tax Credits

As noted earlier, the effect of allowing credits for foreign taxes paid is that foreign income is taxed at the higher of the two effective rates, and the cumulative taxation penalty that would occur if each tax rate were applied in sequence to after-tax income from the earlier tax calculation is eliminated. A very important aspect of tax management arises because allowable tax credits within each basket can be pooled by countries. Combining by countries allows excess tax credits from countries with high effective tax rates on that basket to be used to neutralize taxes on income received from low-tax-rate countries. The effective combining of dividends from several countries to obtain the lowest effective overall rate is a major goal of tax planning.

To illustrate, assume that America Corporation has operating subsidiaries in Sweden, where the income tax rate is 52%, and in Taiwan, where the rate is 25%. Each subsidiary earns $10,000 before taxes in its overall basket. The Taiwan subsidiary pays a 100% dividend to America Corporation, and the Swedish subsidiary pays no dividends. For simplicity assume no dividend withholding taxes.

The current Taiwan situation is as follows.

Taiwan income before taxes		$ 10,000
Taiwan income tax at 25%		–2,500
Available and declared as dividend		7,500
Included in U.S. taxable income		$ 10,000
U.S. (tentative) tax thereon at 34%	$ 3,400	
Less credit for Taiwan taxes	–2,500	
Additional U.S. taxes due	900	
Total taxes paid ($2,500 + $900)		3,400
Taiwan earnings after all taxes		$ 6,600

The current Swedish situation is as follows.

Swedish income before taxes	$ 10,000
Swedish income tax at 52%	–5,200
Net income (no dividends declared)	$ 4,800

Total income taxes paid, each country's contribution to consolidated net income, and cash dividends received are:

	Income Taxes Paid	Contribution to Consolidated Net Income	Cash Dividend to America Corporation After Witholding Taxes
United States	$ 900	—	—
Taiwan	2,500	$ 6,600	$6,600
Sweden	5,200	4,800	—
Total	$8,600	$11,400	$6,600

Dividends from Taiwan lead to $900 of additional U.S. taxes. If dividends were declared from Sweden they would create excess tax credits that could be used to offset U.S. taxes now paid on Taiwan dividends. Each dollar of dividend from Sweden creates an excess tax credit of $1(52% − 34%) = $0.18. If the additional taxes paid on Taiwan dividends are divided by the potential excess tax credit from Sweden, one can determine how much dividend from Sweden should be declared to neutralize U.S. taxes on Taiwan dividends:

$$\text{Neutralizing dividend calculation} = \frac{\text{additional U.S. tax on Taiwan dividends}}{\text{excess tax credit for Sweden, per dollar of dividend}}$$

$$= \frac{\$900}{0.18}$$

$$= \$5,000.$$

In this example the Swedish subsidiary cannot declare a $5,000 dividend because it has only $4,800 of net income available for dividends. (Dividends declared this year out of prior years' earnings create a separate set of calculations.) Nevertheless if the Swedish subsidiary were to declare a dividend of $4,800 the combined results would be as follows.

Combined Swedish and Taiwan income before taxes		$ 20,000
Combined income taxes		−7,700
Combined available and declared as dividends		12,300
Included in U.S. taxable income		$ 20,000
U.S. (tentative) tax thereon at 34%	$ 6,800	
Less credit for all foreign taxes	−7,700	
Additional U.S. taxes due	None	
Total taxes paid		7,700
Remaining in U.S. after all taxes		$ 12,300

Total income taxes paid, each country's contribution to consolidated net income, and dividends received are now:

	Income Taxes Paid	Contribution to Consolidated Net Income	Cash Dividend to America Corporation After Witholding Taxes
United States	$ None	—	—
Taiwan	2,500	$ 7,500	$ 7,500
Sweden	5,200	4,800	4,800
Total	$ 7,700	$12,300	$12,300

On an overall basis, total taxes are reduced from $8,600 to $7,700, a $900 saving. Consolidated income increases from $11,400 to $12,300, an increase of $900, equal to the tax saved. Whether or not it is desirable that more cash end up in the United States than previously depends on America Corporation's cash positioning strategy; if the dollars can be respent anywhere in the world without additional taxation or loss of value, their transfer to the United States would not seem detrimental.

CONTROLLED FOREIGN CORPORATIONS AND SUBPART F

The rule that U.S. shareholders do not pay U.S. taxes on foreign-source income until that income is remitted to the United States was amended in 1962 by the creation of special *Subpart F* income. The revision was designed to prevent the use of arrangements between operating companies and base companies located in tax havens as a means of deferring U.S. taxes and to encourage greater repatriation of foreign incomes. The Tax Reform Act of 1986 retained the concept of Subpart F income but made a number of changes that expanded categories of income subject to taxation, reduced exceptions, and raised or lowered thresholds.

Several definitions are needed to understand Subpart F income: A *controlled foreign corporation* (CFC) is any foreign corporation in which U.S. shareholders, including corporate parents, own more than 50% of the combined voting power or total value. A U.S. *shareholder* is a U.S. person owning 10% or more of the voting power of a controlled foreign corporation. A U.S. *person* is a citizen or resident of the United States, a domestic partnership, a domestic corporation, or any nonforeign trust or estate. The required percentages are based on *constructive ownership*, under which an individual is deemed to own shares registered in the names of other family members, trusts, etc.

Under these definitions a more-than-50% owned "subsidiary" of a U.S. corporation would be a controlled foreign corporation, and the U.S. parent would be taxed on certain undistributed income (Subpart F income) of that controlled foreign corporation. Since 10% ownership is required by each U.S. shareholder, a foreign corporation in which six unrelated U.S. citizens and/or corporations each own 9% of the combined voting power or total value would not be a controlled foreign corporation, even though total U.S. ownership is 54%. Nor would a foreign corporation in which U.S. shareholders own exactly 50% be a controlled foreign corporation.

Subpart F income, subject to immediate U.S. taxation even when not remitted, is income of a type otherwise easily shifted offshore to avoid current taxation. It includes (1) passive income received by the foreign corporation such as dividends, interest, rents, royalties, net foreign currency gains, net commodities gains, and income from the sale of non–income-producing property, (2) income from the insurance of U.S. risks; (3) financial service income; (4) shipping income; (5) oil-related income; and (6) certain related-party sales and service income.

Subpart F, restated, provides that if a foreign corporation is considered to be a controlled foreign corporation (that is, the corporation is more than 50% controlled by U.S. shareholders), each U.S. shareholder owning 10% or more of that controlled foreign corporation must include the shareholder's pro rata share of the controlled foreign corporation's Subpart F income in the shareholder's gross income. Thus Subpart F income is subject to current U.S. taxation at the shareholder level even though not remitted to the United States.

FOREIGN SALES CORPORATION (FSC)

Over the years the United States has introduced into U.S. tax laws special incentives dealing with international operations. To benefit from these incentives, a firm may have to form separate corporations for qualifying and nonqualifying activities. The most important U.S. special corporation is a foreign sales corporation (FSC).

FSCs were introduced in the Tax Reform Act of 1984 as a device to provide tax-exempt income for U.S. persons or corporations having export-oriented activities. FSCs replaced domestic international sales corporations (DISCs), which had been created by the Revenue Act of 1971 for somewhat similar purposes. Under the Tax Reform Act of 1986, FSC distributions and DISC dividends go to separate FSC and DISC baskets.

FSCs Versus DISCs

Briefly, a DISC was a U.S. corporation formed to export U.S.-produced goods to either foreign affiliates or unrelated foreign buyers. A portion of the earnings and profits of a DISC were not taxed to the DISC, but instead were taxed to the DISC's shareholders when distributed or deemed distributed to them.

Almost from their beginning, DISCs were the subject of dispute between the United States and other signatories of the General Agreement on Tariffs and Trade (GATT). The Europeans contended that the DISC allowed an illegal export subsidy in violation of GATT regulations because it permitted indefinite deferral of direct taxes on income earned from U.S. exports. GATT permits indirect taxes such as value-added taxes to be rebated, but the provision on direct taxes such as income taxes is more complicated. Export income may be exempt from a member country's income taxes only if the economic processes by which that income arises occur outside the country. The United States did not concede that DISCs were in violation of GATT, but to avoid further disputes the United States replaced the DISC with the FSC.

A FSC differs from a DISC in that use of a FSC allows *permanent* exemption of certain income from U.S. taxes, whereas the DISC only allowed *deferral* of taxes. A FSC is a foreign corporation, whereas a DISC was a domestic U.S. corporation.

Tax Benefits of a FSC

"Exempt foreign trade income" of a FSC is not subject to U.S. income taxes. Exempt foreign trade income is income from foreign sources that is not effectively connected with the conduct of a trade or business within the United States. Exempt foreign trade income is a portion of total foreign trade income.

A FSC's total foreign trade income is derived from gross receipts from the sale of export property; lease or rental of export property; incidental services provided with the sale or lease of export property; and fees for engineering, architectural, or managerial services. The exempt portion of the FSC's total foreign trade income depends upon the pricing rules used. "Export property" is manufactured, produced, grown, or extracted from the United States by an entity other than the FSC; and is sold, leased, or rented outside the United States.

If foreign trade income is based on arm's length pricing between unrelated parties, or between related parties under the rules of Section 482 of the Internal Revenue Code, then exempt foreign trade income is defined as 34% of the income from the transaction. If prices are set under special administrative rules established for FSCs, exempt foreign trade income is the fraction 17/23 of income from the transaction. That portion of total foreign trade income that is not exempt is regarded as effectively derived from the conduct of trade or business by a permanent business establishment in the United States, and is therefore subject to U.S. income taxes.

Exempt income of a FSC may be distributed to its U.S. shareholders on a tax-free basis. Dividends paid from nonexempt income of a FSC are fully taxable to the U.S. parent.

Creating a FSC

A corporation qualifies as a FSC if it maintains an adequate foreign presence, has foreign management, carries out some economic processes outside the United States that are related to its export income, and complies with appropriate transfer price legislation. These rules are to ensure that the FSC is a bona fide foreign corporation that earns its exempt income from economic activities conducted outside the United States.

Adequate Foreign Presence. To establish an adequate foreign presence, a FSC must satisfy each of the following requirements.

1. The FSC must be a foreign corporation, incorporated under the laws of a foreign country or certain overseas possessions of the United States, such as Guam, American Samoa, the Commonwealth of the Northern Mariana Islands, and the Virgin Islands. Puerto Rico does not qualify because it is within the U.S. customs area. Most FSCs are owned by a single U.S. parent corporation. However, a FSC may have up to a

maximum of 25 shareholders. This provision allows the benefits of FSCs to pass through directly to owners of closely held corporations.

2. A FSC may not issue preferred stock, although under some conditions separate classes of common stock are allowed. Congress was concerned that different classes of stock might be used to direct some dividends to shareholders having taxable income and other dividends to shareholders having net operating losses.

3. The FSC must maintain a permanent establishment outside the United States, including an office, books, and records. The office must be in a fixed location, be equipped for the performance of the firms's business, and be regularly used for business activity of the FSC.

4. At least one member of the FSC's board of directors must be a nonresident of the United States.

5. The FSC must elect to be treated as a FSC, and the FSC may not be a member of an affiliated group of corporations that also includes a DISC as a member.

Foreign Management

The FSC must be managed outside the United States, as indicated by the following requirements.

1. All board of directors meetings and all shareholders meetings must be held outside the United States.

2. The principal bank account of the corporation must be maintained outside the United States.

3. All dividends, legal and accounting fees, and salaries of members of the board of directors must be disbursed from bank accounts outside the United States.

Foreign Economic Process. Certain economic processes must take place outside the United States for each individual transaction for which tax exemption is sought.

1. The solicitation, negotiation, or making of the contract must take place outside the United States.

2. Foreign direct costs incurred by the FSC and attributable to each transaction must be paid by the FSC. Direct transaction costs are for processing customers' orders and arranging for delivery; billing customers and receiving payment; arranging and paying of transportation, advertising, and sales promotion; and assuming credit risk. The FSC must pay either 50% of each of the cost categories above, or 85% of the direct costs in any two categories.

Transfer Pricing Rules. Taxable income of the FSC must be determined from transfer prices that are either based on arm's-length pricing between unrelated parties or on use of Section 482 of the Internal Revenue Code for transactions between related parties.

An alternative is for the FSC to price under certain "safe harbor" rules designated "administrative pricing rules."

POSSESSIONS CORPORATION

A business carried on to a substantial extent in a U.S. possession can be carried on by a separate U.S. corporation, which, if it meets the requirements for a possessions corporation, is not subject to U.S. tax on income earned outside the United States unless the income is *received* in the United States. Although technically a U.S. corporation, a possessions corporation is treated like a foreign corporation in nearly every respect. U.S. corporate shareholders of a possessions corporation may claim deemed-paid foreign tax credit if they own 10% of its stock. Its dividends do not qualify for the dividends-received deduction, and it may not be included in a consolidated U.S. return.

Requirements

To qualify as a possessions corporation, a corporation must satisfy the following requirements.

1. It is a domestic U.S. corporation.
2. At least 80% of its gross income is derived from within a U.S. possession.
3. At least 75% of its gross income is derived from the active conduct of a trade or business in a U.S. possession.

Requirements 2 and 3 must be met for the three years preceding the end of the tax year or from date of incorporation for a new corporation.

Possessions of the United States include the Commonwealth of Puerto Rico, the Panama Canal Zone, Guam, American Samoa, and Wake and Midway Islands.

The U.S. Virgin Islands, although a U.S. possession, are excluded from possessions corporation benefits because of their peculiar tax situation. A U.S. corporation operating in the U.S. Virgin Islands pays its taxes, as computed under the U.S. Internal Revenue Code, to the Islands Treasury. However, under the Islands' incentive legislation, a qualifying corporation would receive a subsidy from the Islands of up to 75% of the tax paid. Thus, in effect, qualifying corporations would pay tax of about 8.5% (25% of 34%) on Virgin Islands income. In order to qualify, the corporation must meet requirements similar to 2 and 3 above and must also satisfy the incentive legislation requirements.

Exclusion from Gross Income

A corporation meeting the above requirements excludes from U.S. gross income amounts earned outside the United States unless the income is received in the United States. Thus a possessions corporation should arrange to *receive* income initially outside the United States, although it may subsequently transfer it from a foreign bank account to a bank account in the United States.

Prior to 1976 a possessions corporation was exempt from U.S. tax until the income was paid as a dividend to the U.S. parent company.[1] The exemption was granted in an indirect way by subjecting the income to U.S. tax and then allowing a credit equal to the U.S. tax. The 1986 tax revisions retain but tighten up certain 1982 changes in the possessions tax credit. The essence of these is that any portion of the income of a possessions corporation that is attributable to intangibles developed in the United States must be paid or allocated to a U.S.-related party in order for any of the income allocated to the intangible to be eligible for the possessions credit.

Thus the possessions corporation's income is subject to U.S. tax, but a tax-sparing credit is allowed for U.S. taxes on foreign-source income attributable to the conduct of a trade or business in a U.S. possession and qualified possessions-source investment income. The net result is that nonqualified income is subject to U.S. tax, but possessions income is exempt from tax.

The income qualifying for this credit is as follows:

- Income from foreign sources that is attributable to the conduct of a trade or business in a possession.

- Qualified possessions-source investment income that is defined as investment income (a) from sources within the possession in which the business is carried on, and (b) which the taxpayer establishes is attributable to the funds derived from the business or investment in such possession.

Other investment is taxable in the United States on a current basis. No foreign tax credit is available to possessions corporations except to the extent that a foreign tax is imposed on income subject to U.S. tax but not eligible for the tax-sparing credit.

As regards the U.S. parent company of a possessions corporation, foreign taxes paid with respect to distributions from the possessions subsidiary are neither creditable nor deductible.

Dividends from possessions corporations are eligible for the 100% or 85% dividends-received deduction, regardless of when the income was earned. Thus accumulated earnings from prior years can be repatriated by the possessions corporation to the U.S. parent with little or no U.S. tax.

An *election* is required to be filed to obtain the tax benefit of possessions corporation status. The election is for a ten-year period and may be revoked during that period only with the consent of the commissioner. An electing corporation is not includable in a consolidated return. Income accumulated by a possessions corporation is not subject to the accumulated earnings tax.

NOTES

1. The rest of this section is quoted from Price Waterhouse, *Tax Reform Act of 1976,* November 1976, pp. 34–36.

Glossary

Glossary

A.B. *Aktiebolag.* Swedish word for incorporated or stock company.

A.G. *Aktiengesellschaft.* German word for incorporated or stock company.

Accounting exposure. The potential for an accounting-derived change in owners' equity resulting from exchange rate changes and the need to restate financial statements of foreign affiliates in the single currency of the parent corporation. Also called "translation exposure."

ACU. *See* Asian currency unit.

ADB. Asian Development Bank.

Adjusted present value. A type of present value analysis in capital budgeting in which operating cash flows are discounted separately from (1) the various tax shields provided by the deductibility of interest and other financial charges, and (2) the benefits of project-specific concessional financing. Each component cash flow is discounted at a rate appropriate for the risk involved.

ADR. *See* American Depositary Receipt.

Ad valorem duty. A customs duty levied as a percentage of the assessed value of a product.

AfDB. African Development Bank.

Affiliate. A foreign operation, formed as either a branch or a foreign-incorporated subsidiary.

Agency for International Development (AID). A unit of the U.S. government dealing with foreign aid.

AID. *See* Agency for International Development.

All-equity discount rate. A discount rate in capital budgeting that would be appropriate for discounting operating cash flows if the project were financed entirely with owners' equity.

American Depositary Receipt (ADR). A certificate of ownership, issued by a U.S. bank, representing a claim on underlying foreign securities. ADRs may be traded in lieu of trading in the actual underlying shares.

American selling price (ASP). For customs purposes, the use of the domestic price of competing merchandise in the United States as a tax base for determining import duties. The ASP is generally higher than the actual foreign price, so its use is a protectionist technique.

American terms. Foreign exchange quotations for the U.S. dollar, expressed as the number of U.S. dollars per unit of non-U.S. currency.

A/P. In international trade documentation, abbreviation for "authority to purchase" or "authority to pay." In accounting, abbreviation for "accounts payable."

Appreciation. In the context of exchange rate changes, a rise in the foreign exchange value of a currency that is pegged to other currencies or to gold. Also called "revaluation."

Arbitrage. The purchase of a commodity, including foreign exchange, in one market at one price while simultaneously selling that same currency in another market at a more advantageous price, in order to obtain a risk-free profit on the price differential.

Arbitrageur. A individual or company that practices arbitrage.

Arm's-length price. The price at which a willing buyer and a willing unrelated seller freely agree to carry out a transaction. In effect, a free market price. Applied by tax authorities in judging the appropriateness of transfer prices between related affiliates.

Asian currency unit. A section of a Singaporean bank that deals in foreign currency deposits and loans.

Ask price. The price at which a dealer is willing to sell foreign exchange, securities, or commodities. Also called "offer price."

ASP. *See* American selling price.

Back-to-back loan. A loan in which two companies in separate countries borrow each other's currency for a specific period of time, and repay the other's

655

currency at an agreed maturity. Sometimes the two loans are channeled through an intermediate bank. Back-to-back financing is also called "link financing."

Balance of payments. The measurement of all economic transactions (both trade and financial) between residents of a given country and residents of all other countries.

Balance of trade. An entry in the balance of payments measuring the difference between the monetary value of merchandise exports and merchandise imports.

Balance on current account. *See* current account.

Bankers' acceptance. An unconditional promise of a bank to make payment on a draft when it matures.

Barter. International trade conducted by the direct exchange of physical goods, rather than by separate purchases and sales at prices and exchange rates set by a free market.

B/E. *See* Bill of exchange.

Bearer bond. Corporate or governmental debt in bond form that is not registered to any owner. Possession of the bond implies ownership, and interest is obtained by clipping a coupon attached to the bond. The advantage of the bearer form is easy transfer at the time of a sale, easy use as collateral for a debt, and what some cynics call "taxpayer anonymity," meaning

that governments find it hard to trace interest payments in order to collect income taxes. Bearer bonds are common in Europe, but are seldom issued any more in the United States. The alternate form to a bearer bond is a registered bond.

Beta. Second letter of Greek alphabet, used as a statistical measure of risk in the Capital Asset Pricing Model. Beta is the covariance between returns on a given asset and returns on the market portfolio, divided by the variance of returns on the market portfolio.

Bid. The price which a dealer is willing to pay for (i.e., buy) foreign exchange or a security.

BID. *Banco Interamericano de Desarrollo.* Spanish name for the Inter-American Development Bank.

Bid-ask spread. The difference between a bid and an ask quotation.

Big Bang. The October 1986 liberalization of the London capital markets.

Bill of exchange (B/E). A written order requesting one party (such as an importer) to pay a specified amount of money at a specified time to the order of the writer of the bill of exchange. Also called a "draft."

Bill of lading (B/L). A contract between a common carrier and a shipper to transport goods to a named destination. The bill of

lading is also a receipt for the goods.

B/L. *See* Bill of lading.

Black market. An illegal foreign exchange market.

Blocked funds. Funds in one country's currency that may not be exchanged freely for foreign currencies because of exchange controls.

Border tax adjustments. The fiscal practice, under the General Agreement on Tariffs and Trade, by which imported goods are subject to some or all of the tax charged in the importing country and reexported goods are exempt from some or all of the tax charged in the exporting country.

Branch. A foreign operation not incorporated in the host country, in contradistinction to a "subsidiary."

Bretton Woods Conference. International conference in 1944 that established the international monetary system in effect from 1945 to 1971. Bretton Woods is a resort town in the state of New Hampshire.

Bulldogs. Sterling-denominated bonds issued within the United Kingdom by a foreign borrower.

CAD. "Cash against documents." International trade term.

Call. An option to buy foreign exchange or financial contracts. *See* Option.

Capital account. That portion of the balance of payments that measures public and private international lending and investment.

Capital Asset Pricing Model (CAPM). A model of equilibrium rates of return and asset values determined in competitive and efficient financial markets.

Capital budgeting. The analytical approach used to determine whether investment in long-lived assets or projects is viable.

Capital flight. Movement of funds out of a country because of political risk.

Capital markets. The financial markets in various countries in which various types of long-term debt and/or ownership securities, or claims on those securities, are purchased and sold.

CAPM. *See* Capital Asset Pricing Model.

CFC. *See* Controlled foreign corporation.

C&F. *See* Cost and freight.

Cia. *Companía.* Spanish word for company.

CIF. *See* Cost, insurance, and freight.

CHIPS. *See* Clearinghouse Interbank Payments System.

CKD. "Completely knocked down." International trade term for components shipped into a country for assembly there. Often used in the automobile industry.

Clearinghouse Interbank Payments System (CHIPS). A computerized clearing system used by banks to settle interbank foreign exchange obligations.

Collar option. The simultaneous purchase of a put option and sale of a call option, or vice versa. Thus a form of hybrid option.

COMECON. Council for Mutual Economic Assistance. An association of the Soviet Union and Eastern European governments formed to facilitate international trade among European Communist countries.

Commercial risk. In banking, the likelihood that a foreign debtor will be unable to repay its debts because of business (as distinct from political) events.

Common market. An association through treaty of two or more countries that agree to remove all trade barriers between themselves. The best known is the European Common Market.

Comparative advantage. A theory that everyone gains if each nation specializes in the production of those goods that it produces relatively most efficiently and imports those goods that other countries produce relatively most efficiently. The theory supports free trade arguments.

Concession agreement. An understanding or contract between a foreign corporation and a host government defining the rules under which the corporation may operate in that country.

Consolidation. In the context of accounting for multinational corporations, the process of preparing a single "reporting currency" financial statement that combines financial statements of affiliates that are in fact measured in different currencies.

Controlled foreign corporation (CFC). In the U.S. tax code, a foreign corporation in which U.S. shareholders own more than 50% of the combined voting power or total value.

Convertible currency. A currency that can be exchanged freely for any other currency without government restrictions.

Correspondent bank. A bank that holds deposits for and provides services to another bank on a reciprocal basis.

Cost and freight (C&F). Price, quoted by an exporter, that includes the cost of transportation to the named port of destination.

Cost, insurance, and freight (CIF). Exporter's quoted price including the cost of packaging, freight, or carriage, insurance premium, and other charges paid in respect of the goods from the time of loading in the country of export to their arrival at the named port of destination or place of transshipment.

Cost of capital. *See* Weighted average cost of capital.

Countertrade. A type of international trade in which parties exchange goods directly rather than for money. Hence a type of barter.

Countervailing duty. An import duty charged to offset an export subsidy by another country.

Country risk. In banking, the likelihood that unexpected events within a host country will influence a client's or a government's ability to repay a loan. Country risk is often divided into sovereign (political) risk and foreign exchange (currency) risk.

Covered interest arbitrage. The process whereby an investor earns a risk-free profit by (1) borrowing funds in one currency, (2) exchanging those funds in the spot market for a foreign currency, (3) investing the foreign currency at interest rates in a foreign country, (4) selling forward, at the time of original investment, the investment proceeds to be received at maturity, (5) using the proceeds of the forward sale to repay the original loan, and (6) having a remaining profit balance.

Cross rate. An exchange rate between two currencies derived by dividing each currency's exchange rate with a third currency. For example, if ¥/$ is 140 and DM/$ is 1.5000, the cross rate between ¥ and DM is ¥140/$ ÷ DM1.5000 = ¥93.3333/DM.

CTA account. *See* Cumulative translation adjustment account.

Cumulative translation adjustment (CTA) account. An entry in a translated balance sheet in which gains and/or losses from translation have been accumulated over a period of years.

Current account. In the balance of payments, the net flow of goods, services, and unilateral transfers (such as gifts) between a country and all foreign countries.

Current rate method. A method of translating the financial statements of foreign affiliates into the parent's reporting currency. All assets and liabilities are translated at the current exchange rate.

Current/noncurrent method. A method of translating the financial statements of foreign affiliates into the parent's reporting currency. All current assets and current liabilities are translated at the current rate, and all noncurrent accounts at their historical rates.

D/A. "Documents against acceptance." International trade term.

Deemed-paid credit. A portion of taxes paid to a foreign government that is allowed as a credit (reduction) in taxes due to a home government.

Depreciate. In the context of foreign exchange rates, a drop in the spot foreign exchange value of a floating currency, i.e., a currency the value of which is determined by open market transactions. *See* Devaluation. In the context of accounting, a periodic charge (expense) that represents the allocation of the cost of a fixed asset to various time periods.

Devaluation. A drop in the spot foreign exchange value of a currency that is pegged to other currencies or to gold. *See* Depreciate.

Direct quote. The price of a unit of foreign exchange expressed in the home country's currency. The term has meaning only when the "home country" is specified.

"Dirty" float. A system of floating (i.e., market-determined) exchange rates in which the government intervenes from time to time to influence the foreign exchange value of its currency.

DISC. *See* Domestic International Sales Corporation.

Domestic International Sales Corporation (DISC). Under the U.S. tax code, a type of subsidiary formed to export U.S.-produced goods. A portion of the earnings and profits of DISCs is not taxed to the DISC but is instead taxed directly to its shareholders.

D/P. "Documents against payment." International trade term.

Draft. An unconditional written order requesting one party (such as an importer) to pay a specified amount of money at a specified time to the order of the writer of the draft. Also called a "bill of exchange." Personal checks are one type of draft.

D/S. "Days after sight." International trade term.

Dumping. The practice of offering goods for sale in a foreign market at a price that is lower than that of the same product in the home market or a third country. As used in GATT, a special case of "differential pricing."

Economic exposure. Another name for operating exposure. *See* "operating exposure."

ECU. *See* European Currency Unit.

Edge Act and Agreement Corporation. Subsidiary of a U.S. bank incorporated under federal law to engage in various international banking and financing operations, including equity participations which are not allowed to regular domestic banks. The Edge Act subsidiary may be located in a state other than that of the parent bank.

Efficient market. A market in which all relevant information is already reflected in market prices. The term is most frequently applied to foreign exchange markets and securities markets.

EOM. "End of month." International trade term.

Eurobond. A bond originally offered outside the country in whose currency it is denominated. For example, a dollar-denominated bond originally offered for sale to investors outside of the United States.

Euro-Commercial Paper. Short-term debt obliga-

tions of a corporation or bank, sold on a discount basis in the Eurocurrency market.

Eurocurrency. A currency deposited in a bank located in a country other than the country issuing the currency.

Eurodollar. A U.S. dollar deposited in a bank outside the United States.

Euronote. Short- to medium-term debt instruments sold in the Eurocurrency market.

European Currency Unit (ECU). Composite currency created by the European Monetary System to function as a reserve currency numeraire. The ECU is used as the numeraire for denominating a number of financial instruments and obligations.

European Monetary System (EMS). A monetary alliance of twelve (1991) European countries, formed to maintain member exchange rates within specified margins about fixed central rates.

European terms. Foreign exchange quotations for the U.S. dollar, expressed as the number of non-U.S. currency units per U.S. dollar.

Exchange rate. The price of a unit of one country's currency expressed in terms of the currency of some other country.

Ex dock, followed by the name of a port of import. International trade term in which the seller agrees to pay for the costs

(shipping, insurance, customs duties, etc.) of placing the goods on the dock at the named port.

Exim Bank. *See* Export-Import Bank.

Export-Import Bank (Eximbank). A U.S. government agency created to finance and otherwise facilitate imports and exports.

Expropriation. Official government seizure of private property, recognized by international law as the right of any sovereign state provided expropriated owners are given prompt compensation and fair market value in convertible currencies.

FAF. "Fly away free." International trade term.

FAQ. "Free at quay." International trade term.

FAS. "Free alongside." International trade term in which seller's quoted price for goods includes all costs of delivery of the goods alongside a vessel at the port.

FCIA. *See* Foreign Credit Insurance Association.

FDI. *See* Foreign direct investment.

FI. "Free in." International trade term meaning that all expenses for loading into the hold of a vessel are for the account of the consignee.

FIFO. "First in, first out." An inventory valuation approach in which the cost of the earliest inventory purchases is charged against current sales. The opposite is LIFO, or "last in, first out."

Fisher Effect. A theory that nominal interest rates in each country are equal to the required real rate of return to the investor plus compensation for the expected amount of inflation.

Fixed exchange rates. Foreign exchange rates set and maintained by government support.

Floating exchange rates. Foreign exchange rates determined by demand and supply in an open market that is presumably free of government interference.

FOB. "Free on board." International trade term in which exporter's quoted price includes the cost of loading goods into transport vessels at a named point.

Foreign Credit Insurance Association (FCIA). Private U.S. insurance association that insures exporters in conjunction with Eximbank.

Foreign bond. A bond issued by a foreign entity (corporate or government) for sale in a particular country and denominated in the currency of that particular country.

Foreign direct investment (FDI). Purchase of physical assets, such as plant and equipment, in a foreign country, to be managed by the parent corporation. FDI is in contradistinction to foreign portfolio investment.

Foreign exchange risk. The likelihood that an unexpected change in exchange rates will alter the home currency value of foreign currency cash payments expected from a foreign source. Also, the likelihood that an unexpected change in exchange rates will alter the amount of home currency needed to repay a debt denominated in a foreign currency.

Foreign sales corporation (FSC). Under U.S. tax code, a type of foreign corporation that provides tax-exempt or tax-deferred income for U.S. persons or corporations having export-oriented activities.

Foreign tax credit. The amount by which a domestic firm may reduce (credit) domestic income taxes for income tax payments to a foreign government.

Forfaiting. A technique for arranging nonrecourse medium-term export financing, used most frequently to finance imports into Eastern Europe. A third party, usually a specialized financial institution, guarantees the financing.

Forward differential. The difference between spot and forward rates, expressed as an annual percentage.

Forward discount or premium. The same as "forward differential."

Forward rate. An exchange rate quoted today for settlement at some future date. The rate used in a forward transaction.

Forward transaction. A foreign exchange transaction agreed upon today but to be settled at some specified future date, often one, two, or three months after the transaction date.

Freely floating exchange rates. Exchange rates determined in a free market without government interference, in contradistinction to "dirty" float.

Free trade zone. An area within a country into which foreign goods may be brought duty free, often for purposes of additional manufacture, inventory storage, or packaging. Such goods are subject to duty only when they leave the duty-free zone to enter other parts of the country.

Fronting loan. A parent-to-affiliate loan channeled through a financial intermediary such as a large international bank.

FSC. *See* Foreign sales corporation.

Functional currency. In the context of translating financial statements, the currency of the primary economic environment in which a foreign affiliate operates and in which it generates cash flows.

Futures, or futures contracts. Exchange-traded agreements calling for future delivery of a standard amount of any good, e.g., foreign exchange, at a fixed time, place, and price.

GATT. *See* General Agreement on Tariffs and Trade.

General Agreement on Tariffs and Trade (GATT). A framework of rules for nations to manage their trade policies, negotiate lower international tariff barriers, and settle trade disputes.

Glasnost. Russian language word for the political reform policies of President Mikhail S. Gorbachev in the Soviet Union.

G.m.b.H. *Gesellschaft mit beschraenkter Haftung.* German term for limited liability company.

Gold standard. A monetary system in which currencies are defined in terms of their gold content, and payment imbalances between countries are settled in gold.

Gross up. *See* Deemed paid credit.

Group of Five. France, Japan, United Kingdom, United States, and West Germany. Central bankers and finance ministers of these countries met in the mid-1980s to discuss coordinating economic policies.

Group of Seven. Canada, France, Germany, Italy, Japan, United Kingdom, and the United States. Political leaders of these countries met in 1990 and 1991 to discuss, among other topics, economic aid to the Soviet Union and whether to intervene in the foreign exchange markets to try to stop the rise in the international value of the U.S. dollar.

Group of Ten. The ten most industrialized countries in the non-Communist world, meeting in the mid-1980s to establish the Basle Accord as well as deal with other common economic issues.

Hedge. The purchase of a contract (including forward foreign exchange) or tangible good that will rise in value and offset a drop in value of another contract or tangible good, thus protecting the owner from loss.

Hijo(s). Spanish word for son(s).

Hnos. *Hermanos.* Spanish word for brothers.

Hot money. Money that moves internationally from one currency and/or country to another in response to interest rate differences, and moves away immediately when the interest advantage disappears.

Hybrid foreign currency options. Purchase of a put option and the simultaneous sale of a call (or vice versa) so that the overall cost is less than the cost of a straight option.

Hyperinflation countries. Countries with a very high rate of inflation. Under United States FAS#52, these are defined as countries where the cumulative three-year inflation amounts to 100%.

IBRD. *See* International Bank for Reconstruction and Development.

IMF. *See* International Monetary Fund.

IMM. International Monetary Market. A division of the Chicago Mercantile Exchange.

Inc. "Incorporated." American English word for a business formed as a corporation. *See also* Limited.

Indirect quote. The price of a unit of a home country's currency expressed in terms of a foreign country's currency.

Interest rate parity. A theory that the differences in national interest rates for securities of similar risk and maturity should be equal to but opposite in sign to the forward exchange rate discount or premium for the foreign currency.

International Bank for Reconstruction and Development (IBRD, or World Bank). International development bank owned by member nations that makes development loans to member countries.

Internal rate of return (IRR). A capital budgeting approach in which the discount rate is found that matches the present value of expected future cash inflows with the present value of outflows.

International Banking Facility. A separate banking operation within a domestic U.S. bank, created to allow that bank to accept Eurocurrency deposits from foreign residents without the need for domestic reserve requirements, deposit insurance premiums, or interest rate ceilings.

International Fisher Effect. A theory that the spot exchange rate should change by an amount equal to the difference in interest rates between two countries.

International Monetary Fund (IMF). An international organization created in 1944 to promote postwar exchange rate stability.

IRR. *See* Internal rate of return.

Joint venture. A business venture that is owned by two or more other business ventures. Often the several business owners are from different countries.

Jumbo loans. Loans of $1 billion or more.

Kangaroo bonds. Australian dollar-denominated bonds issued within Australia by a foreign borrower.

KK. *Kabushiki-Kaishi.* Japanese term for stock company.

Lag. In the context of leads and lags, payment of a financial obligation later than is expected or required.

L/C. *See* Letter of credit.

Lead. In the context of leads and lags, payment of a financial obligation earlier than is expected or required.

Letter of credit (L/C). An instrument issued by a bank, in which the bank promises to pay a beneficiary upon presentation of documents specified in the letter of credit.

LIBOR. *See* London Interbank Offered Rate.

LIFO. "Last in, first out." An inventory valuation approach in which the cost of the latest inventory purchases is charged against current sales. The opposite is FIFO, or "first in, first out."

Limited (Ltd). British English word for a business formed as a corporation.

Link financing. *See* Back-to-back loan.

London Interbank Offered Rate (LIBOR). Deposit rate applicable to interbank loans in London. Used as a base rate for many international interest rate transactions.

Ltd. *See* Limited.

Managed float. *See* "Dirty" float.

MFN. *See* Most-favored-nation treatment.

Monetary/nonmonetary method. A method of translating the financial statements of foreign affiliates into the parent's reporting currency. All monetary accounts are translated at the current rate, and all nonmonetary accounts are translated at their historical rates. Sometimes called "temporal method" in the United States.

Money market hedge. Use of foreign currency borrowing to reduce transaction or accounting foreign exchange exposure.

Money markets. The financial markets in various countries in which various types of short-term

debt instruments, including bank loans, are purchased and sold.

m.n. *Moneda nacional.* Spanish language term for "national money," the local currency.

Most-favored-nation treatment. Application of duties on the same, or "most favored," basis to all countries accorded such treatment. Any tariff reduction granted in a bilateral negotiation must be extended to all other nations that have been granted most-favored-nation status.

Negotiable instrument. A draft or promissory note that is in writing, signed by the maker or drawer, contains an unconditional promise or order to pay a definite sum of money on demand or at a determinable future date, and is payable to order or to bearer. A "holder in due course" of a negotiable instrument is entitled to payment despite any personal disagreements between drawee and maker.

Net present value. A capital budgeting approach in which the present value of expected future case inflows is subtracted from the present value of outflows to determine the "net" present value.

Nominal exchange rate. The actual foreign exchange quotation, in contradistinction to "real exchange rate," which is adjusted for changes in purchasing power.

Nontariff barrier. Trade restrictive practices other than custom tariffs. Examples are import quotas, "voluntary" restrictions, variable levies, and special health regulations.

Note issuance facility (NIF). An agreement by which a syndicate of banks indicate a willingness to accept short-term notes from borrowers and resell those notes in the Eurocurrency markets. The discount rate is often tied to LIBOR.

NPV. *See* Net present value.

n.s.f. "Not sufficient funds." Term used by a bank when a draft or check is drawn on an account not having sufficient credit balance.

N.V. *Naamloze vennootschap.* Dutch term for stock company or corporation.

O/A. "Open account." Arrangement in which the importer (or other buyer) pays for the goods only after the goods are received and inspected. The importer is billed directly after shipment, and payment is not tied to any promissory notes or similar documents.

Offer. The price at which a trader is willing to sell foreign exchange, securities, or commodities. Also called "ask."

Operating exposure. The potential for a change in expected cash flows, and thus in value, of a foreign affiliate as a result of an unexpected change in exchange rates. Also called "economic exposure."

Option. In foreign exchange, a contract giving the purchaser the right, but not the obligation, to buy or sell a given amount of foreign exchange at a fixed price per unit for a specified time period. Options to buy are "calls" and options to sell are "puts."

Order bill of lading. A shipping document through which possession and title to the shipment reside with the owner of the order bill of lading.

Outright quotation. The full price, in one currency, of a unit of another currency. *See* Points quotation.

Parallel loan. Another name for a back-to-back loan, in which two companies in separate countries borrow each other's currency for a specific period of time, and repay the other's currency at an agreed maturity.

Parallel market. An unofficial foreign exchange market tolerated by a government but not officially sanctioned. The exact boundary between a parallel market and a black market is not very clear, but official tolerance of what would otherwise be a black market leads to use of the term parallel market.

PEFCO. *See* Private Export Funding Corporation.

Perestroika. Russian language word for the economic reform policies of President Mikhail S. Gorbachev of the Soviet Union.

P/N. "Promissory note."

Points quotation. A forward quotation expressed only as the number of decimal points (usually four decimal points) by which it differs from the spot quotation.

Political risk. The possibility that political events in a particular country will have an influence on the economic well-being of firms in that country. *See also* Sovereign risk.

Portfolio investment. Purchase of foreign stocks and bonds, in contradistinction to "foreign direct investment."

Possessions corporation. Under U.S. tax code, a type of corporation organized to conduct business in U.S. possessions. Certain tax benefits exist for income of possessions corporations.

Private Export Funding Corporation (PEFCO). A private U.S. corporation, established with government support, that helps finance U.S. exports.

Protectionism. A political attitude or policy intended to inhibit or prohibit the import of foreign goods and services. The opposite of "free trade" policies.

Pty. Ltd. "Proprietary Limited." Term used in Australia, Singapore, and other countries for a privately owned corporation.

Purchasing power parity. A theory that the price of internationally traded commodities should be the same in every country, and hence the exchange rate between the two currencies should be the ratio of prices in the two countries.

Put. An option to sell foreign exchange or financial contracts. *See* Option.

Quota. A limit, mandatory or "voluntary," set on the import of a product.

Quotation. In foreign exchange trading, the pair of prices (bid and ask) at which a dealer is willing to buy or sell foreign exchange.

Real exchange rate. Spot foreign exchange quotation adjusted for relative price level changes since a base period. Sometimes referred to as "real effective exchange rate," it is used to measure purchasing-power-adjusted changes in exchange rates.

Registered bond. Corporate or governmental debt in a bond form in which the owner's name appears on the bond and in the issuer's records, and interest payments are mailed to the owner. Transfer, as at the time of sale or if the bond is being possessed as collateral for a loan in default, requires power of attorney and the return of the physical bond to a transfer agent. The transfer agent replaces the old bond with a new one registered to the new owner.

Reinvoicing center. A central financial subsidiary used by a multinational firm to reduce transaction exposure by having all home country exports billed in the home currency and then reinvoiced to each operating affiliate in that affiliate's local currency.

Rembrandt bonds. Dutch guilder-denominated bonds issued within the Netherlands by a foreign borrower.

Reporting currency. In the context of translating financial statements, the currency in which a parent firm prepares its own financial statements. Usually this is the parent's home currency.

Revaluation. A rise in the foreign exchange value of a currency that is pegged to other currencies or to gold. Also called "appreciation."

SA. *Sociedad Anónima* (Spanish), or *Société Anonyme* (French). Term meaning corporation.

SACI or SAIC. *Sociedad Anónima de Capital e Industria.* Spanish term for company of capital and industry.

Samurai bonds. Yen-denominated bonds issued within Japan by a foreign borrower.

SARL. *Società a Responsabilità Limitada* (Italian), or *Société a Responsabilité Limitéé* (French). Term for company with limited liability.

S/D. "Sight draft." International trade term.

S/D-B/L. "Sight draft and bill of lading attached." International trade term.

SDR. *See* Special drawing right.

S. de R.L. *Sociedad de Responsabilidad Limitada.* Spanish term for limited partnership.

Section 482. The set of U.S. Treasury regulations governing transfer prices.

S. en C. *Sociedad en Comandita.* Spanish term for silent partnership.

Shogun bonds. Foreign currency-denominated bonds issued within Japan by Japanese corporations.

SIBOR. Singapore interbank offered rate.

SIMEX. Singapore International Monetary Exchange.

Snake. Informal name for European Narrow Margins (or Joint Float) Agreement, in which European governments agreed to keep their currencies within a ±2.25% trading band around an agreed central value. As of 1991 the governments of Belgium, Denmark, France, Germany, Ireland, Italy, Luxembourg, Netherlands, Spain, and the United Kingdom participated.

Society for Worldwide Interbank Financial Telecommunications (SWIFT). A dedicated computer network providing funds transfer messages between member banks around the world.

Sovereign risk. The risk that a host government may unilaterally repudiate its foreign obligations or may prevent local firms from honoring their foreign obligations. Sovereign risk is often regarded as a subset of political risk.

SPA. *Società per Azioni.* Italian term for corporation.

Special Drawing Right (SDR). An international reserve asset, defined by the International Monetary Fund as the value of a basket of five currencies.

Speculation. An attempt to make a profit by trading on expectations about future prices.

Spot rate. The price at which foreign exchange can be purchased or sold in a spot transaction. *See* Spot transaction.

Spot transaction. A foreign exchange transaction to be settled (paid for) on the second following business day.

SPRL. *Sociéte dé Personnes a Responsabilité Limitéé.* Belgian term for company of persons with limited liability.

Stripped bonds. Bonds issued by investment bankers against coupons or the maturity (corpus) portion of original bearer bonds, where the original bonds are held in trust by the investment banker. Whereas the original bonds will have coupons promising interest at each interest date (say June and December for each of the next twenty years), a given stripped bond will represent a claim against all interest payments from the entire original issue due on a particular interest date. A stripped bond is in effect a zero coupon bond manufactured by the investment banker.

Subpart F. A type of foreign income, as defined in the U.S. tax code, which under certain conditions is taxed in the United States even though it has not been repatriated to the United States.

Subsidiary. A foreign operation incorporated in the host country, in contradistinction to a "branch."

Sushi bonds. Eurodollar, or other non-yen denominated, bonds issued by a Japanese corporation for sale to Japanese investors.

Swap. This term is used in many contexts. In general it is the simultaneous purchase and sale of foreign exchange or securities, with the purchase being effected at once and the sale back to the same party to be carried out at a price agreed upon today but to be completed at a specified future date. Swaps include interest rate swaps, currency swaps, and credit swaps. A "swap rate" is a forward foreign exchange quotation expressed in terms of the number of points by which the forward rate differs from the spot rate.

SWIFT. *See* Society for Worldwide Interbank Financial Telecommunications.

Syndicated loan. A large loan made by a group of banks to a large multinational firm or government. Syndicated loans allow the participating banks to maintain diversification by not lending too much to a single borrower.

Systematic risk. In a portfolio, the amount of risk that cannot be diversified away.

T/A. "Trade acceptance." International trade term.

Tariff. A duty or tax on imports that can be either a percentage of cost or a specific amount per unit of import.

Tax haven. A country with very low tax rates that uses its tax structure to attract foreign investment or international financial dealing.

Temporal method. In the United States, term for a codification of a translation method more commonly called the "monetary/nonmonetary method."

Terms of trade. The weighted average exchange ratio between a nation's export prices and its import prices, used to measure gains from trade. Gains from trade refers to increases in total consumption resulting from production specialization and international trade.

Trade acceptance. A draft accepted by a commercial enterprise, instead of by a bank.

Transaction exposure. The potential for a change in the value of outstanding financial obligations entered into prior to a change in exchange rates but not due to be settled until after the exchange rates change.

Transfer pricing. The setting of prices to be charged by one unit (such as a foreign affiliate) of a multiunit corporation to another unit (such as the parent corporation) for goods or services sold between such related units.

Translation exposure. *See* "Accounting exposure."

Unbiased predictor. A theory that spot prices at some future date will be equal to today's forward rates.

Unbundling. Dividing cash flows from an affiliate to a parent into their many separate components, such as royalties, lease payments, dividends, etc., so as to increase the likelihood that some fund flows will be allowed during economically difficult times.

Unsystematic risk. In a portfolio, the amount of risk that can be eliminated by diversification.

Value-added tax. A type of national sales tax collected at each stage of production or sale of consumption goods, and levied in proportion to the value added during that stage.

Value date. The date when value is given (i.e., funds are deposited) for foreign exchange transactions between banks.

VAT. *See* Value-added tax.

WACC. *See* Weighted average cost of capital.

Weighted average cost of capital (WACC). The sum of the proportionally weighted costs of different sources of capital.

World Bank. *See* International Bank for Reconstruction and Development.

Yankee bonds. Dollar-denominated bonds issued within the United States by a foreign borrower.

Y.K. *Yugen-Kaisha.* Japanese term for limited liability company.

Zero coupon bond. A bond that pays no periodic interest, but simply returns a given amount of principal at a stated maturity date. Zero coupon bonds are sold at a discount from the maturity amount to provide the holder a compound rate of return for the holding period.

Zoonen. Dutch word for sons.

Indexes

Author Index

Subject Index

FINANCIAL QUOTATIONS FROM THE WALL STREET JOURNAL

EXCHANGE RATES
Tuesday, June 11, 1991

The New York foreign exchange selling rates below apply to trading among banks in amounts of $1 million and more, as quoted at 3 p.m. Eastern time by Bankers Trust Co. and other sources. Retail transactions provide fewer units of foreign currency per dollar.

Country	U.S. $ equiv. Tues.	U.S. $ equiv. Mon.	Currency per U.S. $ Tues.	Currency per U.S. $ Mon.
Argentina (Austral)	.0001010	.0001010	9900.01	9900.01
Australia (Dollar)	.7560	.7530	1.3228	1.3280
Austria (Schilling)	.08015	.08035	12.48	12.44
Bahrain (Dinar)	2.6522	2.6522	.3771	.3771
Belgium (Franc)				
Commercial rate	.02740	.02750	36.50	36.37
Brazil (Cruzeiro)	.00354	.00355	282.56	281.49
Britain (Pound)	1.6580	1.6700	.6031	.5988
30-Day Forward	1.6504	1.6627	.6059	.6014
90-Day Forward	1.6381	1.6501	.6105	.6060
180-Day Forward	1.6235	1.6352	.6160	.6115
Canada (Dollar)	.8736	.8737	1.1447	1.1445
30-Day Forward	.8717	.8718	1.1472	1.1470
90-Day Forward	.8681	.8683	1.1519	1.1517
180-Day Forward	.8636	.8635	1.1579	1.1581
Chile (Peso)	.002997	.002832	333.68	353.09
China (Renmimbi)	.186916	.186916	5.3500	5.3500
Colombia (Peso)	.001738	.001738	575.25	575.25
Denmark (Krone)	.1466	.1472	6.8235	6.7916
Ecuador (Sucre)				
Floating rate	.000966	.000966	1035.51	1035.51
Finland (Markka)	.23872	.23973	4.1890	4.1713
France (Franc)	.16625	.16703	6.0150	5.9870
30-Day Forward	.16572	.16653	6.0343	6.0050
90-Day Forward	.16483	.16561	6.0670	6.0382
180-Day Forward	.16373	.16450	6.1075	6.0790
Germany (Mark)	.5639	.5658	1.7735	1.7675
30-Day Forward	.5625	.5645	1.7778	1.7715
90-Day Forward	.5599	.5618	1.7859	1.7800
180-Day Forward	.5567	.5585	1.7964	1.7906
Greece (Drachma)	.005169	.005185	193.45	192.85
Hong Kong (Dollar)	.12942	.12940	7.7270	7.7280
India (Rupee)	.04762	.04762	21.00	21.00
Indonesia (Rupiah)	.0005165	.0005165	1936.03	1936.03
Ireland (Punt)	1.5115	1.5140	.6616	.6605
Israel (Shekel)	.4258	.4268	2.3483	2.3430
Italy (Lira)	.0007587	.0007625	1318.01	1311.51
Japan (Yen)	.007082	.007060	141.20	141.65
30-Day Forward	.007071	.007050	141.43	141.85
90-Day Forward	.007053	.007033	141.78	142.19
180-Day Forward	.007039	.007018	142.07	142.49
Jordan (Dinar)	1.4684	1.4684	.6810	.6810
Kuwait (Dinar)	z	z	z	z
Lebanon (Pound)	.001091	.001091	917.00	917.00
Malaysia (Ringgit)	.3600	.3599	2.7775	2.7785
Malta (Lira)	2.9586	2.9586	.3380	.3380
Mexico (Peso)				
Floating rate	.0003317	.0003317	3015.00	3015.00
Netherland (Guilder)	.5004	.5020	1.9986	1.9920
New Zealand (Dollar)	.5750	.5765	1.7391	1.7346
Norway (Krone)	.1444	.1451	6.9237	6.8932
Pakistan (Rupee)	.0420	.0420	23.82	23.82
Peru (New Sol)	1.2015	1.2231	.83	.82
Philippines (Peso)	.03697	.03697	27.05	27.05
Portugal (Escudo)	.006455	.006538	154.92	152.96
Saudi Arabia (Riyal)	.26663	.26663	3.7505	3.7505
Singapore (Dollar)	.5615	.5610	1.7810	1.7825
South Africa (Rand)				
Commercial rate	.3511	.3512	2.8483	2.8473
Financial rate	.3000	.3030	3.3330	3.3000
South Korea (Won)	.0013805	.0013805	724.35	724.35
Spain (Peseta)	.009116	.009153	109.70	109.25
Sweden (Krona)	.1569	.1575	6.3740	6.3489
Switzerland (Franc)	.6601	.6623	1.5150	1.5100
30-Day Forward	.6588	.6612	1.5178	1.5124
90-Day Forward	.6569	.6593	1.5222	1.5168
180-Day Forward	.6549	.6569	1.5270	1.5222
Taiwan (Dollar)	.036792	.036792	27.18	27.18
Thailand (Baht)	.03880	.03880	25.77	25.77
Turkey (Lira)	.0002414	.0002418	4142.00	4135.02
United Arab (Dirham)	.2723	.2723	3.6725	3.6725
Uruguay (New Peso)				
Financial	.000518	.000518	1930.00	1930.00
Venezuela (Bolivar)				
Floating rate	.01836	.01847	54.47	54.15
SDR	1.32089	1.32142	.75707	.75676
ECU	1.16093	1.16193	....	....

Special Drawing Rights (SDR) are based on exchange rates for the U.S., German, British, French and Japanese currencies. Source: International Monetary Fund.

European Currency Unit (ECU) is based on a basket of community currencies. Source: European Community Commission.

z = Not quoted.

OPTIONS
PHILADELPHIA EXCHANGE

Option & Underlying	Strike Price	Calls-Last Jun	Calls-Last Jul	Calls-Last Sep	Puts-Last Jun	Puts-Last Jul	Puts-Last Sep
50,000 Australian Dollars-European style.							
ADollr	77	r	0.22	r	r	r	r
50,000 Australian Dollars-cents per unit.							
ADollr	74	r	r	r	r	0.42	1.10
75.23	75	r	0.92	r	0.12	0.86	r
75.23	76	0.10	r	r	r	r	r
31,250 British Pounds-European Style.							
BPound	160	r	r	r	r	r	2.42
166.96	162 1/2	r	r	r	r	1.40	r
166.96	170	r	r	r	r	5.05	r
166.96	172 1/2	r	r	r	r	7.05	r
166.96	175	r	r	r	8.83	r	r
31,250 British Pounds-cents per unit.							
BPound	162 1/2	r	r	r	r	1.40	r
166.96	165	1.35	r	r	0.55	2.35	4.70
166.96	167 1/2	0.35	r	2.93	1.72	3.95	r
166.96	170	r	1.00	r	4.00	5.42	r
166.96	172 1/2	r	0.60	r	6.48	7.60	r
166.96	175	r	r	r	8.75	r	r